Professional
Xen® Virtualization

Professional
Xen® Virtualization

William von Hagen

WILEY

Wiley Publishing, Inc.

Professional Xen® Virtualization

Published by
Wiley Publishing, Inc.
10475 Crosspoint Boulevard
Indianapolis, IN 46256
www.wiley.com

Copyright © 2008 by Wiley Publishing, Inc., Indianapolis, Indiana

Published simultaneously in Canada

ISBN: 978-0-470-13811-3

Manufactured in the United States of America

10 9 8 7 6 5 4 3 2 1

Library of Congress Cataloging-in-Publication Data is available from the publisher.

For Dorothy, my wife and best friend. As always, and forever.

About the Author

William von Hagen (Bill) has been a UNIX system administrator for over 20 years and a Linux fanatic since the early 1990s. He has worked as a systems programmer, system administrator, writer, applications developer, drummer, and documentation manager. Bill has written or co-written books on such topics as Ubuntu Linux, GCC, Linux server hacks, Linux filesystems, SUSE Linux, Red Hat Linux, SGML, Mac OS X, and hacking the TiVo. He has also written numerous articles on Linux, embedded computing, Mac OS X, Unix, and open source technology.

Credits

Acquisitions Editor
Jenny Watson

Senior Development Editor
Tom Dinse

Technical Editors
Dan Magenheimer
Richard Artz

Production Editor
Eric Charbonneau

Copy Editor
Nancy Rapoport

Editorial Manager
Mary Beth Wakefield

Production Manager
Tim Tate

Vice President and Executive Group Publisher
Richard Swadley

Vice President and Executive Publisher
Joseph B. Wikert

Project Coordinator, Cover
Lynsey Stanford

Proofreader
Kathryn Duggan

Indexer
Johnna VanHoose Dinse

Acknowledgments

First, I'd like to thank my wife and best friend forever, Dorothy Fisher, who has been more supportive than any human could be expected to be. Fish, the best day of my life was the day I met you! There's no way to thank you enough for the life that I have today.

Next, friends like Jim Morgan, Dr. Joe O'Lear, Larry Rippel, and Kim Walter are an amazing bonus to life itself. Similarly, incredible relatives such as Morgan Gable, Elise Platz, and Luke Platz are the real hope of the future. My life is richer for having all of you as a part of it. Lucky me, indeed!

Thanks to Dan Magenheimer and Richard Artz, who did the technical edit on this book, and made it far better than it would have been without their insightful involvement. Thanks to Kit Kemper, ex-Wiley, who helped me promote the idea for this book in the first place, and thanks to the amazing (and patient) people at Wiley who helped make it a reality: Tom Dinse, Carol Long, Rebekah Gholdson, Jenny Watson, and others that I probably don't even know. It takes a team to create a book, and I'm lucky to have worked with all of you. All errors and omissions are mine alone, but this book would be poorer without all of your contributions.

Contents

Contents

Contents

Contents

Introduction

Virtualization and emulation are inherently fascinating topics. Why should you need to have multiple computers running multiple operating systems when one computer can run them all? Even better, if you have a sufficiently powerful machine, why limit yourself to running only one operating system at a time?

Savvy IBM mainframe users greet virtualization with a yawn and a statement like "That old thing?" Thousands of IBM systems have been running critical business tasks in virtual machines on mainframes for a few decades now. Originally introduced as a mechanism to simultaneously support legacy and more modern operating systems on newer hardware without requiring software changes, virtualization has been a part of enterprise computing since the 1960s.

The emergence of powerful, affordable, open source virtualization has taken a long time. As this book illustrates, today's virtualization technologies have an important place in today's powerful, 24/7 enterprise computing environments. Virtualization can help you get the most out of your existing hardware; reduce data center costs; help guarantee the seamless availability of critical systems; help support "occasional-use" legacy applications without requiring aging, hard-to-replace hardware; and much, much more.

I refer to today's virtualization technologies as "commodity" virtualization technologies because they run on standard, off-the-shelf hardware using a variety of readily available operating systems such as Linux — no mainframe, special hardware, or proprietary service contract is necessary. The powerful, open source virtualization technology of Xen is the perfect complement to the flexibility and reliability of the Linux kernel and the enterprise and end-user application infrastructure that it powers. Just as Linux has taken over most server and many desktop tasks, virtualization is the technology of the future, and Xen is the most interesting and capable virtualization technology available today. (If you disagree with any of the last few statements, feel free to send me an e-mail message from a UNIX-like system using the command `cat > /dev/null`.)

I wrote this book because virtualization is a powerful and cost-effective technology that deserves explanation and promotion. Virtualization can save system administrators time and effort, increase system and service availability, reduce ongoing infrastructure costs, and help minimize future hardware expenses, all while maximizing the return on investment from your existing hardware. Not too shabby for something that is free.

Commodity virtualization technology is still relatively young. As technologies such as Xen and associated tools mature, the potential applications of virtualization in enterprise computing will continue to expand. Xen's approach to virtualization provides performance and capabilities that no other commodity virtualization solution can match. Processor vendors such as Intel and AMD now provide hardware support for virtualization in their latest processors, enabling virtual machines to make the most of multiple cores, CPUs, and your systems' other hardware resources. At the time of this writing, the mainline Linux kernel (2.6.23.1) already includes built-in support for Xen virtual machines (domainU), and support for Xen's administrative interfaces (domain0). The Xen hypervisor is actively being incorporated.

This book can help you take advantage of commodity virtualization with Xen. It takes a while to explore and master a new technology — I've already done that for you. This book will help you explore, understand, and implement virtualization as part of your enterprise computing infrastructure. You, your CTO, and your CFO will be glad that you did.

Who Should Read This Book

The primary audience for this book is system administrators who are interested in implementing and using Xen in the computing environments that they manage. However, this book is also designed to be useful for MIS managers or anyone else who is interested in virtualization, but needs specific information about the differences between various approaches to virtualization and their associated advantages and disadvantages. For example, the first two chapters of this book are written for anyone who is interested in virtualization as a general technology and needs a clear explanation of the different virtualization technologies that are available today, and how they compare.

After the first two chapters, the content of this book becomes increasingly targeted to system administrators, but without any assumptions about your level of experience. For example, when explaining the boot process on a Xen host system in Chapter 4, I explain how standard Linux systems perform various hardware and software checks and start system servers, and I explain the alternate (but compatible) startup mechanisms used on Linux distributions such as Ubuntu. If you already know all that, feel free to skip over it, but it's there for those who need it. Along the same lines, some sections of this book focus on detailed Xen topics that you may not care about. For example, Chapter 9 includes a large section on trusted platform computing and its implementation in a virtual machine environment. Most people will not care, but it is required in some environments, so I've explained how to set it up and use it. (Plus, it's a fascinating topic!)

Some chapters of this book will be of more or less interest to you depending on where you have obtained the version of Xen that you want to run on your systems. For example, Chapter 3 discusses both getting distribution-specific Xen packages as well as building and installing Xen from source code. You'll probably want to do only one of those, but both sections are present to satisfy both types of Xen implementations. Similarly, like most of this book, Chapter 7 focuses on open source tools for managing Xen that work out-of-the-box on all Linux distributions. If you already have a system management tool in place and that tool provides support for Xen, then you may not be particularly interested in a detailed explanation of vanilla open source tools.

What This Book Covers

This book focuses on the open source Xen hypervisor (in version 3.1.1 at the time of this writing) and the open source tools that accompany it. I find the open source Xen tools to be sufficient for most enterprise computing environments. However, new tools for Xen are appearing every day, and enterprise-wide system administration environments for Xen are still emerging and maturing. The "one true tool" for Xen may be just beyond the horizon.

What makes Xen and other open source technologies so compelling is their rate of improvement and the incredible amount of information about them that is available on the Internet. Although I've tried to address the most important concepts, tasks, and techniques associated with using and configuring Xen, there are probably many detailed hardware or system-specific questions that I haven't experienced and can't anticipate. I've tried to summarize both common techniques and common troubleshooting tips to make your experience with Xen as rich and rewarding as mine has been, but the Internet may be your new best friend if you are having problems getting your Acme 666 network fiber channel hardware working.

As I mentioned earlier, this book covers every aspect of Xen: building it, installing it, creating (or simply obtaining) virtual machines that will run on the Xen host system, networking Xen systems, managing Xen systems, and so on. A quick glance at the table of contents should show that I've tried to address all of the topics that you might need to install, configure, and manage a Xen-based, enterprise-quality, virtualization environment. However you, I'm still learning. If there's some topic that was important to you, but which I've overlooked, please let me know via e-mail (wvh@vonhagen.org).

How This Book Is Organized

This book is organized to mirror the process of learning about, installing, configuring, and using Xen hosts and virtual machines in your computing environment. The first two chapters are a general introduction to virtualization and Xen, to provide you with a firm foundation in the terminology and concepts that you will be working with. The following chapter describes how to install the Xen hypervisor and a Linux kernel that can communicate with it on a Linux system (known as domain0 in Xen parlance), and how Xen changes the boot process on that system.

The next few chapters explain how to create and experiment with virtual machines that run on your domain0 system (known as domainU systems in Xen-speak). Separate chapters discuss managing virtual machines, and different approaches to networking between Xen virtual machines, your domain0 system, and the outside world.

The last two chapters focus on advanced virtual machine configuration and usage, and some of the things that you will need to consider and implement in order to create a manageable and responsible enterprise computing environment that makes the most of Xen.

The book concludes with two appendixes that provide a reference for two key aspects of using Xen: the xm command, which is the primary command-line tool for creating, monitoring, and managing Xen domain0 and domainU systems; and the configuration file format used to define and fine-tune Xen virtual machines. These provide in-depth information that improves upon the standard Xen documentation, and serve as a convenient, one-stop-shopping location for common questions about these critical Xen-related topics.

What You Need To Use This Book

The primary requirement for reading this book is curiosity about new technologies. The introductory and overview chapters don't require anything beyond a general familiarity with today's computing technology. For the more technical chapters, I expect you to have a Linux system and know how to perform basic programming and sysadmin tasks such as using a text editor, using make, and using a C compiler (GCC, of course). If your distribution doesn't provide Xen in its package repositories or you need the latest and greatest Xen features, you'll need to build Xen yourself. I've explained the general kernel build process and how to customize your configuration before building Xen and the domain0 Linux kernel, but previous experience building kernels is always a good thing.

I have tried to be completely agnostic regarding the Linux distributions that run on a Xen host and as virtual machines. As discussed in the previous section, this book focuses on open source, distribution-independent tools for building Xen virtual machines and managing Xen in general. Although some sections of various chapters list distribution-specific creation and management tools for Xen, the book does not focus on using them. The techniques and procedures discussed throughout this book should work on any Linux distribution. Similarly, when discussing software packages outside of the core Xen distribution, I focused on distribution-independent installation and configuration. Where different Linux distributions work differently, such as with system logging or system startup, I tried to cover all of the alternatives. However, I am personally and professionally a fan of the Ubuntu and SUSE distributions, in that order, and I'm sure that my allegiances have slipped through in a few places.

Source Code

As you work through the examples in this book, you may choose either to type in all the code manually or to use the source code files that accompany the book. All of the source code used in this book is available for download at www.wrox.com. Once at the site, simply locate the book's title (either by using the Search box or by using one of the title lists) and click the Download Code link on the book's detail page to obtain all the source code for the book.

Because many books have similar titles, you may find it easiest to search by ISBN. This book's ISBN is 978-0-470-13811-3.

Once you download the code, just decompress it with your favorite compression tool. Alternately, you can go to the main Wrox code download page at www.wrox.com/dynamic/books/download .aspx to see the code available for this book and all other Wrox books.

Errata

We make every effort to ensure that there are no errors in the text or in the code. However, no one is perfect, and mistakes do occur. If you find an error in one of our books, such as a spelling mistake or faulty piece of code, we would be very grateful for your feedback. By sending in errata, you may save another reader hours of frustration, and at the same time, you will be helping us provide even higher quality information.

To find the errata page for this book, go to www.wrox.com and locate the title using the Search box or one of the title lists. Then, on the book details page, click the Book Errata link. On this page, you can view all errata that has been submitted for this book and posted by Wrox editors. A complete book list, including links to each book's errata, is also available at www.wrox.com/misc-pages/booklist.shtml.

If you don't spot "your" error on the Book Errata page, go to www.wrox.com/contact/techsupport .shtml and complete the form there to send us the error you have found. We'll check the information and, if appropriate, post a message to the book's errata page and fix the problem in subsequent editions of the book.

p2p.wrox.com

For author and peer discussion, join the P2P forums at p2p.wrox.com. The forums are a Web-based system for you to post messages relating to Wrox books and related technologies and interact with other readers and technology users. The forums offer a subscription feature to e-mail you topics of interest of your choosing when new posts are made to the forums. Wrox authors, editors, other industry experts, and your fellow readers are present on these forums.

At http://p2p.wrox.com you will find a number of different forums that will help you not only as you read this book, but also as you develop your own applications. To join the forums, just follow these steps:

1. Go to p2p.wrox.com and click the Register link.
2. Read the terms of use and click Agree.
3. Complete the required information to join as well as any optional information you wish to provide and click Submit.
4. You will receive an e-mail with information describing how to verify your account and complete the joining process.

You can read messages in the forums without joining P2P but in order to post your own messages, you must join.

Once you join, you can post new messages and respond to messages other users post. You can read messages at any time on the Web. If you would like to have new messages from a particular forum e-mailed to you, click the Subscribe to this Forum icon by the forum name in the forum listing.

For more information about how to use the Wrox P2P, be sure to read the P2P FAQs for answers to questions about how the forum software works as well as many common questions specific to P2P and Wrox books. To read the FAQs, click the FAQ link on any P2P page.

Overview of Virtualization

Virtualization is one of the hottest topics in information technology today. The increasing speed and capabilities of today's x86 processors have made virtualization possible on commodity hardware, and virtualization provides an attractive way of making the most of that hardware.

As happens with most popular IT buzzwords in their heyday, virtualization is frequently touted as *the* solution to all of your IT woes. I'm sure we'd all like to find some one true technology that enables us to set up a powerful, reliable, and highly available IT infrastructure once and for all, so that we can all go home or at least throttle down our hours so that we can work 9-to-5. I have both good news and bad news. The good news is that virtualization is a cool and powerful technology that can indeed simplify your computing infrastructure and help you get the most bang for your buck out of the latest, fastest processors, networking, and storage technologies. The bad news is that, like anything in the real world, successfully implementing, deploying, and supporting a new IT infrastructure based on virtualization requires the same level of planning and system design that any basic shift in infrastructure always has. That's why we're all here and why this book was written in the first place — to define basic concepts, explain basic issues, and explore how to successfully make the most of the best of today's virtualization technologies while providing the capability and availability guarantees that today's often-complex IT infrastructure requires.

This chapter provides an overview of the history of virtualization and the different types of virtualization that are in use today. Following this foundation, I'll discuss the pros and cons of virtualization — regardless of what hottechnologybuzzword.com may say, there are downsides, or at least issues that you have to be aware of when thinking about introducing virtualization into your computing environment. Although this book is about Xen, this chapter primarily focuses on providing a thorough background on virtualization concepts and theory rather than any specific technology; it remains relatively agnostic to any specific approach to virtualization or its implementation. Don't worry — as you might expect (and hope), the rest of this book focuses on Xen, why it is the most attractive of today's virtualization solutions, and how to successfully make the most of Xen in your computing environment.

What Is Virtualization?

Virtualization is simply the logical separation of the request for some service from the physical resources that actually provide that service. In practical terms, virtualization provides the ability to run applications, operating systems, or system services in a logically distinct system environment that is independent of a specific physical computer system. Obviously, all of these have to be running on a certain computer system at any given time, but virtualization provides a level of logical abstraction that liberates applications, system services, and even the operating system that supports them from being tied to a specific piece of hardware. Virtualization's focus on logical operating environments rather than physical ones makes applications, services, and instances of an operating system portable across different physical computer systems.

The classic example of virtualization that most people are already familiar with is virtual memory, which enables a computer system to appear to have more memory than is physically installed on that system. Virtual memory is a memory-management technique that enables an operating system to see and use noncontiguous segments of memory as a single, contiguous memory space. Virtual memory is traditionally implemented in an operating system by paging, which enables the operating system to use a file or dedicated portion of some storage device to save pages of memory that are not actively in use. Known as a "paging file" or "swap space," the system can quickly transfer pages of memory to and from this area as the operating system or running applications require access to the contents of those pages. Modern operating systems such as UNIX-like operating systems (including Linux, the *BSD operating systems, and Mac OS X) and Microsoft Windows all use some form of virtual memory to enable the operating system and applications to access more data than would fit into physical memory.

As I'll discuss in the next few sections, there are many different types of virtualization, all rooted around the core idea of providing logical access to physical resources. Today, virtualization is commonly encountered in networking, storage systems, and server processes, at the operating system level and at the machine level. Xen, the subject of this book, supports machine-level virtualization using a variety of clever and powerful techniques.

As a hot buzzword, it's tempting for corporate marketing groups to abuse the term "virtualization" in order to get a bit more traction for their particular products or technologies. The use of the term "virtualization" in today's marketing literature rivals the glory days of terms such as "Internet" and "network-enabled" in the 1990s. To try to cut through the haze surrounding what is and what is not virtualization, the next few sections discuss the most common classes of virtualization and virtualization technology today.

> *Whenever possible, references in this section to virtualization technologies refer to centralized resources for that term or technology. I've tried to use the Wikipedia entries as a primary reference for most terms and technologies because in most cases, the Wikipedia provides a great, product-agnostic resource that doesn't promote any single technical solution for a given technology. When looking things up on Wikipedia, be aware that terms there are case-sensitive — and that Wikipedia is only a starting point for good information.*

Application Virtualization

The term "application virtualization" describes the process of compiling applications into machine-independent byte code that can subsequently be executed on any system that provides the appropriate virtual machine as an execution environment. The best known example of this approach to virtualization is the byte code produced by the compilers for the Java programming language (http://java.sun .com/), although this concept was actually pioneered by the UCSD P-System in the late 1970s (www.threedee.com/jcm/psystem), for which the most popular compiler was the UCSD Pascal compiler. Microsoft has even adopted a similar approach in the Common Language Runtime (CLR) used by .NET applications, where code written in languages that support the CLR are transformed, at compile time, into CIL (Common Intermediate Language, formerly known as MSIL, Microsoft Intermediate Language). Like any byte code, CIL provides a platform-independent instruction set that can be executed in any environment supporting the .NET Framework.

Application virtualization is a valid use of the term "virtualization" because applications compiled into byte code become logical entities that can be executed on different physical systems with different characteristics, operating systems, and even processor architectures.

Desktop Virtualization

The term "desktop virtualization" describes the ability to display a graphical desktop from one computer system on another computer system or smart display device. This term is used to describe software such as Virtual Network Computing (VNC, http://en.wikipedia.org/wiki/VNC), thin clients such as Microsoft's Remote Desktop (http://en.wikipedia.org/wiki/Remote_Desktop_Protocol) and associated Terminal Server products, Linux terminal servers such as the Linux Terminal Server project (LTSP, http://sourceforge.net/projects/ltsp/), NoMachine's NX (http://en.wikipedia.org/ wiki/NX_technology), and even the X Window System (http://en.wikipedia.org/wiki/X_ Window_System) and its XDMCP display manager protocol. Many window managers, particularly those based on the X Window System, also provide internal support for multiple, virtual desktops that the user can switch between and use to display the output of specific applications. In the X Window System, virtual desktops were introduced in versions of Tom LeStrange's TWM window manager (www.xwinman .org/vtwm.php, with a nice family tree at www.vtwm.org/vtwm-family.html), but are now available in almost every other window manager. The X Window System also supports desktop virtualization at the screen or display level, enabling window managers to use a display region that is larger than the physical size of your monitor.

In my opinion, desktop virtualization is more of a bandwagon use of the term "virtualization" than an exciting example of virtualization concepts. It does indeed make the graphical console of any supported system into a logical entity that can be accessed and used on different physical computer systems, but it does so using standard client/server display software. The remote console, the operating system it is running, and the applications you execute are actually still running on a single, specific physical machine — you're just looking at them from somewhere else. Calling remote display software a virtualization technology seems to me to be equivalent to considering a telescope to be a set of virtual eyeballs because you can look at something far away using one. Your mileage may vary.

Network Virtualization

The term "network virtualization" describes the ability to refer to network resources logically rather than having to refer to specific physical network devices, configurations, or collections of related machines. There are many different levels of network virtualization, ranging from single-machine, network-device virtualization that enables multiple virtual machines to share a single physical-network resource, to enterprise-level concepts such as virtual private networks and enterprise-core and edge-routing techniques for creating subnetworks and segmenting existing networks.

Xen relies on network virtualization through the Linux bridge-utils package to enable your virtual machines to appear to have unique physical addresses (Media Access Control, or MAC, addresses) and unique IP addresses. Other server-virtualization solutions, such as UML, use the Linux virtual Point-to-Point (TUN) and Ethernet (TAP) network devices to provide user-space access to the host's network. Many advanced network switches and routers use techniques such as Virtual Routing and Forwarding (VRF), VRF-Lite, and Multi-VRF to segregate customer traffic into separately routed network segments and support multiple virtual-routing domains within a single piece of network hardware.

Discussing virtual private networks and other virtual LAN technologies is outside the scope of this book. Virtual networking as it applies to and is used by Xen is discussed in Chapter 8.

Server and Machine Virtualization

The terms "server virtualization" and "machine virtualization" describe the ability to run an entire virtual machine, including its own operating system, on another operating system. Each virtual machine that is running on the parent operating system is logically distinct, has access to some or all of the hardware on the host system, has its own logical assignments for the storage devices on which that operating system is installed, and can run its own applications within its own operating environment.

Server virtualization is the type of virtualization technology that most people think of when they hear the term "virtualization", and is the type of virtualization that is the focus of this book. Though not as common, I find the term "machine virtualization" useful to uniquely identify this type of virtualization, because it more clearly differentiates the level at which virtualization is taking place — the machine itself is being virtualized — regardless of the underlying technology used. Machine virtualization is therefore the technique used by virtualization technologies such as KVM, Microsoft Virtual Server and Virtual PC, Parallels Workstation, User Mode Linux, Virtual Iron, VMware, and (of course) Xen. See the section "Other Popular Virtualization Software" in Chapter 2 for an overview of each of these virtualization technologies, except for Xen, which (as you might hope) is discussed throughout this book.

In the maddening whirlwind of terms that include the word "virtual," server virtualization is usually different from the term "virtual server," which is often used to describe both the capability of operating system servers such as e-mail and Web servers to service multiple Internet domains, and system-level virtualization techniques that are used to provide Internet service provider (ISP) users with their own virtual server machine.

The key aspect of server or machine virtualization is that different virtual machines do not share the same kernel and can therefore be running different operating systems. This differs from system-level virtualization, where virtual servers share a single underlying kernel (discussed in more detail later in this chapter) and provide a number of unique infrastructure, customer, and business opportunities. Some of these are:

❑   Running legacy software, where you depend on a software product that runs only on a specific version of a specific operating system. Being able to run legacy software and the legacy operating system that it requires is only possible on virtual systems that can run multiple operating systems.

❑   Software system-test and quality-assurance environments, where you need to be able to test a specific software product on many different operating systems or versions of an operating system. Server virtualization makes it easy to install and test against many different operating systems or versions of operating systems without requiring dedicated hardware for each.

❑ Low-level development environments, where developers may want or need to work with specific versions of tools, an operating system kernel, and a specific operating system distribution. Server virtualization makes it easy to be able to run many different operating systems and environments without requiring dedicated hardware for each.

For more information about specific uses for server virtualization and its possible organizational advantages, see the section "Advantages of Virtualization," later in this chapter.

Server and machine virtualization technologies work in several different ways. The differences between the various approaches to server or machine virtualization can be subtle, but are always significant in terms of the capabilities that they provide and the hardware and software requirements for the underlying system. The most common approaches to server and machine virtualization today are the following:

❑ **Guest OS:** Each virtual server runs as a separate operating system instance within a virtualization application that itself runs on an instance of a specific operating system. Parallels Workstation, VMWare Workstation, and VMWare GSX Server are the most common examples of this approach to virtualization. The operating system on which the virtualization application is running is often referred to as the "Host OS" because it is supplying the execution environment for the virtualization application.

❑ **Parallel Virtual Machine:** Some number of physical or virtual systems are organized into a single virtual machine using clustering software such as a Parallel Virtual Machine (PVM) (www.csm.ornl.gov/pvm/pvm_home.html). The resulting cluster is capable of performing complex CPU and data-intensive calculations in a cooperative fashion. This is more of a clustering concept than an alternative virtualization solution, and thus is not discussed elsewhere in this book. See the PVM home page (www.csm.ornl.gov/pvm/) for detailed information about PVM and related software.

❑ **Hypervisor-based:** A small virtual machine monitor (known as a hypervisor) runs on top of your machine's hardware and provides two basic functions. First, it identifies, traps, and responds to protected or privileged CPU operations made by each virtual machine. Second, it handles queuing, dispatching, and returning the results of hardware requests from your virtual machines. An administrative operating system then runs on top of the hypervisor, as do the virtual machines themselves. This administrative operating system can communicate with the hypervisor and is used to manage the virtual machine instances.

The most common approach to hypervisor-based virtualization is known as paravirtualization, which requires changes to an operating system so that it can communicate with the hypervisor. Paravirtualization can provide performance enhancements over other approaches to server and machine virtualization, because the operating system modifications enable the operating system to communicate directly with the hypervisor, and thus does not incur some of the overhead associated with the emulation required for the other hypervisor-based machine and server technologies discussed in this section. Paravirtualization is the primary model used by Xen, which uses a customized Linux kernel to support its administrative environment, known as domain0. As discussed later in this section, Xen can also take advantage of hardware virtualization to run unmodified versions of operating systems on top of its hypervisor.

❑ **Full virtualization:** Very similar to paravirtualization, full virtualization also uses a hypervisor, but incorporates code into the hypervisor that emulates the underlying hardware when necessary, enabling *unmodified* operating systems to run on top of the hypervisor. Full virtualization is the model used by VMWare ESX server, which uses a customized version of Linux (known as the Service Console) as its administrative operating system.

❏ **Kernel-level virtualization:** This type of virtualization does not require a hypervisor, but instead runs a separate version of the Linux kernel and an associated virtual machine as a user-space process on the physical host. This provides an easy way to run multiple virtual machines on a single host. Examples of this are User-Mode Linux (UML), which has been supported in the mainline Linux kernel for quite a while but requires a special build of the Linux kernel for guest operating systems, and Kernel Virtual Machine (KVM), which was introduced in the 2.6.20 mainline Linux kernel. UML does not require any separate administrative software in order to execute or manage its virtual machines, which can be executed from the Linux command line. KVM uses a device driver in the host's kernel for communication between the main Linux kernel and the virtual machines, requires processor support for virtualization (Intel VT or AMD-v Pacifica), and uses a slightly modified QEMU process as the display and execution container for its virtual machines. In many ways, KVM's kernel-level virtualization is a specialized version of full virtualization, where the Linux kernel serves as the hypervisor, but I think that UML and KVM are unique enough to merit their own class of server virtualization. For more information about the Intel and AMD hardware that supports hardware virtualization, see the section "Hardware Requirements for Xen" in Chapter 3.

❏ **Hardware virtualization:** Very similar to both paravirtualization and full virtualization, hardware virtualization uses a hypervisor, but it is only available on systems that provide hardware support for virtualization. Hypervisor-based systems such as Xen and VMWare ESX Server, and kernel-level virtualization technologies such as KVM, can take advantage of the hardware support for virtualization that is provided on the latest generation of Intel (Intel VT, aka Vanderpool) and AMD (AMD-V, aka Pacifica) processors. Virtual machines in a hardware virtualization environment can run unmodified operating systems because the hypervisor can use the hardware's support for virtualization to handle privileged and protected operations and hardware access requests, and to communicate with and manage the virtual machines. For more information about the Intel and AMD hardware that supports hardware virtualization, see the section "Hardware Requirements for Xen" in Chapter 3.

As you can see from the previous list, hypervisor-based virtualization is the most popular virtualization technique in use today, spanning the best-known server and machine virtualization technologies, including IBM's VM operating system, VMWare's ESX Server, Parallels Workstation, Virtual Iron products, and Xen. The use of a hypervisor was pioneered by the original commercial virtual-machine environment, IBM's CP/CMS operating system (http://en.wikipedia.org/wiki/CP/CMS), introduced in 1966, was popularized by IBM's VM/370 operating system (http://en.wikipedia.org/wiki/VM_%28operating_system%29), introduced in 1970, and remains a great idea today.

Standardizing Linux Server Virtualization

Although Xen is an open source project, keeping up with both the Xen patches and the latest revision of the Linux kernel is tough. The increasing popularity of Xen has made many people hope for the direct inclusion of the Xen patches into the mainline kernel sources. However, the folks from VMware aren't among them because the inclusion of Xen-specific patches could conceivably give Xen (and thus XenSource) a commercial edge over the VMware technologies. As you might hope, the Linux kernel is a truly open effort whose goal is open APIs and general, vendor-agnostic functionality, and should therefore be capable of supporting more than one hypervisor-based virtualization solution.

In 2006, VMware proposed a generic Virtual Machine Interface (VMI) that would enable multiple hypervisor-based virtualization technologies to use a common kernel-level interface. This didn't quite suit the Xen folks, so much wailing, gnashing of teeth, and rattling of swords ensued. Finally, at the 2006 USENIX meeting, VMware and Xen agreed to work together (with others) to develop a more generic interface, known as paravirt_ops, which is being developed by IBM, VMware, Red Hat, and XenSource and is being coordinated by Rusty Russell, a well-known Linux kernel hacker. For a detailed discussion of paravirt_ops, see the section "Other Popular Virtualization and Emulation Software" in Chapter 2.

The upshot of all of this is that the eventual inclusion of the paravirt_ops patches into the mainline kernel will enable any compliant hypervisor-based virtualization technology to work with a vanilla Linux kernel, while kernel projects such as KVM will enable users to run virtual machines, themselves running any operating system, on hardware that supports them, without requiring a hypervisor. UML will continue to enable users to run additional Linux virtual machines on a single Linux system. Though this may appear confusing, increasing richness in mainline Linux support for virtualization simply falls in the "more is better" category, and enables hypervisor-based virtualization technologies to compete on their technical and administrative merits.

Storage Virtualization

Storage virtualization is the logical abstraction of physical storage. In conjunction with different types of filesystems, storage virtualization is the key to making flexible, expandable amounts of storage available to today's computer systems.

Storage virtualization has been around for many years, and should be familiar to anyone who has worked with RAID storage (http://en.wikipedia.org/wiki/Redundant_array_of_independent_disks), logical volumes (http://en.wikipedia.org/wiki/Logical_volume) on systems such as Linux or AIX, or with networked filesystems such as AFS (http://en.wikipedia.org/wiki/Andrew_file_system) and GFS (http://en.wikipedia.org/wiki/Global_File_System). All of these technologies combine available physical disk drives into pools of available storage that can be divided into logical sections known as volumes on which a filesystem can be created and mounted for use on a computer system. A volume is the logical equivalent of a disk partition.

The core features that make storage virtualization so attractive in today's enterprise environments is that they provide effectively infinite storage that is limited only by the number and size of drives that can be physically supported by the host system or host storage system. The reporting and discovery requirements imposed by standards such as Sarbanes-Oxley, the Department of Homeland Security, or basic corporate accountability make it important to be able to store more and more information forever. Storage virtualization enables greater amounts of physical storage to be available to individual systems, and enables existing filesystems to grow to hold that information without resorting to an administrative shotgun blast of symbolic links and interdependent mount points for networked storage.

Technologies such as RAID (Redundant Array of Inexpensive Disks) and logical volumes as provided by the Linux LVM, LVM2, and EVMS packages are usually limited to use on the system to which the actual storage devices are physically attached. Some RAID controllers are dual-ported, allowing multiple computers access to the same volumes and associated filesystems through that RAID controller, although how well this works depends on the type of filesystem in use on the shared volume and how that filesystem is mounted on both systems.

To use a logical volume manager, you must define the disk partitions that you want to use for logical volumes, create logical volumes on that physical storage, and then create a filesystem on the logical volumes. You can then mount and use these filesystems just as you would mount and use filesystems that were created on physical disk partitions.

Like standard disk controllers, RAID controllers provide block-level access to the storage devices that are attached to them, although the size of the storage available from any set of disks depends on the RAID level that is being used. The devices attached to the RAID controller are then made available to the system as though they were a single disk, which you can then partition as you wish, create filesystems on those partitions, and mount and use them just as you would use single physical partitions.

Operating systems such as Linux also support software RAID, where no physical RAID controller need be present. The software RAID system functions exactly as a hardware RAID controller would, providing block-level access to available storage, but it enforces the characteristics of different RAID levels in software rather than in hardware. Software RAID is very efficient and has only slightly lower performance than many hardware RAID controllers. Many system administrators actually prefer software RAID over hardware RAID because hardware RAID controllers are very different from manufacturer to manufacturer and even controller to controller. The failure of a RAID controller typically requires a replacement controller of the same type from the same manufacturer in order to access the data on the storage device that was attached to the failed controller. On the other hand, software RAID is completely portable across all Linux systems on which the software is installed as long as they support the same physical disk drive interfaces (IDE, EIDE, SATA, and so on).

Distributed filesystem technologies such as AFS and GFS have their own internal logical-volume creation and management mechanisms, and also make it possible to share the filesystems on these logical volumes between multiple computer systems because AFS and GFS provide locking mechanisms to synchronize simultaneous writes to shared filesystems over the network. NFS, the default Network File System for most UNIX-like operating systems, also makes it possible to share logical storage across multiple computer systems, although it does this by exporting a directory from a filesystem on the logical storage rather than by directly mounting a system-specific volume or networked filesystem. Distributed filesystems such as AFS and GFS provide filesystem-level access to logical volumes. In this, they are conceptually similar to Network Attached Storage (NAS, `http://en.wikipedia.org/wiki/Network-attached_storage`) devices, which provide filesystem-level access over a network to the filesystems that they contain.

Storage virtualization has become much more accessible across multiple computer systems with the advent of Storage Area Networks (SAN, `http://en.wikipedia.org/wiki/Storage_area_network`), which support block-level I/O and therefore enable multiple systems to share low-level access to various types of storage devices over the network. Most SANs use expensive, high-power network technologies such as Fibre Channel (http://en.wikipedia.org/wiki/Fibre_Channel) and InfiniBand (http://en.wikipedia.org/wiki/InfiniBand) to provide the high levels of throughput and general performance that are most desirable when many systems share access to block- or protocol-level networked storage.

Newer technologies such as iSCSI (Internet Small Computer Systems Interface, http://en.wikipedia .org/wiki/ISCSI) and AoE (ATA over Ethernet, http://en.wikipedia.org/wiki/ATA_over_ Ethernet) provide less expensive mechanisms for getting block-level access to networked storage devices. As the name suggests, iSCSI supports the use of the SCSI protocol over TCP/IP networks, and requires a special type of network controller. AoE provides block-level access to suitable ATA devices using only a standard Ethernet connection. As you'd expect, both of these perform better on higher-bandwidth networks such as Gigabit Ethernet networks, although they are certainly usable on 100-megabit networks. iSCSI and AoE are making networked storage a very real possibility for most of today's data centers and IT infrastructure of any size, and are discussed in more detail in the section "Using Xen and Networked Storage Devices" in Chapter 10.

System-Level or Operating System Virtualization

The system-level virtualization, often referred to as, operating system virtualization, describes various implementations of running multiple, logically distinct system environments on a single instance of an operating system kernel. System-level virtualization is based on the change root (chroot) concept that is available on all modern UNIX-like systems. During the system boot process, the kernel can use root filesystems such as those provided by initial RAM disks or initial RAM filesystems to load drivers and perform other early-stage system initialization tasks. The kernel can then switch to another root filesystem using the chroot command in order to mount an on-disk filesystem as its final root filesystem, and continue system initialization and configuration from within that filesystem. The chroot mechanism as used by system-level virtualization is an extension of this concept, enabling the system to start virtual servers with their own sets of processes that execute relative to their own filesystem root directories. Operating within the confines of their own root directories and associated filesystem prevents virtual servers from being able to access files in each others' filesystems, and thereby provides basic protection from exploits of various server processes or the virtual server itself. Even if a chroot'ed server is compromised, it has access only to files that are located within its own root filesystem.

The core differentiator between system-level and server virtualization is whether you can be running different operating systems on different virtual systems. If all of your virtual servers must share a single copy of an operating system kernel, as shown in Figure 1-1, this is system-level virtualization. If different virtual servers can be running different operating systems, including different versions of a single operating system, this is server virtualization, sometimes also referred to as machine virtualization. Virtualization solutions such as FreeBSD's chroot jails, FreeVPS, Linux VServer, OpenVZ, Solaris Zones and Containers, and Virtuozzo are all examples of system-level virtualization. FreeBSD jails can run logically distinct versions of FreeBSD user-space on top of a single FreeBSD kernel, and can therefore use different instances or versions of libraries, server processes, and applications. Solaris containers and zones all share the same underlying version of Solaris, and can either use completely distinct root filesystems or share portions of a filesystem. Linux-VServer, FreeVPS, and OpenVZ can run different Linux distributions in their virtual servers, but all share the same underlying kernel. All of these are discussed in more detail in the section "Other Popular Virtualization Software" in Chapter 2.

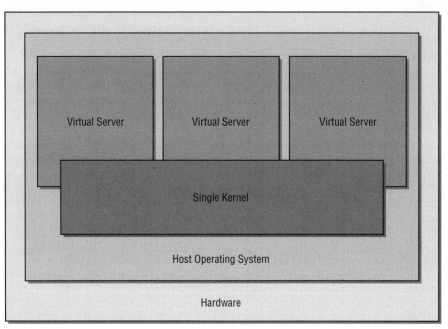

Figure 1-1

System-level virtualization provides some significant advantages over server or machine virtualization. The key to all of these is that, because they share a single instance of an operating system kernel, system-level virtualization solutions are significantly lighter weight than the complete machines (including a kernel) required by server virtualization technologies. This enables a single physical host to support many more "virtual servers" than the number of complete virtual machines that it could support. System-level virtualization solutions such as FreeBSD's chroot jails, Linux-VServer, and FreeVPS have been used for years by businesses such as Internet Service Providers (ISPs) to provide each user with their own virtual server, in which they can have relatively complete control (and, in some cases, administrative privileges) without any chance of compromising the system's primary security configuration, system configuration files, and filesystem. System-level virtualization is therefore most commonly used for server consolidation. The primary disadvantage of system-level virtualization is that a kernel or driver problem can take down all of the system-level virtual servers supported on that system.

Why Virtualization Today?

This section (and the rest of this book) focuses on server and machine virtualization, where a single host system supports multiple, independent instances of virtual machines running various operating systems. Unless otherwise identified, subsequent references to virtualization refer to machine virtualization.

Virtualization is not a new concept, and has been in use for decades in the different ways highlighted in the previous section. However, virtualization is more popular now than ever because it is now an option for a larger group of users and system administrators than ever before. There are several general reasons for the increasing popularity of virtualization:

❏ The power and performance of commodity x86 hardware continues to increase. Processors are faster than ever, support more memory than ever, and the latest multi-core processors literally enable single systems to perform multiple tasks simultaneously. These factors combine to increase the chance that your hardware may be underutilized. As discussed later in this chapter, virtualization provides an excellent way of getting the most out of existing hardware while reducing many other IT costs.

❏ The integration of direct support for hardware-level virtualization in the latest generations of Intel and AMD processors, motherboards, and related firmware has made virtualization on commodity hardware more powerful than ever before. See the section "Hardware Requirements for Xen" in Chapter 3 for an overview of virtualization support in commodity hardware.

❏ A wide variety of virtualization products for both desktop and server systems running on commodity x86 hardware have emerged, are still emerging, and have become extremely popular. Many of these (like Xen) are open source software and are attractive from both a capability and cost perspective. The section "Other Popular Virtualization Software" in Chapter 2 provides an overview of well-known virtualization products (other than Xen) that support commodity hardware.

More accessible, powerful, and flexible than ever before, virtualization is continuing to prove its worth in business and academic environments all over the world. The next two sections explore some of the specific reasons why virtualization can benefit your computing infrastructure and also discuss some of the issues that you must consider before selecting virtualization as a solution to your infrastructure requirements.

Basic Approaches to Virtual Systems

The section "What Is Virtualization?" highlighted the different ways in which the term "virtualization" is popularly used today and discussed different approaches to virtualization in each domain. This section provides a slightly different view of these same concepts, focusing on the type of virtualization that is the topic of this book, where a single physical machine can host multiple virtual machines. This section makes it easier to compare different approaches to running virtual machines on physical hardware by focusing on the underlying technology rather than on terminology and by providing a cheat sheet for general approaches to these types of virtual machines.

The most common approaches to virtual computer systems used today are the following:

❏ **Shared kernel:** A single operating system kernel supports multiple virtual systems. Each virtual system has its own root filesystem. Because all virtual machines share the same operating system kernel, the libraries and utilities executed by these virtual machines must also have been compiled for the same hardware and instruction set as the physical machine on which the virtual systems are running. For more details on this approach to virtualization and some examples of virtualization software that use this approach, see Figure 1-1 and the section earlier in this chapter entitled "System-Level or Operating System Virtualization." For details on any of these software packages, see the section "Other Popular Virtualization Software" in the next chapter.

❑ **Guest OS:** Virtual machines run within an application that is running as a standard application under the operating system that executes on the physical host system. This application manages the virtual machines, mediates access to the hardware resources on the physical host system, and intercepts and handles any privileged or protected instructions issued by the virtual machines. Figure 1-2 illustrates this approach to virtualization. This type of virtualization typically runs virtual machines whose operating system, libraries, and utilities have been compiled for the same type of processor and instruction set as the physical machine on which the virtual systems are running. However, it can also run virtual machines, libraries, and utilities that have been compiled for other processors if the virtualization application can perform instruction-set translation or emulation, as is the case with products such as Microsoft's Virtual PC product. For more information about this approach to virtualization and some examples of virtualization software that uses this approach, see the section "Server or Machine Virtualization" earlier in this chapter. For details on any of these software packages, see the section "Other Popular Virtualization Software" in the next chapter.

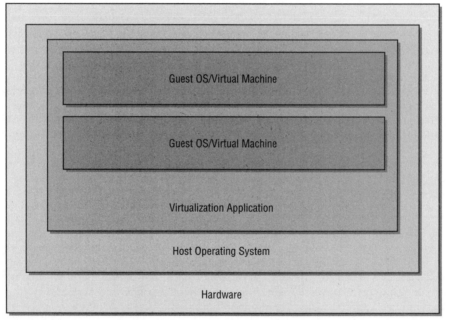

Figure 1-2

❑ **Hypervisor:** A hypervisor is a low-level virtual machine monitor that loads during the boot process, before the virtual machines, and runs directly on the physical hardware, as shown in Figure 1-3. The hypervisor handles requests for access to hardware resources on the physical host system, traps and handles protected or privileged instructions, and so on. Hypervisor-based virtualization runs virtual machines whose operating system, libraries, and utilities have been compiled for the same hardware and instruction set as the physical machine on which the virtual systems are running.

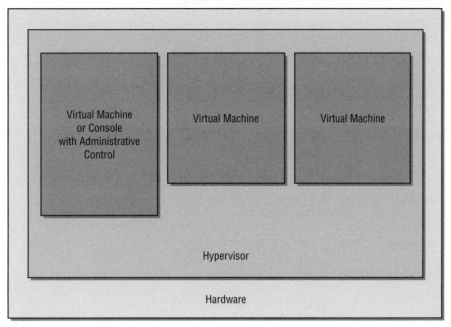

Figure 1-3

Hypervisors are used to support virtual machines in "paravirtualization," "full virtualization," and "hardware virtualization" environments. Depending on the type of hypervisor used and the specific approach to virtualization that it takes, the source code of the operating system running in a virtual machine may need to be modified to communicate with the hypervisor. Figure 1-4 shows hypervisor-based virtual machines that leverage hardware support for virtualization, but also require a hypervisor for some types of administrative interaction with the virtual machines. For more information about hypervisor-based approaches to virtualization and some examples of virtualization software that uses this approach, see the section "Server or Machine Virtualization" earlier in this chapter. For details on any of these software packages, see the section "Other Popular Virtualization and Emulation Software" in Chapter 2.

❑ **Kernel-level:** The Linux kernel runs the virtual machines, just like any other user-space process, as shown in Figure 1-5. This type of virtualization runs virtual machines whose operating system, libraries, and utilities have been compiled for the same hardware and instruction set as the Linux kernel that is running them, which was compiled for the physical machine on which the virtual systems are running. For more information about this approach to virtualization and some examples of virtualization software that uses this approach, see the section "Server or Machine Virtualization" earlier in this chapter. For details on any of these software packages, see the section "Other Popular Virtualization and Emulation Software" earlier in this chapter.

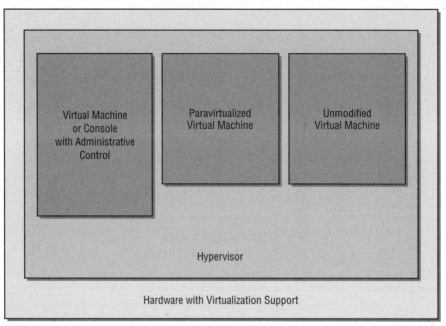

Figure 1-4

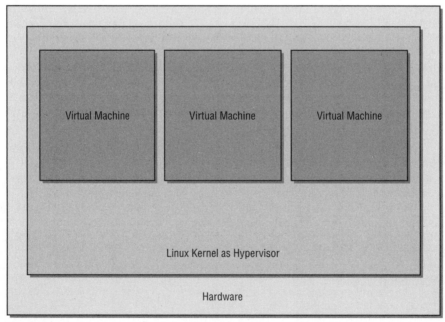

Figure 1-5

❑ **Emulation:** An emulator runs virtual machines by simulating a specific type of processor, its associated instruction set, and mandatory peripheral hardware, and can therefore run operating systems and associated software that have been compiled for processors and instruction sets other than the one used by the physical hardware on which it is running. The terms "emulation" and "server/machine virtualization" are easily confused because both of these enable multiple instances of different operating systems to run on a single host system. The key difference between the two is whether they execute virtual machines that are compiled for the native instruction set of the physical hardware on which the virtual machines are running, or those that have been compiled for some other processor and instruction set. The best-known emulation technology today is QEMU, which can emulate 32- and 64-bit x86, 32- and 64-bit Power PC, Motorola 68000, 32 and 64-bit SPARC, SH, MIPS, and ARM processors and run associated operating systems in those emulated environments. Microsoft's Virtual PC is actually an emulation environment because it emulates the PC instruction set and hardware, enabling it to boot and run x86 operating systems such as Linux and Microsoft Windows on both x86 and PPC Macintosh platforms. For more information about popular emulation software such as QEMU and Virtual PC, see the overviews of various packages provided in the section "Other Popular Virtualization Software" in Chapter 2.

Now that you have virtualization terminology firmly in hand and have explored some of the general reasons why it is such a hot topic today, it's time to look at some of the specific ways in which virtualization can be used to save time and money, simplify infrastructure, and so on.

Advantages of Virtualization

Virtualization can provide many operational and financial advantages as a key technology for both enterprise-computing and software-development environments. The following sections highlight these core advantages and discuss how they can save you time and money, and can help avoid or minimize many types of infrastructure, usage, and availability problems.

Better Use of Existing Hardware

Over the past few decades, processors have gone from 8 bits to 16 bits to 32 bits and now to 64 bits. Each of these increases in processor size has come with an associated increase in the amount of memory and the size of the storage that these processors can address and access. Similarly, processor speed and processor density continue to increase, where today's processors easily exceed 2 GHz and feature multiple processor cores per chip.

Sorry for the buzz kill, but much of that speed and processing power simply goes to waste for most computer systems. Heavily used Web servers, rendering systems, game machines, and the mainframes that are still searching for extraterrestrial intelligence may actually be using all of their processing power, but for most machines, all of that power is like doing your daily half-mile commute in a Lamborghini.

Enter virtualization. Running multiple virtual machines on your existing servers enables you to make good use of your spare processing power. Multiprocessor or multi-core systems can even run different virtual machines on different processors or CPU cores, taking full advantage of each portion of each processor that is available on your system. You can even get more use out of the devices, such as network interfaces, that are present on your existing servers by sharing them across your virtual machines.

Running multiple virtual servers on a single physical hardware system is generally known as "server consolidation." Historically, this meant hosting multiple server processes and their associated services on a single, physical system, increasing the importance of that system but heightening its potential to be a single point of failure for multiple services. Today, server consolidation means running multiple virtual machines on a single physical system. As you'll see throughout this book, server virtualization software such as Xen can help eliminate single points of failure in your IT infrastructure by providing portable virtual servers that can easily be moved from one physical host to another in the event of emerging problems, or which can quickly be restarted on other physical systems in the event of sudden, catastrophic failures.

Reduction in New Hardware Costs

The flip side of getting more mileage out of your existing servers is that, in many cases, you will not have to buy new physical hardware in order to deploy additional servers or services. As your business grows, deploying additional servers to better support the online capabilities that your users and customers require is a cost of being successful. Additional Web servers, new file servers for different groups or to handle increased load, new content management or intranet systems, and other similar systems are frequently added to enterprise environments as both the loads on existing systems and the number of users in general expands.

Combining server consolidation with capacity planning can reduce the number of new machines that you have to buy to support new and existing services by making better use of existing systems. In some cases, server consolidation may not eliminate the cost of new hardware, but it can simply reduce that cost. For example, buying additional memory or additional network interface cards for existing systems can enable you to expand their capabilities so that they can support additional virtual machines, without having to buy complete, new systems.

Reduction in IT Infrastructure Costs

The previous sections discussed how server consolidation can help you make the most of your existing hardware investments and reduce new hardware costs by enabling you to run multiple virtual servers on single hardware platforms. However, saving the cost of purchasing and deploying new servers isn't the only IT cost reduction associated with virtualization.

Machine rooms have a variety of per-machine infrastructure costs that you can reduce (or at least avoid increasing) by getting more mileage out of your existing hardware rather than adding new systems. Each new physical server uses a certain amount of power and places additional load on your cooling system. Virtual machines added to existing computer systems do not add to either of these loads, enabling you to add more servers with no increase in power and cooling requirements. Similarly, if you are able to consolidate multiple existing servers onto a lesser number of server systems, you can actually reduce your immediate power and cooling costs.

During server consolidation, you can often combine hardware from physical servers to increase the capacity of the remaining machines. For example, you can add the memory from a decommissioned system to another server that now supports multiple virtual machines. Similarly, hard drives that formerly provided local storage in decommissioned machines can be reused as spares, for backups, in RAID systems, and so on.

Depending on how many services and server processes you must support and how successful you are in terms of server consolidation, virtualization can reduce space requirements in any systems that you host in a cage at your ISP or that you collocate. It may even provide space savings if you need to move your machine room, although building or allocating space that is tied to your current space requirements is rarely a good idea in the IT space. You should always prepare for some amount of future growth, even if virtualization enables you to minimize or optimize that growth.

In addition to power, cooling, and space savings, reducing the number of physical machines that you manage can reduce remote-access and reliability costs by requiring fewer Keyboard-Video-Mouse (KVM) systems, fewer connections to uninterruptible power supplies, and so on. Depending on how you configure networking on the physical hardware that supports your virtual machines and the number of network interface cards installed in each system, you may even be able to simplify your network cabling and reduce the number of hubs and switches that are required in the machine room.

Simplified System Administration

Using virtualization to reduce the number of physical systems that you have to manage and maintain doesn't reduce the number of systems that you are responsible for. However, it does segment the systems that you are responsible for into two groups of systems: those that are associated with specific physical resources and those that are completely virtual. The physical systems that host your virtual machines are the primary example of the first group, but this group also includes virtual machines that make specific and unique use of physical resources such as additional network cards, specific local storage devices, and so on. Running multiple virtual machines on single physical systems makes the health of those systems more critical to your business functions and introduces some new software infrastructure for virtual machine migration or cloning in the event of emerging hardware problems.

Most enterprise IT groups run some sort of centralized system status or heartbeat software, enabling you to remotely monitor the status of all of your hardware without checking each console. Depending on the capabilities of the monitoring package that you are running, you may be able to create separate sections or alert levels for systems with an explicit physical dependency on local hardware, systems with a dependency on centralized storage systems, and systems that are purely virtual. In addition, many Linux sites use the network support that is built into syslog (the system message log daemon) to consolidate system logs on specific systems in order to simplify identification of emerging hardware or software problems. Because virtual machines believe that they are running on physical hardware, you will need to group hardware-related messages from virtual machines in order to be able to identify any problems in virtual/physical machine communication. Similarly, you will want to group software logs from your virtual machines, so that you can identify emerging or immediate problems in software services such as Web servers, which may be supported on multiple machines for load balancing and redundancy reasons. For more information about consolidating system and process logs, see the sections "Centralized Logging for Virtual Machines" and "Centralized Warning Systems for Virtual Machines" in Chapter 10.

Finally, virtualization may enable you to streamline or simplify other time-consuming but standard system administration tasks, such as backups. Many virtual machines use networked storage to make themselves as independent as possible of the physical system on which they are running, as well as to improve centralization in general. The use of centralized storage such as a SAN, iSCSI, ATA-over-Ethernet, or networked filesystems can reduce the number of machines and storage systems that require physical backups. Similarly, if you choose to use thin clients or "desktop virtualization" so that your users all actually log in and work on centralized servers, you will not need to back up desktop systems that only run remote desktop software and on which no local storage is used.

Increased Uptime and Faster Failure Recovery

As mentioned in the previous section, increasing the isolation of virtual machines from specific physical hardware increases system availability by increasing the portability of those virtual machines. The portability of virtual machines enables them to be migrated from one physical server to another if hardware problems arise on the first system. Xen virtual machines can be migrated from one physical host to another without any interruption in availability — the migration process is transparent to users as well as to any processes running on those virtual machines.

Adopting virtualization and a strategy for automated problem detection and virtual machine migration can lower the costs that are traditionally associated with redundancy and failover because much of the hardware that was formerly required to ensure availability by having redundant physical systems can now be provided by being able to migrate multiple virtual machines to other, suitable hardware platforms in the event of emerging problems. You can migrate virtual systems without interrupting service, and can physically increase availability during power failures by reducing the load on your uninterruptible power supplies because they are supporting fewer physical machines, enabling you to maintain the same level of system availability for a longer period.

When partitioning and deploying software and services for high availability, one key to high availability is to efficiently divide physical and virtual machines in terms of the services that they provide. For example, in a completely virtualized environment, the primary purpose of your physical machines should be to support your virtual machines; they should not provide any external software services themselves. This enables you to respond to emerging hardware problems on your physical hardware by migrating your virtual machines to other physical hardware without having to worry about any software services that are provided by the physical machines themselves (other than support for Xen, of course). For example, you do not want to both run a Web server and support virtual machines on a physical system if you can avoid it because the failure of that physical system will make the Web server unavailable even after you have successfully migrated your virtual machines to other physical hosts. In general, you want to keep your IT infrastructure as independent as possible of the physical systems on which any portion of it is currently executing.

Simplified Capacity Expansion

Virtualization solutions such as virtual machines and storage virtualization remove the hard limits that are often imposed by physical machines or local-storage solutions. Virtual machines can be moved from one physical piece of hardware to another to enable them to benefit from hardware improvements, such as more powerful CPUs, additional CPU cores, additional memory, additional or faster network cards, and so on. Similarly, storage virtualization makes it possible to transparently increase the amount of available storage and the size of existing partitions and filesystems.

Simpler Support for Legacy Systems and Applications

Virtualization is an excellent solution to the need to run legacy software. Many businesses have certain applications that they depend on, but which may no longer be available from a specific vendor or which may not yet have been upgraded so that they can run on newer operating systems or hardware. Although depending on old software that itself depends on a specific version of an operating system is problematic from a business standpoint, it still may be a business reality.

Support for legacy software and operating environments was one of the primary motivations for virtualization when it was first introduced in an operating system by IBM in the 1960s. By running operating systems within logical partitions (known as LPARs in mainframe-speak), customers could upgrade to a newer operating system and newer, more powerful hardware without losing the ability to run the existing software and associated operating system that their businesses depended on.

Using virtualization to solve legacy software problems is a simple process. It consists of installing the appropriate legacy operating system in a virtual machine, installing the legacy software, and ensuring that the legacy software functions correctly in the new environment. Installing and using legacy software that is keyed to a traditionally unique hardware platform identifier such as the MAC address of an Ethernet card is actually simplified by virtualization software such as Xen, which enables you to set the MAC address that is associated with any virtual machine. For example, the need for occasional access to software that only runs on older Microsoft Windows operating system releases can be met quite nicely by creating a virtual machine on which the old version of Windows and your target software package is installed, and using Xen's built-in VNC support to enable remote connections to the virtual machine's desktop.

Of course, addressing legacy software issues through virtualization is only possible for legacy software that runs on the same processor architecture as the virtualization software. For example, you can't support legacy software for SPARC platforms in virtualization software for x86 platforms. In this case, you may be able to use a multi-architecture emulator such as QEMU to support the legacy operating system. Similarly, you should make sure that your virtualization solution supports the older operating systems. Xen is quite flexible in this respect, but many other virtualization solutions are not.

Simplified System-Level Development

A traditional solution to kernel and driver development testing, which often requires frequent reboots to test new kernels, is to do such development in the context of traditional Linux virtual machine solutions such as User-Mode Linux (UML). Being able to restart a virtual machine to test new kernels and drivers is much faster and less of an interruption to the development process than rebooting a physical machine. This approach can also provide significant advantages for low-level debugging if you are working on a desktop system that supports virtual machines because your development environment, development system, and the virtual machine can all coexist on one desktop platform. Virtualization solutions such as Xen provide a similarly easy-to-use development environment.

> *Hypervisor-based virtualization solutions are rarely the right environment for final testing of hardware drivers because they introduce a level of indirection that affects performance to some extent, which also masks a level of access to the bare hardware that such drivers may require. However, virtualization is a great development environment for higher-level drivers and system software such as networked filesystems. Similarly, hardware drivers should be tested against hypervisor-based virtualization solutions whenever possible to verify compatibility.*

Development and testing in virtual machines is a common use of LPARs on IBM mainframes today, where developers can work with and develop for Linux distributions running in logical partitions that are physically hosted on a mainframe.

Simplified System Installation and Deployment

The previous section discussed using virtual machines as a mechanism for testing kernel or driver development efforts. Virtualization also provides a fast, flexible, and cost-effective solution for deploying new systems, depending on the speed and memory available on your server system. Using virtual machines can simplify deploying new systems by enabling you to use a single filesystem image as the basis for all new installations. To install a new system, you can simply create a new virtual machine by cloning that filesystem and starting a new instance of a virtual machine that uses the new filesystem.

The ability to host users and customers on private virtual machines can also be used to simplify infrastructure for businesses that require large numbers of systems that are often extensively customized by their users. For example, linode.com (`www.linode.com/`) uses User-Mode Linux to provide completely customizable servers to their customers. This type of virtualization enables each user to have root access to his or her machine and complete control over the machine's execution and software environments. This is a significant step up from hosting environments that simply provide operating system–level virtual hosts to their customers. The use of full virtual machines also makes it possible to offer any virtualizable operating system to such customers, rather than having to share a kernel and thus limiting customers to various flavors of Linux, BSD, and so on.

When using full virtual machines to deploy new systems, the ability to migrate virtual machines from one host to another can also prove an asset when you're using virtual machines as a system deployment mechanism. Having a development system that is independent from a specific physical hardware platform can make life simpler and more productive for developers by making it easy to migrate those systems to be hosted in faster, more powerful machines, systems with better peripherals, and so on. Of course, whether or not migration is possible depends on the configuration and specific hardware requirements of each virtual machine, but can easily be guaranteed through clever planning and good virtual system design.

Finally, desktop virtualization simplifies deploying new systems by reducing the amount of software that needs to be installed locally. Enabling users to share a common set of software that is installed on a central server system requires careful attention to licensing issues to ensure that you do not violate the terms of each software license. These types of issues can often be solved through the use of open source software, eliminating the licensing issue, or through the use of floating licenses, which are on-demand licenses that are stored in a central pool and are temporarily assigned to users as they actually use the software.

Increasing centralization of shared resources and the standardization of deployed systems can provide significant advantages for system administrators. Regardless of whether you feel that "desktop virtualization" is a bandwagon use of the term or a true example of virtualization, deploying light-weight desktop systems and using rdesktop, Microsoft's Terminal Server, or similar packages to connect to a central server simplifies per-system software installation, reduces downtime because all desktop systems are completely interchangeable, and simplifies system administration tasks such as backups by ensuring that no important, required, or personal files are stored on local disks.

Simplified System and Application Testing

Besides server consolidation and associated savings in hardware and infrastructure costs, software system test and quality assurance environments are the biggest beneficiaries of virtualization. System-test and quality-assurance groups typically need to be able to test a specific software product on many different operating systems or versions of an operating system. Server virtualization is extremely time- and cost-effective in such situations, reducing the amount of hardware required, and also reducing or eliminating much of the time required for system installation, reinstallation, and subsequent configuration.

Server virtualization makes it easy to install software products and test against many different operating systems or versions of operating systems without requiring dedicated hardware for each. By combining virtual machines with storage virtualization solutions such as logical volume management, you can eliminate the need to reinstall these test versions of an operating system in most cases by creating snapshots of pristine operating system distributions and then falling back to the snapshot for your next test run. Using a saved snapshot of a virtual machine is not only faster than reinstalling an entire virtual or physical system, but it can make reinstallation unnecessary if you can roll a virtual machine back to a pristine state via snapshots or the use of the non-persistent disks that are supported by some virtualization solutions.

An interesting use of virtualization in system testing outside the quality assurance or system test groups is using virtualization to test new releases of an operating system and associated software. As a specific example, newer versions of Microsoft Windows often expose or introduce incompatibilities with existing disk layouts, boot loaders, and so on. Testing a new operating system inside a virtual machine, as many of my friends have done with various releases of Microsoft Vista, provides a great sandbox in which to experiment with the new operating system, test and verify application compatibility, and so on, all without permanently disturbing the disks, partitions, and applications on their existing systems.

Virtualization Caveats

This books primarily focuses on the advantages of virtualization. As the previous section discussed, there are many good reasons for integrating virtualization into a computing environment. At the same time, virtualization is not a panacea for all IT woes — it is not appropriate for all scenarios, and it introduces real costs and concerns all its own. When considering integrating virtualization into your computing environment, you should take issues such as the ones discussed in the next few sections into account. Sayings like "An ounce of prevention is worth a pound of cure" and "forewarned is forearmed" aren't just fortune cookies to look for, they are as appropriate in IT management circles as they were when planning next season's crop rotations.

Single Point of Failure Problems

As discussed in the previous section, server consolidation leads to better use of your existing hardware by enabling you to use spare processing power to run multiple virtual machines on a single host. In a typical IT organization, each of these virtual machines runs a single server or set of related services, such as mail servers and associated anti-SPAM software, DNS servers, print servers, file servers, and so on.

The downside of server consolidation is that it increases the potential for the failure of a single physical machine, which hosts multiple virtual servers, to significantly impact your organization. If multiple servers and associated services are running on individual machines, the failure of a single machine has an impact on only a single server. When multiple servers are running as virtual machines on a single piece of hardware, the failure of that hardware can take down all of those servers.

The solution to this sort of problem is detailed planning. When designing a virtual machine–based IT infrastructure, it is very important to make sure that you plan for availability and failover whenever possible. Some common approaches are the following:

❏ Set up redundant hardware such as network interface cards in the host system and bond them together so that the failure of a single card is transparent to the virtual machines.

❏ Purchase and maintain duplicate hardware for the physical systems that host important virtual machines. The cost of having a spare power supply, motherboards, network interface cards, and so on sitting on a shelf is insignificant compared to the costs to your organization of having to wait until a vendor ships you replacement parts.

❏ Replicate virtual machines that host critical services across multiple physical systems so that you can survive the failure of a single physical machine and associated downtime by failing over to alternate servers.

❏ Run centralized system-monitoring software to alert you to emerging hardware and software problems before they become critical. This provides a window of opportunity for you to migrate existing virtual machines to other physical hosts, bring up new physical hosts if needed, and so on.

Centralized failures, such as power or network outages in your cage or machine room, will always be potential problems, and are not significantly different in virtualization environments. Your disaster recovery plans should already include information about how to deal with these types of problems through redundancy and collocation.

Server Sharing and Performance Issues

Planning for growth and increased demands is easy to overlook when creating any IT infrastructure. "Cost-conscious corporate computing" is a phrase that easily rolls off the tongue of bean counters, and it is important to make the case for capacity planning when specifying hardware requirements and designing any associated IT infrastructure. Capacity planning can be even more important when designing a virtualization-based IT infrastructure because the extent to which your virtual servers can handle increased loads and are portable across multiple physical host systems is largely dependent on how they are configured.

While approaches to server virtualization such as paravirtualization provide significant abstraction of the underlying hardware, you must be careful to design your virtual servers so that they are as independent of specific physical constraints as possible. For example, using local physical storage will always be relatively inflexible. The storage requirements of virtual servers can always provide a potential problem unless they, too, are abstracted from physical systems, either through the use of networked filesystems or through some storage virtualization technique. Similarly, applications that depend on the latest, greatest processor extensions may run slowly in a virtualization environment because they cannot get direct access to the hardware that they require.

In terms of capacity planning, the type of work that your users do on virtual servers can change the requirements for those virtual servers. For example, adding more users to existing virtual machines or performing more processor-intensive tasks on those systems can significantly increase the amount of memory that a virtual machine requires, as well as the amount of memory that the physical host system can allocate to it. Similarly, performing more data-intensive tasks on your virtual servers can change the storage requirements of those servers, as well as the way in which they use that storage, requiring additional storage space, changes to how and where swap and paging space is allocated, and so on.

You also need to consider software licensing issues when using virtualization to host multiple user accounts on a single server or when cloning virtual machines. If you cannot afford site-wide licenses for software that your organization depends on, the use of flexible licensing schemes such as floating licenses is critical for servers that host large numbers of users. Another possible licensing problem can be caused by software vendors who do not support their software in virtualization environments — you should check your software license to be sure.

Even areas of virtualization such as desktop virtualization are not appropriate for all users. For example, remote and laptop users will need significantly more local software installed on their systems to guarantee their ability to get work done without continuous dependencies on remote access to your centralized systems.

Per-Server Network Congestion

Most full virtual machines use virtual network interfaces, subnets, and bridging packages to map those virtual interfaces (and virtual networks) to the physical hardware. If your physical host system provides only a single network interface, running multiple virtual machines that are performing network-intensive tasks can make too many demands of your physical network hardware. This can result in network performance problems for a single host or for all hosts that are sharing the same physical network interface. One obvious solution is to install multiple network interfaces in your physical host system and assign these to specific virtual machines. Unfortunately, this type of configuration can make it more complex to migrate these virtual machines from one host to another in order to work around emerging hardware problems or general performance issues.

Increase in Networking Complexity and Debugging Time

Networking on full virtual machines uses virtual network interfaces, subnets, and bridging software to make each host appear to have a unique network interface. Using full virtual machines that each have their own network interface (virtual or physical), IP address, and so on can be more complex than managing multiple physical hosts with the same characteristics. This is not only because of the extra level of software that bridging or other approaches to virtual networking require, but also because firewalls and other network control mechanisms need to be configured to allow specific traffic in specific directions and between specific virtual hosts.

Many sites set up virtual machines on their own subnets, which require separate DHCP servers in order to manage the associated ranges of IP addresses. These subnets also simplify firewalling and routing issues because the firewall or router can easily be configured to handle the blocks of IP addresses associated with those subnets differently.

Other potential issues that you must take into consideration are possible problems such as hardware MAC (Media Access Control) address collisions. In the real world, each physical Ethernet device has a unique MAC address, but most full virtual machines can be assigned specific MAC addresses. Unless you are careful when cloning and customizing your virtual machines' configuration data, it is easy to accidentally bring up multiple hosts whose network interfaces have the same MAC address. This can cause packet routing and forwarding problems, and it is a difficult problem to identify. (A specific block of MAC addresses that should be used with Xen is discussed in Chapter 8.)

In general, the use of virtual network interfaces and virtual machines can make many network management tasks more complex unless you have spent a significant amount of time considering and working around potential problems during the planning phase of your virtual machine infrastructure.

Increased Administrative Complexity

Simplified system administration was identified earlier as a potential benefit of virtualization, but this may not always be the case if you are already using distributed system-management utilities that don't understand virtual machines. If this is the case, or if you are using multiple virtualization solutions at the same time, you should make sure that any management utilities that you already depend on (or plan to purchase) can understand virtual machines, or you'll have to restrict their use to only those systems that they can communicate with. This may not be a problem, but it's certainly a point to consider.

Identifying Candidates for Virtualization

The goal of most virtualization efforts is to consolidate multiple servers on specific physical hardware platforms. Although it is tempting to approach the question of where to start by identifying specific physical machines that you would like to eliminate, a better starting point is to consider the software that you need to support. Identifying older hardware, machines with unique or aging peripherals and storage systems, and so on is an excellent second step in your planning process, providing an excellent mechanism for cross-checking the physical hosts whose software you plan to move to virtual machines, but it is generally most effective to begin the virtualization planning process by identifying the software that you need to continue to support and its requirements.

Identifying existing software that can be moved from physical hosts to virtual machines involves a number of different factors, including hardware requirements, operating system and execution environment software requirements, the usage pattern of the software, and the load that it will place on its host system.

Collecting hardware, operating system, and execution environment data is most easily done using a checklist of some sort to ensure that you collect the same sort of data about all applications and systems that you are considering for virtualization. A spreadsheet with appropriate columns is typically the most useful framework for collecting this information, because it enables you to sort by various columns and identify software with specific physical constraints or current physical host systems that you may be able to either combine in a single virtual machine or implement in separate virtual machines that are hosted on a single piece of physical hardware that satisfies the requirements for multiple pieces of software.

The following list shows the information that you should collect for each of the applications that you are considering moving to a virtual machine. You may actually want to collect this data for all of the applications that your systems support. This will not only provide a good reference for support and licensing information, but it may also help you spot applications that are candidates for moving to virtual machines.

❏ **Application and version** — The name and specific version number of the application. Each version of an application that you must support should be listed separately because it may have specific operating system requirements, use specific hardware, and so on.

❏ **Current operating system and version** — The operating system under which the application is currently running.

❏ **Operating system patches or service packs** — Any specific patches that have been applied to the running operating system, including service packs for Windows-based applications.

❏ **Other supported operating systems** — Other operating systems and associated version numbers that this version of this application is supposed to run on.

❏ **Software execution environment** — Any auxiliary libraries or software packages that the software requires, including the version numbers. This includes software such as the Java virtual machine or GNU Java runtime; scripting environments such as Perl, awk, sed, and so on; interpreters; and auxiliary programs that the application can start communication with.

Trying to decipher shared and dynamically linked library requirements can be quite complex. On Linux systems, you can use the ldd *(list dynamic dependencies) command to identify libraries that an application requires, including the version of the system's C library that it uses (glibc, uclibc, newlib, and so on). On Microsoft Windows systems, you can use an application such as Dependency Walker, which is included with the free Process Explorer (*www.microsoft.com/technet/sysinternals/ ProcessesAndThreads/ProcessExplorer.mspx*).*

❏ **Required privileges and/or users** — Any privileges required for installation and execution, including any specific user and/or group that the software must run as.

❏ **Associated hardware and drivers** — Any hardware that is specifically associated with this version of this application, such as a specific video card, sound card, network interface card, or storage device. If this hardware required special drivers from the hardware manufacturer, you should note their source and version numbers. If the hardware uses standard system drivers, it is still a good idea to note these to ensure that they are available for and supported on any other operating system that you may want to move the application to. You should also note any video resolution requirements.

❏ **Current video resolution** — The video resolution at which the application is currently running, if appropriate. You can simply mark this field as N/A for server or command-line software.

❏ **Memory requirements** — Any specific memory requirements that are associated with the application. This should include any limits on the maximum amount of information that the server or application can use.

❏ **Memory in the current host system** — The amount of memory that is available in the system on which this version of this application is currently running. You can use this information for virtual machine memory sizing purposes if the application does not have explicit memory requirements.

❏ **Current application performance** — Your own or your users' perception of how well the application runs and performs on its current host. Although it is not an empirical measurement, you can use this information to help assess the memory and processor requirements of any virtual machine to which you consider moving this application. This can help determine if, for example, you may want to pin a virtual machine to a specific processor to minimize administrative overhead and help guarantee the responsiveness of any applications or servers that it supports.

❏ **Current licensing** — Whether the application requires a license and, if so, the type of license: per-copy, floating, node-locked (locked to a specific system based on a board identifier, network IP, or MAC address), and so on.

❏ **Virtualization licensing** — Whether the application can be used in a virtual machine environment, which may not be the case if the software license prohibits the use of the application or the operating system that it requires in a virtual machine. This should also include information about whether the use of the application in a virtual machine requires licensing changes, the purchase of additional licenses, and so on.

As you can see, it can take some time to collect and organize all of this information, but doing so will simplify the process of identifying applications that can (or cannot) be moved to a virtual machine, and any special characteristics that the virtual machine must have in order to provide a successful and robust execution environment for your applications and servers.

Summary

This chapter provides an introduction to virtualization, discussing the many ways in which the term is used, and the different approaches to each that are available. It explains why virtualization is an increasingly popular topic today, and provides an overview of the primary advantages of virtualization. It also discusses some circumstances in which virtualization may not be appropriate.

The chapter concludes with a checklist of information that you should collect for each application, server, or service that you are using, in order to help identify candidates for virtualization and to make sure that the migration process is as smooth as possible for any applications that you are moving to virtual machines.

2

Introduction to Xen

Virtualization is easily today's hottest IT buzzword, for a variety of good reasons that were discussed in Chapter 1. What's not to like about the idea of reducing costs, making better use of existing hardware resources, and viewing your commodity hardware as a pool of computing resources rather than a set of dedicated, single-purpose machines? This doesn't mean that you can drag out a bunch of aging servers, make a deal with the devil, and suddenly transmute them into a state-of-the-art computing facility. The hardware on which you base your virtualization solution must be sufficiently powerful to run multiple operating systems and server instances simultaneously. Similarly, you must choose virtualization software that supports the way in which you want to use virtualization and provides the power to use virtualization effectively.

This chapter provides a detailed introduction to Xen, discussing its history, terminology, and capabilities, and also identifies the best resources for the latest information about Xen and virtualization on the Internet. It concludes by providing an overview of current virtualization and emulation solutions other than Xen. This "competitive" information shouldn't shake your faith in Xen as the best virtualization technology today, but is instead intended to help you make sense of the zillions of available and emerging virtualization technologies. Not all virtualization solutions are orthogonal — some are quite complementary. If you are currently in the planning phases of your virtualization environment, this chapter should help you make informed decisions as it covers different commercial and open source approaches to virtualization and the advantages and disadvantages of each.

History of Xen

The United Kingdom has a long and proud history of creativity and technical innovation in the field of computing. Anyone with a sense of the history of modern computing will recognize innovations such as the Electronic Delay Storage Automatic Computer (EDSAC), the Lyons Electronic Office (LEO) computers, the Cambridge Ring and Distributed Computing System, the SERC Common Base Platform and associated popularization of workstations, and many more. (These are just some of my personal favorites.) Luckily for all of us, these innovations continue.

Chapter 2: Introduction to Xen

Over the years, the Engineering and Physical Sciences Research Council of the UK (UK-EPSRC) has funded and helped drive the adoption of many innovations in engineering and the physical sciences, one of which is a project at the University of Cambridge known as the XenoServers project (`www.xenoservers.net`). The XenoServers project is led by Ian Pratt, a Senior Lecturer at the University of Cambridge Computer Laboratory, Fellow of King's College Cambridge, and a leader of the Systems Research Group at the University of Cambridge.

The aim of the XenoServers project is to develop a powerful, flexible infrastructure for global distributed computing. A key element of the XenoServers project is the ability to enable single machines to run different, or multiple, operating system instances and their associated applications in isolated, protected environments. These operating system instances can then separately account for resource use and provide unique system accounting and auditing information. This could make actual, commercial deployment of a global distributed computing environment feasible by providing a huge pool of computing resources along with mechanisms for requesting specific sets of resources and for charging users for the resources that they actually use from that pool.

The flexibility to support and run different operating systems, perhaps concurrently, is a core concept for enabling physical hardware to truly collaborate in a global computing environment. The Xen virtual machine monitor (`www.cl.cam.ac.uk/research/srg/netos/xen/`) was originally developed to support this capability for the XenoServers project. Xen provides the resource management, accounting and auditing capabilities, and operating system independence required by each node in the XenoServer pool.

Xen was first described in the University of Cambridge Computer Laboratory Technical Report 553, which wasn't exactly found on newsstands everywhere (`www.cl.cam.ac.uk/TechReports/UCAM-CL-TR-553.pdf`, by Paul Barham, Boris Dragovic, Keir Fraser, Steven Hand, Timothy Harris, Alex Ho, Evangelos Kotsovinos, Anil Madhavapeddy, Rolf Neugebauer, Ian Pratt, and Andrew Warfield). The first widely available paper on the Xen research efforts is "Xen and the Art of Virtualization," a paper presented at the ACM Symposium on Operating System Principles (SOSP) in 2003 (`www.cl.cam.ac.uk/~kaf24/papers/2003-xensosp.pdf`, by Paul Barham, Boris Dragovic, Keir Fraser, Steven Hand, Timothy Harris, Alex Ho, Rolf Neugebauer, Ian Pratt, and Andrew Warfield). The first public release of Xen (1.0) was in October 2003.

By enabling significant research into techniques for virtualizing physical CPU, memory, disk, and network resources, Xen quickly took on a life of its own, independent of the successes or requirements of the XenoServers project. In 2005, Ian Pratt, Simon Crosby (a former faculty member at the University of Cambridge and a Xen evangelist), and others founded XenSource, Inc. (`www.xensource.com`) to further the open source Xen community, and to sell and support enterprise solutions based on Xen technology. XenSource and its products are discussed later in this chapter.

Today, Xen is in use in thousands of commercial and research environments, and is commercially supported by XenSource and a number of other firms. Aside from the commercial firms that sell and support Xen-based solutions, Xen is used commercially as a powerful, cost-effective solution to control and manage in-house IT infrastructure and related costs, and as an enabling technology for a variety of ISPs and similar service providers, where Xen simplifies providing privileged access to per-customer virtual servers.

Overview of Xen and x86 Virtualization

The holy grails of virtualization on commodity hardware are:

❑   To be able to execute multiple virtual machines (VMs) on a single piece of hardware in isolation from one another so that each one can support its own sets of processes; uniquely address, access, and lock system resources; and be independently managed and administered.

❑   To enable multiple virtual machines to run on a single piece of physical hardware, sharing access to and managing resources on that physical hardware with no degradation in performance over a single machine running a single, dedicated instance of an operating system.

❑   To enable unmodified operating systems to run as virtual machines on a host system.

❑   To be able to centrally administer isolated virtual machines within the context of a physical machine or an IT infrastructure, enabling the administrator to dynamically reallocate resources or even relocate the virtual machines from one host to another with no interruption in service.

All user-space processes on UNIX-like operating systems execute relative to a root directory, which is the directory that represents the top-level of their filesystems. The simplest approach to isolating different sets of processes from each other is to execute different sets of processes relative to their own root directories. This is done using a system call and related wrapper program known as chroot, which can be executed by the root user only. A chroot call affects the execution environment of the current process and all subsequent child processes. Once you have executed a chroot call, all libraries, temporary directories, device nodes, system privilege and configuration files, and so on must be available relative to the directory that you chrooted into. This is the virtual server approach introduced by FreeBSD jails and is the basic approach behind the operating system–level virtualization products discussed later in this chapter.

If done correctly, the chroot approach provides a simple way of isolating and managing separate sets of hierarchical processes, but all chrooted systems still share a single kernel and associated set of physical resources. Although different chrooted systems cannot see others' processes, all chrooted systems on a single machine are being managed as sets of processes by the host system's kernel. Although you can adjust the individual priorities of these processes, there is no elegant way to associate specific resources with them.

Once the benefits of the chroot approach have been exhausted, a common technique is to retrofit performance isolation into the operating system that is hosting the virtual servers. This is the approach taken by many virtual server offerings such as FreeVPS, Linux-VServer, OpenVZ, Virtuozzo, Solaris Containers and Zones, and so on.

All of the solutions discussed so far in this section are UNIX-only and single-kernel solutions. Being UNIX-only solutions means that all of these require UNIX/Linux/BSD system calls, filesystems, process data structures, and so on. Being single-kernel solutions means that a single operating system kernel is managing all requests to/from the virtual machines and arbitrating between them. Both of these facts prevent you from running other operating systems in your virtual machines for two basic reasons: only native UNIX/Linux/BSD processes can execute natively on a UNIX/Linux/BSD kernel, and running multiple, complete operating systems at the same time on commodity x86 hardware would quickly fail due to conflicts in the privilege modes at which various operating system instructions must execute.

X86 Protection Levels: One Ring to Rule Them All

Processors typically run in different protection modes to prevent against unauthorized access to the physical processor and device resources. The original x86 processors featured a single mode of operation, known as real mode. As more sophisticated capabilities, such as additional memory addressing and management capabilities, were added to the 32-bit x86 instruction set, various modes of operation were defined for the processor. These differentiate between the types of resource access that are required versus those that are allowed but not required by various types of processes. The best known of these are:

- ❑ **Real mode:** A process has direct access to all aspects of the hardware, but is limited to the memory addressing capabilities of an 8088 processor: a whopping 1MB of RAM.

- ❑ **System management mode (SMM):** A 16-bit mode that provides direct, short-term access to hardware resources for internal system-maintenance purposes.

- ❑ **Protected mode:** Multiple protection levels, known as rings, are supported in order to differentiate between the types of memory and general hardware access required by an operating system and by higher-level applications. In protected mode, modern Intel x86 and compatible processors support four protection levels, known as rings, which are numbered 0 through 3 in the best C programming language tradition.

Other modes also exist, such as unreal mode, virtual real mode (aka virtual 8086 mode), and long mode, but they aren't relevant here. This section offers a high-level introduction to implications of the different rings provided by protected mode, and discusses the type of code that runs in each ring and its hardware- and memory-access capabilities. For more information than most people would ever want to know about working in protected mode, search Sandpile.org (www.sandpile.org) or see the incredibly detailed document "Working in the Protected Mode Environment" by T.R. Prashant, which is available at http://members.tripod.com/protected_mode/prashant/protmode.html.

In standard operating system environments, the operating system kernel runs in ring 0 and can thus execute all privileged instructions, manage memory, and directly specify the range of memory addresses available to an operating system. The ability to manage memory beyond the physical addressing capabilities of a 32-bit x86 processor through the use of memory segments was one of the primary motivations for protected mode. Ring 0 is typically referred to as "supervisor mode" or "kernel mode" because it controls all direct hardware and memory access. Applications and server processes typically run in ring 3, known as "user mode." Rings 1 and 2 are typically unused in vanilla operating system environments, except by the 14 Luddites who are still running IBM's OS/2.

Internally, protection-level checks are triggered whenever a new code segment is loaded. The code that is executing when a processor enters protected mode has a current privilege level (CPL) of 0, and therefore runs in ring 0. Each code segment that is subsequently loaded has a two-bit descriptor privilege level (DPL) that identifies the privilege level of that segment. One code segment can never load another that has a DPL with more privileges than the CPL. Clear as mud? An easy way to remember this is to say that the current protection level must always be less than or equal to the protection level of any new code segment that it loads. Trying to violate this rule raises a machine exception that punts the offending segment. Code running in ring 0 is responsible for assigning the protection levels of each code segment. An excellent source of detailed information about protection levels, code and data segment isolation, and so on is a series of articles by Jean Gareau for *Embedded Systems Programming* magazine, the most relevant section of which is available at www.embedded.com/98/9805fe2.htm.

In order to mediate hardware access between virtual machines, Xen runs its hypervisor in ring 0, while patched kernels run in higher, less-privileged rings. (Applications still run in ring 3.) On 32-bit hardware, the patched Xen kernels run in ring 1, while on 64-bit systems, the patched kernels run in ring 3 along with applications because it isn't possible to protect ring 0 from processes running in ring 1. The fact that Xen runs in a higher ring than "supervisor mode" operating system code is the origin of the term "hypervisor."

See the section "Xen Domains and the Hypervisor" later in this chapter for more detailed information about how the Xen hypervisor interacts with the Linux kernel in different ways to provide an Uber-kernel that provides virtual hardware resources to other operating Linux kernels and operating systems that are running on top of the Xen hypervisor.

X86 Protection Levels and Virtualization

The previous section provided a quick overview of the protection and privilege levels in which certain instructions execute on commodity x86 hardware. The classic problem with some privileged x86 instructions is that they do not trap when they are executed with insufficient privileges, typically failing without complaining, dooming subsequent instructions to executing in the wrong mode or in some unknown state. Guest-OS solutions, such as VMware Workstation, Parallels Workstation, and VirtualBox, enable you to run unmodified operating system instances simultaneously because the application environment in which the virtual machines is running constantly monitors the instructions that the virtual machines are attempting to execute, and rewrites privileged instructions that would otherwise fail, replacing them with local implementations that either trap or simply do the right thing.

While Guest-OS virtualization packages are excellent desktop solutions when you need to run multiple, unmodified x86 operating systems on a single physical system, the downside is fairly obvious. Guest OS virtualization solutions require that the system must be running a complete operating system itself. Both the virtualization application and each unmodified operating system running within it must contend with the primary operating system and with each other for resources. Finally, examining the instruction stream from each virtual operating system and rewriting it when necessary requires significant processing power.

An alternate, higher-performance approach to virtualization that supports running multiple, different operating systems on a single physical machine is to boot a small Virtual machine monitor on your hardware rather than a higher-level, more resource-intensive operating system. The monitor runs directly on your hardware, manages all low-level resource allocation for the VMs, and provides interfaces that higher-level administrative applications can hook into to perform various administrative tasks. Virtual machine monitors are often referred to as hypervisors because they effectively execute with more privileges than the x86 supervisor code in a higher-level operating system. This is the approach taken by virtualization solutions such as VMware ESX Server and Xen. The hypervisor used by VMware ESX Server performs the same sort of instruction-stream monitoring and management performed by VMware's Workstation product, but provides substantially higher performance because it is running at a much lower level that is much closer to the hardware and contends with no higher-level processes.

On the other hand, the hypervisor used by Xen is very different. When running on hardware that does not provide hardware support for virtualization, the Xen hypervisor requires that the virtual machines running on top of its hypervisor use a customized version of the operating system. These customized versions have been modified to avoid privileged instructions by using an abstract hardware model that differs from the specific hardware that is available on the physical machine, and which can therefore execute at a lower privilege level than the hypervisor. The hypervisor handles memory management, CPU exception handlers, system calls, hardware interrupts, timers, and all direct device I/O. This approach to virtualization is known as "paravirtualization" because modifications to an operating system are required in order to handle privileged operations by communicating with the hypervisor or a less-privileged, administrative Xen-modified kernel.

The operating system changes required for interaction with the hypervisor do not change the kernel's higher-level Application Binary Interface (ABI), and thus the kernel (and kernel-level code such as device drivers) are the only things that require modification for paravirtualization. This also means that no changes to user applications are required in order to run applications in a virtualized environment, which is one of the key aspects of a successfully virtualized environment.

Xen Domains and the Hypervisor

The previous sections introduced common Xen terms such as "hypervisor" and "paravirtualization," but Xen wouldn't be much of a modern computer product if it didn't come with additional jargon that is either specific to Xen or has specific meaning in the Xen environment. The most significant term you'll encounter in Xen literature is the idea of a "Xen domain," which is a specific instance of a Xen virtual machine running on a specific physical piece of hardware. Xen supports two basic types of domains, with different uses and capabilities.

As discussed in the previous section, Xen manages access to memory and hardware resources through a combination of its hypervisor and a specially privileged Xen-modified kernel that is used to manage, monitor, and administer all other Xen virtual machines running on a specific physical piece of hardware. This specially privileged Xen kernel is known as domain0 (or domain-O, or dom0 to its friends). The domain0 kernel and the Linux system that runs on it hosts a Xen daemon (/usr/sbin/xend, written in the Python programming and scripting language) and administrative software that uses the Xen daemon to communicate with the hypervisor. Out of the box, Xen provides a command-line administrative application, known as xm (for Xen Management), in which you can initiate commands to create, connect to, and shut down other domains, and control the amount of memory that is allocated to a domain, associated scheduling parameters, and so on.

The domains started by a domain0 system are known as guest domains, unprivileged domains, or simply domainU domains. When a domain0 system creates, connects to, modifies, or terminates any domainU domain, it uses a configuration file that provides detailed information about the guest domain, such as the physical memory that is initially allocated to that domain, the access that the guest domain had to physical disks and network devices on the domain0 system, how networking is configured on the guest domain, any graphical support that you can use to connect to the console of the guest domain, and so on. Xen domain configuration files are introduced in the first section of Chapter 5 and are explored in complete detail in Appendix B.

When Xen was first released, the kernels used by domain0 and domainU systems had to be compiled with different kernel configuration options in order to differentiate between them. This is no longer the case: a standard Xen kernel can detect whether it is being loaded by the hypervisor or through a domain0 system, and behaves accordingly.

Interacting with the Hypervisor

One of the goals of Xen has always been to separate implementation requirements from policy decisions, leaving administrative and configuration options to the domain0 system rather than hardwiring them into the hypervisor. This is a significant factor in the power and popularity of Xen. Low-level CPU and memory allocation and management is done by the hypervisor because this is a physical requirement for running multiple virtual machines on a single physical system. Similarly, the hypervisor is responsible for creating, managing, and deleting the virtual network interfaces and virtual block devices associated with each guest domain, because each of these contains access-control information that is a requirement for successfully running distinct virtual machines on a single physical hardware platform without violating their separate control and data policies.

Domains use a special type of synchronous call, known as a hypercall, which functions as a software trap to request privileged operations in the hypervisor, much like a traditional system call. Responses from the hypervisor are returned asynchronously via an event mechanism because the hypervisor may be servicing hypercalls from multiple domains at any given time. These events work much like traditional UNIX signals, supporting both the notification of data-related events such as completed I/O or incoming network data, and high-level administrative notification of things like system termination or migration requests.

Controlling Hypervisor Scheduling

A scheduler is the portion of an operating system that determines which processes are available for execution and which should run, in which order. In the case of a hypervisor scheduler, the scheduler determines which virtual machines should get physical CPU and system resources, which physical CPUs they should be associated with, and in which order. The configuration files for Xen domains provide a mechanism for binding one or more CPUs to specific Xen domains in order to guarantee available processing power for Xen domains that are running heavily used services. In addition, the Xen hypervisor supports a standard API for the schedulers that it uses internally to load-balance and service requests from multiple domains. The Xen hypervisor comes with multiple schedulers that you can select from by specifying the name of a specific scheduler as a command-line option to the hypervisor boot option in the configuration file for your bootloader. If you are using the GRUB bootloader, this configuration file is the file `/boot/grub/menu.lst`. Modifying these boot options is discussed in detail in Chapter 4, in the section "Configuring GRUB for Xen." This section summarizes the different types of schedulers that are relevant to the Xen hypervisor and the command-line options that are available to invoke them.

A scheduler can be specified using the `sched=name` option on the boot command line for the Xen hypervisor, where `name` identifies the scheduler that you want to use. Xen 3.*x* supports the following schedulers:

- ❑ **sedf:** Simple Earliest Deadline First scheduler, which supports weighted CPU sharing and uses a priority queue to analyze requests from different domains to try to guarantee responsiveness. You can set parameters for this scheduler from the xm command line using the `xm sched-sedf` command (or through other Xen management tools) by identifying the domain you want to set a policy for, followed by five parameters:

  - ❑ `period`: The maximum scheduling period in nanoseconds.

  - ❑ `slice`: The time slice that should be associated with each request in nanoseconds.

❑   `hint`: An optional scaling value for the period if heavy I/O is in progress.

❑   `extra`: A flag indicating whether a domain can extend the time slice.

❑   `weight`: The relative weight of the virtual CPU for the specified domain.

❑ **credit:** A proportional fair share scheduler that dynamically adjusts CPU and domain priority by measuring use. You can set parameters for this scheduler from the xm command line using the `xm sched-credit` command (or through other Xen management tools) by identifying the domain you want to set a policy for, followed by two parameters:

❑   `weight`: The relative priority of a specified domain. Possible values range from 1 to 65535; the default is 256.

❑   `cap`: The maximum of a CPU that a domain will be able to consume, even if the host system has idle CPU cycles. The cap is expressed as a percentage of one physical CPU. More than one CPU can be specified by using values greater than 100. A value of 0 implies no limit.

Previous versions of Xen supported other hypervisor schedulers such as bvt (Borrowed Virtual Time) and rrobin (Round Robin), but these are in the process of being removed from the Xen code base.

Advanced Topics in Operating System Schedulers

Beyond the scheduler used by Xen's hypervisor, each virtual machine implements its own scheduling policy for processes running within that domain and to service I/O requests within its kernel. In the 2.6 Linux kernel, available process scheduling types are:

❑   **SCHED_FIFO:** First In First Out, where processes are left in their current position in the run queue when they are serviced, enabling the process to use the CPU for as long as it needs to, or until a higher-priority real-time process becomes runnable.

❑   **SCHED_RR:** Round Robin, where processes are move to the end of the run queue after servicing, enabling fair sharing of the CPU between all runnable processes.

❑   **SCHED_NORMAL:** Conventional time-sharing scheduling, known to POSIX fans as SCHED_OTHER.

❑   **SCHED_BATCH:** For batch jobs that are assumed to be CPU-intensive but generally lower priority than interactive processes.

These can be explicitly set for specific processes by using the `sched_setscheduler()` system call in the domain where the specified process is running. If you need to change the priority of a running process and find that standard system commands such as `renice()` don't suffice, it's easy enough to write a little wrapper program to change the scheduler used by a running process rather than modifying an application's source code to do this.

In addition to process scheduling, 2.6 and greater Linux kernels also provide an I/O scheduler that is associated with each storage device on your system. Because the Xen hypervisor handles the actual I/O for your virtual machines, you may not see a great benefit from tweaking per-machine I/O parameters, but it's certainly worth a try if you are experiencing performance problems.

The I/O schedulers that are available for a Linux virtual machine, and the one that is currently selected for a specific block device, are identified in the file /sys/block/device-name/queue/scheduler, where device-name is the base name of a storage device, such as sda, hda, and so on. The available I/O schedulers on Linux systems are noop (simply attempts to merge scheduled requests to minimize I/O), anticipatory (merges requests and also returns to user space after each read, pausing for a few milliseconds in hopes of a subsequent read request to a proximate location on the specified device), deadline (imposes a timed deadline on all requests and prioritizes reads over writes), and cfq (divides the bandwidth of a block device evenly among the processes performing I/O to that device). If you display this file, the name of the currently active I/O scheduling for the specified device is surrounded by square brackets.

You can also change the I/O scheduler associated with a specific device as seen by a domain by writing the name of the scheduler that you want to use to this file, as in the following example, which changes the scheduler to anticipatory for the device hdc:

```
echo "anticipatory" > /sys/block/hdc/queue/scheduler
```

When changing I/O scheduling policies for RAID devices, you must set the same policy on all of the physical drives in the array.

Depending on the disk usage patterns of the applications running in your domains, you may want to experiment with different I/O schedulers, which will change the way in which I/O is requested through the Xen hypervisor. You can do this globally by using the elevator=value option on your VM's Linux kernel command line, setting the value to as, cfq, deadline, or noop.

Some Linux distributions (such as Debian) enable you to specify default I/O scheduling policies for different devices at boot-time, through the file /etc/sysfs.conf.

If you are using the cfq I/O scheduler, you can manually set real-time I/O scheduling policies for specific processes by using the ionice command that is provided by many Linux distributions.

Types of Virtual Machines Supported by Xen

Because of its popularity, flexibility, power, and open source licensing model, Xen is a fast-moving, constantly evolving software package. Combined with similar evolution in the capabilities of commodity x86 processors and related hardware, the state of Xen (and the state of x86 virtualization in general) is a hard thing to pin down. A fairly safe rule is "Things will always get better."

A good example of this is the extent to which Xen can support both 32-bit and 64-bit virtual machines of different types on a single system. Until hardware support for virtualization was added into processors with the Intel VT (Virtualization Technology) and AMD SVM (AMD Secure Virtual Machine) capabilities, you could only run 32-bit Xen domainU domains on a physical host that was also running a 32-bit Xen hypervisor and domain0. Luckily, this is changing, but there are still a number of kernel-level concerns that you must take into account when designing your Xen infrastructure and, especially, inter-machine considerations such as domain migration and failover.

Paravirtualized Systems

As mentioned in the section "Overview of Xen and x86 Virtualization," Xen traditionally uses paravirtualization in its virtual machines because of the performance and administrative advantages that it provides. Paravirtualization means that the guest operating system is modified so that it can interface with the hypervisor and that privileged operations that the operating system would perform in protection ring 0 are translated into hypercalls to the hypervisor. The hypervisor is responsible for direct access to the physical host's hardware, for managing the memory allocated to and used by each domain, and for managing virtual-disk and network access from all guest domains including domain0, Xen's specially privileged administrative domain.

As we are all painfully aware, x86 and compatible systems have been hobbled for years by problems related to memory-access models. Even on Linux systems running the 2.6 Linux kernel, the kernel can generally access only 4GB of main memory, and applications are generally limited to much less. To resolve this problem, Intel introduced a set of Physical Address Extensions (known as PAE) that enable modern systems to access up to 64GB of main memory by viewing physical memory as up to 16 4GB ranges. Both the kernel and applications must be specially compiled to be able to use this memory model, but doing so makes relatively huge amounts of memory available to the system and to applications, improving performance, capacity, and scalability in general.

When running Xen domains on physical hardware that does not provide hardware support for virtualization, all of the kernels for all of those domains must use the same memory model and the same instruction size. For example, if the hypervisor and paravirtualized domain0 kernel that you booted are 64-bit, all other kernels running on that machine must also be 64-bit. If the hypervisor and paravirtualized domain0 kernel that you booted are 32-bit and support the PAE memory extensions, all other kernels running on that machine must also be 32-bit PAE kernels.

This changes drastically if your system is using a processor that has hardware support for virtualization, such as processors with Intel VT and AMD SVM support. These processors enable you to run unmodified guest operating systems, and also extend the types of paravirtualized domains that you can run on your hardware, as described in the next section.

Unmodified Guest Systems

If your system is using a processor that has hardware support for virtualization, such as the Intel VT and AMD SVM processors, you can run unmodified operating systems as virtual machines under domain0. Hardware support for virtualization enables you to run Windows as a domain on a Xen host, and it also means that you can use a vanilla Linux installation disk and install a standard Linux distribution as a virtual machine, without modification. At the time of this writing, processors that provide hardware support for virtualization are the following:

❑ **Intel VT (Virtualization Technology, aka Vanderpool):** Selected Pentium 4 and Pentium D, Xeon 5000 and later, Xeon LV, Core Duo, Core 2 Duo, and Core 2 Quad processors

❑ **AMD-V/SVM (Virtualization/Secure Virtual Machine, aka Pacifica):** Selected Athlon, Opteron, and Turion Socket F and AM2 processors

To determine whether the processor in a given system supports virtualization, you can check the `flags` entry in the file `/proc/cpuinfo`, which looks something like the following:

```
# cat /proc/cpuinfo | grep flags
flags : fpu tsc msr pae mce cx8 apic mtrr mca cmov \
pat pse36 clflush dts acpi mmx fxsr sse sse2 ss ht tm \
syscall lm constant_tsc pni monitor ds_cpl est cid cx16 xtpr
```

If you are using an Intel CPU, you would look for the field vms in the `flags` field. If you are using an AMD CPU, you would look for the field vmx in the `flags` field.

Beyond whether your CPU supports hardware virtualization in the first place, the ultimate arbiter of the general types of operating systems that you can run on a specific Xen domain0 host is the file `/sys/hypervisor/properties/capabilities`. Entries in the `/sys` filesystem provide hardware and system-level information about the state of your Linux system. You can use the standard `cat` command to view the contents of this file, as in the following example from a 64-bit Intel-VT system:

```
# cat /sys/hypervisor/properties/capabilities
xen-3.0-x86_64 hvm-3.0-x86_32 hvm-3.0-x86_32p hvm-3.0-x86_64
```

The contents of the file say that this system can run paravirtualized 64-bit domains (xen-3.0-x86_64), unmodified 32-bit operating systems as hardware virtual machine (hvm-3.0-x86_32), paravirtualized 32-bit domains as hardware virtual machines (hvm-3.0-x86_32p), and unmodified 64-bit operating systems as hardware virtual machines (hvm-3.0-x86_64).

A good general rule is that systems with hardware support for virtualization that are running Xen are generally backward compatible. In other words, a Xen system with more capabilities can generally run a Linux kernel with the same or lesser capabilities. A 32-bit Xen kernel with PAE support can run a Linux kernel without PAE in a hardware virtual machine. A 64-bit Xen system can run any 32-bit Linux kernel in a hardware virtual machine. And so on.

Combining 32-Bit and 64-Bit Kernels, Filesystems, and Applications

Given that both the hypervisor and the domain0 kernel are responsible for managing memory allocation and use by other domains, it's not surprising that you would encounter conflicts when trying to combine paravirtualized 32-bit and 64-bit domains running on a single physical host system. Actually, the problem is not related to whether the filesystem and applications are 32-bit or 64-bit, but is instead specific to the kernel. You can use a 32-bit filesystem with a paravirtualized 64-bit Xen kernel without any problems, as long as any 64-bit loadable kernel modules that it needs can be located in the root filesystem. (Of course, the kernel will usually still run without them, but specific peripherals, internal hardware, and related subsystems will probably not be usable.) You can also manually build 32-bit kernels for use with paravirtualized VMs on a 64-bit system, but this requires significant extra effort and maintenance time.

Similarly, 64-bit Linux kernels can generally run specific 32-bit applications from a 64-bit machine, assuming that the application is statically linked or that it uses shared libraries and that the 32-bit compatibility libraries have been installed on your 64-bit system. Most x86_64 Linux systems today follow the Filesystem Hierarchy Standard (FHS) to some extent, which dictates that 32-bit libraries are installed in `/usr/lib` and that 64-bit libraries are installed in `/usr/lib64`.

Popular Xen and Virtualization Resources on the Internet

A tremendous amount of data about Xen, use cases, success stories, problem reports, and so on, is available on the Internet today. However, the amount of useful and accurate information about Xen on the Internet is much smaller. Xen is evolving so rapidly that you have to be careful to be sure that any information that you locate applies to the version of Xen that you are using. Xen 2.*x* was very different than Xen 3.*x*, and many internals, such as available schedulers and tuning parameters, have changed. Even the contents of Xen configuration files have changed over time, with certain keywords no longer being supported.

All-in-all, the best sources for up-to-date information about Xen on the Internet are the following:

❏ **Xen Wiki:** An open, editable wiki found at `http://wiki.xensource.com/xenwiki`. This wiki contains a tremendous amount of information, some of which is up-to-date. It is the best place to find information about supported and suggested processors that support virtualization, supported and suggested motherboards for use with those processors and Xen, and a huge amount of HOWTO and technical information.

❏ **Open source Xen mailing lists:** Community mailing lists that you can sign up for at `http://lists.xensource.com`. This site provides access to multiple mailing lists that you can either subscribe to or simply browse or search the list archives. These include lists with focus areas such as standard Xen users (xen-users), the Xen developer community (xen-devel), developers of open source tools for Xen (xen-tools), and developers focused on Xen security (xense-devel). Of these, the xen-users mailing list is probably the most useful for most people. As with most mailing lists, you can subscribe to these lists in batch mode, so that you only receive summary digests of recent posts. A real-time subscription to these mailing lists, where you receive every message as it is sent, would probably be quite overwhelming.

❏ **XenSource customer forums:** Mailing lists specific to the commercial Xen products offered by XenSource, but which are still open to the public. You can register for these at `http://forums.xensource.com` or simply browse their contents, although it would be wrong to pose questions here unless you are a XenSource customer. Again, these forums are specific to Xen from XenSource, but they often contain relevant information for open source Xen users.

❏ **Distribution-specific Xen information:** Linux distributions such as Fedora and Novell/SUSE, which are both active proponents of Xen, provide a variety of Xen-related resources. Fedora provides a Fedora-Xen page and associated mailing list, which you can subscribe to at `www.redhat.com/mailman/listinfo/fedora-xen`. Novell provides a Project Xen Technical Preview page at `http://forge.novell.com/modules/xfmod/project/?xenpreview` that contains information about their latest Xen patches and general links to Novell's Xen documentation and other sites. Ubuntu users should check out the Xen Virtual Machine section of the Ubuntu wiki, at `https://help.ubuntu.com/community/XenVirtualMachine`.

If you are just generally interested in virtualization and would like to obtain additional information, there are many sites that provide general-purpose information on virtualization on commodity hardware. Some of my favorites are the following:

❏ **IBM developerWorks, "Virtual Linux" (**`www-128.ibm.com/developerworks/linux/library/l-linuxvirt`**):** This is a great article to begin with if you are interested in general information about virtualization on Linux systems. IBM's developerWorks always provides a huge amount of detailed, technically accurate information. The "Virtual Linux" article provides a good overview and explanation of virtualization on Linux, along with links to many other sites.

❏ **Linux Virtualization Wiki (**`http://virt.kernelnewbies.org`**):** A nice site that provides a good overview of virtualization on Linux and more detailed discussions of various Linux virtualization technologies. It also provides a good introduction to various tools that are available for managing Xen virtual machines, and a good overview of the Xen (and other) virtualization support that is available in various x86 Linux distributions (and in other operating systems, such as OpenSolaris).

❏ **OpenVirtualization.com (**`http://openvirtualization.com`**):** This site, sponsored by Red Hat, is a good source for general information about open source approaches to virtualization.

❏ **SearchServerVirtualization.com (**`http://searchservervirtualization`
`.techtarget.com/`**):** A great TechTarget site that provides a tremendous amount of information about server virtualization, related storage virtualization topics, and so on. One of the advantages of this site is that many vendors make white papers and commercial announcements available there, which makes the site quite useful for keeping track of the pulse of commercial virtualization offerings.

❏ **TheFreeCountry.com (**`www.thefreecountry.com/emulators/index.shtml`**):** A nice summary of free emulation and virtualization software for Intel x86-based (and compatible) machines. This is a great resource, but remember that free does not necessarily mean open source.

❏ **x86 Virtualization Blog (**`http://x86virtualization.com`**):** An interesting blog with some good technical insights. This site provides some good general information about topics such as using networks with virtual machines, desktop and enterprise virtualization, and so on. Unfortunately, Xen often seems to get short shrift here compared to VMware, Parallels, and SWsoft.

❏ **Wikipedia (**`www.wikipedia.com`**):** Big surprise here. Wikipedia has extensive articles about Xen (`http://en.wikipedia.org/wiki/Xen`), virtualization in general (`http://en.wikipedia.org/wiki/Virtualization`), emulation (`http://en.wikipedia`
`.org/wiki/Emulation`), and most of the other terms and players in today's virtualization market. A great source of information, as always. (And Stephen Colbert loves virtualization at Wikipedia!)

Other Popular Virtualization Software

This section provides an overview of most of the other approaches to virtualization that are available on x86 Linux systems today. I can hear you all protesting, "Who cares? We're Xen fans!" — and so am I. Regardless, it is useful to have some idea of the alternatives that are available and their technical approach to virtualization. I find Xen to be the most useful virtualization technology for Linux, by far, but I used other virtualization solutions long before Xen was available. I have also worked in mixed environments, where certain technologies were hosted on different virtualization platforms for cost, support, or legacy reasons.

Each virtualization technology for Linux has its own approach and technical merits — and knowing more about the alternatives will help you be sure that Xen is the right technical solution for you. Although I've tried to be fair, this section provides more information about some of the pure virtualization packages than it does about operating system–level virtualization products because I believe that lower-level virtualization products are more interesting, especially in environments that require the simultaneous use of multiple operating systems, which operating system–level virtualization products do not support, by definition.

FreeVPS

FreeVPS is one of the original operating system–level virtualization solutions for Linux, along with the Linux-VServer project. FreeVPS provides a variety of improvements in system accounting, networking, and a variety of other administrative enhancements. FreeVPS provides complete isolation of the filesystem and processes running on each virtual server, and per-server constraints for resources such as network load, disk space, and memory consumption. FreeVPS also provides separate administrative capabilities for each virtual server as well as more general administrative tasks such as backups and monitoring that can be done across multiple or all virtual servers.

Like other operating system–level virtualization solutions, the primary drawback of FreeVPS is that it limits you to running a single instance of a single Linux kernel, providing both a constraint and a potential single point of failure.

For more information about FreeVPS, see:

❑ **FreeVPS Home Page (**`www.freevps.com`**):** The primary site for information about FreeVPS, the latest downloads, and so on.

❑ **FreeVPS Partner Sites (**`www.freevps.com/partners.html`**):** Links to a number of vendors that are partnering with the FreeVPS project or whose products utilize and extend FreeVPS. Although this is somewhat spare, this is the place to look for FreeVPS fans, partners, and add-ons.

❑ **Wikipedia (**`http://en.wikipedia.org/wiki/FreeVPS`**):** A good summary of general information about FreeVPS.

Kernel Virtual Machine

Many Linux devotees were surprised when Linux Torvalds accepted patches that incorporated a largely unknown virtualization technology called the Kernel-based Virtual Machine (KVM) from a largely unknown company (`www.qumranet.com/`) that is still in stealth mode. I certainly was. These patches were incorporated into the 2.6.20 release of the mainline Linux kernel. However surprising its appearance was, there are good precedents for an in-kernel virtualization technology such as KVM, most notably User-Mode Linux (UML), which is discussed later in this chapter, in the section "User-Mode Linux." Like UML, KVM supports the creation and execution of virtual Linux systems running as a separate process on a Linux system. Unlike UML, KVM requires that the physical host system use a processor that supports Intel Virtualization Technology (VT) or AMD Secure Virtual Machine (SVM/AMD-V). These are the same processors that are required for running unmodified guest-OS systems as Xen, which were discussed earlier in this chapter in the section "Unmodified Guest Systems."

One of the primary reasons for the inclusion of KVM into the mainline kernel (aside from a clean implementation) was the fact that KVM does not require a hypervisor, and therefore is a pure Linux solution, whereas Linux is still the operating system that is running on the bare metal. Internally, KVM works through a device node called /dev/kvm, which is created and managed by CPU-specific loadable kernel modules, intel_kvm.ko and amd_kvm.ko, one of which is loaded as kvm.ko. Opening this device creates a new virtual machine, which can then be managed through ioctl() calls that perform operations such as creating a virtual CPU, allocating memory, intercepting privileged calls, and so on. KVM also requires a user-space application (based on QEMU, which is discussed later in this chapter) to view and interact with each virtual machine.

KVM currently supports Linux virtual machines (x86 and x86_64) and Windows virtual machines. Only 32-bit x86 Windows virtual machines are supported at the moment, although work on 64-bit Windows virtual machines is in progress.

The primary benefit of KVM is the fact that, unlike Xen, it requires no modification to the Linux kernel. However, it therefore does not provide the performance benefits of paravirtualized Linux systems, but is able to take advantage of standard Linux features such as the Linux scheduler rather than the various schedulers that are built into Xen (discussed earlier in this chapter in the section "Controlling Hypervisor Scheduling").

For more information about KVM, see:

❑ **Qumranet's KVM wiki (**http://kvm.qumranet.com/kvmwiki**):** Provides overview information, documentation, and HOWTOs for using KVM on various Linux distributions.

❑ **KVM development mailing list (**kvm-devel@lists.sourceforge.net**):** This list provides up-to-date information about the latest KVM patches and general development efforts. You can subscribe to this list at https://lists.sourceforge.net/lists/listinfo/kvm-devel. This site also provides a great location for viewing the archive of posts to this mailing list.

Linux-VServer

Linux-VServer is the original operating system–level virtualization solution for Linux, predating the FreeVPS project. Linux-VServer provides complete isolation of the filesystem and processes running on each virtual server, and per-server constraints for resources such as network load, disk space, and memory consumption. Linux-VServer also provides separate administrative capabilities for each virtual server. File and directory resources can be shared across virtual servers using specially implemented hard links that can be created with special tools called vunify and vhashify, which also simplify identifying commonly-used files and directories.

> Note that the Linux-VServer project is completely distinct from the Linux Virtual Server project (www.linuxvirtualserver.org), which is a cluster-based Linux solution that provides a single-server interface backed by a load-balancing cluster of physical Linux servers. The Linux Virtual Server project is not a virtualization solution, and is therefore not discussed in this book.

Like other operating system–level virtualization solutions, the primary drawback of Linux-VServer is that it limits you to running a single instance of a single Linux kernel, providing both a constraint and a potential single point of failure.

For more information about Linux-VServer, see:

❑ **Sourceforge project site (**`http://linux-vserver.org`**):** The current location for all up-to-date Linux-VServer patches, documentation, and general information. This site also offers FAQs that provide a great selection of information about how (and why) to get started using Linux-VServer.

❑ **Jacques Gélinas Web site (**`www.solucorp.qc.ca/miscprj/s_context.hc`**):** Jacques was the original author of Linux-VServer, and his site still provides a good deal of general information about getting started with and using Linux-VServer.

❑ **VServer mailing list (**`vserver@list.linux-vserver.org`**):** A mailing list where you can ask questions and interact with other Linux-VServer users. You can view posts to this list at `http://list.linux-vserver.org/archive/vserver`.

❑ **IRC (**`irc.oftc.net`**, channel** `#vserver`**):** An IRC channel for Linux-VServer users, which can be useful in answering questions about installation, configuration, and usage problems.

Microsoft Virtual Server

Microsoft Virtual Server is a virtualization solution that enables you to create and run virtual machines on 32-bit versions of the Windows XP and Windows Server 2003 operating systems. Microsoft Virtual Server was originally developed by Connectix and was quickly acquired by Microsoft. Microsoft Virtual Server is currently free from Microsoft.

I personally can't think of a sillier approach to virtualization than running virtual Linux systems on a Windows system, but your mileage may vary. I don't see any value in running a virtual Jaguar on your Hyundai, but Microsoft Virtual Server is clearly the right choice in enterprise environments that mandate the use of the Windows operating system but when you still wish to take advantage of the power of Linux and associated open source infrastructure software such as the Apache Web server.

Work on the next generation of Microsoft virtualization technologies, code-named Viridian, is actively underway. Interestingly enough, Microsoft is supposedly partnering with Xen (via XenSource) on this effort. Similarly, Microsoft is working with Xen-focused Linux distributions such as Novell (`www.novell.com/linux/microsoft/`) to develop Xen-based solutions for its virtualization technologies.

For more information about Microsoft Virtual Server, see:

❑ **Microsoft Virtual Server page (**`www.microsoft.com/windowsserversystem/ virtualserver/default.mspx`**):** Microsoft's home page for their virtual server product; includes a link to the downloadable version of the most current release.

❑ **Microsoft Virtual Server download (**`www.microsoft.com/windowsserversystem/ virtualserver/software/default.mspx`**):** Free download page for Virtual Server 2005 R2 Enterprise Edition.

❑ **Wikipedia** (http://en.wikipedia.org/wiki/Microsoft_Virtual_Server): A nice summary of general information about Microsoft Virtual Server.

OpenVZ/Virtuozzo

OpenVZ (http://openvz.org) and Virtuozzo (www.swsoft.com/en/products/virtuozzo) are, respectively, the open source and commercial versions of an operating system–level virtualization software package. As discussed in the section "What Is Virtualization?" in Chapter 1, virtualization at the operating system level can provide significant performance improvements over other approaches to virtualization, largely because a single kernel is running on the machine and managing all of the virtual servers on a single physical host. This reduces the memory consumption by each virtual server, and streamlines and optimizes I/O within the virtual servers, because the same kernel is controlling device and resource access. For the same reasons, a single-kernel approach also simplifies resource allocation for different virtual servers, making it easy to associate specific CPUs, memory, and disk space with specific virtual servers. A single-kernel approach also simplifies changing those allocations as needed while virtual servers are running, without needing to "restart" them. For example, the number of CPUs associated with a virtual machine is constrained only by the kernel, not by artificial, implementation-specific constraints such as those that you find in virtualization products such as VMware, Microsoft Virtual Server, and so on. Similarly, the single-kernel approach to virtualization provides many opportunities for optimization. For example, the kernel cache is shared between all virtual servers, and application code and libraries can be shared in memory. This enables OpenVZ and Virtuozzo to efficiently support a large number of virtual servers on a single physical host.

Using an operating system–level virtualization package means that all of your virtual servers must be running Linux, because OpenVZ and Virtuozzo both require the use of a custom Linux kernel that provides the virtualization layer required to differentiate between, support, and manage each virtual machine. However, this does not mean that you are limited to running the same Linux distribution in each of your virtual servers. Operating system–level virtualization products leverage the separation between the kernel and a Linux root filesystem, which contains the runtime and user-space portions of what most people think of as Linux. This enables you to run different Linux distributions in each of your virtual servers, if you so desire. Depending on application and library requirements, different virtual servers can have completely independent filesystems, or can share applications, libraries, and so on, in order to reduce overall system requirements. Different virtual servers can even have separate disk quotas as long as separate disk partitions or volumes are used to hold server-specific sets of files. Operating system–level virtualization solutions such as OpenVZ and Virtuozzo may reduce your overall software licensing costs because applications and the root filesystem can be shared between different virtual servers. As you might expect, the terms of software licenses relating to virtual servers differ for each software package and operating system distribution. For commercial deployments, you may need to lift up a rock or poke some rotting wood with a stick in order to find a lawyer who can verify the terms of your current software and operating system licenses.

To simplify creating unique virtual servers with different runtime characteristics and sets of applications, both OpenVZ and Virtuozzo provide a number of Linux distribution templates, which are sets of packages from different Linux distributions that you can use to quickly populate a filesystem or directory structure that is specific to a virtual server.

OpenVZ provides basic management utilities for resource allocation and management between different virtual servers. As you might expect, the commercial Virtuozzo solution from SWSoft provides a significant number of additional management capabilities that simplify server provisioning, recovery, migration, and so on.

For more information about OpenVZ, see:

❑ **OpenVZ wiki** (`http://wiki.openvz.org/`): a nice site that provides a significant amount of getting started and HOWTO information.

❑ **OpenVZ online documentation** (`http://openvz.org/documentation`): Complete, online versions of all OpenVX documentation.

❑ **OpenVZ FAQs** (`http://openvz.org/documentation/faq`): Frequently asked questions and, more important, answers to them.

For more information about Virtuozzo, see the SWSoft Web site (`www.swsoft.com`).

Parallels Workstation

Parallels (`www.parallels.com`) is a guest-OS virtualization package that runs on 32-bit Linux, Microsoft Windows, and Apple Mac OS X systems. (Support for 64-bit systems has been coming for quite some time.) Introduced in 2005, Parallels quickly became popular as a low-cost commercial alternative to competing products such as VMware Workstation. When Apple switched from PowerPC to Intel processors, Parallels was the first virtualization product available for the Mac, gaining many customers who still needed access to Windows applications but didn't want the hassle and delays inherent in dual-booting via Apple's Boot Camp. VMware's Fusion product, a version of VMware workstation for Mac OS X, recently became available, and it remains to be seen how the virtualization market will shake out on the Mac platform. Parallels is actually owned by SWSoft, Inc., the vendors of the enterprise-level operating system–level virtualization product, Virtuozzo, and its open source version, OpenVZ. (These were discussed in the previous section.)

Cost concerns aside, Parallels is a fast and powerful guest-OS virtualization environment, much like VMware Workstation, VirtualBox, and the Microsoft Virtual PC products from an administrative interface point of view. Figure 2-1 shows the standard Parallels Workstation interface displaying configuration information about a Linux virtual machine.

Parallels uses a number of kernel modules to interface directly with your system's hardware and to efficiently allocate and schedule resource access. Parallels uses the combination of a hypervisor (loaded as a kernel module), other kernel modules for network and general hardware management, and support for hardware virtualization instructions in selected processors to provide a high-performance desktop virtualization environment that can easily run out-of-the-box operating systems. One of its nicest features for desktop users is its clipboard support, which makes it easy to cut and paste between applications running on your desktop operating system and in a virtual machine. Similarly, Parallels' Coherence mode enables you to run applications from a virtual machine side-by-side with applications running on your desktop operating system. Parallels also offers a convenient online update mechanism, enabling you to download and integrate updates as they are available from Parallels.

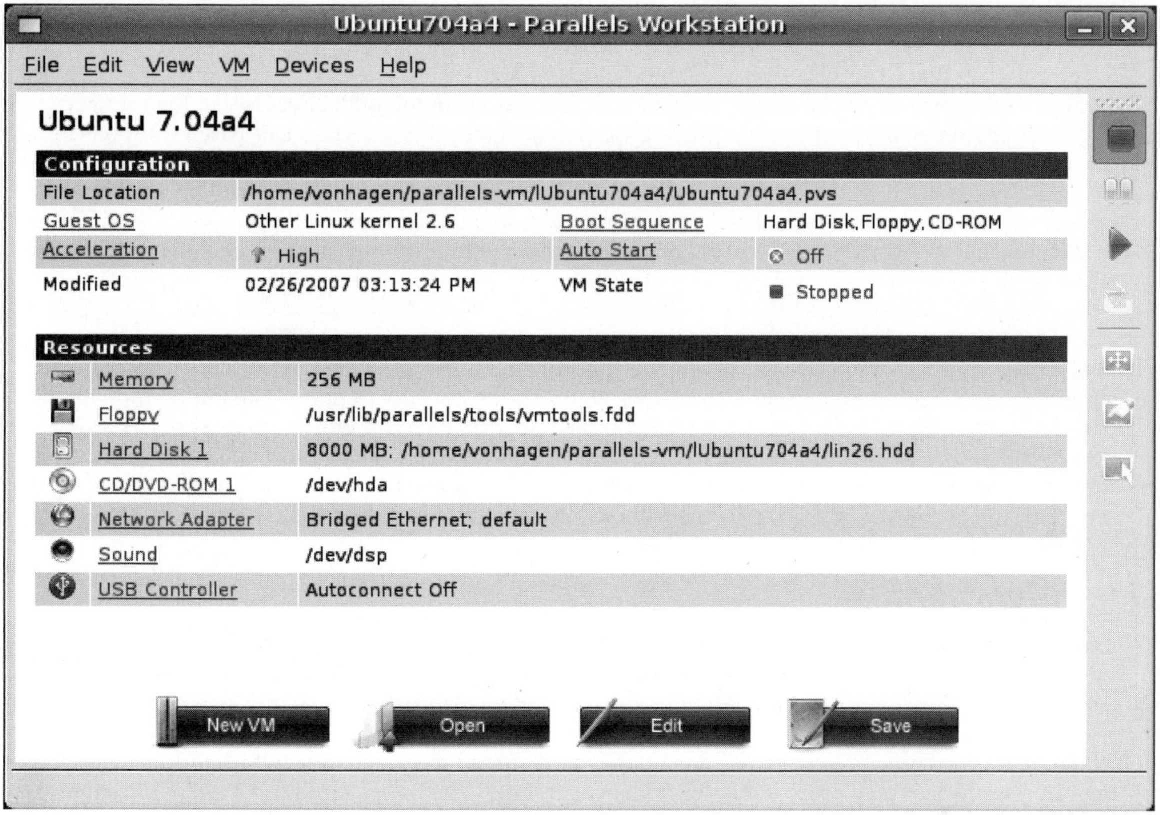

Figure 2-1

As a relatively young solution, Parallels has some growing to do before it can function as an enterprise-level virtualization solution. For example, Parallels does not currently support binding virtual machines to specific cores or virtual CPUs, forcing all virtual machines to share a pool of virtual CPUs as needed. It does not provide easy snapshot support, which therefore precludes rollback to known machine states. Support for some devices, such as DVD/CD burners, is not completely transparent, and support for USB 1.1 devices can be problematic in releases through their 2.2 series. Finally, Parallels' networking support is more restrictive than many of its competitors, supporting only bridged and host-only networking rather than the complete subnet or Network Address Translation (NAT) solutions offered by competitors such as VMware.

Work on a server version of the Parallels products is actively underway. For more information about Parallels' products, go to www.parallels.com.

paravirt ops

Beyond the fact that hypervisor-based solutions such as Xen are not pure Linux virtualization solutions because the hypervisor runs on the bare metal and Linux runs on top of the hypervisor, the primary implementation details that have prevented the wholesale adoption of hypervisor-based solutions into the mainline Linux kernel revolve around the fact that different solutions require different kernel changes. The goal of the paravirt_ops project, while not a virtualization solution itself, is to rectify this problem by developing a standard set of paravirtualization interfaces for the Linux kernel. Vendors such as VMware and Xen can then use a standard set of interfaces to communicate between their hypervisors and a vanilla Linux kernel, which would make everyone happy and allow many virtualization technologies to compete on their own merits.

This project is an important one to call out and follow to get a glimpse of future directions for hypervisor-based solutions such as Xen and VMware. The best source of up-to-date information on the paravirt_ops project is its mailing list, which you can subscribe to or browse at `https://lists.osdl .org/mailman/listinfo/virtualization`. You can also get up-to-date information about the project from the Web site of its leader, Rusty Russell, at `http://ozlabs.org/~rusty`. Rusty has developed a prototype hypervisor, `lguest`, that uses the hooks provided by the paravirt_ops project.

User-Mode Linux

User-mode Linux (UML) provides a safe, secure way of running and testing Linux systems by running a virtual Linux system as a subprocess on an existing Linux system. UML has been a part of the mainline kernel since 2002, when it was merged into a development version of the 2.6 kernel (2.5.34).

Virtual machines running under UML are independent of the Linux system on which they are running, but can execute only on a processor with similar capabilities. The filesystems used by a UML virtual machine are typically contained in a single filesystem image, but you can provide access to shared filesystems through technologies such as the Network File System (NFS). One of the most interesting aspects of UML is that its notion of the hardware on which it is running can be completely different than that of the physical hardware on which it is running. This makes UML a fascinating (and popular) environment for kernel-level development and testing. UML is also used to support virtual Linux servers by a variety of ISPs, most notably linode.com (`www.linode.com`). UML is used as a primary testing environment by many well-known open source projects.

For more information about UML, see the following:

❑ **UML project home page** (`http://user-mode-linux.sourceforge.net`): Provides a vast amount of information about implementing and using UML.

❑ *User Mode Linux* (`www.phptr.com/bookstore/product.asp?isbn=0131865056&rl=1`): A fantastic book on UML by the primary author of UML itself, Jeff Dike. This book is well-written and provides detailed discussions of using UML in a variety of ways. It is well-worth buying for insights into virtualization, even if UML isn't your primary focus.

Virtual Iron

Virtual Iron (www.virtualiron.com) is a virtualization and virtual infrastructure–management firm whose offerings are based on Xen. While not really an "other" virtualization technology (since it is indeed based on Xen virtualization), I'm discussing Virtual Iron here because it is an alternative to the open source version of Xen that this book focuses on.

Like XenSource (discussed later in this chapter), the Virtual Iron folks are focused on delivering commercial, supported Xen-based virtualization solutions and related tools. Virtual Iron focuses on more than just Xen by delivering compatible, integrated storage–virtualization solutions that include things like iSCSI support. Virtual Iron also delivers a policy-driven, virtual infrastructure–management platform, which addresses one of the key issues in implementing an enterprise-wide virtualization solution — how to efficiently manage, track, and evaluate your virtualization infrastructure.

For more information about Virtual Iron, see the following:

❑   **Virtual Iron home page** (www.virtualiron.com): The entry point for a variety of business and technical information about Virtual Iron.

❑   **Virtual Iron Resource Center** (www.virtualiron.com/products/Resource_Center.cfm): Provides white papers and customer case studies.

❑   **Virtual Iron download site** (www.virtualiron.com/products/Free_Download.cfm): You can download a free version of Virtual Iron for personal use or a 30-day free trial of their Enterprise solution.

VirtualBox

VirtualBox (www.virtualbox.org) is an open-source guest-OS virtualization package that runs on and hosts 32-bit Linux and Microsoft Windows systems. A version of VirtualBox that will run on and support 64-bit machines is actively under development, but was not officially released at the time that this book was written.

Although VirtualBox is open source, its development is hosted, sponsored, and commercially supported by InnoTek Systemberatung GmbH (www.innotek.de/), a software company based in Stuttgart, Germany, with offices elsewhere in Germany as well as in the Russian Federation. VirtualBox leverages the open source QEMU emulator, as do other open source Linux virtualization packages.

VirtualBox comes in both commercial and Open Source Edition (OSE) releases. Precompiled commercial binaries are free for personal use or for evaluation purposes according to the terms of the VirtualBox Personal Use and Evaluation License (PUEL), while OSE sources and binaries are freely available under the terms of the GPL. (See www.virtualbox.org/wiki/Downloads for details.) You can also get the latest VirtualBox source code from their Subversion source code repository, using a command like the following:

```
svn co http://virtualbox.org/svn/vbox/trunk vbox
```

VirtualBox provides both command-line and graphical tools for creating, administering, and managing virtual machines. Its graphical administrative environment is much like those provided by tools such as Parallels Workstation, VMware Workstation and Server, and even Microsoft's Virtual PC, enabling you to create and customize virtual machine configurations. The graphical administrative interface for VirtualBox is shown in Figure 2-2.

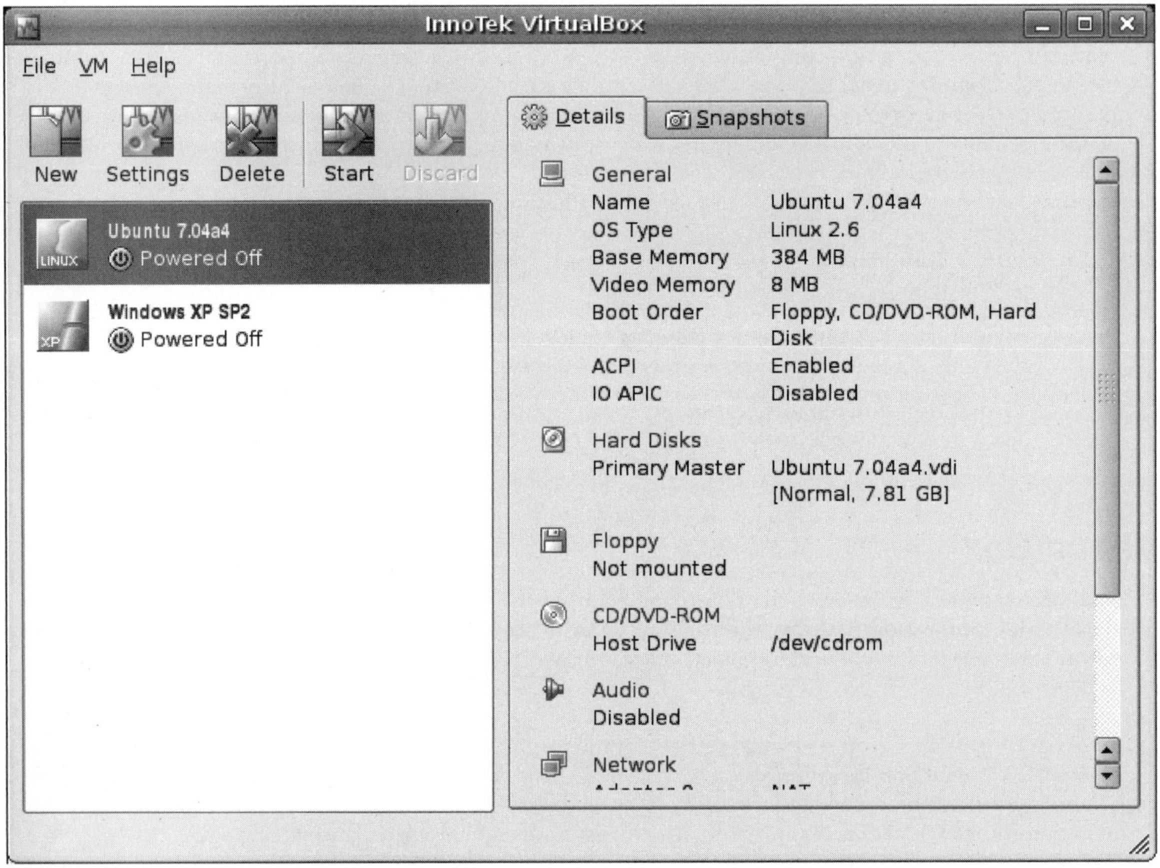

Figure 2-2

The emulation and display environment used by VirtualBox is very similar to that used by VMware Workstation and Parallels Workstation, although the key to release the cursor from being captured is different (and configurable). Internally, VirtualBox uses a kernel module called vboxdrv to communicate with and manage virtual machines and associated resources through the VirtualBox device node /dev/vboxdrv. This node must be publicly writable, or all users who want to run VirtualBox must be members of the `vboxusers` group. (The latter is the default mechanism.) VirtualBox includes a built-in DHCP server and NAT support, to simplify connectivity between multiple machines, whether physical or virtual, while also making it possible to segregate and manage virtual machine network traffic.

VirtualBox is stable and quite responsive, and includes a number of nice features. One of these is the ability to specify the amount of video memory through a slider, which makes it possible to run more graphics-intense applications inside VirtualBox. Another is its built-in support for VirtualBox Remote Desktop Protocol (RDP), which enables you to use a standard RDP client to connect to virtual machines running inside VirtualBox (analogous to VMware's support for remote connections and administration). VirtualBox also supports virtual channels between local devices and RDP-connected virtual machines, enabling you to connect USB devices locally but attach them to remote virtual machines. VirtualBox also supports a nice snapshot feature, which makes it easy to capture the state of a virtual machine at any point, for easy rollback.

For detailed information and documentation about VirtualBox, see the VirtualBox project site at `www.virtualbox.org`.

VMware

VMware (`www.vmware.com`) is the 800-lb gorilla of virtualization on commodity hardware, pioneering the field and providing an excellent, usable, and reliable guest-OS virtualization product for Linux and Windows desktop systems since the late 1990s. I've owned VMware Workstation since version 1-point-something in 1999 (it was a long time ago), have used their server products off and on for years, and have nothing but good things to say about their product line. Their release of VMware Player and Server as free software (not to be confused with open source software) was both a boon to zillions of SOHO (Small Office, Home Office), SMB (Small and Medium Business), and other acronym users, and a clever marketing move. If only more commercial software entities would see the benefits of this type of approach, the universe would be a better place. Figure 2-3 shows the administrative interface for VMware Workstation. Figure 2-4 shows the administrative interface for the free version of VMware Server.

> This little paean to VMware does not diminish my belief that Xen is the best virtualization solution around, as I would hope that this book indicates. Open source is "the right thing." The move towards support for paravirtualization solutions such as Xen in the mainline Linux kernel, thanks to the paravirt_ops project, just makes Xen a more attractive and more supportable virtualization solution (as described in detail elsewhere in this chapter and throughout this book.)

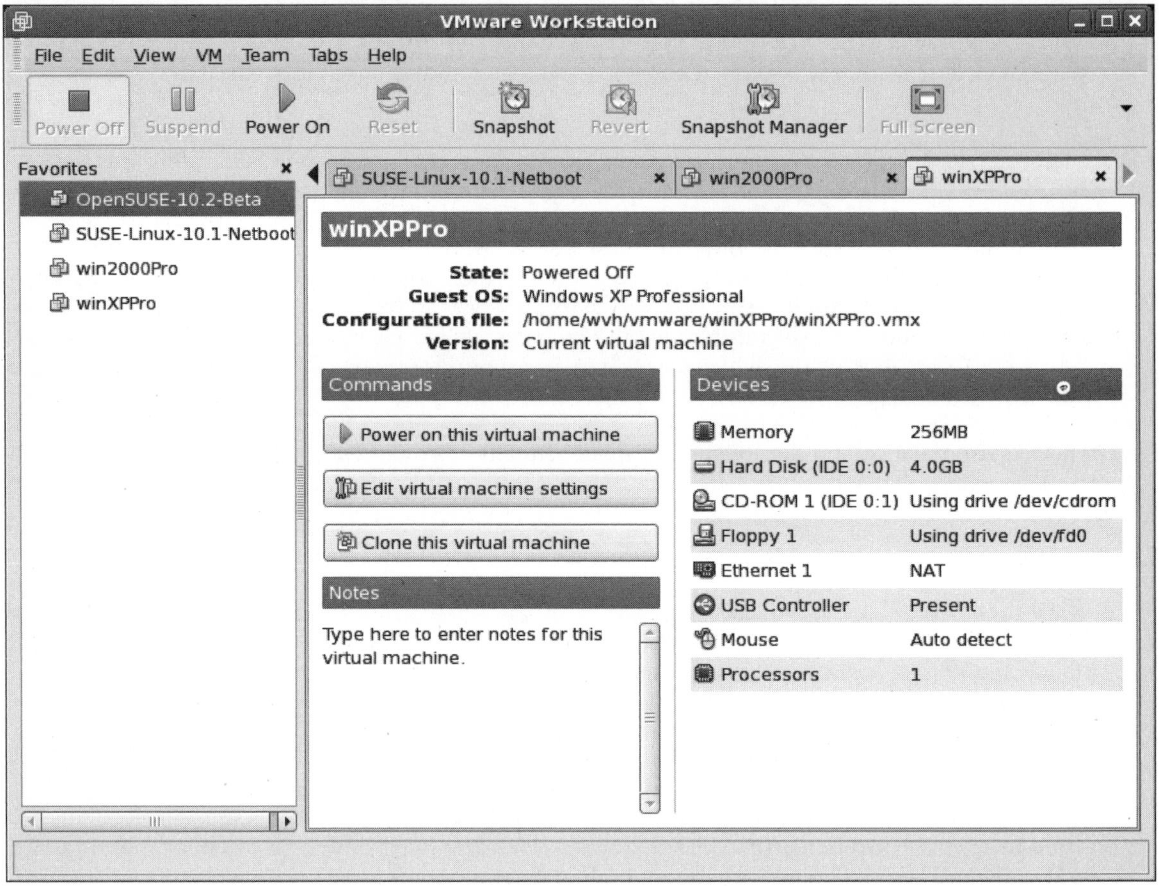

Figure 2-3

VMware has an extensive product line that is knee-deep in marketing language, different performance and support levels, and different permutations of management tools — which is only slightly less complex than a map of the human genome. Without flowcharting the entire thing, it can be conceptually organized as follows:

❑ **Data Center optimization and management products:** Enterprise virtualization and management applications, including VMware Infrastructure 3, a suite of server, management, and optimization software; VMware ESX Server, their core server-level virtualization product, and VMware VirtualCenter, a sophisticated management tool.

❑ **Development and test products:** Virtualization and management applications for desktop systems, including VMware Workstation and VMware Lab Manager, which simplify using VMware in a testing and QA role.

❑ **Enterprise desktop products:** Virtual desktop solutions that provide secure provisioning of desktop systems and data security via virtual machines, as well as more traditional virtual desktop solutions, including VMware ACE (Assured Computing Environment) and VMware Virtual Desktop Infrastructure (VDI).

❑ **Accelerator products:** The VMware Converter utility, which simplifies migrating physical operating system installations to virtual machines (known as Physical-to-Virtual, or P2V, migration), and the conversion of other virtual machine image formats to VMware's image format.

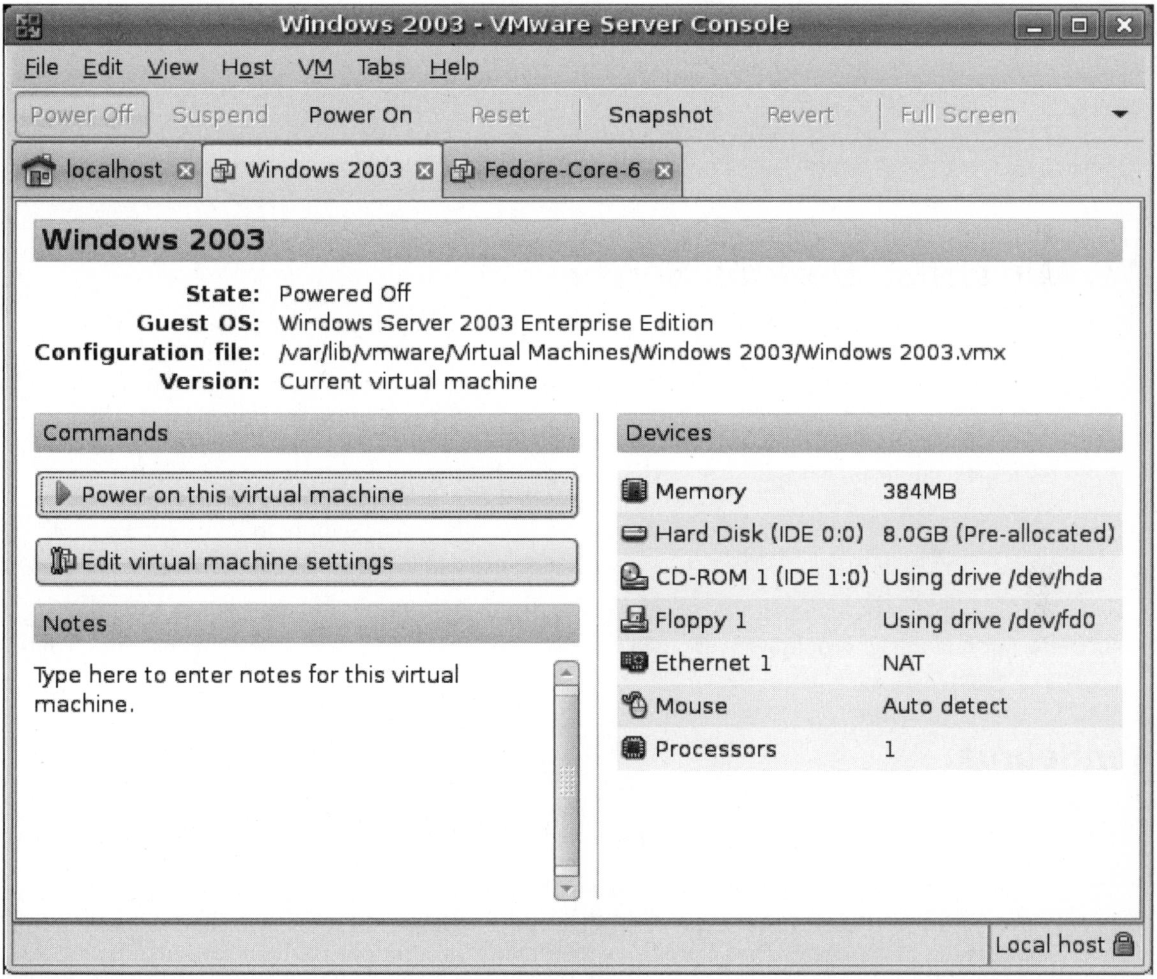

Figure 2-4

Product placement aside, VMware's virtualization products fall into two groups: guest-OS workstation and server products. Both support the installation and execution of unmodified x86-based operating systems, including *BSD, all Linux distributions, all flavors of Microsoft Windows, all x86 Solaris implementations, and even hacked versions of Mac OS X (which are not legal at the moment). The VMware Workstation product supports on-demand execution of various virtual machines, although you can run multiple VMs at the same time. The free and ESX Server products feature automatic VM execution at boot time and some nice remote access and remote management utilities, although the standard free version is more of a guest-OS solution than the high-performance, bare-metal virtualization environment that ESX provides. All VMware virtualization products feature an integrated hypervisor that provides an abstract view of your hardware, which the guest operating systems can leverage without requiring any modifications. VMware's virtualization products can execute unprivileged operating system code natively, which provides intrinsic performance improvements and good opportunities for code sharing between virtual machines, where possible.

Internally, VMware's Workstation and free server products use loadable kernel modules to interface between virtual machines and your physical hardware. They also include a DHCP server and NAT setup that simplifies network administration and segmentation for your virtual machines.

As you might expect, the best source for detailed information about VMware's current products and packaging is the VMware Web site at `www.vmware.com`. For additional information about VMware internals, see `www.vmware.com/interfaces`.

Win4Lin Virtual Desktop Server

Win4Lin (`www.win4lin.com`) delivers a Linux-based solution that provides remote access to Microsoft Windows 2003 and XP virtual machines. It does not deliver or support Linux virtual machines, but provides an interesting solution for Linux environments whose sole virtualization requirement is to satisfy users who still need occasional access to Microsoft Windows systems for some reason. The Win4Lin solution requires the use of a customized Linux kernel, and uses a significant amount of code from the QEMU emulator, which is discussed later in this chapter.

Despite its name, the Win4Lin virtual desktop server product is available for both Linux and FreeBSD systems (where it is known as Win4BSD).

For more information about Win4Lin, see the Win4Lin home page (`www.win4lin.com`), which contains all of the information you could want about Win4Lin and its approach to virtualization, including white papers, customer cases, and so on.

XenSource

XenSource (`www.xensource.com`) was founded by many of the original project members of the Xen project at the University of Cambridge, and is devoted to developing and supporting the use of Xen as a virtualization solution. Although it's not really an "other" virtualization technology (since it is, indeed, Xen virtualization), I'm discussing XenSource here because it is an alternative to the open source version of Xen that this book focuses on. XenSource actively supports and participates in the open source Xen project, and it provides three basic products: XenEnterprise, a supported, high-capacity Xen implementation for enterprise deployments; XenServer, an inexpensive ($99.00) server product designed for SMBs, and which supports up to eight servers on a single physical host; and XenExpress, a free product that supports up to four servers on a single physical host.

In late 2007, XenSource was purchased by Citrix. Citrix has historically specialized in tools that simplify remote access to Microsoft Windows systems, including terminal servers. Xen is a natural extension of this, although at a much lower level. Citrix's purchase of XenSource, the official sponsors of the Xen project, should mean nothing but good things for Xen. Xen is open source, and it has will always been in

Citrix's best interests to promote Xen and its hypervisor technology. The XenSource folks deserve some compensation for their efforts, but the commercial integration of their software will be a good thing for all Xen-related companies.

For more detailed information about XenSource and its products, see www.xensource.com.

Popular Emulation Software

The terms "emulation" and "virtualization" are easily confused because both of these enable multiple instances of different operating systems to run on a single host system. These terms actually describe two very different approaches to running virtual machines. Virtualization technologies typically run software that is compiled for the native instruction set of the physical hardware on which the virtual machines are running, whereas emulation technologies typically emulate an entire physical execution environment, including the processor and hardware subsystems. You can then run different operating systems and related applications that are compiled for that specific type of hardware within the emulated hardware environment.

The best-known emulation package for most systems is probably the Multi-Arcade Machine Emulator (MAME, at www.mame.net), which enables you to play a variety of ancient video games directly from images of their ROMs. On the other hand, the most useful emulation technology in Linux circles is QEMU, which can emulate many different hardware platforms and associated hardware, and which is discussed in detail later in this chapter because open source virtualization packages such as Xen and KVM make heavy use of some of the code from QEMU to avoid reinventing the wheel regarding console emulation, graphics emulation, and so on.

A huge number of emulators are available today, especially on Linux, where many people want to revisit the software glories of their youth (or at least the systems that they ran on). Rather than trying to coax a 20-year-old personal computer from a defunct vendor back to life, writing an emulator can be entertaining, is useful to others who are also interested in that hardware, and provides a fun technical challenge. A quick search for "Linux Emulators" using Clusty (www.clusty.com) or Google (www.google.com) returns hundreds of results. Two especially nice summary pages are Zophar's page of Unix/Linux Emulators at www.zophar.net/unix/unix.phtml, and the Using Linux summary at www.usinglinux.org/emulators/.

This section focuses on emulators that are relevant to virtualization, specifically QEMU and Microsoft's Virtual PC. The latter may be surprising because, as the name suggests, many people view Virtual PC as a virtualization package, rather than the emulation environment that it actually is. Microsoft's Virtual PC is actually an emulation environment because it emulates the PC instruction set and hardware, enabling it to run on both x86 and Macintosh hardware and boot PC operating systems such as various flavors of Linux and Microsoft Windows on both of those platforms. On x86 platforms, little emulation is necessary beyond the capabilities of specific processors, but Virtual PC still works the same way.

Because they must emulate a processor, its instruction set, and related hardware, and then run an operating system and applications on top of this emulated hardware, emulators are usually measurably slower than virtualization environments. Amusingly, some of the systems that can be emulated by software such as QEMU are so slow themselves that emulating them on fast x86 hardware provides performance similar to that of the actual hardware. In general, emulation does not provide a sufficiently high-performance environment to support most of the reasons for which standard virtualization is used, as discussed in Chapter 1.

Microsoft Virtual PC

As mentioned in the introduction to this section, Microsoft's Virtual PC product is an emulation product that also functions as a virtualization product. In this respect, Virtual PC is much like QEMU, discussed in the next section, except that it only emulates the x86 platform. Like Microsoft Virtual Server, Virtual PC was acquired by Microsoft when it purchased Connectix in 2003.

Virtual PC was an extremely popular product back in the days when Apple Macintosh systems used PowerPC chips because they enabled users to install and run Microsoft Windows and related applications on their PPC systems. Now that Parallels Workstation and VMware Fusion are available for Intel-based Macs, Virtual PC is much less popular, and is no longer supported for the decreasing number of PowerPC Macintosh systems that are still in use.

Microsoft Virtual PC is now available as a free download from Microsoft, and enables Windows users to run non-modified operating systems such as Linux distributions and various versions of Microsoft Windows (such as ME, 2000, XP, and Vista) as virtual machines on a Windows XP or Vista system. Virtual PC runs on both 32-bit and 64-bit Windows systems, but does not currently support 64-bit guest operating systems. Figure 2-5 shows the administrative interface for Virtual PC.

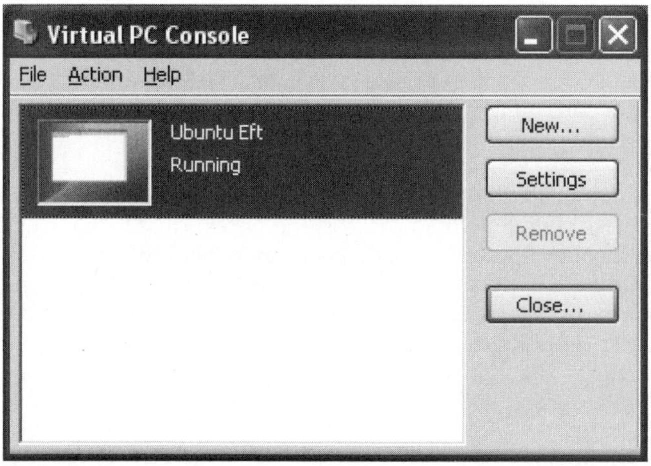

Figure 2-5

The latest version of Virtual PC, Virtual PC 2007, provides direct support for the hardware-based virtualization technology available on the Intel-VT and AMD-SVM processors, which provides significant performance improvements over previous versions.

For more information about Microsoft Virtual PC or access to the freely downloadable version, see www.microsoft.com/windowsxp/virtualpc.

QEMU

QEMU (`http://fabrice.bellard.free.fr/qemu/`) is an amazingly powerful open source CPU emulator developed by Fabrice Bellard and a host of others that can emulate a huge variety of architectures, processors, and related peripheral hardware. QEMU can run operating systems and software that are compiled for platforms including 32- and 64-bit x86, 32- and 64-bit PowerPC, Motorola 68000, 32- and 64-bit SPARC, SH, MIPS, and ARM. QEMU virtualizes a complete hardware environment for each of these processors and architectures, including the CPU and peripheral devices such as one or more serial ports, network interfaces, a PCI bus, VGA graphics adaptors, sound hardware, disk drives, USB components, and more. This enables you to run unmodified guest operating systems for any of these processors or architectures in QEMU. QEMU's hardware emulation is so exceptional that significant parts of QEMU are used to support serial connections, graphics hardware, multi-partition disk images, and so on in the full virtualization implementations of virtualization packages such as Xen and KVM.

At the time of this writing, QEMU provides emulated versions of the following x86 hardware:

❑ IDE hard disk controller supporting up to four drives (each of which is a file containing a disk image)

❑ IDE CDROM device (access to a physical CD-ROM drive or an ISO image)

❑ Floppy disk controller supporting up to two drives (each of which is a floppy disk image)

❑ Graphics card (VGA-VESA or Cirrus Logic GD5446 PCI)

❑ PS/2 Mouse

❑ Ethernet network card (Realtek RTL8139 PCI or NE2000 PCI)

❑ Serial port (COM 1)

❑ Parallel port (LPT 1)

❑ Sound card (Sound Blaster 16 and/or ES1370)

❑ USB-UHCI host controller (Intel SB82371)

Some devices, such as USB devices that are to be attached to the USB controller, must be identified on the QEMU command line.

QEMU uses the Simple DirectMedia Layer (SDL, `www.libsdl.org`) for both video and sound output, and typically executes in the X Window System environment. QEMU also provides an internal DHCP server for network address retrieval from other systems or Xen domains.

QEMU actually supports two emulation modes. The first is system virtualization, where QEMU runs a complete, unmodified operating system and user processes for a specific architecture and processor. The second is user emulation, where QEMU can run a single Linux process from one architecture on another. The focus of this section is on QEMU's system emulation mode, although user emulation mode is actually quite interesting in terms of being able to run single, non-native binaries on other platforms.

For additional information about QEMU, see:

- ❏ **Fabrice Bellard's QEMU page (**`http://fabrice.bellard.free.fr/qemu/`**):** The QEMU page hosted by Fabrice Bellard, the primary author of QEMU.

- ❏ **QEMU home page (**`http://qemu.org`**):** The best starting point for downloads, documentation, or general information about QEMU.

- ❏ **QEMU user documentation (**`http://qemu.org/qemu-doc.html`**):** The primary documentation for QEMU.

- ❏ **QEMU user documentation and more (**`http://fabrice.bellard.free.fr/qemu/user-doc.html`**):** Links to the same user documentation as on the QEMU home page, but also provides links to technical documentation, internals documentation, porting information, information about the disk image format used by QEMU, and much more.

- ❏ **QEMU developers mailing list (**`qemu-devel@nongnu.org`**):** You can subscribe at `http://mail.freesoftware.fsf.org/mailman/listinfo/qemu-devel`.

- ❏ **QEMU users forum (**`http://qemu-forum.ipi.fi/`**):** A great collection of forums discussing how to use QEMU, recent patches, using QEMU on different platforms, and so on.

- ❏ **QEMU IRC** (`#qemu` **channel on** `Freenode.com`**):** A great real-time way of asking questions about QEMU (and, let's hope, getting answers as well).

- ❏ **QEMU wiki (**`http://kidsquid.com/cgi-bin/moin.cgi`**):** An unofficial wiki that provides a good deal of HOWTO information on using QEMU, QEMU networking setup, and so on.

Summary

This chapter provides a history of Xen and related projects, and a detailed look at the paravirtualization approach to virtualization that is Xen's original and primary focus. Next covered are different approaches to virtualization on the x86 platform, and some of the problems associated with x86 virtualization, introducing basic Xen terminology such as domains, domain0, and domainU systems. Then you are provided with a detailed examination of how Xen-based kernels and the Xen hypervisor interact to resolve issues such as privileged commands on x86 and compatible processors. The chapter also covers some of the internal parameters that you can change to modify Xen's scheduling algorithms and similar scheduling algorithms on Linux systems that are running on top of Xen.

The chapter concludes with an examination of competing x86 virtualization solutions, exploring the implementation and capabilities of each, and by discussing popular emulation technologies that are related to virtualization, focusing primarily on the popular QEMU emulator.

The next chapter lets you actually get your hands dirty by giving you the information you need to get Xen in various forms and for various Linux distributions. You learn how to build and install it, and you discover the other software packages that must be present on a Linux system in order to build the Xen hypervisor, a Xen-enabled kernel, and related software.

## 3

Obtaining and Installing Xen

Xen is an open source project that is also actively being incorporated into products by a number of companies. Some, such as Virtual Iron and XenSource, are focused on commercializing Xen itself, independent of a standard Linux distribution. Others, including Linux distribution vendors such as Novell, Red Hat, and Ubuntu are adding Xen and Xen-enabled kernels to their repositories and supported product lines. The commercialization of Xen and the attendant rise in actual end-customer support is indicative of both the maturity of the Xen code base and the value of Xen in enterprise and academic environments.

This chapter starts out by identifying the basic hardware requirements for using Xen. It then discusses how to obtain Xen in a variety of different ways and from a variety of sources, how to build it if necessary, and how to install a usable Xen environment on your computer system. Throughout these discussions, this chapter always identifies any other software, source code, or services that you will need to have on your system in order to build, install, or use Xen.

Hardware Requirements for Xen

As with any operating system, there are big differences between the following:

❑   The absolute minimum hardware that is required to run the Xen hypervisor, a domain0 operating system, and one or more domainU guests

❑   The hardware on which you can run the Xen hypervisor, a domain0 operating system, and one or more domainU guests in a meaningful way for testing and experimentation

❑   The hardware on which you can deploy the Xen hypervisor, a domain0 operating system, and one or more domainU guests in a commercial environment

You're welcome to get Xen running on less-powerful hardware than what's discussed in this chapter and to be excited about it. One of the great selling points of Linux has always been that it will enable you to get more life out of aging hardware. However, aging hardware is not the right place for virtualization unless you are replacing that aging hardware with virtual machines. It always makes sense to strip down both your domain0 virtualization host and your domainU guests so that they are as efficient as possible, starting and running only mandatory processes and thus minimizing memory and resource use at every level, giving you lean, mean virtual machines.

The next section provides a general list of requirements for a system on which you can hope to experiment with Xen in a meaningful way. It also highlights how virtual machines interact with the physical hardware on your host systems, and provides recommendations for additional hardware considerations that can improve virtual-machine performance and usability.

Host System Hardware Requirements

The hardware components of a usable domain0 host, supporting one or more virtual machines, should have the following characteristics:

- ❑ **CPU**: Pentium-4 or compatible system (or better) with a processor speed of 1.5 GHz or better. Xen currently supports systems with up to 32 processors. To run full HardwareVirtualMachine (HVM) systems, a processor must either support the Intel VT or AMD-V extensions. See the "Unmodified Guest Systems" section in Chapter 2 for information about determining whether your CPU supports these extensions. Information about processors that support these extensions is also available on the Xen wiki at `http://wiki.xensource.com/xenwiki/HVM_Compatible_Processors`.

- ❑ **Motherboard:** If you are using a processor that supports the Intel VT instructions, hardware support for virtualization must also be enabled in the BIOS on your motherboard. Any of AMD's Socket AM2 processors with F2 or better stepping should be able to run HVMs on any motherboards with DDR2 memory. (Each unique stepping indicates a revision or change in AMD's CPU manufacturing process.) A small (and unmaintained, and incomplete) list of motherboards that people have gotten some level of hardware/full virtualization working on is available on the Xen wiki at `http://wiki.xensource.com/xenwiki/HVM_Compatible_Motherboards`.

- ❑ **Memory**: 1GB or greater is suggested, and a minimum of 2GB is recommended. The amount of memory that your system requires really depends on the number, type, and size of the virtual machines that you will be running on that system. For example, you could allocate 256MB of memory to some number of non-GUI virtual machines and run them successfully on a non-GUI domain0 host with 1GB of memory. These could support services such as DNS, print servers, or intranet Web servers, but the maximum load and capacity of these virtual machines would be somewhat limited.

- ❑ **Disk**: Disk space requirements vary widely depending on how and where your virtual machines are stored. At an absolute minimum, you will need 1.25 times the amount of local disk space required for your domain0 distribution in order to store multiple kernels, in-progress updates, and so on. I would suggest a general minimum of 15GB of local disk space, excluding swap space. I would personally recommend 250GB disks because these are inexpensive, large enough to be usable, and small enough to be inexpensively backed up (to other 250GB disks). Disk space is ridiculously cheap nowadays. I personally view any disk smaller than 40GB as swap space.

  Your local disk space requirements will increase if you store any portion of any domainU guest as files in your local filesystem or as separate partitions on a local logical volume or physical disk. As discussed in the "Filesystem Choices, Locations, and Flexibility" section in Chapter 6, the physical location of your domainU filesystems has significant implications for disk consumption, performance, failover, migration, backups, and so on.

❑ **Network**: 100 Mbit/second or better, with 1000 Mbit/second (1GB) or better recommended. As discussed in Chapter 8, running multiple virtual machines on a single physical host can significantly impact the network performance of that system. This is not a problem for experimentation purposes, but if you are benchmarking or deploying virtual machines with significant network throughput requirements, a 1GB network is a wise investment.

The various hardware and storage techniques suggested in this list can improve the performance of virtual machines and simplify their administration and use in enterprise environments. A number of specific hardware decisions can help you select hardware that works with Xen and provides sufficient flexibility for successful long-term use in your virtual infrastructure. These are discussed in the next section.

Hardware Issues for Virtual Machines

The previous section focused on minimum and suggested hardware requirements for running the Xen hypervisor, the administrative domain0 operating system, and one or more virtual machines. This section focuses on those aspects of your hardware that have specific implications for virtual machines.

Although virtual machines have no specific hardware requirements, they must share your underlying hardware with domain0 and other guest domainU operating systems. For that reason, it is useful to discuss the ways in which your virtual machines can be bound to specific portions of the host system's hardware. This is especially important to consider during the hardware planning phase. Certain aspects of the hardware that you purchase to support Xen and your virtual machine infrastructure, such as disk devices and network hardware, are inherently flexible and can be changed or expanded at any time. Other aspects of your hardware, such as the number of CPUs and maximum amount of memory supported on your systems, are much harder (and more expensive) to change, making it both wise and cost-effective to think through possible issues in advance.

Performance and ease of administration are the real keys to successfully using virtual machines in enterprise and other 24/7 environments. When discussing "ease of administration" in this section, I'll focus on the physical requirements for administrative tasks such as backups, performance tuning, and high availability. Tools which simplify performing those tasks will be discussed in Chapter 10.

The following list summarizes the hardware-related issues that you should consider when specifying or purchasing the physical systems that will host your virtual machines:

❑ **Processors:** As mentioned in the previous section, Xen supports systems with up to 32 CPUs or cores. The processor requirements of a Xen domainU depend upon the types of applications and services that it is running. High processor or I/O requirements are often one of the key problems in moving certain types of systems to virtual machines. If a virtual machine is experiencing performance problems, one of the easiest ways to address those problems is to bind that virtual machine to a specific CPU on the host system, and to reserve that processor for the exclusive use of the virtual machine. Of course, this only works if your physical host hardware has more than one physical CPU or CPU core. For this reason, if you are planning your virtual infrastructure or simply purchasing new hardware for it, it's a good idea to buy systems that support multi-core processors and/or multiple physical CPUs.

❑ **Memory:** All modern computer systems are memory-hungry. This is especially significant in a virtualization environment, where you are layering the memory requirements of multiple virtual systems atop a single physical host. As you find additional opportunities for moving the services provided by existing physical systems to virtual hosts, the number of hosts that you virtualize will almost always increase. The memory requirements for each virtual host depend on the applications and services that it provides, as well as on the operating system that it is running.

While it is difficult to predict the memory requirements of the physical host for a flexible number of virtual machines, one safe statement is always "as much as possible." When selecting a system, make sure that the motherboard can handle at least 4GB of memory per physical processor, and preferably more. Even a 4GB system may be a bit cramped as you add more and more virtual machines, but anything less will quickly be insufficient. You should also make sure that the motherboard has sufficient slots available to support any networking or networked storage requirements. See subsequent bullets in this list for more information.

Migrating an existing physical server to a virtual machine provides some great data on the amount of memory that the virtual machine will require, because you can watch the performance of the physical system to predict the requirements of its virtual successor. For example, if the machine never swaps, and you never see spikes in the load average of the machine, then the amount of physical memory that is declared in its configuration file is sufficient for a replacement virtual machine. You may even be able to reduce it over time.

❏ **Network:** As with memory and CPU requirements, the network requirements of a virtual machine primarily depend on the applications and services that it is running. Virtual machines that support high-load network services such as high-volume Web servers, centralized mail servers such as POP and IMAP file servers, and so on, can easily overload the capabilities of a single network interface, even a 1GBASE-T or 10GBASE-T. In these cases, you may want to consider putting multiple network interface cards in your system and binding them to the virtual machines with network-intensive requirements.

Similarly, virtual machines whose filesystems are hosted on network devices, whether via NFS, iSCSI, ATA over Ethernet, or on a SAN system, impose significant additional network load each time they boot and subsequently access a non-cached file. In these cases, you may also want to take advantage of multiple network interface cards, binding them to the virtual machines with networked storage or filesystem requirements. Many Xen installations use networked device mirroring solutions such as DRBD (www.drbd.org/) to create network mirrors of the block devices that hold critical filesystems, simplifying recovery and failover in the event of hardware failure. This mirroring can substantially increase the network load on any system, let alone one that already has significant network requirements. See the "Linux Storage and Filesystems" and "Xen and Linux Network Block Devices" sections in Chapter 6 for more information on DRBD.

In any case, having sufficient free slots on your physical virtualization host is a fundamental requirement for being able to add network cards. The motherboard that you select for your physical host should have as many free slots as possible, and these must be of the right type for the interfaces that you want to add. For example, many iSCSI cards are PCI-express cards, which require a different type of slot than a standard PCI card.

❏ **Storage:** The storage requirements for virtual machines vary widely based on the applications and services that they provide. The type of filesystem access required by different types of applications varies from application to application — some applications maintain very little state information (such as log data), whereas others, such as database applications, are completely disk intensive. Somewhere in the middle are file and Web servers, which typically deliver much more data than they create, and mail and print servers, which typically receive incoming data, retain it for some amount of time, and then delete it.

As discussed in Chapter 6, the flexibility of Linux means that the filesystems used by your virtual machines can reside in a number of different locations: single files containing filesystem images, local partitions on physical disks or logical volumes, networked root filesystems, or even on networked block devices access through iSCSI, AoE, or from some other type of SAN. Each of these has its own implications for standard operational tasks such as backups, and for disaster- or failure-recovery scenarios such as migration and failover. Type-specific storage interfaces, such as iSCSI cards or SCSI cards, used to connect to multi-ported RAID storage can be bound to specific virtual machines for performance reasons, as needed.

Nowadays, the physical hosts used for virtualization support should probably support both local IDE and local SATA drives, and those drives should be installed in removable drive trays for easy access and maintenance. Using removable drive trays in an existing system also provides good opportunities for disk-to-disk backups as long as all slots are not actively in use.

It is always important to keep in mind that virtual machines still have physical requirements, and that physical hardware can be dedicated to virtual machines to address performance problems — sometimes in advance, but only after-the-fact if your physical hardware platforms have room for the additional hardware that is required.

Software Packages Required for Running Xen

All software packages have two different types of requirements: compile-time requirements and runtime requirements. Compile-time requirements are composed of the source code and software required to compile all of the software contained in that package. Runtime requirements are any other software packages that are required to execute that software package. Compile-time requirements are also sometimes simply referred to as "build requirements" because they define the source code and software necessary to build a software package.

This section discusses the runtime requirements of the core Xen package and the user-space utilities that are included in that package. The "Software Requirements for Building Xen" section in this chapter discusses compile-time requirements for Xen.

domain0 and domainU systems have different software requirements for running Xen. domainU systems have no specific requirements because they are primarily just self-contained virtual machines. Their requirements are therefore the same as those for the physical machines that they are replacing: appropriate connectivity software (an SSH daemon to handle incoming Secure Sockets Layer (SSL) requests, an X server running XDMCP if remote X sessions are supported, and so on) to support administrative connections, plus whatever software is required by the services and applications that they are providing. However, domain0 systems have a number of specific software requirements because they provide the software glue between the Xen hypervisor and domainU systems.

If you have installed Xen on a Linux system using Xen packages that are provided by the Linux distribution that you are running and have used a packages manager such as apt-get, aptitude, Synaptic, or yum to install them, the packages discussed in this section should have been identified as dependencies or requirements, and should therefore have been automatically installed on your system by the package manager.

If you are rolling your own Xen system or are using a Linux distribution that does not provide official Xen packages, you will need to either verify that these packages are already installed on your domain0 system, or build and install them yourself. This should rarely be necessary because providing complete selections of packages is a key element of a Linux distribution, but YDMV (your distribution may vary).

Software packages that must be present on a domain0 Linux system are the following:

❑ **Bridge utilities:** The bridge-utils package provides utilities, primarily `brctl`, that enable your system to configure virtual network interfaces and set up bridges between your physical hardware and the virtual network interfaces used by your virtual machines. The home page of the Bridge utilities is on Sourceforge, at `http://sourceforge.net/projects/bridge`, from which you can download the source code for the latest version. The Linux Foundation provides a page about these utilities at `http://linux-net.osdl.org/index.php/Bridge` that explains how to get the latest and greatest version from the repository used by the git source code management system.

❑ **GRUB:** GRUB (GRand Unified Bootloader) is the boot loader of choice for modern Linux systems, and is the only Linux boot loader that can deal with loading the Xen hypervisor, a Xen-enabled kernel, and an initial RAM disk for the Xen content. (Sorry, LILO fans — all 16 of you should view this as a forcing function to upgrade to GRUB. The 1990s want their boot loader back anyway.)

❑ **SSL cryptographic libraries:** The SSL cryptographic libraries (`libcrypto.so` and others) are found in the libssl-dev package. A link to the source code for the latest version of this package is available from the OpenSSL home page at `www.openssl.org`.

❑ **iproute:** The iproute (now iproute2) package provides utilities, primarily ip, that enable software to retrieve, set, and manage IP address and routing information on your systems. These utilities are used when configuring communications between your domainU and domain0 systems and other networks. The home page of the iproute project is `http://linux-net.osdl.org/index.php/Iproute2`, which contains a link to the latest version.

❑ **Python:** Python is a popular object-oriented programming (OOP) language. Many of the Xen tools, specifically xm, are written in Python, which is typically provided by most Linux distributions in the python package. You can get the latest version of Python from its home page at `www.python.org`, which includes a link for downloading the latest version. Most versions of Xen require Python 2.4 or better.

❑ **PyXML:** XML, a standard format for exchanging structured information, is used by Xen configuration, data, and log files, as well as for general data exchange within Xen. Support for XML in Python is provided by the PyXML or python-xml package, depending on your Linux distribution. The home page for the PyXML project is `http://pyxml.sourceforge.net`, which also provides a link for downloading the source code for the latest version.

❑ **Python Logging:** Logging has been a standard component of the core Python distribution since Python 2.3, but if you are using an older version of Python for some reason, you may need to separately install the Python Logging package from its home page at `www.red-dove.com/python_logging.html`.

❑ **udev:** udev is a set of applications and rule files that enable a system to create Linux device nodes at boot time, based on the hardware that is detected by probing the system and by subsequent hardware connection and disconnection events. udev is a flexible, intelligent replacement for the problem encountered on classic UNIX and Linux systems, where every possible device node had to exist before a device that used it could be connected and used. Those were the bad old days. Now, only device nodes for the console (`/dev/console`) and the null device (`/dev/null`) must exist when you boot your system — udev handles the rest. In the case of Xen, udev creates nodes for physical devices that are present and any device nodes required for interaction with the hypervisor and its generic hardware resources. The home page for udev is located at `www.kernel.org/pub/linux/utils/kernel/hotplug/udev.html`, but udev is already used by almost every Linux system in existence that uses the 2.6 kernel, and thus is already probably present on your system.

> **If, for some reason, you have to install udev on your system, make sure that your kernel configuration files do not use other mechanisms for dynamic device-node creation, such as the deprecated devfs device filesystem used by many 2.4 and some early 2.6 Linux kernels. You cannot use both of these approaches to device-node creation on a single system at the same time.**

❑ **zlib:** An open source compression library used by Xen for data compression and decompression. The zlib libraries are typically found in the zlib package. The home page for zlib is located at `www.zlib.net`, and provides a link that enables you to download the source code for the latest version.

In addition, the X Window System (`www.x.org`), and one or two of the following packages, is required if you want to have graphical access to the consoles of your domainU systems:

❑ **libvncserver:** A library used by Xen to make the graphical console of a virtual machine viewable in applications that can use the Virtual Network Computing (VNC) protocol (such as vncviewer, xrealvncviewer, xtightvncviewer, and xvncviewer). This library was extracted from the open source code for the X Window System version of VNC to simplify writing applications that could communicate via VNC. This library is typically available in the libvncserver package or as part of the VNC package on most Linux distributions. The home page for libvncserver is `http://sourceforge.net/projects/libvncserver`, which also provides a link where you can download the latest version of the source code.

❑ **libsdl:** The Simple DirectMedia Layer (SDL) is a library used to directly display the graphical console of virtual machines in a graphical X Window System environment without requiring remote connection software such as a VNC viewer. Most Linux distributions provide this library in packages such as SDL or libsdl*version*, where *version* is the specific version number. The home page of the SDL library is `www.libsdl.org`, which also provides a link from which you can download the latest version.

Automated Build Environment Checks

The Xen source code includes a convenient set of scripts that will quickly check your system to see if it satisfies the basic requirements for building Xen. This doesn't catch everything, but it makes it easy to spot obvious omissions. To run this utility, change to the `tools/check` subdirectory of the directory that contains the Xen source code, and execute the following command:

```
# ./chk install
Xen CHECK-INSTALL  Wed Mar 21 06:23:26 EDT 2007
Checking check_brctl: OK
Checking check_crypto_lib: OK
Checking check_iproute: OK
Checking check_libvncserver: unused, OK
Checking check_python: OK
Checking check_python_xml: OK
Checking check_sdl: unused, OK
Checking check_udev: OK
Checking check_zlib_lib: OK
```

Another possible user-space requirement for working with Xen might be a PDF document viewer such as Adobe Acrobat reader, KPDF (the PDF reader provided on Linux systems that use the KDE graphical desktop environment), or evince, the latest PDF reader in a long line of those provided for use on Linux systems that use the GNOME graphical desktop environment. If you did not build Xen from scratch and the documentation for the version of Xen that you are using is not included in the package, you can always get the latest official version from `www.xensource.com/xen/xen/documentation.html`.

Unless you are building your own version of Xen, you should install the software packages required by Xen using your distribution's package management system in order to ensure that your distribution's package management database knows that the other required packages are actually installed. If your system uses a package manager that actually helps with dependencies rather than simply complaining about them (such as the Debian and Ubuntu utilities and, to a lesser extent, yum), required packages will be installed for you when installing Xen packages. If not, you can always install the Xen packages using package management options that tell the package manager to ignore dependency checks, such as RPM's legendary `--force` and `--nodeps` options, but this is much like playing Russian Roulette without first removing one or more bullets from your pistol. A negative outcome is to be expected.

Downloading and Installing Xen from Binaries

Given the popularity of Xen, its relatively tight integration with Linux, and the desire of people to make money, it isn't surprising that you have a wide range of choices when deciding which version of Xen you should experiment with and deploy on your systems. The basic choices are the following:

❑   Download, build, and deploy the open source version of Xen.

❑   Use a set of Xen packages that are provided by the vendor of your Linux distribution.

❑   Use the free versions of Xen that are available from commercial Xen vendors such as XenSource or Virtual Iron.

❑   Purchase a supported, commercial Xen implementation from a commercial Xen vendor such as XenSource or Virtual Iron.

This section discusses the last three of these options, and is provided before the section on building Xen because I think that most enterprise Xen users will want to deploy a set of Xen packages for which some level of support is commercially available. Regardless of the capabilities of your IT staff or how long they've all belonged to the Mensa society, availing yourself of vendor assistance in case you encounter some horrible problem is worth it in most enterprise environments. At some places I've worked, the availability of vendor support is simply a checkbox for IT management when approving new projects.

If you are interested in building and supporting your own set of Xen packages and xen-enabled kernels, feel free to skip the next few sections and go directly to the sections "Getting the Xen Source Code," "Building Xen from Source Code," and "Installing Xen."

Getting and Installing Distribution-Specific Xen Packages

If you have settled on a specific Linux distribution for installation and use throughout your computing environment, it makes sense to seriously consider adopting your Linux vendor as your Xen provider. After all, you already have a service contract with them. They already support Linux (whenever you actually need support, that is) throughout your computing environment. Your IT staff is already familiar with the package management software used with that distribution, and you probably already have maintenance and upgrade policies in place. You already have an existing backup model in place using that distribution — although virtualization changes some aspects of doing and scheduling backups due to system-and network-load issues, the basic process is still the same. Finally, the versions of Xen that they deliver are bound to be in sync with the versions of the standard Linux kernel that they provide, helping ensure that you do not encounter any driver problems or other incompatibilities.

Of course, package management systems differ across almost all Linux distributions. Some of them follow the old Linux blues mantra, "If it wasn't for real bad package management, we wouldn't have no package management at all." Aside from taking sides in the GNOME vs. KDE controversy, the most significant difference between most Linux distributions is the package management philosophy and toolset that they deliver.

Both Red Hat's Fedora project and Novell's OpenSUSE project were early advocates of Xen, and the Fedora, Red Hat, OpenSUSE, and Novell folks have made substantial contributions to the Xen code base.

The following Linux distributions provide Xen packages as part of their default distribution and/or update mechanism:

❑   Debian includes Xen packages in the Debian 4.0 release, in both the unstable and experimental repositories. Xen packages for Debian 3.1 (Sarge) are available through www.backports.org. You can install Xen on a Debian system using the command-line apt-get or aptitude tool, or by using the graphical Synaptic package manager. Included in the Debian packages for Xen are xen-hypervisor-3.0-i386, xen-utils-3.0, linux-image-2.6.*version*-xen-*arch* (where *version* is the latest supported kernel version and *arch* is your system architecture), and libc6-xen.

These install the Xen hypervisor, a Xen-enabled Linux kernel and associated kernel modules, the open source user-space Xen management and administration utilities and associated libraries, and some Debian utilities for creating and working with virtual machine images, which are discussed in the "Other Utilities for Xen Management and Monitoring" section in Chapter 7.

Fedora Core (FC) has officially supported Xen since FC 5, and introduced it along with a README in FC 4. You can install Xen on a FC6 or later system using its yum package manager and a command such as the following:

```
# yum install kernel-xen xen virt-manager
```

You can also install Xen using the graphical package management tool, pirut, that is provided with FC5.

Either of these mechanisms will install the Xen hypervisor, a xen-enabled Linux kernel and associated kernel modules, the open source user-space xen management and administration utilities and associated libraries, Fedora's command-line virt-install tool, and virt-manager, Fedora's graphical tool for creating and managing Xen virtual machines. (These tools are discussed in the "OpenSource Xen Management Utilities" and "Distribution-Specific Xen Management Software" sections in Chapter 7.)

❑   Gentoo supports Xen, but the Xen packages are masked by default. Add the following entries to /etc/portage/package.keywords:

```
app-emulation/xen
app-emulation/xen-tools
sys-kernel/xen-sources
```

On 64-bit systems, you will also need to add sys-devel/dev86 to build the loader for hardware virtual machines that is used by Xen. You can then build and install the hypervisor and Xen applications by executing the following command:

```
# emerge -av app-emulation/xen app-emulation/xen-tools
```

Once this completes, you will need to build the Xen kernel by using the emerge command to install sys-kernel/xen-sources, using the cd command to change to the latest kernel source directory, and doing a Xen kernel build as described in this chapter.

❏ Mandriva has officially supported Xen in a variety of its product offerings since its Mandriva 2006 Powerpack and Corporate Server 4 releases, and offers Xen support in its Mandriva One install-able Live CD offerings. Mandriva provides a standard Xen package and separate kernel-xen0 and kernel-xenU packages containing domain0 and domainU kernels, which are installable using Mandriva's user-friendly rpmdrake package management utility. Mandriva's Corporate Server 4 product provides an interesting cover-the-bases approach to virtualization, actively supporting Xen, OpenVZ, and VMware.

❏ OpenSUSE has officially included and supported Xen longer than any other desktop Linux distribution, adding Xen support before the creation of the OpenSUSE project, in SUSE Professional 9.3. The standard SUSE YaST2 tool provides support for creating and managing Xen virtual machines. YaST2 also provides installation utilities that make it easy to install OpenSUSE into directories or mounted partitions in order to be able to use them as virtual machines. YaST2 and Xen are discussed in the "Novell and SUSE Xen Tools" section in Chapter 7.

❏ Red Hat Enterprise Linux (RHEL) introduced Xen as part of Red Hat's commercially supported enterprise offerings with RHEL 5. This distribution includes the graphical virt-manager tool introduced in Fedora Core, which is discussed in the "Fedora and Red Hat Xen Tools" section in Chapter 7. You can install Xen on RHEL5 as part of your standard installation or subsequently add it to an existing RHEL5 system in the same way as you can on Fedora Core systems, by using yum or the graphical package manager, pirut.

❏ SUSE Enterprise Linux Server (SLES) was the first enterprise Linux distribution to officially include and support Xen, adding Xen support in SLES 10. As with Novell's OpenSUSE distribution, SLES uses the standard SUSE YaST2 tool to create and manage Xen virtual machines. YaST2 also provides installation utilities that make it easy to install SLES into directories or mounted partitions in order to be able to use them as virtual machines. YaST2 and Xen are discussed in the "Novell and SUSE Xen Tools" section in Chapter 7.

❏ Ubuntu Linux has included and supported Xen since their Edgy Eft (6.10) release. You can install Xen on an Eft or later Ubuntu system using the command-line apt-get or aptitude tool, or by using the graphical Synaptic package manager. The Ubuntu meta-package for Xen is the ubuntu-xen-desktop for your system type, which installs the Xen hypervisor, a xen-enabled Linux kernel and associated kernel modules, the open source user-space xen management and administration utilities and associated libraries, and the graphical XenMan (Xen Manager) tool, now known as ConVirt, which is discussed in the "Distribution-Specific Xen Management Software" section in Chapter 7.

Many other Linux distributions and Linux Live CDs provide Xen, but compiling a complete list of these is effectively impossible. If you are just interested in experimenting with Xen, you can try a distribution such as Xenoppix (`http://unit.aist.go.jp/itri/knoppix/xen/index-en.html`), which is not only interesting for its Xen support, but also because it includes support for KVM (Kernel Virtual Machine) virtualization, discussed in Chapter 2, and because it comes with pre-built Xen virtual machines that run open source operating systems other than Linux, such as Plan9 and NetBSD. At one point, you could get Live CDs running Ubuntu and CentOS from XenSource, but those are no longer regularly available.

Commercial Xen Solutions

XenSource, founded by members of the University of Cambridge team that originally created Xen, and Virtual Iron are the two best-known commercial providers of Xen-based virtualization solutions. Both of these firms offer free licenses for developers and IT enthusiasts who are interested in exploring their solutions.

The following sections provide an overview of the free offerings from each of these vendors, as well as an overview of the commercial offerings from these vendors. The goal of these sections is to provide a complete discussion of sources for usable Xen implementations and related packages, not to clone their installation documents or provide free advertising. This book wouldn't exist at all without the tremendous efforts of many of the people who now work at Xensource, and providing commercial, supported solutions is a hallmark of a mature and viable product. Both XenSource and Virtual Iron deserve a close look if you want a supported, commercial version of Xen that includes equally well-supported Xen and VM management utilities.

Downloading Binaries from XenSource

As mentioned previously, XenSource is a commercial entity founded by members of the original Xen development team. Having had the foresight to release Xen under the open source GPL v2.0 license, no one is more aware of Xen's responsibilities to the open source community than the XenSource folks. A significant part of their mission is to participate in, encourage, and nurture the open source Xen community. Therefore, XenSource makes it easy for you to download RPMs of the current release of Xen by clicking the "open source release" link on the page at www.xensource.com/download/index.html. This takes you to a page containing download links for distribution-independent tarballs and RPMs for platforms such as Fedora Core, OpenSUSE, Red Hat Enterprise Linux, and SUSE Enterprise Linux. The download link for the Xen tarballs also includes a link to the tarball of the current source code.

In order to install free RPMs from XenSource, your system will first have to satisfy the runtime package requirements discussed in the "Software Packages for Running Xen" section in this chapter. These software packages are probably available through your Linux distribution's package management system, and are certainly available if the Linux distribution that you are running actively supports Xen itself. As discussed in that same section, if you are installing Xen via RPMs, you should install the other software packages required for Xen using RPM in order to ensure that your distribution's RPM database knows that the other required packages are actually installed. You are playing with fire if you do not do so.

If you are downloading RPMs from XenSource, the number of RPMs differs between platforms in order to more easily integrate with existing software packages provided on different Linux distributions.

The XenSource Xen tarball contains the compiled binaries and documents for the current Xen community release. Because each tarball essentially provides the same binaries that you would get by building Xen using "make world" or "make dist," you will have to unpack the tarball and run the simple installation script described in the "Installing Xen" section of this chapter.

Evaluating XenSource Server Products

XenSource provides three server products, each targeted at a different audience and providing a different set of capabilities:

❑   **XenEnterprise:** An enterprise server solution that supports Linux and Microsoft Windows virtual machines. The XenEnterprise product supports a wide range of device drivers and local and remote storage devices. It includes a graphical virtual-machine-management package that runs on Linux or Windows systems. This product requires a license.

❑   **XenServer:** An enterprise server solution that is targeted towards supporting Microsoft Windows virtualization, supporting Windows Server 2003 and Windows XP VMs. The XenServer product includes a graphical virtual-machine-management package that runs on Windows systems. This product requires a license.

❑ **XenExpress:** A free, entry-level starter package designed for home use or for experimentation with Xen. This product can be used on servers with up to 4GB of RAM and can host up to four Linux or Microsoft virtual machines on that system. No license is required.

All of these XenSource products are available for both 32-bit and 64-bit systems. They are downloadable as an ISO image from which you can create a bootable CD, and install the Xen hypervisor and a small, preconfigured Linux distribution on your server hardware. They all require hardware support for virtualization (Intel-VT or AMD-V) in order to install and run unmodified operating systems, although the XenSource distributions provide some paravirtualized device drivers for Windows domainU guests to improve performance.

As you might expect, the XenSource products are excellent. Providing their own minimal Linux distribution limits the amount of time that they have to spend on supporting pure Linux software issues, enabling them to focus on supporting, extending, and optimizing Xen. The only real downside of the Xen products is that the Linux kernels that they support typically lag the current kernel from kernel.org by several minor revisions. They also cost money, but getting support can be a wise investment, depending on the types of hardware that you are working with and the storage infrastructure behind your virtual machines.

> As mentioned in the discussion of XenSource in Chapter 2, XenSource was acquired by Citrix while this book was being written. This section describes the XenSource products and packaging, which may change as Citrix blends the XenSource products into its existing product line.

Evaluating Virtual Iron Products

Virtual Iron is a provider of Xen-based enterprise virtualization solutions that was founded by a number of industry veterans with significant experience in areas such as enterprise networking, operating systems, and grid and parallel computing, all of which have direct relevance in virtualization-based infrastructures. Virtual Iron's primary competitive focus is on providing a cost-effective alternative to VMWare, although their Xen-based solution also provides the standard performance advantages delivered by paravirtualization.

Virtual Iron also provides impressive graphical tools for managing one or more virtual servers. You can download a free version of Virtual Iron's Xen-based server product (for a single server) from www.virtualiron.com/products/Free_Download.cfm. Installing this requires that the system be running a supported Linux distribution. See the Virtual Iron Web site for information on currently supported Linux distributions.

Getting the Xen Source Code

If there are so many alternatives to the traditional roll-your-own approach to open source software such as Xen, why even bother to build it yourself? There are actually a number of good reasons to do so.

The most common reason to build any open source package is so that you can get the latest and greatest features and fixes to Xen itself, even if they are not yet available from commercial sources, such as from a Xen vendor or in the Xen packages provided by your Linux distribution. If you need feature X and it is only stable in the testing or upcoming release of Xen, you can go and get it yourself, integrate it, and begin using it.

Similarly, you may need to use a specific version of the Linux kernel, which Xen may not support any longer (or yet). Assuming that you are a kernel wizard (or know a few), you can integrate Xen into the latest and greatest kernel. (This is not for the faint of heart or your average Visual Studio programmer!)

A final reason for building Xen packages yourself may be that having the source code for portions of your IT infrastructure and building and maintaining it yourself are requirements for your place of employment, for reasons of security or paranoia (which may be the same thing).

The next few sections discuss the most common mechanisms for getting the latest Xen source code from various locations in preparation for building Xen, the Xen support utilities, and a Xen-enabled kernel. The last section explains how to extract the Xen kernel patches from a Xen source distribution so that you can attempt to apply them to a specific version of the Linux kernel.

Downloading Official Source Tarballs

The classic mechanism for downloading the source code for an open source project is to download a compressed archive file that was created using the tar (and possibly gzip) utilities.

Distribution-independent Xen source code tarballs are available from two primary locations. The first, and best known, is the University of Cambridge Computer Laboratory's Web site. Xen is still an active research project there, and development continues. To see the latest tarballs available there, visit `www.cl.cam.ac.uk/Research/SRG/netos/xen/downloads` using a Web browser and look for the most recent src tarball with the highest version number, which would have a name such as `xen-3.0.3-src.tgz`. If you are feeling adventurous, you could use a testing tarball, which would have a name such as `xen-3.0.4-testing-src.tgz` and is a preliminary version of an upcoming release that is currently being tested.

Unfortunately, the tarballs that are available for downloading from the University of Cambridge site are not updated as regularly as one would like. If you want to retrieve a tarball of up-to-date Xen source code, a better source is XenSource. To retrieve a tarball of the latest official Xen source code from XenSource, go to the page at `www.xensource.com/download` and click the "open source release" link beside the "Open Source Xen RPMs" graphic. This takes you to a page that provides access to RPMs and tarballs of the latest released version of the Xen software, as described in the "Downloading Binaries from XenSource" section in this chapter.

On this page, click the Download button beside the Xen tarballs graphic. This displays a page of Xen downloads, one of which is labeled Source Code. Click the Source Download button to begin retrieving a tarball for the latest release of Xen from XenSource.

Retrieving tarballs provides you with snapshots of specific testing or official releases, which may be exactly what you want and may work fine for you. However, tarballs usually do not include the updates to code that is being tested or the latest fixes to existing releases. Some tarballs are never updated after they are created. To get access to official Xen source code that is as up-to-date as possible and contains the latest fixes and enhancements, you need to retrieve that code directly from the source code control system used by the Xen team, as explained in the next section.

Getting Xen Sources with Mercurial

The Xen project uses a source code control system called Mercurial (`www.selenic.com/mercurial`). The primary interface of Mercurial is provided through an executable called "hg" (the chemical symbol for mercury in the periodic table). Mercurial is a distributed and decentralized source code management package which is released under the GNU General Public License, v2. Mercurial is quite popular and is used for many open source projects, including Xen and OpenSolaris.

Mercurial works by maintaining per-project repositories that, once cloned from another repository, are completely independent of that repository. Changes made in any copy of a repository can be committed back to the repository from which it was cloned, and changes can be pulled in from any other copy of the same repository at any time. Changes to one or more files in a repository are grouped into changesets that can be identified by their revision number, changeset ID, and a string tag. The central concept of Mercurial is branching, where a branch is simply an independent line of development. Each developer effectively has his own branch after he clones a repository and begins making changes. To support this model, Mercurial is very good at merging different branches back into a repository, using HTTP and SSH as its default transport protocols and only transferring diffs to files during commits and local updates, using SHA1 hashes for integrity checking. Mercurial uses the term "heads" to mean the most recently committed changesets on a branch, whereas the term "tip" is the most recently changed head. The tip of a given repository is the default revision for many hg commands, such as clone, update, and so on. For more information about Mercurial, see sites such as `www.selenic.com/mercurial`, which is a wiki that provides a good deal of information about Mercurial as well as access to the latest Mercurial source code.

The Xen project maintains multiple Mercurial repositories, all of which are listed at `http://xenbits.xensource.com`. The names of the active and maintained repositories change from release to release. At the time this chapter was written, Xen 3.0.5 was under active development, so the available repositories were the following:

- ❑ **xen-3.0.4-testing.hg:** A repository for the latest version of Xen 3.0.4, used for testing and kept up-to-date with the latest fixes for that branch.

- ❑ **xen-3.0.3-testing.hg:** A repository for the latest version of Xen 3.0.3, used for testing the latest fixes for that branch.

- ❑ **xen-3.0-testing.hg:** A repository for the latest version of Xen 3.0.2, used for testing the latest fixes for that branch.

- ❑ **xen-2.0-testing.hg:** A repository for the latest version of Xen 2.*x*, used for testing the latest fixes for that branch. Effectively defunct.

- ❑ **xen-unstable.hg:** The development version of Xen. Major code changes may be taking place in this branch at any time, but it is the place to look for specific fixes to problems in the latest official release of Xen. When official Xen releases occur, they are simply cloned from a tagged version of xen-unstable, while forward development continues on xen-unstable itself.

- ❑ **linux-2.6-xen.hg:** A copy of the Linux 2.6 kernel source code with extensions for xen as a sub-architecture. Effectively defunct.

Mercurial is easy to install, configure, and use. The basic command for setting up a Mercurial repository and getting a copy of the latest Xen source code is the following:

```
$ hg clone http://xenbits.xensource.com/repository-name local-repository-name
```

An `hg` command displays status and summary messages as it queries the remote repository and retrieves changes. For example, cloning the `xen-3.0.4-testing.hg` repository to a local directory called `xen-3.0.4-testing` would look something like the following:

```
$ hg clone http://xenbits.xensource.com/xen-3.0.4-testing.hg \
  xen-3.0.4-testing
requesting all changes
adding changesets
adding manifests
adding file changes
added 13140 changesets with 91364 changes to 9471 files
3087 files updated, 0 files merged, 0 files removed, 0 files unresolved
```

After retrieving the source code using Mercurial, change the directory to the local name that you supplied for your copy of the repository. You can then build Xen as described in the next section.

If you have already cloned a repository, you can import the latest changesets at any time by executing the `hg update` command in the directory where your copy of the repository is located.

Patching a Vanilla Linux Kernel for Xen

Xen is a bare-metal paravirtualization solution that currently requires changes to the core Linux kernel source code in order to enable the kernel and drivers to interact with the Xen hypervisor and domain0 kernel. Projects such as the paravirt_ops project discussed in Chapter 2 are focused on simplifying hypervisor and kernel integration in order to minimize kernel changes, but for the time being, we're stuck with them. This isn't necessarily a bad thing — many open source advancements, especially at the kernel level, are provided as patches that update specific portions of the kernel source code. (Patches are text files that describe how to make changes to source code files in order to update the code that they contain, which is known as "applying a patch.")

The overall upside of Xen's kernel modifications is that paravirtualization provides much higher performance than most other server virtualization solutions because the hypervisor can optimize memory handling, processor use and pinning, I/O, and so on. The primary downside of requiring changes to operating system source code is that it requires a fair amount of work to keep patches up-to-date so that they can be cleanly applied to kernel source code that is itself changing.

The rest of this section highlights how to manually create Xen patches and apply them to your favorite Linux kernel — unfortunately, it does not include a kernel programming guide. Unless you are manually creating patches because it is critical that you use a specific version of the kernel that is not supported by Xen, or it is a learning experience for you, I'd strongly suggest that you pursue using a vanilla version of Xen that you either build or obtain from a Linux or Xen vendor.

All parts of the Xen build process are controlled using the make program, which reads build instructions and sequencing dependencies from command files known as makefiles. The make program uses those instructions to build software components in the correct order, minimizing rebuild time after any changes have been made to the associated source code. A makefile contains many sets of instructions, each associated with a user-defined keyword, known as a *make target*, that tells the make program which set of instructions to execute.

The Xen Makefile provides a specific make target, `mkpatches`, that creates a single huge patch for Xen, which you can then manually apply to a specific version of the kernel source code. (See the "Requirement for Building Xen" and "Compiling Xen" sections for more information.) In order to generate this patch file, you must have completed the following:

❑ Installed the Xen source code on your system as described in the previous sections

❑ Built the Xen source code, at least to the point where the source code for the relevant kernel is retrieved from the kernel.org site, uncompressed, and renamed as the reference Linux source for the Xen source directory

You must also execute the `mkpatches` command from the directory that contains the Xen source code and, therefore, the main Xen Makefile. The following is an example of creating a patch file using the `make mkpatches` command:

```
# make mkpatches
for i in linux-2.6 ; do make $i-xen.patch; done
make[1]: Entering directory `/home/xen/mercurial/xen-3.0.4-testing.hg'
rm -rf tmp-linux-2.6-xen.patch
cp -al ref-linux-2.6.16.38 tmp-linux-2.6-xen.patch
( cd linux-2.6-xen-sparse && bash ./mkbuildtree ../tmp-linux-2.6-xen.patch )
diff -Nurp pristine-linux-2.6.16.38 tmp-linux-2.6-xen.patch >\
 linux-2.6-xen.patch || true
rm -rf tmp-linux-2.6-xen.patch
make[1]: Leaving directory `/home/xen/mercurial/xen-3.0.4-testing.hg'
```

As you can see from the output of this command, the `make mkpatches` command created the patch file, linux-2.6-xen.patch.

After you have created a patch file for Xen, you can attempt to apply it to a copy of the source directory for the kernel that you are interested in using with Xen.

Applying patches to source code is relatively simple, thanks to the patch program, which does an incredibly intelligent job of applying patch files. The patch program can even apply patches when the file you are patching is slightly different from the version of the file originally used to produce the patch. The patch program does this by examining a certain number of lines before and after the point at which each change is specified to be inserted, and inserting the modified source code correctly if matching lines are found in this region. For complete information on the patch program, see its online reference page by typing **man patch** on your Linux system.

The general process for applying kernel patches is the following:

1. Use the `su` or `sudo -s` command to become root on the console, in an xterm, or in another terminal window.

2. Change your working directory to the directory created when you installed the kernel source code that you want to patch.

3. Use the `patch` command to apply the Xen patch:

```
# patch -p1 < /path/to/linux-2.6-xen.patch
```

The -p1 option tells the patch command how many of the filenames listed in the patch file to preen in order to correctly locate the files that should be patched. The < shell redirect identifies the file /path/to/linux-2.6-xen.patch as the input patch.

The output of the patch command lists the name of each file that is being patched. If you are extremely lucky, you will see a long series of messages such as the following:

```
patching file include/xen/balloon.h
patching file include/xen/cpu_hotplug.h
patching file include/xen/driver_util.h
patching file include/xen/evtchn.h
patching file include/xen/features.h
patching file include/xen/foreign_page.h
...
```

It is far more likely that some of the updates to individual files that are identified in the patch file cannot be applied cleanly, usually because there have been incompatible changes between the file from which the patch was created and the version of the file that you want to update. These messages will look something like the following:

```
patching file include/net/sock.h Hunk #1 FAILED at 1064. \
    1 out of 1 hunk FAILED -- saving rejects to file include/net/sock.h.rej
```

In this case, you will need to examine the file containing the changes that were rejected, which in this case are stored in the file include/net/sock.h.rej, in order to see if you can manually resolve the problem. Make some strong coffee, get out your thinking cap, and have at it.

After you have integrated all patch-file changes into the appropriate source code files, you're ready to configure, compile, and install the patched kernel.

Configuring the Standard Xen Kernel Source

This section explains how to locate and customize the Xen-related settings in the standard Xen kernel source retrieved from XenSource. If you are looking for information on configuring a mainline Linux kernel that is version 2.6.23 or later, and which therefore has built-in support for Xen, see the next section.

The default configuration settings for the Xen domain0 kernel source are fairly generic, so that they will work correctly on most systems, support most hardware, and so on. At the time that this book was written, the kernel that is patched and built from the standard XenSource source code is based on version 2.6.18 of the mainline Linux kernel. The standard Xen kernel is also often used with paravirtualized domainU guests, where the standard hardware requirements are relatively simple because most of the domainU hardware is actually emulated there. Aside from the standard Xen blktap (block device front/backend driver) and netfront (network front/backend driver) drivers and the drivers for general block device and TCP/IP support, relatively few drivers need to be present in a paravirtualized domainU kernel. These drivers are typically compiled into the kernel for bootstrapping, performance, and portability reasons, rather than being dynamically loaded.

As with any Linux system, you may wish to optimize the kernel used by your domain0 and domainU guests. This can be important for both domain0 and domainU systems because you want the kernel to be as small as possible, both to minimize resource use (so that more memory is available for use by your domainU guests) and for performance reasons. For information about building different Xen kernels automatically, see the "Compiling Xen" section.

If you want to customize the kernel that you are building, the Xen source code distribution provides make targets to simplify the process. You will first want to customize the configuration of your kernel, and then build the kernel using the custom settings. To do this, execute the following commands:

```
# make linux-2.6-xen-config CONFIGMODE=xconfig
# make linux-2.6-xen-build
# make linux-2.6-xen-install
```

The CONFIGMODE variable specifies which kernel configuration interface you want to use, and should be config (to use a completely command-line configuration tool), menuconfig (to use the terminal-oriented configuration tool), xconfig (to use a graphical, X Window System configuration tool based on the Qt graphical library and widgets), or gconfig (to use a graphical X Window system interface base on the GTK+ graphics library and widgets). Of these, menuconfig and xconfig are the best choices. Figures 3-1 shows the xconfig kernel configuration tool, which I highly recommend.

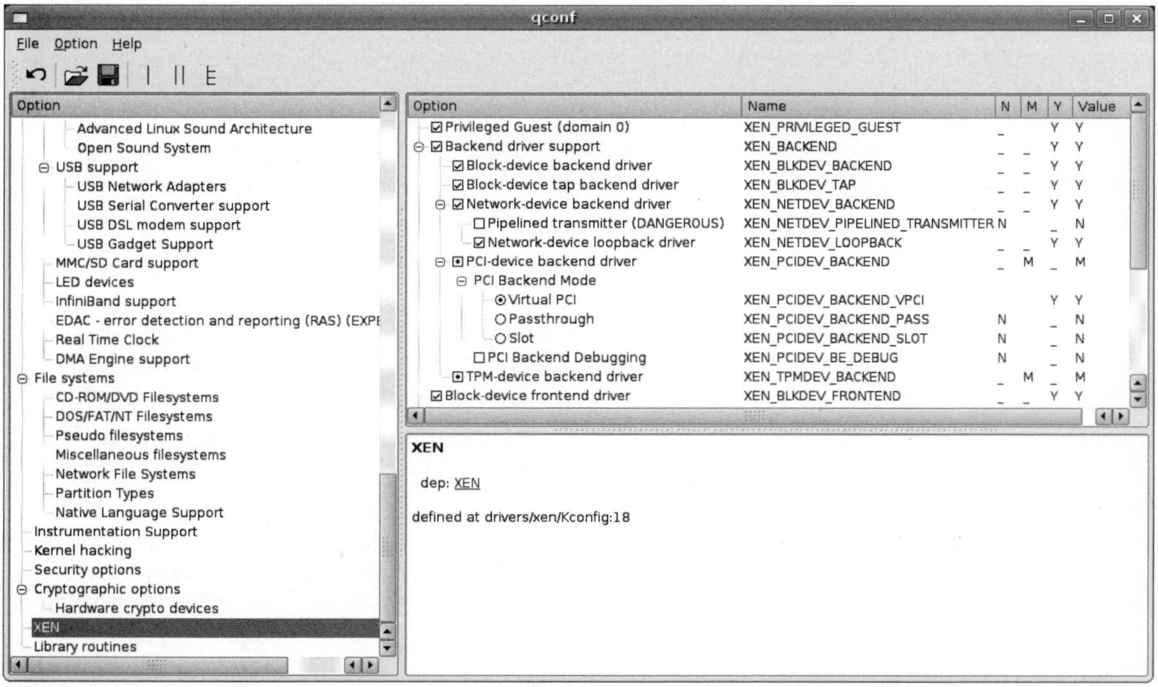

Figure 3-1

Customizing the generic portions of the Xen kernel is exactly like customizing any Linux kernel. You can search for a specific setting using the Edit menu's Find command, or you can simply drill down through the configuration interface by clicking the + (plus) symbols to expand various sections that contain related kernel configuration options. You can select the Show Debug option on the Option menu to display dependency information for any configuration variable or section. You can also select the Option menu's Show All Options setting to display all available configuration options, regardless of whether they can be selected. After changing kernel configuration settings, save your changes using the File menu's Save command, and then rebuild the kernel, as explained previously.

The remainder of this section focuses on the Xen-specific kernel configuration settings. This is not a complete tutorial on generic kernel configuration — that would require an entire book on the subject, which is already available. The best book on kernel configuration is Greg Kroah-Hartman's *Linux Kernel in a Nutshell* (O'Reilly, 2007).

The Xen-related settings for the 2.6.18 Linux kernel as patched by XenSource and the Xen community are all located in a top-level kernel configuration section labeled XEN, as shown previously in Figure 3-1. These settings are the following:

- ❑ **XEN:** Enables Xen support in the kernel. By default, this value is set to true in the 2.6.18 kernel after the Xen patches have been applied.

- ❑ **XEN_BACKEND:** Enables general support for the front/backend drivers used to provide I/O services to paravirtualized domainU guests.

- ❑ **XEN_BLKDEV_BACKEND:** Enables support for the block device backend driver, which enables the kernel to export its block devices to domainU guests using a shared-memory interface.

- ❑ **XEN_BLKDEV_FRONTEND:** Activates the block device frontend driver that enables the kernel to access block devices that are provided within another operating system running as domain0.

- ❑ **XEN_BLKDEV_TAP:** Similar to the block device backend driver, this driver enables block requests from domainU guests to be redirected to user space using a device interface. This driver enables the use of file-based disk images.

- ❑ **XEN_COMPAT_030002_AND_LATER:** Specifies that this kernel is compatible with Xen API versions 3.0.2 and later. This option is only necessary if you are still running paravirtualized virtual machines or associated software created using Xen version 3.0.2.

- ❑ **XEN_COMPAT_030004_AND_LATER:** Specifies that this kernel is compatible with Xen API versions 3.0.4 and later. This option is only necessary if you are still running paravirtualized virtual machines or associated software created using Xen version 3.0.4.

- ❑ **XEN_COMPAT_LATEST_ONLY:** Specifies that the kernel is compatible only with the version of Xen that it was built with. This option provides the best performance, but should be selected only if you are rebuilding all of the kernels used by your virtual machines (or if you are using the same kernel with all of them).

- ❑ **XEN_DISABLE_SERIAL:** Causes Xen to disable the standard serial port drivers normally used for console access, enabling the Xen console driver to provide a serial console at ttyS0.

- ❑ **XEN_FRAMEBUFFER:** Activates a frontend driver that enables the kernel to create a virtual framebuffer that can be viewed in another domain. This option should be selected only if your domain has direct access to a physical video card.

❑ **XEN_INTERFACE_VERSION:** Identifies the version of the Xen interface that this kernel supports. By default, this is set to the hexadecimal value 0x00030205, which essentially means version 3.2.5.

❑ **XEN_KEYBOARD:** Activates the frontend driver for a virtual keyboard, which is typically used with the virtual framebuffer (XEN_FRAMEBUFFER).

❑ **XEN_NETDEV_BACKEND:** Enables support for the network device backend driver, which enables the kernel to export network devices to domainU guests using a shared-memory interface.

❑ **XEN_NETDEV_FRONTEND:** Activates the network device frontend driver that enables the kernel to access network interfaces that are provided within another operating system running as domain0.

❑ **XEN_NETDEV_LOOPBACK:** Enables a two-interface loopback device that emulates a local network front/backend connection.

❑ **XEN_NETDEV_PIPELINED_TRANSMITTER:** Reduces the overhead on communication with the network device backend driver. Enabling this driver can cause problems if the domain0 system is doing packet filtering or other packet manipulation tasks. This option is marked as DANGEROUS, and should rarely be enabled.

❑ **XEN_PCIDEV_BACKEND:** Enables the kernel to export arbitrary PCI devices to paravirtualized domainU guests by supplying a backend driver for PCI devices.

❑ **XEN_PCIDEV_BACKEND_CONTROLLER:** An alternative PCI backend driver that virtualizes the PCI topology by providing one virtual PCI bus for each PCI root device. For systems with complex I/O addressing, this is the only PCI backend mode that supports extended I/O port spaces and MMIO translation offsets.

❑ **XEN_PCIDEV_BACKEND_PASS:** An alternate PCI backend mode that provides a real view of the PCI topology to the front end. This mode may be required for drivers that depend on finding their hardware in certain bus slot locations.

❑ **XEN_PCIDEV_BACKEND_SLOT:** An alternate PCI backend mode that hides the actual PCI topology and makes the front end think there is a single PCI bus that contains only the exported devices. This mode is much like XEN_PCIDEV_BACKEND_VCPI, but it reassigns detected hardware to new slots.

❑ **XEN_PCIDEV_BACKEND_VPCI:** The default PCI backend mode used when XEN_PCIDEV_ BACKEND is selected. This PCI backend driver hides the actual PCI topology and makes the front end think there is a single PCI bus that contains only the exported devices, identified by PCI IDs bus slot numbers.

❑ **XEN_PCIDEV_BE_DEBUG:** Activates additional debugging information for the PCI backend drivers. This can affect performance, so it is usually turned off.

❑ **XEN_PRIVCMD:** Enables Xen to use the /proc filesystem for interprocess communications for privileged commands. This option can only be selected if the /proc filesystem is enabled in the kernel, which is done via the PROC_FS configuration variable.

❑ **XEN_PRIVILEGED_GUEST:** Adds support for the privileged modes of operation required by domain0 Xen systems.

❏ **XEN_SCRUB_PAGES:** Causes Xen to erase memory before returning it to the global allocation pool in domain0. This option is normally enabled for security purposes, but induces some performance overhead.

❏ **XEN_SMPBOOT:** Enables Xen to take advantage of multiple processors, if available. This option depends on whether Symmetric multiprocessing (SMP) was enabled in the Processor Type and Features section of the standard kernel configuration screens.

❏ **XEN_SYSFS:** Causes Xen hypervisor attributes to be stored and displayed under the /sys/ hypervisor hierarchy.

❏ **XEN_TPMDEV_BACKEND:** The backend driver for the Trusted Platform Module device driver. Using this module is explained in the "Xen and TPM Emulation" section in Chapter 9.

❏ **XEN_UNPRIVILEGED_GUEST:** Specifies that the kernel being built is only for use by paravirtualized domainU guests. This option is automatically enabled if you de-select the XEN_PRIVILEGED_GUEST option.

❏ **XEN_XENBUS_DEV:** Enables Xen to use the /proc filesystem for virtual-machine and device-status information. This option can be selected only if the /proc filesystem is enabled in the kernel, which is done via the PROC_FS configuration variable.

During the build process for versions of Xen through 3.1.1, the source code for the 2.6.18 Linux kernel is retrieved from its home location (www.kernel.org), uncompressed, patched, and then compiled. After retrieving and building Xen from XenSource (as described in "Getting the Xen Source Code"), your build directory will contain the following kernel-related directories:

❏ **build-linux-2.6.18-xen_processor:** A build directory used as an output destination when building Xen kernels. If you are building on a 32-bit x86 system, the processor is x86_32. If you are building on a 64-bit x86 or AMD system, the processor is x86_64.

❏ **linux-2.6.18-xen:** The source code for the 2.6.18 Linux kernel with all Xen patches applied.

❏ **linux-2.6-xen-sparse:** A version of the Linux kernel source that contains only the files that are modified for Xen.

❏ **pristine-linux-2.6.18:** The pristine 2.6.18 kernel source code after being extracted from the download tarball.

When using the listed make commands for reconfiguring and building your kernel, the source code in the linux-2.6.18-xen directory will be compiled with your new configuration. The compiled output, however, will be located in the appropriate build-linux-2.6.18-xen_processor directory for the type of processor you are building for.

Xen Support in the Mainline Linux Kernel

As this book demonstrates, virtualization is a hot topic in computing circles today. Although maintaining sets of patches outside the Linux kernel is a reasonable way to begin a project such as Xen, it is hard to maintain and keep up with newer versions of the Linux kernel. This obstacle is the primary reason that the open source Xen distribution available from XenSource is still using the 2.6.18 kernel. Unfortunately, using an older kernel denies Xen users access to the latest device drivers and fixes that are present in newer versions.

With the release of the 2.6.23 Linux kernel, things are much better. Basic support for Xen has been merged into the mainline kernel. Support for the paravirt_ops project is also present, which generally improves life for any hypervisor-based virtualization solution. (The 2.6.23 kernel even comes with a sample hypervisor, Rusty Russell's lguest. For more information about lguest, see the `Documentation/lguest` directory in a 2.6.23 or better kernel source tree.) Figure 3-2 shows the primary Xen-related configuration settings for the 2.6.23 Linux kernel.

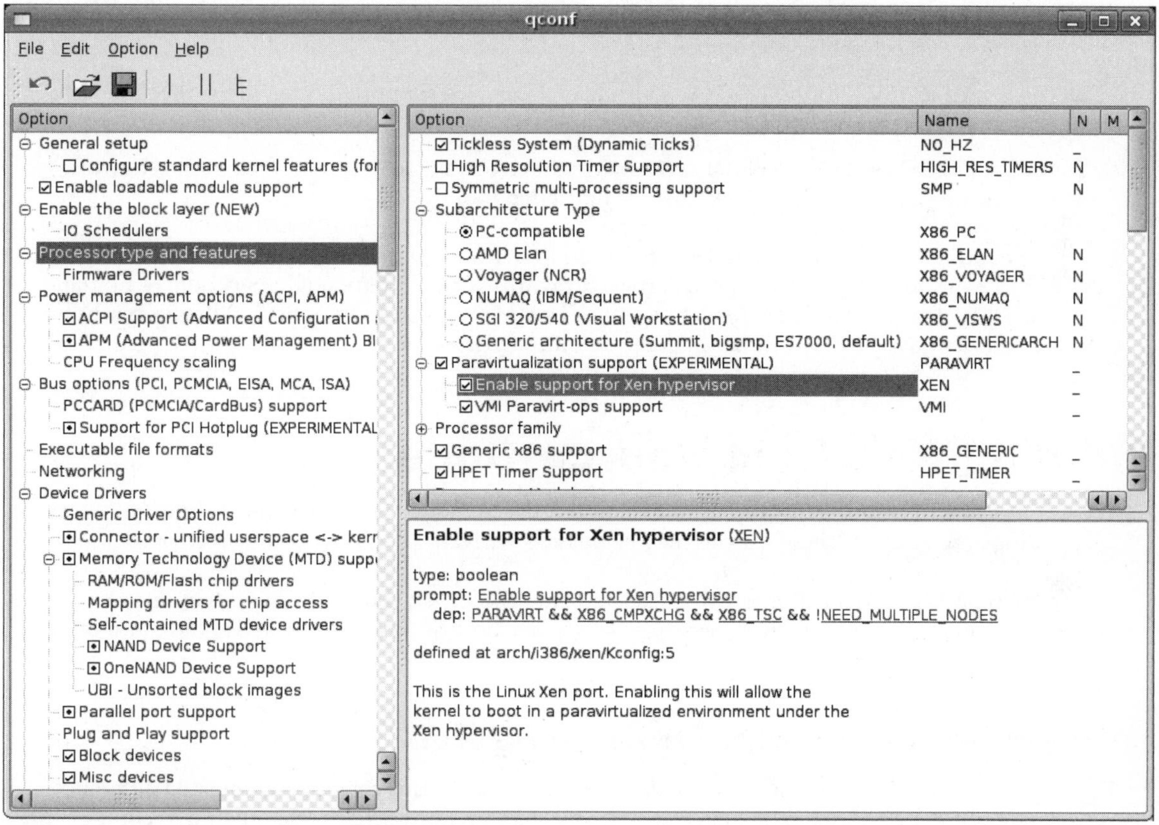

Figure 3-2

At the time of this writing, complete support for Xen is not available in the 2.6.23 kernel. Most important, the 2.6.23 kernel has only limited support for domain0 functionality, but should be fine for use in domainU guests. For domain0, you must use the vmlinux image that is produced during the kernel build process, rather than the more standard compressed vmlinuz image, because of the bzip compression mechanism used in the vmlinuz kernels. You can use the strip and gzip application to reduce the size of the vmlinux image, which should then work fine.

Configuring the 2.6.23 kernel for Xen support requires fewer configuration settings than the patched 2.6.18 kernel used with the open source Xen distribution. The primary setting is XEN, which enables support for Xen. This option is set in the Paravirtualization support section of the Processor type and features configuration area. In order to enable this option, you must specify that your processor is not a 386 or 486 so that options on which it depends are automatically enabled. Building for any Pentium, compatible, or better processor allows you to enable XEN support.

After you select the XEN option, the following others are enabled:

- ❏ **HVC_XEN:** Xen Hypervisor Console support, located in the Device Drivers ⇨ Character devices section of the kernel configuration tool.

- ❏ **XEN_BLKDEV_FRONTEND:** Xen virtual block device support, located in the Block devices section of the kernel configuration tool.

- ❏ **XEN_NETDEV_FRONTEND:** Xen network device frontend driver, located in the Network device support section of the kernel configuration tool.

If you are building a 32-bit version of the kernel, you may want to build with Physical Address Extension (PAE) support in order to get a kernel that works with modern Xen hypervisors (3.1 or later). To activate PAE support, you must first change the High Memory Support option on the Processor type and features section to be 64GB, rather than the default 4GB maximum.

Building Xen from Source Code

The introduction to "Getting the Xen Source Code" earlier in this chapter highlighted some good reasons for building Xen yourself. These reasons may be business-driven, voluntary, or process-driven.

The next few sections discuss the software packages and associated source code files that must be present on your system in order to successfully build Xen, how to compile Xen, and some common problems that you might encounter and their solutions.

Software Requirements for Building Xen

The section "Software Requirements for Building Xen," earlier in this chapter, explains the difference between the software and source code required to build a software package (compile-time requirements), and the software packages required to execute and use a software package (runtime requirements). That section focuses on runtime requirements; this section focuses on compile-time requirements.

As a virtual machine monitor that runs directly on your system's hardware, and which must export the entire hardware model used by a Linux kernel, the most fundamental requirements for building Xen are the same as those for building the Linux kernel itself — a complete toolchain and associated utilities that generate binaries for your target architecture. However, Xen also has a number of higher-level, user-space utilities written in programming languages such as C and Python, each of which adds other requirements.

I've separated the runtime and compile-time requirements for Xen into two different sections because it is quite possible that the machines on which you build software are not the same as those on which you plan to install or test that software. The software and header file packages required for building Xen should be available through the package management system used by your Linux distribution.

In order to build Xen on your system, you need to have the following packages installed on that system:

❏ **C library header and object files:** The C library header files are the include files that define common data types, data structures, macros, and functions for C application development. The C library object files are precompiled object files and libraries that are also required for developing C applications that use the standard C libraries (as almost all do). The packages that contain these files differ depending on your Linux distribution. For example, on Ubuntu and Debian systems, the libc6-dev package provides both the header and object files; on distributions such as Fedora Core, you will have to install both the glibc-headers and glibc-devel packages. The C library used on most Linux systems is known as glibc, the GNU C Library. You can get the source code for the latest version of glibc from the project home page at www.gnu .org/software/libc.

❏ **Curses library and header files:** Curses is an ancient cursor control library that was originally developed when terminals were the most common display devices for computer systems and mainframes that walked the earth. The curses library is still used for cursor control inside terminal-emulation environments such as the X Window System terminal (xterm) and the GNOME and KDE terminal and console applications. The ncurses package is a more modern rewrite of the original curses library, and is used by Xen applications such as xentop. The ncurses library is typically found in the libncurses5 package on most Linux systems; the associated header files are typically found in the libncurses5-dev package.

❏ **GNU binutils:** The binutils package contains utilities that are used when preparing different types of binaries for use on a variety of platforms. The combination of a compiler and the binutils package is typically referred to as a toolchain. The binutils package contains utilities such as the linker (ld) used to assemble object files into executables and libraries, the GNU assembler (as), and the indexer used when creating libraries (ranlib). The binutils package is probably available for your Linux distribution, but you can also get its source code from the project home page at www.gnu.org/software/binutils.

❏ **GNU compiler collection:** The C compiler (gcc) included in the GCC compiler suite is the standard compiler for Linux systems (and most other systems nowadays). Versions of Xen prior to Xen 3 required GCC version 3.*x*, but Xen 3 and later can be built successfully using the latest versions of GCC (4.*x*). Your Linux distribution almost certainly provides GCC packages, but you can get the source code for GCC from http://gcc.gnu.org, as well as precompiled binaries for many systems. The latter can be quite useful because building a compiler without a compiler is an interesting bootstrapping problem.

❏ **GNU make:** All parts of the Xen build process are controlled using the make program, which reads build instructions and sequencing dependencies from command files known as makefiles. The make program uses those instructions to build software components in the correct order, minimizing rebuild time after any changes have been made to the associated source code. A makefile contains many sets of instructions, each associated with a user-defined keyword, known as a make target, that tells the make program which set(s) of instructions to execute. GNU make is the standard version of the make program nowadays, and is probably available as a package for your Linux distribution. You can get the source code for the latest version of GNU make from the project's home page at www.gnu.org/software/make/make.html.

❏ **Patch utility:** The patch utility, discussed earlier in this chapter, is used to apply sets of changes to source code files. The patch program is probably available from your Linux distribution, but you can also get the source code for the latest version from the project home page at www.gnu .org/software/patch.

❏ **Python language and header files:** Python is a popular object-oriented programming (OOP) language. Many of the Xen tools, specifically xm, are written in Python, which is typically provided by most Linux distributions in the python package. When building Xen, you also need the header files for compiling Python applications, which are typically provided in the python-dev package. You can get the latest version of Python from its home page at www.python.org, which includes a link for downloading the latest version.

❏ **SDL library and header files:** The Simple DirectMedia Layer (SDL) is a library used to directly display the graphical console of virtual machines in a graphical X Window System environment without requiring remote connection software such as a VNC viewer. Most Linux distributions provide this library in packages such as SDL or libsdl*version*, and the associated header files in packages such as SDL-devel or libsdl-dev. The home page of the SDL library is www.libsdl.org, which also provides a link for downloading the latest version.

❏ **SSL cryptographic libraries and header files:** The SSL cryptographic libraries (libcrypto.so and others) and the header files used for compiling Linux applications that use SSL are found in the libssl-dev package. A link to the source code for the latest version of this package is available from the OpenSSL home page at www.openssl.org.

❏ **X Window System libraries and header files:** The X Window System is the standard graphical user interface provided on all Linux systems and provides the underpinnings for higher-level desktop environments such as GNOME and KDE. The header files for X Window System development are typically contained in packages such as x11-dev or libX11-devel, depending on your Linux distribution. The home page of the version of the X Window System that is currently used on most Linux systems is www.x.org.

❏ **zlib cryptographic libraries and header files:** zlib is an open source compression library used by Xen for data compression and decompression. The zlib libraries are typically found in the zlib package; the zlib header files are typically located in the zlib-dev package. The home page for zlib is located at www.zlib.net, which provides a link that enables you to download the source code for the latest version.

In addition, if you are building Xen on a 64-bit system, you also need the bbc package to build the loader for hardware virtual machines. The bcc compiler is a 16-bit compiler that produces vanilla 8086 code. This compiler is typically provided in packages such as bcc or dev86, depending on your Linux distribution. If you need to obtain the source code and build it yourself for some reason, the home page for this compiler is http://homepage.ntlworld.com/robert.debath.

The system on which you are compiling Xen will also have various standard utilities, such as the GNU tar utility, which is used to unpack the Linux kernel source code that is downloaded from www.kernel .org. These standard utilities are part of every Linux distribution, so they are not listed in detail here.

Automated Build Environment Checks

The Xen source code includes a convenient set of scripts that quickly check your system to see if it satisfies the basic requirements for building Xen. This doesn't catch everything, but it makes it easy to spot obvious omissions. To run this utility, change to the `tools/check` subdirectory of the directory that contains the Xen source code, and execute the following command:

```
$ ./chk build
Xen CHECK-BUILD  Wed Mar 14 15:55:18 EDT 2007
Checking check_crypto_lib: OK
Checking check_libvncserver: unused, OK
Checking check_openssl_devel: OK
Checking check_python: OK
Checking check_python_devel: OK
Checking check_sdl: unused, OK
Checking check_x11_devel: OK
Checking check_zlib_devel: OK
Checking check_zlib_lib: OK
```

This utility can be especially useful in verifying that you have installed the header files associated with various mandatory packages. If header files are missing, compilation proceeds to the point where they are needed, and then terminates with many messy error messages about undefined values. These can typically be traced back to the absence of a specific header file that is provided by one of the development packages.

The previous list explains all of the utilities, libraries, and header files that you need to install in order to build Xen itself. By default, building Xen (as explained in the next section) also attempts to build the Xen documentation, stopping if mandatory tools are not installed. To build the Xen documentation in PDF form, you need to install the following packages:

❑   **TeX and LaTeX:** The Xen documentation is written in LaTeX, a macro package that provides a markup language that uses the freely-available TeX document processor to create formatted documentation from which PDF documents are generated. These tools are usually provided by your Linux distribution in the tetex and tetex-extra packages. The tetex-extra package typically includes LaTeX support, although you may also have to install the tetex-latex package on some distributions. The home page for tetex is www.tug.org/teTeX.

❑   **Transfig and fig2dev:** The illustrations in the official Xen documentation are created with a tool called xfig (which you do not need), but you will need the Transfig and fig2dev tools to convert these illustrations into a form that can be successfully included in the LaTeX documentation. These are provided by most Linux distributions in the transfig and fig2dev packages. The home page for all utilities related to the xfig drawing package is www.xfig.org/.

After you have built or installed all of the mandatory packages and, optionally, used the chk utility to verify that everything that you need is present, you're ready to build Xen, as explained in the next section.

Compiling Xen

After satisfying all of the dependencies discussed in previous sections, building Xen is somewhat anti-climactic. To build Xen, change to the directory that contains your Xen source code, and type the `make world` command. You must build Xen on a platform that is connected to the Internet, because one of the first steps in the build process is to download a tarball of the version of the Linux kernel that is associated with the version of Xen that you are building. Typically, downloading the vanilla kernel source is done only the first time that you build Xen. Subsequent rebuilds will use an existing, local tarball if one is found in the top-level Xen source code directory.

If you've installed everything that is required for the build process, the Xen build should proceed smoothly. If the build fails for some reason, scroll back through the error messages that are displayed on your screen to find the initial error the occurred. This is typically something easy to fix, such as:

❑   **Missing header file:** Make sure that you installed all of the -dev packages listed in the previous section, or actually installed any packages that you built locally. If you manually built selected packages and they were installed in `/usr/local/bin` rather than `/bin` or `/usr/bin`, you may need to modify the `Config.mk` file in the Xen source code directory to add the `-I/usr/local/include` and `-L/usr/local/lib` options to the `HOSTCFLAGS` variable settings. This variable defines sets of options that are automatically used by the gcc compiler on the host on which you are building Xen.

❑   **Missing utility:** Ensure that the directory in which the missing utility is located is present in the `path` environment variable of the shell from which you began the Xen build. For example, I can remember having to add `/usr/lib64/bcc` to my path to make sure that the bcc compiler could find all of its associated utilities on a 64-bit machine.

If building Xen has failed, you must restart the build process after correcting the problem. However, you don't want to use the `make world` command the second time around because this causes the build process to clean everything, delete the kernel source trees that it has retrieved, and start over from scratch. Instead, you want to use the `make dist` command because this only restarts the build process from the point at which it terminated.

Building Separate domain0 and domainU Kernels

The Xen source code distribution provides automatic support for building separate domain0 and domainU kernels named linux-2.6-xen0 and linux-2.6-xenU by using the KERNELS environment variable, which you can specify when executing the make command. For example, to build the separate domain0 and domainU kernels, you would execute the following commands from your Xen source code directory:

```
# make mrproper
# make kernels KERNELS="linux-2.6-xen0 linux-2.6-xenU"
```

These commands make targets build the standard domain0 kernel and a much smaller domainU kernel that does not contain any physical device drivers. The former may still be too large for your tastes, and the latter may be too minimal. In these cases, you will want to customize the configuration of your kernel, as explained earlier in this chapter.

The Xen build process also provides a number of other make targets that enable you to build subsets of the Xen package rather than the complete thing. For example, make xen builds only the Xen hypervisor. Similarly, make docs builds only the Xen documentation. For a complete list of Xen make targets, change to the directory containing the Xen source code, and execute the make help command.

After the Xen build completes successfully, you're ready to install Xen and then (finally!) begin exploring the world of virtualization.

> **This section focuses on building Xen on Linux systems with standard x86 hardware. Specialized hardware, such as MacTel boxes, has additional caveats and concerns for both Xen and Linux. For information about configuring the Linux kernel and using Xen on MacTel systems, see Web sites such as the MacTel Linux site's information on kernel configuration (**www.mactel-linux.org/wiki/Kernel_Configuration_Guide**) and user sites such as Mark Klein's Xen/MacTel information at** www.scl.ameslab.gov/Projects/mini-xen

Installing Xen

After your Xen build has completed successfully, all of the files associated with Xen are located under the "dist" subdirectory of the directory containing your Xen source code. If you are installing Xen from a precompiled tarball that you've downloaded from XenSource, this tarball contains only the dist directory.

You can then install Xen via the following commands as root or via sudo:

```
# cd dist
# sh ./install.sh
```

If you have installed Xen using packages that are provided by your Linux distribution, these packages generally update your system's boot configuration by adding the correct entries for booting the Xen kernel to /boot/grub/menu.1st. However, after building Xen yourself, installing the free XenSource RPMs, or installing from a XenSource tarball of precompiled binaries, you will still have to manually create the GRUB entries to boot the Xen hypervisor, and load the kernel and initial RAM disk. You do this by creating a stanza in your /boot/grub/menu.1st file that looks like the following:

```
title Xen from XenSource
      root (hd0,0)
      kernel /xen-version.gz
      module /vmlinuz-2.6.version ro root=/dev/root-device
      module /initrd-2.6.version.img
```

You must make sure that the root entry matches the root entry of the other GRUB stanzas in /boot/grub/menu.1st that refer to the device on which your /boot directory is located. You must also replace the version and root-device keywords with the appropriate values for the version of the Xen hypervisor, Xen-enabled kernel, and initial RAM disk that you installed. You can identify the right values for the version by using the ls command to list the contents of your /boot directory.

After installing Xen, make sure that any initial RAM disk image that it refers to actually exists. If it does not, you can create one using tools such as mkinitramfs or yaird. You may need to install the packages that provide these utilities.

> When you're manually modifying the /boot/grub/menu.lst file to add Xen entries, I suggest that you initially make sure that the hidden option is not active, and increase the timeout setting to something like 10 seconds. These two changes will ensure that the GRUB boot menu is displayed on your console and will give you enough time to ensure that the kernel that you actually want to boot is selected. You may also want to ensure that the default value does not identify your Xen kernel as the default kernel for your system, just in case you've made a typo in its GRUB stanza. Remember that GRUB's default entry begins counting at 0, so the number that you provide should refer to a GRUB stanza containing the "standard" kernel for your system. Once your system and Xen are working correctly, you can reintroduce the hidden option and reduce the timeout.

After this is complete, you can reboot your system and test your new Xen installation. Congratulations! You aren't running EUNICE!

Summary

This chapter covers a lot of ground, starting with the hardware requirements for systems running Xen and the relationship between system hardware and virtual machine configuration. The early sections also discuss the ways in which system hardware can affect the types of virtual machine configurations that you can use with Xen. This chapter also discusses requirements for running and building Xen, along with the different sources from which you can obtain and install Xen on your system. The chapter concludes with an explanation of the Xen build and installation processes.

4

Booting and Configuring a Xen Host

Now the fun actually begins! The previous chapters provided background information on virtualization in general and Xen in particular, and discussed how to obtain and install Xen on a Linux system. In this chapter, we finally get to start the Xen hypervisor and boot a paravirtualized Linux kernel under the hypervisor. By the end of this chapter, you'll have a fully functioning administrative domain for Xen (domain0) and will be ready to move on to installing paravirtualized Xen virtual machines and/or fully virtualized Hardware Virtual Machines (HVMs) in your Xen environment, depending upon the capabilities of your hardware.

As in the rest of this book, this chapter focuses on using Xen on Linux systems. Therefore, this chapter focuses on the Xen hypervisor boot process, which is essentially the same on any system, and subsequent interaction between the Linux boot process and Xen domain0 initialization. If you are booting Xen on a Solaris or *BSD system, the startup process will be similar and will perform the same types of tasks, but systems other than Linux are not covered in detail in this chapter.

Overview of Xen and Linux System Startup

As discussed in the previous chapter, the standard Linux boot loader, known as the Grand Unified Bootloader or GRUB to its friends, is a key component of installing and booting the Xen hypervisor on a Linux system. GRUB not only understands how to boot the Xen hypervisor like any other bootable image, but it also understands how to identify a Linux kernel and associated initial RAM disk that your domain0 Linux kernel may require. As you might expect, there are many options, bells, and whistles that you can configure when booting the hypervisor and loading the domain0 kernel and any associated RAM disk. This makes it important to have a good idea of both the Xen and standard Linux boot processes, how Linux systems discover devices and start processes such as system daemons during the boot process, and so on.

The next few sections of this chapter discuss each aspect of the startup process on a Xen domain0 system: BIOS initialization, executing GRUB, starting the Xen hypervisor, and starting a domain0 kernel and associated Linux system. A final section discusses how to use a serial console and serial connection to another system in order to capture system boot information for debugging purposes. This should rarely be necessary, but can be critically important when you do actually need it.

BIOS Initialization and System Startup

When you first turn on a computer system, it loads a boot monitor or BIOS (Basic Input/Output System) from storage on the motherboard. This storage is usually a programmable read-only memory (PROM), chip or a section of flash memory that is present on the board. The BIOS or boot monitor is a very low-level, hardware-oriented application that does some basic hardware initialization, performs some amount of hardware testing and verification (often optional), waits for keyboard or console input for some predetermined period of time, and then usually begins to execute a set of predetermined instructions to load another program into memory. These instructions load another program into memory from a predetermined location such as a portion of flash memory or the Master Boot Record (MBR) of a storage device such as a hard drive or CD-ROM, and then they specify the memory address at which to begin executing the program once it has been loaded successfully.

On most desktop and server computer systems, an intermediate program is loaded into memory from the MBR, which then provides additional configuration and customization options for the boot process. On modern x86, PPC, and SPARC systems, the program that is loaded into memory at this point is known as a boot loader, which is a configurable application that provides higher-level options for loading an operating system on the computer. The boot loader that is most commonly used on modern x86 systems today (including 64-bit systems) is the Grand Unified Bootloader (GRUB), although some Linux distributions still use an older, simpler boot loader known as the Linux Loader (LILO). Xen requires the use of GRUB.

GRUB

Boot loaders traditionally consist of two stages: a minimal first-stage boot loader and a more elegant, second-stage boot loader. The size of a first-stage boot loader is constrained by the size of the MBR on a storage device, which is a single sector (512 bytes). Therefore, the first-stage boot loader primarily contains enough information to locate and load the second-stage boot loader, which is where all the action is.

GRUB uses an intermediate step in the boot process, first loading what GRUB calls a stage 1.5 boot loader that understands a specific type of Linux filesystem, and can therefore load GRUB's text-format configuration file directly from your machine's root filesystem. GRUB provides many different stage 1.5 boot loaders, including the following:

- ❏ e2fs_stage1_5: For booting from a partition containing an ext2 or ext3 filesystem
- ❏ fat_stage1_5: For booting from a partition containing a DOS or Microsoft Windows VFAT filesystem
- ❏ ffs_stage1_5: For booting from a partition containing a Berkeley Fast FileSystem
- ❏ iso9660_stage1_5: For booting from a partition containing an ISO9660 filesystem, such as a CD-ROM
- ❏ jfs_stage1_5: For booting from a partition containing a JFS filesystem
- ❏ minix_stage1: For booting from a partition containing a Minix filesystem
- ❏ reiserfs_stage1_5: For booting from a partition containing a ReiserFS filesystem
- ❏ ufs2_stage1_5: For booting from a partition containing a traditional UNIX filesystem
- ❏ vstafs_stage1_5: For booting from a partition containing a Plan 9 VSTa filesystem
- ❏ xfs_stage1_5: For booting from a partition containing an XFS filesystem

The stage 1.5 boot loaders provided with GRUB depend on the Linux distribution that you have installed and are using for your domain0 system. Most Linux systems include stage 1.5 boot loaders for booting from ext2/ext3, JFS, Minix, ReiserFS, VFAT, and XFS filesystems.

The stage 1.5 boot loader then loads GRUB's second-stage boot loader and associated configuration files directly from the type of filesystem on which they are located.

A second-stage boot loader typically provides access to a menu that enables you to choose between different ways of loading an operating system on your computer. GRUB can be configured to display this menu for a short period of time, to only display it in response to specific keyboard input (such as pressing the Escape key), or not to display it at all. Once your system boots Linux, you can modify the configuration of the boot loader to automatically display a menu by modifying the boot loader's configuration file, which is usually /boot/grub/menu.1st for GRUB. On some Linux distributions, such as Fedora, /boot/grub/menu.1st (which stands for menu list, hence the 1st extension) is actually a symbolic link to the GRUB configuration file /boot/grub/grub.conf.

On many Linux systems, GRUB is configured to boot a default configuration without displaying a menu. If this is the case on your system, you can press the Escape key when GRUB first starts (do it quickly!) to display a menu that shows all of the available GRUB boot options. Figure 4-1 shows an example of a GRUB menu on a Ubuntu system. If you do not press Escape during the boot process, GRUB will automatically boot the default boot configuration that its configuration file directs it to use.

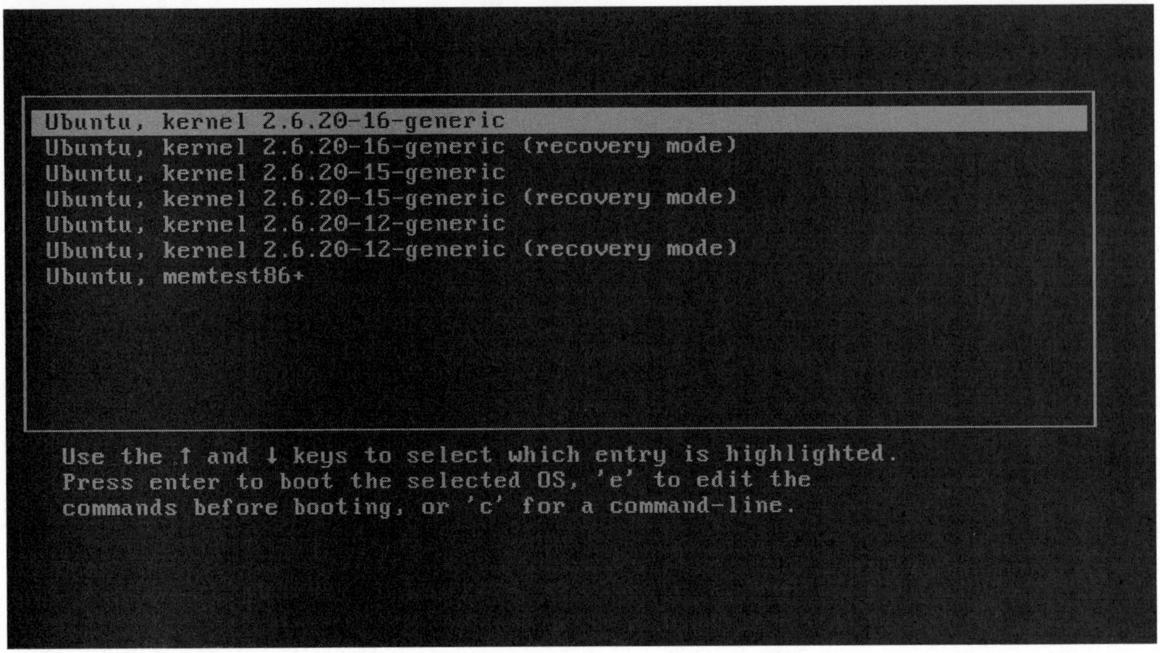

```
Ubuntu, kernel 2.6.20-16-generic
Ubuntu, kernel 2.6.20-16-generic (recovery mode)
Ubuntu, kernel 2.6.20-15-generic
Ubuntu, kernel 2.6.20-15-generic (recovery mode)
Ubuntu, kernel 2.6.20-12-generic
Ubuntu, kernel 2.6.20-12-generic (recovery mode)
Ubuntu, memtest86+




    Use the ↑ and ↓ keys to select which entry is highlighted.
    Press enter to boot the selected OS, 'e' to edit the
    commands before booting, or 'c' for a command-line.
```

Figure 4-1

GRUB configuration files typically contain multiple definitions for ways to boot your system. Each set of related entries is referred to as a stanza. In a standard, non-Xen GRUB stanza, the GRUB entries look like the following:

```
title   Ubuntu, kernel 2.6.15-23-386
        root    (hd0,0)
        kernel /boot/vmlinuz-2.6.15-23-386 root=/dev/hda1 ro quiet splash
        initrd /boot/initrd.img-2.6.15-23-386
```

Extra white space is ignored in entries in a GRUB stanza. Each line in a stanza begins with a keyword that identifies the aspect of the boot process that it described. In the preceding example, these entries have the following meanings:

❏   `title`: Provides the name for this entry displayed on the GRUB menu.

❏   `root`: Identifies the absolute location of the runtime root filesystem using GRUB's own nomenclature.

❏   `kernel`: Identifies the kernel to boot and provides command-line boot parameters for that kernel.

❏   `initrd`: Identifies an initial RAM disk or initial RAM filesystem image that should be loaded by the kernel during the boot process.

In a Xen boot stanza, the syntax is slightly different. A standard Xen boot stanza for GRUB looks like the following:

```
title   Xen 3.0.5 RC2 Serial Console
        root    (hd0,0)
        kernel /boot/xen.gz
        module /boot/vmlinuz-2.6-xen ro root=/dev/hda1
        module /boot/initrd-2.6.18-xen.img
```

In a Xen boot stanza, GRUB loads the Xen hypervisor using its kernel command, and then uses the module keywords to subsequently identify the domain0 kernel and an (optional) initial RAM disk or filesystem. You can pass a variety of options to Xen on the kernel line, all of which are discussed in the "Configuring GRUB for Xen" section later in this chapter. The majority of these only affect the Xen hypervisor, although some are also propagated to the Linux kernel for domain0. These options are discussed in the "Shared Xen and Linux Boot Options" section later in this chapter.

Finally, Xen adds a few new command-line parameters to the Linux kernel itself. These are discussed later in this chapter, in the "Xen-Specific Linux Boot Options" section.

> The GRUB keywords discussed in this section are only a subset of the keywords supported by GRUB. For complete information about GRUB configuration files, see the online documentation for GRUB, which is provided in the grub-doc package, which you must install manually using the Synaptic package manager or the apt-get application. Once you have installed this package, the complete GRUB documentation is available by typing `info grub` from any Ubuntu command line. For even more information about GRUB, see the GRUB home page at `www.gnu.org/software/grub`. This page also discusses the new, improved, family-size version of GRUB, GRUB2, that is currently under development.

The next step in booting your domain0 Xen system is actually loading and executing the hypervisor, which is described in the next section.

The Xen Boot and Initialization Process

When you boot your system and select a Xen boot stanza, the system boots the hypervisor, which probes your system and performs some basic initialization before chain-loading the domain0 Xen kernel and an optional RAM disk. Much of the Xen hypervisor's initialization process can be customized by the options discussed later in this chapter in the section "Configuring GRUB for Xen." This section provides a high-level overview of the vanilla hypervisor boot and initialization processes up to the point where the hypervisor loads the domain0 kernel, at which point the remainder of the boot process is the same as that on any Linux (or other UNIX-like system).

The Xen hypervisor's initialization process primarily consists of probing and initializing your system's hardware so that the hypervisor can correctly map and handle incoming requests from the actual device drivers used by the domain0 kernel, as well as requests from paravirtualized drivers in other domains. The hypervisor begins by reserving internal regions for bookkeeping, interrupt, and device management. It then examines system memory, optionally disabling any pages that have been marked as bad through Xen command line options (explained later in this chapter), and selecting a processor or processor core for its use.

Once a processor has been selected, the hypervisor enables Advanced Programmable Interrupt Controller (APIC) interrupt requests, and allocates physical memory for use, once again optionally limited by Xen hypervisor command-line options. Xen then creates its own memory map for managing memory use by various domains. Finally, the hypervisor loads the Linux kernel that it should boot for domain0 and validates the initial RAM disk (if any) that is associated with the domain0 kernel. It then transfers control to the domain0 kernel.

If you want to see detailed information about the Xen hypervisor boot process, you can either capture Xen information through a serial console (as described later in this chapter in the section "Capturing Xen and Linux Boot and Startup Information") or execute the xm dmesg command as a user with root privileges on your domain0 system after it has booted successfully and started the xend process. The xm dmesg command is exactly like the standard dmesg command, except that it displays the message ring buffer associated with the Xen hypervisor rather than the standard Linux kernel's ring buffer. The following is sample output from the xm dmesg command on one of my systems:

```
 __  __/__ _ __      __ ___ / / | / |
 \ \/ /__  _  __    |   / / | / |
  \ // _ \ '_ \     |_ \ | | | |
  / \  __/ | | |     __) || |_| |
 /_/\_\___|_| |_|    |____(_)_(_)_|

http://www.cl.cam.ac.uk/netos/xen
University of Cambridge Computer Laboratory
Xen version 3.1.1 (root@) (gcc version 4.1.2 (Ubuntu 4.1.2-0ubuntu4)) Thu Oct 11
    09:23:46 EDT 2007
Latest ChangeSet: Thu Oct 11 10:12:07 2007 +0100 15467:d6d3c7856abc
(XEN) Command line: noreboot dom0_mem=1G
(XEN) Video information:
(XEN)  VGA is text mode 80x25, font 8x16
(XEN)  VBE/DDC methods: V2; EDID transfer time: 1 seconds
(XEN) Disc information:
(XEN)  Found 1 MBR signatures
(XEN)  Found 1 EDD information structures
(XEN) Xen-e820 RAM map:
(XEN)  0000000000000000 - 000000000000a0000 (usable)
(XEN)  00000000000f0000 - 0000000000100000 (reserved)
(XEN)  0000000000100000 - 00000000cf688000 (usable)
(XEN)  00000000cf688c04 - 00000000cf68ac04 (ACPI NVS)
(XEN)  00000000cf68ac04 - 00000000cf68cc04 (ACPI data)
(XEN)  00000000cf68cc04 - 00000000d0000000 (reserved)
(XEN)  00000000f0000000 - 00000000f4000000 (reserved)
(XEN)  00000000fec04000 - 00000000fed00400 (reserved)
(XEN)  00000000fed20000 - 00000000feda0000 (reserved)
(XEN)  00000000fee00000 - 00000000fef00000 (reserved)
(XEN)  00000000ffb00000 - 0000000100000000 (reserved)
(XEN) System RAM: 3318MB (3397792kB)
(XEN) Xen heap: 9MB (10132kB)
(XEN) Domain heap initialised: DMA width 32 bits
(XEN) PAE enabled, limit: 16 GB
(XEN) Processor #0 15:4 APIC version 20
(XEN) Processor #1 15:4 APIC version 20
(XEN) IOAPIC[0]: apic_id 8, version 32, address 0xfec04000, GSI 0-23
(XEN) Enabling APIC mode:  Flat.  Using 1 I/O APICs
```

```
(XEN) Using scheduler: SMP Credit Scheduler (credit)
(XEN) Detected 2793.153 MHz processor.
(XEN) CPU0: Intel(R) Pentium(R) D CPU 2.80GHz stepping 07
(XEN) Mapping cpu 0 to node 255
(XEN) Booting processor 1/1 eip 90000
(XEN) Mapping cpu 1 to node 255
(XEN) CPU1: Intel(R) Pentium(R) D CPU 2.80GHz stepping 07
(XEN) Total of 2 processors activated.
(XEN) ENABLING IO-APIC IRQs
(XEN)  -> Using new ACK method
(XEN) Platform timer overflows in 14998 jiffies.
(XEN) Platform timer is 14.318MHz HPET
(XEN) Brought up 2 CPUs
(XEN) acm_init: Loading default policy (NULL).
(XEN) *** LOADING DOMAIN 0 ***
(XEN)  Xen  kernel: 32-bit, PAE, lsb
(XEN)  Dom0 kernel: 32-bit, PAE, lsb, paddr 0xc0100000 -> 0xc0447e3c
(XEN) PHYSICAL MEMORY ARRANGEMENT:
(XEN)  Dom0 alloc.:   000000003c040000->000000003e000000 (253952 pages to be
   allocated)
(XEN) VIRTUAL MEMORY ARRANGEMENT:
(XEN)  Loaded kernel: c0100000->c0447e3c
(XEN)  Init. ramdisk: c0448000->c1847800
(XEN)  Phys-Mach map: c1848000->c1948000
(XEN)  Start info:    c1948000->c194846c
(XEN)  Page tables:   c1949000->c195c040
(XEN)  Boot stack:    c195c040->c195d000
(XEN)  TOTAL:         c0400000->c1c04000
(XEN)  ENTRY ADDRESS: c0100000
(XEN) Dom0 has maximum 2 VCPUs
(XEN) Initrd len 0x13ff800, start at 0xc0448000
(XEN) Scrubbing Free RAM: ......................done.
(XEN) Xen trace buffers: disabled
(XEN) Std. Loglevel: Errors and warnings
(XEN) Guest Loglevel: Nothing (Rate-limited: Errors and warnings)
(XEN) Xen is relinquishing VGA console.
(XEN) *** Serial input -> DOM0 (type 'CTRL-a' three times to switch input to Xen).
(XEN) Freed 96kB init memory.
```

The next section describes the process of booting a Linux kernel, loading its optional RAM disk or RAM filesystem, and performing basic initialization up to the point where the kernel actually starts the first Linux user-space process and begins user-space system startup.

Loading the Kernel and Optional RAM Disk

As with a regular Linux kernel, the kernel specified in a Xen GRUB stanza is typically a compressed kernel image that is loaded directly into memory. This compressed kernel is prefixed by some instructions that perform initial hardware and execution environment setup (stack definition, page table initialization, starting the swapper, and so on), uncompress the kernel image into high memory, store any initial RAM disk or initial RAM filesystem in memory for subsequent access, and then begin execution of the uncompressed kernel. Xen-based kernels use the virtual memory map for the kernel and initial RAM disk or filesystem that have already been laid out by the hypervisor during its initialization.

The kernel then sets up interrupts, performs additional hardware initialization, and then uncompresses and mounts any initial RAM disk or filesystem that was found in the kernel image or specified using GRUB's initrd keyword. If an initial RAM disk or filesystem is found or specified, the system follows the sequence of events described in the next section, "Loading and Using an Initial RAM Disk or RAM Filesystem." If no initial RAM disk or initial RAM filesystem is found in the kernel or identified using the initrd parameter, the kernel mounts the root filesystem identified on the command line using the disk identifiers specified in GRUB's root entry, and then starts the standard system initialization process, as described in "The Linux System Startup Process" later in this chapter.

Loading and Using an Initial RAM Disk or RAM Filesystem

Many Linux systems use a special type of filesystem as part of the boot process, before actually mounting the non-transient storage devices that are attached to your system. These initial filesystems are optional, and come in two different flavors: an initrd (initial RAM disk) or initramfs (initial RAM filesystem). On most desktop and server computer systems, these initial filesystems are typically used to load kernel modules, such as specialized device drivers that the kernel needs but which are not built into the kernel, and to perform specialized hardware and software initialization functions. On most desktop and server systems, an initial RAM disk or initial RAM filesystem is almost always a transient part of the boot process.

Initial RAM disks are the traditional mechanism used by many 2.6 and all earlier Linux kernels to enable the kernel to load drivers and execute processes that must be available in order to boot successfully. Initial RAM disks are compressed files that contain an actual filesystem in a format such as ext2, romfs, and so on. Initial RAM disks are uncompressed into a pre-allocated portion of memory and are then mounted for use by the kernel. The primary problems with initial RAM disks is that they consume a substantial amount of system memory and, because they are actual block devices, require the kernel to contain drivers for whatever type of filesystem they use.

The development series (2.5) preceding the release of the 2.6 Linux kernel introduced the idea of initial RAM filesystems that exist directly in the kernel's file and directory cache. Initial RAM filesystems are identified or built into the kernel in the same way that initial RAM disks are, but consist of compressed archive files in the format produced by the UNIX/Linux cpio command. These archive files contain all of the files and directory entries for the initial RAM filesystem, and are directly unpacked into the kernel's file and directory entry cache, which is then mounted as a filesystem. Using the file and directory cache as a filesystem substantially reduces the amount of memory required for the initial RAM filesystem because files and directories live in the kernel's page and directory entry (dentry) cache, where they would be copied anyway if they were used from a filesystem located on a block device. An initial RAM filesystem is an instance of the Linux tmpfs filesystem.

Linux systems that boot with an initial RAM disk execute the file /linuxrc from that filesystem after uncompressing and mounting the filesystem. This file is typically a command file, but can also be a version of the /sbin/init program that follows the standard initialization process described in the "The Linux System Startup Process" section later in this chapter. (This is typically done when the initial RAM disk will be your runtime filesystem, as in embedded systems.) Linux systems that boot with an initial RAM filesystem execute the file /init from that filesystem after loading it into the file and directory entry cache. As with the /linuxrc file used with initial RAM disks, /init is typically a command file, but can also be a version of the init program that follows the standard runtime system initialization process described in the next section.

On desktop and server systems that use physical root filesystems, the last step in the /linuxrc or /init instructions is to mount the real root filesystem (identified in the kernel or by using the root= kernel boot parameter), begin using that root filesystem as the new root filesystem (by using a pivot_root or chroot command), and starting the init process, as described in the section "The Linux System Startup Process."

Comparing Initial RAM Disks and RAM-Based Filesystems

Some of the more significant ways in which initial RAM disks and initial RAM filesystems differ are the following:

❑   You do not need any special privileges to build an initial RAM filesystem file or a kernel that contains one. Building an initial RAM disk typically requires root privileges unless you do so using an external application such as the genext2fs application.

❑   Initial RAM disks (initrd) are compressed files containing a filesystem in a specific format such as ext2, romfs, cramfs, squashfs, and so on. Initial RAM filesystems (initramfs) are compressed archive files in the format used by the Linux/UNIX cpio application.

❑   Initial RAM disks must be prepared outside the kernel and identified during the kernel build process if you want to link them directly into the kernel. Initial RAM filesystems can be prepared outside the kernel and identified during the kernel build process, but can also be automatically created during the kernel build process. 2.6 and later kernels enable you to identifying a directory that contains the files that you want to have in your initial RAM filesystem or a configuration file that describes their contents.

❑   Initial RAM disks allocate and require a fixed amount of memory that is specified when building the kernel, regardless of the actual size of the files and directories that they contain. Any space not used by files and directories in the initial RAM disk is completely wasted. Initial RAM filesystems are directly allocated in the kernel's page and dentry cache, and therefore only require allocating the amount of memory that is required by the files and directories that they contain.

❑   You can easily add a new script or file to an initial RAM filesystem that is specified as an external file in GRUB by using the gunzip application to uncompress the cpio archive, using the cpio --append command to add the new file to the archive, and using the gzip command to recompress the archive. You should do this only for testing purposes because your modification will go away the next time you build a kernel or receive an update. You can permanently add the file or script to future initial RAM filesystems that you build by adding that file or script to the directory or script pointed to by the CONFIG_INITRAMFS_SOURCE kernel configuration variable for your kernel.

❑   Initial RAM disks automatically execute the file /linuxrc from the RAM disk. Initial RAM filesystems automatically execute the file /init from the RAM filesystem. The /init file in an initramfs filesystem runs with process ID 1, just like the init process in a standard Linux system.

The contents of an initial RAM disk or initial RAM filesystem differ based on the hardware, system capabilities, and type of Linux system that you are using. Desktop Linux systems typically use these filesystems to provide loadable device drivers or mandatory system setup procedures that are required in order to proceed with the boot process. This is especially important for server systems that may need to load drivers for special hardware that enables them to configure and access network-based storage, such as ATA-over-Ethernet (AoE) or iSCSI hardware or filesystems, before the system can actually come all the way up. Both initial RAM disks and initial RAM filesystems provide only transient storage that does not enable you to save files across system restarts, but initial RAM filesystems are much more efficient and place fewer requirements on the kernel.

The Linux System Startup Process

After loading the kernel and mounting a runtime root filesystem, traditional UNIX and Linux systems execute a system application known as the init (initialization) process, which is typically found in /sbin/init on Linux systems. Typically, the init process is process number 1 on the system, as shown in a process status listing produced using the ps command, and is therefore the ancestor of all other processes on your system.

The traditional init binary used on most UNIX and Linux systems is part of a package of applications known as the sysvinit package. The sysvinit package uses a package of related command scripts known as the initscripts package, to identify the processes that are started when a system boots into different runlevels and the order in which they are started. The sysvinit program reads the file /etc/inittab to identify the way in which the system should boot and defines all of the other processes and programs that it should start.

As the name suggests, the sysvinit package and related processes have their conceptual roots in the Sys V version of UNIX — or more properly UNIX System V, Release 4 (SVR4) — which was released in 1989. Although elegant in its simplicity, the sysvinit package suffers from a lack of parallelism and flexibility, which can lead to longer system startup times than are absolutely necessary and can complicate the process of recognizing and using networked and removable devices. Various replacement init packages are available to replace sysvinit with a faster, increasingly parallel, and more responsive system initialization mechanism. The best known of these are initng (Init, the Next Generation — www.initng .org/), Apple's launchd (http://developer.apple.com/macosx/launchd.html), Sun's Predictive Self-Healing architecture and Service Management Facilities (SMF) (www.sun.com/bigadmin/content/selfheal), and upstart (http://upstart.ubuntu.com):

❑ **initng:** Can start multiple processes in parallel, and is designed to be able to start subsequent processes as soon as any dependencies that they have are satisfied. (It is therefore commonly referred to as a "dependency-based" initialization mechanism.) initng is available for many Linux distributions, but is not used by default on any distribution that I'm aware of.

❑ **launchd:** The replacement init system used in Mac OS X, and designed to also replace other system scheduling mechanisms such as cron and xinetd. launchd was not originally an open source project, and its conversion to open source hasn't attracted many users other than those from Mac OS X.

❑ **SMF:** Sun's SMF is a dependency-based and extremely responsive notification system that enables processes to be started and restarted as needed. It is now open source with the rest of Solaris, but is not GPL and therefore no one is using it outside of Solaris. In general, I can't see widespread adoption of this, primarily because it is a complex system that is orthogonal to most of the initialization and notification mechanisms that are currently used by Linux, such as udev, dbus, and hotplug. It would also need another name for anyone to take it seriously — "Predictive Self-Healing" sounds like it should ship with a crystal or some incense.

❑ **upstart:** Developed for the Ubuntu Linux distribution and used only by that distribution at the time of this writing. However, it is designed to be portable and can easily be adopted by other distributions. upstart is an event-driven system initialization package that increases parallelism in system startup tasks and provides a highly responsive framework for starting, stopping, and automatically restarting processes that depend on the availability of services that are started earlier in the system initialization process.

This chapter focuses on discussing the system startup mechanisms that are deployed by default with existing Linux distributions, namely sysvinit and upstart.

The existence of different system initialization mechanisms on different Linux distributions is another good argument for using the set of Xen packages that are provided by whatever Linux distribution you select as the basis for your virtualization environment. These packages will be integrated with your system's startup mechanism, simplifying that aspect of system administration for you. However, you may still need to use a version of Xen that is newer than the one that is available for your distribution. The "Xen-Related Startup Scripts and Processes" section of this chapter identifies the critical Xen and Xen-related processes that must be started on a domain0 system and the scripts that traditionally start them. If you are rolling your own version of Xen, you must make sure that these critical processes are available for successful integration with the Xen hypervisor and the correct initialization of your network environment. You may need to customize the default Xen startup mechanism to work correctly on your system.

System Runlevels

Most desktop and server Linux systems use the concept of *runlevels* to identify the applications that the system executes and the order in which they are executed. Different runlevels are simply a way of defining a set of applications that the system administrator believes should be run when the system is being used in a certain way. For example, runlevel 1 is usually known as single-user mode, and is used for system maintenance. Only the core set of applications required for a system administrator to contact the system and perform maintenance tasks are running when the system is in runlevel 1. The runlevels used by Linux systems are the following:

- ❏ **0:** Halt.
- ❏ **1:** Single-user.
- ❏ **2:** Default multiuser runlevel on Linux systems such as Ubuntu and Debian. On Linux distributions where runlevel 3 or 5 is the default multiuser runlevels, runlevel 2 is a multiuser runlevel without networking support.
- ❏ **3:** Non-graphical multiuser runlevel on Linux distributions such as Fedora, Red Hat, SUSE, Mandrake, and so on.
- ❏ **4:** Reserved for a custom, user-defined runlevel.
- ❏ **5:** Graphical multiuser runlevel on Linux distributions such as Fedora, Red Hat, SUSE, Mandrake, and so on.
- ❏ **6:** Used to reboot a Linux system.

Runlevels are a core concept of the sysvinit package and provide the traditional mechanism for system initialization on Linux systems. The concept of runlevels is therefore well-known and well-understood by most system administrators. Even alternate system initialization and init packages, such as those introduced at the end of the previous section, are typically installed so that they emulate the spirit and behavior of the sysvinit package, while forsaking its internals. For example, Ubuntu's upstart package installs itself in sysvinit compatibility mode so that it still follows the runlevel convention. (More about this in the "Upstart System Initialization" section later in this chapter.)

The startup commands associated with each Linux runlevel are located in the directory /etc/rcN.d, where N is the number associated with a runlevel. The files in these directories have names of the form Snnname or Knnname, and are usually executable shell scripts (or, more commonly, are links to a common set of scripts) that contain lists of other system commands to execute. Files beginning with the letter "S" are executed when the system starts a specified runlevel. Entries beginning with the letter "K" are executed when the system leaves a specified runlevel. Commands are executed in the numerical order specified by the number Variable. The Variable portion of an entry is user-defined, but is generally evocative of the program or subsystem that the file starts.

Because Linux systems start many of the same commands at different runlevels, the entries in the runlevel command directories are usually just symbolic links to the master collection of system startup and shutdown scripts located in the directory /etc/init.d. The names of the symbolic links in the different runlevel directories use the Snnname and Knnname naming convention to impose a sequence on their execution. The names of the scripts in /etc/init.d (that is, the scripts that the runlevel directories link) have generic names. Using symbolic links rather than explicit startup and shutdown scripts for each runlevel makes it easy to add or remove services from a given runlevel without duplicating the master scripts, and leaves /etc/init.d as a single, central location where you can modify any of these scripts to propagate your changes to the startup/shutdown process for all of the associated runlevels.

sysvinit System Initialization

Systems that use both the sysvinit and initscripts packages boot in the following sequence: once the kernel is loaded and begins executing from its runtime root filesystem, it invokes a process known as the /sbin/init (initialization) process, which reads the file /etc/inittab to identify the basic processes and programs that it should start.

In the /etc/inittab file, the default runlevel for your system is identified with a line containing the string "initdefault," as in the following example:

```
id:2:initdefault:
```

In this case, the default runlevel is 2. An additional entry in the /etc/inittab file identifies a command script that is run to initialize the system itself, as in the following example:

```
si::sysinit:/etc/init.d/rcS
```

> On some Linux distributions, such as Ubuntu with sysvinit compatibility, the /etc/init.d/rcS command actually runs the /etc/init.d/rc command with an argument of S which executes all of the scripts in the directory /etc/rcS.d that begin with an upper-case S, as described in the rest of this section. On some other Linux distributions, the system initialization script is a single script to which you manually add any initialization commands that you want to run.

After the system initialization script is run, Linux distributions that use the sysvinit and initscripts packages then define what occurs when the system enters a specific runlevel. For example, a few lines later in the /etc/inittab file, you might see additional information about runlevel 2 in an entry such as the following:

```
l2:2:wait:/etc/init.d/rc 2
```

This line specifies that when the system enters runlevel 2, the /etc/init.d/rc command will be executed with an argument of 2. This causes rc (run command) to execute all of the appropriate files located in the directory /etc/rc2.d, following the S (start) and K (kill) naming convention that was discussed earlier in the section on runlevels.

As the last step of the startup process for any multiuser runlevel, the init process for most Linux distributions runs the script /etc/rc.local, which is provided so that you can customize the startup process for a specific machine without making general changes to the startup scripts and symbolic links for that machine.

Two traditional assumptions that you can make about the startup scripts on your system are the following, regardless of the system initialization mechanism that it uses:

❑ All device drivers have been initialized, local filesystems have been mounted, and networking is available after all of the S40* scripts have completed.

❑ The system clock has been set, NFS filesystems have been mounted (if any are listed in /etc/fstab or you use the automounter, which is started later), and all filesystems have been checked for consistency after all of the S60* scripts have been executed.

You should keep these rules in mind when adding your own startup scripts to the startup sequence for any of your system runlevels.

upstart System Initialization

upstart is an extremely interesting event-driven system initialization system that replaces the traditional init program and (currently) provides compatibility with the sysvinit and initscripts runlevel mechanism. Events are essentially string messages that can be sent by a process in response to a change in the state of something that it is monitoring. Event messages are sent once by a process.

The control files for upstart's version of /sbin/init are known as *job files* and are located in the directory /etc/event.d. Each of these is a text file that must contain at least the following:

❑ One or more events in response to which that job file should perform some action. For example, the start on startup entry states that a job file should be executed when a startup event is received, and the stop on runlevel 2 entry states that a job file should stop whenever a runlevel 2 event is received.

❑ An exec or script stanza that identifies the tasks to be performed in response to the events for which this job file is valid. An exec stanza is used to execute a specific binary and associated command line on the system. A script stanza provides shell script code that should be executed, and must end with an end script statement.

Other keywords can also be used in upstart job files in order to identify output devices, scripts to run before the primary exec or script section is executed, scripts to run after the primary exec or script sections are completed, and so on. The pre- and post-scripts are intended to be able to initialize the environment required for script or exec commands, and to clean up or perform post-processing after they complete. Other upstart commands are also available in job files. See http://upstart.ubuntu .com/getting-started.html for a complete list.

For example, the following is the job file /etc/event.d/rcS, which is used to emulate the behavior of a Linux system at startup time or in single-user mode:

```
start on startup
stop on run level
# Note: there can be no previous run level here, if we have one
# it's bad information (we enter rc1 not rcS for maintenance).
console output
script
        run level --set S >/dev/null || true
        PREVLEVEL=N
        RUNLEVEL=S
        export PREVLEVEL RUNLEVEL
        exec /etc/init.d/rcS
end script
```

The following two conceptual classes of processes are managed by upstart:

❑ **Tasks**: Must complete and therefore essentially transition from stopped, to started, and back to stopped.

❑ **Services**: Must be running, and therefore essentially transition from stopped to started. Services have either respawn or service in their job file.

upstart's init program generates the following system events:

❑ startup: Event issued when the system boots and /sbin/init first starts.

❑ shutdown: Event issued when the system is in the process of being shut down.

❑ stalled: Event issued when there are no jobs running and no pending events are in the queue.

Similarly, the shutdown tool provided with upstart sends one of the following events when the system is being shut down, depending upon the way in which the shutdown command was issued:

❑ reboot

❑ halt

❑ poweroff

❑ maintenance (i.e., single-user mode)

You can also manually send a specific event from the shutdown command by invoking it as:

```
shutdown -e event ...
```

upstart jobs also generate events themselves when they change state, making it easy to chain multiple job files together and guarantee dependencies. Job files issue the following events:

- ❏ jobname/start: Sent when a job is first started.

- ❏ jobname/started: Sent once a job has actually started.

- ❏ jobname/stop: Sent when a job is stopping.

- ❏ jobname/stopped: Sent once a job has stopped.

- ❏ jobname: For services, this event is generated once the associated task is running. For tasks, this event is generated once it has finished.

Processes on the system can send events through the upstart control socket or by invoking initctl trigger event from within a script or job file.

As mentioned earlier in this section, Ubuntu's upstart system is installed in sysvinit emulation mode by default. When you start up a Ubuntu system, /sbin/init issues a startup event. This causes the script /etc/event.d/rcS to run, which executes the run level command, triggering a runlevel event. The script then execs itself again, and stops when the runlevel event is detected. Stopping this script triggers the /etc/event.d/rc-default script.

The /etc/event.d/rc-default script first checks if you booted the system with the single keyword on the kernel command line, indicating that you want to boot the system in single-user mode. If so, the script uses the telinit command to put the system in single-user mode. If not, the script checks for the presence of an /etc/inittab file. This file is not provided by default on Ubuntu 7.04 and later systems, but this check gives you a way to override the system's default runlevel by creating this file with an appropriate initdefault entry (as described in the previous section). If this file is not found, the script automatically executes the run level command to put the system in runlevel 2. This invokes the script /etc/event.d/rc2, which executes the scripts in the directory /etc/rc2.d in the standard order, and away we go!

Ubuntu's upstart mechanism is a breath of fresh air that provides a faster, simpler, and more parallel boot mechanism while (at the moment) preserving the core runlevel concepts and associated startup script model that all Linux system administrators have become one with over the years.

Xen-Related Startup Scripts and Processes

Xen assumes that your Linux system is running a sysvinit-like startup mechanism. Installing Xen domain0 on a system causes two primary scripts to be installed in the directory /etc/init.d:

- ❏ xend: The shell script responsible for starting, stopping, and otherwise managing the primary Xen daemon, /usr/sbin/xend, which is written in the Python programming language. The xend script accepts the following keywords: start, stop, reload, restart, and status. The Xen daemon executes the commands in its configuration file, /etc/xen/ xend-config-xenapi.sxp, when it starts. Among other things, this configuration file identifies the network startup script that xend should run to initialize Xen's bridged networking. By default, this is the script /etc/xen/scripts/network-bridge, although other network startup scripts are available. All of the Xen-specific scripts provided with Xen are located in the directory /etc/xen/scripts. See Chapter 8 for more detailed information about Xen networking and the different networking configurations that are available.

❑   `xendomains`: The script responsible for automatically starting selected Xen domains at boot time. By default, this script sets environment variables from the system configuration file `/etc/sysconfig/xendomains` (if it exists), restarting any stopped domains whose images are located in the directory `/var/lib/xen/save`, and automatically starting any domains whose configuration files are located in the directory `/etc/xen/auto`. All of these options can be configured by modifying the `/etc/sysconfig/xendomains` system configuration file.

On Fedora, Red Hat, SUSE, Mandrake, and similar systems, these startup scripts are installed in the `/etc/init.d` directory and symbolic links are created to them from various `/etc/rc?.d` directories. At a minimum, a symbolic link should be created to these scripts from the directory that is appropriate for your default runlevel, as identified in `/etc/inittab`. (This is usually either runlevel 3 or runlevel 5, and therefore one of the directories `/etc/rc3.d` or `/etc/rc5.d`.) On Gentoo systems, these startup scripts are added to the `/etc/init.d` directory, and symbolic links to them are created from the `/etc/runlevels/default` directory that identifies the system startup scripts for the default runlevel. On Ubuntu and Debian systems, these scripts are added to the `/etc/init.d` directory, and symbolic links to them are created in the `/etc/rc2.d` directory, causing them to be executed at the system's default runlevel, which is 2.

Capturing Xen and Linux Boot and Startup Information

If you encounter problems booting the hypervisor or starting the domain0 kernel, it can be difficult to capture the verbose output from the boot process in order to diagnose the problem. You can resolve this by using a serial console with GRUB and capturing the serial output of the boot process on another system. If the system on which you are running Xen still has a serial port, you can run a serial cable between your Xen system and another system, and use the Xen and Linux boot options described later in this chapter to redirect the Xen system's boot information to the serial port. You can then use minicom or a similar terminal emulation program on the non-Xen system to capture the output from GRUB and the Xen and Linux boot processes for further analysis.

Getting serial output from GRUB when booting Xen is somewhat different than the standard mechanism for using a serial console with GRUB. You will need to add serial port–configuration information to both the GRUB entry for the Xen hypervisor and the entry for the Xen-enabled Linux kernel in the same GRUB boot stanza in `/boot/grub/menu.lst`. A sample GRUB stanza for serial output while booting Xen is the following:

```
title Xen 3.0.5 Serial Console
        root (hd0,0)
        kernel /boot/xen.gz com1=115200,8n1
        module /boot/vmlinuz-2.6-xen ro root=LABEL=/ console=tty0
          console=ttyS0,115200n8r
        module /boot/initrd-2.6.18-xen.img
```

The first line identifies the title of this boot stanza. The second identifies the disk and partition on which the `/boot` directory and associated kernels and initial RAM disks are located. The third line boots the Xen hypervisor `/boot/xen.gz`, configuring its first serial port to communicate at 115,200 baud, using 8-bit communications, no stop bits, and 1 parity bit.

The fourth line is the truly interesting one. Because you are chain-loading the kernel through Xen, this is a module line. The first three arguments on this line identify the domain0 kernel, the fact that it must be mounted read-only initially to check its consistency (and replay its log if it is a journaling filesystem), and the partition that contains the root filesystem (in this case identified by the partition label). The last two items on this line tell the kernel where to send boot output. The first entry, console=tty0, tells the kernel to send output to virtual console 0. The second entry, console=ttyS0,115200n8r, tells the kernel to send output to ttyS0 (the first serial port on most Linux systems) and to do so at 115,200 baud, using no parity, 8 bits, and using hardware flow control (RTS/CTS, hence the r). If there are multiple console declarations on the kernel's module line, the last is the device that will be associated with /dev/console by the kernel.

> *Depending upon the Linux distribution that you are using, you may see other options on a kernel's module line. Red Hat and Fedora Core systems typically include a rhgb option (Red Hat Graphical Boot) that tells GRUB to use a user-space X server during the boot process to show whizzy graphical status screens. Other common options tell the kernel not to display verbose initialization messages (quiet) and to display a graphical splash screen (splash). See the GRUB home page (www.gnu .org/software/grub) and its associated documentation and reference sites for more complete information about GRUB and all available GRUB boot options and configuration settings.*

The last module line in the GRUB boot stanza identifies an initial RAM disk or RAM filesystem archive file that should initially be used by the kernel when it boots.

See the "GRUB Boot Options for the Xen Hypervisor" section later in this chapter for more detailed information about the com1 and console configuration options in GRUB boot entries for Xen.

If you are building your own version of the hypervisor or the domain0 kernel and are using the serial console for debugging, you may also want to ensure that your domain0 kernel starts a getty process on the serial console, so that you can log in there (just in case). The getty process (which stands for "get tty") is a process that communicates over a specified serial port or other terminal connection, displays the login and password prompts, and enables you to log in and create a shell on the system through those connections. This is only useful, of course, if your system actually comes up to the point where it processes /etc/inittab and/or runs all of the system startup scripts.

On Linux systems that use /etc/inittab, you can start a getty process on your serial port by adding a line like the following to the end of /etc/inittab:

```
S0:2345:respawn:/sbin/agetty -L 115200 ttyS0 vt102
```

This starts a 115,200 baud agetty process on serial port S0 at runlevels 2, 3, 4, and 5, restarting the process if it ever terminates (respawn). The specific options that you will need to use depend on the version of getty that your system uses. If it is available on your system, /sbin/agetty is a good choice, because it is well-suited to serial connections. The -L option identifies /dev/ttyS0 as a local line that does not require a carrier detect signal in order for the agetty process to start successfully. The last two arguments identify the entry, relative to /dev/ on your system, on which the agetty process should be started, and the type of terminal that it should expect to encounter there. I typically use vt102 because this is one of the types of terminals that are emulated by the Linux minicom terminal emulator, which is what I typically use to connect to serial consoles from Linux systems.

On Ubuntu systems, you should create the file /etc/event.d/ttyS0 by copying one of the other ttyn files and editing its exec entry to look like the following:

```
exec /sbin/agetty -L 115200 ttyS0 vt102
```

Using a serial console with GRUB and capturing the serial output of the boot process on another system can be very useful during debugging, or simply to keep an accurate record of your system's boot sequence and any messages that are being displayed when booting. Having a `getty` running there can be quite useful for subsequent system exploration or when attempting to correct problems before rebooting.

Configuring GRUB for Xen

Although the Xen hypervisor is not a standalone operating system in the sense that you could boot it and execute applications within that context, it is a standalone operating system in the sense that it has its own set of boot options that define its initial configuration and many aspects of the way that it performs. This section discusses the options that you can pass to the Xen hypervisor within the GRUB stanza for a Xen domain0 kernel and root filesystem.

The following are three basic types of Xen boot options:

❑   Those that you can supply on the GRUB kernel entry for the hypervisor and which are only meaningful to the hypervisor.

❑   Those that you can supply on the GRUB kernel entry for the hypervisor that are also propagated to the Linux domain0 kernel.

❑   Xen-specific options that you supply on the module line for the domain0 kernel and which are only meaningful to the domain0 kernel.

In my experience, few of these boot options (with the exception of the serial console options discussed in the previous section) are necessary for most Xen domain0 systems. However, they can be quite useful to work around specific hardware issues or problems.

GRUB Boot Options for the Xen Hypervisor

This section discusses boot options that are only meaningful to the Xen hypervisor. If used, these are most commonly appended to the kernel line for the Xen hypervisor in the GRUB boot stanza for a domain0 kernel.

If you believe that these boot options are necessary on your system, the easiest way to test them is to manually append them to the Xen hypervisor boot entry during the boot process. To do this, select the entry for the kernel that you want to boot from the initial GRUB boot screen, and press UserInput to edit that stanza. This displays all of the lines associated with the selected GRUB boot stanza. Use the arrow keys to highlight the kernel entry for the Xen hypervisor and press UserInput to edit that command. This enables you to edit that line, automatically placing you at the end of the line so that you can simply append options. If you make an error or want to add options in a specific order, you can use the right and left arrow keys to move the cursor within the line. When you are done adding or editing options, press Enter or Return to return to the stanza edit menu, and press UserInput to boot the system using the modified stanza.

Note that any changes you make or additional options that you add in this fashion are completely transient. They are not written back to your GRUB configuration file. If you are experimenting with large number of options, you should write them down as you add them, so that you can easily remember the exact options that had the desired effect on your system. You can then add them permanently by manually editing the GRUB configuration file once Linux is running correctly in domain0.

The options that are available for configuring the Xen hypervisor are the following:

❑ `apic=platform`: Enables you to specify a particular Non-Uniform Memory Access (NUMA) platform, which selects a specific x86 sub-architecture that in turn determines how APIC types are recognized and configured. Available values for this platform are `bigsmp`, `default`, `es7000`, and `summit`. This can usually be probed automatically when the hypervisor boots, but can be useful if your NUMA platform is being detected incorrectly.

❑ `apic_verbosity=value`: Prints more detailed information about local APIC and IOAPIC configuration during Xen hypervisor initialization. Available values are `verbose`, which simply displays additional information, and `debug`, which displays a great deal of detailed information that is intended to help you diagnose APIC and IOAPIC configuration.

❑ `badpage=pagenumber,pagenumber, ...`: Enables you to specify one or more pages of physical system memory that should not be used because they contain one or more bytes that cannot be written to or read from reliably. By default, each memory page is 4K in size, and the page on which a bad byte is located is therefore identified by the leading five hexadecimal digits from a problem report from your system or a memory tester. For example, if a memory tester says that byte 0x12345678 is bad, you would identify 0x12345 as the bad page by adding the `badpage=0x12345` option to the hypervisor boot entry.

❑ `com1=baud,DPS,io_base,irq` and `com2=baud,DPS,io_base,irq`: Enable you to configure the two UART 16550-compatible serial ports supported by the Xen hypervisor. You need to specify only the options that are not standard and cannot be auto-detected. For example, if the I/O base and IRQ are standard but you want to use a different baud rate or word size, you could specify something such as `com1=115200,8n1` or `com2=9600,8n1`. If the baud rate is preconfigured but you want to be able to change the communications parameters for that port, you can specify `auto` for the baud rate setting, as in `com1=auto,8o0` for a (strange) port that requires 8 data bits, odd parity, and no stop bits.

Because the hypervisor supports only two serial ports directly, you can still use more than two serial ports within a Linux kernel by loading the appropriate drivers for the expansion card that provides the serial ports. This option only refers to two serial ports that Xen can use directly.

❑ `console=list`: Enables you to specify one or more destinations for Xen console I/O as a comma-separated list. If not explicitly defined, the default value for this option is `com1,vga`, which sends console output to both the first serial port and the VGA console, the latter only until domain0 begins booting. Possible values are:

  ❑ `vga`: Uses the VGA console until domain0 boots and then relinquishes it unless the `vga=keep` Xen boot option is also specified.

  ❑ `com1`: Uses the first 16550-compatible serial port.

  ❑ `com2H`: Uses the second 16550-compatible serial port and communicate with the most significant bit (MSB) set.

  ❑ `com2L`: Uses the second 16550-compatible serial port and communicate with the most significant bit (MSB) cleared. The `com2H` and `com2L` options enable you to share a single serial port between two subsystems, such as the console and a debugger, as long as each device can be configured to respect specific communication requirements.

❑ `console_to_ring`: Enables Xen guest domains to write their console output into the same memory buffer that is used by the Xen hypervisor's console. Although disabled by default, this option can be useful to centralize logging or to simplify the retrieval, analysis, and display of Xen domain0 and domainU console data.

❑ `conswitch=switch-char auto-switch-char`: Enables you to identify the character used to switch serial-console input between Xen and domain0. To do this, you must press Ctrl+{switch-char} three times. The default `switch-char` is a, so pressing Ctrl+a three times is the default character sequence for switching between the Xen console and domain0. To disable switching between the Xen console and domain0, specify a backtick (`` ` ``) as the `switch-char`. By default, Xen automatically switches from the Xen console to domain0 when it boots — to disable this, specify x as the `auto-switch-char`.

❑ `dma_bits=xxx`: Enables you to specify the width of a Direct Memory Access (DMA) address. By default, 30-bit DMA addresses are used, enabling you to address up to 1GB via DMA.

❑ `dma_emergency_pool=xxx`: Enables you to specify a lower boundary on the size of the DMA pool. Addresses below this value will fail rather than being allocated from the DMA pool. Many drivers need small DMA-coherent memory regions for DMA descriptors or I/O buffers. Because of their small size, these are allocated from the DMA pool rather than in page units.

❑ `dom0_mem=specifiers`: Sets the amount of memory to be allocated to domain0. `Specifiers` is a comma-separated list containing one or all of the following: `min:amount`, the minimum amount to allocate to domain0; `max:amount`, the maximum amount to allocate to domain0, and `amount`, which is a precise amount to allocate to domain0. Amounts can be specified in numeric units using the B (bytes), K (kilobytes), M (megabytes), or G (gigabytes) suffix. If no units are specified, the default unit is kilobytes. Negative numeric values can also be specified, in which case the associated amount is the full amount of system memory minus the specified numeric value.

If no specific amount of memory is reserved for domain0, the Xen hypervisor allocates all available system memory to domain0, minus 128KB for its own use. Guest domains can request memory from domain0 when they are created.

❑ `dom0_vcpus_pin`: Pins domain0 virtual CPUs to their respective physical CPUs (the default is `false`).

❑ `guest_loglvl=level/level`: Specifies the level of log messages that guest domains should write to the Xen console, and (optionally) any log levels that should be rate-limited. See the `loglvl` option for more information. If you do not specify this parameter, Xen behaves as if you had specified `guest_loglvl=none/warning`.

❑ `hap`: Tells the Xen hypervisor to detect hardware-assisted paging support, such as AMD-V's nested paging or IntelVT's extended paging. If available, Xen will use hardware-assisted paging instead of shadow paging for guest memory management. Shadow paging is a software technique whereby memory is allocated to watch for changes in the per-machine page table and swap pages in and out of VM memory, which uses additional system memory. The `shadow_pagetable` entry in your domainU configuration file option defines the amount of memory reserved for shadow paging, and recommends at least 2KB per megabyte of domain memory, plus a few megabytes for each virtual CPU, for each guest domain.

❑ `ignorebiostables`: Specifying this option disables parsing and the use of BIOS-supplied hardware information tables. This option may be useful if you are having problems running Xen on a specific motherboard or system. Specifying this option also disables SMP (nosmp) and APIC tables (nolapic).

❑   `lapic`: Specifying this option forces the hypervisor to use local APIC assignments even if APIC is disabled in the BIOS.

❑   `loglvl=level/level`: Specifies the level of log messages that the Xen hypervisor should write to the console, and (optionally) any log levels that should be rate-limited. The first specifier identifies the security level of messages that will be printed to the Xen console. Valid levels are `all`, `debug`, `error`, `info`, `none`, and `warning`. Messages of the specified security level and higher will be sent to the console. By default, all messages of level `warning` and above are sent to the Xen console.

The second specifier is optional, and identifies a minimum log level at which messages should be discarded if they arrive too frequently. This enables you to reduce the size of your logs by not having 100,000 messages stating that the system can't read from a floppy drive, for example.

❑   `mem=amount`: Enables you to define the maximum amount of physical memory that can be used by the hypervisor and domain0. Any RAM beyond this address in the memory map will be ignored. Amounts can be specified in numeric units using the `B` (bytes), `K` (kilobytes), `M` (megabytes), or `G` (gigabytes) suffix. If no units are specified, the default unit is kilobytes.

❑   `nmi=reaction`: Enables you to specify how the hypervisor reacts to a non-maskable interrupt (NMI) resulting from a parity or I/O error. Possible values for reaction are `fatal` (the hypervisor prints a diagnostic message and then hangs), `dom0` (send a message to domain0 for logging purposes but continue), and `ignore` (ignore the error). If you do not specify this option, Xen uses the default value `dom0` internally.

❑   `noht`: Enables you to tell Xen to disable hyper-threading. This may be useful if you suspect that hyper-threading is conflicting with Xen's allocations and management of virtual CPUs.

❑   `noirqbalance`: Specifying this option disables software IRQ balancing and affinity, which can be useful on some systems (such as the Dell 1850/2850) that already use hardware support to work around IRQ-routing issues.

❑   `nolapic`: Tells the hypervisor to ignore local APIC settings in a uniprocessor system, even if they are enabled in the BIOS. This may be useful if you are using peripherals with fixed IRQs.

❑   `noreboot`: Tells the hypervisor not to reboot the machine automatically if errors occur. Specifying this option can be useful if you are having problems but are not using a serial console to track debugging and general system messages.

❑   `nosmp`: Specifying this option disables SMP support. This option is implied by the `ignorebiostables` option, and may be useful if you are having problems running Xen on a specific motherboard.

❑   `sched=name`: Specifying this option enables you to manually specify which CPU scheduler the hypervisor should use. Possible values for `name` are `credit` (which is the default), and `sedf`. See the section of Chapter 2 entitled "Controlling Hypervisor Scheduling" for additional information about scheduling in Xen.

❑   `sync_console`: Specifying this option forces Xen to perform synchronous console output. This can slow down the overall performance of your Xen host, but is very useful if your system is failing before all messages are being flushed to the console. The hypervisor generally enters this mode automatically when internal errors occur, but you can specify this option on the Xen GRUB entry to force this behavior if you are experiencing problems and suspect that you are not seeing all possible console output.

❑ `tbuf_size=size`: Enables you to manually set the size of the trace buffers that are available for every physical CPU in your system. The `size` parameter is expressed as the number of memory pages that you want to devote to trace output for each CPU.

❑ `vga=options`: Enables you to specify the resolution at which the hypervisor should use a VGA console, and optionally enables you to tell the hypervisor not to relinquish the VGA console when domain0 begins to boot. Possible values are `text-mode`, where `mode` is `80x25`, `80x28`, `80x30`, `80x34`, `80x43`, `80x50`, or `80x60`. To instruct Xen not to relinquish the VGA console, pass the `keep` option. For example, `vga=text-80x50,keep` would instruct Xen to display text on the console using 80 characters per line, with 50 lines of text, and to keep the console after your domain0 operating system begins to boot.

❑ `watchdog`: Specifying this option enables an internal NMI watchdog function, which can be useful in reporting transient problems or mysterious failures.

Additional options for the Xen kernel entry in a GRUB configuration file may have been added since this book was written, but you will rarely have to use most of these unless you are trying to work around hardware problems or are trying to use Xen with a specific motherboard and associated chipset that is not fully supported. See the documentation for the version of Xen that you are using for information about any additional options that may have been added since Xen 3.0.5, which is the version of Xen that was available when this book was written.

Shared Xen and Linux Boot Options

In addition to the options discussed in the previous section, a few other options are available for the Xen entry in your Xen boot stanza. Unlike those discussed in the previous section, which are only relevant to the Xen hypervisor, the options discussed in this section are first used by the Xen hypervisor and are then automatically passed by the hypervisor to the domain0 kernel when it begins execution. These are therefore standard Linux kernel boot options that the Xen hypervisor also makes use of.

The boot options that are shared by the hypervisor and the Linux kernel are the following:

❑ `acpi=type`: Enables you to specify how the Xen hypervisor and domain0 parse and use the Advanced Configuration and Power Interface (ACPI) tables that are stored in the BIOS. Possible values for `type` are: `force` (enable ACPI even if it is off in the BIOS), `ht` (use sufficient ACPI information to enable hyper-threading), `noirq` (do not use ACPI for IRQ routing), `off` (disable ACPI even if it is on in the BIOS), and `strict` (requires strict compliance with the ACPI specification — this can cause problems if your motherboard is not completely compliant).

❑ `acpi_skip_timer_override`: Tells the Xen hypervisor and domain0 to ignore timer-interrupt override IRQ0/pin2 instructions. These instructions are only necessary on some nForce2 BIOS versions.

❑ `noapic`: Tells the Xen hypervisor and domain0 not to use any IOAPICs that may be present in the system, and to instead continue to use the legacy PIC.

Xen-Specific Linux Boot Options

In addition to the standard Linux kernel boot options that can be used with any Linux kernel, the Xen patches to the kernel also add one kernel boot option. This is the xencons option, which tells the Linux kernel which device node (if any) to attach to Xen's virtual console driver. Possible values are as follows:

- ❏ xencons=off: Disables the virtual console.

- ❏ xencons=tty: Attaches the Xen console to /dev/tty1 once the system is available. The device tty0 is still used during the boot process.

- ❏ xencons=ttyS: Attaches the Xen console to /dev/ttyS0, which is typically the first serial port on a Linux system.

If you do not explicitly specify this option, domain0 will always attach the Xen console to /dev/ttyS1, and all guest domains will attach their Xen consoles to /dev/tty1.

Hiding PCI Devices from domain0

The most common way in which you may want to customize a domain0 Xen host is to customize domain0's knowledge of available I/O devices, which therefore determines which domains can access specific hardware. This is typically done for performance reasons, but can also be used to heighten network security.

As discussed in the "Virtualization Caveats" section of Chapter 1, having to share hardware resources such as network and disk connections between multiple virtual machines can hurt performance in I/O-intensive environments. There are multiple solutions to this problem, which fall into two general classes:

- ❏ Providing dedicated hardware, such as network interfaces, for specific domains so that there is no contention for specific local interfaces.

- ❏ Virtualizing underlying resources, most commonly storage, so that filesystem access is either network-based or logical, avoiding the overhead of increased access to single, local filesystems.

The second of these is covered in detail in the sections of Chapter 5 that discuss creating and using filesystems for virtual machines, and is primarily a driver and infrastructure issue. However, "hiding" specific PCI hardware from domain0 so that it can be dedicated to one or more guest domainU domains is quite common, and is also quite easy to do.

Dedicating PCI devices to specific Xen domains leverages the standard support for PCI driver domains in the Linux kernel. Xen's PCI device backend driver (known as pciback) logically separates PCI driver requests into a front end and back end that use shared memory and an event channel to communicate configuration and access requests. The pciback driver primarily prevents other drivers from attaching to hidden devices in the domain0 kernel. This enables you to still see the hidden devices in domain0 using utilities that probe your hardware (such as the lspci utility), but prevents domain0 from using these devices directly. Specific PCI devices can then be allocated to different domains by identifying their PCI ID in the configuration file for that domain using the pci keyword.

The PCI devices that you want to use exclusively with specific guest domains are hidden from domain0 through the pciback driver in one of two ways:

❑   If the pciback driver is compiled into your domain0 kernel, you can supply GRUB command-line arguments to invoke the driver at boot-time and hide specific devices based on their PCI ID.

❑   If the pciback driver is a loadable kernel module (the most common scenario), you can load the module and hide specific devices based on their PCI ID. Devices should be hidden before the Xen daemon is started and before other startup scripts associated with that hardware might be run. This ensures that the xend daemon has an accurate picture of the hardware on your system that it is responsible for, and eliminates potential problems in related startup scripts that might otherwise attempt to configure the hidden hardware.

Regardless of which scenario you use, the key to hiding a specific PCI device is knowing its PCI identifier (ID). This information is provided by the first field in the entry in lspci output for your device. Consider the following sample lspci output for the Ethernet devices on a sample system (abbreviated slightly for formatting purposes):

```
# lspci | grep -i Ethernet
00:04.0 Ethernet controller: Silicon Integrated Systems [SiS] 190 ...
00:09.0 Ethernet controller: 3Com Corporation 3c905B 100BaseTX ...
```

The first field is the interesting one for the device that you want to hide. This field identifies the number of the PCI bus on which the device is found, the slot in which the device was found, and the function number of this particular service on that bus slot. The slot is actually more of a sequence number for the order in which the PCI device was found when probing, and the function is typically 0 except for multi-function devices such as USB controllers and integrated I/O controllers.

Locating the pciback Driver on Your System

To determine if the Xen pciback driver is compiled into your kernel, already loaded by default on your system, or available as a loadable kernel module, boot your system using the domain0 kernel and look for the directory /sys/bus/pci/drivers/pciback. If this directory exists, the pciback driver is installed, which probably means that it's built into your kernel if you haven't done anything special. Just to be sure, check the kernel modules that are loaded on your system by typing the following:

```
# lsmod | grep pci
```

If you don't get any output but the /sys/bus/pci/drivers/pciback directory exists, the driver is definitely built into your domain0 kernel. If you see something like the following, the pciback driver is indeed a loadable kernel module that is already being loaded:

```
# lsmod | grep pci
pciback                38865  0
```

If you do not get any output from the lsmod command, the pciback module simply may not be loaded on your system (which is normally the case unless you've already experimented with hiding PCI devices). To make sure that the pciback module is available on your domain0 system, try manually loading the pciback module into your kernel using the following command as the root user (depending on the Linux distribution that you are using, you may need to use the sudo command to execute this as root):

```
# modprobe pciback
```

If this command doesn't return anything, this means that the pciback module was successfully located on your system and loaded correctly into the kernel. If you see a message such as "FATAL: Module pciback not found," then you will either have to build the module for your domain0 kernel or rebuild the kernel with the module built in. See the sidebar "Adding pciback Support to Your domain0 Kernel" for more information.

The next two sections describe how to hide a specific PCI device from your domain0 kernel depending on whether the pciback driver is built into your kernel or is available as a loadable kernel module.

Adding pciback Support to Your domain0 Kernel

If you are building your own domain0 kernel and the pciback module is not activated by default as a built-in or loadable kernel module, or the pciback module is not available for the Xen domain0 kernel for your Linux distribution, you'll have to activate the module and rebuild your kernel. Follow the instructions in Chapter 3 for obtaining the source for the kernel that you are using and starting your favorite kernel configuration utility (usually either make menuconfig or make xconfig, as discussed in Chapter 3). Next, scroll down until you see the XEN section, and do one of the following:

❑   If you want to build the pciback module as a loadable kernel module in your domain0 kernel, make sure that the CONFIG_XEN_PCIDEV_BACKEND configuration variable is set to m.

❑   If you want to compile the pciback driver into your kernel, make sure that the CONFIG_XEN_PCIDEV_BACKEND configuration variable is set to y.

If you are using the same kernel for domain0 and your domainU virtual machines, you will also need to set the CONFIG_XEN_PCIDEV_FRONTEND kernel configuration variable to either y (to compile it into your kernel) or m (to make it available as a module).

If you are using a single kernel for both domain0 and domainU systems, it is usually a good idea to make the pciback driver available as a module in your domain0 kernel, and to build the frontend support for this driver into your kernel. If you are using separate kernels, you can do it however you like, but you will have to ensure that the appropriate driver is available before you try to hide a PCI device or use a hidden one.

For more information about configuring and building the kernel and loadable kernel modules, see the "Building Xen from Source Code" section in Chapter 3.

Hiding a PCI Device Using Kernel Command-Line Arguments

If the pciback driver is compiled into your kernel, you can hide PCI devices from a domain0 kernel at boot time by adding the `pciback.hide=(ID)` argument to the module entry for the domain0 kernel in the appropriate stanza of your `/boot/grub/menu.lst` file. You should replace ID with the `bus:slot.function` identifier for the card that you want to hide. If you want to hide more than one PCI card, each ID should appear within its own set of parentheses, as in the following example:

```
pciback.hide=(00:09.0)(00:04.0)
```

This hides the PCI devices whose IDs are 00:09.0 and 00:04.0, as reported by the `lspci` command.

That's all there is to it! As mentioned previously, the pciback driver prevents domain0 from binding other drivers to that PCI device, and does not affect the inclusion of hidden PCI devices in the output from commands that actually probe hardware, such as the `lspci` command.

See the "Creating Xen Configuration Files for Paravirtualization" section in Chapter 5 for detailed information about configuring guest domains to use the hardware that you have hidden from domain0.

Hiding a PCI Device Using a Loadable Kernel Module

If the pciback driver is a loadable kernel module on your system (which is the most common case), you will need to integrate loading this module into your system's startup process. Actually, you will have to do several things:

❑ Unload any driver that your system may already have bound to the device that you want to hide.

❑ Load the pciback kernel module.

❑ Bind the PCI device that you want to hide to the pciback driver.

Depending on the Linux distribution that you are using and your personal preferences, you can do these in three basic ways:

❑ By creating clever module installation entries in `/etc/modprobe.conf` that replace the entry for loading the driver for the device that you want to hide with instructions that load the pciback driver instead

❑ By modifying an existing script that is run as part of your system's startup sequence

❑ By adding a new startup script to the series of scripts that are run as part of your system's startup sequence

Regardless of which of these solutions you select, you will usually want to add a `pciback` options entry to the kernel module configuration file, `/etc/modprobe.conf`. This entry defines the device that you want to hide, and looks like the following:

```
options pciback hide=(00:09.0)
```

Whenever you load the pciback driver, this entry tells the driver to automatically hide the device whose PCI identifier is 00.09.0. As with the `pciback.hide` kernel option discussed in the previous section, you can hide multiple devices by enclosing each of their PCI IDs within its own set of parentheses, as in the following example:

```
options pciback hide=(00:09.0)(00:04.0)
```

After adding an entry like this one (but which uses the PCI identifiers of your cards, not mine), you should select the approach that you're most comfortable with for loading the pciback driver on your system. Remember that this should take place before you start the `xend` daemon.

Of the three approaches listed, I personally prefer the third, adding a custom startup script to the system's startup sequence. The startup script that I use is called `xen_hide_pci.sh`, and looks like the following:

```
#!/bin/sh
#
### BEGIN INIT INFO
# Required-Start: $local_fs
# Default-Start:  2 3 4 5
# Description: Hide an Ethernet card from Xen domain0
### END INIT INFO
check_if_loaded_or_in_kernel() {
if [ -d /sys/bus/pci/drivers/pciback ] ; then
echo "Xen pciback driver already loaded"
exit 0
fi
}
hide_me() {
    /sbin/modprobe -r 3c59x
    /sbin/modprobe pciback
# The following code is not needed if you have an
# entry like the following in /etc/modprobe.conf:
#
#     options pciback hide=(00:09.0)
#
# This is just here as a manual example.
#
#    if [ $? = 1 ] ; then
#      echo "ERROR: Modprobe of pciback module failed"
#    else
#      cd /sys/bus/pci/drivers/3c59x
#      echo -n "0000:00:09.0" > unbind
#      cd /sys/bus/pci/drivers/pciback
#      echo -n "0000:00:09.0" > new_slot
#      echo -n "0000:00:09.0" > bind
#      echo "SUCCESS: 3com Ethernet card hidden from domain0"
#    fi
}
case "$1" in
  start)
    check_if_loaded_or_in_kernel
    hide_me
        ;;
```

(continued)

(continued)

```
    stop)
       echo "Xen pciback: No reason to unhide"
         ;;
    *)
    echo "Usage: $0 {start|stop}"
       exit 1
    esac
    exit $?
```

As you can see, this script first checks if the pciback module is already loaded. I use this script at various runlevels when running and testing a variety of kernels, some of which have pciback compiled in, and some which the module may have already been loaded in a different runlevel. If that's the case, the script simply displays a message and exits. If the driver is not already loaded, the script removes the kernel module for a 3c59x Ethernet card (my favorite standard, inexpensive Ethernet card), and then loads the pciback module. The commented section in the middle of the script shows the steps that you would need to perform in the script if you chose not to put an "options pciback . . ." statement in your /etc/modprobe.conf file.

Once I've created this script, typically in /etc/init.d, and made it executable, I then manually create the symlinks for this script from the startup directories for the appropriate runlevels for the type of system I'm configuring. (Usually runlevel 2 on Ubuntu and Debian systems and runlevels 3 and 5 everywhere else.) The sample script I've provided has the correct entries for use with LSB-compliant startup scripts, and many systems provide tools for graphically integrating these into your startup process. I generally find executing one or two `ln -s` commands from a shell to be faster.

If you would prefer to modify /etc/modprobe.conf to do the correct module loading there, you could add something like the following to /etc/modprobe.conf to load the pciback driver instead of the example 3c59x driver:

```
install 3c59x /sbin/modprobe pciback ;
```

This entry redefines the command that the modprobe utility uses when it thinks that it should load the 3c59x driver. As you can see, it loads the pciback driver instead of the actual 3c59x driver. If you happen to have multiple cards in your system that use this driver, you would still need to load the driver, but it could try to bind to the cards that you've hidden in the option you supplied for the pciback driver in /etc/modprobe.conf. In this case, you would use an entry like the following:

```
install 3c59x /sbin/modprobe pciback ; \
/sbin/modprobe --first-time --ignore-install 3c59x ;
```

This entry should be on a single line but is split here for formatting purposes, and also assumes that you have added the appropriate `options pciback` command earlier in /etc/modprobe.conf.

This entry redefines the command that the modprobe utility uses when it thinks that it should load the 3c59x driver, first loading the pciback module and hiding the cards whose PCI IDs you specified, and then loads the actual 3c59x driver. The `--ignore-install` option prevents it from going into an infinite loop when it sees a command to load a driver whose load process has been redefined. The `--ignore-install` option tells the modprobe utility to ignore module loading (`install`) command redefinitions for a specific drivers, and to simply load the real driver.

I do not like to use this approach because trying to be too clever in `/etc/modprobe.conf` can confuse your system and lead to changes in the discovery sequence and aliases for the devices in your system. It also makes it difficult for other system administrators to see what you've done on a system. Adding a unique startup script is highly visible to other system administrators, and a well-commented script can easily be read to see exactly what it's doing.

Similarly, I do not like to modify existing system startup scripts, such as the `/etc/rc.d/rc.sysinit` script that Fedora systems run at boot time. While tempting, there are two basic problems with this. First, it is hard for other system administrators to locate and maintain modifications that you bury in an existing script. Secondly, modifying scripts that the system delivers as part of its default set of packages may prevent updates from being delivered. Worst-case, forcing the installation of updates that affect these scripts can cause you to lose your changes.

As with all system-administration tasks, the choice is yours, but I believe that every week is "Be Kind to Your Sysadmin Week," and integrating system changes in a visible location is always better than hiding them away somewhere.

Summary

Booting a domain0 Xen host is usually quite straightforward, especially if you've installed Xen packages that were provided by the supplier of your Linux distribution. However, depending on the complexity of how you want to use Xen, you may find that you'll need to do some customization to get things working just the way you want them. This can involve anything from supplying different command-line options in your GRUB configuration file, to creating and modifying startup scripts for your domain0 host, to building and deploying your own kernel.

This chapter explains the startup process on various types of Linux systems, discussing the BIOS, Xen hypervisor, and Linux phases of system initialization and startup. The last section discusses how to modify the boot sequence on your domain0 system to reserve specific hardware for other domains.

Now that you have a domain0 system up and running, the next chapter explains how to configure and boot virtual machines, known as guest domains in Xen parlance. Soon, you'll be getting the most out of your hardware (and having fun with it, too)!

5

Configuring and Booting Virtual Machines

The previous chapter discussed how to get a domain0 system up and running, highlighting some common problems, concerns, and solutions. However, having a domain0 system up and running without any guest domains is pretty equivalent to simply having a Linux system running in the first place. Aside from the fact that the Xen hypervisor gives you even more knobs to twist than a standard Linux system, it's not really all that exciting until you bring up your first virtual machine.

As explained in the first two chapters of this book, Xen supports both paravirtualized systems and hardware virtualization, the latter only if it is supported by your hardware. Once you have a valid HVM domainU configuration file, hardware virtual machines are pretty easy to install and use as a standard domainU system because you install and create them using standard OS installation disks. On the other hand, paravirtualized systems are more interesting for a few reasons, most notably because they typically provide higher performance than hardware virtual machines, and work on a much wider range of hardware than hardware virtual machines can. If all of your systems are brand-new, 64-bit Intel-VT or AMD SVM hardware, I'm proud to know you and somewhat jealous. On the other hand, if your machine room already has a significant investment in powerful 32-bit or non–HVM-compatible 64-bit machines, it's hardly cost-efficient to simply replace that hardware because it doesn't support HVM. Clearly, new purchases should be made with HVM in mind, but why not make the most of what you already have?

This chapter gets to the heart of Xen by discussing how to quickly get your first few paravirtualized domainU systems up and running using Xen virtual machine images that you can easily find on the Internet. I have always found it wise to familiarize myself with new technologies by doing some prototyping, in this case experimenting with preexisting domainU systems before spending significant time and effort building my own. This is useful for both proof-of-concept implementations and to reduce the number of variables when you're getting started with Xen.

Using domainU components that are freely available and which someone else has already debugged is a great bootstrap mechanism for familiarizing yourself with Xen, its configuration files, and its administrative environment. Don't worry — plenty of complexity is available later, when you're ready for it.

This chapter also discusses how to create a simple configuration file for an HVM (assuming, again, that your hardware supports HVM), and how to set up a Xen HVM using a file to contain its filesystems. The goal of this section is to quickly get you up and running with Xen HVMs, not to provide a complete discussion of filesystems and associated storage (discussed in detail in Chapter 6), or every nuance of the Xen configuration file (discussed in detail in Appendix B).

Virtual Machine Requirements

As discussed in Chapters 1 and 2, Xen supports both paravirtualized systems, which require operating system kernel and driver changes, and hardware virtual machines, which can run unmodified operating systems as long as your hardware provides virtualization support. The next two sections summarize the requirements for running each of these types of virtual machines.

Requirements for Paravirtualized Xen Guest Domains

After getting your domain0 system up and running, you will need several basic components for each of your domainU paravirtualized guest domains:

❑ **A Xen-enabled kernel:** A Linux kernel compiled for use as a domainU guest. Earlier versions of Xen often used separate kernels for domain0 and domainU systems, but most Xen kernels today are compiled for use with both domain0 or domainU systems.

❑ **A root filesystem (RFS):** The filesystem that contains the applications, system utilities, and system configuration files for each domainU system. The kernel (described in the previous bullet) is typically external to the root filesystem, but can also be stored inside it, depending on how the root filesystem was constructed. Tools such as Red Hat's Virtual Machine Manager (virt-manager) typically store the kernel inside the root filesystem to simplify organization and clarify the kernel/RFS relationship.

❑ **Any loadable kernel modules (LKMs) required by the domainU kernel that you are running:** These may not be necessary if you have compiled all of the drivers that you need into your Xen-enabled kernel, but it is rare. In most cases, the time required to fine-tune your kernel by building in required modules isn't worth the amount of space that you save in your root filesystem. Your time is usually valuable, whereas disk space is relatively cheap. Loadable kernel modules are especially important if you are dedicating specific PCI devices to specific virtual machines, unless (again) the drivers for that hardware are compiled into the kernel.

❑ **An initial RAM disk or initial RAM filesystem (optional):** If your domainU kernel is compiled to require an initial RAM disk or initial RAM filesystem, you will need to provide one. This is usually unnecessary in paravirtualized environments unless you need to load specific device drivers as loadable kernels modules in order to access certain types of root filesystems, such as block-level networked root filesystems stored on ATA over Ethernet or iSCSI devices.

❑ **A swap file (optional):** As with any Linux system, swapping enables your system to efficiently run more processes than fit in the amount of physical memory that has been allocated to the system. Physical Linux systems traditionally allocate a separate disk partition for use as swap space. In paravirtualized systems, you can do the same thing by using a file formatted for use as swap space, making it available to your VM by identifying it in the domainU configuration file, and identifying that file as a swap partition in the virtual machine's filesystem table file, `/etc/fstab`, which is located in your virtual machine's root filesystem.

❑ **A Xen configuration file:** One that specifically describes how the preceding elements fit together and defines some basic characteristics of the paravirtualized system, such as networking.

Typically, a kernel and the loadable kernel modules that it requires go hand-in-hand, but it is important to think of them separately in the Xen context. On physical Linux systems, building and installing the kernel and any associated loadable kernel modules are integrated steps of the kernel compilation process. Although the kernel and kernel modules are typically built and installed together, they are installed in two different filesystem locations. The kernel is typically installed in the `/boot` directory, whereas loadable kernel modules are always installed in a subdirectory under the `/lib/modules` directory with the basename of the version of the kernel that they are associated with. On physical Linux systems, both the `/boot` and `/lib/modules` directories are located in the same logical filesystem, whereas on paravirtualized systems, your domainU kernel is located in domain0's logical filesystem and each domainU system typically has its own root filesystem.

The root filesystems used by domainU systems can be located in any of the following locations:

❑ A single file that contains an image of a Linux root filesystem

❑ A physical disk partition containing a root filesystem that is not used by the domain0 system

❑ A logical volume that contains a root filesystem that is not used by the domain0 system

❑ A block-level networked root filesystem, such as those exported by various Linux Network Block Device (NBD) drivers or iSCSI and ATA over Ethernet hardware. These types of filesystems are created on storage that is located on remote system over a network, but which can be accessed at the block level, just like a local filesystem.

❑ A networked root filesystem, typically a Network File System (NFS). The Linux kernel supports using an NFS as a root filesystem.

Creating root filesystems in all of these locations is explained in Chapter 6. Single files containing root filesystem images are the easiest to obtain and get started with, and are therefore used in the examples in this chapter.

> **Sharing physical filesystems between virtual machines is a common temptation in any virtualized environment. Unfortunately, this is not just a bad idea, but is technically illegal in Linux. Having multiple kernels and applications accessing the same local filesystem will quickly corrupt the filesystem because each virtual machine will have its own cache of information about that filesystem, with independent ideas of allocated blocks, updated blocks, and so on. Journaling filesystems would compete for both filesystem journals and filesystem updates. You can share networked filesystems (OpenAFS, NFS, GFS, and various clustered filesystems) across multiple virtual machines because networked filesystems are designed to synchronize access and locking at a higher level. However, you should never attempt to share a local, physical filesystem or filesystem image across multiple virtual machines.**

Requirements for Xen Hardware Virtual Machines

The core requirements for a Xen HVM guest are the following:

❑ Disk space sufficient to hold the root, swap, and other filesystems used by your HVM.

❑ Xen configuration file that identifies the disk space that will be used by your HVM and defines some basic characteristics of the paravirtualized system, such as networking, how you connect to the HVM, and so on.

❑ The installation media for the x86 operating system that you want to install in your HVM.

As discussed in the previous section, paravirtualized Xen guests require that you separately identify each partition and device that they will use, assigning each a specific device number and partition letter. When creating Xen HVMs, the storage that you specify is at least one partition (or an equivalent, such as a large image file, logical volume, network block device, and so on), plus at least one additional entry for the installation media for the operating system that you are installing as an HVM (an image file, an installation CD, a bootable network installation location, and so on). The storage that you allocate to the HVM is used as an entire disk and holds the disk image that is created during the HVM installation process. For this reason, you do not associate the name of a partition (such as sda1) with that storage, but instead provide the name of the device that the virtual machines will use as storage (such as sda).

If you do not have a free partition or logical volume available, you can create an image file into which you can install your first HVM. (See Chapter 6 for a discussion of the performance aspects of different types of storage devices, including files mounted as filesystems.) You can easily create a sample image file using the dd *command, as in the following example:*

```
# dd if=/dev/zero of=image_file.img bs=1024k seek=4096 count=0
```

This will create a 4GB file that you can identify as the root filesystem in your HVM configuration file. Remember that your image file must be large enough to hold all of the files associated with whatever operating system you are installing in your HVM, as well as the boot loader, any swap space that the HVM requires, and so on.

Obtaining Sample Xen Filesystem Images

Although it is fairly easy to create your own, customized root filesystem for use with domainU Xen systems (as explained in Chapter 6), it is even easier to simply download an existing root filesystem image that is ready to use. The sites described in the following sections provide a variety of ready-to-use Xen filesystem images that you can download to get up and running quickly.

FreeOsZoo

The Free Operating Systems Zoo (FreeOsZoo) site (www.oszoo.org/wiki/index.php/Main_Page) provides images that are designed for use with QEMU, many of which can also be used with Xen on hardware that provides support for virtualization.

Jailtime.org

The Jailtime.org site (`www.jailtime.org`) is a great source of filesystem images for use with Xen. Most of the images provided on Jailtime.org are compressed, single filesystem images and associated files that are designed for use with paravirtualized Xen systems.

The downloadable files provided by the Jailtime.org site are typically provided as tar files that have been compressed using the bzip2 utility (known as "compressed tarballs"), and usually contain a filesystem image, a swap file image, and one or more Xen configuration files. The following examples use a CentOS 5.0 root filesystem image that was downloaded from Jailtime.org at `www.jailtime.org/` `download:centos:v5.0`.

After downloading the CentOS 5.0 compressed tarball (or any other, for that matter), and before extracting its contents, you should also download its companion MD5 file, which provides an MD5 checksum for the downloaded image so that you can be sure that it downloaded correctly. First, generate the MD5 checksum for the downloaded file, as in the following example:

```
# md5sum centos.5-0.20070424.img.tar.bz2
e11f710c4fddf1f2a5e2360a51286e27   centos.5-0.20070424.img.tar.bz2
```

You can then display the contents of the MD5 file that you downloaded to make sure that it matches the checksum that you got for the downloaded file:

```
# cat centos.5-0.20070424.img.tar.bz2.md5
e11f710c4fddf1f2a5e2360a51286e27   centos.5-0.20070424.img.tar.bz2
```

After downloading and verifying any of these archive files, you can extract its contents using the tar utility, as in the following example:

```
# tar jxvf centos.5-0.20070424.img.tar.bz2
centos.5-0.img
centos.5-0.xen2.cfg
centos.5-0.xen3.cfg
centos.swap
```

Note that the compressed tarballs are much smaller than the files that they contain, primarily because much of the filesystem image is unallocated space. For example, the sizes of the files in a Slackware 11.0 tarball are as follows:

```
# du -h centos*
95M     centos.5-0.20070424.img.tar.bz2
4.0K    centos.5-0.20070424.img.tar.bz2.md5
1002M   centos.5-0.img
4.0K    centos.5-0.xen2.cfg
4.0K    centos.5-0.xen3.cfg
65M     centos.swap
```

This shows that the compressed tarball itself is only 95 megabytes, but the amount of space required for the extracted files is slightly under 1.1 gigabytes. Not a bad compression ratio, but this means that you will need to ensure that you have sufficient free space available to de-archive the contents of the compressed tarball.

In most cases, the root filesystem image files that these archives contain have been preconfigured to work with Xen by pre-populating various configuration files for the filesystem (`/etc/fstab`), networking support (`/etc/sysconfig/network-scripts/ifcfg-eth0`), and user configuration files (`/etc/passwd`) with valid and generic entries.

At the time this book was written, the Jailtime.org site provided filesystem images for CentOS 4.4, CentOS 5.5, Debian 3.1, Fedora Core 6, Gentoo 2006.1, Slackware 11.0, and an interesting set of root filesystems that can be used to set up a miniature Xen-based cluster. Each of the download pages at Jailtime.org provides an MD5 checksum that you can use to verify your download, a list of the packages that are pre-installed in that root filesystem, and various notes about that root filesystem.

The root login is enabled in all of the filesystem images available on the Jailtime.org site, with the default password being "password." This isn't really much of a security problem, because these are provided as "getting started" images — you can either change the root password after updating and before deploying them, or experiment with them in a protected network environment.

The Jailtime.org site also provides HOWTO files containing useful information about Xen-related topics such as creating and populating filesystem image files.

rPath's rBuilder Online

rPath (`www.rpath.com`) is an interesting company whose primary technology, known as rBuilder (`www.rpath.com/rbuilder`), is extremely useful for Xen fans. rPath's corporate goal is to make it easy to create software appliances that perform specific software functions. These software appliances are complete, customized Linux distributions that contain specific applications, typically server applications. These software appliances are designed and built online using rPath's rBuilder tools. Once built, they can be quickly deployed to provide the functionality that you defined for each appliance.

Virtualization is a natural companion technology for rPath's software appliance approach, because virtualization simplifies deploying software appliances. You can deploy software appliances without installing them on physical hardware beyond downloading and uncompressing the software appliances, creating a Xen configuration file for them, and using that to start them as virtual machines. rPath's rBuilder has also been used to create complete Linux distributions targeting the end user, such as Foresight Linux and rPath Linux. Xen makes it just as easy to deploy these as rPath's special-purpose software appliances.

One advantage of getting started with images from rPath is that the rPath site provides both compressed, single filesystem images designed for use with paravirtualized Xen systems, and complete disk images designed for use with HVM Xen systems.

Locating Xen Images on the rPath Site

The rPath Web site provides a convenient integrated search capability that makes it easy to find appliance partition and disk images that have been built for use with Xen. To locate these, go to the rBuilder page (`www.rpath.com/rbuilder/`) and use the search application in the upper-right corner of the page. Enter **Xen** in the text area where you specify what you're looking for, make sure that Project is selected as the type of thing that you're looking for, and click Search. The resulting page displays a list of software appliances that are located on the rPath site and can be used with Xen.

The primary rPath home page, www.rpath.com, also provides a search capability (again, in the upper-right corner). This search can be useful when you're searching for Xen-related items on the rPath site, and is not limited to locating software appliances. Searching for Xen from this page will display Xen-related documents, wiki pages, and press releases, as well as relevant software appliances.

Building Your Own Xen Images with rBuilder

The process of creating a software appliance is quite simple. First, you must create an account on the rPath site. You can then create a project, which requires some general information to label what you're doing and what you'll be building. You then add software groups to the project, which represent sets of packages that you want your software appliance to contain. You can also add specific packages to your group by searching for them and adding them to your group. You then "cook" this group, which means to formalize its definition and resolve any dependencies for any of the packages that it contains. At this point, you must identify the target architecture (32-bit or 64-bit x86 only) for which you are going to build your appliance. This point in the process also gives you the option of explicitly adding Xen domainU support to the group you're defining.

Next, you build the specified group, which is done for you online on rPath's servers. Possible output formats for the results of your build are as follows:

- Installable CD/DVD
- Raw Filesystem Image
- Compressed Tar File
- Demo CD/DVD (Live CD/DVD)
- Raw Hard Disk Image
- VMware (R) Virtual Appliance
- VMware (R) ESX Server Virtual Appliance
- Microsoft (R) VHD Virtual Appliance
- Virtual Iron Virtual Appliance
- Amazon Machine Image

Only choices that are relevant to the contents of your virtual appliance will be selectable. For example, if your virtual appliance does not contain a Linux kernel, no bootable or installable formats will be available. The most useful choice for paravirtualized Xen VMs is Raw Filesystem Image, which will give you a root filesystem image that you can use with Xen. If you want to use your rPath software appliance with a Xen HVM, the most useful choice is Raw Hard Disk Image, which will produce a QEMU hard disk image file, as used by Xen HVMs.

Depending on the number of packages that your group contains, the build can take some time. Once the build completes successfully, you can download your software appliance and use it with Xen.

The rPath site features useful documents on building software appliances for Xen, providing separate documents for domain0 and domainU systems. For information about building domain0 appliances using rPath's rBuilder and Linux distributions, see `http://wiki.rpath.com/wiki/rPath_Linux:Xen_Dom0_on_rPL_HOWTO`. For information about building domainU appliances using rBuilder, see `http://wiki.rpath.com/wiki/Xen_DomU_Guide`.

Defining and Starting a Paravirtualized VM

Once you have a root filesystem for use with a paravirtualized Xen VM, you need only do a few things in order to boot your first paravirtualized VM. This section creates a Xen virtual machine using a CentOS 5.0 root filesystem image that was downloaded from Jailtime.org at `www.jailtime.org/download:centos:v5.0`.

Creating Xen Configuration Files for Paravirtualization

As discussed in more detail in Appendix B, a Xen virtual machine configuration file offers many options for fine-tuning memory use, networking, and your interaction with the VM. Luckily, the majority of these are optional, because Xen will substitute intelligent default values for any unspecified configuration parameters. As mentioned in the "Jailtime.org" section of this chapter, Xen images from Jailtime.org include some template configuration files for paravirtualized Xen VMs. For example, the ones provided in the CentOS5 tarball from Jailtime.org are named `centos.5-0.xen2.cfg` and `centos.5-0.xen3.cfg`. The former is historically interesting, but the latter provides a good starting point. It has the following contents:

```
kernel = "/boot/vmlinuz-2.6-xenU"
memory = 256
name = "centos.5-0"
vif = [ '' ]
dhcp = "dhcp"
disk = ['file:/xen/centos/centos.5-0.img,sda1,w',
        'file:/xen/centos/centos.swap,sda2,w']
root = "/dev/sda1 ro"
```

The key changes that you'll have to make to this file are the following:

❑ Change the kernel entry to point to a valid Xen domainU kernel. For paravirtualized systems, this kernel must be located in a filesystem that your domain0 system can access. You can typically use the same kernel that you're running on your domain0 system to get started with. (You can subsequently fine-tune your own domainU kernels, but let's start with an easy success story.)

❑ Optionally add a `ramdisk` entry if your domainU kernel requires one. If you are using the same kernel on your domain0 and domainU systems, you can also reuse the same RAM disk. If you need to create an initial RAM disk manually for a custom kernel, see "Creating Initial RAM Disks and Filesystems for Your Kernel" later in this chapter.

❑ Change the disk entries to point to the filesystem location of the CentOS root filesystem and swap files that you extracted from the compressed tarball.

That's all there is to it! You could, of course, optionally change or add other parameters in the file, such as the following:

❑ dhcp: Tells the VM to obtain its Ethernet address via DHCP. If desired, you can also use a static IP address and supply other network configuration information by setting this value to no and supplying the proper entries as part of your vif statement.

❑ memory: The amount of memory allocated to the domainU. The optimal value really depends on what your VM will be doing, which may not be something you'll know up front.

❑ name: The name given to the domainU VM. It's a good idea to follow some meaningful convention for these, as discussed in "Documenting Your Virtual Machines" in Chapter 10.

❑ pci: If you are hiding hardware from domain0 and want to use it in your paravirtualized domain (as discussed in "Hiding PCI Devices from domain0" in Chapter 4), you will need to add a pci specification. This looks something like the following:

```
pci= [ '00:09:0' ]
```

This statement declares that the PCI device with the identifier 00.09.0 will be used by this para-virtualized domain. To use a dedicated PCI device, the drivers for that device must be present in the kernel, initial RAM disk, or root filesystem, and the device must be correctly configured within the domainU system.

❑ root: Identifies the root device to the domainU kernel and provides its initial mount arguments (just as found on the kernel line in the GRUB boot stanza for an unmodified kernel).

❑ vif: Identifies the characteristics of the virtual network interface. In this case, its presence tells Xen that a virtual network interface should be created, but its lack of any specific directives tells Xen to use intelligent default values for things such as the virtual interface name, its MAC address, the network bridge to connect to, and so on.

One additional change that you may want to make is to replace the file: prefix for the filesystem image files with the more modern tap:aio: prefix. This tells Xen to use its blktap driver instead of the loopback driver used with file-backed virtual block devices. The blktap driver supports asynchronous I/O (aio) to file-based block devices with higher performance, and in a more scalable and secure environment. The file: prefix was used in earlier versions of Xen and still works (at the time that this book was written), though its use is deprecated. The blktap driver must be present in the initial RAM disk or RFS for both domain0 and your domainU guest in order to be used. Similarly, when you're using the tap:aio: identifier, the name of the devices associated with your disk images should now be xvda? for image files containing single filesystem images (where ? is the partition number), and xvda for complete disk (multi-partition) images.

> If you have problems using the tap:aio: device identifier, try falling back to the file: identifier. Older disk images and Xen-enabled kernels that you are using may not support the new driver and associated options. See the troubleshooting section of this chapter for more information.

This disk entry also enables you to provide access to physical storage devices, such as a CD-ROM drive, from your paravirtualized guest. See the "Identifying Physical Resources for Xen Domains" section later in this chapter for more information.

As an example, consider the following minimal configuration file for a paravirtualized Xen domain. I use the same kernel and initial RAM disk on my domain0 and domainU systems, and store my CentOS images in the centos5 subdirectory of /home/xen. My CentOS configuration file would therefore look like the following:

```
kernel = "/boot/vmlinuz-2.6.18-xen"
ramdisk = "/boot/initrd-2.6.18-xen.img"
memory = 256
name = "centos.5-0"
dhcp = "dhcp"
vif = [ '' ]
disk = ['tap:aio:/home/xen/centos.5-0.img,xvda1,w',
        'tap:aio:/home/xen/centos.swap,xvda2,w']
root = "/dev/xvda1 ro"
```

As mentioned earlier, the initial RAM disk filesystem specification may be unnecessary, depending on the Xen kernel that you are using and the drivers that you need to load in order to access your filesystems and other devices.

The next few sections discuss additional steps that you may need to perform before starting your paravirtualized domainU system. If your system already provides all of the items identified in your domainU configuration and you just want to see Xen in action, you can skip ahead to the section "Manually Starting Paravirtualized Xen Domains."

Integrating Loadable Kernel Modules into Your Root Filesystem

Once you have obtained a filesystem image (or built a filesystem or filesystem image yourself, as described in the next chapter), the next step is to integrate loadable kernel modules associated with the kernel that you will be running in your domainU guest system.

The loadable kernel modules associated with any installed kernel on your system are installed in a subdirectory of the directory /lib/modules that has the same basename as the kernel with which they are associated. For example, the loadable kernel modules associated with the kernel vmlinuz-2.6 .18-xen and located in the directory /lib/modules/2.6.18-xen. You can use the uname command to identify the kernel that your system is running, as in the following example (the output of the uname command would normally appear on one line, but has been split across two here for formatting purposes):

```
$ uname -a
Linux xen.vonhagen.org 2.6.18-xen #1 SMP Fri May 25 06:49:40 EDT 2007 \
  x86_64 x86_64 x86_64 GNU/Linux
```

You can use the `uname -r` command to identify just the kernel version string, which is the same as the name of the directory in `/lib/modules` that holds its loadable kernel modules, as in the following example:

```
$ uname -r
2.6.18-xen
```

In order to copy the loadable kernel modules for your Xen domainU kernel into the root filesystem that a domainU guest will be using, you must temporarily mount that filesystem on another Linux system in order to copy the files into it. This Linux system is typically your domain0 system because that's where your loadable kernel modules are probably located, but this can be done on any Linux system where you have access to the kernel and loadable kernel modules that you want to use.

In the case of a filesystem image, you must mount it on your Linux system using the `mount` command's `-o loop` option, which mounts the filesystem image on a directory. You must do this either by using the `sudo` command to execute the following commands as root, or by becoming the root user via the `su` or `sudo -s` commands, as in the following example:

```
$ su
Password: *********
# mkdir -p /mnt/img
# mount -o loop centos.5-0.img /mnt/img
```

Once the image is mounted, change to the `lib/modules` directory relative to the directory on which you mounted the image, and recursively copy in the correct hierarchy of loadable kernel modules, as in the following example:

```
# cd /mnt/img/lib/modules
# cp -r /lib/modules/`uname -r` .
# ls
2.6.18-xen
```

While the filesystem image is mounted, you should also perform the checks in the next section to ensure that your virtual machine will identify its filesystems and start the network correctly.

Checking Other Configuration Files in the Root Filesystem

While the filesystem image is mounted, you should also check various configuration files in the image to make sure that they match the values that you specified in your domainU configuration file, most notably the names of the virtual devices associated with your filesystems and the way in which your virtual network interface is configured.

Filesystem information is contained in the file `/etc/fstab` (filesystem table) in any Linux root filesystem. To check the contents of the filesystem table in your mounted filesystem, you would examine the version of this file that is relative to the directory on which you mounted your filesystem image, as in the following example:

```
# cat /mnt/img/etc/fstab
/dev/sda1          /          ext3      defaults         1 1
/dev/sda2          none       swap      sw               0 0
none               /dev/pts   devpts    gid=5,mode=620   0 0
none               /dev/shm   tmpfs     defaults         0 0
none               /proc      proc      defaults         0 0
none               /sys       sysfs     defaults         0 0
```

As you can see, the etc/fstab file in your filesystem image file still refers to the devices /dev/sda1 and /dev/sda2. In the section "Creating Xen Configuration Files for Paravirtualization," I changed the names of the devices in the sample configuration file to xvda1 (which would be /dev/xvda1 in the virtual machine) and xvda2 (which would be /dev/xvda2 in the virtual machine). You should therefore use a text editor to rename the etc/fstab file in your filesystem image to reflect this change. (Make sure that you edit the file /mnt/img/etc/fstab, not the file /etc/fstab.) After you have edited it, the corrected file should look like the following:

```
# cat /mnt/img/etc/fstab
/dev/xvda1         /          ext3      defaults         1 1
/dev/xvda2         none       swap      sw               0 0
none               /dev/pts   devpts    gid=5,mode=620   0 0
none               /dev/shm   tmpfs     defaults         0 0
none               /proc      proc      defaults         0 0
none               /sys       sysfs     defaults         0 0
```

Next, you'll want to check how the primary Ethernet interface is to be configured to make sure that it uses dhcp, as you stated in the domainU configuration file. This information is stored in the file etc/sysconfig/network-scripts/ifcfg-eth0 on most Linux systems, again relative to the directory on which the filesystem image is mounted. You can examine the contents of this file as shown in the following example:

```
# cat /mnt/img/etc/sysconfig/network-scripts/ifcfg-eth0
TYPE=Ethernet
DEVICE=eth0
BOOTPROTO=dhcp
ONBOOT=yes
```

In this case, the interface is configured to get its configuration information via DHCP. If your file looks different than this and specifies any fixed IP address, netmask, router, or gateway information, you should change it to look like this example.

Not all Linux systems store their network configuration information in the sysconfig directory. Debian-based distributions such as Debian and Ubuntu store this information in the file etc/network/interfaces, which should look something like this in a mounted Debian or Ubuntu filesystem image:

```
# cat /mnt/img/etc/network/interfaces
auto lo
iface lo inet loopback
auto eth0
iface eth0 inet dhcp
```

Again, this example matches the dhcp requirement that you specified in the configuration file. If your file looks different than this example and you are running a DHCP server, you should change the file in your root filesystem to look like this example.

Once you have completed these checks and made any mandatory changes, you should then change directory to some directory that is not in the mounted filesystem image, flush pending writes to the filesystem image using the sync command, and unmount the filesystem, as in the following example:

```
# cd /
# sync
# umount /mnt/img
```

Creating Initial RAM Disks and Filesystems for Your Kernel

Many different programs and shell scripts are available to help you create initial RAM disks and initial RAM filesystems for use with your Xen kernels. If you are running the same kernel on your domain0 and domainU systems, you can also use the same initial RAM disk filesystem on both. You can look in your GRUB configuration file (/boot/grub/menu.lst) to see which initial RAM disk filesystem your kernel is current using—it will be the initrd entry in the GRUB boot stanza for the kernel that you are running.

Initial RAM disk filesystems are actually optional unless your kernel has been compiled to require one, or unless you need to use them to load special device drivers, such as iSCSI or AoE drivers that are required in order to access the storage devices on which your root filesystem is located.

The best-known program for creating initial RAM disks is mkinitrd, which is a shell script. Unfortunately, the mkinitrd script differs widely from Linux distribution to Linux distribution. Some versions, such as the one available on Debian and Ubuntu systems, are limited in the filesystem formats that they can create (cramfs, by default) and accept very few options:

```
# mkinitrd
Usage: /usr/sbin/mkinitrd [OPTION]... <-o outfile> [version]
 Options:
  -d confdir  Specify an alternative configuration directory.
  -k          Keep temporary directory used to make the image.
  -m command  Set the command to make an initrd image.
  -o outfile  Write to outfile.
  -r root     Override ROOT setting in mkinitrd.conf.
```

Other versions, such as the one used by Fedora, are much more complex:

```
usage: mkinitrd [--version] [--help] [-v] [-f] [--preload <module>]
       [--force-ide-probe] [--force-scsi-probe | --omit-scsi-modules]
        [--image-version] [--force-raid-probe | --omit-raid-modules]
       [--with=<module>] [--force-lvm-probe | --omit-lvm-modules]
       [--builtin=<module>] [--omit-dmraid] [--net-dev=<interface>]
       [--fstab=<fstab>] [--nocompress] <initrd-image>[{{[SPACE]}}]<kernel-version>
```

Given this disparity and the fact that, as discussed in "Loading and Using an Initial RAM Disk or RAM Filesystem" in Chapter 4, initial RAM filesystems are much simpler and more modern, I suggest using initial RAM filesystems with Xen whenever possible. The best applications to create these are mkinitramfs (from the initramfs-tools package) and yaird (from the yaird package). These seem to only be available in the Debian and Ubuntu repositories, so if you are using a Fedora or Fedora-based system, it is easiest to simply use mkinitrd for the time being.

The basic commands that you would use with each of these are very similar. The following commands each produce a usable initial RAM disk filesystem called initrd-2.6.18-xen.img that contains the loadable kernel modules for kernel version 2.6.18-xen, as reported by the uname -r command:

```
# yaird --output initrd-2.6.18-xen.img 2.6.18-xen
# mkinitramfs -o initrd-2.6.18-xen.img 2.6.18-xen
# mkinitrd -o initrd-2.6.18-xen.img 2.6.18-xen
```

The first two of these commands create initramfs archives, whereas the third creates a compressed filesystem archive in traditional initial RAM disk format. All three of the output files produced by these commands can be used by modern (2.6 or later) Linux kernels.

Manually Starting Paravirtualized Xen Domains

Once you've customized the configuration file to reflect your local configuration, you can start your paravirtualized Xen system. You must execute the appropriate xm command with root privileges, either by becoming the root user via the su or sudo -s command, or by using the sudo command to execute the xm commands as root.

The standard command to start a paravirtualized VM is xm create variable, where variable is the name of the configuration file for that virtual machine. When first starting a paravirtualized VM, it's usually a good idea to create an initial connection to the console of that virtual machine, which you do by adding the -c option to your initial xm create command-line. To continue with the previous example, you would type the following to use the modified centos.5-0.xen3.cfg configuration file to start a virtual machine in your current terminal window and open a connection to the virtual machine's console:

```
# xm create centos.5-0.xen3.cfg -c
```

Initially connecting to the console from an existing terminal application has the advantage of enabling you to see all of the system boot messages, including any error messages that might be displayed. Once the VM is up and running successfully, I disconnect from the console by pressing Control-]. Then I use the xm list command to identify its domain ID and the xm console command to reconnect to the console in its own window, as in the following example:

```
# xm list
Name                     ID Mem(MiB) VCPUs State    Time(s)
Domain-0                  0     1752      2 r-----   56978.8
Foresight                46      384      1 -b----    1180.1
OpenSUSE                 17      256      1 -b----    2114.4
Ubuntu                   34      256      1 -b----     591.7
centos.5-0               45      256      1 -b----     302.9
Freespire-HVM            49      256      1 -b----      63.2
# xterm -T "CentOS Console" -e xm console 45 &
```

This displays a simple text-based xterm console labeled "CentOS Console," which I can then use to interact with the virtual machine, monitor it, and start any subsequent process that I'm interested in.

Defining and Starting Xen Hardware Virtual Machines

Configuring and starting HVM domainU guest systems is actually much simpler than creating a paravirtualized domainU guest system. ("Unmodified Guest Systems" in Chapter 2 describes how to determine if your hardware supports HVMs.)

Creating Xen HVM Configuration Files

A very basic Xen domainU configuration file, `freespire.cfg`, for an HVM that runs the Freespire Linux distribution looks like the following:

```
import os, re
arch = os.uname()[4]
if re.search('64`, arch):
    arch_libdir = 'lib64`
else:
    arch_libdir = 'lib'
kernel = "/usr/lib/xen/boot/hvmloader"
builder='hvm'
memory = 256
shadow_memory = 8
name = "FS-IMG-HV"
acpi=1
apic=1
vif = [ 'type=ioemu, bridge=xenbr0`
disk = [ 'tap:aio:/home/xen/HVM/freespire1013.img,hda,w',
    'phy:/dev/hda,hdc:cdrom,r' ]
device_model = '/usr/' + arch_libdir + '/xen/bin/qemu-dm'
boot="dc"
serial='pty'
usb=1
usbdevice='tablet'
```

The entries in this sample HVM configuration file have the following meanings:

❑ The first section is a block of Python code that imports two modules, identifies the architecture on which Xen is running, and sets the library directory used by Xen (standard 32-bit or 64-bit) appropriately.

❑ `kernel`: Defines the initial code that should be loaded when booting the virtual machine. In this case, it's a hardware virtual machine loader that is used to emulate a bare x86 BIOS and to run the target operating system's boot loader from the `boot` block.

❑ `builder`: Defines the function that should be used to construct the domainU system.

❑ `memory`: The amount of memory initially allocated to the HVM.

- ❏ `shadow_memory`: The amount of memory reserved for the internal table used to map domainU memory pages into domain0 memory pages. See Appendix B for more detailed information about this setting.

- ❏ `name`: The name of the virtual machine. It's a good idea to follow some meaningful convention for these, as discussed in "Preparing for Automation" in Chapter 10.

- ❏ `acpi`: Whether or not the ACPI (Advanced Power and Control Interface) is enabled in the virtual machine. A value of 1 specifies that it is enabled.

- ❏ `apci`: Whether or not the APCI (Advanced Programmable Interrupt Controller) is enabled in the virtual machine. A value of 1 specifies that it is enabled.

- ❏ `vif`: Specifies that this network device will use QEMU's ioemu emulation device for the network interface rather than Xen's virtual frontend network driver (netfront). Also specifies that this HVM will be attached to the xenbr0 bridge, the default Xen bridge.

- ❏ `disk`: Identifies the storage to be associated with each local storage device that this HVM has access to. See the next section, "Identifying Physical Resources for Xen Domains," for more information about identifying physical resources. Note that filesystem image file, disk, or other device references in an HVM configuration file are references to storage that the HVM will see as an entire disk, not as a single partition. Each device statement, enclosed within single quotes, identifies a single local storage device using the standard domain0 name, domainU name, and read/write information nomenclature. Any HVM name in a storage specification should provide the name of an entire device, not just a partition of a device.

- ❏ `device_model`: The real-mode instruction emulator used by HVMs, which is the full path to the QEMU device model binary.

- ❏ `boot`: Identifies the order in which the HVM tries to boot from specified devices, where c represents virtual hard disk and d represents a DVD/CD-ROM drive.

- ❏ `serial`: Redirects serial console output from the HVM to a pseudo-TTY, making it possible to collect console boot information by connecting to `/dev/pty/`*`variable`* (where `variable` is the domain ID), which you can connect to using the `xm` command or a terminal emulator such as minicom.

- ❏ `usb`: Enables you to subsequently attach USB devices to an HVM by using commands such as `xm block-attach` (for USB block storage devices) and `xm network-attach` (for USB network devices).

- ❏ `usbdevice`: Identifies how a USB mouse tracks within the HVM. The `tablet` setting forces absolute movement tracking within the HVM window. The other possible value, `mouse`, tracks relative movement and uses standard techniques, such as acceleration.

By default, this configuration file creates an HVM graphical display that you can connect to via a VNC client application, such as vncviewer, which is available for most Linux distributions in their default repositories or directly from vendors, such as TightVNC (`www.tightvnc.com/`) and RealVNC (`www.realvnc.com/`). By default, the VNC port that you connect to is 127.0.0.1:5900 + DomainID. For example, if your HVM is domain 31 as listed by the `xm list` command, you would start your vncviewer with the following command to connect to the graphical console of your HVM:

```
$ vncviewer 127.0.0.1:5931
```

Whether the VNC session(s) to your virtual machine(s) is available through your machine's real IP address or only through the loopback IP address is determined by the `vnc-listen` setting in your xend configuration file. See the section "Configuring the Xen Daemon" in Chapter 7 for more information about customizing this setting.

If you would prefer more immediate feedback from your HVM, enabling you to watch the entire boot process, you can add commands to the Xen HVM configuration file to use the Linux Simple DirectMedia Layer (SDL, www.libsdl.org) to display the console rather than VNC. This will display an SDL window as soon as you start the HVM, in which the graphical console for your HVM will display. The configuration file commands you want to use to do this are the following:

```
sdl=1
vnc=0
```

Identifying Physical Resources for Xen Domains

The disk entry in the configuration files for both paravirtualized and HVM Xen guest domains enable you to provide access to physical storage devices on your domain0 system, such as a CD-ROM drive, from your domainU guests. To do this, you would add an entry such as 'phy:/dev/hda,hdc:cdrom,r' to the comma-separated list of disk devices. (Older versions of Xen used a specific cdrom configuration file, which is now deprecated.) The phy: prefix in this entry identifies it as a physical device, /dev/hda is its location in your domain0 system, hdc is the device that the domainU guest will map to the device, and r means that it is read-only. When specifying the name of the physical device on the domain0 system, you should always use its actual device name, rather than the name of a symbolic link that points to this resource, such as /dev/cdrom or /dev/dvd.

Manually Starting HVM Xen Domains

Starting an HVM Xen guest is almost identical to the process of starting a paravirtualized Xen guest. Once you've customized the configuration file to reflect your local configuration, you can start your HVM Xen system manually by executing the appropriate xm command with root privileges. The most common ways to do this are by becoming the root user via the su or sudo -s commands and executing the xm command within the resulting root shell, or by using the sudo command to execute your xm command as root.

The standard command to start an HVM Xen guest is xm create variable, where variable is the name of the configuration file for that virtual machine. When you're first starting an HVM, it's usually a good idea to create an initial connection to the console of that virtual machine, which you can do either by adding the -c option to your initial xm create command line or by using a terminal emulator, such as minicom, to connect to the PTY that is associated with your HVM. This is /dev/pty/variable, where variable is the domain ID of your system as reported by the xm list command. This will enable you to see and record any error messages that may be displayed by the HVM boot process.

To continue with the previous example, you would type the following to use the modified freespire .cfg configuration file to start a virtual machine in your current terminal window:

```
# xm create freespire.cfg -c
```

As with the examples of starting a paravirtualized system shown earlier in this chapter, initially connecting to the console from an existing terminal application has the advantage of enabling you to see all of the system boot messages, including any error messages that might be displayed.

Once the HVM domainU guest is up and running successfully, disconnect from the console by pressing Control-]. Then use the `xm list` command to identify its domain ID and the `xm console` command to reconnect to the console in its own window, as in the following example:

```
# xm list
Name                    ID Mem(MiB) VCPUs State   Time(s)
Domain-0                 0    1752      2 r-----  56978.8
Foresight               46     384      1 -b----   1180.1
OpenSUSE                17     256      1 -b----   2114.4
Ubuntu                  34     256      1 -b----    591.7
centos.5-0              45     256      1 -b----    302.9
Freespire-HVM           49     256      1 -b----     63.2
# xterm -T "FreeSpire Console" -e xm console 49 &
```

Assuming that your configuration file contains the same `serial="pty"` entry shown in the sample HVM configuration file earlier in this chapter, you could also use a terminal emulator such as minicom and a command such as the following to connect to the text console of your HVM:

```
# minicom -p /dev/pty/49
```

These xterm and minicom commands connect you to the text console of an HVM, not to its graphical display. As mentioned previously, the sample HVM configuration file creates an HVM graphical display that you must connect to via a VNC client application, such as vncviewer.

Automatically Starting Xen Domains at Boot Time

As discussed in Chapter 4, Xen-enabled domain0 systems generally install two startup scripts in /etc/init.d (or the equivalent directory in your Linux system). These are the xend script, which starts the Xen daemon, and the xendomains script, which you can use to automatically start Xen domains each time you boot your domain0 system.

Symbolic links to both of these startup scripts should be present in the startup script directory for your domain0 system's default runlevel to ensure that they run as part of your startup and shutdown processes. The naming convention used for these symbolic links is discussed in detail in Chapter 4. A link to the xend script is almost always present; a link to the xendomains script is optional unless you want to automatically start domainU guests whenever you restart your domain0 system. This is generally a good idea, especially if your domainU guests provide services that are required by your computing environment.

Once you have created or verified that the appropriate symbolic links to the xendomains script are present, all you have to do to enable automatic domainU startup is to create symbolic links in the /etc/xen/auto directory that point to the configuration files for the domainU systems that you want to auto-start.

Once one or more such symbolic links are present, you can execute the xendomains script manually to launch your domainU systems by executing the /etc/init.d/xendomains start command. If some of the domains that you want to auto-start are already running, you may want to stop them before running this script. You can stop them either by terminating them manually using the `xm destroy DOMAIN-ID` command as the root user, or by executing the `/etc/init.d/xendomainsstop` command. Using the script to shut down your domains has the added benefit of verifying that your domainU guests will be correctly terminated when you shut down your system, because `/etc/init.d/ xendomainsstop` is the command that is executed at system shutdown.

> For more information about using this script, see "Configuring and Using the xendomains Init Script" in Chapter 10.

Troubleshooting Configuration Files and Guest Domains

It's relatively easy to divide the types of problems that you may encounter when starting a Xen virtual machine, into several different classes. First, there are configuration file problems that prevent the `xm` command from launching a virtual machine, regardless of whether it is a paravirtualized or hardware VM. Second, there are problems that prevent your virtual machine from booting successfully, whether they are related to the kernel, an initial RAM disk filesystem, the root filesystem, and so on. Finally, there are problems that prevent your virtual machine from functioning correctly once it has booted. The next few sections discuss each of these classes of errors in order, explaining common problems that you may encounter and how to resolve them, and discussing how to identify and address more insidious problems that can range from simply being frustrating to being infuriating.

One good source of troubleshooting information is the Xen FAQ on the XenSource wiki (`http://wiki .xensource.com/xenwiki/XenFaq`). This lists many common problems and suggests solutions. I've minimized duplication between that information and the troubleshooting information in this section, with the exception of some errors that are common enough to merit discussion here.

As with any troubleshooting guide, I wish that I could say that the next few sections are 100-percent complete, but I doubt that I've seen every Xen error (yet). Hopefully, these sections will help you avoid some of my mistakes, or will at least help you resolve them if you happen to make the same ones.

Troubleshooting Xen Configuration Files

Configuration file syntax errors are extremely easy to make and can be quite frustrating to track down. Earlier versions of Xen were fond of displaying the message `Error: 22, Invalid Argument` in response to any configuration file syntax error, which wasn't particularly useful. The types of error messages displayed by the latest versions of Xen are much more useful, actually providing some information about the type of error that was encountered and, most importantly, where the error was encountered. Error messages, such as the following, where *FILENAME* is the name of the configuration file that you are using, actually identify where in the configuration file an error was encountered:

```
Error: EOL while scanning single-quoted string (FILENAME, line 1)
Error: invalid syntax (FILENAME, line 1)
```

Both of these error messages identify syntax errors on line 1 of the configuration file. The first identifies a missing quotation mark, and the second identifies an unrecognized statement on the first line of the configuration file.

Similarly, invalid entries within a valid type of statement can also generate error messages. Error messages such as the following, where Variable is all or part of the value supplied for a valid configuration file parameter, are fairly straightforward:

```
Error: Kernel image does not exist: Variable
Error: Invalid disk specifier: Variable
```

In these types of cases, the error message identifies the offending entry. In the first case, you've probably mistyped the name of the kernel that you want to use. In the second case, you've probably left out some component of a disk declaration or the punctuation that separates each of the components within an entry. Each entry in a disk declaration is enclosed within quotation marks and consists of three portions: the local device and device identifier, the name of the partition or device that the Xen domain sees, and the read/write state of the device.

The most common, and infuriating, error message that you can get when attempting to start Xen is `Error 22, Invalid Argument`. This error was formerly the standard message for all configuration file errors, but has been replaced by the more user-friendly error messages, discussed earlier in this section. However, you may still see this message for more insidious types of errors. When you do, check the xend log file, `/var/log/xen/xend.log`. This may help you identify the syntax problem in your configuration file, which you can then double-check and correct.

A less common, but harder to debug, problem that causes Error 22 is having incompatible Xen installations on the same system. Messages in the `/var/log/xen/xend.log` file that identify problems in construction of the UUID (Universal Unique Identifier) for a domain such as `ERROR (__init__ :1021) (22, 'Invalid argument')` generally mean that inconsistent Python files and libraries are installed on your system. You may see these messages if you have installed your distribution's version of Xen and then have built and installed a newer version of Xen on the same system. The best solution is to use your system's package-management tools to completely remove the distribution version of Xen, and then reinstall the version that you built. Similarly, you could use the Xen source distribution's `make uninstall` command to attempt to remove the hand-built version of Xen. You could then reinstall the version of Xen that is provided by your Linux distribution and hope that this eliminates the error.

Device-related errors that you may encounter, and which can easily be resolved, are the following:

```
Error: Device Variable (2049, vbd) is already connected
```

This error means that you have identified the same partition (where Variable is the name of a partition from the perspective of the domainU system,) in multiple entries in a `disk` configuration statement. This is an easy cut-and-paste error to make.

```
Error: Device 2050 (vbd) could not be connected.
File FILENAME is loopback-mounted through /dev/loop0,
which is mounted in a guest domain, and so cannot be mounted now.
```

Similar to the previous error, this means that you have identified the same `file:` (or `tap:aio:`) entry multiple times in a `disk` configuration statement. Again, this is an easy cut-and-paste error to make.

In the course of using Xen, you will probably encounter other error messages and spend some time resolving them. In the interest of good Xen citizenship and furthering the open source community, you should consider summarizing the message, the related problem, and its resolution, and posting this information to the Xen Users mailing list, as discussed in "Popular Xen and Virtualization Resources on the Internet" in Chapter 2.

Troubleshooting Xen VM Startup

Once you have a valid Xen configuration file and the kernel boots, you have moved on to the next plane of potential error messages, typically problems related to accessing the root filesystem, problems loading device drivers, or problems accessing specific devices.

After the kernel boots and loads any initial RAM disk filesystem that you have specified, the next major step in the boot process is to mount the filesystem that you identified as the root filesystem in your Xen configuration file. The following is a relatively common error that you may see when booting paravirtualized systems:

```
VFS: Cannot open root device "<NULL>" or unknown-block(0,0)
Please append a correct "root=" boot option
Kernel panic - not syncing:
   VFS: Unable to mount root fs on unknown-block(0,0)
```

This error can mean that the entry in your Xen configuration file for your root filesystem is incorrect, which is relatively easy to check. The root filesystem is identified in a combination of the Xen configuration file's `root` statement and the corresponding portion of a `disk` statement. The root directive generally looks like the following:

```
root = "/dev/sda1 ro"
```

This tells the kernel which device to mount as the root filesystem and how to initially mount it. In this example, you should check the portion of the `disk` statement in your configuration file to ensure that a device or file is identified as being mapped to sda1. If this is the case, try mounting that device or file using the loopback command on your domain0 host, which would resemble the following:

```
# mount -o loop /IMAGE/FILE/NAME /mnt
```

If the device or file can be mounted correctly on your domain0 system, then your domainU guest should be able to mount it. This often means that the kernel that you are using needs to load a loadable kernel module in order to be able to mount a root filesystem of the type that you are providing. If you have not identified an initial RAM disk or filesystem in the configuration file for your paravirtualized system, try adding one, creating it if necessary (as explained in "Creating Initial RAM Disks and Filesystems for Your Kernel," earlier in this chapter). If the kernel can now mount your root filesystem, you may want to consider rebuilding the kernel to compile as support for the format used by your root filesystem format.

If the kernel can mount your root filesystem but encounters problems accessing it, you may see a message such as the following:

```
VFS: Cannot open root device "sda1" or unknown-block(0,0)
Please append a correct "root=" boot option
Kernel panic - not syncing:
  VFS: Unable to mount root fs on unknown-block(0,0)
```

I have seen this error message when using older versions of Xen and when testing older root filesystem images that I have downloaded from the Internet. If you are using a root filesystem image, try substituting the `file:` disk-type identifier prefix for the more modern `tap:aio:` prefix. This shouldn't really be a problem (and I doubt that you'll be using downloaded filesystem images for production work), but this can be a useful workaround when testing, prototyping, and so on.

At this point in the boot process, you may also encounter a message such as the following:

```
Waiting for root filesystem...
```

This generally means that your configuration file does not contain a root directive, and the kernel therefore doesn't really know where to boot from. Adding a root directive of the form shown earlier in this section should resolve this problem.

Once the domainU kernel has mounted your root filesystem and begins the Linux startup process, you may see a message such as this:

```
modprobe: FATAL: Could not load FILENAME: No such file or directory
```

This is not a Xen problem, but is actually a root filesystem problem. It simply means that a loadable kernel module required by the kernel was not found. The most common cause of this sort of problem is that you did not copy the loadable kernel modules required by the kernel that you are booting into the root filesystem and the kernel is mounting.

The previous errors in this section were primarily related to paravirtualized systems. Hardware virtualization has its own unique set of potential problems. One of the most interesting problems encountered when using hardware virtualization is that you are able to boot from your installation media, but you encounter problems partitioning the device or file that you identified as your HVM disk. This problem can often be traced to the SELinux (Security-Enhanced Linux) system on the domain0 host. SELinux is a set of Linux add-ons that provide more granular control and substantially higher security on Linux systems by imposing mandatory access controls that determine which users and programs can access specific files and devices. In order to use Xen successfully on a domain0 host, you must either disable SELinux or modify the permissions for all of the files and devices that your domainU guests require access to.

Troubleshooting Virtual Machines

Once a paravirtualized virtual machine has booted cleanly and without errors, you're almost done! However, you may still encounter occasional errors related to the interaction between drivers on your domain0 and domainU systems or even the device node subsystem itself.

Modern 2.6-based Linux systems use a subsystem called udev to automatically create the access points for devices on a Linux system as it boots. Older Linux and Unix systems required that the filesystem entry that identifies each device (known as a "device node") be manually created in the /dev directory. Because device nodes had to exist before a device could be accessed, Linux and Unix systems either shipped with every possible device node or provided instructions for manually creating device nodes before using specific types of devices. Not only is this difficult and completely unscalable, it also wastes disk space by pre-creating device nodes that would never be used. To eliminate this problem, the udev system was integrated into the 2.6 Linux kernel. The udev system is a user-space mechanism for creating device nodes based on sets of rules that ship with the system. Device nodes are created at boot time based on probing the hardware that can be detected on your system. After the boot process is complete, a udev daemon continues to run on the system and automatically creates device nodes in response to the hotplug and similar events that are issued when removable devices are attached to a running system.

If you have problems accessing devices on a domainU system, you should first make sure that the appropriate device nodes exist, and that any mandatory symbolic links to those device nodes have also been created. For example, CD-ROM and DVD devices may be physical devices such as `/dev/hda` or `/dev/hdb`, but are often accessed through symbolic links such as `/dev/cdrom` or `/dev/dvd`. When attaching newer devices for use by existing domainU systems, you may find that you need to update the udev rules on your system because your domainU system may be using an older set of udev rules.

For example, an interesting, udev-related problem that I experienced on systems running earlier versions of SUSE 10.*x* was that the device nodes for my Ethernet devices would be created and used correctly the first time I booted my domainU system, but would increment on each subsequent reboot. In other words, the first time I booted, eth0 was created and worked fine, but the next time I booted, the system wanted to use eth1, the subsequent time eth2, and so on. This was due to a problem in the udev persistent naming rules, contained in the file `/etc/udev/rules.d/30-net_persistent_names`.`rules`, which recorded the MAC address that was being dynamically generated for my domainU system each time it booted and, because it differed each time, assigned the next Ethernet interface to the new MAC address. I solved this problem (which was subsequently fixed) by assigning a specific MAC address in my domainU configuration file, and then modifying the udev rule file to always associate that MAC address with eth0.

Once you are sure that the device nodes associated with any device that you are trying to use exist, you should also make sure that the drivers for that device are either compiled into the kernel or are available in your root filesystem as loadable kernel modules. As mentioned in the previous section, it is easy to forget to install the loadable kernel modules that accompany your kernel into each root filesystem that you are using.

If you are using hardware that you have hidden from your domain0 system and are dedicating to one or more domainU systems, any mandatory drivers must be present and the device must be enabled in the configuration file for each domain that uses it via a `pci = ['XX:XX.0']` configuration statement. If you still have problems with the drivers for hidden cards, you may want to try adding the `pciback.permissive` option for the module entry in your GRUB configuration file for your kernel. This option is used with drivers, such as some NIC drivers, which must be able to write to registers on the PCI device itself.

A final set of common errors have to do with networking. If your domainU system doesn't come up with a network interface, first make sure that a `vif` statement is present in your domainU configuration file. An empty `vif` statement is fine, because this tells the `xm` command to create a network interface for your virtual machine, and to select intelligent default values when doing so.

If your domainU system comes up with an Ethernet device, but that interface is not automatically configured, make sure that your domainU configuration file includes a statement such as `dhcp = 'dhcp'`. This tells the guest domain to attempt to automatically configure its Ethernet interface using the

Dynamic Host Control Protocol (DHCP). You should also try configuring the interface manually, by using a command such as the following:

```
# ifconfig eth0 XXX.XXX.XXX.XXX netmask 255.255.255.XXX up
```

In this example, the first expression is a valid Ethernet interface for the subnet on which your domain0 system is located, and the second is a netmask for your network segment. If you can ping other hosts on your network by their IP address, then the interface is working correctly, but is not being automatically configured correctly. Check that a DHCP client daemon is started by your domainU system at boot time, and check the system logs for any DHCP messages that the system may be receiving.

A final networking problem that is occasionally encountered is when your network interfaces report communication errors and only minimal network applications such as ping work correctly. (You can use a command such as `tcpdump -nvvi eth0` to see packet traffic and associated error messages on the Ethernet device eth0.) If you see checksum errors on your virtual network interfaces, you may want to eliminate transmit checksums on your domainU host by using a command such as `ethtool -K eth0 tx off`. If you are still seeing communication errors, you should also disable the receive checksum by using a command such as `ethtool -K eth0 rx off`.

If your domainU system seems to be working correctly but you are having problems starting user processes, your domainU system may simply not have sufficient memory. If this is the case, try restarting your domainU system after increasing the amount of memory specified in the `memory` configuration statement.

Summary

This chapter discusses some quick recipes for initial success with Xen, using both easily available paravirtualized system components from the Internet, and simple hardware virtual machine configurations. This chapter provides a firm foundation for the more specialized paravirtualized and hardware virtual machines that you may eventually want to build and configure yourself. The next chapter discusses how to build, install, and use your own domainU systems from scratch, providing all of the low-level filesystem, driver, and system configuration information necessary to excite any true Linux fan.

Building Filesystems for Virtual Machines

6

Paravirtualized Xen virtual machines provide substantially better performance than hardware virtual machines, but are inherently harder to create than hardware virtual machines. Although Xen's hardware virtual machines can run only on hardware with specific processors and characteristics, they are easy to install. They require only a valid Xen configuration file, the installation media for the operating system that you want to install, and some storage to install them into. Hardware virtual machines use this storage as a virtual disk drive, partitioning it appropriately, internally, and automatically during the installation process for the operating system that you are installing.

As discussed in Chapter 5, paravirtualized Xen systems usually use specific filesystems rather than using storage as a virtual disk drive. You can use complete disk images with paravirtualized Xen systems, but I find this to be needlessly complex. However, the installation procedure for most operating systems is designed to install to an entire disk drive rather than installing software subsets to a specific partition. For this reason, creating and populating disk images or partitions for use by paravirtualized Xen virtual machines requires a bit more thought than simply installing a complete operating system.

This chapter begins by providing background information about Linux filesystems and associated storage locations. It then discusses filesystems and storage for paravirtualized and hardware virtual machines, discussing how your choice of storage locations affects system administration tasks such as backups and virtual machine migration. It concludes by discussing how to create various types of root filesystems, and how to add specific capabilities to those root filesystems.

This chapter focuses on providing basic, low-level information about building root filesystems using basic Linux tools and techniques, and is therefore distribution-independent wherever possible. It also discusses how to use distribution-specific package management utilities and similar tools to simplify the process of manually creating different types of filesystems.

Linux Storage and Filesystems

A filesystem is the structure imposed on a pool of storage so that Linux systems can access and use that storage through system and user-level commands. In order to use a storage device, the storage that it provides must first be partitioned so that each partition can be used to hold a physical filesystem, or allocated to a logical volume management or storage management system. As a result, the storage that it provides can be allocated to volumes (which are essentially analogous to partitions) or used to hold copies of other data (as in a RAID system). A filesystem can then be created on each partition or volume. Once a filesystem has been created, that filesystem can be mounted on a directory on your Linux system and can be accessed by that system.

Linux supports a large number of different filesystems, including the following:

❑ Local filesystems that were originally developed for Linux, such as Ext2, Ext3, Ext4, ReiserFS, and Reiser4.

❑ Local filesystems that are open-source but which originated on other UNIX-like platforms, such as JFS (IBM) and XFS (SGI).

❑ Local filesystems in well-understood or proprietary formats that are primarily used with other operating systems, such as FAT and NTFS (Microsoft Windows) and HFS and HFS+ (Apple MacOS).

❑ Network filesystems with enhanced volume, locking, and authentication support that multiple Linux systems can mount and share access to. Depending on the type of filesystem and how your Xen guests are configured, these filesystems can be used as root filesystems or by mounting them after using a local root filesystem for the boot process. This type of filesystem includes traditional distributed filesystems such as NFS (originally developed by Sun Microsystems), OpenAFS (based on IBM's AFS product, which was originally developed by CMU and Transarc), GFS (originally developed by Sistina and now open source but marketed by Red Hat). This group also includes filesystems originally developed for clustering such as OCFS2 (Oracle), Lustre, and so on. (For more information about these, see the "Network Filesystems" section later in this chapter.)

Based on the type of filesystem and how it is made available to your Linux system, the storage associated with these filesystems can be files that are themselves located in another filesystem, local storage devices, block-level network storage, or networked file servers that deliver connectivity to more advanced distributed or clustering filesystems.

Because Xen can leverage the basic capabilities and flexibility of Linux, Xen domain0 and domainU systems can use many different types of storage devices, each with their own caveats and issues in terms of device drivers, types of filesystems, and portability. The next few sections provide an overview of the different locations when Xen domainU filesystems can be stored, discussing the advantages, disadvantages, and use of each in terms of flexibility, administration, and general use with Xen.

Filesystem or Disk Images

As discussed in the previous chapter, files that contain an image of a filesystem are the easiest way to get started with paravirtualized Xen virtual machines. Files that contain an image of a hard disk provide a similarly easy way to get started with Xen's support for hardware virtual machines and system virtualization. Files that contain filesystems can be accessed via Xen's blktap driver or the older loopback mechanism, whereas files that are used as disk images make use of hard disk emulation mechanisms that were originally developed for QEMU. Filesystem or disk images accessed using the blktap driver are identified in your virtual machine configuration file by the `tap:` prefix before the full pathname of the image files. Filesystem or disk images accessed using the traditional loopback method are identified in your virtual machine configuration file by the `file:` prefix before the full pathname of the image files. The `tap:` driver was introduced in Xen 3.0.

After ease of use, the primary advantage of using Xen with filesystem or disk image files is their portability. Because they are independent of any physical device, they can easily be manually migrated from one system to another. They can also be easily copied for use with other virtual machines and can be manually migrated from one Xen host to another in the event of system problems or for load-balancing purposes.

On the down side, using Xen with filesystem or disk image files can require significant amounts of memory to mount and access these images, especially when using the older `file:` (loopback) model with filesystem images. Filesystem and disk images are also typically less efficient than physical devices whose performance and access patterns can be optimized. On the other hand, small filesystem images that can remain memory resident can be extremely efficient for dedicated, small-footprint Xen virtual machines.

For information about creating and populating filesystem image files, see "Building Virtual Machine Filesystems" later in this chapter. For information about creating and populating disk images files, see "Creating and Using QEMU Disk Images," also later in this chapter.

Local Filesystems

Using physical storage devices to hold filesystems for paravirtualized Xen guests is the obvious alternative to using files as filesystems, and is quite easy to use when getting started with Xen. The identification prefix for a physical partition in a Xen configuration file is `phy:`.

As explained in detail later in this chapter, you can easily use a physical partition to hold the root filesystem for a paravirtualized Xen guest domain. In this case, the type of filesystem used on that partition must be one that is either directly supported by the kernel, or one for which the drivers are provided on an initial RAM disk or filesystem.

You can also install an HVM Xen guest system into a physical disk partition, in which case the partition is internally formatted into multiple partitions that can use any filesystem format that is supported by the HVM kernel. These partitions are invisible to the domain0 system.

Although easy to use, the primary downside of using local, physical partitions for paravirtualized or HVM Xen guests is that they are tied to a physical disk on a single physical machine. Limiting a virtual machine to a physical partition limits its flexibility by constraining its maximum size to the size of that partition. Similarly, the failure of either that disk or that system will bring down all of the virtual machines that are hosted on it. This eliminates much of the flexibility required to take advantage of Xen capabilities such as migration, as discussed in the "Filesystem Choices, Locations, and Flexibility" section later in this chapter. As discussed in that section, local filesystems can be mirrored to remote systems over a network using techniques such as a Distributed Replicated Block Device (DRBD, www.linux-ha.org/DRBD) to help minimize the impact of local failures during migration.

RAID Storage

RAID (Redundant Array of Inexpensive Disks or Redundant Array of Independent Disks, depending on whom you ask) is a hardware and/or software mechanism used to improve the performance and maintainability of large amounts of disk storage through some extremely clever mechanisms. As the name suggests, RAID makes a large number of smaller disks (referred to as a RAID array) appear to be one or more large disks as far as the operating system is concerned, and can also be used to provide protection against the failure of any single disk in your system. RAID does this by providing its own internal disk management interface.

RAID is typically provided by specialized disk controller hardware, by system-level software, or by some combination of both. The support for software RAID under Linux is known as the multiple device (md) interface. Hardware RAID has performance advantages over software RAID, but can be a problem in enterprise environments because hardware RAID implementations are usually specific to the RAID controller or controller manufacturer that you are using.

A number of different RAID configurations exist, referred to as RAID levels. The capabilities provided by different RAID levels include concatenating disks to maximize partition size, locating different portions of your filesystems on different physical disks or disk partitions to improve performance (known as striping), and using checksums, parity-checking, spare disk partitions, and physical copies of partitions (known as mirroring) to protect against data loss from the failure of some number of participating disks. Once a specific RAID level has been configured, the storage provided by your RAID array can be partitioned and used as you would on any physical storage devices. When used with Xen, paravirtualized or HVM Xen guests generally use these partitions through the domain0 system, so your guest domains do not need to have any special device drivers for your RAID storage.

In the Xen context, RAID is generally used to provide reliability guarantees for your guest domains by protecting them against downtime caused by the failure of one or even two disks. As discussed in the "Filesystem Choices, Locations, and Flexibility" section later in this chapter, RAID provides maximum benefits when combined with logical volume management, delivering maximum location-independence and flexibility for your virtual machines.

Logical Volumes

A fundamental rule of data storage is that storage requirements expand to consume all available space. Traditional solutions to storage management, such as disk quotas, can't solve the actual problem, which is the fixed-size aspect of disk storage. Logical volumes solve this problem in an elegant fashion, by combining available storage into a logical storage pool from which partitions can be allocated. The pool of storage space from which specific volumes are created is known as a volume group. Volume groups are created by first formatting specific physical devices or partitions as physical volumes in a special format used by the Linux volume management systems, and then by creating one or more logical volume groups on those physical volumes. Finally, you create specific logical volumes within a logical volume group, and can then use those logical volumes as if they were physical partitions.

Once in use, logical volumes can be resized as needed, and physical volumes can be flexibly added or removed from volume groups with no interruption in availability. This enables you to quickly add new storage to your system by adding new disks, creating new physical volumes on them, and adding those physical volumes to existing volume groups. Without logical volumes, you could always add new disk storage to your systems in the traditional fashion, by adding new disks, partitioning them, and mounting them at various locations in existing filesystems, but your environment would quickly become an unmanageable administrative nightmare of mount points and symbolic links. You would also still be susceptible to problems caused by the failure of single partitions, disks, and systems.

Portability and flexibility are important concerns for virtual machines, enabling you to maintain Xen guest uptime across disk and system failures. If a disk begins to fail and sufficient space is available in a volume group, the physical volumes on that disk can be removed from a volume group, which automatically migrates data from those physical volumes to others within that volume group. When combined with RAID, logical volumes provide even better support for the uptime and availability guarantees that are required in enterprise environments. Logical volumes can be used on top of RAID storage at certain RAID levels, enabling you to replace failing disks without the need to remove the volumes from a volume group.

Linux provides multiple logical volume management systems, known as LVM (old and deprecated), EVMS (Enterprise Volume Management System, `http://evms.sourceforge.net`), and LVM2, which is the standard logical volume management system used on most Linux systems and the one that this book refers to by default. A clustering logical volume manager, CLVM (`http://sources.redhat.com/cluster/clvm`), is also available to support shared access to logical volumes from multiple systems, but requires other software such as a locking library and a daemon running on each participating system.

As with any filesystems, logical volumes can also be mirrored to remote systems over a network using techniques such as Distributed Replicated Block Devices (DRBD, `www.linux-ha.org/DRBD`) to help minimize the impact of local disk failures and support migration to protect against system failures. If you do not want to use mirroring, you can use CLVM.

Network Filesystems

Network filesystems are filesystems whose storage is actually located on networked file servers. These file servers handle filesystem-level access and allocation requests that are received over a network from client systems. Network filesystems provide protection against disk failures on client systems, and provide built-in support for simultaneous access of a given network filesystem from multiple client systems, with certain caveats. Network filesystems were originally developed to provide flexible, shared access to large amounts of storage from multiple, otherwise stand-alone computer systems. Many newer network filesystems were developed for use in clustering environments, where multiple computer systems can work together as a single virtual system and similarly share access to network filesystem resources.

Popular open source network filesystems for Linux include NFS (`http://nfs.sourceforge.net`), OpenAFS (`http://openafs.org`), and GFS (`www.redhat.com/gfs/`). NFS is purely a filesystem-level network filesystem, while both OpenAFS and GFS provide their own storage and logical volume managers. Popular open source clustering filesystems for Linux include the Lustre File System (`www.lustre.org`) and the Oracle Cluster File System 2 (`http://oss.oracle.com/projects/ocfs2`, now incorporated into the mainline Linux kernel).

> *Although there are many technical differences, network and clustering filesystems generally provide similar functionality for Xen domain0 and domainU systems. Thus, they will be generically referred to simply as network filesystems whenever possible throughout the remainder of this book.*

One primary advantage of networked filesystems is that they were designed to be accessed and shared by multiple systems, and therefore provide built-in support for simultaneous access to both single files and the filesystem as a whole from those systems. None of the storage locations discussed in the previous sections are designed for simultaneous access, and therefore cannot be easily shared by multiple Xen domains as writable filesystems. The Linux kernel tracks the status of writes to all block-level filesystems. Because each Xen domain is running its own kernel, trying to write to the same filesystem from multiple guest domains will quickly cause filesystem corruption. Network filesystems typically provide access at the file and directory level, rather than the block level, and provide their own caching mechanisms.

With the exception of NFS, network filesystems are rarely used as root filesystems, but are commonly used to provide access to shared sets of system binaries, project directories, and user directories. NFS root filesystems can even be shared by multiple Xen guests, although conflicts can still occur in commonly-used directories such as /tmp and /var unless your domainU guests are configured to use their own, unique storage for these directories. (The /proc and /sys directories are not a problem because these are transient, in-memory filesystems that are uniquely created during the boot process of each domainU system.) However, if you are using filesystem or disk images for your domainU systems, networked filesystems provide a convenient location in which to store those filesystems or disk images to simplify the migration of guest domains from one host to another.

To use an NFS root filesystem, you must configure your Xen kernel to enable NFS support in the kernel, not as a module, and then select the CONFIG_ROOT_NFS option. See "Configuring the Standard Xen Kernel Source" in Chapter 3 for additional information about enabling this option. See the "Creating Root Filesystems for Use with NFS" section later in this chapter for additional information about filesystem changes that you will want to make.

Networked Block-Level Storage

As described in the previous section, network filesystems provide filesystem-level access to storage that is located on networked file servers. Filesystem-level access means file and directory access, not access to raw storage devices, virtual partitions, or similar block-level access. Block-level network storage, such as that used in most Storage Area Network (SAN) solutions, is storage that is physically located on other devices on your network, but which your system can access at the block-level using protocols and associated drivers such as ATA over Ethernet (AoE), Internet Small Computer Systems Interface (iSCSI), network block device drivers such as NBD, GNBD, and so on. NBD, GNBD (used by the GFS network filesystem discussed in the previous section), and AoE support is built into the mainline Linux kernel, whereas specific iSCSI hardware requires specific drivers, only some of which are in the mainline kernel.

Block-level network storage is ideal for creating physical partitions or logical volumes that can be used as root filesystems for paravirtualized Xen domains or as disk images for Xen hardware virtual machines. This facilitates the migration of Xen guest domains from one host to another to avoid hardware problems or to facilitate load-balancing. However, as with any block-level storage, block-level network storage does not support sharing writable filesystems between multiple guest domains unless you are using software such as a cluster-aware logical volume manager.

Filesystem Choices, Locations, and Flexibility

The "Virtual Machine Requirements" section in Chapter 5 highlighted the primary differences between how paravirtualized and HVM Xen guests use storage. To recap, paravirtualized Xen guests use storage at the filesystem level, whereas hardware virtual machines use storage at the device level. Paravirtualized guests expect each disk device in their Xen configuration file to contain a filesystem, whereas hardware virtual machines expect each device in their Xen configuration file to be a device that contains a partition table and must provide a boot loader in order to be bootable.

The next sections discuss the filesystem and storage-related decisions that are critical for different enterprise environments.

Single domain0 System Configuration

If you are running a single domain0 system that supports multiple domainU guests, your initial administrative concerns are correctly configuring your domainU guests, configuring the software that they are running, and insuring the uptime of the domain0 host on which they are running. After this point, the reliability and continuous availability of the storage used by those guests is critical. Any hardware redundancy that you have planned for that domain0 host, whether it is a set of identical replacement hardware or a complete, mirrored, replacement host, should be reflected by designing your virtualization environment to rely on flexible, reliable, and redundant storage. Using a combination of software RAID and logical volumes will provide the highest level of flexibility and reliability for quick recovery from unexpected hardware failures.

Besides the partition level, your choice of the type of filesystem that you will use in your domainU systems is the most significant factor in minimizing any downtime on those systems. Using a journaling filesystem such as ext3, JFS, ReiserFS, or XFS will help ensure fast restart of any domainU guests that you have to reboot for one reason or another, as well as on the domain0 system itself. (The ext4 and Reiser4 filesystems are other alternatives. However, at the time of this writing, they are less mature, and therefore aren't good choices for enterprise virtualization at this time.) I typically prefer the ext3 filesystem for domainU guests because of the number of filesystem tuning and debugging tools that are available for it. The filesystem that you use on your domain0 system is a similar decision, but should be influenced by any other tasks that the system will support. In general, I suggest that Xen support should be the primary task of your domain0 system, and preferably its only task.

If you are supporting users in your guest domains, using a networked filesystem to store user directories will simplify your backup efforts and build in flexibility if you need to migrate users from one domainU system to another. Using a networked filesystem to hold directories of shared Linux binaries can save significant space for identical domainU guests,. However, it can be problematic if you are running different Linux distributions in different domainU systems because shared binaries typically also rely on shared libraries, the same versions of which must be available in every domainU system to guarantee identical execution and behavior in your applications.

If you are more concerned about backups and redundancy than with centralized access to filesystems and data resources, local filesystems can be mirrored to remote systems over a network using techniques such as a Distributed Replicated Block Device (DRBD, www.linux-ha.org/DRBD) to help minimize the impact of local failures during migration.

Finally, if block-level networked storage or network filesystems are not options in your environment, you can facilitate manual, emergency migration between guests by using inexpensive hardware such as drive trays in your domain0 systems. In this case, you must provide some logical abstraction for these partitions (such as filesystem labels) to avoid problems with disk renaming when existing disks are installed into a different system.

Running Multiple domain0 Systems

Besides its support for paravirtualization and associated performance improvements, the most significant advantage of Xen over other open source virtualization technologies is its ability to migrate Xen domains from one domain0 system to another. This makes Xen an excellent choice for enterprise-level virtualization where high availability is a fundamental requirement.

When migrating a domainU guest from one domain0 host to another, both domain0 systems must provide identical runtime environments. As far as storage is concerned, this means that all participating domain0 systems must have access to the same storage locations. This makes networked storage of some sort the only viable mechanism for true enterprise-level virtualization. Although accessing and using networked filesystems and block-level storage can incur significant overhead, they can be hosted on highly reliable servers with sufficient redundant hardware to guarantee high availability. domainU systems that use them as their root (and other) filesystems and disks are completely portable across identically configured domain0 hosts.

> At the time of this writing, domainU systems can be migrated only between domain0 hosts on the same class C network, so these network resources must be available on the same class C network segment.

In my experience, a combination of RAID-enabled AoE networked storage and network filesystems provides the maximum amount of flexibility and reliability with the lowest cost and the least amount of frustration. Coraid's AoE storage systems (www.coraid.com) are competitively inexpensive, highly reliable, and provide built-in support for RAID. (I also find using and configuring iSCSI to be a complete hairball, but that could just be me.) Using logical volumes on top of RAID5 storage on an AoE device provides sufficient flexibility and reliability for almost any scenario. One consideration in this scenario is to make sure that backing up networked storage can be integrated into your current backup mechanisms, or you will have to update your backup procedures. As much as we'd all like it to be true, RAID is not a substitute for backups. If you think that this is true, you will be burned at some point in the future.

For domainU systems that run a limited amount of software, I personally prefer using NFS wherever possible. NFS is not as elegant as other network filesystems, but it is simple, well-known, and easily diagnosed when problems occur. If you are already using NFS for file-sharing, you can leverage the reliability you have (hopefully) already built into your enterprise NFS environment. If you are already using another network filesystem technology, using that instead of NFS is the right thing to do. Your fellow administrators will thank you for minimizing the number of system-specific decisions that they have to make, and should already be experts in your existing network filesystem.

When using any sort of networked storage, it's important to consider the impact of using the network as the primary conduit for all system and filesystem interaction on your virtual machines. The impact may not be all that significant for memory-intensive applications, but can be extremely significant for disk-intensive applications such as databases, and even highly interactive applications such as games (which probably isn't an enterprise concern unless you work for a gaming company). Filesystem interaction can also be an important bandwidth consideration if, for example, you are using block-level network storage to support a distributed filesystem. Although this is the normal usage pattern for filesystems such as GFS, you should monitor your network usage to see if this networked storage is appropriate for other filesystems such as NFS. For example, in most cases, NFS filesystems exported from a file server with local storage will be just as maintainable and will consume much less network bandwidth for heavily used filesystems.

Flexibility, ease of administration, performance, and network bandwidth consumption are important concerns for both physical and virtual machines in any modern enterprise-computing environment. Similarly, security is as important for virtual systems as it is for physical systems. When you use distributed filesystems for your domainU guests, access to those filesystems can be locked down so that your file servers accept only mount and file requests from the range of IP addresses that you associate with your domainU and administrative systems. If you are using DHCP, you can further secure your environment by assigning specific MAC addresses to each domainU guest and providing specific DHCP configuration stanzas for each of those MAC addresses. The domainU systems can be further secured by enabling only remote access via SSH (and any client software that they are supporting, of course).

To best support migration between participating domain0 hosts, everything specified in the configuration file for any migratable virtual machine should be identically available on each participating domain0 system. The same kernel and initial RAM disk or filesystem must be available if you ever need to shut down and restart a migrated domainU system. The same network and bridging environment must be available on all participating domain0 systems, especially if you have manually specified bridges or network configuration in the configuration files for your domainU guests.

An easy point to overlook in a migratable environment is the fact that your domainU configuration files should be available from all participating domain0 systems. It is pointless to be able to migrate domainU systems if your filesystem can't subsequently restart them on their new domain0 host whenever necessary. Storing your Xen configuration files in a networked filesystem that is mounted at the same location on all of your domain0 systems will make every system administrator's life better.

As a final tip, you should allocate as much memory as necessary to your heavily-used domainU guests in order to minimize (or eliminate) swapping. The only significant drawback to using networked filesystems or storage exclusively is that they should rarely be used for swap space because the network overhead associated with swapping can significantly impair the performance of a heavily loaded Xen guest.

Building Virtual Machine Filesystems

As discussed in Chapter 5, hardware virtual machines are typically installed from the same installation media that you use when installing the same operating system on a physical computer system or server. Creating the filesystems used by paravirtualized domainU guests can be much more complex. Luckily, the power and flexibility of Linux and the increasing popularity of Xen and other virtual machine solutions have evolved a number of different techniques and tools for creating the root and other filesystems used by virtual machines. The next few sections discuss various ways of creating image files, partitions, and logical volumes, and populating them with the contents of the root filesystem from the Linux distribution of your choice.

Creating Filesystem Image Files

As discussed in Chapter 5, using image files containing the root filesystem for paravirtualized Xen guests is the easiest way to start using and experimenting with Xen. If you do not have a free partition or logical volume available, you can easily create an image file in which you can install a root filesystem or which you can use as a virtual disk when you install your first HVM. You can easily create a sample image file using the dd command, as in the following example:

```
# dd if=/dev/zero of=image_file.img bs=1024k seek=4096 count=0
```

This creates a 4GB file that you can identify as the root filesystem in your HVM configuration file. The size of the image file is the block size (in this case, 1024KB, or 1MB) multiplied by the number of blocks that you want to seek into the file. Seeking to a specified block location in an empty image file is an easy way to quickly create a file of a specified size without actually writing data to it. You can also use the following command to do the same thing, but by writing the specified number of null blocks to the file (which is therefore substantially slower):

```
# dd if=/dev/zero of=image_file.img bs=1024k count=4096
```

The size of the image file that you need to create for use with a Xen virtual machine depends on both the number and size of the files that you want to install there, and the type of virtual machine that you will be using it with. If you are going to use this file to hold a root filesystem for a paravirtualized guest, the image file must be large enough to hold all of the files that you will ever want to put in your root filesystem. If you will be using this file with a HVM, it must be large enough to hold all of the files associated with whatever operating system you are installing in your HVM, as well as the bootloader, any swap space that the HVM requires, and so on. Image files for use with paravirtualized domainU guests are therefore almost always smaller than those used with HVM domainU guests.

Once you have created an image file, your next step depends on the type of virtual machine that you will be using it with. If you will be using it with an HVM, no further action is necessary. You can simply identify this file in the configuration file for your Xen HVM, correctly identify your installation media in that file, and start the guest domain. If, however, you will be using this to hold the root filesystem for a Xen guest, you must next create a filesystem in that file. For information about this process, skip to the "Creating a Filesystem in an Image File, Partition, or Logical Volume" section later in this chapter.

Creating Physical Partitions

Partitions are uniquely addressable portions of a storage device. Partitions are most commonly thought of in relation to storage devices that are physically attached to your computer system, but they can actually be located on any block-level storage device, such as Linux storage accessed via the NBD, GNBD, AoE, or iSCSI protocols and drivers. Partitions are created by using privileged commands to divide up the available storage on a block-level device, a process that is known, cleverly enough, as "partitioning."

Once created, partitions cannot be used by your Linux system for standard file and directory storage until you have formatted them for use as a specific type of Linux filesystem, as explained in "Creating a Filesystem in an Image File, Partition, or Logical Volume" later in this chapter. Many Linux distributions provide different graphical tools for partitioning disks, but the most common tool for creating disk partitions is the command-line `fdisk` tool, which is therefore the tool that is used in this section.

As an example of partitioning, this section shows how to create a single 5GB partition on a previously unformatted disk, and does not show how to do anything with the rest of the disk. In most cases, you would want to allocate all of the space available on a disk by repeating the sequence of commands explained in this section to create multiple partitions on that disk, perhaps with different partition starting locations and size values.

To begin, execute the `fdisk` command as the root user, supplying the name of the hard disk on which you want to create a partition. This disk must obviously have sufficient free space available to create a partition of the size that you specify. The `fdisk` command displays some summary information about your disk, and displays the `Command (m for help):` prompt, letting you know that it is waiting for you to type a command, as in the following example:

```
# fdisk /dev/sdb
Device contains neither a valid DOS partition table,
nor Sun, SGI or OSF disklabel
Building a new DOS disklabel. Changes will remain in memory only,
until you decide to write them. After that, of course, the previous
content won't be recoverable.
 The number of cylinders for this disk is set to 30394.
There is nothing wrong with that, but this is larger than 1024,
and could in certain setups cause problems with:
1) software that runs at boot time (e.g., old versions of LILO)
2) booting and partitioning software from other OSs
   (e.g., DOS FDISK, OS/2 FDISK)
 Command (m for help):
```

To verify that the disk does not currently contain a partition table, enter the p (print) command. This displays summary information about the disk and any partitions that it contains, and will then redisplay its prompt, as in the following example:

```
Disk /dev/sdb: 250.0 GB, 250000000000 bytes
255 heads, 63 sectors/track, 30394 cylinders
Units = cylinders of 16065 * 512 = 8225280 bytes
   Device Boot      Start         End      Blocks   Id  System
Command (m for help):
```

Type **n** to begin creating a new partition. The `fdisk` command will prompt you for the type of partition that you want to create, as in the following example:

```
Command action
   e   extended
   p   primary partition (1-4)
```

Linux disks can have up to four primary partitions, which are physical sections of the disk. This is a legacy feature from older operating systems when disks were smaller (like a recessive gene that you can't help passing on to your kids). If you want to create more than four partitions on a disk, you can identify one or more of the partitions on the disk as extended partitions, which are essentially physical partitions inside which you can create logical partitions. In this example because you are only creating a single partition, enter **p** to create a primary partition.

Next, you will be prompted for the number of the partition that you want to create, the starting point (first cylinder) which should be allocated to that partition, and the size of the partition. The size of a partition can be either expressed as an actual size value, such as +5G for five gigabytes, or in terms of the last cylinder that should be allocated to the partition. In most cases, a size value is easier to supply. The following example shows the fdisk prompts and the values that you would specify to create a 5GB partition as the first partition on a disk:

```
Partition number (1-4): 1
First cylinder (1-30394, default 1):
Using default value 1
Last cylinder or +size or +sizeM or +sizeK (1-30394, default 30394): +5G
```

After entering these values, the fdisk command will redisplay its generic prompt. You can enter the p command to show the new partitions table, as in the following example:

```
Disk /dev/sdb: 250.0 GB, 250000000000 bytes
255 heads, 63 sectors/track, 30394 cylinders
Units = cylinders of 16065 * 512 = 8225280 bytes
    Device Boot      Start         End      Blocks   Id  System
/dev/sdb1              1           609     4891761   83  Linux
```

At this point, the new partition table is stored only in memory. If you exit the fdisk program without writing your changes to the disk, the partition table on the disk will be in the exact state that it was when you first started the fdisk command. To write the updated partition table to the disk, enter the w command. The fdisk command will display the following messages, and will exit:

```
The partition table has been altered!
  Calling ioctl() to re-read partition table.
Syncing disks.
```

As discussed at the beginning of this section, disk partitions cannot be used to store files and directories until you have created a filesystem of some sort in them. For information on creating a filesystem in your new partition, skip to "Creating a Filesystem in an Image File, Partition, or Logical Volume" later in this chapter.

Creating Logical Volumes

As mentioned earlier in this chapter, logical volumes provide a logical layer of abstraction between specific block-level storage devices and the data that is stored on them. Storage that you want to use to hold logical volumes can be existing partitions or complete block-level storage devices, whether local or network-oriented. For an overview of logical volumes, see the "Logical Volumes" section earlier in this chapter.

The initial step in creating and using logical volumes is to use the `pvcreate` command to create physical volumes on those partitions or disks, so that the Linux logical-volume management system can use them.

If you are devoting entire disks to logical volumes, there are several ways to do so:

❑ Make sure that the disk does not contain a partition table, and create a single physical volume on the disk.

❑ Create a single partition on the disk, and create a physical volume on that partition.

❑ Create multiple partitions on your disk, and create physical volumes on each.

Each has advantages and disadvantages, but I prefer the third as a general rule. The first two approaches are simplest, but do not localize disk problems within a disk because the entire disk is a single physical volume. Because sector problems will cause the Linux LVM system to drop a physical volume from a volume group, using entire disks can significantly decrease your available storage when a few sectors go bad on these disks. To protect yourself against this type of problem, create multiple partitions on each disk, and then use the `pvcreate` command to create physical volumes on each. The size of these partitions should strike a balance between the amount of disk space that you are willing to temporarily lose access to if disk problems arise, and the amount of time that you want to spend using the `fdisk` command. I usually create four or five equally sized partitions on each disk, depending on its size.

After creating any partitions that you want to use as physical volumes, use the `pvcreate` command to actually allocate them for use as physical volumes, as in the following example:

```
# pvcreate /dev/hdb1
  Physical volume "/dev/hdb1" successfully created
```

You can then confirm the status and size of your new physical volume by using the `pvdisplay` command:

```
# pvdisplay
  --- NEW Physical volume ---
  PV Name               /dev/hdb1
  VG Name
  PV Size               50.00 GB
  Allocatable           NO
  PE Size (KByte)       0
  Total PE              0
  Free PE               0
  Allocated PE          0
  PV UUID               hy8hck-B5lp-TLZf-hyD4-U9Mu-EFn8-wob9Km
```

Once you've created one or more physical volumes, you need to add them to a specific volume group so that they can be allocated for use in a logical volume. You add a physical volume to a volume group with the `vgcreate` command, as in the following example:

```
# vgcreate VM /dev/hdb1
  Volume group "VM" successfully created
```

You can then confirm the status of your new volume group by using the `vgdisplay` command:

```
# vgdisplay VM
  --- Volume group ---
  VG Name               VM
  System ID
  Format                lvm2
  Metadata Areas        1
  Metadata Sequence No  1
  VG Access             read/write
  VG Status             resizable
  MAX LV                0
  Cur LV                0
  Open LV               0
  Max PV                0
  Cur PV                1
  Act PV                1
  VG Size               50.00 GB
  PE Size               4.00 MB
  Total PE              59618
  Alloc PE / Size       0 / 0
  Free  PE / Size       59618 / 232.88 GB
  VG UUID               SeY0pJ-Q0Ej-AQbT-Fri0-tai6-5oED-7ujb1F
```

After you have created a volume group, you can begin to use some of the storage in the physical volumes that it contains by creating logical volumes within the volume group using the `lvcreate` command. When creating a logical volume, you must specify its size using the `-L` option, the volume group in which you want to create it, and the name of the logical volume that you want to create. As an example, the following command creates a 5GB logical volume named XP in the VM volume group:

```
# lvcreate -L 5G -n XP VM
  Logical volume "XP" created
```

You can then use the `lvdisplay` command to get information about the new logical volume that you just created:

```
# lvdisplay
  --- Logical volume ---
  LV Name               /dev/VM/XP
  VG Name               VM
  LV UUID               yV06uh-BshS-IqiK-GeIi-A3vm-Tsjg-T0kCT7
  LV Write Access       read/write
  LV Status             available
  # open                0
  LV Size               5 GB
  Current LE            1432
  Segments              1
  Allocation            inherit
  Read ahead sectors    0
  Block device          253:0
```

As you can see from this output, the actual access point for the new logical volume is the directory /dev/VM/XP, which was created by the `lvcreate` command. When you create a logical volume, the logical volume system also creates an appropriate entry in the directory /dev/mapper that maps each logical volume to the physical volume that it was created from, as in the following example:

```
# ls /dev/mapper
control  VM-XP
```

These entries are used by the volume management system to mount logical volumes and synchronize updates to them.

At this point, your logical volume is functionally equivalent to a newly created disk partition. It cannot be used to store files and directories until you create a filesystem of some sort in it. For information on creating a filesystem in your new logical volume, see the next section.

Creating a Filesystem in an Image File, Partition, or Logical Volume

As discussed in the "Linux Storage and Filesystems" section at the beginning of this chapter, storage devices cannot be used to hold files and directories until they contain a filesystem. Creating a filesystem on any block-level storage device requires the same steps, regardless of whether that block-level storage is a filesystem image file, disk partition, or logical volume.

The actual commands that you use to create a filesystem differ depending on the type of filesystem that you are creating and any specific options that you want or need to supply. Many Linux distributions provide custom, graphical commands to simplify creating different types of filesystems, but because these commands are distribution-specific, this section focuses on creating filesystems using command-line commands that are found on every Linux distribution.

Creating filesystems under Linux is ordinarily done using the /sbin/mkfs command. The mkfs command's -t option enables you to specify the type of filesystem that you want to create. The mkfs command invokes different filesystem-specific programs based on the type of filesystem that you are creating. For example, executing the /sbin/mkfs -t ext2 /dev/*whatever* command actually invokes the /sbin/mkfs.ext2 command to create a filesystem on /dev/*whatever*. The mkfs command passes any extra arguments to the appropriate filesystem-specific program. Similarly, specifying the /sbin/mkfs -t xfs /dev/*whatever* command invokes the /sbin/mkfs.xfs command, passing all of the command-line options that the mkfs command was called with to that program (except for the -t option, of course).

The commands to create a standard ext3 filesystem on an image file, disk partition, and logical volume differ only in the name of the file or device that you are formatting:

```
# mkfs -t ext3 image_file.img
# mkfs -t ext3 /dev/sdb1
# mkfs -t ext3 /dev/VM/XP
```

The mkfs command (in this case, the mkfs.ext3 command invoked by the mkfs command) displays output such as the following for each of these commands:

```
mke2fs 1.40-WIP (14-Nov-2006)
Filesystem label=
OS type: Linux
```

(continued)

155

(continued)

```
Block size=4096 (log=2)
Fragment size=4096 (log=2)
524288 inodes, 1048576 blocks
52428 blocks (5.00%) reserved for the super user
First data block=0
Maximum filesystem blocks=1073741824
32 block groups
32768 blocks per group, 32768 fragments per group
16384 inodes per group
Superblock backups stored on blocks:
        32768, 98304, 163840, 229376, 294912, 819200, 884736
 Writing inode tables: done
Creating journal (32768 blocks): done
Writing superblocks and filesystem accounting information: done
 This filesystem will be automatically checked every 34 mounts or
180 days, whichever comes first.  Use tune2fs -c or -i to override.
```

When you are creating a filesystem on a partition or logical volume, no further input is required. However, when you are creating a partition on an image file, the mkfs command detects that the file is not an actual device, and prompts you for confirmation before proceeding:

```
image_file.img is not a block special device.
Proceed anyway? (y,n) y
```

This is a fairly simple example of creating an ext3 filesystem, using the minimum number of options required. However, one option that you may always want to use when formatting disk partitions is the -L label option, which takes a text label as an argument and writes that label to the header information for the partition that you are creating. You can then use that label to identify the partition when you want to mount it, rather than providing the name of a specific disk partition. This is not necessary for things like image files or logical volumes, whose names can uniquely identify them and suggest their content and purpose. For disk partitions, where the partition name is simply a numeric identifier based on the device name, disk labels can be extremely handy if you ever need to add other disks to a system or move the disk to another system.

When adding or moving devices, the name of a device may change depending on the other disks that are already present in that system and the controller to which the disk is attached. For example, the disk /dev/sda in one system will be identified by another as /dev/sdb if you attach it to the second port on your SATA controller. The partitions on the disk will have the same contents, but you will have to mount them using different partition names. On the other hand, if you had created a partition with a label such as MUSIC, you could identify the label in your /etc/fstab file in the following way on any system, without needing to know the physical device on which it is found:

```
LABEL=MUSIC   /opt2      ext3     defaults      0 1
```

For example, to label the partition /dev/sdb1 with the label F7-RFS (perhaps indicating that it contains a root filesystem for Fedora 7), you would execute the following command:

```
# mkfs -t ext3 -L F7-RFS /dev/sdb1
```

Once a `mkfs` command is done, you can then mount the image file, partition, or logical volume on the host where you will be creating a root filesystem for use with Xen, so that you can populate it. Mounting image files, partitions, or logical volumes is described in the next section.

Mounting an Image File, Partition, or Logical Volume

Filesystems must be mounted on directories in the Linux filesystem in order for files and directories to be created in them. Mounting a filesystem is done using the `mount` command, identifying the location of the filesystem and the name of the directory on which you want to mount it. The directory on which you want to mount a filesystem must already exist.

As an example, the command to mount the filesystem located on the partition `/dev/sdb1` on the directory `/mnt/tmp` would be the following:

```
# mount /dev/sdb1 /mnt/tmp
```

Linux will do its best to identify the type of filesystem that is located on `/dev/sdb1` and use any default mount options that are associated with that type of filesystem. In some cases, you may need to use the `mount` command's `-t` (type) option to specify the type of filesystem that you are mounting. For example, to tell the `mount` command to mount an XFS filesystem that is located on `/dev/sdb1` on the directory `/mnt/tmp`, you would execute the following command:

```
# mount -t xfs /dev/sdb1 /mnt/tmp
```

The man page for the `mount` command lists all of the supported filesystem type values that the `mount` command understands. To see this information, type the `man mount` command from any Linux shell or terminal session.

In the case of a filesystem image, you must also specify the `-o loop` option of the `mount` command, which tells the `mount` command to use the loopback interface when mounting the filesystem image.

Creating Root Filesystems

Once an image file, partition, or logical volume is mounted, you can begin using it to store files and directories. This chapter focuses on creating root filesystems for use with paravirtualized Xen systems, so the next few sections highlight generic and distribution-specific ways to put all of the files and directories that are required for a root filesystem into a mounted image file, partition, or logical volume.

Cloning Existing Root Filesystems

The easiest way to create a root filesystem on any Linux distribution is to clone an existing root filesystem. For best results, this should be done on a newly installed system that is configured as closely as possible to the configuration that you want to have on your virtual machines. Cloning a root filesystem from a newly installed system will also help ensure that as little extraneous software is present on the system. All systems tend to grow over time, as new packages are installed permanently or for testing purposes.

In order to copy files and directories to your new root filesystem, the image file, partition, or logical volume in which you want to create it must be mounted, as explained in the previous section. The examples in this section assume that it has been mounted on the directory `/mnt/tmp`. You can mount it anywhere, of course, but if you do, you must make appropriate changes to the sample commands given in this section.

The first step in manually creating a new root filesystem by cloning an existing one is to recursively copy a number of directories that must be present in your root filesystem. I typically use the standard `cp` command, but you can also use network-aware commands such as `rsync` to clone filesystems over the network. An example of using the `cp` command is the following:

```
# cp -ax /{bin,dev,etc,lib,root,sbin,usr,var} /mnt/tmp
```

The `-a` option tells the `cp` command to preserve file permissions and ownership when copying files, to preserve symbolic links as symbolic links, and to recursively copy the specified directories. The `-x` option tells the `cp` command to stay in your root filesystem rather than crossing any mount points for other filesystems that it may encounter during the recursive copy.

A similar example using `rsync` would be the following:

```
rsync -ax -e ssh --exclude=/proc --exclude=/sys \
root@server-where-filesystem-lives:/  /mnt/tmp/
```

As with the `cp` command, the `-a` option copies in archive mode — recursively, maintaining protections, and so on — and the `-x` option prevents the `rsync` command from crossing filesystem boundaries. The `-e` option, followed by `ssh`, tells the `rsync` command which shell to use when connecting to the remote system. This command would not normally break across two lines — this is done here for formatting purposes. If you want to use `rsync`, see "Backing Up Selected Files and Directories Using rsync" in Chapter 10 for more information about configuring `rsync` on remote hosts.

Next, use the `mkdir` command to create certain directories that must (or should) exist in any root filesystem, but whose contents you do not want to copy from your actual root filesystem. This includes the `/home` directory, where user accounts are typically created, the `/proc` and `/sys` directories used to hold dynamic information about the state of a running system and its processes, the `/tmp` directory used to hold temporary program and system data files, and the `/opt` directory used to hold system-specific (optional) applications. A sample command to create empty versions of these directories in your new root filesystem is the following:

```
# mkdir /mnt/tmp/{home,proc,opt,sys,tmp}
```

The `/tmp` directory in any root filesystem must be publicly writable, so you should change it to the correct mode in your new root filesystem, as in the following example:

```
# chmod 777 /mnt/tmp/tmp
```

Next, you should make sure that no extraneous temporary data has accidentally been copied into your new root filesystem. The most common location for this is the directory `/var/tmp`, so you could clean out the version of this directory in your new root filesystem using the following command:

```
# rm -rf /mnt/tmp/var/tmp/*
```

Next, you should customize the new root filesystem for use with your virtual machines by making appropriate changes to configuration files such as the following:

❑   `/mnt/tmp/etc/exports`: If the system you are cloning is an NFS server, you will want to ensure that your virtual machines do not attempt to export the same filesystems (unless you want them to, of course).

❑   `/mnt/tmp/etc/fstab`: If necessary, replace the name of the root device with the name of the root device that you will be specifying in your virtual machine configuration file (often `/dev/sda1` or `/dev/hda1`).

❑   `/mnt/tmp/etc/group`: Remove the names of any user- or application-specific groups that you will not need on the virtual machine.

❑   `/mnt/tmp/etc/hostname`: Change any specific hostname that might conflict with other hostnames that are already in use.

❑   `/mnt/etc/network/interfaces` or `/mnt/etc/sysconfig/network`: These are the primary network configuration files on Debian-based and Red Hat–based Linux distributions. You should make sure that these do not duplicate static IP addresses that are in use on other machines or, more commonly, that the Ethernet interfaces on your virtual machines are configured to get the IP address, gateway, DNS, and related information from a DHCP server.

❑   `/mnt/tmp/etc/passwd`: Remove the names of any individual or application-related users that you will not need on the virtual machine.

Be careful when editing these files because it's easy to accidentally end up editing the "real" versions of these files on your host system, rather than editing the versions of these files in your new root filesystem.

Next, copy in the right version of `/lib/modules` for the kernel that you'll be using with your virtual machine. For example, if you will be using the kernel 2.6.18-xen with your virtual machine, you would execute the following command:

```
# cp -a /lib/modules/2.6.18-xen /mnt/tmp/lib/modules
```

Finally, you may want to check that there are no huge applications in the root filesystem that you don't actually want to have in the virtual machine. When cloning a root filesystem, the most obvious of these are things such as the GNOME or KDE desktop environments. If you are using your virtual machines to support users, you may want these, but in many cases you will not. To remove such applications, you can use the `chroot` command to temporarily make the new root filesystem into your working root directory, and then use the standard package management commands for the distribution that you are cloning to remove those packages. For example, if you are sure that you don't want X11, you could remove the X11 Font Server in a root filesystem that you cloned from a Red Hat system using the following commands:

```
# chroot /mnt/tmp
# rpm -e xorg-x11-xfs
# exit
```

Be very careful when doing this, making sure that you execute these commands in the `chroot`'ed environment. You almost certainly do not want to accidentally remove these packages from the physical machine on which you are running!

You should now have a fairly pristine root filesystem that you can use with a Xen virtual machine. If you will be creating multiple virtual machines and want to use this root filesystem with more than one of them, you should create an archived copy of this root filesystem that will simplify creating other root filesystems in the future. For example, you could create an archive of the contents of this root filesystem in the file `/home/xen/rfs_contents.tgz` by executing the following commands:

```
# pushd /mnt/tmp
# tar czf /home/xen/rfs_contents.tgz
# popd
```

After creating this archive file, you could simply extract its contents into any new root filesystems that you want to create based on the same system.

The final step before you can actually use your new root filesystem is to unmount it from the system where you created it. You can do this by executing the following command:

```
# umount /mnt/tmp
```

You are now ready to identify the image file, partition, or logical volume that contains your new root filesystem as the root filesystem in the configuration file for a paravirtualized Xen system, as explained in Chapter 5.

Using debootstrap on Debian and Ubuntu Systems

The debootstrap utility is far and away the best distribution-specific tool for building a root filesystem. In its most basic form, it takes two arguments: the name of the release on which you want to base your root filesystem, and the location where you want the root filesystem to be created. For example, to create a root filesystem on a Ubuntu system, base that root filesystem on Ubuntu's Feisty Fawn (7.04) release, and create the root filesystem in a filesystem mounted at `/mnt/tmp`, you would execute the following command:

```
# debootstrap feisty /mnt/tmp
```

That's all that there is to it! The following example shows the highlights of the voluminous output that this command would produce:

```
I: Retrieving Release
I: Retrieving Packages
I: Validating Packages
I: Resolving dependencies of required packages...
I: Resolving dependencies of base packages...
I: Checking component main on http://archive.ubuntu.com/ubuntu...
I: Retrieving adduser
...
I: Configuring ubuntu-minimal...
I: Base system installed successfully.
```

On a Debian system, you would use the name of a Debian release such as etch, woody, and so on, rather than the name of a Ubuntu distribution.

On a Ubuntu Feisty system, this command only requires a few minutes to populate a basic root filesystem. This root filesystem is approximately 350MB in size, and doesn't include anything but the basics for booting a network-enabled Xen virtual machine. Once booted, you can always use the standard Ubuntu apt-get tool to install other applications.

The xen-tools package for Debian and Ubuntu Xen systems includes a xen-create-image script that will create a Xen filesystem image, swap file image, and Xen configuration file for you at the same time.

Using rpm and yum on Fedora, Red Hat and Similar Systems

Red Hat provides a number of excellent tools for creating and managing virtual machines. (These are discussed in more detail in "Fedora and Red Hat Xen Tools" in Chapter 7.) Unfortunately, all of these focus on creating disk images rather than simple filesystem images, so they are not germane here.

On Red Hat-based systems, you can always use the rpm command to attempt to manually create small root filesystems, using the --root option to specify a different directory (where you mounted your root filesystem) as the root when installing them. Unfortunately, although RPM does a great job of identifying dependencies, it seems unable to use this information to actually resolve them. Therefore, as with most RPM-based installation exercises, this quickly dissolves into a morass of interwoven dependencies that are difficult to resolve. A script entitled rpmstrap (http://rpmstrap.pimpscript.net) was under development to simplify bootstrapping systems from RPM packages, but its development seems to have stopped.

Luckily, you can use a combination of RPM and yum (a successor to RPM with better dependency handling) to populate a root filesystem on Red Hat, Fedora, and similar systems as follows (this example assumes that the image file for your root filesystem is mounted at /mnt/loop):

1. Initialize the RPM database in the mounted filesystem image using a command such as the following:

```
# rpm --root /mnt/loop --initdb
```

2. Obtain an rpm file that contains a general release description from a location such as www.rpmfind.com. To install a Fedora release, search for the string fedora-release and download the rpm file for the version of Fedora that you want to install.

3. Execute the following commands to create the log directory in the mounted image and create the log file used by yum, so that you have a record of what was installed:

```
mkdir -p /mnt/loop/var/log
touch /mnt/loop/var/log/yum.log
```

4. Install the rpm file that you download to initially populate the mounted filesystem image, using a command such as the following:

```
rpm -ivh --nodeps --root /mnt/loop fedora-release-8.2.noarch.rpm
```

5. You can then use yum to do a basic installation via a command such as the following:

```
yum --installroot=/mnt/loop/ -y groupinstall Base
```

6. You can then change root to the new filesystem and do some fine-tuning, using commands such as the following:

```
chroot /mnt/loop
mount -t proc /proc /proc
mount -t sysfs /sys /sys
```

7. You should then create the `/etc/fstab` file (while still `chroot`'ed) to reflect the filesystem names used in your Xen domainU configuration file, set the root password, create a user account, and so on.

At this point, you can exit from the `chroot`, and copy the libraries for your Xen kernel into the `/lib/modules` directory of your filesystem image (`/mnt/loop/lib/modules`, in this example). You can then umount the root filesystem image, and test it with your Xen configuration file.

Using yast2 on SUSE Linux Systems

The YaST and YaST2 system administration utilities used by Novell's SUSE Linux products and the open source OpenSUSE distribution include an "Installation into Directory" tool that makes it easy to create root filesystems from your SuSE or OpenSUSE installation media. They also include features for creating and managing Xen virtual machines, as discussed in detail in "Novell SUSE Xen Tools" in Chapter 7. This section focuses on using the graphical YaST2 utility, though the YaST utility can perform exactly the same function, but in a terminal-oriented, rather than graphical, environment.

To create a root filesystem for use with Xen on a SUSE or OpenSUSE Linux system, first mount the image file, partition, or logical volume that you want to use on your system, as described earlier in this chapter. By default, YaST2's "Installation into Directory" module populates a root filesystem in the directory `/var/tmp/dirinstall`, so you should mount your file, partition, or logical volume there to simplify things.

Next, start Yast2 and select "Installation into Directory" from the dialog box shown in Figure 6-1.

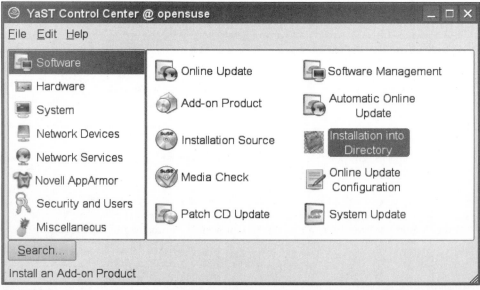

Figure 6-1

The dialog box shown in Figure 6-2 appears.

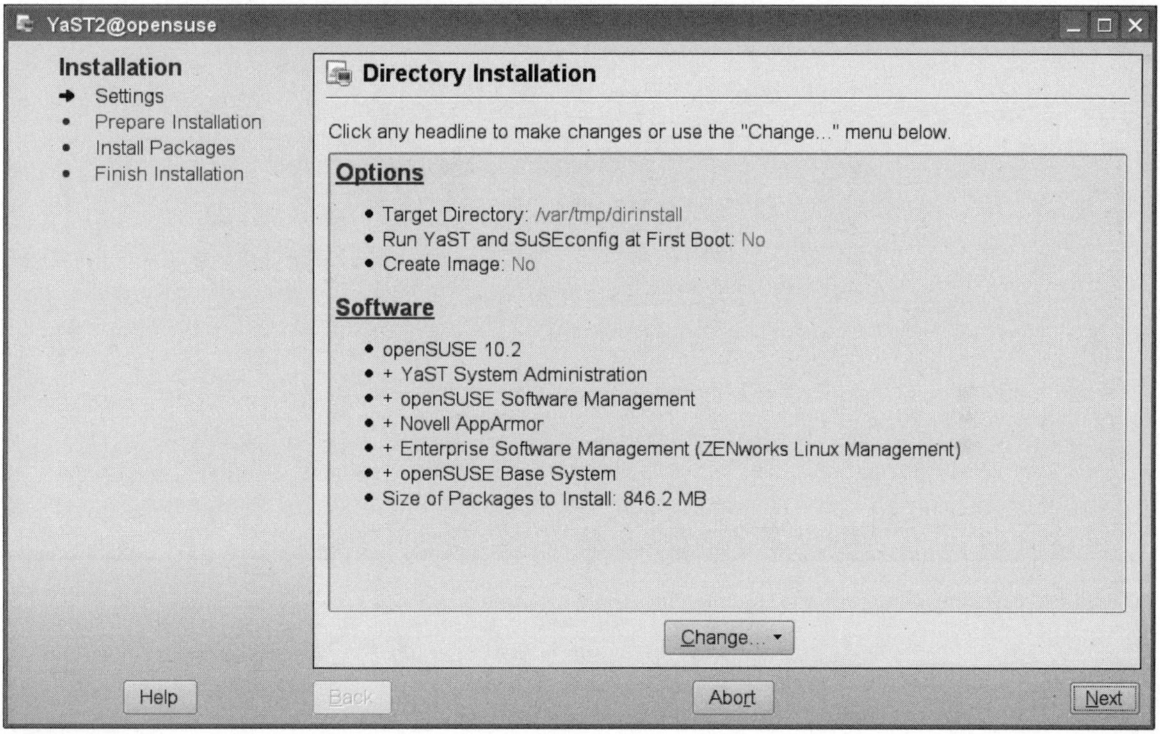

Figure 6-2

Click Options to display the dialog box shown in Figure 6-3. This dialog box enables you to change the directory where you will be installing the selected software to create a root filesystem or to also create a filesystem image file. The installation directory that you specify should be the name of the directory on which you mounted your image file, partition, or logical volume. You can also select the "Run YaST and SuSEconfig on First Boot" option to automatically run SuSE's standard "first time" configuration utilities to complete the configuration of the system whose filesystem that you are creating.

Once you are done making any changes that you want on this dialog box, click Accept to return to the dialog box shown in Figure 6-2.

If you want to customize the software that will be installed into your root filesystem, select Software to display a dialog box that enables you to search for packages that match a specific pattern, so that you can add software to the packages that are currently planned for installation. To see the packages that are currently selected for installation, click Filter and select Patterns from the drop-down box. This displays the dialog box shown in Figure 6-4.

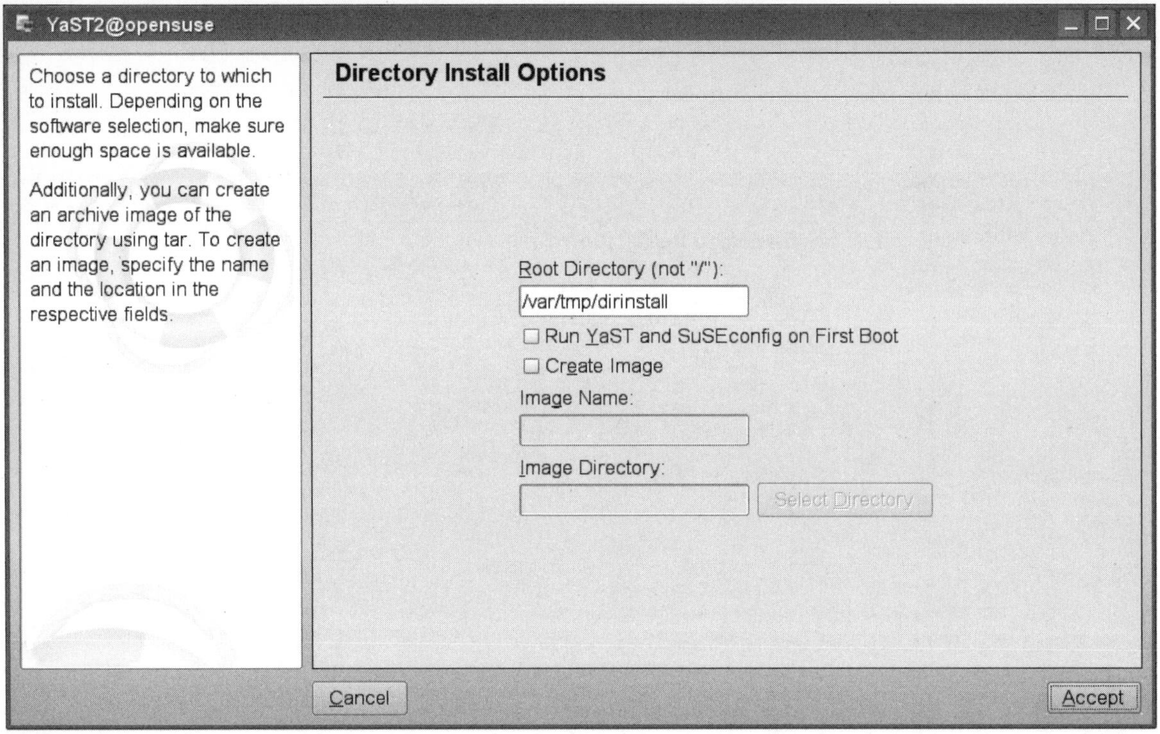

Figure 6-3

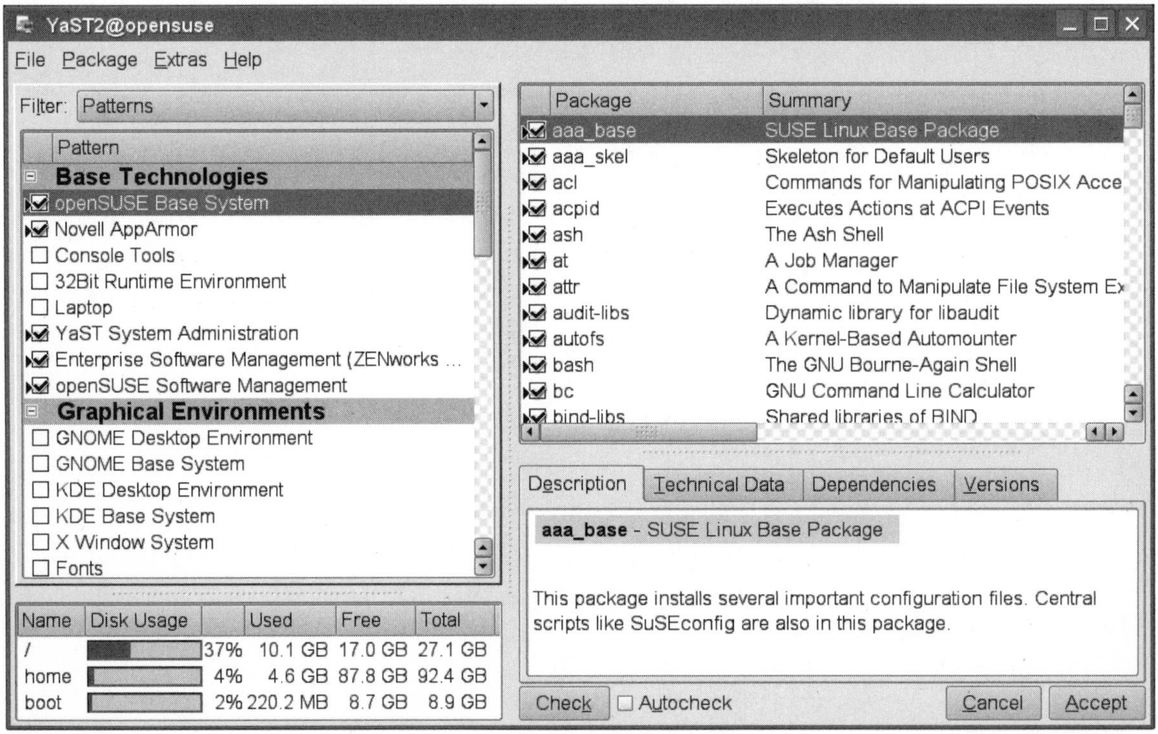

Figure 6-4

From this dialog box, you can deselect packages such as Novell AppArmor, Enterprise Software management (ZenWorks), Games, and others that you may not want in a virtual machine, and select packages that you may want, such as the KDE Desktop environment and C/C++ Development tools, depending on your goal for the virtual machine whose filesystem you are creating. Click Accept to close this dialog box and accept any license agreements necessary for the currently selected packages. The installer then recalculates dependencies, prompts you to accept new packages, and returns to the Directory Installation dialog box.

To begin installing a root filesystem into the directory shown on the Options panel (which is /var/tmp/dirinstall by default), click Next. When the installation completes, exit YaST2 and unmount the image, partition, or logical volume that holds your new root filesystem. The root filesystem is now ready for use with Xen.

Creating Root Filesystems for Use with NFS

Root filesystems for use with Xen systems that boot via NFS are simply directories that have been populated using the mechanisms described in the previous sections, and are then added to the /etc/exports file on your domain0 system so that domainU guests can mount and use them. A sample section of an /etc/exports file looks like the following:

```
/home/xen/nfs-fc7                    *(rw,no_root_squash,async)
```

The first field identifies a directory that is being exported (/home/xen/nfs-fc7). The second identifies the hosts that can access it (in this case *, meaning all hosts, which is not very secure). The parenthesized options specify how it is being exported — read-write (rw) , with root access enabled (no_root_squash), and with writes being done asynchronously (async). If you want the root user to be able to log in, the entries for any directories that Xen NFS root filesystems export must specify the no_root_squash option.

The following are a few caveats to remember when configuring your domainU kernel and the system files in these directories:

❑ As mentioned previously, your kernel must have NFS server support compiled in, and the CONFIG_NFS_ROOT options must have been enabled in that kernel.

❑ If you are using DHCP in your Xen configuration file, the system will already have an IP address by the time the root filesystem's startup files are executed. Make sure that the Ethernet configuration in your NFS root filesystem does not attempt to re-obtain an IP address. This is done differently on different Linux distributions. For example, on Red Hat, Fedora, and similar systems, you will want to set BOOTPROTO to none in the /etc/sysconfig/network-script directory script for your Ethernet interface, typically ifcfg-eth0.

❑ Update your /etc/fstab file to identify /dev/nfs as the device associated with your root filesystem.

A simple configuration file for a paravirtualized domainU guest would look something like the following:

```
kernel = "/boot/vmlinuz-2.6.18-nfs"
memory = 256
name = "FC6-NFS-PV"
vif = [ '' ]
dhcp = "dhcp"
```

(continued)

(continued)

```
nfs_root="/home/xen/nfs-fc7"
nfs_server="192.168.6.64"
root="/dev/nfs"
```

Of these, the critical entries for using an NFS root filesystem are the following:

- ❑   `nfs_root`: Identifies the directory that is being exported by your NFS server that you want to use as the root filesystem.

- ❑   `nfs_server`: Identifies the hostname or IP address of the NFS server.

- ❑   `root`: Setting this to `/dev/nfs` identifies the fact that the root filesystem is an NFS root filesystem.

I find NFS root filesystems to be sufficient for most purposes. They are easily migrated from one domain0 host to another (assuming that the root filesystems are not being exported by either domain0 host, which would be problematic) and easily administered.

Manually Creating Minimal Filesystems

A number of tools and related information are available to help you manually create extremely minimal root filesystems for use with Linux systems. These were traditionally developed for embedded systems, where a small root filesystem is a good root filesystem. The best known of these is Buildroot (`http://buildroot.uclibc.org/`), which will quickly and easily create a very small root filesystem for you.

This chapter has assumed that you will be basing your virtual machines on one or more existing distributions that you may already be using in your computing environment. If this is not the case and you want to develop your own, home-grown Linux distribution entirely from scratch, the Linux From Scratch project (`www.linuxfromscratch.org`) will be your new best friend. You may also be able to get some useful information from Tom Fawcett's Linux Boot Disk HOWTO (`www.tldp.org/HOWTO/Bootdisk-HOWTO`), which is available from the Linux Documentation Project. This HOWTO is a bit dated, but provides a good foundation in the basics of creating bootable, small-footprint Linux systems.

Creating Swap Filesystems for Xen

As discussed in Chapter 5, you may also want to specify a swap device in the configuration files for your paravirtualized Xen systems. Swap space is used by Linux systems to enable more applications to run than will fit in available physical memory. In the case of a Xen virtual machine, this is the amount of memory specified in each virtual machine's configuration file.

Swap partitions can be created in image files, on physical disk partitions, or even in logical volumes. Once you have allocated whichever of these you want to use, you simply execute the `mkswap` command to format it for use as swap space, as in the following examples:

```
# mkswap image_file.img
# mkswap /dev/sdb1
# mkswap /dev/VM/SWAP1
```

As with root filesystems, swap files cannot be shared across different virtual machines. The Linux kernel's memory manager writes memory regions directly to these files when swapping out a process, and copies portions of the swap file directly into memory when swapping them back in. Having multiple kernels sharing the same swap file would quickly cause a system crash.

Adding Applications to a Xen Root Filesystem

As with any root filesystem for a physical Linux system, the root filesystems used with Xen virtual machines may also need to be updated over time. This enables you to install updated versions of existing applications or add new applications and associated capabilities. This process is only slightly different from the process of updating a standard Linux desktop or server system.

After you have booted a virtual machine using a root filesystem, you can update that root filesystem using the standard package management utilities that are used by the distribution on which your virtual machine is based. The only major point that you must keep in mind is that space is at a premium on most virtual machine root filesystems. You should therefore always use your package management utility's options to prevent local copies of installed packages from being saved after they have been installed.

Common packages that you may want to add to minimal root filesystems are packages such as the vncserver, which enables you to run a window manager on your virtual machine that you can connect to remotely.

Creating and Using QEMU Disk Images

As discussed in the "Filesystem or Disk Images" section earlier in this chapter, the fact that Xen uses the QEMU device model and uses some of QEMU's device emulation code enables Xen domain0 and domainU guests to take advantage of much of QEMU's disk and filesystem image-handling support. QEMU supports disk and filesystem images in various types:

- ❑ cloop: Linux compressed loop image, used by some Live Linux distributions to provide access to compressed CD-ROM images.

- ❑ cow: A deprecated copy on write format primarily used by User-Mode Linux.

- ❑ qcow: QEMU copy on write, which is a QEMU image format that provides support for sparse files, compression, encryption, and snapshots, regardless of what is provided by the underlying filesystem or operating system.

- ❑ raw: A standard, portable disk image format that is the QEMU default. This format is a raw copy of a disk or filesystem and uses underlying filesystem concepts such as sparse files, where only sectors that have actually been written will reserve disk space.

- ❑ vmdk: An image format that is compatible with VMware 3 and 4.

The raw and qcow image formats are the most meaningful disk image formats for Xen users, whereas vmdk support is useful for converting those old VMware disk images to better formats that Xen can use.

The blktap driver supports qcow (tap:qcow:), raw (as tap:aio: or tap:sync:), and vmdk (tap:vmdk:), although it does not support some of the latest VMDK features.

> **For a great discussion of converting VMware disk images to QEMU formats so that they can be used as Xen hardware virtual machines, see Ian Blenke's writeup at** http://ian.blenke.com/vmware/vmdk/xen/hvm/qemu/vmware_to_xen_hvm.html.

QEMU disk images typically either contain a single filesystem or an image of an entire disk, with multiple partitions. Using a QEMU disk that only holds the root partition with Xen doesn't provide significant advantages over simply using a raw filesystem image in standard Linux format. However, QEMU disk images can be used with paravirtualized domainU guests to provide a mechanism for you to store your kernel inside the root filesystem for a paravirtualized domainU guest. I typically store the kernels for paravirtualized guests on my domain0 host, so I can reuse the same kernels for multiple domainU guests, but storing the kernel in the root filesystem can simplify administration, migration, and cloning. The remainder of this section explains how to create a QEMU disk image, how to install a paravirtualized guest in a QEMU image, and how to modify your Xen configuration file to locate and boot the paravirtualized kernel inside the image.

Creating a QEMU Disk Image

Disk images are created using the qemu-img application that is part of the QEMU package. This application is also included with most Xen distributions. Its source code is also provided with the source code for the open source version of Xen. To build this application for the open source version of Xen, execute the make tools and make install-tools commands from your top-level Xen source code directory.

When creating a disk image, the basic syntax of the qemu-img application is the following:

```
qemu-img create [-b base_image] [-e] [-f fmt] filename [size]
```

The parameters have the following meanings:

❑   -b *base_image*: (Optional) When you are creating a QEMU copy-on-write (qcow) image, this option enables you to specify a read-only base image that will be used to identify changed data that must be written to the copy-on-write image. This enables you to create many copy-on-write copies of a single permanent image, each of which will contain only the data that has been modified by the kernel using that particular copy. This option is useful only if you are creating a qcow disk image.

❑   -e: (Optional) Specifies that the disk image that you are creating must be encrypted. This option is useful only if you are creating a qcow disk image for use with QEMU itself, and should not be specified for disks that you want to use with Xen.

❑   -f *fmt*: (Optional) Enables you to specify the format in which the image will be created. This must be cloop, cow, qcow, raw, or vmdk, though only qcow is commonly explicitly specified. The default format in which a QEMU disk image will be created is the raw format.

❑   *filename*: (Required) The name of the image file that you want to create.

❑   *size*: (Required) The size of the disk image in kilobytes (K), megabytes (M), or gigabytes (G).

For example, to create a 10GB disk image file named `test1.img` in `raw` format, you would execute the following command:

```
qemu-img -f raw test1.img 10G
```

Once you have a QEMU disk image, you're ready to proceed to installing a paravirtualized guest there.

Installing a Paravirtualized domainU Guest

The simplest approach to installing a Linux distribution inside a QEMU disk image is to simply use QEMU. This enables you to use the graphical installer provided with your Linux distribution, and simplifies installing the paravirtualized kernel and associated modules during the installation process, assuming that they are provided by your operating system distribution. If they are not, this section also explains how to mount a specific partition of a QEMU disk image and install them manually.

Starting QEMU to boot and install an operating system from a CD-ROM onto your disk image file is essentially equivalent to booting a new computer with a blank hard drive from an installable CD-ROM. The basic command to do this with `qemu` is the following:

```
qemu -hda image-file -cdrom file-or-device -boot d -m 256 -localtime
```

The options to this command are the following:

❑ `-hda` *image-file*: Identifies the QEMU disk image file that you created in the previous section as your primary hard drive.

❑ `-cdrom` *file-or-device*: Identifies the device file (such as `/dev/cdrom`) or ISO image that you want to use as your CD-ROM drive.

❑ `-boot d`: Tells QEMU to boot from device d, which is the CD-ROM drive or image.

❑ `-m 256`: Memory in megabytes. This is the amount of memory that will be associated with this emulated machine for this run of QEMU. 256MB is a suggested value that should suffice for any Linux distribution.

❑ `-localtime`: Tells QEMU to set the real-time clock to local time rather than Coordinated Universal Time (UTC). This is mandatory for Windows systems, so I typically always use this option for systems that don't use NTP directly.

Executing this command boots into the standard installer on the CD or ISO image that you're using as your CD-ROM drive, and you can then follow the standard installation procedure to install your system.

When formatting the disk image file, jot down the number of the partition that contains the `/boot` and `/` filesystems in the disk image as it is formatted because you may need this information later. In general, I do not create separate `/boot` partitions in QEMU disk images because this can make installing new kernels and associated modules more complex. It's also a good idea to use a traditional filesystem such as ext2 or ext3 when creating and formatting the partition that contains the `/` directory (and `/boot` partition, if you insist on creating that separately) in a QEMU image file, to simplify direct access to the filesystem from your domain0 system if you subsequently need that capability. I tend to use ext3 for all filesystems in a QEMU image to guarantee ease of access because using logical volumes in a fixed-size image file isn't as useful as I'd like it to be.

If a Xen domainU kernel is available as part of the standard installation process on the Linux distribution that you're installing, install that kernel and the associated modules. The installation process should create the appropriate GRUB entries for the domainU kernel. (If it does not, see "Configuring GRUB for Xen" in Chapter 2 for detailed information on creating an appropriate GRUB boot entry.) Because you are installing a domainU system, you do not need (or want) to install the hypervisor or any of the standard domain0 tools in the virtual machine.

Once the installation process has completed, you can exit from QEMU by typing the following command:

```
qemu -boot c -hda image-file
```

This boots Linux from the specified image file, using an SDL console. Make sure that you select a standard, non-Xen kernel for this test because QEMU will be running the virtual machine in emulation mode, rather than Xen running it as a virtual machine. After the system comes up correctly, you can simply shut it down using your favorite graphical or command-line system shutdown command.

If the distribution that you are installing contains a Xen kernel and modules and you were able to see them on the GRUB boot menu when testing, skip the next section and proceed to "Using pygrub to Locate and Boot the Xen Kernel."

Manually Installing the Xen Kernel in a QEMU Disk

If your distribution doesn't provide a paravirtualized kernel or if you want to install a specific version of the Xen kernel (such as one that you've built yourself), you can install a Xen kernel and the associated modules manually. You can do this by using the lomount command that is provided with Xen. You can use lomount only with QEMU disk images that contain a partition table.

The lomount command mounts the filesystem contained in a specified partition inside the QEMU disk image on a specified mountpoint on your domain0 system. The basic syntax of the lomount command is the following:

```
lomount -diskimage image-file -partition NUM mount-point -verbose [OPTIONS]
```

The options to the lomount command are the following:

❑　-diskimage *image-file*: (Required) Identifies *image-file* as the QEMU disk image that contains the partition that you want to mount.

❑　-partition *number*: (Required) Identifies the *number* of the partition containing your /boot directory. This is typically the first partition (number 1). If you do not specify a partition number (or specify partition 0), the lomount command displays the list of available partitions in the QEMU disk image.

❑　*mount-point*: (Required) Specify the directory on your domain0 system on which you want to mount the specified partition.

❑　-verbose: (Optional) Causes the lomount command to display additional information such as the mount options that it uses by default, the offset into the disk image file at which the partition is located, and so on.

❑   *OPTIONS*: (Optional) Can provide any other options that you want to pass to the mount command that is internally being invoked by `lomount`, such as the `-t` *TYPE* option to identify a non-standard partition type, and so on.

Once the partition containing the `/boot` partition is mounted on your domain0 system, you can copy in the Xen kernel and initial RAM disk, and then manually create a GRUB boot entry in the GRUB configuration file inside the QEMU disk image. If the `/boot` directory is located on a partition other than the root partition for your system, you will also have to use `lomount` to mount your system's / partition so that you can copy the modules required by the domainU kernel into the `/lib/modules` directory.

Once you have installed the domainU kernel, initial RAM disk, and modules for Xen in your QEMU disk image, execute the `sync` command to flush pending writes to all mounted filesystems, and then unmount the partitions that you mounted using `lomount` via the standard `umount` command. Proceed to the next section.

> **The kpartx utility is similar to the lomount utility, enabling you to list the partitions in a QEMU disk image and automatically create device mappings between those partitions and loopback devices. I personally prefer lomount, but you may find that kpartx is more intuitive for you.**

Using pygrub to Locate and Boot the Xen Kernel

Booting a paravirtualized Xen kernel from within a QEMU disk image is done by specifying the pygrub boot loader in the configuration file for the domainU system. The pygrub utility is a Python utility that uses a filesystem access library to read GRUB configuration data and the images and RAM disks, which it specifies and boots from domain0 using the standard domain builder. The pygrub utility displays a standard GRUB boot screen in the console for your domainU system, as shown in Figure 6-5.

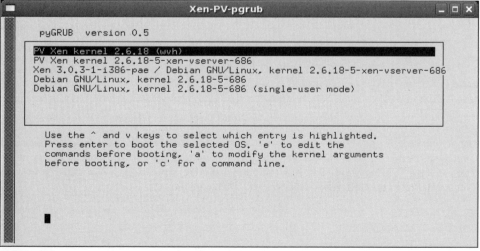

Figure 6-5

domainU configuration files that use pygrub are much closer to the configuration files for Xen hardware virtual machines than they are to more traditional Xen domainU configuration files. They do not need a kernel, initial ram disk, or swap partition specification because all of these are contained within the disk image. The following is an example of a Xen domainU configuration file that I use to boot a 32-bit Debian system from a QEMU image on one of my 64-bit domainU systems:

```
import os, re
arch = os.uname()[4]
if re.search('64', arch):
    arch_libdir = 'lib64'
else:
    arch_libdir = 'lib'
bootloader="/usr/bin/pygrub"
maxmem = 1024
memory = 256
shadow_memory = 8
name = "DEB-QE-PV"
acpi=1
apic=1
disk = [ 'tap:aio:/home/xen/HVM/Etch_HD_10G.raw,hda,w' ]
device_model = '/usr/' + arch_libdir + '/xen/bin/qemu-dm'
boot="c"
```

Note that the disk specification identifies the QEMU disk image file as a device, not as a partition, as it would on a more traditional domainU configuration file. Similarly, HVM configuration files identify the kernel as the hvmloader utility, which reads the boot block in a virtual disk, whereas the configuration files for paravirtualized systems using a QEMU disk image identify the boot loader, in this case pygrub.

> On 64-bit systems, depending on the version of Xen that you are running and the versions of the utilities that it provides, I often have to modify the pygrub utility to search the 64-bit python libraries for its filesystem access library. This is done by editing /usr/bin/pygrub, replacing the line:
>
> ```
> sys.path = [ '/usr/lib/python' ] + sys.path
> ```
>
> with the line:
>
> ```
> sys.path = [ '/usr/lib64/python' ] + sys.path
> ```

Interestingly enough, if your hardware supports hardware virtual machines, you can use a single QEMU image as both a HVM and a paravirtualized system (though certainly not at the same time). The following is a Xen HVM configuration file that boots from the same image — in which you would select a non-Xen kernel from the GRUB boot menu in the SDL console:

```
import os, re
arch = os.uname()[4]
if re.search('64', arch):
    arch_libdir = 'lib64'
```

```
else:
    arch_libdir = 'lib'
kernel = "/usr/lib/xen/boot/hvmloader"
builder='hvm'
maxmem = 1024
memory = 512
shadow_memory = 8
name = "DEB-QE-HV"
acpi=1
apic=1
vif = [ 'bridge=xenbr0' ]
disk = [ 'file:/home/xen/HVM/Etch_HD_10G.raw,hda,w',
         'phy:/dev/hda,hdc:cdrom,r' ]
device_model = '/usr/' + arch_libdir + '/xen/bin/qemu-dm'
boot="cd"
sdl=1
usb=1
usbdevice='tablet'
```

You'll note that I've allocated additional memory to the hardware virtual machine, specified an SDL console, and set the standard USB settings for HVMs, but otherwise the configuration files are very similar.

As you can see from the past few sections, QEMU disk images can be used with Xen as both paravirtualized and hardware virtual machines. I find it more convenient to use separate kernels, initial RAM disks, and filesystems, but there are certainly cases when QEMU disk image provide an easily administered and convenient migration mechanism, especially when used in conjunction with networked storage.

Summary

This chapter provides detailed information and suggestions about using different types of storage with paravirtualized and HVM Xen guest systems. It explores basic Linux filesystem and storage concepts, and then explains how to create root filesystems for use with paravirtualized Xen guests in a variety of different ways.

7

Managing and Monitoring Virtual Machines

Xen provides a number of tools for creating, managing, and monitoring the status of domainU guests. Some of these are used internally by other Xen utilities, and some are intended for use by the system administrators, operators, and automated utilities that manage your enterprise IT infrastructure.

As Xen continues to grow in popularity and enterprise adoption, the number of virtual machines that are being used continues to expand, and the scenarios in which it is deployed become more complex. Effectively monitoring and managing a virtual infrastructure is a brass ring that many open software efforts and commercial software vendors are actively pursuing. In addition to Xen-specific management tools, many existing open-source system management and monitoring tools can easily be applied to Xen environments without requiring you to adopt and incorporate an entire new suite of multisystem management utilities.

This chapter focuses on providing a detailed discussion of the tools that are included with all standard Xen distributions, in order to provide information that will be useful to you regardless of which Linux distribution you are using in domain0 and your domainU guests. However, it would be doing everyone a disservice to ignore the excellent Xen-related work being done by specific Linux distributions, most notably in the Fedora and OpenSUSE environments that eventually feed into the commercial Red Hat Enterprise Linux (RHEL) and Novell's SUSE Linux Enterprise Server (SLES) distributions. This chapter therefore provides an overview of distribution-specific administrative software for Xen, and provides links to more detailed information. It also provides an overview of the open source tools that are being developed and used to help manage and monitor Xen in enterprise environments.

Overview of the Xen Daemon

The Xen daemon, `xend`, is written in Python and runs as a background process (a daemon, in UNIX parlance) on all domain0 Xen systems. The Xen daemon must run as root in order to be able to execute privileged system management, domain creation and management, network control, and resource management functions. The `xm` command is the primary source of these on a running domain0 system, but any other privileged, administrative application can also communicate with the Xen daemon using the Xen APIs.

The Xen daemon is started by the script `/etc/initd.d/xend`, typically near the end of the boot process on any domain0 Linux system.

Configuring the Xen Daemon

Configuration information for the Xen daemon is a combination of default values and values specified in the Xen daemon's configuration file, `/etc/xen/xend-config.sxp`. This file contains values for all of the configuration variables that you can set for the Xen daemon, and shows the default values for these variables in commented-out values where the default value is actively being used. Lines in this file that begin with a hash mark (#) are commented out, and are ignored by the Xen daemon when it is started, as are blank lines. Values in this configuration file that are actively being used are defined in S-expression (SXP) format, a standard way of representing semi-structured data in human-readable form. (For more information about S-expression format, see `http://en.wikipedia.org/wiki/S-expression`.) This format basically consists of name-value pairs inside parentheses. For example, `(logfile /var/log/xen/xend.log)` sets the variable `logfile` to the value `/var/log/xen/xend.log`.

> **The most commonly changed values in this file are VNC-related values, network/vif-related values, migration/relocation-related values, and domain0 values, such as the default number of CPUs and minimum amount of memory that domain0 will allow.**

The configuration values that you can set for the Xen daemon are the following:

❑ **API server:** Set by the `xen-api-server` variable, this configures the ports, interfaces, and access controls for the Xen API server used to communicate with the Xen daemon. The value of this variable consists of a set of parentheses enclosing one or more server configuration sets, each of which is itself defined within parentheses. The first entry in each set is `unix` (a Unix UDP socket), a port number, or an address:port pair. The second entry in each set is optional and can be `none` (unconditional access) or `pam` (access is managed by the system's Pluggable Authentication Module configuration, which is the default). If `pam` is specified in some way, a third entry can be present, which consists of a whitespace-separated list of regular expressions that host names or IP addresses must match in order to communicate with this server. Common examples would be a regular expression for all hosts in a given domain by name (for example, `'^.*\\.vonhagen\\.org$'`), all hosts on a given network segment by IP address (for example, `'192.168.6.*'`), or both (`'^.*\\.vonhagen\\.org$ 192.168.6.*'`). If the third argument is not present or is empty, connections are accepted from any source. The default value for this variable is `((unix))`, which accepts connections to its UNIX domain socket from any host and uses PAM for authentication.

❑ **Console buffer size:** Set by the `console-limit` variable, this is the maximum size of the console buffer for each domain in kilobytes. The default value is `1024`. Limiting the size of this buffer on a per-domain basis is designed to prevent any given domainU system from overwhelming the Xen console server.

❑ **domainU CPUs:** Set by the `dom0-cpus` variable, this value is the number of CPUs (including CPU cores) that domain0 will initially use. At least one CPU is used by default. If `dom0-cpus` is set to `0`, domain0 will use all CPUs. The default value is `0`.

❑ **domainU minimum memory:** Set by the `dom0-min-mem` variable, this is the lowest amount of memory in megabytes that domain0 can have when freeing memory from its pool of allocated memory (ballooning) to give that memory to a domainU system. Setting this variable to `0` prevents ballooning, in which case domain0 will never free memory for domainU systems. The default value is `196`.

❑ **Enable core dumps:** Set by the `enable-dump` variable, this determines whether a domainU crash will cause a core dump to be generated. The default value is `no`.

❑ **HTTP address:** Set by the `xend-address` variable, this is the IP address on which the Xen daemon's HTTP interface should listen. The default value is `' '` (two single quotation marks with no value between them), which means that the HTTP server will listen on all available interfaces. You can specify `localhost` to allow only local connections. This value is meaningful only if the HTTP server is enabled.

❑ **HTTP port:** Set by the `xend-port` variable. This is the number of the port on which the Xen daemon's HTTP interface is listening. The default value is `8000`. This value is meaningful only if the HTTP server is enabled.

❑ **HTTP server:** Set by the `xend-http-server` variable, this is a yes or no value that determines whether the Xen daemon runs an internal HTTP server that can be used to communicate with the Xen daemon. The default value is `no`. The use of this server is deprecated.

❑ **Log file name:** Set by the `logfile` variable, this identifies the name of the log file to which the Xen daemon will write error and status messages. The default value is `/var/log/xen/xend.log`.

❑ **Log level:** Set by the `loglevel` variable. This is the default lowest level of Xen daemon log messages that will be written to the log file. Possible values (in descending order of significance) are `CRITICAL` (critical conditions), `ERROR` (error conditions), `WARNING` (warning conditions), `NOTICE` (normal, but significant, conditions), `INFO` (informational messages), and `DEBUG` (debug-level messages). The default is `DEBUG`, which causes all available messages for all conditions to be written to the log because all of them are more significant than `DEBUG` messages. Setting the `loglevel` to a lower value filters out less significant messages. For example, setting `loglevel` to `NOTICE` would cause only `CRITICAL`, `ERROR`, `WARNING`, and `NOTICE` messages to be written to the Xen daemon's log file. `INFO` and `DEBUG` messages would be discarded.

❑ **Network configuration script:** Set by the `network-script` variable. This script identifies the name of the shell script that is called when setting up the network environment for domain0 and any domainU guest. Standard values are `network-bridge` (all domains are hosted on a bridge that uses your physical Ethernet device to communicate with the network), `network-nat` (all domains are hosted on a bridge, use their own subnet, and use NAT through your physical Ethernet device to talk to the external network), and `network-route` (all domains simply route traffic through your physical network interface, and domain0 handles IP forwarding and ARP proxying). The default value is `network-bridge`. You can specify a nonstandard Ethernet device by passing its name to whatever script you want to call by using the `netdev` option, such as (`network-script 'network-bridge netdev=eth1'`). The bridge is named xenbr0 by default. Similarly, you can also specify a nonstandard bridge by passing its name to whatever script you want to call by using the bridge option, such as (`network-script 'network-bridge bridge=mybridge'`).

❑ **Relocation hosts:** Set by the `xend-relocation-hosts-allow` variable. This is a whitespace-separated list, within single quotes, of zero or more regular expressions that host names or IP addresses, which must match in order to communicate over the relocation port. If no regular expression is provided (the default), all hosts can connect to this port. Common examples of `relocation-hosts` values include a regular expression for all hosts in a given domain by name (for example, `'^.*\\.vonhagen\\.org$'`), all hosts on a given network segment by IP address (for example, `'192.168.6.*'`), or both (`'^.*\\.vonhagen\\.org$ 192.168.6.*'`). This value is meaningful only if the relocation server has been enabled.

❑ **Relocation port:** Set by the `xend-relocation-port` variable. This is the number of the port on which the Xen daemon listens for relocation requests. The default value is `8002`, which is meaningful only if the relocation server is enabled.

❑ **Relocation server:** Set by the `xend-relocation-server` variable. This is a yes or no value that determines whether the Xen daemon supports relocation of domainU guests from this system (aka migration). The default value is `no`.

❑ **Socket location:** Set by the `xend-unix-path` variable. This is the full pathname of the socket used when communicating with the Xen daemon. The default value is `/var/lib/xend/xend-socket`.

❑ **Migration tool:** Set by the `external-migration-tool` variable. This is the name of the script or application that actually handles external device migration and is called from the `/etc/xen/scripts/external-device-migrate` script. By default, no device migration script is defined.

❑ **UNIX server:** Set by the `xend-unix-server` variable. This is a yes or no value that determines whether the Xen daemon runs an internal HTTP server that can be used to communicate with the Xen daemon over a UNIX socket. The default value is `no`. The use of this server is deprecated.

❑ **Virtual interface script:** Set by the `vif-script` variable. This identifies the name of the shell script that will be called when creating or destroying any virtual network interface, such as those used by all domainU guests. Standard values are `vif-bridge` (standard bridged networking, used with the `network-bridge` script), `vif-route` (routed network traffic, used with the `network-route` script), and `vif-nat` (native address translation, used with the `network-net` script). The default value is `vif-bridge`. All of these predefined scripts are located in the directory `/etc/xen/scripts`.

❑ **VNC interface:** Set by the `vnc-listen` variable. This is the interface on which domainU virtual machines will listen for VNC connections. The default value for this is `127.0.0.1`, which means that virtual machines will listen over different ports on the local machine's loopback interface. To cause the VNC consoles to listen on all available interfaces, set this variable to `0.0.0.0`. The default behavior in earlier versions of Xen was listening anywhere.

❑ **VNC password:** Set by the `vncpasswd` variable. This is the default password for a VNC console on any HVM domain. The default value is the empty string, `''` (two single quotation marks with no value between them). Thus, authentication is not required to contact a VNC console server.

❑ **XMLRPC address (TCP):** Set by the `xen-tcp-xmlrpc-server-address` variable. This is the IP address on which the Xen daemon's XMLRPC interface should listen. The default value is `' '` (two single quotation marks with no value between them). As a result, the TCP XMLRCP server will listen on all available interfaces. You can specify `localhost` to allow only local connections. This value is meaningful only if the TCP XMLRCP server is enabled.

❑ **XMLRPC certificate (TCP):** Set by the `xend-tcp-xmlrpc-server-ssl-cert-file` variable. This is the full pathname of the file containing the SSL certificate for the legacy TCP XMLRPC server. The default value is `/etc/xen/xmlrpc.crt`. Setting this value and the associated key value means that the TCP XMLRPC server will accept only SSL connections, rather than the standard, unencrypted connections.

❑ **XMLRPC key file (TCP):** Set by the `xend-tcp-xmlrpc-server-ssl-ckey-file` variable. This is the full pathname of the file containing the SSL key for the legacy TCP XMLRPC server. The default value is `/etc/xen/xmlrpc.key`. Setting this value and the associated certificate value means that the TCP XMLRPC server will accept only SSL connections, rather than the standard, unencrypted connections.

❑ **XMLRPC port (TCP):** Set by the `xen-tcp-xmlrpc-server-port` variable. This is the number of the TCP port on which the Xen daemon's legacy TCP XMLRPC interface is listening. The default value is `8006`. This value is meaningful only if the TCP XMLRPC server is enabled.

❑ **XMLRPC server (TCP):** Set by the `xend-tcp-xmlrpc-server` variable. This is a yes or no value that determines whether the Xen daemon runs an internal, TCP-only XMLRPC server that can be used to communicate with the Xen daemon. The default value is `no`. The use of this server is deprecated.

❑ **XMLRPC port (UNIX):** Set by the `xend-unix-xmlrpc-server-port` variable. This is the number of the port on which the Xen daemon's HTTP/UNIX socket XMLRPC interface is listening. The default value is `8000`. This value is meaningful only if the XMLRPC server is enabled.

❑ **XMLRPC server (UNIX):** Set by the `xend-unix-xmlrpc-server` variable. This is a yes or no value that determines whether the Xen daemon runs an internal, HTTP/UNIX socket XMLRPC server that can be used to communicate with the Xen daemon. The default value is `yes`.

The `/etc/xen/xend-config.sxp` script is well-commented and provides a good deal of additional information about many of these variables. It is certainly the best place to look if new variables have been introduced or you suspect that new default values are used when you install a new version of Xen.

After changing any of the values in this file, you must restart the Xen daemon for the new values to be used.

Xen Daemon Log Files

By default, the Xen daemon logs events to the following log files:

❑ `/var/log/xen/xend.log`: This log file contains domainU error and status messages. The status messages can be quite useful in seeing exactly how each domainU has been configured, especially if you are using a Fedora or other system where domainU configuration information is actually stored in the XenStore. (See the "XenStore and Related Utilities" section later in this chapter for more information.) The location and default debugging level (`DEBUG`) for this log file can be set in the Xen daemon configuration file, as described in the previous section.

❑ `/var/log/xen/xend-debug.log`: This log file contains high-level domainU status and error messages that are often more readable than those written to `/var/log/xen/xend.log`. This file also contains tracebacks for `xend` errors. This file is a good first place to look when you are experiencing problems starting a domain or the Xen daemon itself.

Other log files in `/var/log/xen` are created by QEMU when using HVM- or QEMU-format disk images (`/var/log/xen/qemu-dm.PID.log`), by the Xen hotplug script `/etc/xen/scripts/xen-hotplug-common.sh` when adding or removing devices (`/var/log/xen/xen-hotplug.log`), and by the Xen control interfaces when creating domains (`/var/log/xen/domain-builder-ng.log`).

Xen daemon errors generally manifest themselves as errors in an administrative application, such as `xm`. For more information about the types of errors that you may find in the Xen daemon's log files, see "Common xm Errors" later in this chapter.

Using the xm Command

The `xm` (Xen management) command is the primary command used to create, examine, and terminate domains, obtain information about domain0 and other domains, dynamically add and remove block and network devices from running domains, and so on, from a console or terminal application. Usually installed as `/usr/sbin/xm`, the `xm` command is the only command that you truly need in a Xen environment that consists of a single domain0 system and any number of domainU guest systems. Because the `xm` command requires access to privileged, system-level information and resources, it must be run as a user with root privileges on your domain0 system.

The next few sections illustrate how to perform common maintenance and monitoring tasks using the `xm` command. See Appendix A for a complete list of available `xm` commands and associated options.

Getting Information About Virtual Machines

One of the most commonly used `xm` commands is the `xm list` command, which lists all Xen domains (including domain0) that are running on the local machine and provides various information about each. Each row of information provides the following information about a domain:

❑ **Name:** The name assigned to the domain in its configuration file, XenStore entry, or using the `xm rename` command

❑ **ID:** The numeric identifier for the domain

❑ **Mem:** The amount of memory currently allocated to the domain in megabytes

❑ **VCPUs:** The number of virtual CPUs allocated to the domain

❑ **State:** The current state of the domain, which is b (blocked), c (crashed), p (paused), r (running), or s (shutdown)

❑ **Time(s):** The amount of CPU time (in seconds) that the domain has used

Sample output from this command looks like the following:

```
# xm list
Name                    ID   Mem VCPUs     State   Time(s)
Domain-0                 0  1302    1     r-----    5809.3
WinXP-LVM-HVM            4   256    1     -b----      31.8
fedora.fc6.nfs          1   256    1     -b----      11.2
```

You can also use the -l (the lowercase letter L preceded by a dash) option with the xm list command to get verbose output that provides complete information about all domains in the Xen daemon's SXP configuration file format.

Starting Virtual Machines

Although getting information about virtual machines is probably the most common use of the xm command, its most critical function is the ability to start Xen domainU guests, which Xen calls "creating" domains, by using the xm create command. This section uses the term "starting" to differentiate between creating virtual machine configuration information and actually starting the virtual machines that you've defined.

As you might expect, the xm create command takes more options than most xm commands. These are the following:

❑ -c: Connect to the console of the VM once it is created. This option can also be specified as --console_autoconnect for those who wish to type more characters.

❑ -f=FILE: Identifies a Python configuration script to load after all arguments to the xm create command and the domainU configuration file have been processed. This option can also be specified as --defconfig=FILE for those who wish to type additional characters. This option enables you to provide a set of default values that you can use when creating multiple domains. The order of precedence is:

   ❑ Configuration values set in the configuration file

   ❑ Configuration values specified as variable=value pairs on the xm create command line

   ❑ Configuration values set in the Python configuration file.

❑ -F=FILE: An explicit option for identifying the SXP-format domain configuration file that you want to use. This option can also be specified as --config=FILE.

❑ -h: Displays a help message that lists all available xm create options. This option can also be specified as --help.

❑ --help_config: Displays a help message that lists all available domainU configuration variables.

❑ -n: Performs a dry run of domainU configuration using the specified SXP configuration file and the current set of xm create options without actually creating a new Xen domain. This option can also be specified as --dryrun.

❑ -p: Creates the domain but leaves it in a paused state. This option can also be specified as --paused.

❏ `--path=PATH`: Enables you to specify the search path to be used when looking for domainU configuration files. The search path is specified as a colon-separated list of directory names. For example, `--path=/home/xen/PARAVIRT:/home/xen/HVM:/home/xen/default` would search the directories `/home/xen/PARAVIRT`, `/home/xen/HVM`, and `/home/xen/default` for configuration files, in that order.

❏ `-q`: Suppresses any output from the `xm create` command. This option can be useful when you're scripting domainU creation, and can also be specified as `--quietm`.

❏ `-s`: Skips DTD checking when creating a domain from an XML-format configuration file. Using this option can decrease domain creation time, but it can also cause domain creation to fail if your XML configuration file is specified incorrectly. This option can also be specified as `--skipdtd`.

❏ `-x`: Performs a dry run of domainU configuration using the specified XML-format configuration file and the current set of `xm create` options without actually creating a new Xen domain. This option can also be specified as `--xmldryrun`.

By default, the `xm create` command produces very little output. It initially displays a message of the following form:

```
Using config file "./feisty_lvm.cfg".
```

This message identifies the configuration file that is being used. If the domain can be created successfully, the `xm` command simply exits after creating and starting the domain. If errors are detected in the configuration file or when creating the domain, the `xm create` command displays an error message and exits without creating the domain. For a discussion of some common error messages, see "Common xm Errors" later in this chapter.

Connecting and Disconnecting from Xen Domain Consoles

When using the `xm` command to create a domain, you can specify the `-c` option to immediately connect to that domain's console. This can be quite useful when debugging configuration, connectivity, or root filesystem problems. However, you rarely want the shell from which you start a domain to be permanently connected to a domainU console — this can also be extremely confusing for your fellow system administrators if you leave shells around that are connected to the consoles of other machines. To disconnect from the console of a virtual machine, you can type the Ctrl+[key sequence.

After starting virtual machines, you can manually connect to their consoles by using the `xm console DomID` command, where `DomID` is the domain ID of the domainU guest that you want to connect to. This is primarily useful for Linux and other UNIX-like Xen guests because operating systems, such as different versions of Microsoft Windows, display very little output to a text-format system console.

The `xm console DomID` command can be useful in a number of different situations. One of the most common is when you are seeing performance problems in a domainU guest and want to check whether critical system messages are being sent to the console. Similarly, it is also quite easy to forget the `-c` option when starting a guest domain. Using this option when starting a domain isn't necessary, but it is certainly useful when you're initially deploying new virtual machines to verify that networking is being initialized correctly (especially when you're using a dedicated network controller), that the root filesystem is being mounted correctly, and that the system initialization process is running as expected.

If your domain0 system is running a graphical console, it can often be convenient to establish console connections to various virtual machines by executing the xm console DomID command within an xterm or other X Window system console window. A simple command to do so is the following:

```
# xterm -T name-of-domain -e xm console DomID &
```

This creates an xterm whose title bar displays name-of-domain and which contains a console connection to the domain identified by DomID.

The xm create command takes a single, optional argument. This is the -q option, which suppresses the error message that would typically be displayed if the domain identified by DomID does not exist. This option can also be specified as --quiet.

Adjusting Memory Use in Virtual Machines

The amount of memory allocated to a domain is specified by the memory = value option in the configuration file for a virtual machine. In most cases, you can guesstimate the appropriate amount of memory required by a specific Xen domain based on the number processes that you will be running within that domain, the size of those executables, the long-term memory requirements of those processes, and so on. Unfortunately, it can be difficult to predict the long-term memory consumption of server processes with variable amounts of activity, such as mail servers, Web servers, and so on.

If you are running HVM domains or paravirtualized domains that use QEMU disk images with a pre-allocated swap partition or explicit swap files, exchanging optimal performance with the ability of the system to swap to virtual memory is a standard sysadmin tradeoff. However, swapping in virtual machines can cause performance problems because of the fact that disks are rarely local to a virtual machine. To minimize the impact of memory and swapping-related problems, Xen provides you with the ability to dynamically change the amount of memory allocated to a domain without requiring that you restart the domain. This can be very useful in scenarios such as the following:

❑   A domain is experiencing performance problems due to frequent swapping.

❑   You want to start additional processes in a domain that is currently performing well without increasing the chance that the system will begin swapping.

❑   A domain never swaps and never uses all of the memory that you have pre-allocated to it.

The xm mem-set command enables you to increase or reduce the amount of memory that is allocated to a domain identified by DomID. This command takes advantage of Xen's memory ballooning technique to deallocate pages from one domain and return to the pool from which other virtual machines can allocate memory. This reallocation is transient. The next time you start a modified domain, it will allocate the amount of memory specified in its configuration file.

Once you have identified a domain that requires more memory, you can obtain the domain ID of that domain using the xm list command, as in the following example:

```
# xm list
Name                      ID    Mem VCPUs      State   Time(s)
Domain-0                   0   1161     1      r-----  11195.1
WinXP-LVM-HVM              4    256     1      -b----    186.8
fedora.fc6.nfs             1    256     1      -b----     52.0
fedora.fc6.ym.nfs          5    256     1      -b----    289.5
```

To be able to increase the amount of memory available to a domain, your domain configuration file must contain a maxmem value, which specifies the maximum amount of memory that can be assigned to that domain. You must specify this in advance to ensure that the page tables and other data structures for the domain are large enough to potentially handle the amount of memory specified by maxmem. The domain configuration file's memory variable specifies the initial amount of memory that is assigned to the domain at boot time. For example, the following configuration file entries specify that a domain should initially allocate 256MB, but specifies that the maximum amount of memory that can be assigned to the domain is 1GB:

```
memory = 256
maxmem = 1024
```

If you do not specify a value of maxmem that is larger than the value of memory (or do not specify a maxmem value at all), the value of the memory variable is used to set maxmem, and you will not be able to increase the amount of memory allocated to that domain. In these cases, you will see an error message such as the following when trying to increase the size of available memory:

```
Error: memory_dynamic_max must be less than or \equal to memory_static_max
```

To increase the amount of memory allocated to a domain where memory < maxmem, specify the ID of that domain, followed by the new amount of memory that you want to allocate to that domain, as follows:

```
# xm mem-set 5 384
# xm list Name      ID    Mem VCPUs     State    Time(s)
  Domain-0           0   1033    1     r-----    11204.2
WinXP-LVM-HVM        4    256    1     -b----     187.2
fedora.fc6.nfs       1    256    1     -b----      52.2
fedora.fc6.ym.nfs    5    384    1     -b----     289.7
```

Similarly, you can decrease the amount of memory available to a domain by specifying the ID of that domain and the new amount of memory that you want to allocate to that domain, as in the following example:

```
# xm mem-set 5 192
# xm list
Name                 ID    Mem VCPUs     State    Time(s)
Domain-0             0   1161    1     r-----    11204.2
WinXP-LVM-HVM        4    256    1     -b----     187.2
fedora.fc6.nfs       1    256    1     -b----      52.2
fedora.fc6.ym.nfs    5    192    1     -b----     289.7
```

Note that the amount of memory shown as being allocated to domain0 is not actually reduced until the domain whose memory allocation you have increased or reduced actually begins to use the new memory that is available to it.

Memory reallocation should only be done for tuning and emergency purposes in running domains. Because of its transient nature, you should always remember to update the configuration file or XenStore information for domains that require additional memory. You should also remember to update the configuration information for domains that require less memory in order to avoid allocating it in the first place and also to maximize the size of the pool of memory that is available for use on your domain0 systems.

Getting Xen System and Configuration Information

You may occasionally need to obtain general information about the version of Xen that is running on a specific system, such as version information, capability information, how it was built and the tools used to do so, and so on. You can easily obtain this information from the command line, as shown in the following example:

```
# xm info
host                  : xen.vonhagen.org
release               : 2.6.18-xen
version               : #1 SMP Thu Jul 5 11:00:06 EDT 2007
machine               : x86_64
nr_cpus               : 1
nr_nodes              : 1
sockets_per_node      : 1
cores_per_socket      : 1
threads_per_core      : 1
cpu_mhz               : 2200
hw_caps               : 078bfbff:ebd3fbff:00000000:00000010:\
                        00002001:0000001d:0000001d
total_memory          : 1983
free_memory           : 257
xen_major             : 3
xen_minor             : 1
xen_extra             : .0
xen_caps              : xen-3.0-x86_64 xen-3.0-x86_32p \
                        hvm-3.0-x86_32 hvm-3.0-x86_32p \
                        hvm-3.0-x86_64
xen_scheduler         : credit
xen_pagesize          : 4096
platform_params       : virt_start=0xffff800000000000
xen_changeset         : Fri May 18 16:59:32 2007 +0100
cc_compiler           : gcc version 4.1.2 20070626
cc_compile_by         : wvh
cc_compile_domain     : vonhagen.org
cc_compile_date       : Thu Jul  5 09:52:55 EDT 2007
xend_config_format    : 4
```

Common xm Errors

One of the more frustrating aspects of using the xm command is that the error messages that it displays can be cryptic, even on a good day. This section doesn't provide a complete list of possible error messages, but it does list the most commonly encountered messages, their causes, and what you can do about them.

Of all the messages displayed by the xm command, Error 22 is the most daunting:

```
Error: (22, 'Invalid Argument')
```

This error message means that an error has been found when parsing an SXP configuration file. Unfortunately, it doesn't identify the line on which the error was encountered or even the variable for which an incorrect value was specified. The first thing to check is that the values specified for the disk and `vif` variables are correct. The values that define multiple disks can be quite complex, each specific disk definition must be enclosed within quotation marks of some sort and separated from the next by a comma. Each disk definition contains three fields, each of which must also be separated from the next by a comma.

You may also see this message if one of the disk type identifiers is unrecognized. This was a common problem when, for example, the blktap driver introduced in Xen 3.0.3 provided higher performance for filesystem images than the older loopback mechanism. If you are using an older version of Xen (for some reason), you may need to make sure that you specify the file disk type rather than the `tap:aio type/ driver` combination. This particular example should rarely occur nowadays, but similar problems may surface as new disk types are introduced for Xen and configuration file updates may precede system software updates.

A common legacy error message that was often seen when using the `file:` disk type identifier was the following:

```
"Error: vbd: Segment not found: uname=file:/path/to/image"
```

This message meant that no additional loopback devices could be created to handle accessing a disk in a newly created domain. By default, Linux allows up to eight loopback devices to be active. You can increase this number by setting `max_loop=NN` on the domain0 kernel command line in GRUB and rebooting, where *NN* is the new number of loopback devices that you want the kernel to support. Because the `file:` disk type is deprecated in Xen 3.1, you should not encounter this message, but you could still see it if you have a large number of domainU guests and have not yet updated their configuration files to use the newer blktap driver.

Other common error messages are memory-related, such as the following:

```
Error: (12, 'Cannot allocate memory') 'The privileged domain did not balloon!'
```

These messages mean that memory could not be allocated to a new domain, and typically occur when you are using the `xm create` command to first start a new domain. To eliminate both of these error messages, you can use the `xm mem-set` command to reduce the amount of memory associated with existing domains, freeing up memory so that the hypervisor can allocate it to the new domain.

XenStore and Related Utilities

XenStore is a collection of hierarchical name/value pairs stored in a standard Linux Trivial Database (TDB, `http://sourceforge.net/projects/tdb`) file in the directory `/var/lib/xenstored`. Xen uses the XenStore database and related utilities to store configuration, event, and status information about Xen domains and device drivers. The XenStore is used by Xen much like the standard `procfs` directory hierarchy is used by Linux systems in general.

For paravirtualized drivers, Xen uses a bus abstraction known as XenBus to communicate between domains. Xen virtual device drivers register themselves with the XenBus at initialization time, storing information in keys in the XenStore database and setting watches on the appropriate keys so that they can respond. Domains can therefore use the XenStore to exchange event information for significant, low-level events such as memory management and frontend/backend device driver activity requests.

Each domain has its own directory hierarchy in the XenStore that contains data related to its configuration. All active domains have access to the XenStore and apply any changes that they make to the XenStore transactionally, meaning that they are either made completely or not at all.

Traditional tools for accessing TDB databases such as tdbdump and tdbtool can still be used with the XenStore, but all Xen installations also provide a set of custom utilities that provide the different functions that Xen domains need to use to access the XenStore more directly. These utilities communicate with the daemon (/usr/sbin/xenstored) that manages access to the XenStore. These utilities are as follows:

❑ /usr/bin/xenstore-chmod: Changes the access/protection mode of a specified node in the XenStore

❑ /usr/bin/xenstore-exists: Verifies that a specified key exists in the XenStore

❑ /usr/bin/xenstore-list: Lists the values associated with a specific node in the XenStore

❑ /usr/bin/xenstore-ls: Provides a hierarchical listing of the key/value pairs under a specific node in the XenStore

❑ /usr/bin/xenstore-read: Reads the value of a single node in the XenStore

❑ /usr/bin/xenstore-rm: Removes a specific key/value pair from the XenStore

❑ /usr/bin/xenstore-write: Writes a specific key/value pair to the XenStore

The three top-level nodes in the XenStore hierarchy are as follows:

❑ /vm: Stores configuration information about each Xen domain on the current system. The information for each domain is stored hierarchically under a node whose name is the UUID generated for each domain.

❑ /local/domain: Stores detailed information about the current execution and driver state for each Xen domain on the current system. The information for each domain is stored hierarchically under a node whose name is the domainID for each domain.

❑ /tool: Stores information for Xen-related tools.

The XenStore and related commands are rarely accessed directly by users or administrators. They are primarily used by administrative applications and Xen itself to examine and manipulate Xen's internal status information. The Xen wiki provides the following shell script (at http://wiki.xensource.com/xenwiki/XenStore), which you can use to hierarchically dump the contents of the XenStore:

```
#!/bin/sh : unction dumpkey() {
    local param=${1}
    local key
    local result
    result=$(xenstore-list ${param})
    if [ "${result}" != "" ] ; then
        for key in ${result} ; do dumpkey ${param}/${key} ; done
      else
        echo -n ${param}'='
        xenstore-read ${param}
    fi
}
for key in /vm /local/domain /tool ; do dumpkey ${key} ; done
```

For detailed information about the XenStore and each node in its hierarchy, see `http://wiki.xensource.com/xenwiki/XenStoreReference`.

Xen Tracing and Performance Monitoring

Identifying the source of performance problems and optimizing system performance can be a complex task on standard Linux systems. Virtualization makes performance analysis and tuning even more complex because it introduces additional factors into the problem set, some of which are difficult to measure or address. Network and disk driver performance analysis is made more complex by the introduction of paravirtualized drivers, bridged networks with virtual interfaces, different storage abstractions and emulation, and so on. Hardware support for virtualization can slow down the operation of virtual machines, especially in highly interactive, disk-intensive, or network-intensive processes.

Xen and other virtualization technologies cannot succeed if the benefits (more efficient and flexible use of existing systems) do not outweigh the drawbacks (significant performance problems). Although Xen began as a research project, its growing success in commercial markets and its continuing popularity as a research and development environment mean that significant time and money is being invested in Xen performance analysis and problem identification. Many commercial Xen vendors are producing product-specific performance tuning and analysis tools. Companies that traditionally focus on enterprise system administration, such as Computer Associates and Tivoli, are adding Xen-specific modules to their software suites.

Luckily, you don't have to spend megabucks to manage and monitor an enterprise-caliber Xen environment. Xen comes with a good set of basic performance monitoring and analysis tools, and its Linux foundation means that standard Linux analysis and tuning tools are still extremely valuable in the Xen environment. The next few sections discuss the Xen-specific performance analysis tools that are provided as part of the open source Xen distribution.

XenMon

XenMon is a performance monitor for Xen that serves as a front end for the Xen tracing features exported by the xenbaked daemon. Originally developed at Hewlett-Packard, XenMon is now included as part of the standard Open Source Xen distribution. Although XenMon was originally developed to enable researchers to compare Xen performance under different CPU weightings for Xen's Borrowed Virtual Time scheduler, it provides a variety of performance-related data that can be quite useful when simulating different levels of per-domain load. (See "Controlling Hypervisor Scheduling" in Chapter 2 for more information about the schedulers used by the Xen hypervisor.) XenMon can also be quite useful in identifying the domains with the highest execution and I/O load, helping you identify domains whose active processes you may want to distribute to other domains, or to which you may want to dedicate additional resources.

> A technical paper on the development and initial use of XenMon at Hewlett-Packard is available at `www.hpl.hp.com/techreports/2005/HPL-2005-187.html`.

The executable for XenMon is named xenmon.py, and is typically installed as /usr/sbin/xenmon.py. This executable must be run with root privileges in order to be able to access Xen performance statistics.

For each domain (and a general category of idle time), the default XenMon output displays three rows of summary information collected over intervals of 10 and 1 seconds. These provide data about the amount of time spent actually executing instructions (Gotten), the amount of time spent sleeping (Blocked), and the amount of time spent waiting to run (Waited). Three values are provided for each of the 10- and 1- second intervals: the time spent in that state over the measurement interval; the time spent in that state expressed as a percentage of the measurement interval; and the average CPU time (Gotten), average blocked time per I/O event (Blocked), or average waiting time (Waited), depending upon the line that you're looking at. Figure 7-1 shows a sample output screen from the xenmon.py application.

```
                                    wvh@xen:/home/xen
CPU = 0              Last 10 seconds (99.87%)                  Last 1 second (99.90%)
==========================================================================================
   0   134.71 ms   13.47%   190.33 us/ex    97.30 ms    9.73%   177.02 us/ex   Gotten
   0   858.85 ms   85.89%     0.00 ns/io   897.65 ms   89.77%     0.00 ns/io   Blocked
   0     6.37 ms    0.64%     9.00 us/ex     4.98 ms    0.50%     9.07 us/ex   Waited
 Idle 814.61 ms   81.46%   534.99 us/ex   854.50 ms   85.45%   730.82 us/ex   Gotten
 Idle   0.00 ns    0.00%     0.00 ns/io     0.00 ns    0.00%     0.00 ns/io   Blocked
 Idle 185.03 ms   18.50%   121.52 us/ex   144.30 ms   14.43%   123.42 us/ex   Waited
  18     7.63 ms    0.76%   120.91 us/ex     7.62 ms    0.76%   121.02 us/ex   Gotten
  18   991.09 ms   99.11%     0.00 ns/io   991.85 ms   99.18%     0.00 ns/io   Blocked
  18     1.29 ms    0.13%    20.44 us/ex   536.31 us    0.05%     8.52 us/ex   Waited
  21    26.78 ms    2.68%    19.84 us/ex    24.97 ms    2.50%    25.01 us/ex   Gotten
  21   907.27 ms   90.73%     0.00 ns/io   929.77 ms   92.98%     0.00 ns/io   Blocked
  21    65.35 ms    6.54%    48.42 us/ex    44.72 ms    4.47%    44.79 us/ex   Waited
  23     3.12 ms    0.31%   108.60 us/ex     2.75 ms    0.27%   101.82 us/ex   Gotten
  23   976.81 ms   97.68%     0.00 ns/io   980.58 ms   98.06%     0.00 ns/io   Blocked
  23    20.06 ms    2.01%   698.84 us/ex    16.66 ms    1.67%   617.49 us/ex   Waited
  20    11.88 ms    1.19%    28.85 us/ex    11.83 ms    1.18%    28.87 us/ex   Gotten
  20   956.42 ms   95.64%     0.00 ns/io   963.56 ms   96.36%     0.00 ns/io   Blocked
  20    21.67 ms    2.17%    52.64 us/ex    17.75 ms    1.78%    43.33 us/ex   Waited
   *                        99.87%                               99.90%
```

Figure 7-1

To start XenMon, execute the xenmon.py command. This displays the output for CPU 0 that is shown in Figure 7-1, updating this information continuously. Type **q** to exit from XenMon. You can also type **c** to toggle between data for different physical CPUs, or the **n** or **p** command to move to the next or previous physical CPU. The CPU-specific commands are relevant only if you have more than one physical CPU.

When you exit from the XenMon command, it displays summary information about systems on which XenMon was running and the events that occurred while running XenMon, as in the following example:

```
# xenmon.py
xenbaked: no process killed
ms_per_sample = 100
Initialized with 1 cpu
CPU Frequency = 2200.10
Event counts:
```

(continued)

(continued)

```
11196451        Other
00000000        Add Domain
00000000        Remove Domain
00000000        Sleep
00946672        Wake
00808420        Block
01540020        Switch
00000000        Timer Func
01540024        Switch Prev
01540022        Switch Next
00004571        Page Map
00004571        Page Unmap
00000000        Page Transfer
processed 17580751 total records in 376 seconds (46757 per second)
woke up 23036 times in 376 seconds (61 per second)
```

These summaries provide an interesting overview of the events that took place while XenMon was running, including administrative operations such as creating or destroying domains, time spent switching between and servicing different domains, and the time spent exchanging driver-related data between different domains and the hypervisor by page-flipping.

XenMon provides a number of options to control its execution, where it collects data, and the type of data that it collects. To display these options, execute the following command with root privileges:

```
# python 'which xenmon.py' -h
```

This displays the following usage message:

```
usage: xenmon.py [options]
options:
  -h, --help       show this help message and exit
  -l, --live       show the ncurses live monitoring frontend (default)
  -n, --notlive    write to file instead of live monitoring
  -p PREFIX, --prefix=PREFIX
                   prefix to use for output files
  -t DURATION, --time=DURATION
                   stop logging to file after this much time has
                   elapsed(in seconds). set to 0 to keep logging
                   indefinitely
  -i INTERVAL, --interval=INTERVAL
                   interval for logging (in ms)
  --ms_per_sample=MSPERSAMPLE
                   determines how many ms worth of data goes in a
                   sample
  --cpu=CPU        specifies which cpu to display data for
  --allocated      Display allocated time for each domain
  --noallocated    Don't display allocated time for each domain
  --blocked        Display blocked time for each domain
  --noblocked      Don't display blocked time for each domain
  --waited         Display waiting time for each domain
  --nowaited       Don't display waiting time for each domain
```

```
--excount        Display execution count for each domain
--noexcount      Don't display execution count for each domain
--iocount        Display I/O count for each domain
--noiocount      Don't display I/O count for each domain
```

Most of these are self-explanatory, but one especially interesting set of options enables you to write performance data to per-domain output files rather than to the interactive display. To do this, specify the -n option to disable the interactive display, and then specify the -t (time) option followed by the amount of time for which you want to collect data, expressed in seconds. By default, XenMon creates per-domain output files with names of the form log-domID.log, including an additional output file for overall idle time. You can change the names of these files by specifying the -p option followed by a new prefix to replace the default log prefix.

XenPerf

XenPerf enables you to capture and display Xen performance data that is recorded by a number of counters within the Xen source code. As with all software performance measurements, populating and tracking these counters causes a slight degradation in performance. In order to capture this information, you must therefore recompile the Xen hypervisor with performance counters enabled.

To modify your Xen source code distribution to enable the performance counters used by XenPerf, edit the file SRCDIR/xen/Rules.mk, and set the perfc and perfc_arrays variables to y. These variables are set to n by default, and are located near the beginning of the file. You must then change directory to your main Xen source code directory (SRCDIR), and execute the make clean command before executing make dist or make world to rebuild your Xen distribution.

> *When building a version of a Xen distribution for performance measurement, I typically also modify the kernel and hypervisor makefiles, adding -perf to the end of the EXTRAVERSION declarations so that I can easily identify performance-related versions and do not accidentally overwrite my main Xen hypervisor and domain kernel binaries. The setting for the hypervisor is in SRCDIR/xen/Makefile, to which I typically make the following modification:*
>
> export XEN_EXTRAVERSION ?= .0$(XEN_VENDORVERSION)-perf
>
> *The setting for the kernel is in SRCDIR/kernel-xen/Makefile, to which I typically make the following modification:*
>
> EXTRAVERSION =$(XENGUEST)-perf
>
> *This is optional, but can save you some grief if you have already heavily tuned your existing hypervisor and kernel binaries, and don't want to risk having to recreate them.*

Once you have rebuilt your Xen distribution, install it as described in "Installing Xen," in Chapter 3, and create a new GRUB stanza for that hypervisor, kernel, and initial RAM disk filesystem. After rebooting and selecting the performance-enabled boot stanza, you can run the xenperf command at any time to show the values that are currently contained in the performance counters. As with other administrative

Xen commands, the XenPerf command (executed as `xenperf`) must be executed with root privileges. When run without options, the output of the `xenperf` command looks like the following:

```
# xenperf
exceptions                       T=  52982797
vmexits                          T=         0
cause vector                     T=         0
SVMexits                         T= 188994044
segmentation fixups              T=         0           0
apic timer interrupts            T=  21208186    21208186
domain page tlb flushes          T=         0           0
calls to mmuext_op               T=  19949725    19949725
mmuext ops                       T=  39319278    39319278
calls to mmu_update              T=    639697      639697
page updates                     T=    671975      671975
calls to update_va_map           T=   8932963     8932963
page faults                      T=  12867066    12867066
copy_user faults                 T=    274457      274457
[much additional output not shown]
```

The `xenperf` command provides several options to produce better looking and more detailed output, such as the following:

❑ `-f`: Print full performance arrays- and histograms

❑ `-p`: Print full arrays and histograms in a (supposedly) better-looking format

❑ `-r`: Reset counters

Of these, the most useful is probably the `-r` option, which resets all counters. This can be useful when you want to measure performance under certain types of load or activity, or over specific periods. You can reset the counters, take a generic performance measurement, reset the counters again, apply load, and then recapture the performance counters so that you can compare the results.

XenTop

The standard Linux `top` command, which provides a dynamic view of process execution and resource use, is one of the system administrator's best friends on any Linux system. The `top` command uses the same information as the standard Linux `ps` command, but displays system information in a curses-based graphical display that is constantly updated and, by default, sorts this information based on the percentage of the CPU and available memory that various processes are using.

The XenTop command, originally developed at IBM and installed as `/usr/sbin/xentop` by default, is a domain-oriented Xen equivalent for the `top` command. The XenTop command shows general information about the Xen domains that are running on a given system (including domain0), sorting this output based on the amount of CPU time and available memory that these domains are using. As with other administrative Xen commands, the XenTop command (executed as `xentop`) must be executed with root privileges. Figure 7-2 shows sample XenTop output in an xterm window.

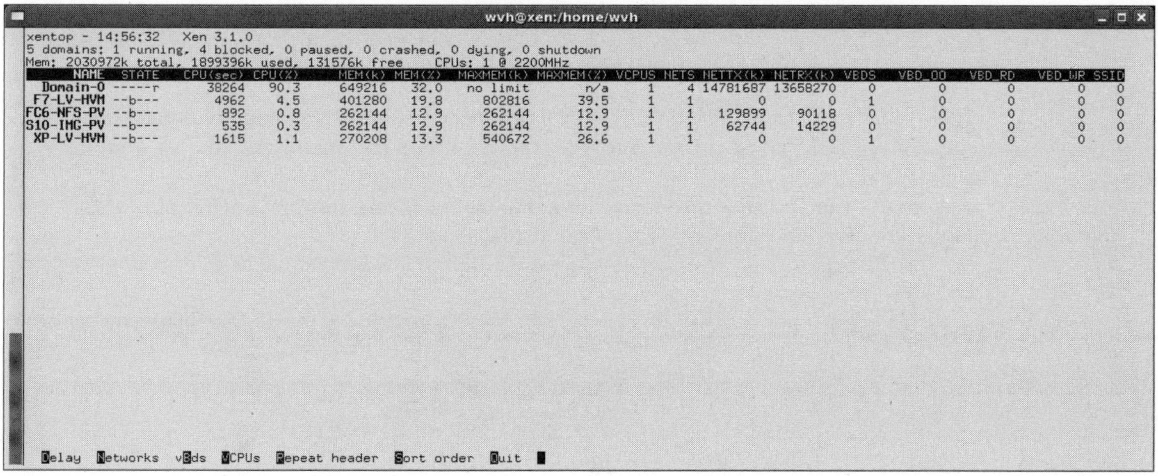

Figure 7-2

The `xentop` command provides the following command-line options, which you can display by executing the `xentop -h` command:

```
# xentop -h
Usage: xentop [OPTION]
Displays ongoing information about xen vm resources
-h, --help             display this help and exit
-V, --version          output version information and exit
-d, --delay=SECONDS    seconds between updates (default 3)
-n, --networks         output vif network data
-x, --vbds             output vbd block device data
-r, --repeat-header    repeat table header before each domain
-v, --vcpus            output vcpu data
-b, --batch            output in batch mode, no user input accepted
-i, --iterations       number of iterations before exiting
Report bugs to <dsteklof@us.ibm.com>.
```

You can exit from the XenTop display at any time by typing **q** or pressing the Escape key.

The options for displaying selected types of data are actually more interesting when activated within XenTop's interactive display by pressing the following keys while the XenTop command is running:

❑ **D:** Prompts you to set the delay between updates

❑ **N:** Toggles whether detailed, per-domain network information is displayed. By default, this information is not displayed unless you execute the `xentop` command with the `-n` option.

❑ **R:** Toggles whether the XenTop header is repeated before the summary information for each domain. By default, only a single header is shown unless you execute the `xentop` command with the `-r` option.

❑ **S:** Cycles through the various columns in this display, using the values in the current column as the basis on which the XenTop output is sorted. By default, the XenTop display is sorted based on the domain that is using the most CPU on the host system.

❑ **V:** Toggles whether detailed virtual CPU (VCPU) information is displayed. By default, this information is not displayed unless you execute the xentop command with the -v option.

All of these interactive commands are case-insensitive. Figure 7-3 shows sample XenTop output that includes virtual network interface information in the display.

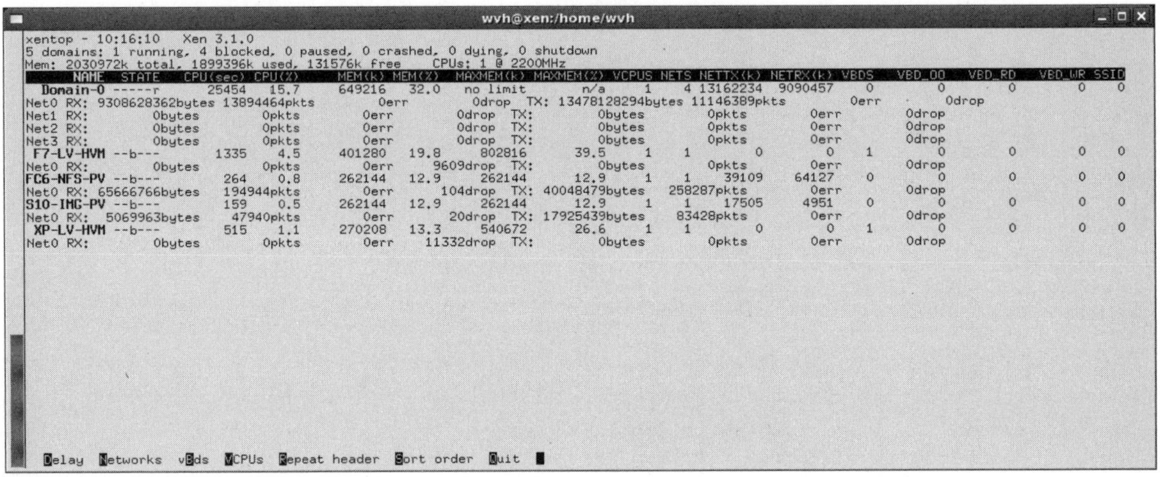

Figure 7-3

As you can see from the figures in this section, the XenTop command produces fairly long lines of output, which can be somewhat inconvenient on small or fixed-width consoles. However, it provides a useful snapshot of the general state of a Xen server system that makes it very easy to identify heavily used domains that may be causing overall performance problems in your Xen environment. Similarly, the memory usage and maximum memory columns can help you identify domains whose memory allocation can be adjusted (in their configuration files) to more efficiently use available system memory the next time you start those domains.

XenTrace

The XenTrace application enables you to capture Xen trace buffer information from a running hypervisor. Although primarily of interest to hypervisor developers, it may be useful to system administrators in identifying the events that lead up to repeatable problems and submitting problem reports. Because of the volume of the information that it captures, and the fact that this output is in binary, the XenTrace application can only write its output to a pipe or to stdout for redirection into a file. XenTrace will not write output to a TTY.

The XenTrace application is typically installed in /usr/bin/xentrace by a standard Xen distribution. As with other commands that require direct access to the hypervisor and other privileged information, the XenTrace command (executed as xentrace) must be executed with root privileges.

By default, the XenTrace command writes binary output data in the following form:

```
CPU(uint) TSC(u64) EVENT(u32) D1 D2 D3 D4 D5 (all u32)
```

CPU is an unsigned integer that gives the processor number. TSC is an unsigned, 64-bit value containing the timestamp of the record (the value of the CPU cycle counter). EVENT is an unsigned 32-bit value containing the event ID. D1 through D5 are unsigned 32-bit values containing the actual trace data. The endian-ness of the output depends on that of the host on which you are capturing the data.

The XenTrace command provides options that:

❑ Set the polling time for new data (-s *VAL*, where *VAL* is an integer number of milliseconds)

❑ Set the number of new records required to trigger writing output data (-t *VAL*, where *VAL* is an integer)

❑ Enable you to specify a CPU mask to filter results so that you capture data only for a specific CPU (-c *VAL*, where *VAL* is a mask that prevents XenTrace from generating trace data from specific CPUs)

❑ Enable you to specify an event mask to filter results so that you can filter out unwanted events and associated trace data to reduce the size and complexity of your trace data (-e *MASK*, where *MASK* is a hexadecimal or predefined value)

Because XenTrace is rarely used by system administrators, the possible event masks are not listed here. See the XenTrace command's man page (man xentrace) for detailed information on possible event mask values.

Once you have captured information using xentrace, you will want to use the associated xentrace_format command to display the binary data in a human-readable format. In order to use the xentrace_format command, you will need to provide a file containing formatting rules for the different types of data found in XenTrace output. Luckily, a sample trace format–definition file is included with the Xen source code distribution, and can be found in the file SRCDIR/tools/xentrace/format. You then format and display the data using a command such as the following, where xentrace.out is a file containing output from the xentrace command and xentrace.fmt is the name of the file containing your trace formatting rules:

```
# cat xentrace.out | xentrace_format xentrace.fmt | more
```

This command would display formatted xentrace output to a screen. You could also redirect the output to a file or printer to permanently capture formatted data. The default formatted output that is produced is quite wide. You will want to use a smaller font or print in landscape mode when actually printing xentrace output.

Reporting Bugs in Xen

As much as anyone hates to admit it, all software has bugs. Once you've determined that a problem you are experiencing is actually a bug, you should always report such problems. A big part of the value of the open source community lies in working together to develop and debug great, free software.

Submitting problem reports on existing software can be just as useful as submitting code — you're just contributing at a different level.

Xen distributions include the `xen-bugtool` command, which provides an interactive, command-line interface for collecting system information and relevant log files that may be useful in diagnosing and resolving reported problems. As with other commands that require direct access to privileged information, the `xen-bugtool` command must be executed with root privileges. The `xen-bugtool` tool is typically installed as `/usr/sbin/xen-bugtool`.

> The `xen-bugtool` command collects only information that can be attached to existing bugs. It does not enable you to create bug reports in the Bugzilla bug-tracking system used by XenSource and the Xen project. You must be a registered Bugzilla user at the XenSource site in order to file bugs. You can create a Bugzilla account at the XenSource site by selecting the Open a new Bugzilla Account link at `http://bugzilla.xensource.com/bugzilla/index.cgi`.

The `xen-bugtool` command collects Xen diagnostic message (dmesg) output, details of your machine's hardware configuration, and information about the build of Xen that you are using, and prompts you to include system and Xen log files such as `/var/log/messages`, `/var/log/xen/xend-debug.log`, `/var/log/xen/xen-hotplug.log`, and `/var/log/xen/xend.log`. Log files such as `/var/log/syslog` and `/var/log/debug` can also be appended if they exist on your system.

> The `xen-bugtool` command displays a message cautioning that the log files that it is collecting may contain private information, and that you should either not use the tool or explicitly exclude selected log files from the archive that it creates.

Open Source Xen Management Utilities

As discussed throughout this book, the development of good administrative and managerial software for virtualization products such as Xen is going to be one of the keys to its success. This book focuses on the software that is part of the official Xen project, all of which is command-line oriented. However, many open source projects, commercial software manufacturers, and Linux distribution vendors are working hard to create sophisticated, graphical software that simplifies creating and managing Xen environments. This section provides an overview of Xen-related open source projects, noting distribution dependencies and providing general status information whenever possible.

The best general source on the Web for information about Xen administration tools is the Virtualization and Grid Computing Web site at `www.gridvm.org/xen-remote-management-interfaces.html`. This site provides a great list of open source and commercial software projects dedicated to deploying, monitoring, managing, and administering Xen virtual machines and enterprise Xen environments. Another useful site for locating Xen-related software is the SourceLabs SWiK site at `http://swik.net/virtualization+monitoring`.

Specific open source Xen administration projects that are promising and growing in popularity are as follows:

❑ **XenMan:** The Controlling Virtual Systems (ConVirt) project's XenMan package supports creating and managing Xen virtual machines on one or more hosts. XenMan is available from the ConVirt project's page at SourceForge (`http://xenman.sourceforge.net`). The XenMan software requires Xen 3.0.2 or later and requires that a package known as python-paramiko, a Python SSH library, be installed on your system. (See `www.lag.net/paramiko` for more information about this package.) XenMan is currently supported and tested only on Fedora Core and OpenSUSE systems.

❑ **Enomalism:** Provides a virtual machine management dashboard that is supported and tested only on the Fedora Linux distribution (FC6, at the time that this book was written). The Enomalism software is available for free download at `www.enomalism.com`. Enomalism has many dependencies and software requirements, but offers to install all of these packages during the Enomalism installation process.

❑ **MLN:** The Manage Large Networks project provides a command-line oriented package for creating and managing Xen and User-Model Linux (UML) virtual machines. MLN is available from `http://mln.sourceforge.net`.

❑ **OpenQRM:** The OpenQRM project is an open source system management package that provides a usable, Web-oriented interface for managing Xen systems and related services such as TFTP, DHCP, NFS, and many more. Management and monitoring of each of these services is done by separate plugins that work together thanks to the flexible OpenQRM framework. OpenQRM is available from `www.openqrm.org`. Commercial support for OpenQRM and additional Xen-related plugins are available from OpenQRM's sponsor company, Qlusters, Inc., at `www.qlusters.com`.

In addition to these open source packages for Xen, commercial vendors such as IBM (`www-03.ibm.com/systems/management/director/extensions/vm.html`) and Platform Computing (`www.platform.com/Products/Platform.VM.Orchestrator/Product.Information/Overview.How.it.Works.htm`) are also working on products to support deploying and managing Xen as well as other virtualization solutions.

Distribution-Specific Xen Management Software

Distributions such as Debian and Ubuntu provide a good selection of command-line tools for creating Xen filesystems images, such as the `debootstrap` command discussed in Chapter 6. Although these tools are useful, they are not administrative environments. Distributions such as Fedora and OpenSUSE include graphical tools that make it easy to create and monitor the status of Xen virtual machines. The following sections introduce the tools provided by each of these Linux distributions and provide pointers to more detailed information.

Fedora and Red Hat Xen Tools

Fedora and Red Hat provide several custom tools for creating and managing local Xen virtual machines. They provide the command-line virsh and virt-install tools to facilitate creating Xen images and starting, stopping, and managing Xen virtual machines. They also provide a graphical tool, the Virtual Machine Manager, that truly simplifies creating and working with local virtual machines. The Virtual Machine Manager is executed as the `virt-manager` command, and must be run with root privileges. Figure 7-4 shows the main screen for the Virtual Machine Manager, showing the execution status of domain0 and a domainU Fedora 7 guest.

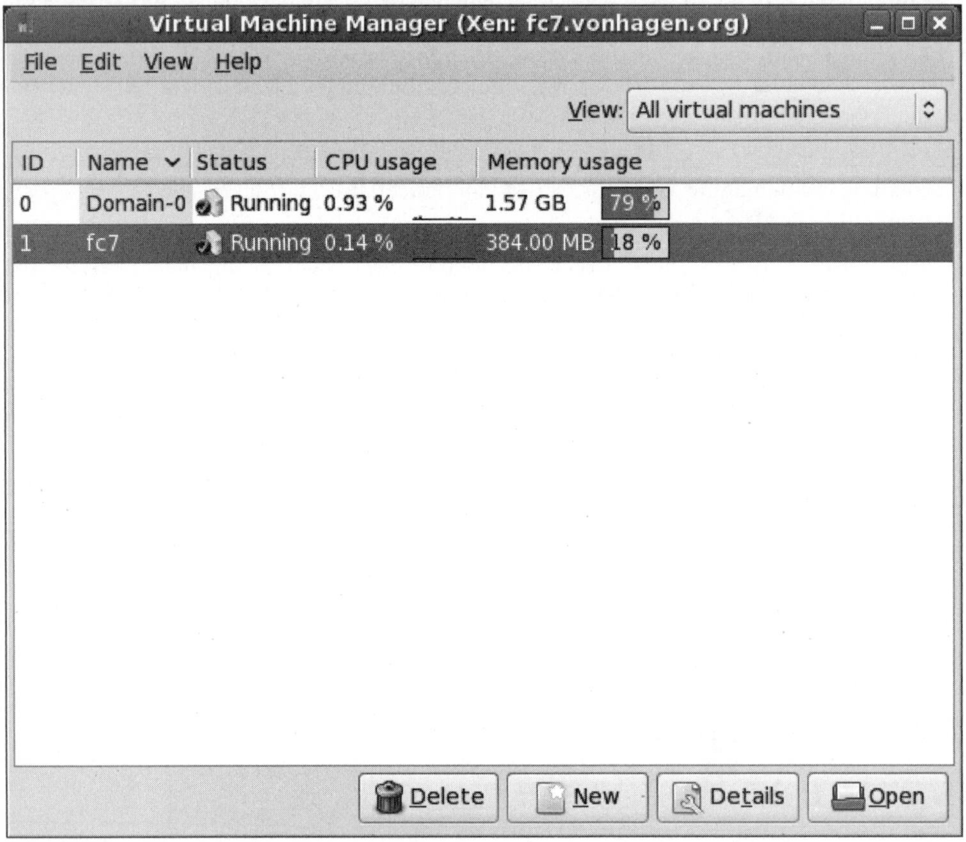

ID	Name ∨	Status	CPU usage	Memory usage	
0	Domain-0	Running	0.93 %	1.57 GB	79 %
1	fc7	Running	0.14 %	384.00 MB	18 %

View: All virtual machines

Virtual Machine Manager (Xen: fc7.vonhagen.org)

File   Edit   View   Help

Delete   New   Details   Open

Figure 7-4

Fedora and Red Hat have taken a slightly more flexible approach to virtualization than other Linux distributions. They have implemented an intermediate virtualization library, libvirt, that provides a relatively virtualization-neutral interface for their tools. Although the Fedora virtualization tools currently work only with Xen and KVM virtual machines, this approach provides a flexible management environment with plenty of room for future expansion.

At the moment, the primary limitations of the virt-manager are that it does not support more advanced operations such as migration, and that its creation and use of disk images and partitions is tailored towards whole-disk QEMU images into which an operating system must be installed, rather than simply supporting using existing partitions, filesystem images, standalone kernels, and so on.

SUSE Xen Tools

As discussed in Chapter 6, the standard YaST2 administrative framework used by Novell's SUSE Linux distributions makes it easy to install SUSE distributions into a directory. These directories can easily be used as filesystems for paravirtualized Xen systems. However, SUSE also provides a YaST2 module designed solely for creating and managing Xen virtual machines. You can start this module by executing the yast2 xen command as root from any command prompt, or by starting YaST2, selecting System from the Groups list, and clicking the Xen Hypervisor module. Figure 7-5 shows the initial screen for this YaST2 module.

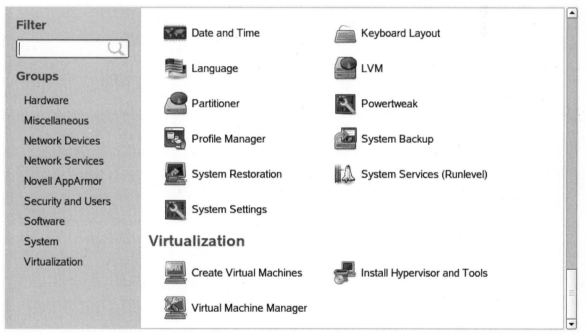

Figure 7-5

Novell's YaST2 module for Xen is much more flexible than Fedora's Virtual Machine Manager, although it is specifically tailored toward Xen. It enables you to create virtual machines using operating system install disks, existing partitions, existing disk images, and so on. Unfortunately, as with the Virtual Machine Manager, it is currently limited to creating and managing domainU guests running on the local system. It does not provide a complete, network-aware virtualization management solution that includes support for advanced operations such as migration, which are required in enterprise Xen environments.

Summary

The development of good administrative and managerial software for virtualization products such as Xen is going to be one of the keys to the long-term success of these technologies. The enterprise-wide adoption and success of Xen will require sophisticated, out-of-the-box management and monitoring solutions that can automatically detect problems, notify administrators and, if necessary, migrate virtual machines from one host to another.

This chapter discusses the Xen administration and management utilities that are included as part of open source Xen distributions and highlights promising open source and commercial software products for Xen monitoring and management. The chapter also discusses graphical Xen management software that has been developed by Linux distribution vendors such as Red Hat and Novell, and is included with both their open source and commercially supported distributions.

8

Xen Networking

Creating, configuring, and managing physical networks can be extremely complex. Routing, performance, and security issues can combine to require fairly complex networking topology to support restricted-access networks, hosts in a demilitarized zone between public and private networks, and so on.

Although virtual machines on a single physical host typically share network interfaces, using virtual machines doesn't free you from worrying about networking and security issues. All virtual machines on a given physical host require unique network addresses, just as physical hosts do. Xen virtual machines use virtual network interfaces to connect their emulated network devices to a network. Xen provides you, as a system administrator, with a great deal of flexibility in how you configure network interfaces, create virtual networks, and how your virtual machines communicate with the physical network. This makes it very easy for you to logically connect multiple virtual machines in different ways — such as segregating them on their own virtual network and using multiple Ethernet interfaces on your domain0 system to route different types of virtual and physical traffic — and to efficiently and securely connect virtual networks to your physical network.

This chapter discusses the various ways that Xen supports connecting domainU (and domain0) hosts to your network. It discusses the different types of networking configurations provided out-of-the-box with Xen, the configurable aspects of the Xen daemon and a virtual machine's networking setup, and provides some general tips for creating different types of secure, manageable networks of domain0 and domainU hosts.

> This chapter discusses Xen networking as implemented in the open source Xen distribution. Some Linux distributions, most notably Fedora and therefore Red Hat, have extensively customized Xen by adding intermediate virtualization libraries, which change the way that Xen networking is configured and used. If Xen network configuration doesn't work for you as described in this chapter, check any Xen and virtualization-related release notes for your distribution and the Xen daemon configuration file for information about any ways in which Xen's networking may have been "improved" by your distribution.

Overview of Xen Networking

Out of the box, the open source version of Xen supports three basic ways of configuring network connectivity between your domainU hosts and an external network:

❑   **Bridged networking:** Your domain0 and domainU hosts are connected to a virtual network (one virtual network per physical network interface). The virtual network is then connected to your physical network. This is Xen's default networking configuration. Bridging and the scripts used by Xen to configure this approach to networking your domainU guests are discussed in more detail in the "Bridged Networking" section later in this chapter.

❑   **NAT networking:** Your domain0 host is configured to forward IP packets. Iptables are used to configure your domain0 kernel to do masquerading using IP packet filter rules that are configured in your domain0 kernel. Optionally, Dynamic Host Configuration Protocol (DHCP) can be used to assign IP addresses to your domainU guests from a different network address family than the one used on your domain0 system. NAT and the scripts used by Xen to configure this approach to networking your domainU guests are discussed in more detail in the "NAT Networking" section later in this chapter.

❑   **Routed networking:** Your domain0 host is configured to forward IP packets. A static route, for routing packets addressed to each domainU's IP address, is added as each domainU host comes up. Routed networking and the scripts used by Xen to configure this approach to networking your domainU guests are discussed in more detail in the "Routed Networking" section later in this chapter.

As discussed in Chapter 7, the `network-script` parameters in the Xen daemon's primary configuration file (`/etc/xen/xend-config.sxp`) determine which of these approaches to networking you are using. The choices provided with a standard Xen installation are the following:

❑   `network-bridge`: Bridged networking (the default)

❑   `network-nat`: NAT networking

❑   `network-route`: Routed networking

If you don't want to use one of the out-of-the-box approaches to Xen networking, the `network-script` parameter can also be set to the name of your own configuration script. If you need to extensively customize one of these scripts, it's a good idea to make a copy of the default script with a different name in the `/etc/xen` directory, configure the Xen daemon to use your new script by changing the value of the `network-script` parameter to the name of your new script, and then modify the copy. This enables you to keep a pristine copy of the original script on your system for reference purposes as well as providing a copy for your modifications.

All of these approaches to networking require that your domainU guests have an IP address, whether assigned statically or dynamically, and that the Ethernet device with that address on each domainU guest is associated with a unique virtual network interface on your domain0 host. The next section provides an overview of virtual network interfaces and how they are mapped to the primary Ethernet interface in your domainU guests.

Virtual Network Interfaces

As discussed in Chapter 7, the `vif-script` parameter in the Xen daemon's primary configuration file (`/etc/xen/xend-config.sxp`) identifies the script that is used to create the virtual network interface for each Xen virtual machine. Each of the three default Xen networking scripts (`network-bridge`, `network-nat`, and `network-route`) have an associated script (`vif-bridge`, `vif-nat`, and `vif-route`, respectively) that is used to create and configure a virtual network interface for a Xen virtual machine when the associated type of networking is being used. However, the default naming convention for these virtual network interfaces is the same regardless of which script is being used.

By default, the virtual network interface in domain0 that is used by each virtual machine is named `vifDomID.Interface`, where `Interface` identifies a specific network interface. For example, on domain0 systems with a single Ethernet interface, the virtual network interface associated with domain0 is typically named `vif0.0`, showing that it is the virtual interface for the domain whose ID is 0 and that it is associated with the first Ethernet interface (eth0 on Linux systems) on that machine (because we all count from 0).

Each time that you start a domainU system, the hotplug system creates a new virtual network interface named `vifDomID.Interface` on domain0, based on the ID of the domain that you are starting and the Ethernet interface on that domainU system with which that virtual network interface is associated. The hotplug system then maps that interface to the domainU system's Ethernet interface. For example, the first domainU guest started on that system will use the virtual network interface vif1.0, showing that it is the virtual interface for domain 1 and that it represents the first Ethernet device on the domainU guest. If you create another Ethernet device on your domain 1 system, the virtual interface on your domain0 system that it will be associated with is vif1.1. All of the network interfaces associated with a domainU system persist until that domainU system is shut down, at which point they are deleted by the same `vif-script` that created them in the first place.

How traffic from domainU guest systems is handled on your domain0 host and routed to outside networks depends on the type of networking that you are using on your domain0 system. This is explained in the next few sections.

Bridged Networking

Linux includes built-in support for bridging, which is a mechanism to connect multiple networks and network segments. A good analogy for a bridge is a network hub to which multiple systems and networks can be connected, but which has a single connection to the rest of the network. Packets are forwarded across a bridge based on Ethernet address rather than IP address, which means that all Ethernet protocols can travel over a bridge. The user-space software for creating and configuring bridged networks on Linux systems is the brctl tool, which is part of the Bridge Utilities package that was discussed as a Xen prerequisite in Chapter 3.

Figure 8-1 shows a simple Xen bridge using the bridge and virtual network names used by the open source version of Xen.

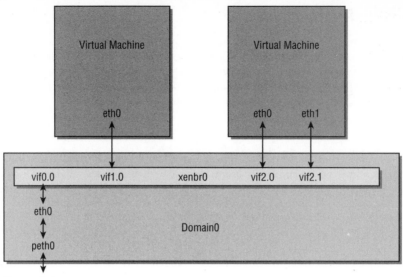

Figure 8-1

When using bridging with Xen, the `network-bridge` script performs the following actions when the Xen daemon starts on your domain0 host:

❏   Uses the `brctl` utility to create a new bridge named xenbr0. (This bridge is known as virbr0 on Fedora and Red Hat systems.)

❏   Uses the `ip` command to copy all IP address information from the physical Ethernet interface (for example, eth0) to the associated virtual network interface (for example, veth0).

❏   Uses the `ip` command to shut down the physical Ethernet interface.

❏   Uses the `ip` command to rename the existing physical Ethernet interface (for example, eth0) to another, more obvious, physical Ethernet interface name (for example, peth0). This enables you to continue to differentiate between the actual physical Ethernet device for domain0 and the bridged domain0 interface that feeds traffic to your domainU guests.

❏   Uses the `ip` command to rename the virtual network interface (for example, veth0) to the default physical Ethernet interface name (for example, eth0). The Linux networking subsystem and many network applications require that physical Ethernet devices with default names such as eth0 exist on a system.

❏   Uses the `brctl` command to add the new name of the original physical Ethernet interface (for example, peth0) and the user-level virtual network interface (for example, vif0.0) that is associated with the internal virtual network interface (for example, veth0) to the bridge.

❏   Brings up the bridge, the new physical Ethernet interface (for example, peth0), and the virtual network interface (for example, vif0.0).

❏   Deletes all routes associated with the original physical Ethernet interface (for example, eth0) and recreates them as being attached to the bridge.

Once the bridge and domain0 connections are available, bringing up any domainU guest causes the Xen daemon to run the `vif-bridge` script, which does the following:

❑ Associates the Ethernet device in the domainU guest with `vifDomID.Interface` (for example, vif1.0).

❑ Attaches `vifDomID.Interface` to the bridge (for example, xenbr0).

❑ Brings up the `vifDomID.Interface` for the guest (for example, vif1.0).

❑ If antispoofing is enabled (which it is by default in Xen 3.0), uses the `iptables` command to set up kernel packet forwarding rules so that incoming packets are forwarded to the bridge.

When using bridged network and the default `network-bridge` script, you can display status information about your system's networking using the `network-bridge status` command, which displays output like the following:

```
# /etc/xen/scripts/network-bridge status
============================================================
3: eth0: <BROADCAST,MULTICAST,UP,LOWER_UP> mtu 1500 qdisc noqueue
    link/ether 00:16:ec:ca:ae:20 brd ff:ff:ff:ff:ff:ff
    inet 192.168.6.64/24 brd 192.168.6.255 scope global eth0
    inet6 fe80::216:ecff:feca:ae20/64 scope link
        valid_lft forever preferred_lft forever
13: xenbr0: <BROADCAST,MULTICAST,UP,LOWER_UP> mtu 1500 qdisc noqueue
    link/ether 2e:c0:5f:6d:6d:00 brd ff:ff:ff:ff:ff:ff
  bridge name     bridge id          STP enabled         interfaces
xenbr0          8000.2ec05f6d6d00         no              vif5.0
                                                          tap1
                                                          vif4.0
                                                          tap0
                                                          vif3.0
                                                          vif2.0
                                                          vif1.0
                                                          peth0
                                                          vif0.0
  192.168.6.0/24 dev eth0  proto kernel  scope link  src 192.168.6.64
169.254.0.0/16 dev eth0  scope link
default via 192.168.6.1 dev eth0
      echo 1 >/proc/sys/net/ipv4/ip_forward
iptables -t nat -A POSTROUTING -o ${netdev} -j MASQUERADE
        [ "$dhcp" != 'no' ] && dhcp_start
Kernel IP routing table
Destination   Gateway       Genmask         Flags Metric Ref  Use Iface
192.168.6.0   0.0.0.0       255.255.255.0   U     0      0      0 eth0
169.254.0.0   0.0.0.0       255.255.0.0     U     0      0      0 eth0
0.0.0.0       192.168.6.1   0.0.0.0         UG    0      0      0 eth0
============================================================
```

In order to produce this particular information, the script ran the following commands:

❑ `ip addr show eth0`: To get IP information about the current default Ethernet device

❑ `ip addr show xenbr0`: To get IP information about the default bridge

❑   `brctl show xenbr0`: To display information about the interfaces that are associated with the default bridge

❑   `ip route list`: To display basic IP routing information for the default Ethernet device

❑   `route -n`: To quickly display kernel routing information by using network addresses rather than names

Bridged networking can seem complex if you aren't used to it, but it is traditionally a great mechanism for linking different networks together, whether physical or virtual. When using Xen virtualization, bridged networking provides a great deal of flexibility that can simplify routing packets between Xen domains, virtual networks, and external networks.

> **If you manually create and delete bridges, you may find that Xen will recreate some of them for you each time that you reboot, depending on the state of your system when you last restarted it. The Xen daemon stores persistent state information in file in** `/var/lib/xend/state`**. If deleted bridges are being recreated automatically, purge them from the file** `/var/lib/xend/state/network.xml`**, delete the bridge manually, and then restart the Xen daemon.**

NAT Networking

Network Address Translation (NAT, also known as Native Address Translation or Masquerading) is a technique by which computer systems that do not have externally visible IP addresses can route their traffic through a Linux host that does. As this traffic is forwarded by the externally visible system, that system uses specific port numbers to keep track of the internal system from which the traffic originated. Return traffic for those ports is then routed back to the internal host from which it actually originated. As you might expect, this requires that packet addresses and checksums be recomputed and rewritten in outgoing packets from the internal hosts and in incoming packets that need to be forwarded to those internal hosts.

The user-space software for creating and configuring NAT networking on Linux systems is the iptables tool, which is installed by default on most Linux systems and therefore was not identified as a Xen prerequisite in Chapter 3 because NAT networking is not the default networking mechanism for Xen. You can install the iptables package using your Linux distribution's package management system.

Xen's NAT networking is much simpler than bridged networking, but is much less powerful. NAT can cause problems or prevent connectivity in network services that require all participants to have "real" IP addresses, and can also make the use of stateless protocols such as UDP more complex because UDP routing works at a completely different level than TCP.

If you are already running a DHCP server when using NAT networking with Xen, you can optionally configure the DHCP server on your domain0 host to hand out IP addresses on the 10.0.0.0 subnet to domainU hosts via DHCP by modifying the `dhcp=${dhcp:-no}` entry in the `/etc/xen/scripts/network-nat` file to be `dhcp=${dhcp:-yes}`.

When using NAT networking with Xen, the `network-nat` script performs the following actions when the Xen daemon starts on your domain0 host:

❑   Activates IP forwarding on your system using the following command:

```
# echo 1 > /proc/sys/net/ipv4/ip_forward
```

❑   Sets up a post-routing rule in your kernel that activates masquerading on the physical network interface for your domain0 system (for example, eth0).

❑   Optionally restarts DHCP with a new configuration file entry that will enable all domainU guests to get IP addresses on the 10.0.0.0 subnet via DHCP.

Once NAT has been configured in the domain0 kernel, bringing up any domainU guest causes the Xen daemon to run the `vif-nat` script, which does the following:

❑   Associates the Ethernet device in the domainU guest with `vifDomID.Interface` (for example, vif1.0).

❑   Configures routing for the `vifDomID.Interface` (for example, vif1.0) and its associated IP address to flow through the domain0 host.

❑   Configures the domain0 host to also handle (proxy) Address Resolution Protocol (ARP) requests for the `vifDomID.Interface` (for example, vif1.0) using a command such as the following:

```
# echo 1 > /proc/sys/net/ipv4/conf/vif1.0/proxy_arp
```

❑   Optionally writes an entry for your domainU host to your DHCP configuration file and restarts DHCP so that the domainU host will get the IP address used when configuring routing.

Xen's NAT networking script does not provide a general status information option because you can check your domain0 system's system log (`/var/log/messages`) or the DHCP leases file (usually `/var/lib/dhcpd/dhcpd.leases`) to determine the status of DHCP on your system. You can also use the `iptables -L` command to view information about the masquerading rules that are in use in your kernel.

Routed Networking

Routing enables packets for one host to be sent through another host that understands how to send those packets to their destination and also how to redirect responses to the host for which they are intended.

Support for routing is built into the Linux kernel. The user-space software for configuring routing on Linux systems is the `route` command, which is installed by default on all Linux systems where TCP/IP networking is used, and therefore was not identified as a Xen prerequisite in Chapter 3 because TCP/IP networking is not the default for Xen. The `route` command is found in the net-tools package.

Using routed networking with Xen is very similar to using NAT, except that traffic to your domainU guests is directly routed through your domain0 host, and that a static route to each domainU guest must exist in the domain0 kernel's routing table.

When using routed networking with Xen, the `network-route` script performs the following actions when the Xen daemon starts on your domain0 host:

❑   Activates IP forwarding on your system using the following command:

```
# echo 1 > /proc/sys/net/ipv4/ip_forward
```

❑   Configures the domain0 host to also handle (proxy) ARP requests for domainU using a command such as the following:

```
# echo 1 > /proc/sys/net/ipv4/conf/eth0/proxy_arp
```

Once routing has been configured in the domain0 kernel, bringing up any domainU guest causes the Xen daemon to run the `vif-route` script, which does the following:

❑   Copies the IP address from the gateway interface (for example, eth0) to `vifDomID.Interface` (for example, vif1.0).

❑   Brings up `vifDomID.Interface` (for example, vif1.0).

❑   Adds a static route for domainU's IP address to the `vifDomID.Interface` (for example, vif1.0).

Routed networking is a common networking model for Xen systems that avoids the connectivity problems that NAT networking can introduce for systems that require specific IP addresses or that use stateless protocols such as UDP.

Specifying Parameters for Xen Network Startup

The preceding sections discussed the scripts used for different types of Xen networking, both for initial networking setup and for per-domainU virtual networking interface configuration. All of these scripts can be edited to change their default behavior, but they can also be called with specific arguments in order to customize specific aspects of their behavior without modifying the scripts themselves.

The next two sections describe the arguments with which the general networking setup and per-domain virtual interface configuration scripts can be called, and discuss where you must make changes in order to automate calling the appropriate scripts with the parameters that describe your specific networking environment.

General Parameters for Xen Networking Startup

As suggested in the "Overview of Xen Networking" section at the beginning of this chapter, the easiest way to make extensive changes in the default behavior of any of the standard Xen networking setup scripts (`network-bridge`, `network-nat`, or `network-route`) is to create a copy of one of these scripts, make your changes in the copy, and then modify your Xen daemon's configuration file (`/etc/xen/xend-config.sxp`) to invoke your new script rather than the default one. However, there are actually two other ways of customizing Xen's default networking setup:

❑   By passing parameters to the existing network scripts inside the `network-script` entry in the Xen daemon's configuration file

❑   By creating a custom script that simply calls the existing scripts multiple times with different parameters

The approach you take depends on how extensively you are customizing Xen's default networking. If you are simply changing aspects of a standard networking configuration that are already available as parameters to the script that creates it, you should simply pass those parameters in your Xen daemon's configuration file. However, if you are configuring multiple bridges, using multiple Ethernet interfaces, or something similar, you should create your own script from scratch and use it to call the default Xen networking setup scripts one or more times, changing the behavior of each call to the default scripts by passing parameters to them. The following table shows the parameters that are available and which of the default Xen networking scripts accept them.

Parameter	Meaning	Default Value	network-bridge	network-nat	network-route
vifnum	The number of the virtual device to associate with this bridge	0	Yes	No	No
bridge	The name of the bridge to use	xenbr$vifnum	Yes	No	No
netdev	The physical network interface to use to a bridge or as a gateway	eth$vifnum	Yes	Yes	Yes
antispoof	Whether to use iptables to prevent spoofing	no	Yes	Yes	Yes
dhcp	Whether to directly modify the local DHCP configuration	no	No	Yes	No

In both of the customization approaches, passing parameters to the existing scripts enables you to leverage the capabilities that they already provide and eliminates needing to modify them directly. This, in turn, eliminates the chance of accidentally losing your modifications after an upgrade.

If you are making changes only to the default behavior of an existing script, those changes are available as parameters to that script, and you are only setting up a single bridge or gateway, you can change the entry in the Xen daemon's configuration file to pass those parameters to an existing script when it is being called, as in the following example. This configuration file change tells the Xen daemon to use the `network-bridge` script to initiate networking, using the Ethernet interface eth1 when creating the default bridge xenbr0 instead of the default Ethernet interface eth0:

```
(network-script 'network-bridge netdev=eth1')
```

Note that you need to enclose the name of the script and the parameters that you want to pass to it within single or double quotation marks because the Xen daemon's `network-script` configuration parameter accepts only a single argument.

If you need to call the existing scripts multiple times, you will still need to create your own script, even if you can configure the behavior of an existing script by specifying parameters. As an example, suppose that you want to use bridged networking but need to set up two bridges, one on each of two Ethernet interfaces. Your replacement Xen network setup script could then simply look like the following:

```
#!/bin/sh
dir=$(dirname "$0")
$dir/network-bridge" "$@" vifnum=0 netdev=eth0 bridge=xenbr0
$dir/network-bridge" "$@" vifnum=1 netdev=eth1 bridge=xenbr1
```

Assuming that this script was written to a file named `dual-bridge.sh`, you would make that file executable (`chmod 755 dual-bridge.sh`) and then modify the Xen daemon's configuration file to use this script by commenting out any existing `network-script` statements in the configuration file and adding the following line:

```
(network-script dual-bridge.sh)
```

If you have changed basic aspects of Xen's networking configuration, you will also need to ensure that different domains are aware of those changes when they start. Making this information available to Xen guest domains when they start is done by passing parameters in the virtual interface (vif) statement in the domainU configuration files. Parameterizing vif statements is discussed in the next section.

Parameters for domainU Networking Startup

Customizing how the virtual networking interface for each Xen domainU guest is configured is done by specifying parameter/value pairs in the Xen configuration file or by setting explicit values in the XenStore if you are using a version of Xen that permanently stores per-domain information in the XenStore. This section focuses on configuration file changes in standard SXP format because this is the standard mechanism for making such changes that is used by the standard open source Xen distribution.

The parameters that you can specify as part of a vif statement in a domainU configuration file are the following:

❑   **Bridge name:** Specified using the command `bridge=variable`, where variable is the name of the bridge that you want to use. This parameter enables you to specify a specific bridge on which the host should appear.

❑   **IP:** Specified using `ip=variable`, this enables you to permanently associate specific IP addresses with specific domainU guests. If you are using DHCP for network information assignment, you have to ensure that any addresses that you permanently assign are outside the DHCP allocation ranges for your network.

In DHCP environments, it is usually unnecessary to use this parameter because you can hardwire the Media Access Control (MAC) address for a domainU guest and then associate a specific IP address with that MAC address in your DHCP configuration file. See the "DHCP Tips for Xen Environments" section later in this chapter for more information about easily identifying and working with Xen domainU guests in DHCP configuration files.

❏ **MAC address:** Specified using the command `mac=variable`, where variable is two hexadecimal digits that represent the contents of a byte in the Ethernet interface's MAC address. If you do not specify a MAC address, the Xen daemon generates a random address from the range 00:16:3E: variable. This address range has been assigned by IEEE to XenSource as an Organizationally Unique Identifier (OUI). Having a MAC address range that is dedicated to Xen virtual machines provides some interesting opportunities for DHCP Ethernet address configuration, as discussed in "DHCP Tips for Xen Environments" later in this chapter.

> Note that the MAC address range used by Xen domainU hosts does not apply to physical Ethernet devices on domain0 systems or which are passed through to domainU systems. Physical Ethernet devices have their own MAC addresses, determined by their manufacturer. The 00:16:3E MAC address range only applies to virtual network interfaces created in Xen on Xen virtual machines.

❏ **Model:** Specified using `model=variable`, where variable is one of the specific types of network cards emulated by QEMU. This option is therefore only useful if you are using ioemu as the type of network driver you are using. Valid values are `lance`, `ne2k_isa`, `ne2k_pci`, `rtl8139`, and `smc91c111`. The default value is `ne2k_pci` if you are using QEMU (i.e., ioemu) network drivers.

❏ **Script:** Specified using `script=variable`, this enables you to identify a particular script as the one used to set up the network interface for a domainU guest, by overriding the `vif-script` directive in your Xen daemon configuration file.

❏ **Type:** Specified using `type=variable`, where variable is `ioemu` (using QEMU's network drivers), `netfront` (the default, which uses the split Xen frontend/backend network drivers), or (rarely) an arbitrary string identifying a specific network emulation/driver mechanism that you want to use. When running non-Linux domainU guests, you usually want to specify `type=ioemu` to ensure that Xen uses QEMU network device emulation rather than trying to use the standard Xen split `netfront` network drivers.

❏ **Virtual interface (vif) name:** Specified using `vifname=variable`, where variable is typically something in the standard Xen virtual interface name format, such as fc60.1. These names are traditionally auto-generated each time a domain is started — being able to hardcode them to specific virtual machines simplifies many administrative and reporting operations because it provides logging continuity across system restarts.

> The DHCP and IP settings are meaningful only in paravirtualized virtual machines because hardware virtual machines use the system-specific network configuration mechanisms specified during HVM installation to obtain and specify their IP address.

Regardless of the operating system you are running in your virtual machine, it is generally useful to manually assign a specific MAC address and vifname to each domainU guest, to simplify network tracking and logging throughout your network environment. Similarly, if you use multiple bridges and want a domainU to appear on only one of them, it is necessary to specify the bridge name. A sample configuration file statement that sets all of these would look like the following:

```
vif = [ 'vifname=llamp0.1,mac=00:16:3E:00:00:66,bridge=local' ]
```

This setting is from the domainU configuration file for a Linux LAMP Web server that assigns it a specific vifname that can be used for high-level network monitoring such as the monitoring performed by SNMP. SNMP is a specific MAC address that enables integration with a DHCP server and assigns this guest's virtual network connection to a specific virtual bridge to simplify routing, localize certain types of traffic, and expedite inter-domainU communication.

A similar vif configuration file declaration for a hardware virtual machine running Microsoft Windows XP might be the following:

```
vif = [ 'vifname=xp0.1,mac=00:16:3E:00:00:12,type=ioemu' ]
```

This specifies that the vifname would be xp0.1 (to help identify communication through this virtual network interface as coming from an XP system, to give it a specific MAC address to help identify requests coming from this network interface in the system logs, and to specify that QEMU's ioemu network driver be used).

You can also specify multiple sets of parameters if you want to create multiple network interfaces for a single domainU guest, but put each on a separate bridge, as in the following example:

```
vif=[ 'mac=00:16:3e:00:00:13',
      'mac=00:16:3e:00:00:14,bridge=local ]
```

This would create two network interfaces, putting the interface with the MAC address 00:16:3e:00:00:13 on the default bridge (usually xenbr0), and putting the interface with the MAC address 00:16:3e:00:00:14 on the bridge named local.

> **For fine-tuning the network bandwidth associated with your domainU guests, you can use the vif statement's rate option, which looks like** `rate=10BM/s`**. This would limit this domainU guest to 10 megabytes per second. By limiting the rate on some domainU guests, you can effectively provide more bandwidth to a domainU guest whose rate you do not limit.**

Using Multiple Ethernet Cards with Xen

The previous section discussed the parameters that you can specify in the vif entry of your domainU configuration files in order to modify the network configuration for each Xen guest. You can take advantage of this parameterization to efficiently use multiple Ethernet cards in your Xen environment.

Bridged networking is the default networking implementation of Xen because it is administratively simple, requiring no manual changes to your routing tables, existing firewall and iptable rules, and so on. However, when using bridged networking with a single Ethernet card in your domain0 system, all domainU guests can see the packet traffic from all domains running on that system. This may not be an issue in pure server environments, where domainU guests only run server processes and their only authorized users are therefore system administrators. However, if you have actual user accounts on any of your domainU systems, you may want to better segregate your domainU guests so that users on those systems do not have access to all traffic on a single bridge.

Using multiple Ethernet cards in a single domain0 host to eliminate access to selected network traffic from other domains is as simple as installing multiple Ethernet cards in your domain0 host, creating a custom `network-script` that creates separate bridges, each of which is associated with a specific Ethernet card, and then manually modifying the configuration files for your Xen domainU guests so that they are located on specific bridges. For a domain0 system with three Ethernet cards, your custom `network-script` would look something like the following:

```
#!/bin/sh
dir=$(dirname "$0")
"$dir/network-bridge" "$@" vifnum=0 netdev=eth0 bridge=xenbr0
"$dir/network-bridge" "$@" vifnum=1 netdev=eth1 bridge=xenbr1
"$dir/network-bridge" "$@" vifnum=2 netdev=eth2 bridge=xenbr2
```

The Xen configuration file for each host that you want to attach to a specific bridge would therefore contain at least something like the following:

```
vif = ['bridge=xenbrvariable']
```

You would replace variable with the number of the bridge to which you wanted to attach that domainU guest. For reporting purposes, you probably want to hardwire the MAC address and perhaps the vifname (as discussed in the previous section). Specifying a bridge for each guest would enable you to manually distribute your domainU guests across the available bridges as you see fit for both security and load-balancing purposes.

When using multiple Ethernet cards on a single subnet, you will need to ensure that each gets a unique Ethernet address on that subnet. If you are using multiple Ethernet cards, multiple subnets, and DHCP for network information assignment, you will need to make sure that your DHCP server is correctly configured to hand out IP addresses based on the subnet associated with the bridge to which specific Xen guests are attached. See the "DHCP Tips for Xen Environments" section later in this chapter for more detailed information.

Virtual, Non-Routable Subnets for Xen Guests

For additional security, you may want to attach some number of domainU guests to a virtual network that uses its own non-routable IP addresses and is completely local to a specific domain0 system. You can do this by setting up a bridge on your domain0 host that is not associated with a physical Ethernet device. Using this model, no one can access your domainU guests unless they add a specific route to their machine's routing table that identifies the specific IP address on a specific domain0 system as the gateway for your virtual network. This also enables you to manually distribute your domainU guests across multiple available bridges as you see fit for both security and load-balancing purposes.

To do this, you would create a local bridge on your domain0 system using commands such as the following:

```
# brctl addbr local
# brctl setfd local 0
# brctl stp local off
# ip link set local arp off
# ip link set local multicast off
# ip link set local up
# ifconfig local 10.0.0.1 netmask 255.255.255.0 broadcast 10.0.0.255 up
# echo "1" > /proc/sys/net/ipv4/ip_forward
```

These commands do the following:

1. Create a bridge named local. This name is completely arbitrary, but should be illustrative, so I tend to use "local" as the name for local, virtual bridges.

2. Set the forwarding delay for packets from this bridge to 0 so that they will be instantly forwarded.

3. Turn off spanning tree protocol, which can slow down performance and is only necessary if you have multiple potential paths between single hosts.

4. Turn off ARP caching on the bridge itself.

5. Turn off multicasting so that broadcasts will not be sent across the bridge.

6. Bring up the bridge.

7. Assign the IP address 10.0.0.1 to the bridge so that this can easily be used as a gateway to and from the virtual subnet 10.0.0.X.

8. Guarantee that your system will forward packets between Ethernet interfaces.

Once you have done this, you would simply modify the domainU configuration files for the Xen guests that you want to put on the virtual subnet to contain at least the following:

```
vif = ['bridge=local']
```

As mentioned in previous sections, you probably want to hardwire the MAC address and perhaps the vifname for your domainU guests for reporting and tracking purposes. You will also need to make sure that your DHCP server is correctly configured to distribute IP addresses to your domainU guests based on the subnet associated with the local bridge, rather than getting IP addresses on your public network segment. See the "DHCP Tips for Xen Environments" section later in this chapter for more detailed information.

Assuming that you want hosts other than your domain0 host to be able to access hosts on the bridge, you will also need to configure your domain0 host to do IP packet forwarding. This is easily done through the following command:

```
# echo "1" > /proc/sys/net/ipv4/ip_forward
```

Finally, you will need to integrate the bridge setup commands and IP forwarding activation into your domain0 system startup mechanism. If you are using the default bridging for some domainU guests and a virtual bridge for others, you can simply create your own `network-script` that calls the standard `network-bridge` script and then executes the commands to set up your local bridge. This could be as simple as the following:

```
#!/bin/sh
dir=$(dirname "$0")
"$dir/network-bridge" "$@" vifnum=0 netdev=eth0 bridge=xenbr0
brctl addbr local
brctl setfd local 0
brctl stp local off
ip link set local arp off
ip link set local multicast off
ip link set local up
ifconfig local 10.0.0.1 netmask 255.255.255.0 broadcast 10.0.0.255 up
echo "1" > /proc/sys/net/ipv4/ip_forward
```

The Linux bridging mechanism automatically sets up the correct routes to access domains on any bridge as part of the bridge setup. However, only the domain0 host knows about any virtual networks that are present on that machine but are not associated with a physical Ethernet interface. Therefore, you must manually set up a route to your virtual network on any other system that needs access to the virtual machines located on that virtual subnet. You can do this by issuing a `route` command like the following on each machine:

```
# route add -net 10.0.0.0 netmask 255.255.255.0 dev eth0 gw 192.168.6.64
```

You should change `10.0.0.0` in this example to the actual Class B or C IP address of your virtual network. You may need to change the Ethernet device, depending on how that system connects to the host on which the virtual subnet is located. You must also specify a gateway address that is an externally visible IP address on the domain0 host where the virtual subnet is located.

Virtual LANs and Xen Guests

Traditional local area networks (LANs) consist of a set of systems, wireless access points, and connectivity equipment (such as hubs and switches) that are physically connected to a single local area network and are therefore part of a single address family and broadcast domain. Virtual LANs (VLANs) enable systems to participate in multiple LANs at the same time by creating logical networks that these hosts can belong to, independent of physical connectivity and location. The VLAN standard, 802.1q, is an open standard for 100-Mbps or faster Ethernet networks, and has been supported in Linux systems since the days of the 2.4 kernel.

VLANs work by tagging network frames with a 4-byte VLAN identifier that identifies the VLAN with which they are associated. VLAN-enabled switches and Linux bridges use this VLAN identifier to determine the VLAN to which packets should be sent, which therefore makes the packet available to the appropriate host on that VLAN. Only hosts on the same VLAN will see broadcast packets on that VLAN.

Using VLANs can simplify the topology of a network by replacing traditional segmentation hardware, such as switches and hubs. The most common use of VLANs today is to enable remote systems to participate in multiple networks at the same time, which allows remote office, home office workers, and road warriors to share network resources independent of their physical location and local network configuration.

In order to use VLANs on Linux systems, your kernel must be built with the CONFIG_VLAN_8021Q configuration symbol set to y (built-in) or m (built as a loadable kernel module). The open source Xen distribution kernels are built with this option as a module. You must also build or install the package containing user-space VLAN configuration tools, which is usually the vlan package. This package should be available in your Linux distribution's package management system. If it is not, you can get information about recent changes at www.candelatech.com/~greear/vlan.html, and you can download the latest version of the VLAN source code from www.candelatech.com/oss/.

> **Before setting up a VLAN or a VLAN connection on any Xen system, make sure that the 8021q kernel module is available on that system. If it is compiled into the kernel, you don't need to do anything. If it is compiled as a loadable kernel module, you need to load it by executing the** modprobe 8021q **command.**

To create a VLAN on a domain0 system, you typically do something such as the following:

1. Create a virtual network interface for the VLAN using a command like the following:

```
# /sbin/vconfig add eth0 66
```

This will create a virtual network device named eth0.66 for the VLAN.

2. Associate a unique IP address with the new virtual network interface, using a command like the following:

```
# /sbin/ifconfig eth0.66 172.16.0.1 netmask 255.255.255.0 up
```

3. Create a bridge with which the VLAN traffic will be associated using a command like the following:

```
# /etc/xen/scripts/network-bridge netdev=eth0.66 bridge=xen-vlan
```

4. Create and bring up similar Ethernet interfaces inside each domainU system that you want to connect to the VLAN. (Steps 1 and 2)

5. In the configuration file for each domainU system that you want to be on the VLAN, modify the vif entry so that it looks something like the following:

```
vif = [ 'bridge=xenbr0',
        'bridge=xen-vlan' ]
```

If you are using a Linux distribution that supports `/etc/sysconfig`, you can create the following `ifcfg-eth0` and `ifcfg-eth0.66` network configuration files in `/etc/sysconfig/network-scripts`, to automate the creation of the right Ethernet device in the future:

❑   `ifcfg-eth0`:

```
DEVICE=eth0
BOOTPROTO=dhcp
ONBOOT=yes
TYPE=Ethernet
```

❑   `ifcfg-eth0.66`:

```
DEVICE=eth0.10
BOOTPROTO=static
IPADDR=172.16.0.1
NETMASK=255.255.255.0
ONBOOT=yes
TYPE=Ethernet
VLAN=yes
```

You need to modify the Ethernet address in the second example to reflect the Ethernet address family that you are using on your VLAN.

Once you have your VLAN working, make sure that you add the necessary configuration steps to the Xen networking startup scripts on the domain0 system to ensure that the VLAN and bridge will come up automatically in the future.

Vnets

In addition to private, non-routable virtual networks and standard VLANs, Xen also supports vnets. Vnets emulate private LANs that domains can use, much like virtual private subnets or VLANs, but different from both in two significant ways.

First, vnets persist across domain0 restarts until they are explicitly deleted. This is because Xen vnets are created using an `xm` command and an external configuration file, but the information about the vnet is permanently stored in the XenStore until it is deleted.

Second, domainU guests that are connected to a vnet remain connected if domains are migrated. This is because Ethernet traffic on a vnet is actually tunneled inside packets on the physical network, and is therefore independent of per-domain0 network configuration.

Unfortunately, vnet support is not ready for prime time in the current open source Xen distribution available at the time of this writing. It is discussed in the official "Xen User's Manual" that accompanies the source code distribution of Xen. Vnets are a promising and powerful technology. You should check to see if the version of Xen that you install and build actually includes the Xen `vn` command that is used to configure vnets. If it is, check the Xen User's Manual for information on using them.

DHCP Tips for Xen Environments

One consequence of the different types of virtual networking that Xen supports is the need for different virtual hosts to be able to receive network configuration information that assigns them network addresses and related network configuration information for different networks. DHCP servers are the most common way of distributing IP address and related configuration information, but Xen and the use of multiple physical and virtual networks can make configuring your DHCP server more complex than it has been before.

This section is not intended to be a complete tutorial on DHCP server configuration. For some excellent online tutorials, see:

❑   Linux DHCP Server Configuration: `www.yolinux.com/TUTORIALS/DHCP-Server.html`

❑   How To Set Up A DHCP Server For Your LAN:
    `www.howtoforge.com/dhcp_server_linux_debian_sarge`

This section assumes that you are familiar with the syntax of basic DHCP configuration files (`dhcpd.conf`), such as the following example that distributes IP addresses and related network configuration information to 150 hosts on the 192.168.6. subnet:

```
ddns-update-style interim;
deny client-updates;
authoritative;
option domain-name "vonhagen.org";
option domain-name-servers  192.168.6.13, 208.67.222.222;
option routers 192.168.6.1;
option ntp-servers ntp-1.mcs.anl.gov;
default-lease-time 14400;
max-lease-time 172800;
subnet 192.168.6.0 netmask 255.255.255.0 {
  range 192.168.6.80 192.168.6.230;
}
```

To keep this example as simple as possible, I've left out the key, zone, and ddns-hostname information used to enable dynamic DNS updates and dynamically create hostnames. As you can see, this `dhcpd.conf` file makes most network configuration settings global, and simply identifies 192.168.6.80 through 192.168.6.230 as the range of available IP addresses that it will distribute to requests coming in through the 192.168.6.0 network.

When DHCP servers need to hand out addresses on different subnets, one common and simple solution is to run multiple DHCP servers, each listening to a single port or network number. However, this is not only inelegant, but can be hard to set up, maintain, and verify. A simpler solution is to modify a single DHCP server so that it can handle different types of incoming requests. For example, to support two networks, 192.168.6.0 and 10.0.0.0, you could change your configuration file to something like the following:

```
ddns-update-style interim;
deny client-updates;
authoritative;
option domain-name-servers  192.168.6.13, 208.67.222.222;
option ntp-servers ntp-1.mcs.anl.gov;
```

```
option domain-name "vonhagen.org";
default-lease-time 14400;
max-lease-time 172800;
subnet 192.168.6.0 netmask 255.255.255.0 {
  range 192.168.6.80 192.168.6.230;
  option routers 192.168.6.1;
}
 subnet 10.0.0.0 netmask 255.255.255.0 {
  range 10.0.0.80 10.0.0.230;
  option routers 10.0.0.1;
}
```

With this configuration file, you can insure that DHCP requests coming in from the 192.168.6.0 network receive IP addresses and gateway information for that network, while DHCP requests coming in from the 10.0.0.0 network receive network configuration information that is relevant to that network.

You can also force specific domainU guests to receive specific network configuration information based on their MAC address, which is important for domainU guests that are running server processes. For example, suppose the vif entry in the domainU configuration file for your domainU host looks something like the following:

```
vif = [ 'mac=00:16:3E:00:00:66', 'bridge=local' ]
```

You could assign that host a specific IP address by adding a stanza to your dhcpd.conf file like the following:

```
host samba {
      hardware ethernet 00:16:3E:00:00:66 ;
      fixed-address 10.0.0.66 ;
      option routers 10.0.0.1;
      option host-name "samba.vonhagen.org";
}
```

When adding specific host-stanzas to your DHCP configuration file, you must make sure that the fixed IP addresses that they contain are not in the range of IP addresses that you are dynamically allocating on that network.

You can also use some of the features that are supported by the DHCP configuration file to identify general classes of MAC addresses and handle them differently. This is especially convenient when working with Xen because all of Xen's dynamically allocated MAC addresses are of the form 00:16:3E:variable, as mentioned earlier. For example, suppose that you want all Xen domainU guests to get IP addresses on the 10.0.0.0 network, regardless of the network interface over which the request was received. You could do this with the following entries in your dhcpd.conf file:

```
class "xen" {
  match if (
    (substring(hardware,1,3) = 00:16:3E) );
}
subnet 10.0.0.0 netmask 255.255.255.0 {
    pool {
        allow members of "xen";
        range 10.0.0.80 10.0.0.230;
    }
}
```

In this example, the `class` statement puts requests into a class named `xen` if the first three bytes of their MAC address matches the standard Xen MAC address prefix, 00:16:3E. The pool statement in the 10.0.0.0 subnet stanza limits the hosts that will receive IP addresses in the range 10.0.0.80 to 10.0.0.230 to hosts that are members of the `xen` class.

Your completed DHCP configuration file would therefore look like the following:

```
ddns-update-style interim;
deny client-updates;
authoritative;
option domain-name-servers  192.168.6.13, 208.67.222.222;
option ntp-servers ntp-1.mcs.anl.gov;
option domain-name "vonhagen.org";
default-lease-time 14400;
max-lease-time 172800;
subnet 192.168.6.0 netmask 255.255.255.0 {
  range 192.168.6.80 192.168.6.230;
  option routers 192.168.6.1;
}
class "xen" {
  match if (
    (substring(hardware,1,3) = 00:16:3E) );
}
subnet 10.0.0.0 netmask 255.255.255.0 {
    pool {
        allow members of "xen";
        range 10.0.0.80 10.0.0.230;
    }
}
host samba {
    hardware ethernet 00:16:3E:00:00:66 ;
    fixed-address 10.0.0.66 ;
    option routers 10.0.0.1;
    option host-name "samba.vonhagen.org";
}
```

As you can see, this small DHCP configuration file actually contains a fair bit of intelligence. Many other conditionals are available to help you further customize a single DHCP configuration file so that it can efficiently serve a number of networks and different types of hosts.

Fine-Tuning Services on Xen Guests

Xen domainU guests provide a great way of reducing the demands on single servers by dedicating virtual hosts to providing specific services and handling specific types of requests. However, Xen guests are just as sensitive to the demands of multiple services and associated processes competing for a finite amount of network bandwidth as physical Linux hosts are. The next few sections provide some general guidelines that you can use to identify and eliminate extraneous services and associated network traffic on your Xen domainU guests, domain0 hosts, or any Linux host.

> Some of the network analysis tools discussed in the next few sections may not be installed on all of your domainU hosts by default, but the small amount of disk space that they require is well worth it if they can provide long-term performance and throughput benefits in per-system network load and general networking infrastructure.

Open Port and Active Server Minimization

Any open network port on your system indicates a potential entry point to that system. In this context, an open network port is a port on which some server is listening for and responding to requests. Two common ways of listing open ports when logged in on a machine are by using the lsof and netstat commands.

The lsof (list open files) command lists all open files on a Linux system. Its -i option tells the command to list all IP (Internet protocol) related files, and the -n option suppresses the mapping of IP addresses to host names for any established connection. (Avoiding these lookups improves the speed with which results are returned.) You then pipe the output of this command to the egrep command, selecting only those results that contain COMMAND (which gives you the headings for the various columns), TCP (a daemon that uses TCP to listen), and UDP (a daemon that uses UDP to listen). The following is sample output from the lsof command on a Red Hat Enterprise Linux (RHEL) 4 system:

```
# lsof -i -n | egrep 'COMMAND|TCP|UDP'
COMMAND     PID    USER   FD    TYPE DEVICE SIZE NODE NAME
portmap     1871    rpc   3u   IPv4   4428       UDP  *:sunrpc
portmap     1871    rpc   4u   IPv4   4431       TCP  *:sunrpc (LISTEN)
rpc.statd   1891 rpcuser  4u   IPv4   4468       UDP  *:32768
rpc.statd   1891 rpcuser  5u   IPv4   4457       UDP  *:795
rpc.statd   1891 rpcuser  6u   IPv4   4471       TCP  *:32769 (LISTEN)
sshd        2082   root   3u   IPv6   4945       TCP  *:ssh (LISTEN)
xinetd      2097   root   5u   IPv4   5007       TCP  *:auth (LISTEN)
xinetd      2097   root   6u   IPv4   5008       TCP  *:telnet (LISTEN)
xinetd      2097   root   8u   IPv4   5009       TCP  *:vnc (LISTEN)
ntpd        2113    ntp   4u   IPv4   5108       UDP  *:ntp
ntpd        2113    ntp   5u   IPv6   5109       UDP  *:ntp
ntpd        2113    ntp   6u   IPv4   5110       UDP  127.0.0.1:ntp
ntpd        2113    ntp   7u   IPv4   5111       UDP  192.168.6.233:ntp
sendmail    2132   root   3u   IPv4   5136       TCP  127.0.0.1:smtp (LISTEN)
cupsd       3427   root   0u   IPv4  10857       TCP  127.0.0.1:ipp (LISTEN)
cupsd       3427   root   2u   IPv4  10858       UDP  *:ipp
```

This output shows that the daemons running directly on this systems are portmap (RPC port mapper), rpc.statd (RPC status monitoring), sshd (secure shell), ntpd (network time protocol), sendmail (mail server), gdm (GNOME display manager), and cupsd (CUPS print daemon). In addition, the xinetd Internet services daemon is running the auth (remote identification daemon), telnet (network terminal), and vnc (virtual network computing) servers.

The netstat (network statistics) command provides very similar output when run on the same system. The -t option produces output for all TCP/IP ports, and the -u option produces output for all UDP ports. The -l option restricts the output to ports that are actively listening for connections. The -p option shows the program and process ID that owns the network connection. The following is sample output from the netstat command on a Red Hat Enterprise Linux (RHEL) 4 system:

```
# netstat -tulp
Active Internet connections (only servers)
Proto Recv-Q Send-Q Local Address             Addr    State   PID/Program name
tcp      0      0 *:32769                      *:*     LISTEN 1891/rpc.statd
tcp      0      0 *:sunrpc                     *:*     LISTEN 1871/portmap
tcp      0      0 *:auth                       *:*     LISTEN 2097/xinetd
tcp      0      0 *:vnc                        *:*     LISTEN 2097/xinetd
tcp      0      0 localhost.localdomain:ipp    *:*     LISTEN 3427/cupsd
tcp      0      0 *:telnet                     *:*     LISTEN 2097/xinetd
tcp      0      0 localhost.localdomain:smtp   *:*     LISTEN 2132/sendmail: acce
tcp      0      0 *:ssh                        *:*     LISTEN 2082/sshd
udp      0      0 *:32768                      *:*            1891/rpc.statd
udp      0      0 *:795                        *:*            1891/rpc.statd
udp      0      0 *:sunrpc                     *:*            1871/portmap
udp      0      0 *:ipp                        *:*            3427/cupsd
udp      0      0 rhel4.vonhagen.org:ntp       *:*            2113/ntpd
udp      0      0 localhost.localdomain:ntp    *:*            2113/ntpd
udp      0      0 *:ntp                        *:*            2113/ntpd
udp      0      0 *:ntp                        *:*            2113/ntpd
```

This list provides a bit more detail, but shows the same open ports and associated services as the lsof command.

A machine's internal view of the services that it provides should match those that an outside machine would see. To verify this, you can use the nmap (network mapping) command from another system. The -sT option does a TCP port scan, whereas the -sU option does a UDP port scan. Scanning the same machine from another system produces output such as the following:

```
# nmap -sTU 192.168.6.233
Starting nmap 3.81 ( http://www.insecure.org/nmap/ ) at 2006-07-30 16:42 EDT
Interesting ports on rhel4.vonhagen.org (192.168.6.233):
(The 3131 ports scanned but not shown below are in state: closed)
PORT         STATE            SERVICE
22/tcp       open             ssh
23/tcp       open             telnet
111/tcp      open             rpcbind
111/udp      open|filtered    rpcbind
113/tcp      open             auth
123/udp      open|filtered    ntp
631/udp      open|filtered    unknown
795/udp      open|filtered    unknown
32768/udp open|filtered       omad
MAC Address: 00:E0:18:76:C0:B4 (Asustek Computer)
Nmap finished: 1 IP address (1 host up) scanned in 1475.249 seconds
```

Although the `nmap` command can't identify the services associated with ports 631 and 795, the local machine output from the `lsof` and `nmap` commands shown previously identifies these as a print daemon and the `rpc.statd` command, respectively.

Given that all of this output agrees, the next step is to analyze the services that are available to determine whether they are all necessary and, if not, what to do about them:

❑   The cupsd (print) and sendmail (mail server) daemons shown in the `netstat` and `lsof` output are not visible in the `nmap` output. The `netstat` and `lsof` output confirms that they are only listening on the local loopback interface, and are therefore not accessible from outside the machine, and thus should not pose a security problem. If performance is an issue for the machine you're analyzing, sendmail is useful for local mail delivery, but you may want to terminate the CUPS daemon if no one will be printing from this machine.

❑   The ssh (secure shell) daemon provides a secure mechanism for remote logins and supports encrypted communication, so that's fine.

❑   The telnet daemon (network terminal) represents an older protocol used to establish remote connections, and typically uses unencrypted communications. Some newer versions of telnet support secure authentication and communication mechanisms such as Kerberos, but regardless, this is an unnecessary service because SSH is also supported, and you should therefore shut this down.

❑   The rpcbind (port mapper) and rpc.statd (port 795) daemons are useful in NFS environments only. If the machine you're analyzing is not an NFS client, these should be shut down.

❑   The auth daemon can be useful in analyzing problems with network clients, but can also provide intruders with information about the users of your systems. However, some FTP and other network clients essentially require it. It should either be disabled or started with its -n option, which causes it to display numeric user IDs rather than user names.

❑   The ntp (network time) daemon is used to synchronize the clock across systems on a network, but has been exploited in the past. You can replace this daemon with running the `ntp -q` command at boot time, which queries and synchronizes with a time service once and then exits.

❑   The omad daemon on port 32768 is initially puzzling, but cross-checking against the `lsof` and `netstat` output shows that port 32768 is being used for `rpc.statd` queries, and therefore should be eliminated by shutting down the rpc.statd daemon.

The next step in this process is to go to the virtual machine that you're analyzing and determine where and when these daemons are being started, so that you can terminate the extraneous services (auth, cupsd, portmap, rpc.statd, telnet, and vnc).

Disabling xinetd-Based Network Services

The `lsof` and `netstat` output discussed in the previous section identified the auth, telnet, and vnc services as being run by the xinetd Internet services daemon. This daemon is a general-purpose network daemon that waits for incoming requests on selected ports and then starts the services associated with those ports. The xinetd daemon is an enhanced, more secure, and more flexible descendant of a similar daemon, known as inetd, that was used on many earlier Linux and Unix systems.

The concept of "TCP wrappers" was originally introduced with xinetd. This is a library that is transparent to the end user but provides system administrators with fine-grained control over the hosts that can (or cannot) access a specific network service and associated daemon. The TCP wrappers library does this by checking the files /etc/hosts.allow and /etc/hosts.deny for any restrictions on the hosts that can access a service before allowing a connection to be established. The TCP wrappers concept has proven to be so useful that most modern Linux distributions compile all network daemons, including stand-alone daemons such as sshd and NFS daemons such as portmap, with the TCP wrappers library.

The configuration files for all daemons managed by the xinetd daemon are located in the directory /etc/xinetd.d. This directory contains the following files on a sample RHEL system:

```
# ls
amanda          daytime       gssftp                 rexec   tftp
amandaidx       daytime-udp   klogin                 rlogin  time
amidxtape       dbskkd-cdb    krb5-telnet            rsh     time-udp
auth            echo          krb5-telnet.rpmsave    rsync   vnc
chargen         echo-udp      kshell                 swat
chargen-udp     eklogin       ktalk                  talk
cups-lpd        finger        ntalk                  telnet
```

The files in this directory are text files that contain startup instructions for each associated service. Each of these files contains an entry that identifies whether the associated service is disabled on the target machine. To double-check which of these services are actually enabled, you would execute commands such as the following:

```
# cd /etc/xinetd.d
# grep disable * | grep no
auth:           disable = no
krb5-telnet:    disable       = no
vnc:            disable       = no
```

The output will be different on your system, but it should look fairly similar to this example. This shows that the auth daemon, a Kerberos-enhanced version of the telnet daemon, and the vnc server are all started in response to incoming requests on the ports that they are associated with. As noted earlier, you need to disable these servers.

To disable services so that they are not started by xinetd, simply edit each file in a text editor and change no to yes in each disable entry.

You will need to restart (or stop and start) xinetd to pick up the changes to the services that it will support. You can do this by executing the following command:

```
# /etc/init.d/xinetd restart
```

Reducing the number of running processes and available services on a given system also has the fringe benefit of returning the amount of memory required by those services to the pool that is available to the system itself.

Troubleshooting Xen Networking

Troubleshooting Xen networking is essentially the same as debugging networking in a non-virtual environment, except that the use of virtual interfaces and, optionally, various types of bridges simply adds a few extra places that you need to check. This section provides some general suggestions for diagnosing, debugging, and resolving common network problems in the Xen environment. This section focuses on resolving bridged networking problems.

When attempting to diagnose connectivity problems between domain0 and domainU hosts, the first thing to check is that the domains that you're interested in are either in the block (b, waiting for input) or running (r) state, which you can see by using the xm list command, as in the following example:

```
# xm list
Name                   ID   Mem VCPUs     State   Time(s)
Domain-0                0   900    1      r-----  36349.9
FC6-IMG-PV              5   256    1      -b----     16.4
FC6-YUMIMG-PV           6   256    1      -b----     20.7
XP-LV-HVM               9   256    1      -b----     91.6
```

In this case, everything is okay, but if the domain you're having problems communicating with is marked as paused (p), you can unpause it by executing the xm unpause *DomainID* command, where *DomainID* is the ID of the domain you're interested in. Once the domain shows that it is blocked or running, try communicating with it again (using the ping *IPADDRESS* command is the simplest test, where *IPADDRESS* is the IP address of your host). If you can ping the host successfully, congratulations! If not, read on.

The next thing to check is that there are no firewall rules on your domain0 host that may be interfering with communication between your hosts. You can use the iptables -L command as the root user to see all of the iptables rules that are currently active on your domain0 system, as in the following example:

```
# iptables -L
Chain INPUT (policy ACCEPT)
target     prot opt source       destination
Chain FORWARD (policy ACCEPT)
target     prot opt source       destination
ACCEPT     all  --  anywhere     anywhere     PHYSDEV match --physdev-in vif5.0
ACCEPT     all  --  anywhere     anywhere     PHYSDEV match --physdev-in vif5.1
ACCEPT     all  --  anywhere     anywhere     PHYSDEV match --physdev-in vif6.0
ACCEPT     all  --  anywhere     anywhere     PHYSDEV match --physdev-in vif9.0
Chain OUTPUT (policy ACCEPT)
target     prot opt source                   destination
```

Unless you've manually specified a vifname in your domainU configuration file, the name of the virtual interface for your domain will be vif*DOMAINID*.*ETHERNETINTERFACE*. (You can also use the xm network-list *DOMAINID* command to verify the virtual network interface being used by a specific domain. See Appendix A for more information.)

In this example output from the `iptables` command, the only relevant rules are forwarding rules that accept traffic to and from anywhere, so that isn't a problem. If you see other rules that reject or reroute traffic, you can drop them temporarily using the `iptables -F` command. If you can communicate with the domain in question, then you simply need to examine your system's iptables configuration and either identify and modify an existing rule or add a new rule that accepts communication to and from that domain's network interface. One common problem is that you must permit packets on TCP port 590*variable*, where *variable* is the number of the display for your domainU guests (usually, the DomainID). VNC servers listen for connections from a VNC viewer on these ports and, depending on the IP address for VNC that is specified in your Xen daemon's configuration file (127.0.0.1, the loopback interface, by default), you should check that no rules interfere with these ports on that Ethernet interface.

When modifying iptables rules, remember that unless you specify the vifname for a domain in that domain's configuration file, the vifname will change the next time you start that domain, and its virtual interface will be named based on its new DomainID. You can either make your rules flexible enough to support any Ethernet interface, or you can permanently add any new rules by specifying the vifname in the vif entry in your domain's configuration file, and then use that vifname in your iptables rules.

The subject of creating and deciphering iptables rules is both large and outside the scope of this book. For more detailed information about iptables rules, take a look at the following tutorials:

❑ Oskar Andreasson's iptables tutorial: `http://iptables-tutorial.frozentux.net/iptables-tutorial.html`

❑ Yolinux.com's iptables tutorial: `www.yolinux.com/TUTORIALS/LinuxTutorialIptablesNetworkGateway.html`

As a sidenote, if you want to set up iptables-like rules on a bridge, you want to use ebtables (Ethernet bridge tables) rather than iptables. See `http://ebtables.sourceforge.net` for detailed information about ebtables. This Web site provides good introductory documents as well as HOWTOs and links to various articles about the interaction between bridging, ebtables, and iptables.

The next thing to check is that the virtual interface for your domainU host is actually bound to a bridge. You can use the `brctl show` command to identify the bridges that are available on your system and the virtual interface attached to each of them, as in the following example:

```
# brctl show
bridge name     bridge id               STP enabled     interfaces
local           8000.ffffffffffff       no              vif5.1
                                                        vif5.0
                                                        vif6.0

xenbr0          8000.b28151d627c3       no              tap0
                                                        vif9.0
                                                        peth0
                                                        vif0.0
```

If your domain's virtual Ethernet interface doesn't appear in this list, try attaching it to the bridge manually by using the `brctl addif BRIDGE INTERFACE` command, where *BRIDGE* is the name of the bridge on which the interface should appear and *INTERFACE* is the name of your virtual interface. Once you get communications working, you can check your network and vif startup scripts (specified by the network-script and vif-script variables in your Xen daemon's configuration file) to determine why your virtual interface wasn't automatically added to the correct bridge.

When checking your network and vif startup scripts, it is often useful to modify them so that they display each command as they execute it. You can do this by changing the first line of each script from the standard #!/bin/bash entry to #!/bin/bash -x. This will cause them to run verbosely, so that you can see each command as it executes, and more easily determine where a problem is being caused. You should, of course, change them back to run silently when you're finished debugging.

The next thing to check is the Ethernet device configuration on your domainU guest. If you're using bridged networking and its virtual interface wasn't connected to a bridge, it is probably not configured at all, but checking the configuration is a debugging necessity anyway. You can use the ifconfig command to get interface configuration information if your domainU guest is a Linux system, or use the ipconfig command if you're having networking problems with a domainU Microsoft Windows HVM.

Remember that you need to check this on the guest, not on your domain0 system. Linux output will look like the following sample:

```
# ifconfig eth0
eth0      Link encap:Ethernet  HWaddr 00:16:3E:00:00:66
          inet addr:192.168.6.66  Bcast:192.168.6.255
Mask:255.255.255.0
          inet6 addr: fe80::216:3eff:fe00:66/64 Scope:Link
          UP BROADCAST RUNNING MULTICAST  MTU:1500  Metric:1
          RX packets:411 errors:0 dropped:0 overruns:0 frame:0
          TX packets:463 errors:0 dropped:0 overruns:0 carrier:0
          collisions:0 txqueuelen:1000
          RX bytes:33566 (32.7 KiB)  TX bytes:85652 (83.6 KiB)
```

Windows output looks like this sample:

```
C:\> ipconfig
Ethernet adapter Local Area Connection:
        Connection-specific DNS Suffix  . : vonhagen.org
        IP Address. . . . . . . . . . . . : 192.168.6.84
        Subnet Mask . . . . . . . . . . . : 255.255.255.0
        Default Gateway . . . . . . . . . : 192.168.6.1
```

You can get more detailed information on a Windows system by running ipconfig /all, but the basic ipconfig command provides enough information to see your basic networking configuration.

In both of these examples, eth0 is configured (and was assigned via DHCP), so all is well regarding basic connectivity. However, if your Ethernet interface does not have an IP address, try restarting networking on the domainU guest, either by executing the command /etc/init.d/network restart on a Linux system or by using the Control Panel's Network Connections applet on a Windows system. If restarting networking resolves the problem, you should check your startup scripts and the Xen daemon's logs (/var/log/xen/xend.log and /var/log/xen/xend-debug.log) to see if any errors occurred that can help you diagnose the problem.

If your domainU guest is still not getting an IP address and you are using DHCP, first check that your DHCP server is actually running. If it is, check the domain0 system log (/var/log/messages) to see if there is any information about DHCP requests from your domainU guest. Successful messages will look like the following and will also include timestamp and host information:

```
dhcpd: DHCPDISCOVER from 00:16:3e:00:00:66 via local
dhcpd: DHCPOFFER on 10.0.0.66 to 00:16:3e:00:00:66 via local
dhcpd: DHCPREQUEST for 10.0.0.66 (10.0.0.1) from 00:16:3e:00:00:66 via local
dhcpd: DHCPACK on 10.0.0.66 to 00:16:3e:00:00:66 via local
```

If you are using DHCP and do not see messages like these, then your domainU guest is still not communicating with your domain0 system. Try terminating the domainU system (xm destroy DomainID) and then starting a utility such as tcpdump to watch for traffic on your system's physical Ethernet interface when you restart the domain. To do this, open a separate terminal window and, as the root user or via sudo, execute the tcpdump -vv -i INTERFACE command, where INTERFACE is the name of the bridge that your domainU guest is connecting to. You should see output like the following as the client attempts to obtain an IP address via DHCP:

```
# tcpdump -vv -i local
tcpdump: listening on local, link-type EN10MB (Ethernet)
13:07:57.052270 IP (tos 0x0, ttl  64, id 0, offset 0, flags [DF], \
  proto: UDP (17), length: 576) 0.0.0.0.bootpc > \
  255.255.255.255.bootps: [no cksum]
  BOOTP/DHCP, Request from 00:16:3e:00:00:66 (oui Unknown), \
  length: 548, xid:0x92c68383, flags: [none] (0x0000)
      Your IP: 255.255.255.255
      Server IP: 255.255.255.255
      Client Ethernet Address: 00:16:3e:00:00:66 (oui Unknown) [|bootp]
```

If you do not see any traffic on this bridge, then your domain's Ethernet interface is still not being connected to the virtual interface, or the virtual interface is still not being set up on the bridge. If your domainU guest is a HVM Windows system, make sure that you specified ioemu networking because Windows guests need to emulate networking connectivity via QEMU's networking emulation. If this is the case, try specifying another Ethernet driver (such as ne2k_pci) using the model=CARD vif configuration item discussed in "Parameters for domainU Networking Startup" earlier in this chapter.

If you can communicate between your domainU guest and domain0 but not with any other hosts, check the routing table on your domainU guest. On a Linux system, you can do this using the route command, as in the following example:

```
# route -n
Kernel IP routing table
Destination     Gateway     Genmask         Flags Metric Ref   Use Iface
10.0.0.0        0.0.0.0     255.255.255.0   U     0      0     0 eth0
169.254.0.0     0.0.0.0     255.255.0.0     U     0      0     0 eth0
```

The output of this command shows that there is no default route to hosts outside the 10.0.0.0 subnet. To correct this problem, add a default route using a command such as the following where variable is the IP address of your gateway):

```
# route add default gw GATEWAYIP
```

You should now be able to ping external hosts.

On a Windows system, you can use the `route print` command from a DOS shell, as in the following example:

```
C:\> route print
===========================================================================
Interface List
0x1 ........................... MS TCP Loopback interface
0x2 ...00 16 3e 31 1f 18 ...... Realtek RTL8139 Family PCI Fast Ethernet NIC
===========================================================================
Active Routes:
Network Destination        Netmask          Gateway       Interface  Metric
          0.0.0.0          0.0.0.0      192.168.6.1    192.168.6.84     20
        127.0.0.0        255.0.0.0        127.0.0.1       127.0.0.1      1
      192.168.6.0    255.255.255.0     192.168.6.84    192.168.6.84     20
     192.168.6.84  255.255.255.255        127.0.0.1       127.0.0.1     20
    192.168.6.255  255.255.255.255     192.168.6.84    192.168.6.84     20
        224.0.0.0        240.0.0.0     192.168.6.84    192.168.6.84     20
  255.255.255.255  255.255.255.255     192.168.6.84    192.168.6.84      1
Default Gateway:         192.168.6.1
===========================================================================
Persistent Routes:
  None
```

This particular host is located on the 192.168.6.0 subnet, and therefore uses 192.168.6.1 as its gateway (obtained through DHCP). However, if you are using local subnets on your domain0 host, you will need to add a rule that provides a route to them because you don't want them going through your default gateway. You could do this with a command like the following, assuming that you want to add a route for a 10.0.0.0 subnet that is local to your domain0 host:

```
C:\> route add 10.0.0.0 mask 255.255.255.0 192.168.6.64
```

In this example, 10.0.0.0 is the subnet that you want to be able to connect to, and 192.168.6.64 is the IP address of your domain0 host, on which the local subnet is located.

If you are routing between subnets on your domain0 host, make sure that IP forwarding is enabled on the domain 0 host. As mentioned earlier, this is done using the following command:

```
# echo "1" > /proc/sys/net/ipv4/ip_forward
```

Finally, if networking is working correctly but you are seeing weird problems, such as incrementing names for your Ethernet devices after each reboot, you should look in files such as `/etc/iftab` or `/etc/udev/rules.d/30-net_persistent_names` for entries for the Ethernet interfaces that are not being used, and delete or rename them appropriately. This was a problem in some older Xen distributions, especially when using udev, but it may still appear, depending on the type of system that you are using for your domain0 host. Similarly, some systems store MAC or IP address mappings in files in `/etc/sysconfig/network`. You may need to rename or delete these to guarantee that the right network interface is getting the IP address that you expect.

Network debugging can be complex, but the basic techniques explained in this section should help you figure out where to look, use the appropriate commands to obtain network and connectivity information, and find solutions to the most commonly encountered Xen networking problems.

Summary

This chapter explores the approaches to Xen networking that are provided with the open source Xen distribution, explaining how each works and providing a detailed discussion of Xen's virtual network interfaces. It discusses using parameters in startup scripts and Xen domain configuration files to customize Xen networking and virtual interface startup, and using multiple Ethernet cards, virtual private networks, and VLANs with Xen. Subsequent sections discuss DHCP configuration for Xen and multiple networks, and various ways of guaranteeing that your domainU systems aren't running any network-related processes that you aren't actually using. The chapter concludes by discussing various tools and techniques for debugging and resolving networking and connectivity problems to and from domain0 and domainU guests.

9

Advanced Virtual Machine Configuration

Up to this point, most of this book has focused on providing background information, helping you get Xen installed on your domain0 system, and getting your first few domainU guests up and running. Assuming that all of this has been successful, this section dives into some advanced topics. Some of these topics are optimization-related (tweaking GRUB settings, managing memory, and so on), and others are procedural topics about tasks that you don't have to worry about right away, but which will probably become important to you as you expand and fine-tune your Xen implementation (how to add new hardware in domain0 and use it in domainU systems, how to work with X, and how to use Xen security policies). This chapter is still hands-on. The next chapter focuses on the more theoretical aspects of rolling out Xen: integrating it with your policies, SLAs, and procedures; and so on.

> This chapter discusses many different configuration settings for paravirtualized and HVM Xen guests. If you are using Xen's lifecycle management from the command line or a configuration tool (such as virt-manager) that stores its configuration information in the XenStore, you will need to update the XenStore configuration information for a domain before this new setting will actually take effect. This is most easily done from the command line by backing up your configuration information in XML or SXP format, deleting the old configuration by domainU name, and then reloading your configuration file into the XenStore.

domain0 and domainU Memory Management in Xen

On vanilla Linux systems, the amount of physical memory that is present in a system is detected during the boot process. Some of this memory is allocated as contiguous sections for the use of the running kernel and device drivers, some is allocated for internal purposes such as DMA buffers, and the remainder is divided into pages that can subsequently be allocated to user-space processes. This process is very similar in Xen, except that the hypervisor performs the initial sizing and allocation of memory, initially allocating all unused memory to domain0. When additional memory is required by a domainU system (or when domainU memory is freed if a domainU system is terminated), physical memory can be reclaimed by the hypervisor through a technique known as memory ballooning, which moves pages of memory from one virtual machine to another, as required.

It is important to detect the total amount of physical memory on a system so that the kernel can use this value to correctly size some of its internal data structures. However, memory detection works very differently on domainU systems, which do not actually probe physical memory, because the memory that they use is memory that is allocated to them by the hypervisor based on initial and maximum memory parameters. For domainU systems, this is the reason that the xm command and Xen configuration files enable you to set both the maximum amount of memory that can ever be allocated to a domain and the current amount of memory that is used by a domain.

When creating or starting a domainU guest, the kernel's memory-related data structures are sized to the value of the maxmem variable (if it is set in your domainU configuration). If this variable is not set, the maximum amount of memory available to that domainU guest is set to the same value as its initial memory allocation (the value of the memory variable in its configuration). Graphical tools for defining virtual machines also enable you to set both of these values, but they don't expose the internal names of the variables that you are setting.

Controlling domain0 Memory Use

When allocating memory to domainU guests, the Xen hypervisor initially tries to allocate free memory on your system, and then attempts to allocate memory that is currently associated with domain0. Reallocating memory from domain0 to a domainU guest is done via the memory ballooning driver, and will continue until any minimum memory size that has been set for domain0 is reached. Correctly sizing the amount of memory that can be used by domain0 can help eliminate the need to resize the amount of memory available to domain0, which results in increased performance and eliminates the chance that deallocating memory from a running domain0 will cause applications or domain0 itself to crash.

If you can determine the amount of memory that your domain0 system will use, you can specify the amount of memory that will be allocated to that system by using the dom0_mem=*VALUE* parameter on the GRUB kernel command line for the Xen hypervisor. For example, the following GRUB entry specifies that domain0 will be allocated 1GB of memory:

```
title XEN 3.1.0
root (hd0,5)
kernel /boot/xen-3.1.0.gz noreboot dom0_mem=1G
module /boot/vmlinuz-2.6.18-xen root=/dev/sda6 ro
module /boot/initrd-2.6.18-xen.img
```

The units in which domain0 memory can be specified are B (bytes), K (kilobytes), M (megabytes), or G (gigabytes). If no units are specified, the value is assumed to be expressed in kilobytes.

The maximum amount of memory that you want to allocate to domain0 can be specified in one of four ways:

❏ As a minimum value, such as dom0_mem=min:384M. This guarantees that domain0 is initially allocated 384MB of memory, but does not place any upper limit on memory allocation to domain0.

❏   As a maximum value, such as `dom0_mem=max:1G`. This places a limit of 1GB on the amount of memory that can be allocated to domain0, but does not impose any initial or minimum allocation restrictions.

❏   As a range of values, such as `dom0_mem=min:384M,max:1G`. This defines both upper and lower limits on the amount of memory that can be allocated to domain0.

❏   As an explicit value, such as `dom0_mem=1G`. This specifies the amount of memory that will be initially allocated to domain0. This value is also a maximum and minimum value — domain0 memory will not be reclaimed by the hypervisor for reallocation to domainU guests.

> **When specifying the amount of memory for domain0, it is important not to confuse the `dom0_mem=VALUE` GRUB option with Xen's `mem=VALUE` GRUB option. The latter sets an explicit limit on the amount of physical memory that Xen will see in your machine. Any physical memory above this limit will be permanently ignored (until you adjust this value and reboot the system, of course).**

See the "GRUB Boot Options for the Xen Hypervisor" section in Chapter 4 for detailed information about other Xen-related boot options for GRUB.

Fine-Tuning Linux Memory Use

Appendix A discusses all of the available `xm` commands, including the `mem-set` command. If you are running out of sufficient memory to start all of the domainU guests that you want to run on a given domain0 system, the best solution is to purchase and install additional memory. However, it is also important that you use memory as efficiently as possible in domain0 and the domainU guests that you are running on a physical machine. This section discusses some ways in which you can see how much memory a system is using and whether or not it really needs all of the memory that is currently allocated to it.

The most detailed guide to memory use on a Linux system is the file `/proc/meminfo`. This file provides up-to-date information about the total amount of physical memory that is visible on a given system, the amount of memory that is currently in use, the amount of swap space used and available on a given system, and much more. On a newly started domainU guest, you can get a good idea of the minimum amount of memory required by a system by subtracting the `MemFree` value from the `MemTotal` value. Similarly, the `free` command (`/usr/bin/free`) provides another view of this same information. The `free` command is part of the procps package, and is therefore installed on almost every modern Linux desktop or server system.

You can use the `free` command's `-o` option to hide buffer usage information, and the `-m` option to summarize memory usage in megabytes, for ease of interpretation, as in the following example:

```
# free -o -m
            total    used    free  shared  buffers   cached
Mem:         1417    1406      10       0      301      497
Swap:        2000       0    1999
```

This sample output shows that, of 1417MB of physical memory, this system is currently using 1406MB. It also shows that the system has hardly used any of the 2GB of swap space that is available to it. Unless throughput is absolutely critical, this suggests that the amount of memory allocated to this system could be decreased, so that the system will use its swap space (virtual memory) rather than keeping everything in physical memory. This also suggests that the system may not need as much swap space as you have allocated to it. Freeing up 1GB of swap space is not very significant unless you are using `file` or `tap:aio` devices to hold the swap space for a given domainU system.

In addition to the output of the `free` command, the `top` command (also a part of the procps package) provides some useful summary information about system resource usage at the "top" of its output, which looks like the following:

```
top - 12:38:48 up 34 days, 14:41, 17 users, load average: 0.00, 0.02, 0.00
Tasks: 176 total,  2 running, 174 sleeping,  0 stopped, \ 0 zombie
Cpu(s): 1.6%us, 0.5%sy, 0.3%ni, 96.1%id, 1.5%wa, 0.0%hi, \ 0.0%si, 0.1%st
Mem:   1451008k total,  1402520k used,    48488k free, \ 306676k buffers
Swap:  2048276k total,      312k used,  2047964k free, \ 474528k cached
```

This displays similar output to the `free` command, but provides some additional information. For example, this shows that a relatively large number of processes are running, but sleeping, on this system. This suggests that you may want to examine your system's startup scripts or active processes (also shown by the `top` command), to see if there are any unnecessary processes being started on your system. Minimizing the number of running processes is a straightforward way of reducing memory use on a given system.

When attempting to optimize memory use on a system, you should check memory usage when the system first comes up, and compare this to memory usage a day or two after it has been running whatever services you want to run on the system. Active processes typically allocate additional memory as they run, and you will want to have a clear picture of how much memory a given Xen domain needs when it is first started (the memory setting), and how much it may eventually need after running for a while (the `maxmem` variable).

When working with Xen, you may eventually encounter a situation where the domain0 kernel does not see all of the physical memory that is actually present in your system. This typically occurs on 32-bit systems when booting a version of Xen and a domain0 Linux kernel that were not compiled with PAE (Physical Address Extension) support. By default, 32-bit Linux kernels can access only 4GB of memory, whereas 64-bit systems can theoretically access up to 16 Exabytes of memory, although 64GB of memory is the limit built into recent Linux kernels. 32-bit Linux kernels use PAE to see up to 64GB of physical memory, although individual processes can have no more than 4GB of memory per process.

To see the maximum amount of physical memory available on a 32-bit system, make sure that the `XEN_TARGET_X86_PAE` option is set to `y` when building Xen. See the "domain0 and domainU Kernel and Binary Considerations" section later in this chapter for more information on potential limitations on the amount of memory that is visible to different Linux kernels and user-space programs.

Accessing New and Removable Storage in domainU Guests

As discussed in "XenStore and Related Utilities" in Chapter 7, the ability to monitor name/value pairs in the XenStore enables the use of the XenStore as an event-driven mechanism for sharing status and device information between domain0 and your domainU guests. One excellent example of this is the ability to dynamically add and remove different types of devices from domainU guests using `xm` subcommands such as `block-attach`, `block-configure`, `block-detach`, `network-attach`, and `network-detach`. When you attach, detach, or modify a block (storage) or network device, the associated `xm` command actually modifies the XenStore and then notifies the target domainU of what is effectively a hotplug, "new hardware" event.

The sections of Appendix A on the `xm block-attach`, `xm block-configure`, and `xm network-attach` commands provide detailed information about these commands and their syntax, along with a few examples. This chapter provides task-oriented, HOWTO information to help you use these commands to perform the most common types of tasks that you may want to do when using Xen.

Mounting and Unmounting Additional Block Devices

The `xm block-attach` command enables you to attach block devices that were not part of the initial configuration of a domainU system so that the domainU system can mount them and access their contents. In traditional UNIX terms, block devices are random-access storage devices as opposed to character devices, which can only be read sequentially. In practical terms, block devices are things such as physical disk partitions (IDE, PATA, SATA, SCSI, and so on), removable storage media (such as CDs, DVDs, and the occasional floppy disk), and network storage accessed via the network block device drivers.

Attaching an additional block device is usually done for temporary purposes, such as installing software, making local copies of files and directories without impacting the network, and so on. However, if your domainU hosts are using Xen's lifecycle management support, information about block devices that have been associated with domainU guests are also stored in the XenStore, and are therefore "permanent," maintaining that association until they are detached using the `xm block-detach` command. Like any filesystem on Linux domainU guests, partitions and other storage that have been manually mounted must be manually mounted again after a reboot, but the domainU guest will still recognize the block device after a restart without reissuing an `xm block-attach` command.

Attaching an additional block device to a domainU guest is very different from dedicating hardware to a domainU guest. In the former case, you must issue commands in domain0 to export a device that domain0 knows about to one or more domainU guests. When dedicating hardware to a domainU guest, domain0 is essentially unaware of that hardware, and the hypervisor's virtualization layer maps a specific device to a specific domainU guest. Although storage interfaces and associated storage can be used by a domainU guest by either exporting them to the guest or by dedicating them to a specific guest, exporting block devices provides greater flexibility than dedicated hardware, enabling block devices to be used by a number of domainU guests, one at a time, without requiring that you load or unload drivers, restart the guests, and so on.

To make a new block device available to a domainU guest, some basic conditions must be satisfied:

❏ The block device must not already be mounted as a writable device in your domain0 system.

❏ The block device must not already be attached as a writable device to any other domainU system.

❏ The domainU guest must provide a driver for whatever filesystem is located on the block device (unless you are going to reformat the block device in the domainU guest).

If these conditions are satisfied, you can export a block device to a domainU guest using a command like the following:

```
# xm block-attach 4 phy:/dev/sda1 /dev/xvda1 w
```

As discussed in detail in Appendix A, the arguments to the xm block-attach command are: the domain to which you want to attach the block device, a *type:device* identifier for the block device that you want to export, the name that the device should have on the target domainU guest, the read/write mode with which you want to export the device, and (optionally) the identifier for the domain that hosts the device (which defaults to domain0).

The read/write mode in which you export a device is typically one of r (read-only) or w (read/write). When using fixed storage devices and specifying the name of the device on the target system, make sure that you do not specify the name of a device that is already in use on that system. As discussed in the next section, "Changing CDs and DVDs," fixed and removable block devices work slightly differently when they are attached to a new domainU system because CD/DVD drives are usually predefined on domainU guests, and you are therefore changing the media associated with an existing device definition rather than creating a new one.

Once you have exported a new block device to a Linux domainU guest, you must mount that block device in that virtual machine so that you can access it, just like any Linux disk partition or other block device. This is done with the mount command, as follows:

```
# mount -t FSTYPE DEVICE MOUNTPOINT
```

FSTYPE is the filesystem type, and is optional, although specifying the *FSTYPE* will minimize the time required to mount the filesystem. If no *FSTYPE* is specified, the mount command will attempt to guess the filesystem type by examining the superblock and, if that is still inconclusive, will try all of the types of filesystems listed in /proc/filesystems. The *DEVICE* is the name of the device of the domainU system that you specified in the xm block-attach command. The *MOUNTPOINT* is the name of the domainU directory on which you want to mount that device.

For temporary directory mounts, I typically create subdirectories of the standard /mnt directory that reflect what I am using them for. For example, for a mount point used to install software that I'm installing, I typically make the directory /mnt/install and use that as a mount point. In this case, the command to mount the block device used in the previous example would be something like the following:

```
# mount -t ext3 -o noatime /dev/xvda1 /mnt/install
```

In this example, I've mounted the filesystem on the directory /mnt/install using the -o (options) flag to specify the noatime option. This mounts the filesystem such that access times will not be updated for any files or directories in the filesystem. This will minimize any updates to the mounted filesystem to consist of just newly created, edited, or deleted files or directories, rather than wasting time updating the time that each file or directory was accessed.

Using subdirectories of the /mnt directory with meaningful names makes it easy to identify temporarily mounted filesystems in the standard output of commands such as df. When the df command is invoked with no arguments, it lists mounted filesystems, as in the following example:

```
# df
Filesystem      1K-blocks      Used Available Use% Mounted on
/dev/sda1        6192704    695724   5182408  12% /
varrun            131168        36    131132   1% /var/run
varlock           131168         0    131168   0% /var/lock
udev              131168        24    131144   1% /dev
devshm            131168         0    131168   0% /dev/shm
/dev/xvda1         56068      7900     48168  15% /mnt/install
```

Once you are finished using a block-attached filesystem in a domainU system, you must unmount it before you can cleanly detach that filesystem from the domainU system. Before unmounting any filesystem that you have imported as a writable filesystem, you should first use the sync command to ensure that any pending updates to that filesystem have been completely written to disk. This may be necessary even if you have not created or deleted files, because file and directory access timestamps may need to be updated (if you didn't mount the filesystem using -o noatime), and is never a bad idea.

Once you've synced the filesystem, you can unmount it in domainU using the umount command, as in the following example:

```
# umount /mnt/install
```

Once the filesystem has been unmounted, you should use the xm block-detach command on your domain0 host to disassociate the block device with the domainU system in which you had been using it. This command has the following syntax:

```
# xm block-detach DOMAIN DEVICEID [-f]
```

This command disassociates the block device identified by DEVICEID from the DOMAIN. To find the DEVICEID for a block device that has been manually associated with a given domainU guest, use the xm block-list command to list the block devices associated with that domain, as in the following example which lists the block devices for the domainU guest whose ID is 11 (line breaks have been inserted for formatting purposes):

```
# xm block-list 11
Vdev   BE handle state evt-ch ring-ref BE-path
2049    0    0     4      6       8 \
    /local/domain/0/backend/tap/11/2049
2050    0    0     4      7       9 \
    /local/domain/0/backend/tap/11/2050
51713   0    0     4      9     804 \
    /local/domain/0/backend/vbd/11/51713
```

The output from this command shows that this domain knows about three block devices, two of which are tap devices (in this case, filesystem and swap images), and one that is a virtual block device whose device identified is 51713. In this case, you could disassociate the virtual block device with domain 11 using a command like the following:

```
# xm block-detach 11 51713
```

As mentioned previously, the block device must not be mounted in the target domainU guest. If it is, you will see a message like the following on the domainU console, and the `block-detach` command will fail:

```
vbd vbd-51713: 16 Device in use; refusing to close
```

You can eliminate this message and successfully detach the block device by umounting it in the domainU guest. If you cannot do this for some reason, such as when the domainU guest is unresponsive, you can use the `block-detach` command's `-f` (force) option to forcibly disassociate the block device from that domainU. After block-detaching writable media, you should use the appropriate version of `fsck` to verify and potentially repair the filesystem on the block device before attaching it to any other domain.

> As mentioned earlier in this section, manually attaching and detaching block devices from various domains is generally intended for transient purposes. If you plan to use a given block device with a specific domainU guest for an extended period of time, you may want to add that block device to the configuration file or other configuration information for that domain. If you are using Xen's lifecycle management support for paravirtualized domains and are also using domain configuration files in Python variable format, you will need to delete (`xm delete`) and reinitialize (`xm new`) the domain configuration information that is stored in the XenStore.

Changing CDs and DVDs

As mentioned in the previous section, the block device commands that you use to work with removable media differ slightly from those that you use when simply attaching and removing a single block storage device from a domain. This is because CD/DVD devices are typically predefined in the domain configuration information for hardware machines (for software installation purposes) and in paravirtualized systems (simply for convenience). In such cases, it is more important to be able to change the media in the drive than to repeatedly attach and detach the same physical device. You can do this easily by using the `xm block-configure` command to reconfigure the device or media associated with an existing device.

> This section applies to CDs and DVDs that are being automatically accessed by some application, such as an installation program, or are being automatically mounted on operating systems such as Microsoft Windows. If you manually mount CDs or DVDs in a Linux domainU guest using the `mount` command, you must manually unmount them before you can change or detach them, just as if you were working with nonremovable block devices as described in the previous section. If you do not do this, you risk invalidating the contents of the kernel's cache of mounted filesystem data and completely confusing your Linux system.

For the purposes of this section, let's assume that the disk entry for the configuration file for a domainU guest contains the following statement to define a CD drive:

```
'phy:/dev/hda,hda:cdrom,r'
```

After booting a paravirtualized guest or hardware virtual machine containing this declaration, you can easily cause the CD drive to recognize new media by executing the following commands from your domain0 system:

```
# xm block-configure 1 phy:/dev/null hda:cdrom r
# xm block-configure 1 phy:/dev/hda hda:cdrom r
```

The first command maps a different physical device to the CD drive and effectively simulates an `eject` command because the physical device associated with the CD drive is empty. The second command simulates inserting a new CD.

When using multiple CDs to install software or an operating system and you must manually select an eject button, you would execute the first of these commands for each CD, before selecting the `eject` command. Alternately, you could use the `xm block-detach` command to manually detach the CD drive before each `eject` command, select the `eject` command, insert the new CD, and use the `xm block-attach` command to manually attach the new CD again before continuing.

If the `xm block-configure` command cannot modify the device that is attached to your domain, you will see a message like the following:

```
Error: Refusing to reconfigure device vbd:768
       to {'uname': '/dev/cdrom', 'mode': 'r', 'dev': 'hda'}
```

This error message lists the arguments that were passed to the `xm block-configure` command and how they were interpreted. The most common cause of this error is that either the name of the domain0 device was incorrectly specified (as in this example, where the name of the backend device did not include a device type prefix, such as `phy:` or `file:`), or the name of the frontend device in the target domain was incorrectly specified. The name of the device in the target domain must be the same as the name used in the Xen configuration file for the target domain. This is often a problem in Windows HVMs, where the name of the device specified in the configuration file does not necessarily correspond to the drive letter that the device was assigned when the domainU guest is created. For example, CDROM drives will show up as `C:` or `D:` even if they have been assigned to devices such as hda or hdb.

Using Dedicated Hardware in Guest Domains

The most common reason for dedicating hardware to a domainU system is increased performance. The most common type of dedicated PCI hardware is a network card. Dedicating a network card to a domainU system enables direct network communications from that system without having to multiplex a single Ethernet connection on you domain0 system. This can substantially increase the throughput and general usefulness of Web servers, print servers, and file servers running on domainU systems. Similarly, storage-related cards for external storage devices such as SCSI, FireWire, and even e-SATA are often dedicated to domainU systems to provide faster throughput for database tasks, data requests on file servers, or other storage-intensive tasks.

At the time of this writing, you can use only dedicated hardware on paravirtualized Xen guests, primarily because hardware devices typically expect to access registers and data at specific memory addresses. Non-virtual systems can provide this information for PCI devices, which require it for bus mastering and successful communication, but virtual Xen guests can't get this information without hardware such as an IOMMU (input/output memory management unit), which is still under development for commodity x86 processors. IOMMU hardware will be able to redirect the memory addresses at which Xen guests believe that hardware can be found to the actual physical addresses that are known by the hypervisor. See the Linux Weekly News (`http://lwn.net/Articles/229864`) for more information about upcoming hardware improvements for virtualization support.

The primary downside of using dedicated hardware on a domainU system is that requiring this hardware makes the domainU guest much less flexible than when it is completely virtualized. For this reason, migrating virtual machines that use dedicated hardware is impossible unless you are migrating a virtual machines between two physical domain0 hosts that are completely identical, down to the PCI addresses of any dedicated hardware that the VM is using, which is highly unlikely.

Using Dedicated PCI Devices in domainU Guests

The "Hiding PCI Devices from domain0" section in Chapter 4 explains various ways to hide a PCI device from domain0 so that it can be exclusively used by a paravirtualized domainU system. Once it is hidden from domain0, it is actually quite simple to use such a "hidden" PCI device in a domainU system.

As discussed in Chapter 4, one important thing to remember is that hidden PCI devices will still be visible in domain0 when you use utilities such as lspci that probe your hardware. Hidden devices use the pciback driver to prevent device-specific drivers from attaching to that device in domain0, making them unavailable to the domain0 kernel. They remain visible in domain0, but cannot be used there.

Adding a dedicated PCI device to a domainU system is simple. Edit that domain's configuration file and add an entry for the hidden device to that file, as in the following example:

```
pci=[ '00:09.0' ]
```

This is essentially the same information that you used when hiding the PCI device, as explained in Chapter 4. This example statement assigns the PCI device identified by the PCI identifier 00:09.0 to the domainU guest associated with this configuration file. After starting the domain using this configuration file, running `lspci` inside that domain will show the dedicated PCI device as the only physical PCI device that is present on the system, as in the following example:

```
# lspci
00:09.0 Ethernet controller: 3Com Corporation 3c905B 100BaseTX...
```

Once a domain is started with dedicated PCI hardware, the guest must provide a driver for the specified device in order for the domain to actually use the PCI device in that domainU guest. Like any other driver, the driver for the dedicated PCI device can either be built into the domainU kernel or available as a loadable kernel module in the initial RAM disk filesystem or root filesystem used by the domainU guest.

Using USB Devices in domainU Guests

In domainU guests, Xen provides built-in support for USB pointer devices such as mice and tablets, and leverages the USB support in the QEMU emulator to provide support for other types of USB devices. In order to use USB devices in domainU guests, you must have the following line in the configuration file for your domainU guest:

```
usb=1
```

Because pointing devices and other USB devices, such as storage devices and printers, are configured differently in a domainU configuration file, the next few sections provide detailed information about attaching, configuring, and using these different types of USB devices.

USB Pointer Device Support

This section discusses using different types of pointer-device emulation inside domainU guest systems. Your domain0 system doesn't require special configuration or settings for using standard PS/2 or USB mice. Support for these is provided by your domain0 kernel. In Xen domainU virtual machines, USB pointer devices are meaningful only when you are using a virtual frame buffer with a paravirtualized domainU guest, or when you are using an SDL or VNC graphical console with a Xen hardware virtual machine.

Xen provides support for both relative and absolute pointer devices in domainU guests. The drivers for relative pointer devices, such as mice, usually take factors such as speed and acceleration into account when moving the pointer on the screen, enabling you to work more efficiently than if your movement of the pointing device mapped directly to the distance that the pointer moves on the screen. Absolute pointer devices, such as tablets, provide a limited surface area over which a pen or puck can move, and can therefore move the pointer precisely based on the movement of the pointer device.

By default, Xen assumes that your pointer device is a PS/2 mouse, which is inherently supported by all of the graphical operating systems that you can run in Xen virtual machines. If you don't specify usb=1 in your domainU configuration file, any graphical domainU systems that you are using will work fine. However, because Xen supports a PS/2 mouse as a relative pointer device, you may find the mouse hard to control or notice that the mouse pointer inside your graphical console or virtual frame buffer is out of sync with the actual position of the mouse on your screen. (This is an extremely common problem when using VNC to access and display a graphical console.) In these cases, you can leverage Xen's USB mouse emulation to provide better control of the cursor.

The usbdevice entry in a domainU configuration file supports two keywords that enable you to control whether Xen treats its emulated mouse device as an absolute or relative pointer device. The default, which is a relative pointer, is usbdevice='mouse'. To tell your domainU guests to treat the cursor as an absolute pointer device, add the entry usbdevice='tablet' after the usb=1 entry in your domainU configuration file.

If you are using a virtual frame buffer or graphical console with any of your domainU guests, I strongly suggest that you always configure them with USB support and usbdevice='tablet'. However, this only controls how the kernel perceives the mouse, not necessarily how any graphical desktop environment or window manager that you are using interacts with the mouse. See the section "The Many Moods of Graphics for domainU Guests" later in this chapter, for additional information about controlling cursor movement and behavior in graphical domainU guests.

Using USB Storage Device Partitions in PV Guests

There are several different ways of using specific partitions of a USB storage device with a paravirtualized (PV) domainU system. The approach that you take depends on whether you plan to permanently associate that USB storage with a specific domainU guest, or whether you only want to occasionally use USB storage with a specific domainU guest.

If you want to permanently use a partition of a USB storage device with a paravirtualized guest, the easiest thing to do is to add that partition to the disk entry in your virtual machine's configuration file. As discussed in the sections of Chapter 5 on the requirements for paravirtualized and hardware virtual machines, paravirtualized systems usually access only partitions or partition images, rather than the entire devices or device images used by hardware virtual machines. You can therefore simply add another entry to your virtual machine's disk specification for each partition that you want to use from your USB storage device. For example, suppose that you wanted to add the partition /dev/sdc1 to a virtual machine's disk entry. The original entry looks like the following:

```
disk = ['tap:aio:/home/diskimage-fc6.ext2,sda1,w',
        'tap:aio:/home/xen/fedora.swap,sda2,w']
```

After adding an entry for /dev/sdc1, your disk entry would look like the following:

```
disk = ['tap:aio:/home/diskimage-fc6.ext2,sda1,w',
        'tap:aio:/home/xen/fedora.swap,sda2,w',
'phy:/dev/sdc1,sda3,w']
```

If you only occasionally want to be able to access USB storage from a virtual machine, such as when installing software or doing backups, you can simply use the xm block-attach command to attach specific partitions from your USB storage device to that virtual machine. Only paravirtualized kernels provide the Xen virtual block device drivers, so this approach is only relevant for paravirtualized systems. The following is an example:

```
# xm block-attach 25 phy:/dev/sdc1 /dev/sda3 w
```

This is the equivalent of the disk entry modification shown earlier. In both cases, you will have to mount the new disk partition (/dev/sda3) before you can actually access its contents. However, modifying only the disk entry is persistent across restarts of the paravirtualized system.

Using USB Devices in HVM Guests

Xen provides two basic ways of accessing USB devices such as storage devices or printers from a domainU hardware virtual machine. Just like the techniques for paravirtualized machines discussed in the previous section, the approach that you select depends on whether you want a long-term or short-term binding between your domainU system and the USB device. Also, as in the previous section, one modification is done in the configuration information for your domainU guest, while the other is done interactively.

For long-term associations between your domainU guest and a USB device, you can add a host: vendor:product entry to the usbdevices entry in your domainU configuration file. This makes the specified device available to the target domain.

For short-term associations between your domainU guest and a USB device, you must be running your domainU HVM with an SDL graphical console and must also have enabled the QEMU monitor in your domainU configuration file . You can then use the VNC QEMU monitor to manually add the device to your domainU system using the `usb_add host:vendor:product` command in the QEMU monitor.

The key to both of these approaches is to be able to determine the vendor ID and product ID of the USB device that you want to attach to your HVM domain. The easiest way to do this is by using the `lsusb` command on your domain0 system, as in the following example:

```
# lsusb
Bus 004 Device 001: ID 0000:0000
Bus 004 Device 002: ID 152d:2338
Bus 001 Device 001: ID 0000:0000
Bus 002 Device 002: ID 04b8:0005 Seiko Epson Corp. Stylus Printer
Bus 002 Device 001: ID 0000:0000
Bus 003 Device 001: ID 0000:0000
```

The ID string identifies the vendor ID and the product ID of a specific USB device, separated by a colon. This ID string is followed by the name of the device if that particular vendor ID and product ID is present in the file `/usr/share/hwdata/usb.ids` (or the file `/usr/share/usb.ids` on some older Linux distributions). In this example output, `ID 152d:2338` corresponds to an external USB disk that is not listed in this file, and `ID 04b8:0005` corresponds to a USB printer.

If the `lsusb` command is not available on your domainU system, it is available in the usbutils package, which you can install using your system's package management tool. If you don't want to install this package for some reason, you can still obtain this information by examining the file `/proc/bus/usb/devices` on your domain0 system, which will show entries like the following for each USB device:

```
T:  Bus=02 Lev=01 Prnt=01 Port=01 Cnt=01 Dev#=  3 Spd=12   MxCh= 0
D:  Ver= 1.10 Cls=00(>ifc ) Sub=00 Prot=00 MxPS= 8 #Cfgs=  1
P:  Vendor=04b8 ProdID=0005 Rev= 1.00
S:  Manufacturer=EPSON
S:  Product=USB Printer
S:  SerialNumber=L11P105505280955070
C:* #Ifs= 1 Cfg#= 1 Atr=c0 MxPwr=  2mA
I:  If#= 0 Alt= 0 #EPs= 2 Cls=07(print) Sub=01 Prot=02 Driver=usbfs
E:  Ad=01(O) Atr=02(Bulk) MxPS=  64 Ivl=0ms
E:  Ad=82(I) Atr=02(Bulk) MxPS=  64 Ivl=0ms
```

This example shows the entry for the printer that was also listed in the `lsusb` output.

To add an entry for the printer to your domainU configuration, your configuration file would contain entries like the following:

```
usb=1
usbdevice=[ 'host:04b8:0005' ]
```

The `host` prefix on the USB device ID is important because it tells the QEMU subsystem that the specified USB device is present on the domainU system and should be mapped to the guest.

At the time of this writing, this mechanism for attaching USB devices works only for select USB devices. This number will certainly increase over time.

The alternate mechanism for attaching USB devices to a HVM domainU guest is to use the QEMU monitor to manually attach the device to your domainU guest. To do this, the following entries must be present in your domainU configuration file:

```
vnc=0
sdl=1
monitor=1
usb=1
```

As you can see, this only works if you are using an SDL graphical console for your domainU HVM. The ability to access the QEMU monitor from a VNC connection to a graphical monitor is disabled for security reasons.

After starting your domainU guest normally, press the Left-Ctrl, Left-Alt, and 2 keys at the same time to display the QEMU monitor, which looks like the screen shown in Figure 9-1.

Figure 9-1

This figure shows the list of available commands in the QEMU monitor, available by typing the `help` command. If you are already familiar with QEMU, you will note that these commands are very different than the standard QEMU monitor commands. (For complete documentation on QEMU, see http://fabrice.bellard.free.fr/qemu/qemu-doc.html.) After the help output, Figure 9-1 shows the use of the following command to make the USB printer device available to my domainU guest:

```
usb_add host:04b8:0005
```

After executing this command, you must press the Left-Ctrl, Left-Alt, and 1 keys simultaneously to return to your virtual machine. Do not use the `quit` command, because this will terminate your virtual machine!

Once you return to the virtual machine, the printer is visible to the guest domain, as shown in the following figures. Figure 9-2 shows the Microsoft Windows XP New Hardware Wizard about to install the appropriate drivers. Figure 9-3 shows the System ⇨ Administration ⇨ Printers dialog box on a Ubuntu Feisty HVM running GNOME, illustrating that the printer was also automatically recognized in a Linux domainU HVM.

Figure 9-2

Figure 9-3

Passing USB devices to domainU guests is still a hot topic in Xen development circles. The latest development versions of Xen also offer a `usbport` statement that you can specify in your domainU configuration file, passing it a value that represents a USB port on your system.

Using USB Devices Over the Network

The previous sections discussed various ways of physically allocating specific USB devices to specific paravirtualized and HVM hosts. Another mechanism for connecting specific USB devices to virtual machines is by attaching them to a networked USB hub and installing the drivers for the networked hub within the virtual machine. Two of these devices are available at the time of this writing:

❑ Belkin F5L009 5-Port Networked USB 2.0 Hub (www.belkin.com/search/?q=F5l009&sid=1)

❑ Agilent Unveils E5813A Networked USB Hub (www.home.agilent.com, search for "Networked USB Hub")

The Belkin hub is USB-only, whereas the Agilent hub also supports GPIB and RS-232 devices in case you need to hook up a flatbed plotter from the 1980s (or, more seriously, if you are using scientific instrumentation or measuring devices). A wireless networked USB hub will be available soon from Belkin, but the current one can be combined with any wired-to-wireless Ethernet device to use these hubs in a wireless environment.

Using networked USB hubs completely avoids the USB allocation and pass-through issues in paravirtualized and HVM virtual machines, and works surprisingly well. Unfortunately, Linux drivers for these devices are not yet available, so this is only a solution for virtualized Microsoft Windows systems at the moment. However, if you are running Windows virtual machines, a networked USB hub is a great solution for accessing USB printers, storage devices, and so on from Windows HVMs which you can easily migrate because they are therefore not tied to specific USB Variable IDs or physically attached devices.

Working with Sound on domainU Guests

Xen's use of QEMU as the underlying device model for HVM domainU guests enables Xen HVMs to take advantage of QEMU's sound support. Although QEMU supports a number of different sound devices, its support for the Ensoniq AudioPCI ES1370 sound card is probably the easiest to use on a variety of platforms. To enable sound on an HVM guest, simply add the following entry to your domainU HVM guest's configuration file:

```
soundhw='es1370'
```

The next time that you start this virtual machine, you should hear your system's startup sounds (assuming that they are enabled).

Other possible values for soundhw are 'sb16' (Sound Blaster 16), 'alsa', and 'all'. Selecting 'alsa' should eventually enable you to share sound devices between your domain0 and domainU systems. At the time of this writing, direct use of the sound emulation hardware on a domainU HVM guest blocks the domain0 system from accessing the sound hardware. Other alternatives are to use a networked sound mechanism such as Enlightenment Sound Daemon (esound, http://ftp.gnome.org/pub/gnome/sources/esound/0.2), GNOME's GStreamer package (http://gstreamer.freedesktop.org/apps/), KDE's aRts (analog Real time synthesizer, www.arts-project.org/), or a similar mechanism. If you need to use sound from both Linux and Windows HVM systems, you will need to find a solution that works on both platforms. For information about a WinAMP plugin for esound that you can use on your Windows HVMs to send sound to an esound server, see www.linuxfan.dk/index.php?page=esound. An older esound driver is also available at www.clingman.org/winesd.

Time Synchronization in domain0 and domainU

Most enterprise environments today run a time server that uses the Network Time Protocol (NTP) to synchronize the clocks on multiple systems. NTP uses UDP port 123 to communicate between systems and time servers, and provides a platform-independent mechanism for synchronizing individual system clocks with individual servers or a hierarchy of delegating, centralized time servers.

Beyond simple accuracy, time synchronization is critical in enterprise environments where timestamps have any significance. This is especially true in networked build environments where multiple developers share a central set of files and timestamps are used to identify updated source code, but it is equally important in any shared filesystem environment.

By default, the clock in domainU guests is always synchronized with the clock in the domain0 system that is hosting them. However, if you want to run a time server in a domainU system or want to maintain a separate time zone for a given virtual machine, you can divorce it from the domain0 clock in one of several ways:

❑ Add `xen.independent_wallclock = 1` to the `/etc/sysctl.conf` file on the domainU guest, if present.

❑ Write the value `1` to the file `/proc/sys/xen/independent_wallclock`. If you choose this solution, you may want to automate this by adding a command like the following to one of your system's startup files:

```
echo 1 > /proc/sys/xen/independent_wallclock
```

❑ Add `independent_wallclock=1` to your kernel command line via the `extras` option in your domainU configuration file.

To re-enable synchronization with the domain0 system clock, you can execute the following command:

```
echo 0 > /proc/sys/xen/independent_wallclock
```

domain0 and domainU Kernel and Binary Considerations

Executing, managing, interacting with, and supporting virtual machines is a complex process, both at the hardware and software level. The section "Overview of Xen and x86 Virtualization" in Chapter 2 covers x86 processor execution and protection modes, and explains some of the complexity involved in running different types of virtual machines on different types of hardware. The next few sections discuss kernel considerations for different types of virtual machines and hardware, and summarize the issues involved in combining 32-bit and 64-bit virtual machines and filesystem executables in a single virtualization environment.

Using Different Kernels for Different Domains

Older releases of Xen used separate kernels for domain0 and paravirtualized domainU systems. Although you can still use this approach, it is much more common in Xen 3.0 and later to use the same kernel for both types of systems. This simplifies installation and maintenance, making it easy to upgrade many domain0 and domainU hosts with a single rebuild.

Of course, using the same kernel in domain0 and domainU guests applies only to paravirtualized systems, not Xen HVMs. HVMs install and execute their own kernels without knowing that they are virtual machines. Any modern or legacy systems that you have installed and are running in a domainU HVM guest should work fine under Xen.

If you decide to use different kernels in different domainU guests, the primary requirement is that these kernels must not be built against Xen distributions that are newer than the distribution that you are running on domain0. Attempting to run newer kernels against an old domain0/hypervisor combination could cause the domainU kernels to make calls to domain0 or the hypervisor that they do not support.

Similarly, you cannot run an HVM whose hardware requirements are higher than those provided by the domain0/hypervisor that you are running. The sections "Paravirtualized Systems" and "Unmodified Guest Systems" in Chapter 2 discuss compatibility between different types of paravirtualized and HVM guests. The following table summarizes the different types of hardware and the types of kernels that will run on each.

Hypervisor	dom0	domU(PV)	domU(HVM)
32-bit	32-bit	32-bit	32-bit
32-bit PAE	32-bit PAE	32-bit PAE	32-bit or 32-bit PAE
64-bit	64-bit	64-bit or 32-bit PAE	32-bit, 32-PAE, or 64-bit

As shown in this table, 64-bit hardware with VT/SVM support will run almost anything. 64-bit hardware cannot run 32-bit domainU guests directly because of the differences in the amount of memory that is installed in these types of systems and how it is addressed. However, as explained in the next section, you can run 32-bit legacy systems on 64-bit hardware as long as the kernel that you are using is a 32-bit PAE or 64-bit kernel.

Running 32-Bit Paravirtualized Guests on 64-bit Hardware

Linux distributions that directly support both 32-bit and 64-bit hardware must provide both 32-bit and 64-bit system and user libraries, as well as the compilers and other parts of a toolchain used to build and execute those binaries. However, most Linux distributions install only the set of libraries that is necessary for a specific hardware system. The key issue in the type of root filesystem that you have is therefore where you built or obtained that root filesystem.

It is easiest to build a 32-bit root filesystem on a 32-bit machine, because all of the right libraries will already be installed and available. In most cases, a 32-bit root filesystem or root filesystem image will work fine with a 64-bit domainU kernel. The reverse is not true.

As shown in the table in the previous section, hardware virtual machines can run on systems with VT/SVM support as long as the physical hardware that they are running on is greater than or equal to the hardware requirements of the HVM.

The Many Moods of Graphics for domainU Guests

Supporting graphics on virtual machines is a hot-button issue for many people, especially those who are using virtual Windows guests or who want to access Xen virtual machines remotely as though they were physical Linux hosts, complete with a window manager or desktop system. The next few sections explain the graphical capabilities of HVMs and paravirtualized systems, and how to use them with the X Window system in different ways.

Using SDL and VNC Consoles for HVM Guests

As discussed in the section "Creating Xen HVM Configuration Files" in Chapter 5, Xen HVMs can display a graphical console in either a Simple DirectMedia Layer (SDL) or Virtual Network Computing (VNC) window. Each of these has its own advantages and disadvantages.

SDL is a cross-platform multimedia library that provides an abstraction of the graphics, sound, and input devices on specific platforms. Writing code to its APIs enables graphical software written on one platform to run on other supported platforms simply by recompiling it against their versions of the SDL library. The SDL library and its subsystems provide functions to manage and synchronize things such as digital audio, CDs, events, networking, sound, threads, timers, and more. SDL maps its generic interfaces to underlying functionality on each operating system where it is supported, such as DirectX on Microsoft Windows systems or Xlib and the X11 Window system on Linux systems. SDL is often used to simplify porting multimedia software, such as games, from one platform to another.

VNC is a cross-platform graphical desktop sharing system that uses a network, the RFB protocol, and a client/server model to remotely communicate with and control another computer. VNC sends keyboard, mouse, and screen update events from clients back to the server that they are connected to. VNC viewers are optimized to minimize network traffic and provide good-quality graphics. VNC is often used to provide graphical access to desktop computer systems from remote locations, such as when you're traveling or working from home.

SDL graphical consoles for Xen provide superior graphics performance and more accurate and immediate tracking of input events because they use a domain0 system's native graphical support to display the console and track input and update events. VNC was designed as a remote console display and control system, so it provides better performance, minimal network traffic, and greater flexibility in remote display environments. VNC clients are also available for Windows systems, which you could therefore use to display the graphical console of your Xen HVM on a Windows desktop. You could do this with SDL consoles, too, but you would have to install the X11 Windows system on your Windows systems.

There are two primary downsides of using VNC for your graphical consoles. First, VNC's tracking of mouse movements can easily get out of sync with the actual mouse cursor (although there are some workarounds, as discussed in "X11 Tips and Tricks for VNC" later in this chapter). Second, you cannot access the QEMU monitor from a VNC console because it has been disabled for security reasons.

To use SDL for your graphical console, the configuration file for your domainU guest must include the following entries:

```
sdl=1
vnc=0
```

One advantage of SDL consoles is that they appear immediately on your screen when you start an HVM that uses SDL. You do not need any other software (beyond SDL, which is a fundamental Xen requirement) in order to display or use your graphical console. Xen's use of SDL also leverages QEMU's screen emulation, which means that you must often click the mouse inside the graphical console in order to use it. This locks the mouse to the Xen graphical console. To free the mouse from the SDL console, press the Left-Ctrl and Left-Alt keys at the same time.

To use VNC for your graphical console, the configuration file for your domainU guest must include at least the following entries:

```
sdl=0
vnc=1
```

You can also set a number of other options for a VNC display, including `vncconsole`, `vncdisplay`, `vnclisten`, `vncpasswd`, and `vncunused`. See Appendix B for more information on these options.

Connecting to a Graphical Console Using VNC

Once you have started an HVM that uses VNC for its graphical console, you must use a VNC client to connect to it. The best known VNC clients are TightVNC (`www.tightvnc.com`) and RealVNC (`www.realvnc.com`), which both provide VNC clients for Windows and most Linux distributions. Of the two, I prefer TightVNC because it makes better use of network bandwidth, utilizing JPEG compression for the display and differentiating between local cursor movement and cursor movement that needs to be communicated back to the VNC server. TightVNC also features automatic SSH tunneling for security purposes.

VNC servers export their virtual displays via ports starting at 5900 plus the number of the display that they are exporting. For example, a VNC server running on the X Window system display :1 will use port 5901. As discussed in "Configuring the Xen Daemon" in Chapter 7, the `vnc-listen` variable in the Xen daemon's configuration file identifies the IP addresses on which the Xen daemon should listen for incoming VNC connections — by default, this is only the loopback address on your domain0 host, 127.0.0.1.

Once you have installed a VNC client (usually `/usr/bin/xrealvncviewer`, `/usr/bin/xtightvncviewer`, or simply `/usr/bin/vncviewer`), you can connect to your domain's graphical console using a command like the following:

```
$ vncviewer 127.0.0.1:1
```

This would connect to the first available VNC port (port number 5901) via your system's loopback address.

Graphics aren't only for HVM Xen domains, although they only work "out of the box" in HVM environments. The next section explains how you can display a graphical console or generally run the X11 Window system on paravirtualized Xen domainU systems.

The X Window System and Paravirtualized Guests

There are two options for graphical access to X Window system desktops and applications on paravirtualized domainU guests:

❑ **Use a virtual frame buffer:** Versions of the open source distribution of Xen later than 3.0.3 support a graphical console through the use of a virtual frame buffer, much like the graphical consoles used on HVM domainU guests. If configured correctly, you can run an X Window server and window manager/desktop directly on this graphical console.

❑ **Use a VNC-aware X server:** An equivalent but somewhat more flexible approach to getting graphical access to a paravirtualized guest is to run a VNC-aware X Window server on the guest, to which remote users can connect using a standard VNC client.

The approach that you use to provide graphical access to paravirtualized guests is completely up to you. Graphical Xen administration tools such as virt-manager use a virtual frame buffer so that they can provide a captive view of the graphical console for domainU guests. Using a virtual frame buffer is also attractive if your domain0 system has a graphical console to which you have access or if your domainU console is being made available from other systems by running an X11-aware VNC server. In general, I find that running an X11-aware VNC server on paravirtualized systems requires fewer resources yet provides the same usability as a virtual frame buffer, and that is the approach that I usually take.

The next section explains how to start a graphical console for a paravirtualized domainU system in a virtual frame buffer. The section after that explains how to start an X server directly in that virtual frame buffer. Subsequent sections explain how to install and configure an X11-aware VNC server, and provide some suggestions for working with an optimizing X11 and VNC on your domainU systems.

Starting a Graphical Console for a Paravirtualized Guest

Graphical consoles for paravirtualized guests can use SDL or VNC, just like those on HVM guests. Using a virtual frame buffer on a paravirtualized guest involves making a few changes to the configuration file for that domain.

To use an SDL graphical console on a paravirtualized domainU guest, add the following line to the configuration file for that domain:

```
vfb = [ 'type=sdl' ]
```

Once you have done that (and reloaded that domain's configuration information into the XenStore, if you are using Xen's lifecycle management), starting that domain displays a boot console like the one shown in Figure 9-4.

Once you have verified that the graphical console works correctly, you can install and configure an X Window system server on the system as explained in the next section, "Configuring and Starting an X Server in a Virtual Frame Buffer."

```
usbcore: registered new driver hub
Loading uhci-hcd.ko module
USB Universal Host Controller Interface driver v3.0
Loading ohci-hcd.ko module
Loading ehci-hcd.ko module
Loading jbd.ko module
Loading ext3.ko module
Loading ide-disk.ko module
Loading sis5513.ko module
Loading scsi_mod.ko module
SCSI subsystem initialized
Loading sd_mod.ko module
register_blkdev: cannot get major 8 for sd
Loading libata.ko module
Loading sata_sis.ko module
Loading dm-mod.ko module
device-mapper: ioctl: 4.7.0-ioctl (2006-06-24) initialised: dm-devel@redhat.com
Loading dm-mirror.ko module
Loading dm-zero.ko module
Loading dm-snapshot.ko module
Creating root device.
Mounting root filesystem.
kjournald starting.  Commit interval 5 seconds
EXT3-fs: mounted filesystem with ordered data mode.
Setting up other filesystems.
Setting up new root fs
no fstab.sys, mounting internal defaults
Switching to new root and running init.
unmounting old /dev
unmounting old /proc
unmounting old /sys
 * Setting preliminary keymap...
```

Figure 9-4

To use a VNC graphical console on a paravirtualized domainU guest, add a line like the following to the configuration file for that domain:

```
vfb = [ 'type=vnc' ]
```

Although this is the only entry that is required in order to use a VNC-viewable graphical console on a paravirtualized domainU guest, you will probably actually want to specify additional VNC configuration options at the same time, as in the following example:

```
vfb = [ 'type=vnc,vncdisplay=13,vncpasswd=foobar' ]
```

This specifies a VNC-based virtual frame buffer, starts the VNC server for that console on port 13, and sets the VNC server password to `foobar`.

Once you have done that (and reloaded that domain's configuration information into the XenStore, if you are using Xen's lifecycle management), starting that domain displays a boot console like the one shown previously in Figure 9-4.

Once you have verified that the graphical console works correctly, you can install and configure an X Window system server on the system as explained in the next section, "Configuring and Starting a VNC X Server."

> **When using a virtual frame buffer on a paravirtualized guest, you may not be able to access the text-only console. If you are using a VNC graphical console, you can access the text-only console by temporarily modifying the** `vfb` **statement in your domainU configuration file to look like the following:**
>
> ```
> vfb=['type=vnc,vncunused=1']
> ```
>
> **If you are using** `virt-manager` **on Red Hat or compatible Linux distributions,** `virt-manager` **routes all serial output to the graphical console, which does not enable you to connect to your system's text console. By default, this is the device** `/etc/xvc0`**, which is the device that the** `xm console` **command attaches to. To be able to log on to this console, you must start a getty process on** `/dev/xvc0`**. You can do this by adding the following entry to your system's** `/etc/inittab` **file:**
>
> ```
> co:2345:respawn:/sbin/agetty xvc0 9600 vt100-nav
> ```
>
> **You must also add the entry** `xvc0` **to the end of the file** `/etc/securetty`**. After doing this, you can reload your system's** `/etc/inittab` **and start/restart required processes by executing the** `telinit q` **command. If your system does not use an** `/etc/inittab` **file (such as in Ubuntu Linux distributions), you will need to make equivalent modifications to the system startup file that actually starts** `getty` **processes (the file** `/etc/event.d/tty*` **on Ubuntu distributions).**

Configuring and Starting an X Server in a Virtual Frame Buffer

Once you have verified that the graphical console in a virtual frame buffer for a paravirtualized domain is working correctly, you can start an X Window system server directly on that graphical console. To do this, you must install the basic X server, the fonts that it uses, and a window manager or graphical desktop system on your paravirtualized system using your Linux distribution's package management system (or by building everything yourself if you are a masochist). For example, I install the following packages in Ubuntu virtual machines:

- ❑   `xserver-xorg-core`: The core X.Org X server
- ❑   `xfonts-100dpi`: 100 dpi fonts for X
- ❑   `xfonts-75dpi`: 75 dpi fonts for X
- ❑   `xfonts-base`: Standard fonts for X
- ❑   `xfonts-scalable`: Scalable default fonts for X
- ❑   `fluxbox`: A lightweight window manager for X

Once you have installed these packages, you must stop the virtual machine and add the following entry to the configuration file for that domain:

```
extra="xencons=off"
```

This disables Xen's console access so that the standard device nodes created by udev on a vanilla Linux system are created when the system boots.

Next, you should modify the configuration file for the X.org X Window system server, which is the file /etc/X11/xorg.conf. You will need to replace the Device, InputDevice, Monitor, Screen, and ServerLayout sections with the following entries:

```
Section "Device"
        Identifier          "Para virtual Framebuffer"
        Driver              "fbdev"
        Option              "fbdev" "/dev/fb0"
EndSection
Section "InputDevice"
        Identifier "Xen Mouse"
        Driver "mouse"
        Option "Protocol"      "PS/2"
        Option "Device"        "/dev/input/mouse0"
EndSection
Section "Monitor"
        Identifier      "Generic Monitor"
EndSection
Section "Screen"
        Identifier      "Default Screen"
        Device          "Para virtual Framebuffer"
        Monitor         "Generic Monitor"
EndSection
Section "ServerLayout"
        Identifier      "Default Layout"
        Screen          "Default Screen"
        InputDevice     "Xen Mouse"
EndSection
```

These values were suggested on the XenSource wiki long ago, and I still find them to be useful as a starting point when getting X working in a virtual frame buffer. You can subsequently tweak them to suit your requirements, but I find these to be the right starting point for all of the paravirtualized guests on which I've used the X Window system with a virtual frame buffer.

Once you have done these things (and have reloaded that domain's configuration information into the XenStore, if you are using Xen's lifecycle management), you can restart the domain, which will enable you to log in on the domain's graphical console.

Once you have logged in, first note the system's IP address in case something goes wrong and you need to terminate the X server by using SSH or a similar program to connect to the machine. Next, start the X server using the startx command. (The startx command does a more robust job of searching for window managers than the xinit application, which requires that you preconfigure an .xinitrc file to start your window manager and other X11 applications.) If you've configured things correctly, you should see the standard X11 fluxbox screen, which should look something like Figure 9-5.

Figure 9-5

If the X Window system does not start correctly, one common error message that you may see is the following:

```
Fatal server error:
  xf86OpenConsole: Cannot open /dev/tty0 \
  (No such file or directory)
```

This message generally means that Xen is still using both a text console and the graphical console on your system. Check that you added the `extra="xencons=off"` entry to your domainU configuration data, and that you deleted your old configuration data and reloaded the updated configuration information into the XenStore if you are using Xen's lifecycle management.

If the X Window system still does not start correctly, you may need to install other packages, depending on the Linux distribution that you are using in your domainU system. If missing packages or libraries are not identified in error messages, see the X11 documentation for your Linux distribution.

> If you want to run X Window system applications that are installed on your
> domainU guest but don't want to actually run an X server there, you can ignore
> everything about setting up a graphical console on the Xen guest, and simply
> connect to it using the `ssh -X` command, which forwards X Window system
> connections through a Secure Shell (SSH) tunnel back to the system from which you
> connected. You can then run X Window system applications such as xterm by simply
> executing them on the remote host inside the `ssh` session. The graphical applications
> will appear on the system from which you connected, assuming that the X11 ports
> are not blocked and that remote applications are allowed to contact your display. You
> may also need to set the `DISPLAY` environment variable to point to the display of the
> system from which you executed the `ssh -X` command.

Some interesting work is being done by various people to provide more sophisticated graphics in the
virtual frame buffer used by Xen. See `www.cs.toronto.edu/~andreslc/xen-gl` for information about
support for Accelerated 3D OpenGL for Xen, and `www.diku.dk/hjemmesider/ansatte/jacobg/gfx`
for GFX support for X under Xen.

Configuring and Starting a VNC X Server

An X11-aware VNC server is my preferred method for connecting to paravirtualized domainU guests.
VNC is lightweight and fast. Because you are running the X-aware VNC server directly on the
paravirtualized domain, its impact on your domain0 system is minimized. For example, you connect to
an X-aware VNC server by using the IP address of the guest and the VNC display number. These
connections do not go through the Xen daemon and do not require that it start VNC servers on a specific
localhost (127.0.0.1) or other connections.

To run an X-aware VNC server on your domainU system, you must install a variety of packages there.
These include the basic X/VNC server, the fonts that it uses, and a window manager or graphical desktop
system. You can do this by using your Linux distribution's package management system (or by building
everything yourself). For example, I install the following packages in Ubuntu virtual machines:

- ❑ **vnc-server:** The X11-aware VNC server
- ❑ **xfonts-100dpi:** 100 dpi fonts for X
- ❑ **xfonts-75dpi:** 75 dpi fonts for X
- ❑ **xfonts-base:** Standard fonts for X
- ❑ **xfonts-scalable:** Scalable default fonts for X
- ❑ **fluxbox:** A lightweight window manager for X

The actual VNC server binary, Xvnc, is contained in the vnc-server package. It is usually started by a Perl
script called `vncserver`. The `vncserver` script provides a flexible mechanism for passing arguments to
the server, displays status information once the server has started and detached, and also builds in the
ability to use a startup script to identify the window manager and any X applications that the VNC

server should start. The VNC server's startup script is the file ~/.vnc/xstartup. If this directory and the startup file do not exist the first time that you start a VNC server, the directory is created and the startup script is cloned from the default X Window system startup file /etc/X11/xinit/xinitrc.

On Red Hat, Fedora Core, Centos, and similar systems, the default ~/.vnc/xstartup script simply executes the startup script for the xinit program, which is the file /etc/X11/xinit/xintrc. This enables VNC on Red Hat, Centos, Fedora Core, and other similar systems to follow the same (somewhat convoluted) chain of X Window startup files that are normally used: ~/.Xclients, ~/.Xclients-$HOSTNAME$DISPLAY, ~/.Xclients-default, /etc/X11/xinit/Xclients. Xclient files can start various desktop environments and window managers by using environment variable settings, and execute the twm window manager (www.plig.org/xwinman/vtwm.html).

On SUSE systems, the ~/.vnc/xstartup script is a little more straightforward:

```
#!/bin/sh
xrdb $HOME/.Xresources
xsetroot -solid grey
xterm -geometry 80x24+10+10 -ls -title "$VNCDESKTOP Desktop" &
twm &
```

This sort of startup script makes it easy for you to start the window manager of your choice by commenting out the twm entry and adding the full pathname of your favorite window manager as the last line in the file, followed by an ampersand.

In multiuser environments, where multiple people need graphical connections to the domainU system, you will probably want to install and start Xvnc via the inetd or xinetd Internet daemon on your domainU system rather than directly executing an X server from the console. You can then install and start a display manager (such as xdm, gcm, or kdm) to respond to XDMCP requests to the domainU system. This is more of an X Window system issue than a Xen issue, so that isn't discussed here, but this information can be found on the Web or in any good Linux and X11 system administration text.

Once you've started the vncserver and supplied any passwords that it requires, the vncserver script displays a message like the following whenever a server is successfully started:

```
New 'X' desktop is centos5.vonhagen.org:1
Starting applications specified in /home/wvh/.vnc/xstartup Log file is
/home/wvh/.vnc/home.vonhagen.org:1.log
```

These messages identify the hostname and port number that you should use to access the X server.

If your system does kernel packet filtering or your network uses a firewall, you must make sure that you do not block ports 590x (used to export VNC server displays), port 6000 (used to communicate with the X Window system server), or ports 580x (if you want to communicate with a VNC server over the Web).

X11 and Xen Tips and Tricks for VNC

One nice thing about SDL consoles is that they appear immediately on your screen as soon as your start an HVM that uses SDL. Connecting to a VNC console can be trickier because VNC consoles do not always show up on the port that you expect.

In theory, the VNC server for your graphical console determines the port that it should listen on by using either the domain ID or the value you specified using the `vncdisplay` configuration file option. In reality, neither of those is always the case. The folks at SUSE wrote a great little script to automatically figure out the port to connect to, which I have modified slightly to be a bit more flexible. This looks like the following:

```
#!/bin/sh
function usage {
        echo "Usage: $0 DOMAIN-ID/DOMAIN-NAME"
        exit 1
}
if [ $# = 0 ] ; then
usage
fi
domid=`xm domid $1`
port=`xenstore-read /local/domain/${domid}/console/vnc-port`
if [ $port .gt. 5900 ] ; then
port=`expr $port - 5900`
fi
host=`grep vnc-listen /etc/xen/xend-config.sxp | sed -e \
    "s;.*'\(.*\)');\1;"`
echo "Starting viewer for $1 ($domid): host $host port $port"
vncviewer $host:$port
```

This script takes the ID or name of a HVM domainU guest as an argument, and examines the XenStore to look up the VNC port that the domain is using. This script will therefore only work for HVM domains, because only they set the `vnc-port` name/value key in the XenStore. The script then looks at the Xen daemon configuration file to determine the IP address on which the Xen daemon listens for VNC connections, and starts a VNC viewer to connect to the specified port and address. This script doesn't do sufficient error-checking, but it's primarily here as an example. Feel free to add your own error-checking for cases such as when the specified domain is a paravirtualized domain, and therefore doesn't set the `vnc-port` key, if multiple `vnc-listen` entries exist in the Xen daemon's configuration file, and so on. Distributions such as Fedora 7 that use recent versions of the libvirt virtualization library provide tools such as virt-viewer that officially replace scripts such as this one for a variety of virtual machines, including Xen, but it is still useful to understand how to use the XenStore if Xen is your focus.

Regardless of the window manager or desktop environment that your X11 VNC server is starting, minimizing the amount of in-screen or desktop updates is always a good idea for both speed and network performance reasons. Here are some tips to minimize graphical updates and the network bandwidth required to communicate them:

❏   Minimize the color depth of the desktop.

❏   Eliminate window highlighting when windows get focus.

❏   Don't automatically raise windows when they get focus.

❏   Don't use opaque moves when moving windows. Configure your window manager or desktop environment to move window outlines instead.

Xen Lifecycle Management

Lifecycle management is the phrase used to describe managing the creation, deployment, use, maintenance, and eventual disposal, retirement, or replacement of some entity. There are many different lifecycle management domains, each with its own set of special considerations related to that domain: product lifecycle management, application lifecycle management, information lifecycle management, and so on. In the area of virtual machines and enterprise computing environments, the cornerstones of lifecycle management are the ability to create, suspend, migrate, monitor, resume, shut down, and otherwise manage virtual machines.

Older open source releases of Xen required that virtual machines be started manually (created) using a configuration file in Python variable format. Virtual machines could be started automatically at boot time (using the `xm create` command) by putting a symbolic link to their configuration files in the directory `/etc/xen/auto`. Information about these virtual machines was created in the XenStore when they were started, but this information was not persistent across system restarts. During system shutdown, these virtual machines would be shut down, migrated, or checkpointed automatically, depending on settings in the file `/etc/sysconfig/xendomains`. This mechanism still works with current Xen distributions if you do not use the current lifecycle management approach explained in the rest of this section. No state information about these virtual machines was preserved across system restarts except for the names of the different domains provided in the `/etc/sysconfig/xendomains` file, plus any checkpoint files that had been preserved when the system was shut down.

With Xen 3.0.3, Xen configuration files can be loaded into the XenStore (using the `xm new` command) and that configuration information persists across system restarts. Systems that have configuration information present in the XenStore are started using the `xm start` command rather than the `xm create` command. Storing domain information in the XenStore immediately permits listing information about domains that are available on a given domain0 host rather than just those that are currently running.

Xen's lifecycle management is still actively under development, but it is fundamental to more advanced administrative tools that interact with central resources such as the XenStore. This enables such tools to cooperate rather than each using its own data structures and information repositories.

The developers of Linux distributions that include Xen as well as vendors and open source projects that are working on Xen administration and monitoring software are actively involved in helping expand the lifecycle management capabilities of Xen. Standards organizations such as the Distributed Management Task Force (DMTF, `www.dmtf.org`) provide guidelines for systems management of IT environments in enterprises and the Internet. Such standards enable operating system and software vendors to develop platform-independent, compatible, and interoperable systems management software. As commercial deployments of Xen increase, the need for software that documents, monitors, and manages enterprise Xen environments will become even more pressing.

Xen Access Control and Security Policies

Xen provides an optional low-level access control framework based on the Secure Hypervisor (sHype) security architecture that was originally developed by IBM research (`www.research.ibm.com/ssd_shype`). This framework permits and denies resource access and communication between domains at the hypervisor level based on a security policy. Linux resource and access control mechanisms such as SELinux (Security Enhanced Linux, www.nsa.gov/selinux/ or http://selinux.sourceforge.net/) provide similar protection at the operating system level.

Applying access policies at the hypervisor level provides fundamental protection against rogue domains in the Xen environment. More important, it provides an operating system–independent policy mechanism that enables the application of identical policies across different Xen domains regardless of the degree to which they are supported in any given operating system. Hypervisor access and resource policies are not limited to use on a single machine. The same policies can be copied and used on multiple domain0 systems to guarantee equivalent policies and protections to all Xen guest domains that are participating in distributed computing tasks. Hypervisor-level security models provide security at a level that is independent of the physical or network configuration of a given domain0 system, and can therefore migrate to other machines where the same policies are in effect without requiring higher-level reconfiguration.

The next section explains how to build a version of Xen that supports security policies and provides the tools necessary to work with them. Subsequent sections explain how to create a security policy and associate it with your domains and the resources that they use.

Xen, Tools, and Package Requirements for Access Control

To use Xen's access control framework, you must be using a version of Xen that has been built with support for the sHype access control module (ACM). If you are building Xen from source code, you can enable the ACM in the Xen kernel by modifying the file Config.mk, located in the main Xen source code directory. By default, ACM security is disabled (ACM_SECURITY ?= n). To enable ACM security, change the value of this variable to y:

```
ACM_SECURITY ?= y
```

An additional variable in the Config.mk file that you should consider is the ACM_DEFAULT_SECURITY_POLICY variable. This variable defines the default policy used by Xen if security is enabled but no policy file is specified, or the specified policy file cannot be accessed for some reason. The default value of this variable is ACM_NULL_POLICY, as shown in the setting delivered in the vanilla Config.mk file:

```
ACM_DEFAULT_SECURITY_POLICY ?= ACM_NULL_POLICY
```

As the name suggests, the ACM_NULL_POLICY value tells Xen not to use security. The other possible value, CHINESE_WALL_AND_SIMPLE_TYPE_ENFORCEMENT_POLICY, tells Xen to use a Chinese wall model for determining which domains can run simultaneously and controlling resource sharing. The term "Chinese wall" refers to a basic security model in which read/write access to data is governed by whether users and data belong to classes that are used to identify mutually exclusive interests.

After configuring your kernel for ACM security, you can then rebuild the Xen kernel using your standard make command, typically make dist.

Once you build the kernel, you must also build the tools required to define and save policies. To do this, execute the following command from the main Xen source code directory:

```
make tools
```

You can then install the new Xen kernel in the standard fashion (as discussed in "Installing Xen" in Chapter 3). Once the updated kernel and associated modules are installed, you must also install the tools required to define and save policies. To do this, execute the following command from the main Xen source code directory:

```
make install-tools
```

The tool that Xen source distributions provide to enable you to create and save policies is called `xensec_ezpolicy`, and is installed in the directory `/usr/sbin`. This graphical tool uses the wxPython package (`http://wxpython.org`) to provide Python bindings for the cross-platform wxWidgets library (`http://wxwidgets.org/`). You must install these packages before you can proceed. If your Linux distribution provides a package management tool, the wxWidgets library will usually be installed automatically in order to satisfy the requirements of the wxPython package.

The next few sections explain how to create and use an access control policy. The following is an overview of the process:

1. Create an access control policy and add it to the GRUB boot stanza for your Xen installation.

2. Reboot your system so that the hypervisor starts with the new policy.

3. Associate each of your Xen domains with a specific entity (known as a workload) in the policy file.

4. Associate all of the resources for each of your domains with the appropriate entity in the policy file.

5. If you are using Xen's lifecycle management, delete the old entries for your domains and reload the configuration files for your domains.

6. Restart your domainU guests.

Unfortunately, but by design, Xen access controls and security policies are an all-or-nothing proposition. Once you restart the hypervisor with a security policy, you will not be able to start any domains without their being associated with a valid entity in the policy file that the hypervisor is using.

Creating an Access Control Policy

Once you have built Xen, the ACM tools, and the packages that these tools require, executing the command `/usr/sbin/xensec_ezpolicy` should bring up the graphical application shown in Figure 9-6.

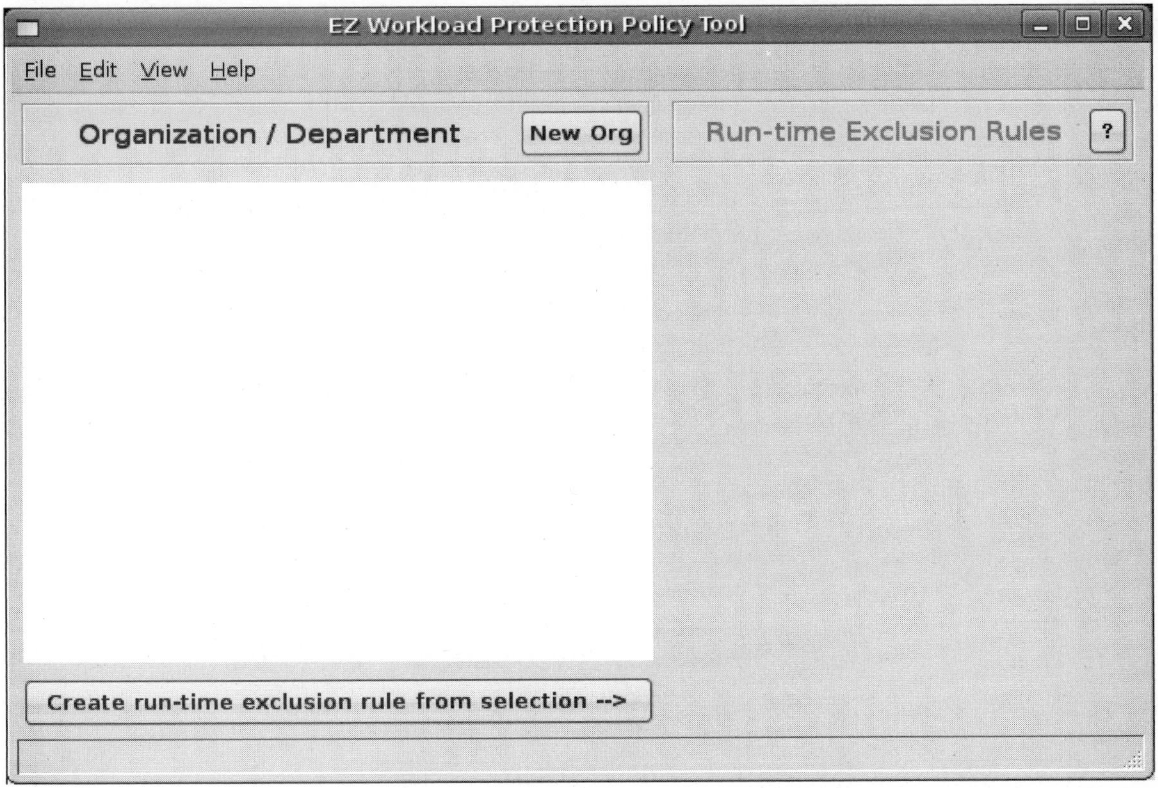

Figure 9-6

The following is the general process of creating a policy using this tool:

1. Define each entity that you want to be able to uniquely identify in your security policy. The xensec_ezpolicy terms for these are *organizations,* which are top-level entities, and *departments,* which are entities within organizations. Each of these is generically referred to as a workload because it represents a specific class of VM activity.

2. Define runtime conflicts between those workloads.

3. Save your workload and runtime conflict definitions as a workload definition, for future reference.

4. Generate a Xen access control policy from the workload definition.

The following example creates two organizations (workloads): Internal and External. It then creates a runtime conflict rule that will be used to prevent virtual machines from different organizations from running at the same time on the same machine. If you are interested in using Xen's access control framework and are also using migration to support high-availability systems, a simple rule such as this one can be quite useful to prevent virtual machines with privileged or proprietary data from running in a networked environment where they might be fair game for hackers, such as in a DMZ or on the Internet itself.

To use the xensec_ezpolicy tool to create a simple policy file that implements this rule, do the following:

1. As the root user, start the xensec_ezpolicy tool, which should look like the screen shown in Figure 9-6.

2. Click New Org and create a workload named Internal, as shown in Figure 9-7. Click OK to save the new organization. In the example, the workload will be associated with virtual machines that are visible only from computers within your enterprise, presumably because they may contain source code, privileged information such as personnel or finance information, and so on.

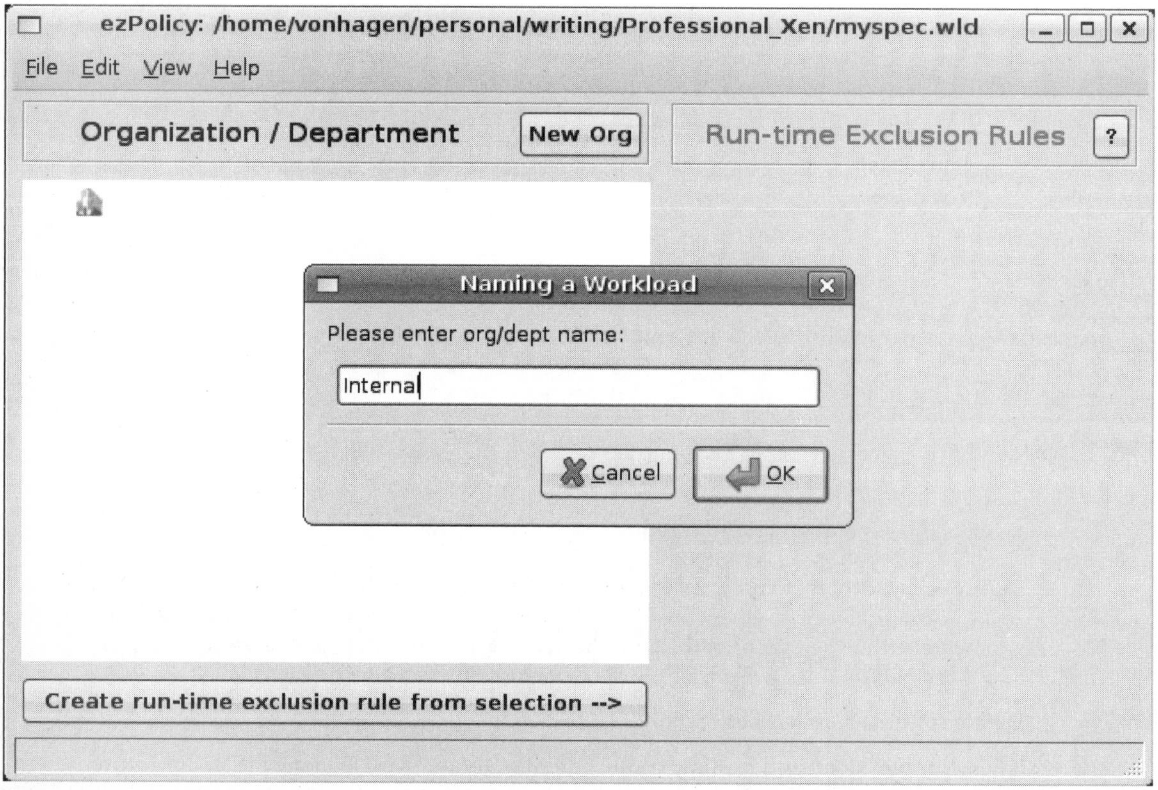

Figure 9-7

3. Click New Org again and create a workload named External. Conceptually, this workload will be associated with virtual machines that are visible from computers that are external to your enterprise.

4. Hold down the Ctrl key and select the names of both of these organizations. Click the button at the bottom of the screen that says Create run-time exclusion rule from selection. A dialog box appears, prompting you for the name that you want to assign to this rule, as shown in Figure 9-8.

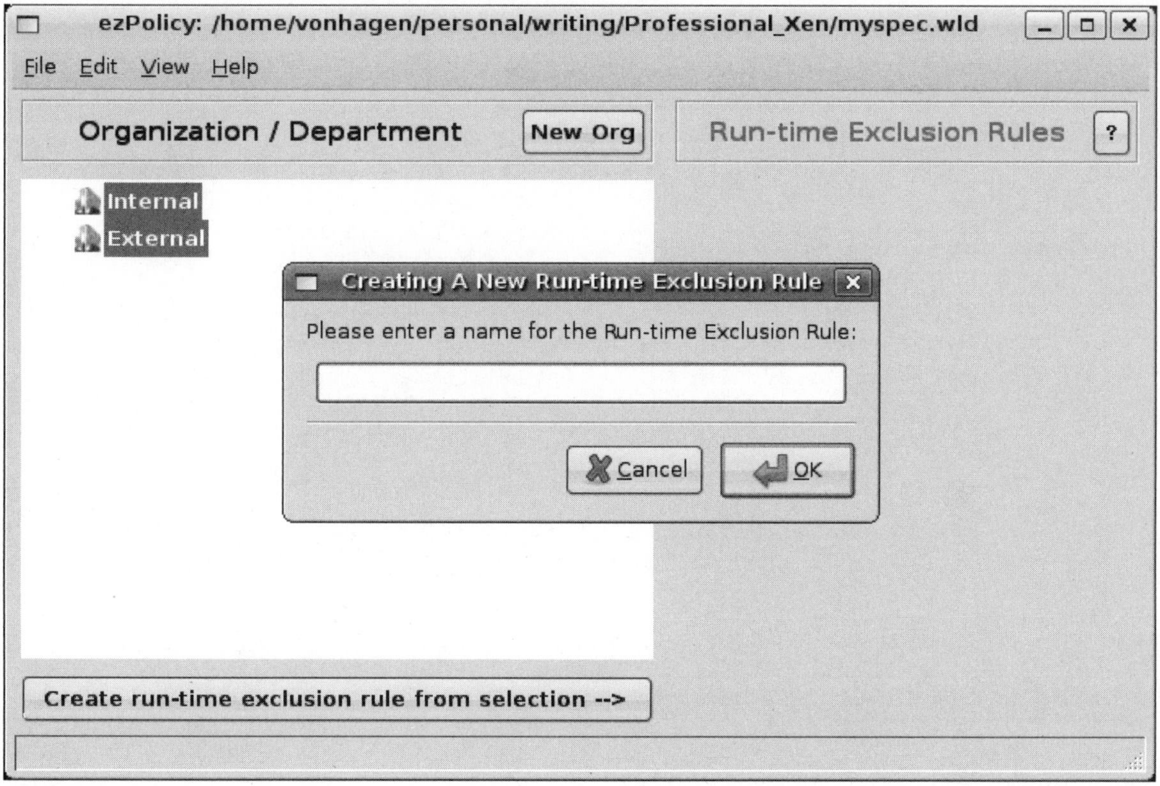

Figure 9-8

5. Enter the name of the rule and click OK to save it. Your screen should now look like Figure 9-9.

6. Select File ⇨ Save (or press Ctrl-S) to save your workload and rule definitions. Because this is the first time that you have saved this data, you will be prompted for the name that this file should have.

7. Select File ⇨ Save as Xen ACM Security Policy. A dialog box appears, prompting you for the name of the policy that you are creating. Note that this is not the name of the file that you are saving to, but is a label for the policy itself. This should usually be composed of alphanumeric characters, dashes, underscores, and so on. This policy name should not contain spaces, because (by default) it will be used in the name of the file in which the policy will be stored. This example uses the sample policy name Internal-or-External.

8. Enter a name and click OK. A second dialog box appears, prompting you for the location in which you want to save this file, which is the directory `/etc/xen/acm-security/policies` by default. The suggested name of the file containing your policy will be created by appending `_security_policy.xml` to the name of the policy that you are saving. In this example, the name of this file would therefore be `Internal-or-External_security_policy.xml`.

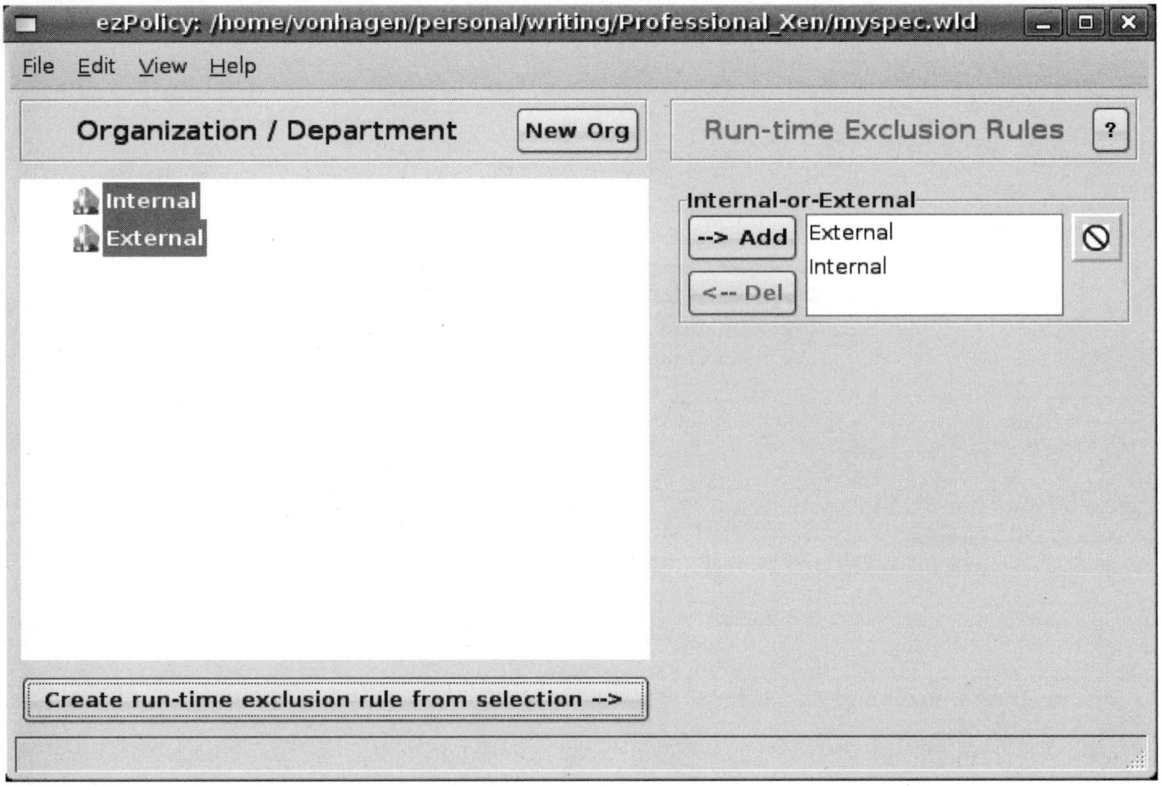

Figure 9-9

9. Exit the xensec_ezpolicy tool and use the `xm makepolicy` command to create a binary policy file that the hypervisor can load. By default, this command looks for files in the directory `/etc/xen/acm-security/policies`, so you can simply execute the following command to create binary policy files that can be used by the hypervisor:

```
# xm makepolicy Internal-or-External
```

After executing this command, listing the directory `/etc/xen/acm-security/policies` shows the following files:

```
# ls -1 -t
Internal-or-External.bin
Internal-or-External.map
Internal-or-External-security_policy.xml
example
security_policy.xsd
```

As you can see, the `xm makepolicy` command creates two files from the XML policy definition file:

❑ `POLICY.bin`: A binary policy-definition file suitable for loading by the hypervisor

❑ `POLICY.map`: A text file that maps logical names to entries in the `POLICY.bin` file

This is just a simple example. In real enterprise environments, you would probably want more granular exclusion rules. This could easily be done by creating multiple departments within an organization and defining inter-department or inter-organization exclusion rules.

> The actual Xen documentation, installed in `/usr/share/doc/xen` in most Xen distributions or if you built and installed Xen yourself, contains a tutorial on creating a policy file using this tool.

The next section explains how to deploy policy files and associate them with your domain0 and domainU systems.

Deploying Policy Files

After creating policy files as described in the previous section, deploying Xen to use them is fairly straightforward. The `xm cfgbootpolicy` command automates this process. This command requires two arguments: the name of the policy that you want to add, and a unique portion of the title entry for the GRUB boot stanza that you want to add it to.

As an example, assume that the entries in your GRUB configuration file are the following on a random system:

```
# grep title /boot/grub/menu.lst
title    XEN 3.1.0
title    XEN 3.1.0 with Policy
title    Ubuntu, kernel 2.6.20-16-386
title    Ubuntu, kernel 2.6.20-16-386 (recovery mode)
title    Ubuntu, memtest86+
```

In this case, you could execute the following command to add a boot policy to the GRUB stanza labeled "XEN 3.1.0 with Policy":

```
# xm cfgbootpolicy Internal-or-External Policy
```

Trying to add a boot policy using a non-unique identifier for a GRUB stanza (such as XEN, in this example) displays an error message like the following:

```
ACMError: Following boot entries matched:
    ['XEN 3.1.0', 'XEN 3.1.0 with Policy'].
Please specify unique part of the boot title.
```

If this doesn't work for some reason, you can accomplish the same thing manually:

1. Copy the binary file for your policy into your system's boot directory, as in the following example:

```
# cp /etc/xen/acm-security/policies/Internal-or-External.bin /boot
```

2. Add a module entry to the target GRUB boot stanza that loads this policy file at boot time:

```
module /boot/Internal-or-External.bin
```

This entry must agree with your other entries in terms of whether or not it needs to include the name of the /boot directory.

At this point, you can reboot your machine, select the appropriate entry from the GRUB menu, and boot into the security-enabled Xen hypervisor with this policy loaded. To verify that the policy file has been loaded, use the xm list command with the --label option to display all security labels that are currently active, as in the following example:

```
Name               ID   Mem VCPUs State    Time(s) Label
LAMP-VM                  256    1              0.0 ERROR
OpenSUSE                 256    1              0.0 ERROR
centos.5-0              256    1              0.0 ERROR
Ubuntu                  256    1              0.0 ERROR
slackware.11-0          128    1              0.0 ERROR
Foresight               384    1              0.0 ERROR
Domain-0           0   1024    2 r-----     789.0 SystemManagement
```

> **If the Label field displays INACTIVE, the hypervisor did not load your security policy file, and the access control framework is inactive. In this case, double-check that the GRUB boot stanza was updated correctly and that the policy file is present in /boot. Then reboot your system, making sure that you select the correct GRUB stanza.**

If Domain-0 shows a Label field value of SystemManagement, this indicates that the newly installed policy framework is working. The SystemManagement label is a default label that is always associated with domain0 when a security policy is being used with Xen.

If you are using Xen's lifecycle management (and therefore have domain information stored in the XenStore), you will also see a few error messages of the following form:

```
ACMError: Security information not found in info struct.
```

In addition, all such domains will display ERROR in their Label field (as shown in the output example). This is because those existing domains have been registered with the XenStore but do not have policy entries in the XenStore because they are not yet associated with any policy.

The remainder of this section explains how to add mandatory labels to each of your domains. The configuration file for the domainU guest used as an example throughout the rest of this section is as follows:

```
kernel = "/boot/vmlinuz-2.6.18-xen"
ramdisk = "/boot/initrd-2.6.18-xen.img"
memory = 256
name = "Ubuntu"
vif = [ '' ]
dhcp = "dhcp"
```

```
disk = ['tap:aio:/home/xen/ubuntu704.img,sda1,w',
        'tap:aio:/home/xen/ubuntu704.swap,sda2,w',
        'phy:/dev/hda,hda:cdrom,r']
root = "/dev/sda1 ro"
serial='pty'
usb=1
usbdevice='tablet'
```

The next section explains how to associate a policy with each of your domainU guests.

Associating Policies with domainU Guests

As mentioned previously, if you are running a Xen hypervisor that uses a security policy file, you will not be able to start any domains that are not associated with a valid entry in that file. Trying to start any domain using the standard xm create command will display a message like the following:

```
# xm create ubuntu704.cfg
Using config file "./ubuntu704.cfg".
   Ubuntu: DENIED
   --> Domain not labeled
Checking resources: (skipped)
Error: 'Security Configuration prevents domain from starting'
```

The new domain could not be created because it is not associated with an entity in your policy file. At the time of this writing, trying to use the xm start command to start a domain that is registered with Xen's lifecycle management but is not associated with a policy will display the following less-than-useful error message:

```
Error: (12, 'Cannot allocate memory')
```

There are certainly cases when this is a valid error message, such as when you actually do not have enough free memory available to start a new domain, but this isn't one of them. In this case, the error message means that the domain could not be started, but the actual cause of this failure isn't being correctly propagated to the xm command. If you are using Xen's lifecycle management, you should delete the current entries for any domains that are not associated with a security policy, as in the following example:

```
# xm delete Ubuntu
```

This domain can be re-registered with Xen's lifecycle management once it is configured correctly.

It is often useful to be able to check the list of security policies that are available to the running hypervisor. You can use the xm labels command to list all of the labels that are available in the current policy file, as in the following example:

```
# xm labels
External
Internal
SystemManagement
```

To label a domain configuration file with one of these labels, use the xm addlabel command, as in the following example:

```
# xm addlabel Internal dom ubuntu704.cfg
```

This associates the domain defined in the ubuntu704.cfg configuration file with the label Internal. (See Appendix A for detailed information on the xm addlabel command.)

Trying to restart your domain at this point displays a new set of error messages:

```
# xm create ubuntu704.cfg
Using config file "./ubuntu704.cfg".
   phy:/dev/hda: DENIED
   --> res: __NULL_LABEL__ (NULL)
   --> dom: External (Internal-or-External)
   file:/home/xen/ubuntu704.img: DENIED
   --> res:__NULL_LABEL__ (NULL)
   --> dom: External (Internal-or-External)
   file:/home/xen/ubuntu704.swap: DENIED
   --> res:__NULL_LABEL__ (NULL)
   --> dom: External (Internal-or-External)
Error: 'Security Configuration prevents domain from starting'
```

Don't worry — this is actually progress. This shows that the domain is now correctly labeled, but that it cannot start because the resources required by that domain are not labeled.

The next section explains how to label the resources associated with a domain.

Labeling Resources

The last step in setting up and using security policies with Xen is to label the resources associated with each of your virtual machines. These resources must be labeled with the same policy that is associated with the domain that uses them. Labeling resources is done with the same xm addlabel command used in the previous section, using the res keyword to identify the fact that you are labeling a resource.

Resources must be labeled so that Xen can identify the policy with which they are associated. Allowing domains to use unlabelled resources would violate basic security principles, because this would potentially enable domains to access resources that are associated with systems that use a different security policy.

Domain label information is stored in a domain's configuration file and propagated to the XenStore if you are using Xen's lifecycle management. Resource label information is stored in the file /etc/xen/acm-security/policies/resource_labels, which is created the first time that you assign a resource label. You will see a message to this effect if this is the case.

To label a resource with the same label as the domainU guest that uses it, type a command like the following:

```
# xm addlabel External res file:/home/xen/ubuntu704.img
Resource file not found, creating new file at:
/etc/xen/acm-security/policies/resource_labels
```

As mentioned previously, because this is the first resource label that has been defined on this system, the file in which resource labels are stored is created automatically.

You would then use the same command to label the other resources required by the domain identified in your configuration file. To continue with the example used throughout this section, you would type the following commands:

```
# xm addlabel External res  file:/home/xen/ubuntu704.swap
# xm addlabel External res  phy:/dev/hda
```

If you see error messages such as "Invalid Resource," make sure that you have specified the full pathname to the resource, and that you correctly identified the type of resource (phy, file, and so on).

You can use the xm resources command to list the resources that have been associated with security policies on your system, as in the following example:

```
# xm resources
file:/home/xen/ubuntu704.swap
    policy: Internal-or-External
    label:  External
file:/home/xen/ubuntu704.img
    policy: Internal-or-External
    label:  External
phy:/dev/hda
    policy: Internal-or-External
    label:  External
```

At this point, if you are using Xen's lifecycle management, you should reload its configuration information into the XenStore (assuming that you previously deleted it) by using the following command:

```
# xm new ubuntu704.cfg
```

Running the xm addlabel --label command shows that the domain is correctly labeled and is present in the XenStore:

```
Name            ID    Mem VCPUs State    Time(s) Label
LAMP-VM               256   1            0.0 ERROR
OpenSUSE              256   1            0.0 ERROR
centos.5-0            256   1            0.0 ERROR
Ubuntu                256   1            0.0 External
slackware.11-0        128   1            0.0 ERROR
Foresight             384   1            0.0 ERROR
Domain-0         0   1024   2 r-----   789.0 SystemManagement
```

You can then start the domain using the xm start command (or the xm create ubuntu704.cfg command, if you are not using Xen's lifecycle management). The xm list --label command would then show results similar to the following:

```
Name            ID    Mem VCPUs State    Time(s) Label
LAMP-VM               256   1            0.0 ERROR
OpenSUSE              256   1            0.0 ERROR
centos.5-0            256   1            0.0 ERROR
```

(continued)

(continued)

```
Ubuntu                  256     1 -b----      3.6 External
slackware.11-0          128     1             0.0 ERROR
Foresight               384     1             0.0 ERROR
Domain-0          0    1024     2 r-----    789.0 SystemManagement
```

> If you are using security policies in a Xen environment where you are using migration to avoid downtime, make sure that you copy those policies and the resource file to all of the domain0 systems that might be involved in migration. You must also make the necessary changes to the GRUB configuration file on all of the domain0 systems that might be involved in migration, and restart them to use the policy framework before attempting migration. Older versions of Xen required that you remove labels from a domainU system and its resources before attempting migration, but this should not be necessary if all of the domain0 systems that could be involved in the migration have identical policy and resource definitions.

Removing Policies from a Xen System

After experimenting with policies, you may find that you do not want to use them on certain hosts because they can be somewhat inflexible (by design, of course). To remove the use of policies from a given domain0 system, I typically do the following:

❑ Clone the boot entry for Xen in `/boot/grub/menu.1st`, creating an identical one that does not load the ACM module. This makes it easiest to revert to using policies as needed, by setting the correct GRUB boot default. If you do not want to use policies, make sure that you set the GRUB boot default to the non-ACM Xen boot entry.

❑ Move the file `/etc/xen/acm-security/policies/resource_labels` file to something like `/etc/xen/acm-security/policies/resource_labels.SAVE` so that you still have this information if you want to restore the use of policies.

❑ Comment out the `access_control` entries in the configuration files for your virtual machines so that you still have this information if you want to reinstitute policies.

❑ Reboot your domain0 system and restart the domainU guests.

Xen's implementation of an access control model and framework is one of the many contributions to Xen that IBM has made, both directly (as in this case) and indirectly (as in relevant research, or pioneering the whole "virtual machine thing" in the first place). Another good example of IBM's contributions to Xen is their virtual TPM implementation, which is discussed in the next section.

Xen and Trusted Computing

Trusted Computing is both a popular and despised topic, depending on whom you ask. The term "trusted computing" refers to technology, both hardware and software, that is intended to provide increased security for computer systems. A Trusted Platform Module (TPM) is a hardware device, generally a microprocessor-based chipset present on a computer system's motherboard, that provides built-in cryptography support and associated storage for security-oriented digital key/value pair generation, storage, and retrieval. The TPM specification (`https://www.trustedcomputinggroup.org/specs/TPM/`) identifies the requirements of TPM devices and modules, and was developed by the Trusted Computing Platform Alliance (now the Trusted Computing Group, `www.trustedcomputinggroup.org/`) which comprised industry vendors such as AMD, Hewlett-Packard, IBM, Intel, Microsoft, Sun Microsystems, and others. TPMs are just one aspect of modern computer security mechanisms, generally known as trusted computing, that are designed to provide a higher level of security through hardware support than traditional motherboard, BIOS, and operating system security mechanisms can deliver. For additional information about trusted computing in general, see the TrustedForum at `www.trustedforum.org`.

Compliant TPMs support hashing, random number generation, asymmetric key generation, and asymmetric encryption/decryption (via an on-board 2048-bit RSA encryption/decryption engine). TPMs permanently associate a unique identifier with each computer system, and can be used to verify the identity of that system, verify that the software running on that system is unmodified, and so on. Unfortunately, they can also be misused to support odious technologies such as Digital Rights Management (DRM) and the conceptually flawed Digital Millennium Copyright Act (DMCA). TPMs are already in use in many secure corporate and government environments and in end-user systems such as Microsoft Windows BitLocker Drive Encryption.

As you can infer from the emphasis on hardware support and unique identifiers for individual computer systems, TPMs provide an interesting problem for virtualized environments, where multiple operating systems are simultaneously running on a single hardware platform. An even more interesting problem is the requirements that TPMs in virtualized environments must also support the secure migration of the TPM state from one physical system to another when domainU guests are migrated from one system to another.

Current TPMs support only single TPM owners (the unique identifier for the system associated with a TPM); a single set of platform configuration registers; single key sets for signing, decryption, and encryption; and so on. To resolve problems such as these, IBM developed extensions to the command set defined in version 1.2 of the TPM specification in order to support virtual TPMs (`http://domino.research.ibm.com/comm/research_projects.nsf/pages/ssd_vtpm.index.html`). These extensions provide virtual TPM management commands that support the secure creation and deletion of TPM instances, which can then be associated with and used by specific virtual machines. These extensions have been integrated into the open source Xen software, which also provides a virtual TPM manager that coordinates virtual TPM activities and coordinates protected key storage in a hardware TPM and frontend and backend drivers. This enables virtual machines to communicate with the virtual TPM manager through a TPM software stack and TPM emulator that can be used for Xen development and testing on systems without TPM hardware. The sample TPM software stack used is known as TrouSerS, which was created and released by IBM, and is available at `http://sourceforge.net/projects/trousers`.

> The TPM emulator provided with Xen is not suitable for deployment, which should only be done on hardware with Linux-supported TPMs on the motherboard (such as motherboards from NSC, Atmel, Infineon, and so on).

If you are going to use Xen's vTPM support, you should also investigate TrustedGRUB, a version of the GRUB bootloader that supports multiboot kernels such as Xen and provides trusted platform module support. TrustedGRUB can be downloaded from SourceForge (`http://sourceforge.net/projects/trustedgrub`). TrustedGRUB supports Xen by enabling the analysis of arbitrary files during the boot process (kernel, initial RAM disk/filesystem, hypervisor, and so on) and the comparison of the results of that analysis against Platform Configuration Registers (PCRs) located on the TPM. Although it is only suitable for use with hardware TPMs, TrustedGRUB provides an additional level of TPM support in secure environments where a flexible bootloader is still required.

Building Xen with TPM Support and Associated Tools

As you might expect, not everyone needs (or wants) TPM support in Xen, so building Xen with TPM support requires that you make minor configuration changes to the default settings in a Xen source distribution. The drivers used for TPM support in Xen are built as modules in the default kernel configuration used by Xen source distributions. However, you will need to modify Xen's default build settings to build the TPM-related tools for Xen, and will have to make some additional modifications if you want to use the TPM emulator.

At the time of this writing, the following kernel configuration variables are relevant when building Xen with TPM support:

```
CONFIG_XEN_TPMDEV_BACKEND=m
CONFIG_TCG_TPM=m
CONFIG_TCG_ATMEL=m
CONFIG_TCG_INFINEON=m
CONFIG_TCG_NSC=m
CONFIG_TCG_TIS=m
CONFIG_TCG_XEN=m
```

The first of these entries builds the backend driver required for TPM support in the domain0 kernel as a module. The others build TPM-specific modules. The `CONFIG_TCG_TPM` configuration variable is associated with the driver that provides the basic support required for the Trusted Computing Group's TPM specification (hence the name of the variable). The `CONFIG_TCG_XEN` configuration variable activates the driver that provides the frontend support required by Xen for TPM support in Xen domainU guests. The other TPM-related configuration variables activate the drivers for specific TPM hardware chip sets.

> As shown in the previous example, the drivers used for TPM support in Xen and for general TPM support are built by default when building the Xen kernel, but are built as modules. This is usually sufficient for development and testing purposes, but you probably want to compile them into your kernel when you actually deploy Xen systems that require TPM support. You can do this by setting the `CONFIG_XEN_TPMDEV_BACKEND`, `CONFIG_TCG_TPM`, and `CONFIG_TCG_XEN` kernel configuration variables to `y`, as well as any variables associated with the particular TPM chipset in the hardware that you are deploying on. If you are building separate kernels for domain0 and domainU systems, you should set the `CONFIG_XEN_TPMDEV_BACKEND` and `CONFIG_TCG_TPM` variables to `y` in your domain0 kernel configuration file, and set the `CONFIG_TCP_TPM` and `CONFIG_TCG_XEN` variables to `y` in your domainU kernel configuration file.

> Building required modules into your kernels will provide a minimal performance improvement. More important, it simplifies deployment and provides increased security because it eliminates the possibility of someone maliciously replacing TPM-related kernel modules. Similarly, if you are deploying on a specific hardware platform with a known TPM chipset, you may want to compile the driver for that chipset into your kernel. Continuing to build the modules for other chipsets can simplify testing on other platforms that use those chipsets, but deploying in that fashion may violate the policies of many secure environments.

After making any desired changes to your kernel configuration, you will also need to modify the primary Xen configuration file so that the tools required to use the virtual TPM will be built. To do this, modify the file `Config.mk` in the root directory of your Xen source distribution, and activate the `VTPM_TOOLS` entry, which will then look like the following:

```
VTPM_TOOLS ?= y
```

If you want to use the TPM emulator for development and testing, you will also need to modify the file `tools/vtpm/Rules.mk` in order to activate building the TPM emulator. The updated entry should look like the following:

```
BUILD_EMULATOR = y
```

You must also update an entry in the file `tool/vtpm manager/Rules.mk` so that the vTPM management daemon communicates via a FIFO rather than the `/dev/tpm` device used with physical TPM chipsets. To do his, remove the comment character at the beginning of the following line in this file:

```
CFLAGS += -DDUMMY_TPM
```

You can now build the Xen kernel, modules, and related tools using your favorite build commands. (See "Building Xen from Source Code" in Chapter 3 for detailed information about available Xen build commands.

> Building the TPM emulator requires that the GNU Multi-Precision Library (libgmp, `http://gmplib.org`) and header files be installed on your build system. The libgmp library is a free library for arbitrary precision arithmetic in which the precision of rational and floating point math is essentially only limited by the capabilities of your system. As such, libgmp is commonly used in cryptographic and computational applications and related research. Linux distributions that use a package management system typically provide this library and related header files as packages with names such as libgmp3 and libgmp3-dev.

The following build command will create an installable Xen distribution in the `dist` subdirectory of your Xen source distribution and will also install the TPM-related tools and emulator on the system where you are building:

```
make dist install-tools
```

Once this completes successfully, you will need to regenerate any initial RAM disk filesystem used by your domain0 system. You can then reboot your system using your standard graphical or command-line reboot process.

> If you are working in a stable or production Xen environment, you may want to build the kernel again, modifying the kernel's makefile to specify a unique extension via the EXTRAVERSION variable. This will change the name of your default kernel and its associated modules directory. You will then have to create a new GRUB entry for this new kernel, but this will preserve your existing Xen kernel, modules, and GRUB boot entry, enabling you to switch back to your default Xen installation when rebooting, if necessary.

Requirements for Running the vTPM Manager

The virtual TPM manager daemon is the file `vtpm_manager`, which is installed in `/usr/bin` by default. This process must be running on any domain0 system where you want to use Xen's TPM support. This daemon uses the device `/dev/vtpm` to communicate with TPM devices (or the emulator). This device must therefore exist on your domain0 system. If it does not, you can create it manually using the following command:

```
# mknod /dev/vtpm c 10 225
```

If you did not compile the vTPM backend driver into your kernel, you must manually load the module that provides this driver before you can start any domainU system that requires TPM support. To do this, execute the following command:

```
modprobe tpmbk
```

If you did not compile the vTPM backend driver into your kernel, you may want to integrate loading this module into your system's default startup process. You can do this by adding a command to load it in the file `/etc/modprobe.conf` or any similar module configuration/load file used by the Linux distribution that you are using on your domain0 system.

Starting the TPM Emulator

If you are doing development using the TPM emulator, you must start the emulator on your domain0 system before starting the virtual TPM manager there. The first time that you start the emulator, you must start it using the following command:

```
# tpm_emulator clear
```

This will produce verbose output such as the following:

```
Initializing tpm: clear
TPMD: tpm/tpm_cmd_handler.c:4137: Debug: tpm_emulator_init()
TPMD: tpm/tpm_startup.c:30: Info: TPM_Init()
TPMD: tpm/tpm_testing.c:242: Info: TPM_SelfTestFull()
TPMD: tpm/tpm_testing.c:42: Debug: tpm_test_prng()
TPMD: tpm/tpm_testing.c:70: Debug: Monobit: 10078
TPMD: tpm/tpm_testing.c:71: Debug: Poker:    14.1
TPMD: tpm/tpm_testing.c:72: Debug: run_1:    2458, 2446
TPMD: tpm/tpm_testing.c:73: Debug: run_2:    1272, 1250
TPMD: tpm/tpm_testing.c:74: Debug: run_3:    641, 637
TPMD: tpm/tpm_testing.c:75: Debug: run_4:    309, 318
TPMD: tpm/tpm_testing.c:76: Debug: run_5:    149, 151
TPMD: tpm/tpm_testing.c:77: Debug: run_6+:   144, 171
TPMD: tpm/tpm_testing.c:78: Debug: run_34:   0
TPMD: tpm/tpm_testing.c:112: Debug: tpm_test_sha1()
TPMD: tpm/tpm_testing.c:156: Debug: tpm_test_hmac()
TPMD: tpm/tpm_testing.c:183: Debug: tpm_test_rsa_EK()
TPMD: tpm/tpm_testing.c:185: Debug: rsa_generate_key()
TPMD: tpm/tpm_testing.c:190: Debug: testing endorsement key
TPMD: tpm/tpm_testing.c:196: Debug: rsa_sign(RSA_SSA_PKCS1_SHA1)
TPMD: tpm/tpm_testing.c:199: Debug: rsa_verify(RSA_SSA_PKCS1_SHA1)
TPMD: tpm/tpm_testing.c:202: Debug: rsa_sign(RSA_SSA_PKCS1_DER)
TPMD: tpm/tpm_testing.c:205: Debug: rsa_verify(RSA_SSA_PKCS1_DER)
TPMD: tpm/tpm_testing.c:209: Debug: rsa_encrypt(RSA_ES_PKCSV15)
TPMD: tpm/tpm_testing.c:213: Debug: rsa_decrypt(RSA_ES_PKCSV15)
TPMD: tpm/tpm_testing.c:217: Debug: verify plain text
TPMD: tpm/tpm_testing.c:220: Debug: rsa_encrypt(RSA_ES_OAEP_SHA1)
TPMD: tpm/tpm_testing.c:224: Debug: rsa_decrypt(RSA_ES_OAEP_SHA1)
TPMD: tpm/tpm_testing.c:228: Debug: verify plain text
TPMD: tpm/tpm_testing.c:260: Info: Self-Test succeeded
TPMD: tpm/tpm_startup.c:45: Info: TPM_Startup(1)
```

At this point, you can put the TPM emulator in the background.

After the first time that you run the TPM emulator (when you are making sure that everything is actually working), you can start the TPM emulator using the `tpm_emulator save` command, which will reuse saved information from a previous run. You may also want to redirect its output into a file because it is quite verbose.

Starting the vTPM Manager

Once you have created the device used by the virtual TPM backend driver and loaded its kernel module, you can start the vTPM manager daemon. This daemon must be running before you can start any TPM-enabled domainU guests. You can start this daemon using the following command:

```
# /usr/bin/vtpm_managerd
```

This will produce output such as the following:

```
ERROR[VTPM]: Failed to load NVM
TPMD[1]: tpmd.c:126: Info: Initializing tpm state: clear, type: pvm, id: 1
TPMD[1]: tpm/tpm_cmd_handler.c:4137: Debug: tpm_emulator_init()
TPMD[1]: tpm/tpm_startup.c:30: Info: TPM_Init()
TPMD[1]: tpm/tpm_testing.c:242: Info: TPM_SelfTestFull()
TPMD[1]: tpm/tpm_testing.c:42: Debug: tpm_test_prng()
TPMD[1]: tpm/tpm_testing.c:70: Debug: Monobit: 9987
TPMD[1]: tpm/tpm_testing.c:71: Debug: Poker:   12.6
TPMD[1]: tpm/tpm_testing.c:72: Debug: run_1:   2505, 2520
TPMD[1]: tpm/tpm_testing.c:73: Debug: run_2:   1222, 1202
TPMD[1]: tpm/tpm_testing.c:74: Debug: run_3:   637, 637
TPMD[1]: tpm/tpm_testing.c:75: Debug: run_4:   298, 309
TPMD[1]: tpm/tpm_testing.c:76: Debug: run_5:   164, 166
TPMD[1]: tpm/tpm_testing.c:77: Debug: run_6+:  160, 153
TPMD[1]: tpm/tpm_testing.c:78: Debug: run_34:  0
TPMD[1]: tpm/tpm_testing.c:112: Debug: tpm_test_sha1()
TPMD[1]: tpm/tpm_testing.c:156: Debug: tpm_test_hmac()
TPMD[1]: tpm/tpm_testing.c:183: Debug: tpm_test_rsa_EK()
TPMD[1]: tpm/tpm_testing.c:185: Debug: rsa_generate_key()
TPMD[1]: tpm/tpm_testing.c:190: Debug: testing endorsement key
TPMD[1]: tpm/tpm_testing.c:196: Debug: rsa_sign(RSA_SSA_PKCS1_SHA1)
TPMD[1]: tpm/tpm_testing.c:199: Debug: rsa_verify(RSA_SSA_PKCS1_SHA1)
TPMD[1]: tpm/tpm_testing.c:202: Debug: rsa_sign(RSA_SSA_PKCS1_DER)
TPMD[1]: tpm/tpm_testing.c:205: Debug: rsa_verify(RSA_SSA_PKCS1_DER)
TPMD[1]: tpm/tpm_testing.c:209: Debug: rsa_encrypt(RSA_ES_PKCSV15)
TPMD[1]: tpm/tpm_testing.c:213: Debug: rsa_decrypt(RSA_ES_PKCSV15)
TPMD[1]: tpm/tpm_testing.c:217: Debug: verify plain text
TPMD[1]: tpm/tpm_testing.c:220: Debug: rsa_encrypt(RSA_ES_OAEP_SHA1)
TPMD[1]: tpm/tpm_testing.c:224: Debug: rsa_decrypt(RSA_ES_OAEP_SHA1)
TPMD[1]: tpm/tpm_testing.c:228: Debug: verify plain text
TPMD[1]: tpm/tpm_testing.c:260: Info: Self-Test succeeded
TPMD[1]: tpm/tpm_startup.c:45: Info: TPM_Startup(1)
Loading NVM.
Sending LoadNVM command
Reading LoadNVM header
```

Like the TPM emulator, the vTPM manager daemon is quite verbose. Once you are sure that it is working correctly, you may want to restart it, redirecting its output to a file. Subsequent restarts of the vTPM manager are less noisy than its initial run, producing messages like the following:

```
INFO[VTPM]: Starting VTPM.
INFO[TCS]: Constructing new TCS:
INFO[TCS]: Calling TCS_OpenContext:
INFO[VTSP]: OIAP.
INFO[VTSP]: Loading Key into TPM.
INFO[VTSP]: Unbinding 256 bytes of data.
INFO[VTPM]: Loaded saved state (dmis = 1).
INFO[VTSP]: Loading Key into TPM.
INFO[VTPM]: Creating new DMI instance 0 attached.
INFO[TCS]: Calling TCS_OpenContext:
INFO[VTPM]: [Backend Listener]: Backend Listener waiting \ for messages.
INFO[VTPM]: [VTPM Listener]: VTPM Listener waiting for \ messages.
INFO[VTPM]: [Hotplug Listener]: Hotplug Listener waiting \ for messages.
```

If you are using migration in your Xen implementation, any domain0 system that you want to be able to function as a TPM-enabled migration destination must also be running the virtual TPM migration daemon. This daemon is the file `vtpm_migratord`, and is also installed in `/usr/bin` by default. You can therefore start this daemon on target domain0 systems using a command like the following:

```
# /usr/bin/vtpm_migratord
```

Once the vTPM manager is running, the vTPM can be accessed by loading the frontend driver in a domainU guest, as explained later in this chapter. Before you can do so, you must modify the configuration file for your domainU guests, as explained in the next section.

> **Once you have loaded the backend driver and are running the vTPM manager daemon on a domainO system, you can use the** `xm vtpm-list` **command at any time to identify any virtual TPM devices that are being used by domainU guests.**

Adding vTPM Support to Guest Domains

The configuration information for any domainU guests that require TPM support must be modified so that they can find the vTPM manager and the domain in which it is running. This requires that you add a single line to their configuration files. These new entries have the following form:

```
vtpm = ['instance=number, backend=domainTD']
```

The parameters to the `vtpm` statement are as follows:

❑   `instance` (optional): Identifies the specific vTPM instance that the domainU guest should communicate with which must be 1 or greater (instance 0 is used internally by domain0). Each domainU guest that requires TPM support must use a different, unique instance. The value of the instance parameter is interpreted as a request, not a mandatory value, and may not be the actual instance number that is assigned to the domainU guest if another domainU guest is already using the requested instance. If a requested instance is already in use, the next available instance will be used. The associations between TPM instances and domain IDs are stored in the file `/etc/xen/vtpm.db` on a domain0 system.

❑   `backend`: Identifies the ID of the domain in which the vTPM manager daemon is running. At the time of this writing, the vTPM manager has to be running in domain0.

Although the instance number is optional and the backend is always 0 (at the time of this writing), the configuration files for domainU guests that need TPM functionality must include a `vtpm` entry to identify that fact. You can therefore disable TPM support in a domainU guest simply by removing the `vtpm` entry in its configuration file. A standard `vtpm` entry is therefore the following:

```
vtpm = ['backend=0']
```

If you are using Xen's lifecycle management, don't forget to delete your old configuration information and load the updated file into the XenStore using the `xm new` command.

Finally, if you built TPM support for your domainU guest as a module, you must make sure that you update the root filesystem for each of your domainU guests to provide the updated kernel modules. These are located in the /lib/modules subdirectory that corresponds to the kernel used by that domainU guest. For example, the default Xen kernel version is still 2.6.18-xen at the time of this writing, so you would need to copy the modules for your domainU kernel into the directory /lib/modules/2.6.18-xen in each root filesystem that uses that kernel.

Once you have updated the configuration file for any domainU guests that require TPM support and updated the kernel modules in each root filesystem, you can then start the updated domainU guest normally.

Using the Virtual TPM in a domainU Guest

After starting a domainU guest with a configuration file that enables it to use Xen's TPM support, entries in its /sys/devices/xen directory make it easy to see if TPM support is enabled and actually working. If TPM support is enabled in a domainU guest, the directory /sys/devices/xen/vtpm-0 will exist. If you did not compile the vTPM frontend driver into your kernel, this directory will contain only the following entries:

```
# ls /sys/devices/xen/vtpm-0
bus  devtype  nodename  power  subsystem  uevent
```

If the vTPM driver has been compiled as module, you must load it using the following command:

```
# modprobe tpm_xenu
```

As with the vTPM backend driver and domain0, if you did not compile the frontend driver into your domainU kernel, you may want to integrate loading this module into your system's default startup process. You can do this by adding a command to load it in the file /etc/modprobe.conf or any similar module configuration/load file used by the Linux distribution that you are using on your domainU system.

After loading this module, the message xen_tpm_fr: Initialising the vTPM driver will be sent to the system log, and you should see the following modules in use on your domainU system:

```
# lsmod | grep tpm
tpm_xenu                20240  0 [permanent]
tpm                     22176  1 tpm_xenu
tpm_bios                12288  1 tpm
```

Once Xen's TPM frontend driver has been loaded successfully, your /sys/devices/xen/vtpm-0 directory will contain additional entries, and will look like the following:

```
# ls /sys/devices/xen/vtpm-0
active   caps      enabled    owned  pubek             uevent
bus      devtype   misc:tpm0  pcrs   subsystem
cancel   driver    nodename   power  temp_deactivated
```

You will also see a new device node, /dev/tpm. This node is a character device with the major number 10 and minor number 224, and is used to communicate with the virtual TPM instance used by that domain.

If everything is working correctly, you can examine the file /sys/devices/xen/vtpm-0/pcrs to see the platform configuration registers that are currently in use by the vTPM, as in the following example:

```
# cat /sys/devices/xen/vtpm-0/pcrs
PCR-00: 00 00 00 00 00 00 00 00 00 00 00 00 00 00 00 00 \ 00 00 00 00
PCR-01: 00 00 00 00 00 00 00 00 00 00 00 00 00 00 00 00 \ 00 00 00 00
PCR-02: 00 00 00 00 00 00 00 00 00 00 00 00 00 00 00 00 \ 00 00 00 00
PCR-03: 00 00 00 00 00 00 00 00 00 00 00 00 00 00 00 00 \ 00 00 00 00
[...]
PCR-21: FF FF FF FF FF FF FF FF FF FF FF FF FF FF FF FF \ FF FF FF FF
PCR-22: FF FF FF FF FF FF FF FF FF FF FF FF FF FF FF FF \ FF FF FF FF
PCR-23: FF FF FF FF FF FF FF FF FF FF FF FF FF FF FF FF \ FF FF FF FF
```

At this point, your domainU has successfully connected to its virtual TPM instance and you are ready to begin developing or testing software with TPM requirements.

Troubleshooting

Software is, well, soft. TPM support on Linux is still in its infancy, and virtual TPM support is somewhat less mature in production environments. The TPM command set is still evolving, and incompatibilities exist between different versions and implementations. Although the TPM emulator discussed in this chapter is designed to enable development on hardware platforms without physical TPM chipsets, it is even more susceptible to command set changes, changes in Xen itself, or additional requirements and code changes exposed by increasing use.

If you experience problems with any aspect of vTPM support outside the kernel, a common solution is to download the source code for the version of Xen that is actively under development, known as the xen-unstable branch. You can download the source code for this branch by using Mercurial to retrieve http://xenbits.xensource.com/xen-unstable.hg. The version of the emulator, vTPM manager daemon, and vTPM migration daemon in this branch contain the latest fixes and enhancements. Building and installing these may resolve any problems that you are seeing. These tools and daemons may not be suitable for deployment, but they may help you proceed with your development efforts until an official Xen release resolves the problems that you are seeing.

If you are experiencing problems with any aspect of TPM support in Xen and can't find a solution to your problem on the Xen user groups or the Web in general, always check the Bugzilla database used to track Xen defects (http://bugzilla.xensource.com/bugzilla). Many of the problem reports there contain information and workarounds that you can use to permanently or temporarily resolve the problem that you are seeing until it is fixed in an upcoming, stable Xen release.

Summary

This chapter covers a number of advanced topics in Xen, including attaching new storage devices and peripherals to running domains, using dedicated hardware in paravirtualized systems, working with sound in HVM domainU guests, and various approaches to using graphical displays in both HVM and paravirtualized domains. The chapter also includes detailed discussions of important security-related topics in Xen: creating and implementing security policies that help control which virtual machines can run simultaneously on the same domain0 host, and Xen's support for trusted computing via a virtual trusted platform module implementation.

The next chapter focuses on enterprise topics for Xen, ranging from discussions of administrative and managerial considerations for virtual machine environments to implementation details such as centralizing logging, integrating domain0 with UPS systems, reacting to power failures, domain0 and domainU monitoring, and so on.

10

Using Xen in the Data Center

As in all technologies, experimentation and deployment are very different things. Experimentation is an obvious first step in examining and evaluating any new technology. Many technologies are interesting for their own sake, and can provide insights into new ways of using hardware and software, and into the business processes that depend on them. Regardless of whether any specific technology is eventually adopted, research into new technologies is an important investment that most successful businesses understand. Even if there is no immediate business benefit from a specific experimental technology, keeping up with the technology curve poises you to successfully understand, implement, and incorporate technologies that can increase productivity, performance, and profitability.

Deploying a new technology as a part of your enterprise infrastructure introduces the same reliability and availability requirements that you have for any other technology that you currently depend on. However, it also introduces new support, maintenance, and education requirements for IT staff to manage and support the day-to-day use of the new technology, as well as the creation, incorporation, and adoption of new IT processes across your enterprise for longer-term issues such as disaster and recovery planning.

This chapter highlights the most important planning and process issues related to adopting Xen as a core part of your enterprise infrastructure. If virtualization is a new technology for your organization, this chapter will help you identify important considerations for successful incorporation, use, and management of any virtualization technology, while focusing on Xen-specific issues.

If you are using Xen to augment or replace existing virtualization technologies, you can probably adapt or expand your existing process for dealing with virtualization technologies. However, as with any technology, Xen has its own unique capabilities and associated requirements that you must make sure are addressed by additions to existing policies and procedures. This chapter may even help you identify any omissions or overlooked aspects of your current policies and procedures.

Documenting Your Virtual Machines

Sadly enough, after over 50 years of growth and progress in software engineering, documentation is still the "most likely to be forgotten" component of software development projects, infrastructure design and build-outs, and most other IT-related projects. Most enterprise IT groups maintain some level of system documentation for asset-tracking purposes, but system and infrastructure documentation have different requirements and a different motivation. Asset tracking data is primarily intended to track capital IT assets at a high level, whereas infrastructure and system documentation are designed to provide information about how these corporate IT assets interoperate. Accurate and usable system and infrastructure documentation does the following:

❑   Identifies the systems that host critical software and services

❑   Identifies critical hardware resources required for specific services

❑   Specifies software and hardware dependencies throughout your infrastructure

❑   Provides location information for critical hardware and software resources

❑   Maps connectivity between different systems and networks

The complete reliance of today's businesses on computer systems has increased awareness of the fact that good, up-to-date documentation of critical systems and your IT infrastructure is a mandatory component of both successful day-to-day operations and any disaster recovery plan. Although not the focus of regulatory legislation such as Sarbanes-Oxley, requirements for risk management have led most companies to design, document, and adopt procedures for IT disaster and recovery planning. Like an insurance policy, you hope to never need it, but it is incredibly valuable when you do.

If you do not already have accurate documentation for your systems and IT infrastructure, migrating portions of your enterprise infrastructure to virtual machines provides a unique opportunity to re-examine and document your existing systems and infrastructure as part of the planning process. Identifying systems that can be virtualized depends on knowing what systems your enterprise requires, identifying dependencies between those systems, and determining how (or if) their resource requirements can be satisfied in a virtual machine environment. The "Identifying Candidates for Virtualization" section in Chapter 1 discusses the most common issues that you should consider when looking for physical systems that you can move to virtual machines.

The system documentation required for virtual machines goes one level deeper than identifying critical hardware resources for specific hardware and software systems. In a purely physical IT environment, where only one operating system runs on each hardware platform, there is a one-to-one mapping between the physical location of a device such as a network or storage interface card and the system that uses it. In virtualized environments, although hardware can still only be physically present in a single location, system and requirement tracking becomes a bit more complex:

❑   Network and storage interfaces are typically shared by multiple virtual machines, and are therefore a requirement for each.

❑   Network and storage interface hardware may be dedicated to a single virtual machine.

❑   Single physical disks may host partitions that contain the root (and other) filesystems for multiple virtual machines.

❏   Removable peripherals such as printers, scanners, and external storage devices may be allocated to and used by specific virtual machines rather than the host to which they are physically connected.

How and where you document your systems depends on the number of systems that you are responsible for. Many small installations can easily manage detailed documentation about their servers in a spreadsheet, with different sheets for physical hosts, virtual machines, interface cards, peripherals, disks, and critical software. Assigning unique identifiers for physical resources makes it relatively easy to map them to both the physical host where they are located and to any virtual machine that depends on them.

Larger installations typically record this same information in a database containing tables for these same classes of information. The number of tables used depends on the granularity of the information that you are recording and the extent to which you want to normalize your data. For example, you may want to store operating system data and processor data in separate tables to centralize that information and simplify the tables for physical and virtual machines. As with any database project, balancing data normalization with the complexity of the queries you must issue to get the information that you need is a judgment call.

The basic rule for a physical and virtual system documentation is that it must enable you to locate any unique aspects of a physical or virtual machine. In physical machines, this generally means tracking at least information such as the following:

❏   Motherboard

❏   Processor

❏   Physical memory

❏   PCI cards

❏   Local disk

❏   Peripherals

❏   Filesystems required to boot the physical host

❏   Operating system

❏   Static network information, such as IP addresses

❏   Locally installed software and its requirements

In virtual machines, you typically need to track information such as the following:

❏   Operating system

❏   Filesystems used and their location

❏   Processor information such as bindings to specific cores and the number of VCPUs used

❏   Initial and maximum memory allocation

❏   Dedicated hardware and peripherals

❑   Static network information, such as IP and MAC addresses, virtual interface names used in SNMP tracking, host connectivity via named bridges, any specialized routing information, and so on

❑   Locally installed software and its requirements

You also need to map your internal and external networks, routing between them, and mandatory network hardware.

If you do not already have this sort of information, there's no time like the present to begin assembling it. Short of opening up every system that you are responsible for, you can obtain much of this information using readily available software such as the following:

❑   **Device Manager:** Available on every Microsoft Windows system, this application provides detailed hardware information.

❑   **HWiNFO32:** A commercial product for all flavors of Microsoft Windows, this tool provides comprehensive and up-to-date information about physical systems (www.hwinfo.com).

❑   **lshw:** For Linux and other Unix-like systems, the lshw (list hardware) program probes your physical hardware and provides detailed reports in text, HTML, and XML output formats. It does a great job of system analysis, all the way down to motherboard analysis including manufacturer, model, and BIOS information (http://ezix.org/project/wiki/HardwareLiSter).

❑   **lspci:** For Linux and most other UNIX-like systems, this utility provides detailed information about PCI devices in your system, including on-board bridges. This utility is part of the pciutils package (http://mj.ucw.cz/pciutils.shtml).

❑   **lsusb:** for Linux systems, this utility provides detailed information about the USB interfaces and attached devices on your system. This utility is part of the Linux-USB project's usbutils package (http://sourceforge.net/projects/linux-usb).

❑   **sg3_utils:** For Linux systems, the sg3_utils packages contains a variety of utilities to help you locate and identify SCSI devices (http://sg.torque.net/sg/sg3_utils.html). A list of other tools for probing devices that use the Linux SCSI interface, such as SATA drives, is available at http://sg.torque.net/sg/tools.html.

Specific Linux distributions provide other tools that can be very useful in providing hardware analysis, such as Debian's discover command, Red Hat's Kudzu system, and Novell SUSE's hwinfo command.

Obtaining information about the configuration of your virtual machines is relatively easy. This information is contained in the configuration data for your virtual machines. This can be a configuration file in Python variable, XML, or SXP format, or may be contained only in the XenStore if you used an administrative tool such as virt-manager to create your virtual machines. If this information is only present in the XenStore, you can use a tool such as virsh to dump this information in a format such as XML, or you can use a simple script such as the one shown in "XenStore and Related Utilities" in Chapter 7.

Recording all of the information that you need about your physical and virtual machines can be time-consuming, and keeping it up-to-date requires a regular commitment that must become part of your IT processes. However, having this sort of information at your fingertips, available via a few database queries or some fancy reporting wizardry, is an incredibly valuable asset. Doing the analysis that is required to obtain this information can help you understand any current performance problems that may exist, identify overlooked dependencies or systems that are not completely integrated into your current procedures, suggest additional candidates for virtualization, and so on.

One important thing to remember is that your system and infrastructure documentation will be a critical part of any disaster recovery or problem analysis efforts, so be careful not to introduce any bootstrapping problems in accessing this data. The best documentation in the world is useless if it is stored in a database that you can't access because of a system failure. Regular backups and regular archival of up-to-date system and infrastructure reports are your friends.

Deploying Virtual Machines

As discussed throughout this book, virtualization enables you to make the most of existing computer systems, optimizing your data center by reducing the number of physical machines that you need to deploy, manage, and maintain. Although minimizing capital expenses and operating costs is important, the reliability, performance, and availability of the computing services that your enterprise requires are the primary concerns of any data center.

Most of this book has focused on the technical aspects of using and configuring Xen. This section provides suggestions for deploying Xen virtual machines and integrating them into your domain0 system startup and shutdown procedures to simplify managing them and to maximize their availability.

Xen is still evolving rapidly, so it's no real surprise that Xen management tools, such as those discussed in "Open Source Xen Management Utilities" and "Distribution-Specific Xen Management Software" in Chapter 7 are still evolving as well. Distribution-specific management utilities are sufficient if you are committed to a specific Linux distribution for all of your domain0 hosts. Unfortunately, although many of the open source Xen management projects are not explicitly distribution-specific, they often have dependencies that can be satisfied only on specific platforms so they may as well be. If mandatory packages are available only for specific Linux distributions, then any tools that depend on them can be considered to be distribution-specific as well.

Your enterprise environment may already be using centralized system management software of some sort, in which case you should contact the vendor to see if they have a Xen support module. If you and your IT staff are already familiar with a specific software management package, forcing everyone to learn an additional, Xen-specific management utility is time-consuming and, frankly, irritating. Similarly, buying or implementing a completely new software package can be expensive.

Preparing for Automation

Xen, and virtualization in general, provide great opportunities for streamlining the server room and increasing the availability and manageability of your computing infrastructure and the services that you deliver. This makes it especially important that you put some thought into the organization of the infrastructure for your Xen environment itself.

As you experiment with virtualizing different operating systems, servers, and associated services, it's easy to leave configuration files, virtual machines images, and virtual machine and hardware documentation scattered across your development systems. Centralizing this information should be a part of your virtual machine implementation from the beginning, and a step in the deployment of each new virtual machine. For example, I find it useful to store all Xen-related configuration files and filesystem images in subdirectories of /home/xen named HVM and PARAVIRT, and all VM and physical machine documentation snapshots and backups under /home/xen/DOC (even though the information itself is stored in a MySQL database). Centralizing your Xen-related data, especially configuration information and filesystems, provides some significant ease-of-use and administrative advantages:

❑ Simplifies navigating to a specific configuration file or image file.

❑ Simplifies looking for information about virtual machines by type. This also makes it easy to write scripts that use information from your configuration files or perform maintenance operations. (As an example, see the fsck_vm_images.sh script discussed in "Automating VM Filesystem Consistency Checks" later in this chapter.)

❑ Makes it easy to back up most of your Xen-related data, although the filesystems for many of your virtual machines themselves may be stored elsewhere, such as on networked storage to enable migration. (Backing up Xen virtual machines themselves is discussed in "Backup Strategies for Xen Domains" later in this chapter.)

❑ Makes it easy for other sysadmins to get up-to-speed by providing a relatively intuitive picture of the use of various virtual machines, configuration files, network interfaces, filesystem images, and logical volumes.

Beyond simply organizing where you store Xen-related data, how you name that data is similarly useful. Adopting naming conventions for configuration files, virtual machines, filesystem image files, and logical volumes can provide immediate information about such items before opening them or examining them in detail. The following are some examples of useful naming conventions:

❑ Configuration filenames that identify the operating system and version, provide information about the storage associated with that virtual machine, and identify the use of that VM make it easy to find the right configuration file without excessive use of the grep utility or a text editor. Some sample filenames that follow the conventions I like to use are the following:

  ❑ hv_u704_netlv_users_live.cfg: The configuration file (.cfg) for a hardware virtual machine (hv) running Ubuntu 7.04 (u704) whose filesystems are located in a networked logical volume (netlv), which is intended for users (users) and is deployed (live).

  ❑ hv_winxpp_netp_users_live.cfg: The configuration file for a hardware virtual machine (hv) running Microsoft Windows XP professional (winxpp) whose filesystem is located in a partition on a network device, is intended for users (users), and is deployed (live).

  ❑ hv_u704s_nfs_web_live.cfg: The configuration file for a hardware virtual machine (hv) that is running an Ubuntu 7.04 server (u704s) whose root filesystem is an NFS filesystem (nfs), provides Web services (web), and is deployed (live).

  ❑ pv_f6_mult_db_dev.cfg: The configuration file (.cfg) for a paravirtualized system (pv) running Fedora Core 6 (f6) which uses multiple filesystems (mult), provides database services, and is still in development or testing (dev).

❑ Virtual machine names provide useful information about the virtual machine when you're listing virtual machines or getting status information through utilities such as xentop. I tend to limit machine names to 10 characters because that is the default width of the machine name field in xentop output. For example, the machine names for the machines in the previous list are as follows:

- ❏ U7-AOEL-HV: In the nomenclature I use, AOEL means a logical volume provided by ATA over Ethernet (AoE) networked storage.

  - ❏ XP-AOEP-HV: Similar to the previous bullet item, except that AOEP indicates a physical partition on an AoE device.

  - ❏ U7-NFS-PV: Ubuntu paravirtualized system using NFS.

  - ❏ F6-MULT-PV: Fedora paravirtualized system with multiple filesystems.

- ❏ Logical volumes that indicate the type of virtual machine filesystems that they contain. For example, I typically simply use the operating system name, the filesystem name (if relevant), and the type of virtual machine that the filesystem is being used with.

- ❏ If you are using network management or monitoring software such as SNMP-based packages, it can be very useful to manually assign MAC addresses and virtual network interface names in your Xen configuration files. Although MAC addresses have a predefined format (and Xen MAC addresses are further predefined as beginning with 00:16:3E), manually assigning them to deployed virtual machines or those that you are stress testing can make it easy to identify the network traffic from specific virtual machines and resolve performance and other problems.

Of course, these are my conventions — you may come up with others that are more useful or intuitive to you. The key idea here is simply to assign filenames, virtual machine names, and network information that is more meaningful than "fedora6.txt," "fedora," and "vif0.2" to make your life easier when looking for configuration information for specific virtual machines, monitoring and managing virtual machines, and watching network traffic for performance, routing, or similar problems. Like many sysadmin tasks, a bit of planning in advance can help eliminate problems down the road — or at least make it easier to track down their source.

This book focuses on the open source version of Xen, and is as distribution-agnostic as possible. For that reason, I tend to use the startup, shutdown, and migration mechanisms provided with the open source version of Xen whenever possible, and find them to be sufficient for most purposes. The next few sections focus on discussing those mechanisms, other considerations for safe virtual machine startup and shutdown, and shared storage mechanisms that enable migration between domain0 hosts in the case of failures or to perform standard system administration tasks such as load-balancing.

Configuring and Using the xendomains Init Script

The "Automatically Starting Xen Domains at Boot Time" section in Chapter 5 introduced the xendomains script as a mechanism for automatically starting Xen domainU guests at boot time. However, this script can also help cleanly terminate virtual machines during system shutdown, and even automatically migrate active virtual machines to other systems as long as they satisfy the criteria for migration.

The /etc/init.d/xendomains script is usually linked into the startup process for your system's default runlevel, as discussed in "The Linux System Startup Process" in Chapter 4. This script uses the configuration file /etc/sysconfig/xendomains to set variables used by both the startup and shutdown processes and to identify virtual machines that should be handled specifically, such as being migrated to another host when a system is shut down. The next few sections discuss the xendomains variables associated with domainU system startup, domainU system shutdown, and domainU system migration.

VM Startup Configuration Options

As discussed in Chapter 5, the xendomains script is used to automatically start domainU guests when a domain0 system is restarted. To configure a domainU guest to be started automatically at domain0 boot time, create a symbolic link in the directory /etc/xen/auto that points to its configuration file. (The name of this directory is actually one of the configuration variables.)

The file /etc/sysconfig/xendomains contains the following configuration variables that are used when a domain0 starts domainU guests through the /etc/init.d/xendomains script:

❑   XENDOMAINS_AUTO: Specifies the name of the directory in which the xendomains script should look for configuration files (or symbolic links to configuration files) that identify domainU guests to start as part of the domain0 system startup process. These are often referred to as *auto-start domains*. The default value of this variable is the directory /etc/xen/auto. If no directory is specified, no domains will be automatically started at boot time. If XENDOMAINS_AUTO is set to a directory and the XENDOMAINS_RESTORE variable is true, autostart domains for which checkpoint files exist will be started first, and then the remaining autostart domains will be started.

❑   XENDOMAINS_CREATE_USLEEP: Specifies the amount of time to wait before starting another domain or returning to the standard system boot process. This value is expressed in microseconds — its default value is 5000000 (that is, 5 seconds). Setting the value gives each virtual machine some amount of dedicated time to load its kernel, RAM disk, and modules, and start its boot process before the next process starts, because system startup is both disk-intensive and processor-intensive.

❑   XENDOMAINS_RESTORE: A Boolean value that determines whether domains saved at shutdown (and for which checkpoint files therefore exist) should be started from those checkpoint files at system startup. By default, this variable is set to true.

VM Shutdown Configuration Options

Some of the variables in the /etc/sysconfig/xendomains configuration file are relevant to how the domain0 system handles running domains when the domain0 system is being shut down or restarted. These variables are as follows:

❑   XENDOMAINS_AUTO_ONLY: A Boolean value that identifies whether shutdown commands such as XENDOMAINS_MIGRATE, XENDOMAINS_SAVE, XENDOMAINS_SHUTDOWN, and XENDOMAINS_SYSRQ apply to only those domainU guests that were started by the xendomains script (true) or all running domainU guests (false).

❑   XENDOMAINS_SAVE: Enables you to specify the name of a directory to which running domainU guests will be checkpointed when a domain0 system is being shutdown. The domains are not shut down if the save operation succeeds, because the save file is assumed to contain valid state information that can be used to resume without corruption. If this variable is empty, any autostart domains will be migrated if XENDOMAINS_MIGRATE is set, or will simply be shut down if not. The default value of this variable is the directory /lib/xen/save.

❑   XENDOMAINS_SHUTDOWN: Enables you to specify a string consisting of options that will be sent to a domain when it is being shut down. These flags are used only if XENDOMAINS_SAVE or XENDOMAINS_MIGRATE is specified. The default value of this variable is --halt --wait, which tells the xm shutdown command to halt each domain but not return to the xendomains script until the domain is completely halted.

❑ XENDOMAINS_SHUTDOWN_ALL: Enables you to specify a string consisting of the options that will be sent to domains that have not been saved, migrated, or shut down according to other rules or statements in the /etc/sysconfig/xendomains file. Passing options such as these to all virtual machines late in the operation of the xendomains init script is typically used to terminate virtual machines that were started manually when XENDOMAINS_AUTO_ONLY has been specified. The default value of this variable is --all --halt --wait.

❑ XENDOMAINS_STOP_MAXWAIT: Enables you to specify a default timeout for the total time spent by the xendomain script's virtual machine save, migration, and shutdown operations. Note that any operations that are in place when this timeout arrives will be terminated abruptly, so you must make sure that this value exceeds the typical save, migration, and shutdown time for your domainU guests. The default value for this variable is 300 seconds.

❑ XENDOMAINS_SYSRQ: Enables you to identify specific system requests that the domain0 host should send to each domain, in order, when the domains are being shut down by the xendomains script. Using this variable to specify system requests is an alternative to using the XENDOMAINS_MIGRATE, XENDOMAINS_SAVE, and XENDOMAINS_SHUTDOWN commands.

The XENDOMAINS_SYSRQ variable must be set to a string value that consists of a space-separated list of letters representing various system requests. These are the same letters that you can manually specify using xm sysrq DOMAINID LETTER as explained in Appendix A. The most common use of this command is to attempt to perform an orderly shutdown, or at least force some specific actions when a domainU guest is being shut down. Common shutdown actions are syncing filesystems (s), generating system status information (m for memory status, t for active tasks and processes, or p for system registers and flags), or a forced shutdown via "s e i u o" (sync, send SIGTERM to all processes except init, send SIGKILL to all processes except init, umount all disks and remount in read-only mode, and turn the system off).

❑ XENDOMAINS_USLEEP: Enables you to specify the period of time between each system request if XENDOMAINS_SYSRQ is set. This gives the domain a specific amount of time to respond to each system request before another arrives. This value is specified in microseconds, and the default value is 100000 (0.1 seconds).

VM Migration Configuration Options

The /etc/sysconfig/xendomains configuration file contains a single value that tells the xendomains script that domainU guests should be migrated to another domain0 host rather than being shut down in one form or another when the domain0 system is being shut down or restarted.

The XENDOMAINS_MIGRATE variable enables you to pass a specific set of options to supply to the xm migrate command. This variable should be set to a string that contains the IP address of the machine to which virtual machines should be migrated and, optionally, the -live flag if you want to migrate a domainU guest without any interruption in service.

xendomains Startup Sequence

The xendomains script uses a lock file as a semaphore to prevent the script from being run multiple times, and thus attempting to start the same domainU guests multiple times. This lock file is the file /var/lock/subsys/xendomains, and is defined as the LOCKFILE variable in the /etc/init.d/ xendomains script.

When a domain0 system is restarted, or the `/etc/init.d/xendomains` script is run manually, the `xendomains` script performs the following actions:

1. It checks for the existence of the lock file and terminates if the file is present.

2. If the `XENDOMAINS_RESTORE` variable is set to `true` and the directory specified in the `XENDOMAINS_SAVE` variable does not exist, the script creates that directory.

3. If the `XENDOMAINS_RESTORE` variable is set to `true` and the directory specified in the `XENDOMAINS_SAVE` variable contains any files, the `xendomains` script attempts to restore a domain from each file in this directory using the `xm restore` command. If the domain is successfully restored, the script deletes the saved file.

4. If the directory specified in the `XENDOMAINS_AUTO` variable contains any files, the `xendomains` script attempts to start a domainU guest from each file in this directory. The `xendomains` script sleeps for the number of microseconds specified in the `XENDOMAINS_CREATE_USLEEP` variable after starting each machine.

As you can see from this explanation, the contents of the directory specified in the `XENDOMAINS_AUTO` variable are very important. If you actually store VM configuration files in this directory, rather than using symbolic links, you must be very careful that any text editor that you use does not create backup or checkpoint files in this directory, or that you delete them if it does. Because backup and checkpoint files for Xen domains are often very similar to the actual files, their presence in the `XENDOMAINS_AUTO` directory could cause Xen to attempt to start the same virtual machines twice. This is always a waste of time, and could cause filesystem corruption and system failures. It could even cause a VM with outdated parameter values to be started.

xendomains Shutdown Sequence

When the `xendomains` script is executed as part of a domain0 system's shutdown sequence, it performs the following actions:

1. If the `XENDOMAINS_AUTO_ONLY` variable is set to restrict the list of domains that the `xendomains` script cares about to those that are identified in `XENDOMAINS_AUTO`, the script builds a list of virtual machine names based on the name entries in the configuration files that are located in the `XENDOMAINS_AUTO` directory.

   The script then loops over the domainU guests that are running (using the output from the `xm list` command), doing the following (in order):

   a. If `XENDOMAINS_AUTO_ONLY` is `true`, it checks whether the host is in the list of autostart domains. If so, the script proceeds to the next step. If not, the script skips this host for the time being.

   b. If `XENDOMAINS_SYSRQ` is set to indicate that virtual machines should do a quick and (one hopes) clean shutdown rather than being migrated, saved, or shut down normally, the system requests identified in the `XENDOMAINS_SYSRQ` variable are sent to the virtual machine.

   c. If `XENDOMAINS_MIGRATE` is set to indicate that domains should be migrated, the script attempts to migrate the domainU system to another host using the IP address and options specified in that variable.

    d. If XENDOMAINS_SAVE is set to indicate that domains should be saved rather than simply being terminated, the script attempts to save the domain to the directory identified in that variable.

    e. If XENDOMAINS_SHUTDOWN is set to provide flags that should be passed when shutting down domainU guests, the script attempts to shut down the domain.

2. The script then checks for any domains that are still running and that are not identified as zombies (which are domains that were not correctly processed in a previous step of the script), and shuts them down using the xm shutdown command along with the flags in the XENDOMAINS_SHUTDOWN_ALL variable.

Although managing hosts using the /etc/init.d/xendomains is not as elegant or flexible as some graphical administrative environments, it does provide an easy-to-use mechanism for handling all of the domains on a given domain0 identically. This makes it very useful in environments where you have a small number of domain0 systems that essentially serve as failover hosts for each other. Sometimes there is indeed elegance in simplicity.

Clean VM Shutdown and Faster Startup

The previous section explained how the /etc/init.d/xendomains script can help terminate machines with some semblance of order any time their domain0 host is being shut down. Unfortunately, not all system shutdowns are planned or provide sufficient time to "do the right thing." This means that your domainU hosts may be shut down (or simply terminated) in ways that do not leave them in a clean, consistent, and well-known state.

At their core, virtual machines are identical to physical machines in terms of basic system requirements such as filesystem consistency, which is explained in detail in the next section. Later sections discuss ways to help guarantee the consistency of your virtual machines' filesystems by integrating checkpoints into the startup sequence of your domain0 systems.

Overview of Filesystem Consistency

As discussed in Chapter 3, a filesystem is a mechanism for successfully storing and retrieving data on a computer system. The data structures that define the organization of a filesystem must be correct when a filesystem is being used. To users, filesystems are hierarchical collections of files and directories. To Linux and other UNIX systems, filesystems consist of large numbers of data structures (known as inodes) that contain information about files and directories (known as filesystem metadata, which is data about data) and the data blocks that actually contain the directory entries and file data. It's easy to see the confusion that would arise if multiple inodes in a filesystem each thought that some specific data block was a part of the file that they represented. Suppose that you were editing a status report for your manager and I was submitting my expense report. If the inodes that identified the blocks in your presentation and the one that pointed to the blocks in my expense report both claimed that a specific data block belonged to our file, one of us is going to be quite surprised when we present our report.

Filesystems whose internal data structures are correct are referred to as being consistent. It is always the responsibility of the system that uses a filesystem to verify the consistency of that filesystem before making it available to the operating system and to users. This is true regardless of whether the filesystem is a traditional local filesystem, a journaled filesystem, or a networked filesystem. In the case of networked filesystems, the server that exports the networked filesystems and manages the physical media on which they are stored must verify their consistency before making them available over the network.

The primary characteristics of consistent filesystems are the following:

❑ A bit in the filesystem's superblock is set to indicate that the filesystem was successfully unmounted when the system was last shut down (known as the "clean bit").

❑ All of the filesystem metadata is correct.

Verifying the consistency of a filesystem would be quite fast if those two points can be verified quickly. Unfortunately, verifying that filesystem metadata is correct involves checking a number of different points:

❑ Each allocation unit (whether it is a block or an extent) belongs only to a single file or directory, or is marked as being unused. The list of which blocks are allocated and unused (free) in a filesystem is usually stored in a bitmap for that filesystem, where each bit represents a specific data block. Filesystems that allocate and manage extents rather than just blocks also maintain information about free extents and their size or range.

❑ No file or directory contains a data block that is marked as being unused in the filesystem bitmap.

❑ Each file or directory in the filesystem is referenced in some other directory in that filesystem. From a user's point of view, this means that there is a directory path to each file or directory in the filesystem.

❑ Each file has only as many parent directories as the reference count in its inode indicates. Although each file exists in only a single physical location on the disk, multiple directories can contain references to the inode that holds information about this file. These references are known as *hard links*. The file can therefore be accessed through any of these directories, and deleting it from any of these directories decrements the link count. A file is actually deleted only when its link count is 0 — in other words, when it is no longer referenced by any directory.

Verifying all of these relationships may take quite a while — if it's necessary to manually check each of them at all. Journaling filesystems such as EXT3, JFS, ReiserFS, and XFS were designed to reduce the frequency with which this sort of check is required, eliminating the need to perform this check entirely in most cases. This is done by tracking changes to the filesystem in a special portion of it, known as a journal. The filesystem remains consistent because changes are transactionally recorded in the journal and then applied to the filesystem. If the system crashes while updates to the filesystem are in progress, filesystem consistency can be restored by replaying all or some of the transaction changes that were recorded in the journal but are not marked as having been completed. When a system that uses a journaling filesystem is shut down cleanly, the journal is emptied and the clean bit is set, as in any other physical filesystem.

In addition to setting the clean bit in a filesystem when it is cleanly unmounted during system shutdown, filesystems such as the EXT2 and EXT3 filesystems (the most popular Linux filesystems in use when this book was written) require that a filesystem be checked for consistency after having been mounted a specific number of times (the default is 32), regardless of whether the filesystem is marked as clean or not. This "mount-count" check guards against the chance that hidden consistency problems may be present that aren't fatal to the filesystem but which are non-optimal, such as unlinked blocks.

All Linux and Windows systems, virtualized or not, perform a basic filesystem consistency check when they boot or when a filesystem is mounted. This usually consists of simply checking the clean bit and replaying any pending transactions from the journal in journaling filesystems. Depending on their severity, corrections that need to be made to your system's root filesystem may cause your system to reboot. Whether or not a reboot is required depends on the severity of the consistency problems and the type of filesystem that you are using.

You can't eliminate filesystem consistency checks from the startup process, but consistency checks are very fast when a filesystem is marked as clean and has not reached its maximum-mount count. The next section discusses how to "pre-perform" filesystem consistency checks for paravirtualized domainU guests, but the best way to eliminate the need for filesystem repair is to ensure that the virtual machine that is associated with a filesystem is shut down normally

Automating VM Filesystem Consistency Checks

As discussed in the previous section, Linux and Windows virtual machines perform a basic filesystem consistency check when they boot, just like any physical Linux or Windows system. Like physical Linux or Windows machines, they may reboot your system if filesystem consistency problems are detected in the root filesystem. As discussed in the previous section, cleanly shutting down virtual machines when you shut down a domain0 system is the best way to ensure that filesystems are cleanly unmounted and that filesystem consistency checks won't be necessary when the virtual machine is restarted.

When problems are detected during a filesystem consistency check, whether or not a reboot is required depends on the severity of the consistency problems and the type of filesystem that you are using. HVM and paravirtualized Linux and Windows systems do the same thing, but paravirtualized systems may not shut down completely or restart correctly.

Paravirtualized domainU guests that use a filesystem image as their root filesystem present an interesting opportunity to resolve filesystem consistency problems before actually starting the paravirtualized VM that they are associated with. To avoid filesystem check and restart problems, I find it convenient to manually check (with the `fsck` command) any filesystem image files that are being used as the root filesystem for a paravirtualized VM. Adding a script to force and repair consistency checks as part of the domain0 startup process largely eliminates the chance that the VM will need to reboot during its startup process.

Assuming that all of the filesystem images for your virtual machines are located in subdirectories of a specific directory, you may want to incorporate a script like the following `fsck_vm_images.sh` script into your domain0 system's startup process:

```
#!/bin/sh
 LOGFILE=/var/log/pv_vm_fsck.log
PVDIR=/home/xen/PARAVIRT
EXTRAS="/dev/VM/U704-ROOT-PV"
function check_fs() {
   filesystem=${1}
   echo -n "*** Checking $filesystem:" >> $LOGFILE
   fsck -p $filesystem 1> $$ 2> $$
   status=`echo $?`
   if [ $status -gt 3 ] ; then
       mail -s "VM FSCK FAILURE" root <<EOF
```

(continued)

(continued)

```
        PV VM Filesystem $filesystem could not be automatically repaired.
        EOF
                echo " problem detected" >>   $LOGFILE
                cat $$ >>   $LOGFILE
                echo "*** Mail sent to root about this problem" >> $LOGFILE
          else
                echo " no problems" >>   $LOGFILE
#               cat $$ >>   $LOGFILE
          fi
          rm $$
    }
    stamp=`date`
    echo "Fscking VM Images during reboot: Start $stamp" >> $LOGFILE
    find $PVDIR -name "*.img" | while read imagename ; do
        check_fs $imagename
    done
    if [ "x$EXTRAS" != "x" ] ; then
        echo $EXTRAS | while read partition ; do
          check_fs $partition
        done
    fi
    stamp=`date`
    echo "Fscking VM Images during reboot: Finished $stamp" >> $LOGFILE
    echo "" >> $LOGFILE
```

This script first runs the `fsck` command manually on each file with the `.img` extension that is found in or below the directory specified in the `PVDIR` variable. It then runs the `fsck` command on every partition specified in the `EXTRAS` variable. All `fsck` operations are logged to the file identified by the `LOGFILE` variable. If any `fsck` operation fails with a return code that indicates that repairs could not be automatically made to a filesystem image or partition, the error message is logged and an e-mail message is sent to the root user.

Integrating a script like this into your domain0 system's startup process before starting the Xen daemon will check (and repair) the consistency of the filesystem images used by your paravirtualized virtual machines before it attempts to start those virtual machines. In order to use this script, you will almost certainly have to change the directory identified in the `PVDIR` and `EXTRAS` variables in the script, and will need to ensure that you follow the image filenaming convention assumed by the script, which is that all filesystem image files (and only filesystem image files) have the extension `.img`.

If you are using the `xendomains` script to manage Xen system startup, shutdown, and migration, you must run the image file consistency checking script before the `xendomain` script is executed during system startup. The `xendomains` script is normally executed as one of the last scripts in the startup process, so you can link it in at any earlier point in the startup process. To do this:

1. Copy the text of this script into a file in your `/etc/init.d` directory. (You can also download it from www.vonhagen.org/xen as the file `pv_vm_fsck.sh`.)

2. Make it executable using a command such as `chmod 755 `*`filename`*, where *`filename`* is the name of your script.

3. Create a symbolic link to this script in your runlevel directory (`/etc/rc.5` if your default runlevel is 5, `/etc/rc2.d` if your default runlevel is 2, and so on) with the correct prefixes and sequence number. I typically create symbolic links with the number 50 to run this script during startup and shutdown, using commands like the following:

```
ln -s ../init.d/pv_vm_fsck.s S50_pc_vm_fsck
ln -s ../init.d/pv_vm_fsck.s K50_pc_vm_fsck
```

This ensures that the script runs after the network and traditional network filesystems such as NFS have been brought up. If you are storing filesystem images in a different network filesystem, such as OCFS2 or GFS, or mounted network-based storage such as ATA-over-Ethernet or GNBD, you must make sure that this script runs after the filesystem storage is accessible to your system.

For more information about startup scripts, see "The Linux System Startup Process" in Chapter 4.

This script is provided as an example, and thus is as short as possible. In actual deployment, I typically add a function that is called when a filesystem check fails, figure out which domain is associated with the inconsistent filesystem, and remove the symbolic link to that domain from the directory used by the `xendomains` script to automatically start domains at boot time. This prevents the `xendomains` script from trying to start a domain with an inconsistent filesystem, conserves the resources that would be allocated to that domain at startup time, and brings up your domain0 system and other domains more quickly. After repairing the filesystem, you can then start it manually and reintegrate it into the `xendomains` startup procedure.

Saving Xen Domain State

In virtualized environments, there are many times when you will want to terminate a running virtual machine, yet save information about its current state to expedite restarting it at some point. This state information consists of the contents of memory at a specific point in time, and therefore includes information about active network connections, storage transactions, and so on. The most obvious times at which you would want to save state information for each virtual machine are in response to imminent hardware failures, power outages, UPS power expiration, and so on. You may even find it necessary to occasionally terminate one or more noncritical virtual machines in order to return the memory being used to the pool of allocatable memory on the domain0 host where it was running. This is especially true during pre-deployment testing, when you could be running test systems on a production domain0 system in order to measure load and performance impact.

Xen's `xm` command provides the `xm save` subcommand to enable you to save the state information for a specified domainU guest to a file. This file can be located on any storage device that a domain0 system can access, and will be slightly larger than the amount of memory that was allocated to the virtual machine because the save file preserves additional information that is used by the hypervisor and domain0 when a domain is restored from the save file. Restoring a domainU guest from a save file is done using the `xm restore` command. See Appendix A for detailed explanations of these commands.

When a standard `xm save` command completes, the domainU guest is no longer running on your domain0 host, and all resources that were allocated to it, specifically memory, are returned to the domain0 host for re-use. You can use the `-c` option to create a save file without shutting down the domain that you are saving. The save file can therefore serve as a checkpoint of the state of a virtual machine at that point in time. Resource handling and save file creation are the primary differences between the `xm save` and `xm pause` commands — no resources are released when a domain is paused, and state information is only preserved in memory when a domain is paused — no permanent record of the state of your virtual machine is made when it is paused. An easy way to think of the `xm save` command is as the conceptual equivalent of hibernating a physical machine, whereas the `xm pause` command is the conceptual equivalent of suspending a physical machine.

In many cases, Xen virtualization environments use migration to support high-availability for virtual machines that are providing core services. However, if this isn't feasible for cost or other reasons, saving virtual machine state information reduces the time required to restart the machine and return it to the approximate point it was at when the save occurred. Depending on the amount of time that elapses between when the state of a virtual machine was saved and when it is restored, the exact state of the virtual machine may not be able to be restored because external resources (such as network connections) that were in use by the virtual machine may have timed out or been terminated. Similarly, a domainU guest restored from a saved file will not have the same domainID that it had before, but it will use the next domainID that is available from the domain0 host.

Saving the state of a running virtual machine is a key option when you use the `xendomains` mechanism that was discussed earlier in this chapter. An important caveat to consider when you use the `xm save` command to save domain state information is that the consistency of the storage location where the save file is being written is critical to being able to restore from the saved image file. If you are saving a domain in response to network problems, writing the save file to local storage is obviously safer than writing to a networked storage resource that could be affected by the same problems that are prompting you to shut down a virtual machine. This may not be the case on multi-hosted systems where network problems are affecting only one network interface, but it's an important point to consider. When restoring paravirtualized systems from state files, you may also want to avoid modifying their filesystems by automatically running the `fsck` command on them (as described in the previous section) because the state file may contain disk state information or buffers that could be invalidated by an `fsck` command.

The `xm save` command can be very useful when you need to temporarily stop one or more domainU guests and return their resources to a domain0 host. It can also be useful in automated shutdown situations, via the `xendomains` startup and shutdown scripts. However, in general sysadmin practice, a clean shutdown of the virtual machine and a subsequent clean restart is generally preferable to using the `xm save` command unless you need to preserve the state of a virtual machine or need to be able to minimize subsequent virtual machine restart time.

Migrating Virtual Machines for High Availability

Migration is the ability to move a running domainU guest from one domain0 system to another, and is one of the key differentiators between Xen and other virtualization solutions. Xen supports two basic types of migration: live and traditional. In live migration, a running domainU guest is migrated to another domain0 host without any noticeable interruption in service (typically only 60–300 milliseconds, to quote the Xen documentation). In traditional migration, where the domain is stopped, its memory image is copied to another domain0 guest, and that image is then restarted on the target domain0 system.

In order to successfully migrate a virtual machine from one domain0 host, the following conditions should all be true:

❑ The target domain0 system must have sufficient available memory to run the migrated virtual machine.

❑ Relocation settings must be enabled in the Xen daemon on both domain0 hosts. Specifically, the `xend-relocation-server` variable must be set to `yes`, and the `xend-relocation-hosts-allow` variable must allow connections from the domain0 hosts (through the use of hostnames, IP addresses, or IP or domain wildcards; or by using an empty string to enable connections from any source). The `xend-relocation-port` and `xend-relocation-address` settings should be unmodified or compatible between the two hosts. See "Configuring the Xen Daemon" in Chapter 7 for more information on these settings.

❑ The target domain0 system must be running the same version of Xen and the Xen daemon. Migration may work if this is not the case, but usually only if the domain0 system to which you are migrating the virtual machine is running a later version of Xen than the domain0 host from which you are migrating.

❑ The source and target domain0 hosts must both be on the same subnet because the guest domainU system's MAC and IP addresses move with the virtual machine. As an alternative, you can use a package such as EtherIP or manually set up tunneling for an IP address on a different subnet so that it appears to be on the same class C subnet, but this is needlessly complex in most Xen deployments.

❑ Both domain0 systems must be using approximately the same processors. Migration may work if the domain0 system to which you are migrating is running a newer processor from the same vendor, and the instruction set of the processor on the target domain0 system is a superset of the one on the source domain0 system.

❑ Both domain0 systems must have access to the root filesystem used by the domainU guest that you are migrating, and that root filesystem must be available from both domain0 hosts by the same pathname. Similarly, any other physical or networked filesystems that are mounted in the domainU guest that you are migrating must also be accessible by the same name from both domain0 hosts. (This does not include in-memory filesystems, such as `/dev/shm`, `/dev/pts`, `/proc`, `/sys`, and so on.)

❑ Authentication information used by the domainU guest that you are migrating must either be local to the guest or be accessible by both domain0 guests.

If these conditions are met, migrating a virtual machine from one domain0 system to another is as easy as executing the `xm migrate` command, as in the following example:

```
# xm migrate DomainID TargetHost -l
```

The `-l` option is optional, but is required in order to do live migration. (This option can also be specified as `--live`.) Other options to this command are the `-p=NUM` (`--port=NUM`) option, which enables you to specify the port used for relocation on the remote server if you have customized the `xend-relocation-port` setting on the remote host, and the `-r=MEGABIT` (`--resource=MEGABIT`) option, which enables you to limit the amount of network bandwidth associated with relocation at the specified number of MEGABITs.

On the host from which you are migrating, this looks something like the following example, which shows a listing of available domains, followed by the `xm migrate` command to initiate a live migration:

```
# xm list
Name              ID    Mem VCPUs     State   Time(s)
Domain-0           0    768    1      r-----  126110.2
FC6-NFS-PV        17    256    1      -b----    22.4
RF-IMG-HV              256    1                  0.0
U7-LVP-HV             256    1                  0.0
XP-AOEL-HV            256    1                 25.2
# xm migrate 17 xen2.vonhagen.org -l
```

Once this command completes, the domain will no longer be running on this domain0 system, and a subsequent xm list command will show the domain as having no state (that is, not running) if you are using Xen's lifecycle management, or will show the domain as nonexistent if you are not.

On the host to which you are migrating, the domainU guest that is being migrated will initially show up as being paused while the memory image of the domain is being transferred, and will then appear to be a normally running domain, as in the following examples:

```
# xm list
Name              ID    Mem  VCPUs      State    Time(s)
Domain-0           0    768    2        r-----      82.1
FC6-NFS-PV         1    256    0        -bp---       0.0
MV-LVP-HV               512    1                    75.0
MX-AOEL-HV              256    1                     0.0
# xm list
Name              ID    Mem  VCPUs      State    Time(s)
Domain-0           0    768    2        r-----      90.8
FC6-NFS-PV         1    256    1        -b----       0.0
MV-LVP-HV               512    1                    75.0
MX-AOEL-HV              256    1                     0.0
```

When a domain migrates, console connections established using the xm console command will be terminated, and must be re-established on the domain0 system to which it migrated. However, any purely networked connections, such as VNC console or SSH connections, should persist.

It is critical to test the ability of domains to migrate successfully before actually counting on migration in a deployment environment. The best test for whether a domainU guest can be migrated from one domain0 host to another is to copy the configuration data for that virtual machine to the target domain0 system, shut down the domainU guest that you want to test, and then attempt to start the domainU guest manually on the target domain0 system. If you can start the same domainU guest with the same configuration information from both domain0 hosts, then the domainU guest that is defined in that file should be able to be migrated. You can then test migration using the xm migrate command. If migration fails, here are a few things you can check:

❑   Make sure that the settings in the Xen daemon's configuration file on both domain0 hosts enable the hosts to communicate with each other, and that no port or address settings have been changed.

❑   Make sure that neither host is running a firewall or a version of SELinux that could interfere with network communication or the migration process at either end.

❑   Make sure that Xen networking has been correctly configured on both hosts.

❑   If you are using bridged networking, make sure that any bridges that you are using are connected to the correct physical Ethernet device on each host so that migration to the bridged network can occur. A bridged network with the same name should exist on both hosts. Make sure that packet forwarding is enabled on the bridges on both domain0 hosts.

❑   If you are not using bridged networking, make sure that the routing table or NAT configuration information on the target domain0 system is updated to enable connections to the migrated virtual machine.

Xen's migration is one of its most interesting capabilities and one of the things that make Xen the best virtualization technology for use in high-availability, enterprise environments. See "Running Multiple domain0 Systems" in Chapter 6 for a discussion of configuration file location, storage choices, and related topics that can help facilitate and simplify migration.

Centralized Logging for Virtual Machines

System logs are important assets for any system administrator, because they enable you to identify usage patterns, monitor some aspects of your network and any intrusion attempts, identify emerging problems before they become critical, and (worst case) identify the potential or explicit causes of a system failure as a postmortem activity. Let's hope the last is rarely necessary, but if it ever is, your system logs should contain the data that you need.

As the number of systems that you are responsible for increases, monitoring their log files for important messages or certain classes of events becomes more difficult. Even if virtualization helps you simplify the physical location of multiple systems, it doesn't help you centralize log data or provide a mechanism that helps you react quickly to important events on your physical or virtual systems.

Luckily, the system logging facilities used on modern Linux systems provide built-in support for centralizing log data. Generically referred to as "syslog," several different system logging facilities are in common use on Linux systems: the traditional syslog facility, an enhanced system and kernel logging package known as sysklogd, and syslog-ng (which stands for "syslog — the next generation") Depending on the Linux distribution that is running on your domain0 system, one of these is almost certainly already installed and running.

> The system logging facilities used on UNIX and Linux system have their roots in 4.2 BSD UNIX, which has been in use for over 20 years. An Internet Engineering Task Force (IETF) working group is now responsible for syslog direction and security issues. See www.ietf.org/html.charters/syslog-charter.html and http://tools.ietf.org/wg/syslog/ for more information.

The next sections explain how to enable the different system logging daemons to send and receive remote log messages. Most Linux distributions ship with the syslogd or sysklogd package installed by default, so I'll focus more on these than on syslog-ng. A final section discusses several logging utilities for your Microsoft Windows systems that direct messages from the Windows event log to a centralized Linux system log server. This enables you to use a centralized log to store information about important events on both Linux and Windows domainU systems.

Configuring syslogd or sysklogd to Receive Networked Log Messages

By default, the UNIX and Linux system logging daemon logs only local messages, but you can easily configure a system logging daemon to also listen for logging messages sent over the network by adding the -r (remote) option to its startup process, and then restarting the daemon. Log messages are sent via

UDP and are received on port 514. An entry like the following must be present in your `/etc/services` file in order for log messages to be received over the network:

```
syslog      514/udp
```

Note that you only have to reconfigure the system logging daemon to receive networked log messages on the system that you want to serve as a centralized logging system. Hosts for which you want to submit log messages over the network require changes to the system logging daemon's configuration file, not to its startup mechanism.

> Your centralized logging system can be any system that you choose. Many sites use domain0 systems as centralized log hosts, which receive log messages from all VMs that each domain0 system supports. Because this can break when virtual machines are migrated, I generally use a dedicated (old) machine with plenty of disk space as a centralized logging host.

On Red Hat–like distributions such as CentOS, Fedora, Mandrake, and (of course) Red Hat, the configuration settings for syslog startup are stored in the file `/etc/sysconfig/syslog`. To enable a syslog daemon to receive log messages from the network, add the `-r` option to the *SYSLOGD_OPTIONS* variable. You may also want to add the `-x` option to this variable, which disables DNS lookups for the source of incoming messages, and simply put the IP address of the remote host in the log message. A modified value for this variable would then look like the following:

```
SYSLOGD_OPTIONS="-m 0 -r -x"
```

This example comes from a Fedora system, where the `-m 0` option is also specified in order to suppress `mark` messages, which are used by default to create log entries that show that the system logging daemon is still running even if no actual loggable events are occurring.

On Debian-like systems such as Knoppix, Linspire, MEPIS, Ubuntu, Xandros, and (of course) Debian, the configuration settings for the system logging daemon are stored in the file `/etc/defaults/syslogd`. On these systems, the variable to change is called SYSLOGD, and a modified value specification for this variable would, look like the following:

```
SYSLOGD="-m 0 -r -x"
```

Once you have changed the system logging daemon's startup options on the host that you want to serve as a centralized logging system, you must restart the server so that it runs with the new options you've specified. On Red Hat–like and SUSE systems, execute the following command as the root user or via the `sudo` command:

```
/etc/init.d/syslog restart
```

On Debian-like systems, execute the following command as the superuser or via the `sudo` command:

```
/etc/init.d/sysklogd restart
```

You will see messages like the following at the end of your standard system log file (typically either `/var/log/messages` or `/var/log/syslog`):

```
Sep 30 19:09:11 xen kernel: Kernel logging (proc) stopped.
Sep 30 19:09:11 xen kernel: Kernel log daemon terminating.
Sep 30 19:09:13 xen exiting on signal 15
Sep 30 19:09:13 xen syslogd 1.4.1: restart (remote reception).
Sep 30 19:09:13 xen kernel: klogd 1.4.1, log source = /proc/kmsg started.
```

Note that the `restart` line shows that the system logging daemon can now receive log messages from remote hosts (`remote reception`). The system logging daemon on your centralized logging system is now ready to receive log messages from other hosts on your network.

If you are running a firewall on a centralized logging server, you may need to add an entry to your firewall configuration file that enables incoming log messages to be received. For example, if you are using iptables for your firewall, you may need to add an entry like the following to one of the input chains of your firewall:

```
iptables -m state --state NEW -m udp -p udp --dport 514 -j ACCEPT
```

You may also want to add entries to limit the Ethernet interface on which log messages can be received (using the `-i` option) or to restrict the networks from which log messages can be received (using the `--source` option).

The next step in configuring networked logging is to modify the configuration file for the system logging daemon on each system that you want to send network log messages, telling it which types of messages to send, and the location to which to send them.

Configuring Networked Log Message Targets for syslogd or sysklogd

The configuration file used by the system logging daemons included in the syslogd and sysklogd packages is the file `/etc/syslog.conf`. This section isn't intended as complete documentation for the contents of this file — I'm focusing only on the critical things that you'll want to know in order to make a host send various types of log messages over the network to a system logging daemon that has been configured to receive them, as described in the previous section. For complete information about the contents and format of this file, use a command such as `man 5 syslog.conf` to display its online documentation.

The standard syslog enables you to identify messages by their source (known as a "facility") and by their priority (also often referred to as their "severity level"), separated by a period. Entries in the syslog configuration file therefore have the following general format:

```
facility.priority      destination
```

For example, `news.emerg` means "all log messages from the news system with emergency priority." You can also use wildcards when identifying messages — for example, `news.*` means "all messages from the news system," and `*.emerg` means "all emergency log messages from any source."

The basic facilities that are supported in Linux are as follows:

- ❑ `auth`: Messages related to system security events.
- ❑ `authpriv`: Messages related to login authentication, access control, and privilege escalation.
- ❑ `cron`: Messages sent by the cron subsystem.
- ❑ `daemon`: Messages sent by system servers and daemons.
- ❑ `kern`: Kernel messages.
- ❑ `lpr`: Messages sent by the print server and spooling mechanism.
- ❑ `mail`: Messages sent by mail servers.
- ❑ `mark`: Timestamp messages generated by the syslog daemon, generally serving as activity messages. I usually turn these off (as explained previously in "Configuring syslogd or sysklogd to Receive Networked Log Messages").
- ❑ `news`: Messages from the Internet news server.
- ❑ `syslog`: Messages from the system logging facility itself.
- ❑ `user`: The default facility used when none is specified.
- ❑ `UUCP`: Messages from UNIX-to-UNIX connection servers.
- ❑ `local0` to `local7`: Locally defined message levels.

In terms of remote logging, the priority of a message is more important than its source. You will want to forward messages of a certain priority level (also often referred to as a "severity level" or simply as "severity"), regardless of the service that they are coming from. The system logging facility supports priority values from 0 to 191, where a smaller number is more important. The following list shows the standard priority levels that are predefined in the system logging facility, the general meaning of each, and their associated numeric priority:

- ❑ `debug`: Non-critical debugging messages (7)
- ❑ `info`: General information messages (6)
- ❑ `notice`: Normal but significant condition (5)
- ❑ `warn`: Warning condition (4)
- ❑ `err`: Error condition (3)
- ❑ `crit`: Critical condition (2)
- ❑ `alert`: Action must be taken immediately (1)
- ❑ `emerg`: System is unusable (0)

I generally find that messages with a priority level of `warn` or lower (more important) are worth forwarding. On each system from which you want to forward log messages, add a line like the following to the end of your `/etc/syslog.conf` file:

```
*.emerg;*.alert;*.crit;*.err;*.warn;     @loghost.vonhagen.org
```

The first portion of this line is a semicolon-separated list of sources and messages that basically boils down to "all messages from any source with a priority level of warn or more important." The second portion of this line uses the @ symbol, followed by a hostname, to specify that remote logging should be performed, and that the specified host should be the recipient of the specified log messages.

After restarting the log server (as described in the previous section), you will then start to see messages from the remote host appearing in your system log, as in the following example:

```
# tail /var/log/messages
Sep 30 19:09:13 xen exiting on signal 15
Sep 30 19:09:13 xen syslogd 1.4.1: restart (remote reception).
Sep 30 19:09:13 xen kernel: klogd 1.4.1, log source = /proc/kmsg started.
Sep 30 19:21:57 192.168.6.88 syslogd 1.4.1#21ubuntu3: restart.
Sep 30 19:22:08 192.168.6.88 exiting on signal 15
Sep 30 19:22:08 192.168.6.88 syslogd 1.4.1#21ubuntu3: restart.
```

The first three messages are from the local system, and the last three messages are from the remote host 192.168.6.88. For additional information about testing system logs, remote logging, and so on, see the sidebar "Generating Log Messages for Testing Purposes".

Of course, configuring remote logging is only interesting by itself if you plan to sit there and monitor the log on your master log system 24/7. Once you've configured remote logging and a central log server, you need to set up one of the many available log monitoring and notification packages to make the most of your central log. The "Centralized Warning Systems for Virtual Machines" section later in this chapter provides more information on monitoring system logs and other automated mechanisms for monitoring system status and health.

Generating Log Messages for Testing Purposes

System logging can provide critical information about the status and general health of your systems, and centralized logging makes it easier for you to receive notification whenever various types of log messages are generated on different types of systems. After configuring a system to send log messages to a central log server, you won't actually know if it works until you've seen it in action, preferably after a complete reboot of the system that is sending the messages, just to be sure that remote logging is correctly integrated into the system's boot cycle. However, waiting for log messages to be generated by a given system is tedious at best.

To help eliminate the wait, most Linux distributions include a utility called logger, which is designed to send messages to the system log. This utility is automatically used by various parts of the boot process on many systems, but it can also be run manually to instantly test any system that has been configured to send log messages to a remote log server.

The logger command has multiple options, all of which are described in its online reference page, available by typing man logger. For simple testing purposes, the only option I generally use is the -p option, which enables you to specify the priority of your message by specifying a numeric or variable pair. I tend to simply test at priority level 3 (error), which is a priority level that I always forward. You then follow the `-p 3` option with the message that you want to the log, as in the following example:

```
logger -p 3 "Remote logging test from 192.168.6.109"
```

Specifying the IP address of the host from which you are sending the message makes it easy to verify the IP address of the source host for the message, which is automatically inserted in the log message by the centralized log server. After executing this command, if log forwarding is correctly configured, you will see a string in your system log like the following:

```
Oct 8 12:49:23 192.168.6.109 wvh: Remote logging test from
192.168.6.109
```

For additional information about the `logger` command, see its online documentation.

Configuring syslog-ng to Receive Networked Log Messages

The syslog-ng package is an enhanced system logging service that is conceptually a drop-in replacement for the standard syslogd package, but provides some significant enhancements and general improvements. One of the primary goals of syslog-ng was to support improved and more granular filtering by supporting message filtering based on both message contents and the traditional variable model. The syslog-ng package also uses a different configuration file format that is much more flexible and powerful than the format used by the traditional syslogd. A final difference between the two logging facilities is that syslog-ng supports logging over TCP, which can help prevent messages from being dropped or otherwise lost. However, this can pose a problem for interoperability with systems running the traditional syslogd package, which uses UDP. Therefore, UDP compatibility must be explicitly enabled in a syslog-ng configuration file, as described later in this section.

The syslog-ng package uses the following four basic concepts to organize, categorize, and filter messages:

❑ **Filter definitions:** These define filters through which specific types of log messages must pass, and can therefore be used to select messages that match different patterns.

❑ **Log definitions:** These connect source, filter, and destination definitions. Log definitions provide a complete specification of where messages come from, which messages should be selected, and where messages should be written.

❑ **Source definitions:** These define the locations from which various types of messages can be received.

❑ **Destination definitions:** These define targets to which certain types of log messages are written. These are typically files, but can also be hostname or IP address, protocol, and port specifications.

The configuration file for your syslog-ng server should already contain definitions of these types, along with an `options` section, which specifies global options that apply to the syslog-ng server itself.

Like the standard syslogd facility, a syslog-ng server can be configured to receive log messages from remote servers, and remote syslog-ng servers can be configured to send log messages to remote servers. This section describes how to configure a syslog-ng server to receive syslog messages from remote servers; the next section explains how to configure syslog-ng servers to send messages to remote servers.

The configuration file for syslog-ng is `/etc/syslog-ng/syslog-ng.conf`. To enable a syslog-ng server to receive remote messages from other systems, you must add an entry like the following to the default source in your syslog-ng configuration file. In many cases, a similar entry is already present, but commented out, so you may just be able to un-comment it.

```
udp(ip("0.0.0.0") port(514));
tcp(ip("0.0.0.0") port(5140));
```

The `udp` line enables syslog-ng to receive syslog messages sent via UDP from any IP address on the default port (514). This entry can be as simple as `udp();`, but I prefer to add the more verbose syntax to remind myself of how to restrict or modify the messages received by the server if this is ever necessary in the future. The `tcp` line enables syslog-ng to receive log messages sent via TCP from any IP address on the default TCP syslog port (5140).

You also need to make sure that the following directives are present in the `options` section of your syslog-ng configuration file or, if you want to restrict them to incoming, remote messages, in a source definition for those:

```
use_dns(no);
keep_hostnames(yes);
```

The first line instructs syslog-ng not to attempt to do DNS lookups of the IP addresses or hostnames in incoming messages. The second line tells the syslog-ng server to preserve any hostname information that is provided in incoming log messages. If none is present, information about the IP address (because I've disabled DNS) from which the incoming messages was received will be logged. The second of these is a somewhat newer command that may not be available in the version of syslog-ng that your system is running.

At this point, you should be able to restart the syslog on your system, and your syslog-ng server should be able to receive remote log messages.

Configuring Log Message Targets for syslog-ng

Sending messages from a syslog-ng daemon to a remote logging facility generally requires the following additions to your syslog-ng configuration file (`/etc/syslog-ng/syslog-ng.conf`):

❑ A destination entry that identifies the host on which the remote log facility is running and, if necessary, the transport protocol to use and the port to send log messages to.

❑ A filter entry that identifies the facilities that originate messages that should be centrally logged, the priority levels of the messages that should be centrally logged, or both.

❑　A log entry that binds the destination and filter with a specific source. In most cases, this is your system's default source entry, which you will not have to modify because it already identifies the valid sources of syslog messages for your host.

As discussed in the previous section, syslog-ng also requires that you identify a source for log messages. In most cases, the default source that is defined in your syslog-ng configuration file will not require any changes because all you are doing is forwarding messages that your system is already receiving. The previous section explained how to configure a syslog-ng server to receive remote log messages. This section explains how to forward log messages to another system. You do not need to, and should not, make the changes described in this section on your centralized logging server. Doing so would cause your system to attempt to forward messages to itself, forward those messages again, and so on until the performance of your network and that system approached absolute zero.

Creating the destination statement depends on the type of remote syslog facility to which you are sending log messages. There are two common enterprise Xen environments: one in which all domain0 and domainU Linux systems run a single Linux distribution, and another in which you are running multiple Linux distributions. If you are running a single Linux distribution and that distribution uses syslog, you may not want to change that. I tend to make as few changes as possible to the configuration of the Linux distributions I run as domainU systems, because these changes have to be redone with any distribution upgrade. Similarly, if I am running multiple Linux distributions, I tend to run my centralized log server using the traditional syslogd because it is the lowest common denominator. In this case, the destination statement in your syslog-ng configuration files needs to redirect logging to that host and use UDP as its transport protocol.

A sample destination definition that sends log messages via UDP to the standard syslog port on the host 192.168.6.64 is as follows:

```
destination loghost { udp("192.168.6.64" port(514)); };
```

If you are running a single Linux distribution and that distribution uses syslog-ng (either by default or by choice), then your log destination need not "downgrade" syslog-ng's logging capabilities, and you can use a destination declaration like the following:

```
destination loghost { tcp("192.168.6.64" port(5140)); };
```

After creating an appropriate destination entry for your centralized system logging mechanism, the next step is to create a filter entry that identifies the facility and the priority level that you want to send to the centralized logging system. I tend to send all messages from any facility with a severity level of warn or more important to my centralized logging systems. A filter entry named f_remote that does this is as follows:

```
filter f_remote    { level(warn,err,crit,alert,emerg); };
```

This filter entry does not specifically identify a facility, and therefore means "all facilities."

The last step in setting up remote logging is to create a log entry that ties together a specific source of log messages, a specific filter entry to use in order to select the messages that you want to forward, and a destination that identifies where you want them to go. Assuming that my default source is named src, a log statement to unify that source, my remote logging filter, and my remote logging destination would be the following:

```
log {source(src); filter(f_remote); destination(loghost); };
```

On most Linux distributions, you should make these changes directly to your /etc/syslog-ng/ syslog-ng.conf file. As discussed in the previous section, if you are using SUSE Linux, you should make these changes to the file /etc/syslog-ng.conf.in, and then use the SuSEconfig command to run the following command as the root user in order to create your actual syslog-ng.conf file:

```
# SuSEconfig -module syslog-ng
```

The syslog-ng logger provides the -s command-line option to tell you if your syslog-ng.conf file is syntactically correct before trying to use it to restart the logger. Before restarting the logger, type a command like the following to check the configuration file:

```
# syslog-ng -v -s syslog-ng.conf
```

If an error is encountered, the syslog-ng application will tell you the line (and filename) where it occurred.

Once you have updated your syslog-ng configuration file and verified that it is syntactically correct, you must restart your syslog-ng server in order for these changes to take effect. To do so, execute the following command as the root user or via the sudo command:

```
/etc/init.d/syslog restart
```

After restarting your syslog-ng log server, you can use the logger command to test whether remote logging is working correctly by sending test messages as described in the sidebar "Generating Log Messages for Testing Purposes" earlier in this chapter.

System Logging for Microsoft Windows Systems

Although most domainU systems in production run Linux servers of various sorts, it is often useful to provide domainU guests that run the versions of Microsoft Windows required in your enterprise computing environment. Windows systems run end-user and server applications that often cannot run in other environments. In combination with remote desktop software, running Windows in virtual machines is also an extremely convenient way to make Windows systems available to developers who need them only occasionally.

The previous sections explained how to consolidate the logs from multiple Linux systems to a single centralized log server, to make it easier to scan the logs manually or use applications that automatically scan logs and send notifications of various events. When running a mixture of Linux and Windows domainU guests, it is useful to be able to send Windows event log messages to that same server, so that you can monitor all of your domainU guests (or other physical machines) from a single, central log. Unfortunately, Windows does not use syslog, but implements its own log formats, messages types, and so on. Fortunately, there are free applications that you can use to forward Windows event log messages to a Linux or UNIX syslog server. You will have to handle log messages from Windows systems differently because they use their own format and nomenclature, but at least all of the information will be in one place.

My favorite free applications for forwarding event log messages to a syslog server are NTsyslog (http://ntsyslog.sourceforge.net) and SNARE (http://sourceforge.net/projects/snare).

Both of these applications install as a system service on most modern Windows systems — both support NT, 2000, XP, and 2003 Server, but only NTSyslog worked on my 64-bit Vista systems.

Both of these applications enable you to identify the remote host to which event log messages should be forwarded in syslog format, and also to identify the sources of the messages that you want to forward. Figure 10-1 shows the NTSyslog configuration dialog box, which enables you to customize the messages that are being forwarded.

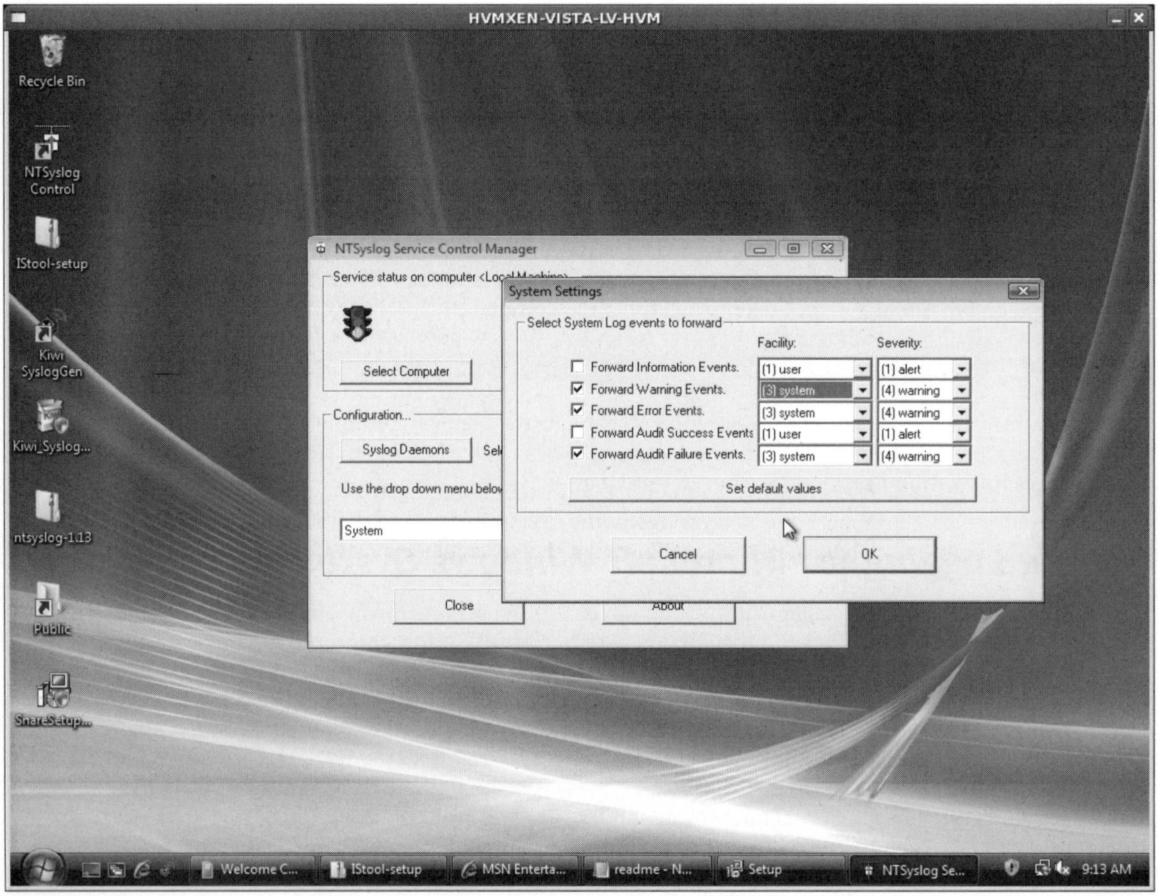

Figure 10-1

I find NTSyslog generally easier to use. You can download the latest version from `http://sourceforge.net/projects/ntsyslog`. Two versions are available:

❑   `IStool-setup.zip`: Uses a graphical installer built with IStool (`www.istool.org/`), and provides a graphical customization utility.

❑   `ntsyslog-1.13.zip`: Must be installed from the command line and configured by modifying registry entries. (Yikes!)

The following are sample messages sent from a Microsoft Windows Vista system to a centralized syslog server via NTsyslog (the first three messages would ordinarily not be split across multiple lines, and are represented that way here for formatting purposes):

```
Oct  5 00:29:37 192.168.6.149 system restore[info] 8194  \
     C:\Windows\system32\svchost.exe -k netsvcs Windows Update
Oct  5 00:30:00 192.168.6.149 system restore[info] 8194  \
     C:\Windows\system32\svchost.exe -k netsvcs Windows Update
Oct  8 00:01:04 192.168.6.149 system restore[info] 8194   \
     C:\Windows\system32\rundll32.exe /d srrstr.dll,\
     ExecuteScheduledSPPCreation Scheduled Checkpoint
Oct  8 00:01:04 192.168.6.149 system restore[info] 8211
Oct  8 00:04:04 192.168.6.149 vss[info] 8224
```

As you can see, these messages are not in the standard syslog format, and will therefore require some special handling when you're working with automated log monitoring and notification software, as described in the next section of this chapter.

SNARE (System iNtrusion Analysis and Reporting Environment) is both a SourceForge product (http://sourceforge.net/projects/snare) and part of a supported, commercial offering from InterSect Alliance (www.intersectalliance.com). SNARE offers a somewhat more complete solution than the NTSyslog application because it is part of an intrusion detection, message processing, and notification suite. Forwarding messages from the Windows Event log is done by the SNARE Agent, which is freely available for Windows and for many other platforms, where it understands their log formats. For additional information about SNARE, see www.intersectalliance.com/projects/SnareWindows/index.html or the SourceForge site (http://sourceforge.net/projects/snare). An improved version of SNARE, known as Epilog, is available from the SourceForge project site, and differs from SNARE primarily in that it can read other log formats, such as IIS logs, flat files, and so on. In the SNARE model, each version of SNARE is tailored to a small number of log formats used on a particular type of system.

For the sake of completeness, an actual syslog server for Windows is available from Kiwi Enterprises (www.kiwisyslog.com). However, this is designed to handle logs from devices that use syslog (such as routers, switches, access points, and so on) in a Windows environment, and is therefore essentially orthogonal to the Windows Event Log without one of the packages discussed earlier in this section.

Centralized Warning Systems for Virtual Machines

The previous section discussed how to centralize the logs of multiple systems (physical or virtual machines) to simplify watching for emerging problems. Few of us have the time or the inclination to monitor the master system log 24/7, so an important adjunct to centralizing system logging is to implement and configure automated monitoring and notification software that will notify you or your admin staff when problems arise.

Many commercial and open source packages exist that can automatically monitor system log files and will send mail or perform other actions in response to specific types of log messages, usually through pattern matching in the system log file. My favorite is the swatch (Simple Watchdog, or Simple Watcher of Logfiles) application, which is a Perl script that supports a powerful and elegant configuration file syntax that makes it simple to watch for any number of patterns in a system log and associate specific actions with each. The Swatch project is hosted on SourceForge at `http://swatch.sourceforge.net`, and the latest official release is 3.2.2 at the time of this writing.

After downloading the latest release, unpack the tarball and change to the directory that is created (swatch-3.2.2 at the time of this writing). Swatch requires that the Date::Calc, Date::Parse, File::Tail, and Time::HiRes Perl modules be installed on the system where it is being built and will run. If packages for these modules are not available in your distribution's package management system, you can easily install these modules via the CPAN online Perl archive using the following command:

```
cpan Date::Calc Date::Parse File::Tail Time::HiRes
```

If you configured CPAN to automatically build any missing prerequisites, the modules that you need and any modules that they require will be downloaded, built, and installed. If not, you may have to answer a few questions first.

Once you have satisfied the prerequisites, you can build, test, and install swatch by issuing the following commands:

```
perl Makefile.PL
make
make test
make install
```

Once swatch is built and installed, the next step is to create a configuration file that tells the program what things to look for in your log files, and what to do when matching log records are found. The man page for swatch provides good documentation for all of the available command-line options and the swatch configuration file format. However, a portion of an actual example swatch configuration file is more useful than just a syntax discussion. The following is a section from a swatch configuration file that I use:

```
# matches syslog lines ($1 is set to everything after the timestamp)
perlcode my $syslog_regex = '^\w{3}\s+\d{1,2}\s+\d{2}:\d{2}:\d{2}.*:(.*)';
# report significant syslog messages immediately
watchfor /crit|emerg|alert/ and /$syslog_regex/
        mail addresses=vonhagen\@vonhagen.org, \
            subject="Important Syslog Message"
# report file system problems
watchfor /file system full/ and /$syslog_regex/
        threshold type=limit,count=3,seconds=600
        mail addresses=vonhagen\@vonhagen.org,
            subject="Syslog: File System Full"
        exec "/usr/local/bin/smsclient 4125551212 $0",when=7-1
# report device errors
watchfor /Buffer I\/O [Ee]rror/ and /$syslog_regex/
```

```
            threshold type=limit,count=3,seconds=600
            mail addresses=vonhagen\@vonhagen.org,
                subject="Syslog: I/O Error",
            exec "/usr/local/bin/smsclient 4125551212 $0",when=7-1
# Report app crashes
watchfor /segfault/ and /$syslog_regex/
            mail addresses=vonhagen\@vonhagen.org,
                subject="Syslog: SegFault"
```

The first un-commented line in this file defines a Perl regular expression that matches basic syslog entries. Defining a pattern that matches the messages that you want to watch for simplifies subsequent configuration.

The remainder of this file consists of four stanzas, each of which watches for a specific type of message. As a simple example, the first stanza watches for syslog messages that match the general syslog pattern I defined and that contain the substring crit, emerg, or alert. If a match is found in a single syslog message, swatch sends an e-mail message to vonhagen@vonhagen.org with the subject "Important Syslog Message." The body of the e-mail is the actual syslog message. Note that you have to escape the @ sign in an e-mail address to avoid Perl interpreting it as an array indicator, and that if you want to break this command across multiple lines for readability purposes, you'll need to escape the newline with a backslash (\). The following is an example of the mail sent by swatch (in response to a match of the third stanza in this configuration file fragment):

```
To: admins@vonhagen.org
Subject: Swatch Syslog Message: I/O Error
Date: Tue,  9 Oct 2007 14:15:34 -0400 (EDT)
From: root@loghost.vonhagen.org
 Sep 17 06:18:50 192.168.6.111 kernel: \
        Buffer I/O error on device sdd, logical block 0
```

The second stanza provides a more interesting and full-featured example of swatch's capabilities. In the second stanza, swatch is looking for matches of the pattern "file system full" and the standard syslog regular expression that was defined earlier in the file. The threshold command enables you to set limits on how often the swatch command will respond to this type of message, which is incredibly useful for recurring error messages (such as "file system full") that can quickly fill a log. The limit keyword tells swatch that it should only perform the specified actions the number of times specified in the count keyword, and then ignore subsequent matches for the remainder of the time interval specified by the seconds keyword. In this particular stanza, swatch will only perform the mail and exec actions the first three times that this message is encountered within a time period of 600 seconds (10 minutes). As in the previous example, the rest of this stanza uses the mail command to tell swatch to send an e-mail message to vonhagen@vonhagen.org with the subject "Syslog: File System Full." The exec command causes swatch to execute a specified program with the specified arguments, and the use of the when keyword enables you to restrict the exec action to occur only on the seventh and first day of the week. In this case, and only on those days, swatch will execute a program that sends a text message to my cell phone, on the off chance that I might not be in the office on those days. The full syntax of possible values for the when keyword is when=day-range:hour-range, which enables you to further restrict certain actions to a specific range of hours on specified days.

After installing and configuring swatch, you need to integrate it into your system's startup and shutdown processes. I use the following file on systems that use the traditional SysV init mechanism:

```
#!/bin/bash
#
# swatch          This starts and stops swatch.
#
# chkconfig: 345 13 13
# description: swatch monitors the syslog and performs \
#              specified actions when patterns are matched.
#
# processname: /usr/local/bin/swatch
# config: /etc/swatch.conf
# pidfile: /var/run/swatch.pid
PATH=/usr/local/bin:/sbin:/bin:/usr/bin:/usr/sbin
# Check for config file
[ -f /etc/swatch.conf ] || exit 0
# Source function library.
. /etc/init.d/functions
# Check that we are root ... so non-root users stop here
  [ `id -u` = 0 ] || exit 1
RETVAL=0
prog="swatch"
pidfile="/var/run/swatch.pid"
start(){
    echo -n $"Starting $prog: "
    daemon $prog --config-file=/etc/swatch.conf --tail-file=/var/log/syslog \
        --pid-file=$pidfile --daemon
    RETVAL=$?
    echo
    return $RETVAL
}
stop(){
    echo -n $"Stopping $prog: "
    PID=`cat "$pidfile" 2>/dev/null `
    /bin/kill "$PID" >/dev/null 2>&1
    RETVAL=$?
    echo
    return $RETVAL
}
restart(){
    stop
    start
}
# See how we were called.
case "$1" in
    start)
start
;;
    stop)
stop
```

```
;;
    restart)
restart
;;
    *)
echo $"Usage: $0 {start|stop}"
RETVAL=1
esac
exit $RETVAL
```

You need to create a similar script for systems that do not run SysV Init. Note that this script runs as startup item 13, which is immediately after the point at which the syslog is started on Linux distributions based on Red Hat or Fedora. This is because the swatch program examines logs by checking the last few lines of the specified system log file (in this case, /var/log/syslog). You need to start swatch as early as possible in order to catch error messages that may be displayed during subsequent phases of the boot process.

Backup Strategies for Xen Domains

Backups are a critical, tedious, and time-consuming operational task. Replacing physical machines with virtual machines obviously doesn't eliminate the need to do backups, but it does require thinking differently about how and when they are done, where backups are stored, and so on.

In many cases, virtualization significantly reduces the amount of data that you need to back up because it is easy to store spare copies of entire virtual machines. These can be deployed and updated quickly if some catastrophe strikes an existing virtual machine. Many of the enterprise environments that I've worked in used applications such as the well-known Symantec/Norton/Binary Research Ghost disk and partition cloning program to provide similar capabilities when deploying new physical machines. The ability to run virtual machines from partition images, disk images, or logical volumes makes it easy to clone the filesystems used by these virtual machines, whether through straightforward copies or the use of techniques such as logical volume snapshots. Similarly, techniques such as DRBD (Distributed Replicated Block Device) make it easy to mirror filesystems over a network, minimizing the amount of data that needs to be backed up because DRBD filesystems are always being backed up.

You can generally divide the types of backups that need to be done on virtual machines into several general classes:

❑ **System and service configuration information and associated data:** On virtual machines that provide only services such as DNS, DHCP, print spooling, outbound mail servers, firewalls, LDAP, VPNs, and so on, the only real information that needs to be backed up is the information that makes it different from any other system. This is usually the system and service configuration data, as well as any databases or file hierarchies used by services that require both state and configuration information (such as the LDAP service).

❑ **Database and other raw filesystem data:** Raw storage devices used by many databases and similar applications can be backed up in multiple ways, including a snapshot or backup operation if they are contained in logical volumes, database-specific mechanisms such as export/import formats, built-in commands such as DB2's backup command, putting a database in a special mode (such as Oracle's BACKUP mode) and doing online backups, application-specific utilities such as Oracle's RMAN or IBM's OnBar for Informix, and commercial backup solutions (depending on your host platform) such as BakBone's NetVault (www.bakbone.com) or Novosoft's Handy Backup (www.handybackup.net/index.html).

❏ **User and fileserver data:** Systems that support actual users must back up any local data that they create or use. This also applies to file servers on which user data is stored, even if users do not have direct access to these machines.

When backing up multiple virtual machines that are located on a single physical host, critical items to consider are the target for the backup operations (the location to which your backups will be written) and the load that backups place on that host. The next two sections discuss these topics. Subsequent sections discuss standard, open source mechanisms for doing the different types of backups identified in this section.

Selecting a Backup Target

The target for backups done in a virtualized environment should usually be a networked storage target because multiple virtual hosts must be able to access the same backup location. Mapping specific PCI or USB controllers and associated devices to paravirtualized domains is an option, but increases both the complexity of your infrastructure and the difficulty of recreating the environment in the event of some catastrophe, such as a fire or permanent hardware failure of your domain0 host. Using dedicated devices for domainU backups is also impractical because they can only be assigned to and used by a single domainU guest.

Identifying the right target for networked backups depends on the size of your virtualization environment, the way that it is implemented, and the network storage targets that are available to you. In smaller virtualization environments or those in which the filesystems for your domainU guests are stored in local logical volumes, it may be practical to do networked domainU backups to removable storage on your domain0 host. Some domain0 involvement is unavoidable for domainU guests whose filesystems are stored in local logical volumes and that use snapshots as the first step of the backup process. In general, using a remote networked storage location other than your domain0 system has significant advantages, including:

❏ Fewer dependencies on your domain0 host.

❏ Reduced domain0 I/O load. Reading data on domainU guests and writing it to domain0 storage can significantly affect overall domainU performance, especially if the domainU guests are using local storage.

❏ Better separation of backup-related activities such as archival, off-site storage, and backup testing and validation.

As mentioned before, I'm a big fan of using networked storage for domainU guests, primarily because system-independent (or network-mirrored) storage is currently mandatory for live migration. My personal preference is ATA over Ethernet (AoE) storage because it is fast and low-level, and does not require the "animal sacrifices" that always accompany iSCSI implementations. Your mileage (and type of sacrifice) may vary.

Identifying and Minimizing Backup Load

Backups always increase the load on the domainU guest, and therefore on the domain0 host. The amount of this increase depends on the type of backups that you are doing and your backup target. When backing up to networked storage, the amount of the increase in network I/O primarily depends on the amount of data that you are backing up, but the existing network load is also a factor because significant backup-related network traffic can saturate your network and degrade overall performance. Processor load and I/O are similarly dependent on the type of backups that you are doing, but are much more variable. Backing up specific files places the minimal load on the system, whereas backups of user, fileserver, or raw filesystem data require substantial computing power and significant disk and filesystem I/O. Incremental backups require that at least file metadata be examined for the complete hierarchy of any directories or filesystems that you are backing up. Full fileserver or raw filesystem dumps typically require less analysis but more I/O because all of the data in the directory structure or raw filesystem must be read and written to the backup target. Database backups done via an export mechanism require both significant I/O and computing power because all of the data must both be read and converted into the export format.

Regardless of your target, backing up multiple domainU guests makes it very important to properly schedule backups. Backups are traditionally done in off-peak hours because this minimizes the extent to which users or applications are modifying your data, and also because system and network load is reduced at these times. domainU backups on a single domain0 host should be done in off-peak hours, but should also be staggered to minimize contention for processor, disk, and network resources. If your domainU guests use dedicated network interface cards, contention for processor and storage resources can still be significant. As you add domainU guests to a domain0 host, it is important to re-examine your backup schedules and adjust them, as needed, to take the new guests into consideration. After adding new domainU guests to a domain0 system, it is good practice to monitor the system and network load while backups are being done for some initial period of time, and to make further scheduling adjustments as needed.

Backing Up Selected Files and Directories Using rsync

The rsync (remote sync) application is a command-line file and directory synchronization program that makes it easy to copy files and directories from one host to another. When both a local and remote copy of a file or directory hierarchy exist, rsync is able to leverage built-in features that help reduce the amount of data that needs to be transmitted in order to ensure that the local and remote copies of those files and directories are identical. The protocol used by the rsync utility to update remote copies of files and directories enables rsync to transfer only the differences between the two sets of files and directories. The rsync program is automatically installed as part of most Linux, Solaris, and other UNIX installations, but requires some configuration on the systems from which you want to copy files and directories to your backup system. Versions of rsync are also available for most versions of Microsoft Windows — see the sidebar "rsync for Windows" later in this section for more information about installing and using rsync on Windows virtual machines.

The ability to work at the file and directory level and its optimized transfer protocol make rsync ideal for backing up virtual machines on which you need to back up a limited number of files and directories. rsync can also be used to push files to virtual machines, but this section focuses on using rsync to pull files from remote systems to a centralized backup system that is running Linux.

The rsync program is suitable for use as a backup mechanism for small numbers of specific files and for portions of mounted filesystems. I tend to use rsync more for system files and directories than for actual filesystem backups because it preserves only the latest versions of files, whereas traditional incremental and full backup applications preserve different versions of files in different backups.

Linux systems that use rsync should have appropriate entries in the /etc/services file that identify the rsync port and protocol. These should already be present on the Linux system that you are using as a backup target, but just in case, they should look like the following:

```
rsync    873/tcp
rsync    873/udp
```

The rsync daemon is usually started in one of two ways:

❑   By an Internet services manager such as inetd or xinetd, in response to incoming requests

❑   During the system startup process as a standalone daemon

Most Linux distributions (including CentOS, Fedora, Mandrake, Red Hat, SUSE, and so on) use an Internet services manager such as inetd or xinetd to manage incoming requests for on-demand services such as ftp, tftp, rsync, and so on. These Internet service managers automatically start the appropriate daemon when an incoming request is received. If you are not already using rsync in your environment, you will have to enable rsync on the system to which you want to back up files, so that the system will respond to incoming rsync requests from your virtual machines. Alhough most systems run xinetd nowadays (the *x* stands for eXtended), I'll explain how to configure both, just in case.

If you are unsure how (or if) your system starts rsync automatically, first check for the presence of a system startup file for the daemon, which is typically the file /etc/init.d/rsync. If this file is not present but the file /etc/init.d/inetd is present, your system uses inetd. If this file is not present and the file /etc/init.d/xinetd is present, your system uses xinetd. If none of these files is present, check whether rsync is installed on your system at all by running the which rsync command as the superuser on the system that you will be using as your backup target. If this command doesn't display the full pathname to rsync on the system, use your system's package management utility to install the rsync package (or build it manually, if you wish). You can get the latest rsync source code from its home page at http://samba.org/rsync. This site also provides binary packages for various Linux distributions if you cannot get rsync from your distribution's primary repositories for some reason.

If the inetd or xinetd startup file is present on your system, you need to make sure that it is actually started at your system's default run level. You can do this using the ps -e command:

```
# ps -e | grep inetd
 3757 ?        00:00:00 xinetd
```

In this case, my target backup host is using xinetd, and it is clearly running at my system's default runlevel. If this command doesn't show inetd or xinetd as running, make sure that the appropriate symbolic link exists in the system startup directory for your system's default runlevel, pointing to the inetd or xinetd startup file in your system's /etc/init.d directory.

The inetd services manager uses the configuration file /etc/inetd.conf to identify the incoming service requests that it should listen for, and to determine how to respond to these. To enable incoming rsync requests on a Linux system running inetd that you are using for backups, you add a line like the following to the /etc/inetd.conf file:

```
rsync stream tcp nowait root /usr/bin/rsync rsyncd --daemon
```

You then need to start (or restart) the inetd process on your system, which you can typically do by using a command like the following as the superuser or via the sudo command:

```
# /etc/init.d/inetd restart
```

The xinetd services manager uses configuration files stored in the directory /etc/xinetd.d to identify the incoming service requests that it should listen for, and to determine how to respond to these. You should see a file named rsync in this directory. This file should look something like the following:

```
# default: off
# description: The rsync server is a good addition to an ftp \
#              server, as it allows crc checksumming etc.
service rsync
{
        disable         = no
        socket_type     = stream
        wait            = no
        user            = root
        server          = /usr/bin/rsync
        server_args     = --daemon
        log_on_failure  += USERID
}
```

To enable incoming rsync requests on a Linux system running xinetd that you are using for backups, make sure that the disable entry in this file is set to no, which therefore enables incoming requests, as shown in the previous example.

The inetd and xinetd Internet service managers are available for other Linux distributions, such as Debian and Ubuntu, but are not installed by default. On these distributions, a specific system startup file that starts rsync in daemon mode is provided as /etc/init.d/rsync. If you subsequently install xinetd and want to use it to manage rsync requests, you need to disable this file and create (or, more probably, edit) the file /etc/xinetd.d/rsync to make sure that the rsync service is enabled on your system.

Regardless of which Linux distribution you are using on the host to which you will be writing backups using rsync, the startup files discussed earlier in this section simply ensure that the rsync daemon will respond to incoming requests. The actual configuration information for rsync itself is stored in the file /etc/rsyncd.conf, which you will have to either create or edit on the systems from which you want to back up files because this configuration file determines which files and directories can be remotely requested from the backup system or automatically pushed to the backup system. The contents of this file are read when any rsync connection is established, so you do not need to restart your Internet services manager or standalone rsync server after modifying this file.

The following is a simple rsync configuration file that contains global parameters and defines two directories that can be synchronized via rsync:

```
uid = root
transfer logging = true
log format = %h %o %f %l %b
log file = /var/log/rsyncd.log
hosts allow = 192.168.6.255/3
secrets file = /etc/rsyncd.secrets
[homes]
path = /home
comment = Home Directories
auth users = admin
[admin]
path=/etc/admin
comment = System Files That are Backed Up
auth users = admin
```

The first section of this file sets parameters for how the rsync daemon runs. In order, the rsync daemon runs as root (`uid`), logs all transfers (`transfer logging`), uses a specific log file format (`log format`) and log file (`log file`), allows access from any host whose IP address is on the 192.168.6.x subnet (`hosts allow`), and uses the password file `/etc/rsyncd.secrets`. The second section of this file identifies two synchronizable entities (known as modules in rsync-speak): `homes`, which maps to the directory `/home` on that system, and `admin`, which maps to the directory `/etc/admin` on that system. Synchronization to or from these directories is done as the user `admin`, whose password must be supplied in the file `/etc/rsyncd.secrets`.

The `/etc/admin` directory is not a standard Linux directory, but reflects a convention that I find useful. I create this directory on any Linux system that I am backing up using rsync, and then create hard links in this directory to the system configuration files that I want to back up. (You can also do this with symbolic links if you always remember to use the `-L` option when running rsync.) I also mirror the directory structure, relative to root, for the configuration files in this directory, so the hard link to `/etc/samba/smb.conf` lives in the directory `/etc/admin/etc/samba/smb.conf`. This provides me with a single directory that I can pull from remote systems that will archive all of their local configuration data. Your mileage may vary, but I find this useful, especially in the case of virtual machines because this gives me a directory structure that I can overlay on a newly created virtual machine if I need to recreate a specific virtual machine, or start with a clone of an existing system.

After saving this file, use your favorite text editor to create the file `/etc/rsync.secrets`. This file should contain an entry for each `auth users` entry in the `/etc/rsync.conf` file, in this case `admin`. Each entry in this file contains the name of a user, a colon, and the plain-text password for that user, as in the following example:

```
admin:hellothere
```

Next, save this file and make sure that it is readable only by the root user on your system using commands such as the following via the `sudo` command or as the root user:

```
chown root:root /etc/rsyncd.secrets
chmod 600 /etc/rsyncd.secrets
```

You can now create local copies of the `/home` and `/etc/admin` directories from the remote system by using a command such as the following, where *remote-system* is the name or IP address of the system on which you just configured:

```
$ rsync -HLavz remote-system-addr::admin remote-system
```

The arguments to the `rsync` command in this example have the following meaning:

- ❑ `H`: Preserve hard links if these exist in any directories that are being copied.

- ❑ `L`: Transform symbolic links into the files that they point to.

- ❑ `a`: Use archive mode, which works recursively, to preserve ownership, symbolic links, device files, and so on. This is essentially a shortcut that saves you from having to specify a large number of other options, but will work only if you run this command as a privileged user because only a privileged user can change the ownership and modes of files.

- ❑ `v`: Be verbose, identifying each file that is copied or considered for copying. You probably want to use this option only when testing.

- ❑ `z`: Use compression when transferring files, which improves throughput.

If you have problems using rsync, you should check the `/var/log/rsyncd.log` file (on the system that you are trying to retrieve files from) for error messages and hints for resolving them. If you are not using the verbose option on the host from which you are retrieving these files, you may want to use it to see if you can identify (and resolve) any other errors that the host that is trying to retrieve files is reporting.

The sync configuration file created in this section is a simple example designed for use on secure networks. You can also run rsync using SSH to both encrypt file transfers for sensitive data and to enable the use of remote key files and associated accounts for authentication purposes. When scripting rsync to pull files from a remote system, you may want to use the `--password-file` command-line option to enable you to use a file on your backup host in which to store password information. If using this approach, this file should be made read-only and owned by the root user.

For details about all of the options available in an rsync configuration file and information about making rsync more secure, see the man page for the `rsyncd.conf` file (`man rsyncd.conf`).

---

rsync for Windows

The rsync application is open source, so it's not surprising that it is also available for Microsoft Windows systems. Because rsync depends heavily on protocols, APIs, and other Linux-isms that aren't natively available for Windows, the only versions of rsync for Windows that I've ever seen all depend on Cygwin (www.cygwin.com), which is a Linux-like environment for Windows consisting of a primary Dynamic Link Library (DLL) and a variety of associated tools.

The folks at ITeF!x Consulting provide a free version of rsync for Windows (www.itefix.no/cwrsync) that is bundled with the Cygwin DLL and a few other DLLs that provide related functionality such as SSH support. This combination

---

runs on Windows 9x, NT, 2000, XP, 2003, and related server products. Installing this package eliminates the need for installing a complete Cygwin environment on your Windows systems, but still enables you to back up files from your Windows systems to a centralized Linux backup server using rsync. This is done by creating batch files that encapsulate the right commands to push files to the backup server using rsync.

Another alternative is to install a complete Cygwin environment on your Windows systems, install the rsync daemon as a service, and perform the same configuration described earlier in this section to define modules that are associated with the directories that you want to be able to pull from your backup server.

Backing Up Logical Volumes Using Snapshots

Chapter 6 discussed the Linux logical volume management system and the use of logical volumes to hold the filesystems and raw partitions used by your paravirtualized domainU guests. Logical volumes provide a flexible approach to allocating storage that removes most of the size and location limitations associated with physical, per-device storage allocation. The use of logical volumes on modern Linux systems also provides some significant advantages in terms of doing backups.

The number one issue when planning and doing backups is the consistency of the data that you are backing up. Doing backups of a filesystem that is actively changing is a problem because there is no single point in time at which the backups can be completely accurate. Filesystem backups typically work in one of two ways: either by scanning a filesystem, creating a list of modified files and directories, and then backing them up; or by actively walking through a filesystem, identifying modified files and directories, and backing them up as they are encountered. If users are actively modifying files and directories while the filesystem is being scanned, changes will occur between the beginning and end of the backups, either because the list of modified files and directories has changed and newly modified files aren't added to the list, or because files and directories that have already been added to the backups may have been subsequently modified. In both of these backup scenarios, it is essentially impossible to predict the size of the backups beforehand because you can't accurately predict the size of the files that you need to back up until you actually add them to the backup.

The Linux Logical Volume Manager (LVM) provides a snapshot capability that makes it easy to guarantee the consistency of a filesystem that is located on a Linux logical volume. As the name suggests, a snapshot reflects the complete state of an existing logical volume at a single point in time. Cleverly, snapshots are not a copy of a logical volume, which would require the same amount of disk space that the original logical volume requires, would be slow to create because all of the data or the raw volume itself would have to be copied, and would interrupt the use of the system while the copy was being created (because it could not change at that time). Instead, snapshots are essentially a copy-on-write duplicate of a logical volume, which means that they are initially empty and data that is changed in the original logical volume is copied to the snapshot whenever the original logical volume is written to. In other word, as changes are made to the original logical volume, the original data that was present at the time the snapshot was made is migrated to the snapshot so that it continues to reflect the exact state of the logical volume when the snapshot was made. For example, suppose that the file foo.txt exists in a logical volume that I have made a snapshot of. If I delete or otherwise modify that file, the original data associated with that file is moved into the snapshot. The snapshot continues to reflect the state of the original logical volume at the time that the snapshot was created, while the contents of the logical volume itself can continue to change.

Using snapshots for backup purposes enables you to back up a logical volume without having to worry about changes being made to the files, directories, or data contained in that volume while the backup is taking place. After creating a snapshot, you can either back it up directly (if it is a raw volume used by a database or similar application) or mount the snapshot and back up the mounted snapshot at the filesystem level. Backing up snapshots rather than the logical volumes that they are based on ensures consistent backups while applications and users are actually modifying the volume that you are backing up.

Backing Up Database Volumes

Backing up snapshots of raw partitions used by databases and similar applications can be problematic because all of the logs used by those databases may not be present in that logical volume. Depending on the database system that you are using and the location of your logs, you will probably want to flush all pending transactions before taking a snapshot if you can. However, this requires that each table be flushed and a read lock obtained, which can take a long time if tables are already locked by other threads due to long-running transactions.

It may not be necessary to flush pending writes if you are using transactional storage such as InnoDB (www.innodb.com/). With InnoDB, snapshots can be taken while the volume is actively in use. If backups from that snapshot have to be restored, InnoDB simply treats the restored volume as needing repair, as if a system crash had occurred, and will correctly replay pending, committed transactions.

If you are using file-backed MySQL and can afford read locks on your databases, you should find the mylvmbackup script (http://lenz.homelinux.org/mylvmbackup/) useful. This is a Perl script that first gets a read lock on all tables, and then flushes all server caches to disk, makes an LVM snapshot of the volume containing the MySQL data directory, and unlocks the tables again while mounting the snapshot and using tar to back up the MySQL files area. You may not be able to take your MySQL server down at all, in which case you may be better doing export/import backups using a utility such as mysqldump or using InnoDB, as described previously.

To create a snapshot of an existing logical volume, execute a command like the following as a user with administrative capabilities:

```
# lvcreate -LSIZE -s -n SNAPSHOT-NAME EXISTING-LOGICAL-VOLUME
```

The -L option specifies the SIZE of the snapshot volume using a standard size specification, such as 100M (100 megabytes), 10G (10 gigabytes), and so on. The -s option identifies the logical volume that you are creating as a snapshot. The -n option enables to you specify the name that you want to assign to the snapshot (SNAPSHOT-NAME), and EXISTING-LOGICAL-VOLUME is the full pathname of the logical volume that you want to make a snapshot of. You must be sure to allocate more than enough space to handle changes during the lifetime of the snapshot because snapshots that are smaller than the size of their "parent" volume will become inconsistent (and therefore useless) if they fill up while they are being used.

The size of the snapshot is based on the amount of change you expect to see in the EXISTING-LOGICAL-VOLUME while you are using SNAPSHOT-NAME. The worst case value for SIZE is therefore the full size of EXISTING-LOGICAL-VOLUME.

After creating the snapshot, you can then mount it somewhere for backup purposes if it is a standard Linux filesystem or back it up in raw form by using an application-specific dump utility if it is a raw partition. Once you are done with the snapshot, you can then umount it (if necessary) and use the lvremove command to remove the snapshot.

Backing Up Filesystems over the Network

The previous two sections discussed rsync, which is a fairly traditional backup utility, and logical volume snapshots, which facilitate the use of traditional local backup utilities such as tar, cpio, and any other local backup tool. One of the best things about open source and its contributors is that it provides a tremendous number of alternatives for any given software task, each of which works in the way that someone thought was "the one true way." This section discusses some of the best-known, network-aware, open source backup utilities, and focuses on my personal favorite, BackupPC.

The best-known, network-aware open source backup utilities that I've encountered in commercial and academic use are the following:

❑ **Amanda:** The Advanced Maryland Automated Network Disk Archiver is an open source distributed backup system that was originally developed for UNIX systems at the University of Maryland in the early 1990s. Amanda makes it easy to back up any number of client workstations to a central backup server, supports Windows Microsoft backups via Samba, and provides a complete backup management system. Amanda supports multiple sets of backups with distinct configurations, supports disc and tape backups, tracks backup levels and dates on its client systems, produces detailed reports that are automatically delivered via e-mail, and keeps extensive logs that make it easy to diagnose and correct the cause of most problems. Communication between Amanda clients and servers is encrypted to heighten security. If it is available in your Linux distribution's repositories, Amanda typically consists of two packages: amanda-server and amanda-client. Amanda's home Web site is at www.amanda.org.

❑ **BackupPC:** BackupPC (http://backuppc.sourceforge.net) is a nice backup system that provides a Web-based interface, which enables you to back up remote systems using SMB (Server Message Block protocol), tar, or rsync. Figure 10-2 shows the Web page of a sample BackupPC server. BackupPC creates backups of your remote systems that are stored and managed on your BackupPC server, and also enables authorized users to restore their own files from these archives (removing the number-one source of migraines for system administrators). Configuration data for each client system is stored on the BackupPC server, which enables you to back up different types of systems using different commands or protocols, and to easily identify which remote directories or filesystems you want to back up. One especially nice feature of BackupPC is that it uses standard Linux commands on the server to create backups, and therefore doesn't require the installation of any software on client systems, although some client-side configuration may be necessary for certain backup commands.

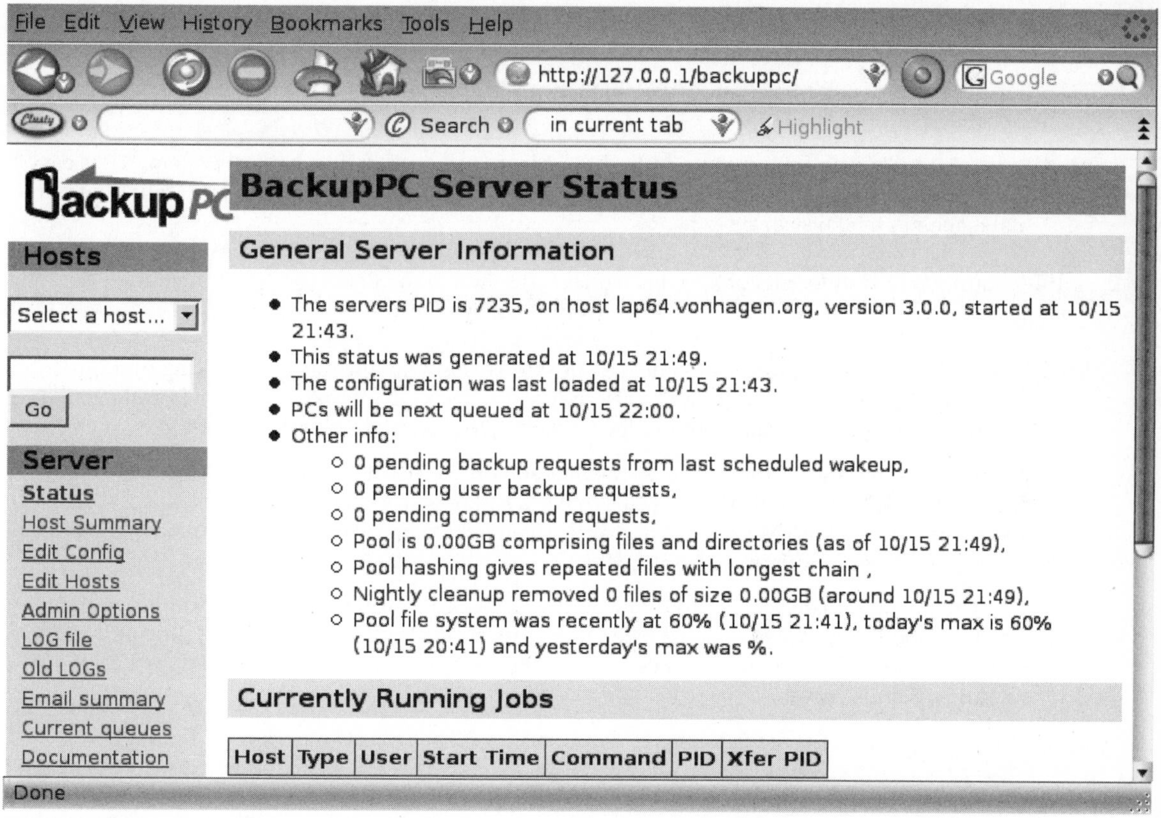

Figure 10-2

❑ **Bacula:** Bacula is an extremely powerful set of programs that provide a scalable network backup and restore system that supports Linux, UNIX, and Microsoft Windows systems. Its power and flexibility easily match that of Amanda, but it is more flexible in terms of how and where backups are stored. Bacula is quite powerful, but can be complex — if you're interested in exploring Bacula, you may want to start by installing the bacula-doc package and reading its documentation to determine if it is right for your environment. Bacula is primarily command-line oriented, but provides a graphical console as a wrapper around its command-line interface. Bacula's home page is www.bacula.org.

Many more network-aware, open source backup utilities are available, but these are probably the best known. Of these, I find BackupPC to be the easiest to use, for several reasons:

❑ It requires no remote configuration on the systems that you are backing up, making it perfect for use with existing virtual machines because it requires no additional configuration.

❑ Because it uses existing remote access mechanisms to do backups, it can easily be used to back up Linux, UNIX, Microsoft Windows, and Mac OS X virtual machines. (Looking forward, of course, to the day when it will be legal to use Mac OS X in a virtual machine, rather than just being possible.)

❑ Its Web-based interface is easy to set up and use.

❏ It enables authorized users to restore their own files from backups, which should delight any system administrator.

❏ It is robust, well-supported, and available for most Linux distributions in their standard repositories.

❏ Because it pulls data from remote virtual machines (and optionally, physical systems), it is easy to schedule along with other types of backups, such as rsync, that also pull data from other virtual machines or physical systems.

BackupPC supports four different backup mechanisms (known in the BackupPC documentation as *backup transports*) to back up the following different types of systems:

❏ `rsync`: Back up and restore via rsync, rsh, or ssh. This is a good choice for backing up Linux, UNIX, or Mac OS X systems, and can also be used to back up Microsoft Windows systems that support rsync, such as those running the Cygwin Linux emulation environment.

❏ `rsyncd`: Back up and restore via an rsync daemon on the client system. This is the best choice for Linux, UNIX, and Mac OS X systems that are running an rsync daemon. This mechanism can also be used to back up Microsoft Windows systems that support rsyncd, such as those running the Cygwin Linux emulation environment.

❏ `smb`: Back up and restore using the smbclient and the SMB protocol on the BackupPC server. This is the best (and easiest) choice when you're using BackupPC to back up Microsoft Windows systems, and can also be used to back up Mac OS X systems or Linux and UNIX systems that are running a Samba server.

❏ `tar`: Back up and restore via tar, tar over ssh, rsh, or NFS. This is an option for Linux, UNIX, and Mac OS X systems. This mechanism can also be used to back up Microsoft Windows systems that support tar, ssh, rsh, and/or NFS, such as those running the Cygwin Linux emulation environment.

A default backup transport value for all backups is set in the primary backuppc configuration file, `/etc/backuppc/config.pl`. The specific mechanism used to back up any particular host can be identified in that host's configuration file, as discussed in "Defining a Backup Using rsyncd" and "Defining a Backup Using SMB" later in this chapter.

Although BackupPC does a great job of backing up systems running Microsoft Windows and Mac OS X, you should be aware of a few issues. First, BackupPC is not suitable for backing up Windows systems so that you can do a bare-metal restore. BackupPC uses the smbclient application on your Ubuntu system to back up Windows disks, so it doesn't back up Windows ACLs and can't open files that are locked by a Windows client that is currently running (such as Microsoft Outlook mailboxes). Similarly, BackupPC doesn't preserve Mac OS file attributes. See `http://backuppc.sourceforge.net/faq/limitations.html` for a list of current limitations in using BackupPC.

For additional information about BackupPC, you can join various mailing lists that are available through the SourceForge BackupPC site:

❏ **backuppc-announce:** A low-traffic list where announcements of new versions are posted (`http://lists.sourceforge.net/lists/listinfo/backuppc-announce`).

❏ **backuppc-devel:** The mailing list for BackupPC developers (`http://lists.sourceforge
.net/lists/listinfo/backuppc-devel`).

❏ **backuppc-users:** The standard mailing lists where you can ask and answer questions about
using BackupPC (`http://lists.sourceforge.net/lists/listinfo/backuppc-users`).

The next few sections explain how to install, configure, and use BackupPC to back up a variety of
physical and virtual machines to a central backup server.

Installing and Configuring BackupPC

Special-purpose backup solutions such as BackupPC aren't installed by default on most Linux
distributions. However, BackupPC is available in the repository for most distributions. If it is not, the
source code for BackupPC is always available from its SourceForge project site at `http://
sourceforge.net/projects/backuppc`. At the time of this writing, the official release is version 3.0.0,
but a beta version of 3.1 is also available. Versions of BackupPC for various Linux distributions generally
provide some incremental patches, so the version for your system may actually be something like 3.0.0-3.

In order to use BackupPC's graphical, Web-based interface, your backup server will have to be running a
version of the Apache Web server. BackupPC also has dependencies on a number of other Perl modules,
so I strongly suggest that you use a package management system to install BackupPC. This section uses
an Ubuntu backup system as an example because I generally find that Ubuntu's graphical package
management utility (Synaptic) best simplifies installing packages, prompting for mandatory
configuration information when necessary. For example, Synaptic will automatically integrate BackupPC
with your Web server (installing Apache if necessary), automatically create and set default passwords,
and so on.

> If you are downloading the BackupPC tarball and building it yourself, execute the
> following commands as an administrative user (these examples are for version 3.0.0
> of the software):
>
> ```
> # tar zxf BackupPC-3.0.0.tar.gz
> # cd BackupPC-3.0.0
> # perl configure.pl
> ```
>
> See the BackupPC installation and configuration documentation (`http://backuppc
> .sourceforge.net/faq/BackupPC.html`) for information on configuring BackupPC
> and integrating it with your Web server.

BackupPC stores its configuration information in two locations. General BackupPC configuration
information and passwords are stored in files in the directory `/etc/backuppc` on Ubuntu systems
(or `/etc/backupPC` on some other Linux distributions). Backup files themselves and host-specific
backup configuration information is stored in subdirectories of `/var/lib/backuppc` (or `/var/lib/
backupPC` on some Linux distributions).

Depending on what you back up, backups of even a single system can take a significant amount of space. This is compounded when you begin to back up other virtual machines (or physical hosts, for that matter) to a central backup server. If your centralized backup server does not already use logical volumes, you may want to add a new disk to your system before starting to use BackupPC, and format that disk as a logical volume. You can then copy the default contents of /var/lib/backuppc to the new disk (preserving file permissions and ownership), and mount that disk on the directory /var/lib/backuppc on the system that you are using for backups. Using logical volumes will enable you to increase the size of your backup area when you need more space to store backups in the future, by adding other disks to your system and allocating them to the volume group that underlies the logical volume used to store backups. You will then be able to increase the size of that logical volume. The BackupPC utility also provides an archive capability that enables you to migrate old backups to other hosts for archival purposes, freeing up disk space on your primary backup server. I tend to simply copy old backups to removable hard drives and use these for archival purposes.

The first thing that you should do is to change the BackupPC password to something easier to remember than the random string generated during the BackupPC installation process. You can do this by issuing the following command as the root user or via the sudo command:

```
htpasswd /etc/backuppc/htpasswd backuppc
```

The htpasswd command changes the password for the user backuppc in the file /etc/backuppc/htpasswd. When you are prompted for a new password, enter something easier to remember than "TLhCi25f," which was the default password generated for my BackupPC installation. You will be prompted to re-enter the new password to make sure that you typed it correctly.

> All of the commands in the subsequent sections on BackupPC should be executed via the sudo command or as root. I'll spare you the pain of reading that for each command.

Identifying Hosts to Back Up

Each host that you want to back up must be identified in the file /etc/backuppc/hosts. Like all BackupPC configuration files, this file is easy to update. Any characters in any line in this file that follow a hash mark are comments, which help explain the meaning of the various fields used in the file. A minimal BackupPC configuration file looks like the following:

```
host            dhcp    user            moreUsers
localhost       0       backuppc
```

The first non-comment line in /etc/backuppc/hosts defines the names of the various fields in each line, and should therefore not be modified. (This is the line beginning with host in the example.) All other lines represent entries for hosts that will be backed up. The first actual host entry is for localhost. It is a special entry used for backing up system configuration information on the BackupPC server, and should not be changed.

The fields in each entry that define a host have the following meanings:

❑ The first field identifies a particular machine, either by hostname, IP address, or NetBIOS name.

❑ The second field should be set to 0 for any host whose name can be determined by DNS, the local hosts file, or an nmblookup broadcast. This field can be set to 1 to identify systems whose names must be discovered by probing a range of DHCP addresses, as is the case in some environments where DHCP and WINS are not fully integrated. Setting this field to 1 requires changes in the host-specific configuration file's $Conf{DHCPAddressRanges} variable to define the base IP address and range of IP addresses that should be probed.

❑ The third field identifies the name of the person who is primarily responsible for backing up that host. This primary user will receive e-mail about the status of any backup that is attempted. I tend to leave this as the backuppc user, so that this user maintains an e-mail record of all backup attempts, but you can set this to a specific user if you wish.

❑ The fourth field consists of one or more users who also have administrative rights to initiate backups or restore files for this machine. The names of multiple users must be separated by a comma.

As an example, a portion of the hosts file on my BackupPC server looks like the following:

```
host            dhcp      user            moreUsers
localhost       0         backuppc
xen             0         backuppc        admin
64bit           0         backuppc        admin
mail            0         backuppc        admin
win2k           0         backuppc        admin
```

In this example, xen happens to be the name of my domain0 system, and 64bit, mail, and win2k are three virtual machines running on that system.

The BackupPC program checks the timestamp on the /etc/backuppc/hosts files each time the BackupPC process wakes up, and reloads this file automatically if the file has been updated. For this reason, you should not save changes to the hosts file until you have created the host-specific configuration files, as described in the examples in the next two sections. If the BackupPC process reloads the hosts file before you have created the host-specific configuration data, and another authorized user initiates a backup of this system, you will either back up the wrong thing or a backup failure will occur. You can always make changes to the hosts file and leave them commented out (by putting a # as the first character on the line) until you have completed the host-specific configuration.

Defining a Backup Using rsyncd

The section "Backing Up Selected Files and Directories Using rsync" earlier in this chapter explained how to set up rsync to respond to incoming requests and how to define synchronization entries that can be remotely accessed via rsync. The sample rsync configuration file created in that section defined two synchronization entries, one of which was called home, and would enable an authorized user to synchronize the contents of all directories under /home on a sample system. I use that same configuration file in the example in this section.

The previous section showed how to define entries in the `/etc/backuppc/hosts` file for the various hosts that you want to back up via BackupPC. The first step in host-specific configuration is to create a directory to hold host-specific configuration data, logs, and so on. Throughout this section, I use the sample host entry `mail`, which I defined in the hosts configuration file in the previous section.

Continuing with this example, the first step in host-specific configuration is to create the directory `/var/lib/backuppc/mail` using the following command:

```
mkdir /var/lib/backuppc/mail
```

Next, use your favorite text editor to create a host-specific configuration file named `config.pl` in that directory using the following command:

```
emacs /var/lib/backuppc/mail/config.pl
```

The contents of this file should be something like the following;

```
$Conf{XferMethod} = 'rsyncd';
$Conf{CompressLevel} = '3';
$Conf{RsyncShareName} = 'admin';
$Conf{RsyncdUserName} = 'admin';
$Conf{RsyncdPasswd} = 'hellothere';
```

The first line identifies the backup mechanism used for this host as rsyncd, which overrides the default backup mechanism specified in the generic `/etc/backuppc/config.pl` file. The second line sets the compression level for this host's backups to level 3, which provides a good tradeoff between the CPU load and time required to do compression and the amount of compression that you actually get. The last three entries in this file correspond to the synchronization entry for the `admin` directory that was shown in the sample `rsyncd.conf` and associated password file created in "Backing Up Selected Files and Directories Using rsync" earlier in this chapter.

When using BackupPC to do automated backups, I like to create a separate authorized user to use rsync for backup purposes so that the system logs show who actually requested a remote sync operation. To do this, you would add this user (I usually use BackupPC) to the `auth users` entry in the remote host's `/etc/rsyncd.conf` file and create an appropriate username/password pair in the remote host's `/etc/rsyncd.secrets` file. You would then modify the host-specific BackupPC configuration file to use this username and password. For simplicity's sake, I didn't do that here, but doing so would provide more accurate log data on the client system.

If the remote system uses an rsync binary other than the default `/usr/bin/rsync`, or the rsync program is listening on a port other than the standard port (873), you should add correct definitions for these to the host-specific configuration file. The default settings for the associated configuration parameters are as follows:

```
$Conf{RsyncdClientPort} = 873;
$Conf{RsyncClientPath} = '/usr/bin/rsync';
```

Next, change the ownership and group of the `/var/lib/backuppc/mail` directory to `backuppc` and change the protection of the configuration file `/var/lib/backuppc/mail/config.pl` so that it is not publicly readable (because it contains password information) using the following commands:

```
chmod -Rv backuppc:backuppc /var/lib/backuppc/mail
chmod 600 /var/lib/backuppc/mail/config.pl
```

The last step in creating a host-specific backup definition for BackupPC is to cause the BackupPC process to re-read its configuration data, which you can do by explicitly reloading the configuration file, explicitly restarting the BackupPC process, or sending the associated process a hangup (HUP) signal. You can force BackupPC to reload its configuration file using the following command:

```
/etc/init.d/backuppc reload
```

The definition for your backup host can now be selected via the BackupPC Web interface. At this point, you can follow the instructions in the section "Starting Backups in BackupPC" to back up this host.

The example in this section backs up only the admin directory on the remote machine. To recursively back up other directories, you would simply create other synchronization entities for those directories in the remote host's /etc/rsyncd.conf file, and then add entries for those synchronization entities to the host-specific configuration file. For example, to back up the synchronization entries named admin and homes, you would change the host-specific RsyncShareName entry to look like the following:

```
$Conf{RsyncShareName} = ['admin', 'homes'];
```

If you back up multiple filesystems or synchronization points, you may create a custom set of arguments to the rsync command in the host-specific configuration file. This enables you to add options such as --one-file-system, which causes BackupPC to back up each filesystem separately, simplifying restores. You can also add options to exclude certain directories from the backups, which you will certainly want to do if you are backing up a remote system's root directory (/), as in the following examples:

```
$Conf{RsyncArgs} = [
        # original arguments here
        '--one-file-system',
        '--exclude', '/dev,
        '--exclude', '/proc',
        '--exclude', '/media',
        '--exclude', '/mnt',
        '--exclude', '/lost+found',
    ];
```

These settings would prevent backups of /dev, which contains device nodes and is dynamically populated at boot time on modern Linux systems; /proc, which is the mount point for an in-memory filesystem that contains transient data; directories such as /media and /mnt on which removable media is often temporarily mounted; and /lost+found, which is a directory used during filesystem consistency checking. You can also exclude directories from rsync backups using the BackupFilesExclude directive, as in the following example:

```
$Conf{BackupFilesExclude} = ['/dev', /proc', '/media', '/mnt', '/lost+found'];
```

The BackupPC program reads the configuration settings in /etc/backuppc/config.pl first and then loads host-specific configuration settings, which enables the /etc/backuppc/config.pl file to provide default settings for all backups. After you have used BackupPC for a while and are comfortable with various settings, you may want to consider modifying the default settings in the `/etc/backuppc/config.pl` file for configuration variables such as `$Conf{RsyncArgs}`, `$Conf{BackupFilesExclude}`, and `$Conf{CompressLevel}`, in order to minimize the number of entries that you have to create in each of your host-specific configuration files.

Defining a Backup Using SMB

The section "Identifying Hosts to Back Up" earlier in this chapter showed you how to define entries in the `/etc/backuppc/hosts` file for the various hosts that you want to back up via BackupPC. The first step in host-specific configuration is to create a directory to hold host-specific configuration data, logs, and so on. Throughout this section, I use the host entry `win2k` from the sample hosts file as an example. As you might gather from its name, this is indeed a hardware virtual machine running Microsoft Windows 2000.

The first step in host-specific configuration is to use the `sudo` command to create the directory `/var/lib/backuppc/win2k`, as in the following command:

```
mkdir /var/lib/backuppc/win2k
```

Next, use the `sudo` command and your favorite text editor to create a host-specific configuration file named `config.pl` in that directory, using a command like the following:

```
emacs /var/lib/backuppc/win2k/config.pl
```

The contents of this file should be something like the following;

```
$Conf{XferMethod} = 'smb';
$Conf{CompressLevel} = '3';
$Conf{SmbShareName} = ['wvh', 'djf'];
$Conf{SmbShareUserName} = 'backuppc';
$Conf{SmbSharePasswd} = 'hellothere' ;
```

The first line identifies the backup mechanism used for this host as `smb`, which overrides the default backup mechanism specified in the generic `/etc/backuppc/config.pl` file. The second line sets the compression level for this host's backups to level 3, which provides a good tradeoff between the CPU load and time required to do compression and the amount of compression that you actually get. The last three entries in this file define the Windows shares that you want to back up, the name of an authorized user who has access to these shares, and the password for that user.

When using BackupPC to back up Microsoft Windows systems, you should create a Windows user that you will only use to do backups, and then add this user to the standard Windows Backup Operators group. This prevents you from having to put your Windows administrator password in the BackupPC configuration files. Even though you should protect those files so that random users can't read them (and access to your backup server should be restricted to IT staff anyway), the fewer places where you write down a password, the better.

Next, change the ownership and group of the `/var/lib/backuppc/win2k` directory to `backuppc` and change the protection of the configuration file `/var/lib/backuppc/win2k/config.pl` so that it is not publicly readable (because it contains password information) using the following commands:

```
chmod -Rv backuppc:backuppc /var/lib/backuppc/win2k
chmod 600 /var/lib/backuppc/win2k/config.pl
```

The last step in creating a host-specific backup definition for BackupPC is to cause the BackupPC process to re-read its configuration data, which you can do by explicitly reloading the configuration file, explicitly restarting the BackupPC process, or sending the associated process a hangup (HUP) signal. You can force BackupPC to reload the configuration file using the following command:

```
/etc/init.d/backuppc reload
```

The definition for your backup host can now be selected via the BackupPC Web interface. At this point, you can follow the instructions in the section "Starting Backups in BackupPC" to back up this host.

The example in this section only backs up shares that correspond to the home directories of selected users on the remote machine. As mentioned earlier in this chapter, BackupPC backups do not support bare-metal restores of Windows systems, and I therefore typically don't back up shares such as C$, which is a default Windows share that represents your system's boot drive. This is especially the case for Windows HVMs because you can back them up by simply copying the image file or creating an image of the partition or logical volume in which they were installed by using commands such as dd. You can then deploy a new Windows system (assuming that you have sufficient licenses) by creating a configuration file that references the cloned image file or a partition or logical volume of the same size to which you have written your dd backup. Once you start the new virtual machine, you can correctly reconfigure its networking (if you are not using DHCP).

The BackupPC program reads the configuration settings in /etc/backuppc/config.pl first and then loads host-specific configuration settings, which enables the /etc/backuppc/config.pl file to provide default settings for all backups. After you have used BackupPC for a while and are comfortable with various settings, you may want to consider modifying the default settings in the /etc/backuppc/config.pl file for configuration variables such as $Conf{CompressLevel}, in order to minimize the number of entries that you have to create in each of your host-specific configuration files.

Starting Backups in BackupPC

Thanks to BackupPC's Web orientation, starting backups, viewing the status of those backups, and checking the backup history for any host is impressively easy. To start a backup in BackupPC, connect to the BackupPC Web interface using the URL http://hostname/backuppc, where hostname is the name of the host on which the BackupPC server is running. A dialog box appears in which you are prompted for the login and password of an authorized user. Once you enter the user/password combination for a user listed in the file /etc/backuppc/htpasswd, the BackupPC server's home page is displayed, as shown earlier in Figure 10-2.

On this BackupPC Server page, click the Select a host drop-down box and select one of the hosts from the list. Selecting the name of any host takes you to a summary page for that host, which provides status information, lists authorized users who can back up and restore files to this host using BackupPC, and displays the last e-mail that was sent about this host, as shown in Figure 10-3.

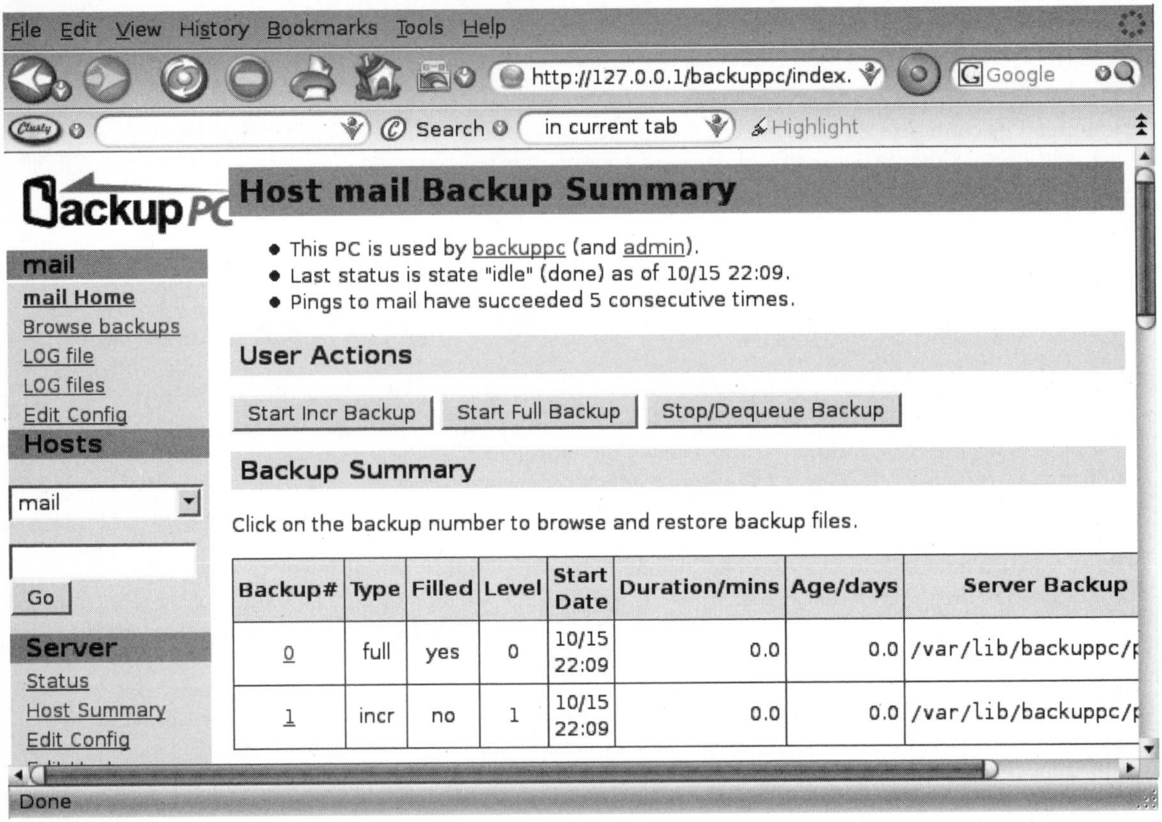

Figure 10-3

Each system's home page displays the subject of the last e-mail sent to the owner of this host. E-mail is only sent occasionally, so seeing a historical problem report does not mean that this problem is still occurring.

You can scroll down on this page to see additional status information about available backups, any transfer errors that occurred during backups, and other tables that show the status of the pool where backup files are archived and the extent to which existing backups have been compressed to save disk space.

To start a backup, click either Start Full Backup to start a full (archive) backup of the system, or Start Incr Backup to start an incremental backup containing files that have changed since the last full backup. A confirmation page is displayed.

Clicking Start Full Backup (or Start Incr Backup for an incremental backup) queues the backup and displays a link that you can click to return to the main page for that host in order to monitor the state of the backup.

Restoring from Backups in BackupPC

Thanks to BackupPC's Web orientation and the fact that BackupPC backups are stored online on the backup server, restoring files from BackupPC backups can be done online, by any authorized user whose name is associated with that host in the /etc/backuppc/hosts file. BackupPC enables you to browse through online backups, interactively select the files and directories that you want to restore, and restore them in various ways.

To begin restoring files or directories, click the name of the full or incremental backup in which they are located. A screen like the one shown in Figure 10-4 is displayed.

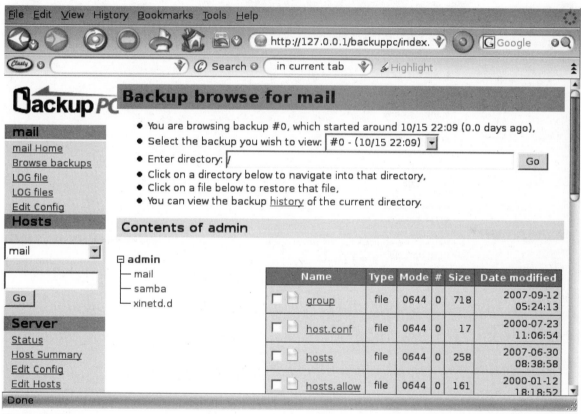

Figure 10-4

The bottom of the screen shown in Figure 10-4 displays a hierarchical listing of the files and directories that are contained in the full or incremental backup that you selected. If you selected an incremental backup, the contents of that incremental backup are overlaid on the contents of the previous full backup to give you an accurate snapshot of the contents of your system when the backup was done. You can drill down into the backup by selecting directories from the tree view to the left of the file listing or you can drill down into individual directories by selecting from the view of the current directory shown at the right of the main window.

To mark files and directories for restoration, select the corresponding check box. Once you have selected all of the files and directories that you want to restore, scroll to the bottom of the restore page and click "restore selected files." A page that enables you to specify how you want to restore those files is displayed, as shown in Figure 10-5.

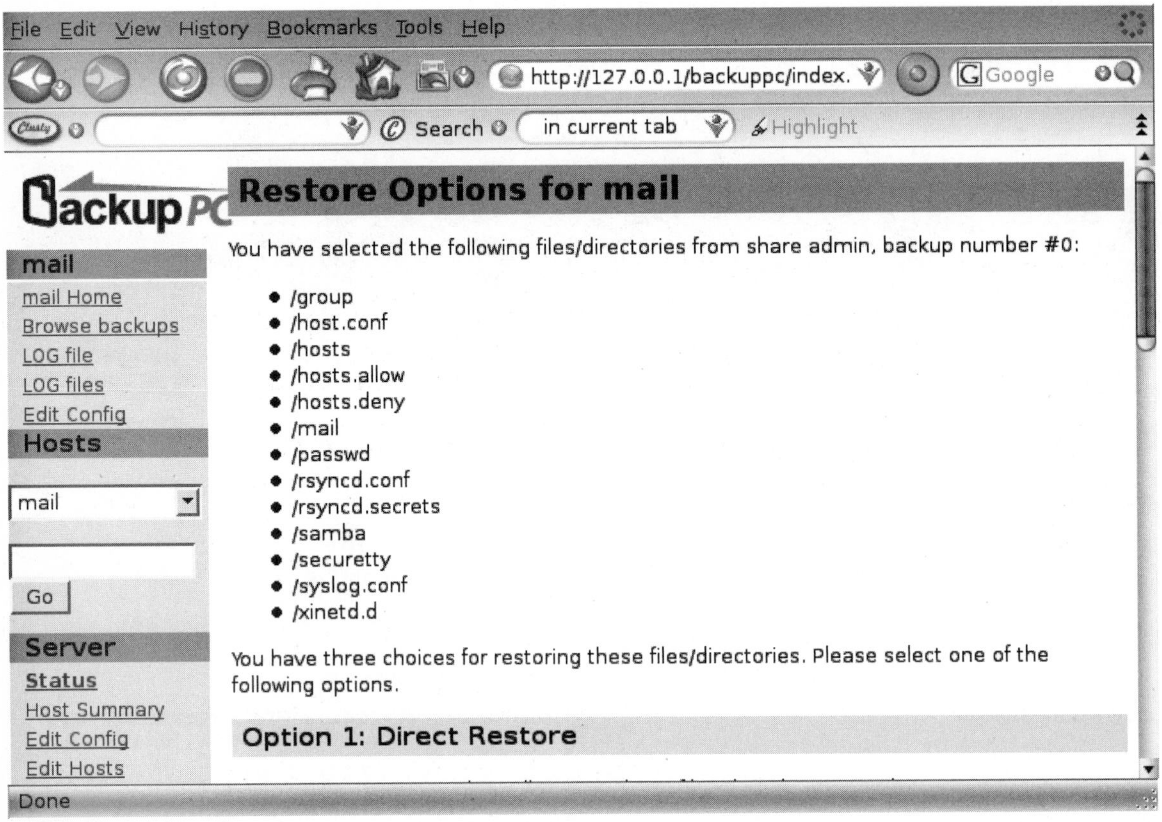

Figure 10-5

You have three options when restoring files using the BackupPC Web interface:

❏ **Direct Restore:** Selecting this option restores files directly to the host from which they were backed up. When doing a direct restore, you have the option of restoring files in the locations from which they originally backed up, or into a subdirectory that BackupPC will create for you if it does not already exist. (The latter is almost always a good idea so that you don't accidentally overwrite any files that you don't actually mean to.) To select this option, enter the name of any subdirectory that you want to use (I usually specify one called tmp) and click "Start restore."

❏ **Download Zip Archive:** Selecting this option restores the selected files and directories into a Zip-format archive that you can download to your desktop and manually extract its contents. When you select this option, you can optionally specify the compression level used in the Zip file, which can be important if you are restoring large numbers of files. To select this option, click "Download Zip file."

❑ **Download Tar Archive:** Selecting this option restores the selected files and directories into a tar-format archive that you can download to your desktop and manually extract its contents. To select this option, click "Download Tar file."

If you selected the Direct Restore option, BackupPC displays a confirmation screen like the one shown in Figure 10-6.

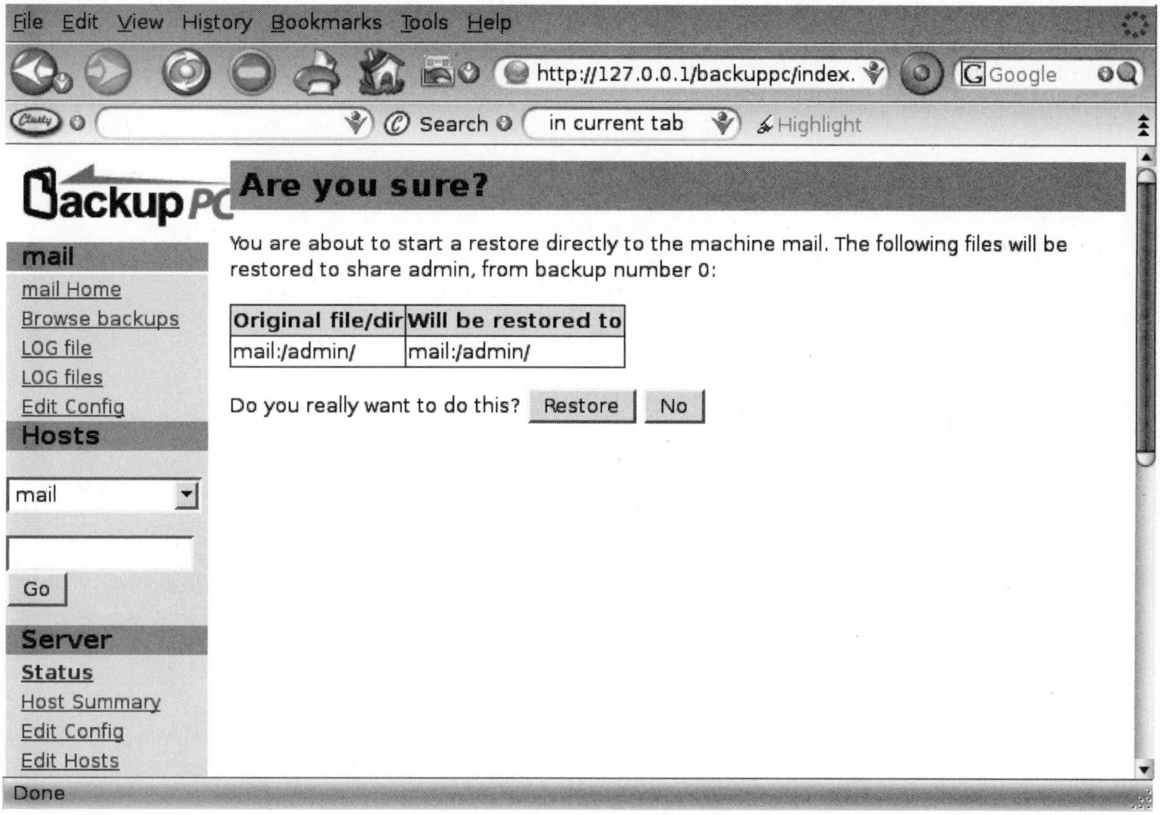

Figure 10-6

This lists the files and directories that you selected for restoration and confirms the location to which they will be restored, including the name of any subdirectory that you specified. To proceed, click Restore.

If you selected the Download Zip Archive or Download Tar Archive option, the BackupPC application displays your Web browser's standard file download dialog box after the archive file has been created.

As you can see from this section (and the preceding sections), BackupPC provides a powerful, flexible interface for backing up and restoring files on many different systems to a single BackupPC server. All you need are a few configuration files and sufficient disk space, and lost files (and the lost time that is usually associated with them) can be a thing of the past.

Summary

Virtualization environments can reduce power consumption and hardware costs, help you make better use of your existing hardware, and provide a high-availability enterprise computing environment. However, running multiple systems on one system requires some changes to your existing infrastructure. Documenting your virtual machines, preparing for and configuring migration, backing up mandatory data on your virtual machines, and monitoring a complex environment can require tools and techniques that are not currently part of your system administration procedures. Any new technology brings with it new techniques. The combination of Xen and the processes and procedures discussed in this chapter can give you a more productive, more stable, and more cost-efficient enterprise computing infrastructure — the golden fleece of enterprise system administration.

xm Command and Option Reference

As discussed throughout this book, the xm command is the core Xen command for interacting with the hypervisor, controlling resource allocation and availability, creating and terminating Xen domainU guests, and so on.

The xm command is essentially a command suite that actually performs many different functions. To perform any of these subcommands, you type **xm subcommand** and supply the options that are necessary for that particular subcommand.

You can display a list of the most commonly used xm subcommands by typing the xm command with no arguments. To see a complete list of all available subcommands, type **xm help**.

This appendix describes all of the available xm subcommands, what they do, the options that each subcommand requires in order to perform a specific task, and any optional arguments that you can supply when executing any of these subcommands.

addlabel: Add a Security Label to a Domain or Resource

Security labels support the Xen/sHype access control framework, which was discussed in "Xen Access Control and Security Policies" in Chapter 9. When security policies and access controls are enabled in the hypervisor, you cannot start a domain that is not labeled with the name of the security policy that it will use. You must label both the domain (in its configuration file) and the file-system and swap resources that it uses. Domain labels are added to a domain's configuration file, and resource labels are stored in the file /etc/xen/acm-security/policies/resource_labels.

The basic syntax of the xm addlabel command is as follows:

```
# xm addlabel LABELNAME dom CONFIGFILE [POLICY]
```

This command adds the specific label *LABELNAME* to the domain configuration file *CONFIGFILE*. This command displays no messages when it completes successfully. The following is an example of using this command:

```
# xm addlabel WordSmiths dom fedora.fc6.xen3.cfg
```

If you do not specify a policy, the default policy from the hypervisor's current policy file will be used. You can optionally identify the specific policy with which you want to label the domain configuration file by identifying the name of that policy in the optional *POLICY* argument at the end of the command line.

Using the xm addlabel command to label all of the resources required by a domain is very similar:

```
# xm addlabel LABELNAME res RESOURCE [POLICY]
```

This command displays no messages when it completes successfully. The following is an example of using this command:

```
# xm addlabel vonhagen res phy:/dev/VM/XP
```

This command adds the specific label *LABELNAME* to the resource *RESOURCE*. The first time that you run this command, you will also see the following message:

```
Resource file not found, creating new file at:
/etc/xen/acm-security/policies/resource_labels
```

If you do not specify a policy, the default policy from the hypervisor's current policy file will be used. You can optionally identify the specific policy with which you want to label the domain configuration file by identifying the name of that policy in the optional *POLICY* argument at the end of the command line. You must apply a label for the same policy to all of the filesystem resources used by a domain.

> You cannot label a domain or resource that is already labeled. You must use the xm rmlabel command to remove an existing label from both domain configuration files and resources before they can be relabeled with a different security policy.

block-attach: Create a New Virtual Block Device

The xm block-attach command enables you to identify an existing block device on one domain and make it available to a domainU guest. The block device can be a filesystem image file or any physical block device or logical volume that contains a filesystem.

The basic syntax of the `xm block-attach` command is as follows:

```
# xm block-attach TARGETDOMAIN LOCALDEVICE TARGETDEVICE MODE [HOSTDOMAIN]
```

This command will make the block device `LOCALDEVICE` in domain0 (or `HOSTDOMAIN`, if specified) available within the domain `TARGETDOMAIN` as `TARGETDEVICE`, with the write mode `MODE`.

The `xm block-attach` command is most commonly used to export block devices from domain0 to a domainU guest. Once block devices have been exported to a domain by the `xm block-attach` command, they must still be mounted in the domainU guest so that they can be accessed. Once they are attached to another domain, block devices remain available to that domain until they are detached, even across domain0 and domainU restarts, because the information about attached block devices is permanently stored in the XenStore.

Consider the following examples:

```
# xm block-attach 6 tap:aio:/home/xen/fc6.img /dev/xvda3 w 0
```

This command attaches the filesystem image `/home/xen/fc6.img` (found in domain 0) to the domain whose ID is 6 using the `tap:aio` device identifier (blktap driver, asynchronous I/O). That device will be available as `/dev/xvda3` in domain 6, and will be writable by domain 6, once it is mounted.

```
# xm block-attach 11 phy:VM/fc6-lamp hda1 r
```

This command attaches the logical volume `fc6-lamp` from the `VM` volume group as a physical device found in domain 0 to the domain whose ID is 11. This device will be available as `/dev/hda1` in domain 11, and can only be mounted as a read-only device.

```
# xm block-attach 4 phy:/dev/cd-rom /dev/hdb ro
```

This command attaches the physical device `/dev/cd-rom` found in domain 0 to the domain whose ID is 4. The device will be available as `/dev/hdb` in domain 4, and can only be mounted as a read-only device.

You must unmount or eject exported block devices in the `TARGETDOMAIN` before you remove, change, or detach them in the `HOSTDOMAIN`. This is especially important when using CDs exported via `xm block-attach` to install software in guest domains.

block-configure: Change Block Device Configuration

The `xm block-configure` command enables you to modify the definition of an existing block device that has already been attached to another domain.

This command takes the same type of arguments, in the same order, as the `xm block-attach` command. The basic syntax of the `xm block-configure` command is as follows:

```
# xm block-configure TARGETDOMAIN LOCALDEVICE TARGETDEVICE MODE [HOSTDOMAIN]
```

This command will modify the current settings for this block device (as shown by xm block-list *DOMAINID*) to match the specified values.

block-detach: Destroy a Domain's Virtual Block Device

The xm block-detach command enables you to disconnect a block device that you have previously made available to a domain using the xm block-attach command.

The basic syntax of the xm block-detach command is as follows:

```
# xm block-detach TARGETDOMAIN DEVICEID [-f|--force]
```

This command will make the block device identified by *DEVICEID* unavailable to the domain *TARGETDOMAIN*. To identify the *DEVICEID* for an attached block device, use the xm block-list *TARGETDOMAIN* command to identify the block devices that are available to the *TARGETDOMAIN*.

Normally, you cannot detach an attached block device while it is mounted in *TARGETDOMAIN*. Attempting to do so will display a message such as the following on the *TARGETDOMAIN* console and in its system log file:

```
vbd vbd-DEVICEID: 16 Device in use; refusing to close
```

You can use the -f (or equivalent --force) option to detach a drive while it is mounted in the target domain. However, doing so may cause filesystem inconsistencies in writable block devices because they are not being cleanly unmounted.

block-list: List Virtual Block Devices for a Domain

The xm block-list command displays a list of the virtual block devices associated with a specified domain. This command provides the device ID information that commands such as xm block-detach require.

The basic syntax of the xm block-list command is as follows:

```
# xm block-list TARGETDOMAIN [-l|--long]
```

This command displays information about all of the virtual block devices associated with the domain whose ID is *TARGETDOMAIN*, as in the following example:

```
# xm block-list 31
Vdev  BE handle state evt-ch ring-ref BE-path
2049   0    0      4     6      8     /local/domain/0/backend/tap/31/2049
2050   0    0      4     7      9     /local/domain/0/backend/tap/31/2050
```

After attaching another block device to a specified domain, you will also see an entry for the new block device, as in the following example:

```
# xm block-attach 31 phy:/dev/sda2 xvda2 r
# xm block-list 31
Vdev  BE handle state evt-ch ring-ref BE-path
2049   0    0     4     6       8     /local/domain/0/backend/tap/31/2049
2050   0    0     4     7       9     /local/domain/0/backend/tap/31/2050
51714  0    0     4     9      780    /local/domain/0/backend/vbd/31/51714
```

If you specify the -l (or equivalent --long) option, the virtual block device information will be displayed in SXP format, as in the following example:

```
# xm block-list 31 -l
(2049
    ((backend-id 0)
        (virtual-device 2049)
        (device-type disk)
        (state 4)
        (backend /local/domain/0/backend/tap/31/2049)
        (ring-ref 8)
        (event-channel 6)
        (protocol x86_32-abi)
    )
)
(2050
    ((backend-id 0)
        (virtual-device 2050)
        (device-type disk)
        (state 4)
        (backend /local/domain/0/backend/tap/31/2050)
        (ring-ref 9)
        (event-channel 7)
        (protocol x86_32-abi)
    )
)
(51714
    ((backend-id 0)
        (virtual-device 51714)
        (device-type disk)
        (state 4)
        (backend /local/domain/0/backend/vbd/31/51714)
        (ring-ref 780)
        (event-channel 9)
        (protocol x86_32-abi)
    )
)
```

cfgbootpolicy: Add Policy to Boot Configuration

The xm cfgbootpolicy command adds a module entry to a specified GRUB boot configuration file stanza that defines an access control policy which that stanza should use when booting Xen.

The basic syntax of the xm cfgbootpolicy command is as follows:

```
# xm cfgbootpolicy POLICYNAME [STANZA]
```

This command adds a module entry for the access control policy *POLICYNAME* to the GRUB boot configuration file. Specifying *STANZA* will add this module entry to the stanza whose title is *STANZA*. If no *STANZA* is specified, this command will add the module entry to the stanza beginning with XEN. If multiple stanzas begin with the word XEN, a specific *STANZA* title must be supplied.

Sample output from this command when multiple matching stanzas are encountered is as follows:

```
# xm cfgbootpolicy vonhagen "Xen 3.1"
ACMError: Following boot entries matched: [
    '\tXen 3.1',
'\tXen 3.1.0rc10',
'\tXen 3.1.0 / Ubuntu, kernel 2.6.18-xen-wvh'].
Please specify unique part of the boot title.
```

Sample, successful output from this command after resolving the stanza title conflicts (by using a text editor to change titles in the file /boot/grub/menu.lst) is as follows:

```
# xm cfgbootpolicy vonhagen "Xen 3.1"
Boot entry 'Xen 3.1' extended and 'vonhagen.bin' copied to /boot
```

See "Xen Access Control and Security Policies" in Chapter 9 for more information about Xen access control policies.

console: Attach to <Domain>'s Console

The xm console command enables you to attach to the console of a paravirtualized Xen guest. Running console processes persist across connections, so you can easily use this command to reestablish a connection to a shell on the console from any shell on domain0.

The basic syntax of the xm console command is as follows:

```
# xm console DOMAINID [-q|--quiet]
```

This command opens a connection to the Xen console for *DOMAINID* under the current shell. You can identify the *DOMAINID* of the domain that you want to connect to by using the xm list command. Specifying the -q command-line option (or the equivalent --quiet option) suppresses an error message if the specified domainU guest does not exist.

To disconnect from the console of a Xen domainU guest, press Ctrl+] (hold down the Control key and press]).

When running in the graphical X Window system environment, it is often more convenient to open a Xen console connection in a separate window, as in the following example:

```
# xterm -T "Xen Console" -e xm console 8 &
```

In this case, you would not need to use the Ctrl+] sequence to return to a parent shell because `xterm` is dedicated to the domainU console and can simply be minimized when not needed.

create: Create a Domain Based on a Configuration File

The `xm create` command is one of the core Xen commands, enabling you to start a Xen domain based on the contents of a Xen configuration file. The `xm create` command enables you to create a non-persistent domainU system, which means that domains started by using the `xm create` command are only transiently stored in the XenStore, and do not persist in XenStore across system reboots. They are, therefore, not associated with the Xenmon's lifecycle management support. See Chapter 9 for more information about Xen lifecycle management.

The basic syntax of the `xm create` command is as follows:

```
# xm create CONFIGFILE [-c] [variable=VALUE] [Other Options]
```

This command creates and starts the domainU guest defined in *CONFIGFILE*. Specifying the `-c` option opens a connection to the domainU console so that you can monitor the boot process, log in once the domainU guest is running successfully, and so on.

Xen domain configuration files come in three different flavors:

❑   **Python variable settings:** The most common type of Xen configuration files. These files look something like the following:

```
kernel = "/boot/vmlinuz-2.6.18-xen"
ramdisk = "/boot/initrd-2.6.18-xen.img"
memory = 384
name = "fedora.fc6"
vif = [ '' ]
dhcp = "dhcp"
disk = ['tap:aio:/home/xen/fedora.fc6.img,xvda1,w',
        'tap:aio:/home/xen/fedora.swap,xvda2,w']
root = "/dev/xvda1 ro"
```

❏ **Xen SXP files:** Configuration files in S-Expression format, which resemble the following:

```
(vm
    (name fedora.fc6)
    (memory 384)
    (vcpus 1)
    (on_xend_start ignore)
    (on_xend_stop ignore)
    (image
        (linux
            (kernel /boot/vmlinuz-2.6.18-xen)
            (ramdisk /boot/initrd-2.6.18-xen.img)
            (ip :1.2.3.4::::eth0:dhcp)
            (root '/dev/xvda1 ro')
        )
    )
    (device (tap (uname tap:aio:/home/xen/fedora.fc6.img)
            (dev xvda1) (mode w)))
    (device (tap (uname tap:aio:/home/xen/fedora.swap)
            (dev xvda2) (mode w)))
    (device (vif)) )
```

❏ **Xen XML files:** Configuration files that use a special XML schema defined by the libvirt project (www.libvirt.org/format.html), which look something like the following:

```
<domain type='xen'>
  <name>fedora.fc6</name>
  <os>
    <type>linux</type>
    <kernel>/boot/vmlinuz-2.6.18-xen</kernel>
    <initrd>/boot/vmlinuz-2.6.18-xen.img</initrd>
    <root>/dev/xvda1</root>
  </os>
  <memory>393216</memory>
  <vcpu>1</vcpu>
  <devices>
    <disk type='tap:aio'>
      <source file='/home/xen/fedora.fc6.img'/>
      <target dev='xvda1´/>
    </disk>
    <disk type='tap:aio'>
      <source file='/home/xen/fedora.swap'/>
      <target dev='xvda2´/>
    </disk>
  </devices>
</domain>
```

The `xm create` command is functionally equivalent to executing the `xm new` command, followed by the `xm start` command, except that domains created and started using the `xm create` command do not persist in the XenStore after they terminate. See Chapter 9 for more information about Xen lifecycle management.

The xm `create` command has many options other than the common `-c` option:

- ❏ `-f=FILE`, `--defconfig=FILE`: Specifies *FILE* as the name of a Xen domain configuration file in Python variable format. The values specified in this file will be read after all command-line arguments and `variable=VALUE` pairs have been processed. Variable settings in the configuration file will not override ones that have been set on the command line.

- ❏ `-F=FILE`,`--config=FILE`: Specifies *FILE* as the name of a Xen domain configuration file in S-Expression format. The values specified in this file will be read after all command-line arguments and `variable=VALUE` pairs have been processed. Variable settings in the configuration file will not override ones that have been set on the command line.

- ❏ `-h`, `--help`: Prints a help message and then exits.

- ❏ `--help_config`: Prints all of the available domain configuration variables for a configuration file in Python variable format and then exits.

- ❏ `-n`, `--dryrun`: Enables you to generate a Xen domain configuration file from one in Python configuration variable format without actually starting a domain.

- ❏ `-p`, `--paused`: Specifies that the domain should be left in a paused state after it has been created.

- ❏ `--path=PATH`: Uses *PATH* as a colon-separated list of directories to search, in order, for Xen configuration files. For example, specifying the option `--path=/home/vonhagen/xen:/home/corporate/xen:/home/xen` would look for a specified configuration file, first in the directory `/home/vonhagen/xen`, then in the directory `/home/corporate/xen`, and finally in the directory `/home/xen`.

- ❏ `-q`, `--quiet`: Suppresses any error messages that would otherwise be displayed.

- ❏ `-s`, `--skipdtd`: Skips checking an XML-format domain configuration file against the Document Type Definition (DTD) that defines the structure, valid, elements, and element nesting rules that must be followed in a Xen domain configuration file.

- ❏ `-x`, `--xmldryrun`: Enables you to generate a Xen domain configuration file from one in Python configuration variable format without actually starting a domain.

As mentioned earlier, most of the Python variables for domain creation can also be specified as `variable=VALUE` pairs on the command line, and will take precedence over any settings in the Xen configuration file. For example, consider the following command:

```
# xm create name=newlamp lamp.cfg
```

In this example, the name of the new domain will be `newlamp`, regardless of any name specified in the configuration file, as shown in the following output:

```
# grep name lamp.cfg
name = "LAMP-VM"
# xm list
Name                 ID   Mem VCPUs     State   Time(s)
Domain-0              0  1400     2     r----- 233496.5
Foresight            24   384     1     -b----   5633.1
Ubuntu               31   256     1     -b----     59.6
newlamp              33   256     1     -b----     13.0
```

debug-keys: Send Debug Keys to Xen

The xm debug-keys command sends keys to the hypervisor, which causes it to display low-level debugging and status information via the printk() function.

The basic syntax of the xm debug-keys command is as follows:

```
# xm debug-keys KEY
```

This command would send the letter represented by *KEY* to the hypervisor. The most commonly used *KEY* is h, which displays a list of available debug outputs.

To see the output of the xm debug-keys command, you must either be using a serial console or you must execute the xm dmesg command to see recent Xen and domain0 system messages. The following is sample output from the xen debug-keys command, showing the active debug-key handlers and extracted from xm dmesg output:

```
(XEN) 'h' pressed -> showing installed handlers
(XEN)  key '%' (ascii '25') => Trap to xendbg
(XEN)  key 'C' (ascii '43') => trigger a crashdump
(XEN)  key 'H' (ascii '48') => dump heap info
(XEN)  key 'N' (ascii '4e') => NMI statistics
(XEN)  key 'R' (ascii '52') => reboot machine
(XEN)  key 'a' (ascii '61') => dump timer queues
(XEN)  key 'd' (ascii '64') => dump registers
(XEN)  key 'h' (ascii '68') => show this message
(XEN)  key 'i' (ascii '69') => dump interrupt bindings
(XEN)  key 'm' (ascii '6d') => memory info
(XEN)  key 'n' (ascii '6e') => trigger an NMI
(XEN)  key 'q' (ascii '71') => dump domain (and guest debug) info
(XEN)  key 'r' (ascii '72') => dump run queues
(XEN)  key 't' (ascii '74') => display multi-cpu clock info
(XEN)  key 'u' (ascii '75') => dump numa info
(XEN)  key 'z' (ascii '7a') => print ioapic info
```

This message will be followed by several screens of Xen status information.

The combination of the xm debug-keys and xm dmesg commands provides a simple way of obtaining low-level information about the state of the hypervisor and domain0 from a running system without requiring a serial connection to that system. This can be especially useful on modern systems that do not have a serial port.

delete: Remove a Domain from xend Domain Management

The xm delete command removes a domain from the Xen daemon's lifecycle management mechanism, removing all information about that domain from the XenStore.

The basic syntax of the xm delete command is as follows:

```
# xm delete DOMAINNAME
```

This command would remove all information about the domainU DOMAINNAME from the Xen daemon and the XenStore. The xm delete command cannot be used to remove a domain that is running, paused, or suspended because information about such domains must still be present in the XenStore. The xm delete command can only be used with domains that have been registered for lifecycle management by the xm new command, through the Xen API, or through a third-party administration tool that uses the xm new command or Xen API.

Consider the following example:

```
# xm list
Name                        ID   Mem VCPUs      State   Time(s)
Domain-0                     0  1400     2      r----- 226490.9
Foresight                   24   384     1      -b----   5211.0
TEST                             256     1                  0.0
Ubuntu                      31   256     1      -b----     36.1
newlamp2                    36   256     1      -b----     69.0
# xm domid TEST
None
# xm delete TEST
# xm list
Name                        ID   Mem VCPUs      State   Time(s)
Domain-0                     0  1400     2      r----- 226495.8
Foresight                   24   384     1      -b----   5211.2
Ubuntu                      31   256     1      -b----     36.1
newlamp2                    36   256     1      -b----     69.6
```

See Chapter 9 for more information about Xen lifecycle management.

destroy: Terminate a Domain Immediately

The xm destroy command terminates a running, suspended, or paused domain immediately. If the domain has not been registered for lifecycle management through the xm new command (or through the Xen API), the domain will no longer be visible in an xm list listing.

The basic syntax of the xm destroy command is as follows:

```
# xm destroy DOMAINID
```

This command terminates the domainU guest DOMAINID and releases all allocated resources associated with that domain. If the domain has been registered for Xen lifecycle management, it will still be visible in an xm list command, but will not have a domain ID because it is not running or paused.

In most cases, using the xm shutdown DOMAINID command is preferable to using the xm destroy DOMAINID command because the former attempts to do an orderly shutdown, whereas the latter is the equivalent of simply turning the machine off, and can therefore cause filesystem corruption and lost data due to incomplete filesystem updates.

See Chapter 9 for more information about Xen lifecycle management.

dmesg: Read and Optionally Clean the Xen Daemon Message Buffer

The Xen daemon keeps track of the most recent hypervisor and domain0 kernel messages in a ring buffer, similar to the behavior of the standard Linux kernel. The xm dmesg command enables you to display, and optionally clear, the contents of the Xen daemon's message buffer.

The basic syntax of the xm dmesg command is as follows:

```
# xm dmesg [-c]
```

This command can be very useful in getting status information about the Xen boot process, in diagnosing problems when they occur, or in seeing debugging and low-level status information generated by the xm debug-keys command. The optional -c argument enables you to clear the contents of the ring buffer after displaying it.

Sample output from the xm dmesg command is as follows:

```
 __  __            _____   ___    ___
 \ \/ /___ _ __    |___ /  / |   / _ \
  \  // _ \ '_ \     |_ \  | |  | | | |
  /  \  __/ | | |   ___) | | |  | |_| |
 /_/\_\___|_| |_|  |____(_)_(_)___/

http://www.cl.cam.ac.uk/netos/xen
University of Cambridge Computer Laboratory
Xen version 3.1.0 (wvh@vonhagen.org) (gcc version 4.1.2)
Latest ChangeSet: Fri May 18 16:59:32 2007 +0100 15042:c0b0974fb055
(XEN) Command line: /boot/xen-3.1.0.gz
(XEN)  0000000000000000 - 000000000009f000 (usable)
(XEN)  000000000009fc00 - 00000000000a0000 (reserved)
(XEN)  00000000000e6000 - 0000000000100000 (reserved)
(XEN)  0000000000100000 - 000000007bfc0000 (usable)
(XEN)  000000007bfc0000 - 000000007bfce000 (ACPI data)
(XEN)  000000007bfce000 - 000000007bff0000 (ACPI NVS)
(XEN)  000000007bff0000 - 000000007c000000 (reserved)
(XEN)  00000000ff780000 - 0000000100000000 (reserved)
(XEN) System RAM: 1983MB (2030972kB)
(XEN) Xen heap: 13MB (14228kB)
(XEN) Domain heap initialised: DMA width 32 bits
(XEN) Processor #0 15:15 APIC version 16
[much output deleted]
(XEN) Xen trace buffers: disabled
(XEN) Std. Loglevel: Errors and warnings
(XEN) Guest Loglevel: Nothing (Rate-limited: Errors and warnings)
(XEN) Xen is relinquishing VGA console.
(XEN) *** Serial input -> DOM0 (type 'CTRL-a' three times to switch
```

domid: Convert a Domain Name to a Domain ID

The xm domid command displays the domain ID associated with a domain name, or displays "None" for inactive domains that have been registered for Xen lifecycle management but not started.

The basic syntax of the xm domid command is as follows:

```
# xm domid DOMAINNAME
```

Sample output is as follows:

```
# xm list
Name                      ID   Mem VCPUs     State   Time(s)
Domain-0                   0  1400    2     r----- 227799.7
Foresight                 24   384    1     -b----    5270.6
Ubuntu                    31   256    1     -b----      39.5
newlamp2                       256    1                  0.0
# xm domid Foresight
24
# xm domid newlamp2
None
```

domname: Convert a Domain ID to a Domain Name

The xm domname command displays the domain name associated with a domain ID.

The basic syntax of the xm domname command is as follows:

```
xm domname DOMAINID
```

Sample output is as follows:

```
# xm list Name                ID   Mem VCPUs     State   Time(s)
Domain-0                   0  1400    2     r----- 227799.7
Foresight                 24   384    1     -b----    5270.6
Ubuntu                    31   256    1     -b----      39.5
newlamp2                       256    1                  0.0
# xm domname 24
Foresight
# xm domname 64
Error: Domain '64' does not exist.
```

dry-run: Test If a Domain Can Access Its Resources

The xm dry-run command uses the sHype/ACM mechanism to test whether a domain conforms to the security policy that is in effect on a given system, and also whether the domain can access the resources specified in a configuration file in Python variable format.

The basic syntax of the xm dry-run command is as follows:

```
xm dry-run CONFIGFILE
```

The xm dry-run command examines any policy label defined in the configuration file and determines whether this is sufficient to create the domain and access the filesystem resources specified in that file. This command always succeeds on a system where no boot policy has been configured. (See the "cfgbootpolicy: Add Policy to Boot Configuration" section for information about configuring Xen's GRUB boot stanzas to enforce a security policy.)

Sample output from a successful run of this command is as follows:

```
# xm dry-run opensuse.cfg
Using config file "./opensuse.cfg".
Checking domain:
    OpenSUSE: PERMITTED
Checking resources:
Dry Run: PASSED
```

dump-core: Dump the Core for a Specific Domain

The xm dump-core command dumps all memory owned by a domain into a default or specified file. This command dumps memory through the hypervisor and domain0, and therefore does not require any direct interaction with the target domain. The xm dump-core command is especially useful for obtaining core dumps of domains that are hung or otherwise incommunicative, or for subsequent analysis if debugging tools or devices are currently unavailable.

The basic syntax of the xm dump-core command is as follows:

```
xm dump-core DOMAINID [FILENAME] [-L] [-C]
```

This command dumps all of the memory used by DOMAINID. Specifying FILENAME writes this output to the specified file in the current working directory. If no FILENAME is specified, the core dump is written to a file in the directory /var/xen/dump whose name is derived from a timestamp and the name of the domain being dumped. For example, executing the xm dump-core 31 command to dump the core for domain 31 named Ubuntu at 16:58 on July 24, 2007 creates the file /var/xen/dump/2007-0724-1658.35-Ubuntu.31.core.

Specifying the -L (or equivalent --live) option causes the dump to be executed without pausing the specified domain. By default, the xm dump-core command pauses the domain, does the dump, and then unpauses the domain. Specifying the -C (or equivalent --crash) option immediately terminates the domain after the dump has completed.

dumppolicy: Print Hypervisor ACM State Information

The xm dumppolicy command displays information about the access control policies that are in effect in the running hypervisor. See "Xen Access Control and Security Policies" in Chapter 9 for more information about creating and configuring policies and access control mechanisms.

The basic syntax of the xm dumppolicy command is as follows:

```
xm dumppolicy
```

If no ACM security policy is set in the current hypervisor, you see the following messages:

```
ACMError: 'INACTIVE' policy. Nothing to dump
Error: "'INACTIVE' policy. Nothing to dump."
```

getlabel: Show the Security Label for a Domain or Resource

The xm getlabel command displays the security label associated with a domain or resource. Security labels support the Xen/sHype access control framework that was discussed in "Xen Access Control and Security Policies" in Chapter 9.

The basic syntax of the xm getlabel command is as follows:

```
# xm getlabel dom CONFIGFILE | res RESOURCE
```

When you're working with domains, the xm getlabel dom CONFIGFILE command displays any security label present in the domain configuration file CONFIGFILE, as in the following example:

```
# xm getlabel dom fedora.fc6.xen3.cfg
policy=example.chwall_ste.vonhagen,label=WordSmiths
```

If no security label is present in the specified configuration file, the xm getlabel command displays an error message, as in the following example:

```
# xm getlabel opensuse.cfg
Error: 'Domain not labeled'
```

When you're working with resources, the `xm getlabel res RESOURCE` command displays any security label associated with the resource *RESOURCE*, as in the following example:

```
# xm getlabel res file:/home/xen/PARAVIRT/fc6/fedora.fc6.img
policy=example.chwall_ste.vonhagen,label=WordSmiths
```

Note that the *RESOURCE* must be fully qualified, exactly as it is in any configuration file that describes that resource. If this syntax is incorrect, the `xm getlabel` command displays a somewhat cryptic error message, as in the following example:

```
# xm getlabel res opensuse.img
ACMError: Resource spec 'opensuse.img' contains no ':' delimiter
Error: "Resource spec 'opensuse.img' contains no ':' delimiter"
```

help: Display Information about xm Subcommands

The `xm help` command displays a list of commonly used, or all, xm subcommands.

The basic syntax of the `xm help` command is as follows:

```
xm help [--long]
```

By default, the `xm help` command displays output such as the following:

```
# xm help
Usage: xm <subcommand> [args]
Control, list, and manipulate Xen guest instances.
xm full list of subcommands:
  console              Attach to <Domain>'s console.
  create               Create a domain based on <ConfigFile>.
  new                  Adds a domain to Xend domain management
  delete               Remove a domain from Xend domain management.
  destroy              Terminate a domain immediately.
[much output deleted]
  shell                Launch an interactive shell.
<Domain> can either be the Domain Name or Id.
For more help on 'xm' see the xm(1) man page.
For more help on 'xm create' see the xmdomain.cfg(5)  man page.
```

This output lists the most commonly used xm subcommands. Specifying the `--long` option displays a complete list of all of the xm subcommands that are available in the version of the xm command that you are using.

info: Get Information about a Xen Host

The `xm info` command displays a variety of information about the domain0 system on which it is executed. This includes information about the hardware, information about Xen's capabilities and configuration on that system, and information about the compilation environment used to build Xen on that system.

The command to display information about domain0 takes no arguments:

```
xm info
```

Sample output from a 64-bit, HVM-capable system is as follows:

```
host                  : xen.vonhagen.org
release               : 2.6.18-xen
version               : #1 SMP Thu Jul 5 11:00:06 EDT 2007
machine               : x86_64
nr_cpus               : 1
nr_nodes              : 1
sockets_per_node      : 1
cores_per_socket      : 1
threads_per_core      : 1
cpu_mhz               : 2200
hw_caps               : 078bfbff:ebd3fbff:00000000:00000010:\
                        00002001:0000001d:0000001d
total_memory          : 1983
free_memory           : 261
xen_major             : 3
xen_minor             : 1
xen_extra             : .0
xen_caps              : xen-3.0-x86_64 xen-3.0-x86_32p \
                        hvm-3.0-x86_32 hvm-3.0-x86_32p \
                        hvm-3.0-x86_64
xen_scheduler         : credit
xen_pagesize          : 4096
platform_params       : virt_start=0xffff800000000000
xen_changeset         : Fri May 18 16:59:32 2007 +0100 15042
cc_compiler           : gcc version 4.1.2 20070626 (4.1.2-13)
cc_compile_by         : wvh
cc_compile_domain     : vonhagen.org
cc_compile_date       : Thu Jul  5 09:52:55 EDT 2007
xend_config_format    : 4
```

The most commonly used entries in xm info output are the xen_caps entry, which describes the types of virtual machines that are supported by the current domain0 system (as does the file /sys/hypervisor/properties/capabilities), and the xen_changeset entry, which defines the Mercurial changeset that your system was built from. This can be useful in determining if your system has certain capabilities or patches. The free-memory entry can also be useful because it identifies the amount of memory that is not currently allocated to any Xen domain on your system.

labels: List Labels for an Active Policy

The xm labels command enables you to display all of the labels that are present in a security policy file.

The basic syntax of the xm labels command is as follows:

```
# xm labels [POLICY] [TYPE]
```

If no security policy is provided on the command line, the command references the security policy file that is currently being used by the hypervisor. If no policy is active in the running hypervisor, you will see an error message, as in the following example:

```
# xm labels
Error: No policy active, you must specify a <policy>
```

The following is a successful example of running this command on a system where the hypervisor has loaded a policy file at boot time:

```
# xm labels
SystemManagement
WordSmiths
WordSmiths.Accounting
WordSmiths.Extranet
WordSmiths.Intranet
vonhagen
vonhagen.Accounting
vonhagen.Extranet
vonhagen.Intranet
```

The `SystemManagement` label is automatically created in all policy files, and is always associated with domain0.

See the section "Xen Access Control and Security Policies" in Chapter 9 for more information about Xen access control policies.

list: List Information about All or Some Domains

The `xm list` command is one of the core Xen commands, enabling you to display information about all running, paused, suspended, or halted Xen domains on the current domain0 system. (The list of running domains also includes blocked domains, which are technically still running even though they are currently waiting for something.)

The basic syntax of the `xm list` command is as follows:

```
xm list [DOMAINS] [-l] [--label] [--state=STATE]
```

With no options or *DOMAINS*, the `xm list` command simply provides status information about all domains that exist on the system, as in the following sample output:

```
# xm list
Name               ID   Mem VCPUs      State   Time(s)
Domain-0            0   900    1       r-----  48450.4
FC6-IMG-PV         10   256    1       --p---    300.2
FC6-YUMIMG-PV       6   256    1       -b----    373.8
XP-LV-HVM           9   256    1       -b----   1253.6
centos.5-0             256    1                    4.9
```

You can limit the output of the `xm list` command to one or more domains by listing their domain IDs on the command line, as in the following sample output:

```
# xm list 10 9
Name                 ID   Mem VCPUs      State   Time(s)
FC6-IMG-PV           10   256    1       -b----    300.2
XP-LV-HVM             9   256    1       -b----   1253.6
```

The `ID` field lists the domain ID of each running or paused domain. If no domain ID is displayed, the domain is either halted or suspended.

The `Mem` field displays the amount of memory requested by each domain, or any value specified by then `xm mem-set` command when it has been used to manually modify the memory allocation for a domain.

The `VCPUs` field identifies the number of virtual CPUs that the domain has requested or is currently using.

The `State` field identifies the state of each Xen domain. Each - in this field can be replaced by a letter, enabling domains to be in multiple states at the same time. (This is infrequent and generally not recommended — see the examples later in this section.) Available states are the following, reading from left to right:

❑   r **(running):** The domain is currently running on a CPU. On a uni-processor, single-core system, only domain0 will ever be shown as being in this state because it must be running in order to display the `xm list` output. On a multi-processor or multi-core system, other domains will only be shown to be running if they are actually doing something.

❑   b **(blocked):** The domain is blocked, typically waiting for an interrupt or a timer.

❑   p **(paused):** The domain has been paused, usually by the `xm pause` command. Paused domains still consume the resources that they have been allocated, but cannot be scheduled by the hypervisor.

❑   s **(shutdown):** The domain is in the process of shutting down. It is difficult to catch a domain in this state unless the shutdown process is temporarily suspended, as when a filesystem cannot be unmounted.

❑   c **(crashed):** The domain has crashed and is not configured to automatically restart on a crash. See Appendix B for information about the domain configuration file `on_crash` setting that enables you to specify what a domain should do after a crash.

❑   d **(dying):** The domain is in the process of exiting, but hasn't completely shutdown or crashed, probably because it is in the middle of a non-interruptible task. This state is typically caused by the `xm destroy` or `xm shutdown` command.

Specifying the -1 (or equivalent --long) option displays output in SXP format, which is typically useful only as input to other administrative tools or for capturing domain configuration information. A sample of this output (for domain 0, in this case) is as follows:

```
(domain
    (domid 0)
    (on_crash restart)
    (uuid 00000000-0000-0000-0000-000000000000)
    (bootloader_args )
    (vcpus 2)
    (name Domain-0)
    (on_poweroff destroy)
    (on_reboot restart)
    (bootloader )
    (maxmem 4194303)
    (memory 1400)
    (shadow_memory 0)
    (cpu_weight 256)
    (cpu_cap 0)
    (features )
    (on_xend_start ignore)
    (on_xend_stop ignore)
    (cpu_time 236047.799004)
    (online_vcpus 2)
    (image (linux (kernel ) (rtc_timeoffset 0)))
    (status 2)
    (state r-----)
)
```

If --label is specified, the domain security labels are displayed and the xm list output is sorted by those labels. This can be very handy when multiple domains are using different security policy labels, and you therefore want them to be grouped together. Using the --label option when labels are active displays output like the following on a system that has been labeled with a policy named "vonhagen":

```
# xm list
Name               ID    Mem VCPUs     State   Time(s) Label
Domain-0            0    900     1     r-----  48450.4 SystemManagement
FC6-IMG-PV         10    256     1     --p---    300.2 vonhagen
FC6-YUMIMG-PV       6    256     1     -b----    373.8 vonhagen
XP-LV-HVM           9    256     1     -b----   1253.6 vonhagen
centos.5-0               256     1                 4.9 vonhagen
```

Requesting labels in your output when labels are not in use displays output such as the following:

```
# xm list
Name               ID    Mem VCPUs     State   Time(s) Label
Domain-0            0    900     1     r-----  48450.4 INACTIVE
FC6-IMG-PV         10    256     1     --p---    300.2 INACTIVE
FC6-YUMIMG-PV       6    256     1     -b----    373.8 INACTIVE
XP-LV-HVM           9    256     1     -b----   1253.6 INACTIVE
centos.5-0               256     1                 4.9 INACTIVE
```

The --state=*STATE* option enables you to restrict the domains listed by the xm list command to those that are in a certain state. Supported values for *STATE* are all (lists domains in all states, and therefore, all domains), halted, paused, running, suspended, and shutdown. Capitalization is ignored in *STATE* values, although spelling is not. Some sample output when specifying *STATE* values is as follows:

```
# xm list
Name                        ID   Mem VCPUs      State   Time(s)
Domain-0                     0  1400     2      r----- 234910.5
Foresight                   24   384     1      --p---   5694.3
Ubuntu                      31   256     1      -b----     63.2
newlamp2                    47   256     1      ----cd      0.5
centos.5-0                       256     1                  4.9
# xm list --state=Running
Name                        ID   Mem VCPUs      State   Time(s)
Domain-0                     0  1400     2      r----- 234910.5
Ubuntu                      31   256     1      -b----     63.2
# xm list --state=paused
Name                        ID   Mem VCPUs      State   Time(s)
Foresight                   24   384     1      --p---   5694.3
# xm list --state=halted
Name                        ID   Mem VCPUs      State   Time(s)
centos.5-0                       256     1                  4.9
```

The --state=*STATE* option can be very useful in scripted, high-availability tools that need to examine machine state to restart halted or crashed domains, take core dumps for diagnostic purposes, and even migrate virtual machines to other systems in the event of system hardware or software problems.

loadpolicy: Load a Binary Policy Into a Hypervisor

The xm loadpolicy command enables you to load a compiled security policy file into a running hypervisor that has been compiled with sHype/ACM security support.

The basic syntax of the xm loadpolicy command is as follows:

```
xm loadpolicy POLICY
```

Loading a compiled *POLICY* file into a running hypervisor is an alternative to configuring the hypervisor to load a compiled policy file at boot time via the xm cfgbootpolicy command.

See "Xen Access Control and Security Policies" in Chapter 9 for more information about creating, compiling, and using Xen access control policies.

log: Print the xend Log

The `xm log` command displays the current contents of the Xen daemon's log file. By default, this is the file `/var/log/xen/xend.log`, but this file can be changed by uncommenting the `logfile` directive in the Xen daemon configuration file (`/etc/xen/xend-config.sxp`) and specifying an alternate file name.

The command to display the Xen daemon's log file takes no arguments:

```
# xm log
Sample output from this command is the following:
[2007-07-15 23:00:02 3742] DEBUG (XendDomainInfo:1414) \
           XendDomainInfo.constructDomain
[2007-07-15 23:00:02 3742] DEBUG (balloon:113) \
Balloon: 14164 KiB free; need 2048; done.
[2007-07-15 23:00:02 3742] DEBUG (XendDomain:434) \
Adding Domain: 26
[2007-07-15 23:00:02 3742] DEBUG (XendDomainInfo:1468) \
XendDomainInfo.initDomain: 26 256
[2007-07-15 23:00:02 3742] DEBUG (XendDomainInfo:1500) \
_initDomain:shadow_memory=0x0, \
           memory_static_max=0x10000000, \
memory_static_min=0x0.
[2007-07-15 23:00:02 3742] DEBUG (balloon:119) \
Balloon: 18236 KiB free; 244388 to scrub; \
need 262144; retries: 20.
[2007-07-15 23:00:02 3742] DEBUG (balloon:127) \
Balloon: waiting on scrubbing
[2007-07-15 23:00:02 3742] DEBUG (balloon:113) \
Balloon: 262632 KiB free; need 262144; done.
[2007-07-15 23:00:02 3742] INFO (image:129) \
buildDomain os=linux dom=26 vcpus=1
[2007-07-15 23:00:02 3742] DEBUG (image:198) \
domid        = 26
[2007-07-15 23:00:02 3742] DEBUG (image:199) \
memsize      = 256
[2007-07-15 23:00:02 3742] DEBUG (image:200) \
image        = /boot/vmlinuz-2.6.18-xen
[2007-07-15 23:00:02 3742] DEBUG (image:201) \
store_evtchn  = 1
[2007-07-15 23:00:02 3742] DEBUG (image:202) \
console_evtchn = 2
[2007-07-15 23:00:02 3742] DEBUG (image:203) \
cmdline = root=/dev/sda1 ro ip=:1.2.3.4:::::eth0:dhcp
[much additional output deleted]
```

These log file entries show memory allocation for a new domain and the first few log messages associated with starting a new domain.

makepolicy: Build Policy and Create .bin and .map Files

The xm makepolicy command uses an XML policy definition file and associated tools to create a binary policy file that can be loaded by the hypervisor. These policy files enable the hypervisor to support the Xen/sHype access control framework that was discussed in "Xen Access Control and Security Policies" in Chapter 9.

The basic syntax of the xm makepolicy command is as follows:

```
xm makepolicy POLICY
```

POLICY is the name that you selected for your policy and workload definition file after creating it, using the xensec_ezpolicy tool. By default, Xen policy files are stored in subdirectories of the directory /etc/xen/acm-security/policies, and have names of the form *POLICY*-security_policy.xml. For example, if you specified vonhagen as the name of your security policy, that policy would be stored in the file /etc/xen/acm-security/policies/vonhagen-security_policy.xml by default.

The xm makepolicy command creates two files from the XML policy definition file:

❑ *POLICY*.bin: A binary policy definition file suitable for loading by the hypervisor.

❑ *POLICY*.map: A text file that maps logical names to entries in the *POLICY*.bin file.

mem-max: Set the Maximum Amount Reservation for a Domain

The xm mem-max command enables you to specify the maximum amount of memory that a domain is able to use.

The basic syntax of the xm mem-max command is as follows:

```
xm mem-max DOMAINID MEMORY
```

This command sets the maximum amount of memory available to the domain whose ID is *DOMAINID* to *MEMORY*, which is an integer amount of memory in megabytes. Specifying a new *MEMORY* value does not cause immediate reallocation, and does not necessarily reflect the amount of memory actually used by the domain because the domain may not need that much memory at the moment.

mem-set: Set the Current Memory Usage for a Domain

The xm mem-set command enables you to specify the amount of memory that is currently allocated to a domain.

The basic syntax of the xm mem-set command is as follows:

```
xm mem-set DOMAINID MEMORY
```

This command uses the balloon driver to set the amount of memory that is currently allocated to the specified domain available to the domain whose ID is DOMAINID to MEMORY, which is an integer amount of memory in megabytes. The memory value displayed in xm list output is immediately updated to reflect the new MEMORY value. This may not take effect immediately within the domain if, for example, more memory than MEMORY is currently in use.

This option should be used with caution because reducing the amount of memory available to a running domain can cause it to crash or terminate running processes when trying to enforce the new memory limit. Using the xm mem-set command can be especially problematic for running domains without swap partitions.

migrate: Migrate a Domain to Another Machine

The xm migrate command enables administrators to take advantage of one of Xen's most powerful and exciting capabilities: the ability to migrate a Xen domain from one domain0 host to another, while the domain is running and with no visible interruption in service.

The basic syntax of the xm migrate command is as follows:

```
xm migrate DOMAINID TARGET [-l] [-p=PORT] [-r=MEGABITS]
```

This command migrates the domain identified by DOMAINID to the host whose hostname or IP address is TARGET. The -l (or equivalent --live) option causes the migration to occur without interrupting the availability of the domain or any of the services that it supports. The -p (or equivalent --port) option enables you to specify the network port on the TARGET that will be used for migration, in case you are using a port other than the default (8002). The -r (or equivalent --resource) option enables you to limit the amount of network bandwidth than can be consumed by the migration by specifying MEGABITS.

Migrating a domain can take quite a while because it requires substantial allocation, network bandwidth, and verification before the migration can complete. As discussed in detail in "Running Multiple domain0 Systems" in Chapter 6, "Configuring the Xen Daemon" in Chapter 7, and "Migrating Virtual Machines for High Availability" in Chapter 10, a number of things must be true in order to successfully migrate a domain from one domain0 to another. In a nutshell:

❑   Both systems must be running a version of the Xen daemon that supports migration.

❑   Relocation must be enabled for both Xen daemons so that the hosts can communicate with each other.

❑   The root filesystem used by the domain that you want to migrate must be visible from both domain0 systems, using the same path, device, and volume names and permissions.

❑   Sufficient resources must be available on the *TARGET* system to support the new domainU guest.

Migration is a complex process with many caveats before and during the migration process. It has many security issues that must be considered during and after the migration process, and it has a variety of system administration and management issues that must be addressed throughout the entire process. See "Migrating Domains for High Availability" in Chapter 10, for additional information.

network-attach: Create a New Virtual Network Device

The xm network-attach command enables you to define a new virtual network device for a given domain with specific characteristics.

The basic syntax of the xm network-attach command is as follows:

```
xm network-attach TARGETDOMAIN [backend=HOSTDOMAIN] \
     [bridge=BRIDGE] [ip=IPADDRESS] [mac=MACADDR] \
  [model=MODEL] [rate=RATE] [script=SCRIPT] \
  [type=TYPE] [vifname=VIFNAME]
```

This command creates a new virtual network device in the domain *TARGETDOMAIN*. The optional backend, bridge, ip, mac, model, rate, script, type, and vifname name=value pairs enable you to specify any of the virtual network interface parameters discussed in "Parameters for domainU Networking Startup" in Chapter 8.

The following is sample output listing virtual network interfaces before and after executing this command:

```
# brctl show
bridge name        bridge id            STP enabled      interfaces
xenbr0             8000.feffffffffff    no               vif0.0
                                                         peth0
                                                         vif31.0
                                                         vif24.0

# xm network-attach 31
# brctl show
bridge name        bridge id            STP enabled      interfaces
xenbr0             8000.feffffffffff    no               vif0.0
                                                         peth0
                                                         vif31.1
                                                         vif31.0
                                                         vif24.0
```

On the domainU system, the new interface shows up immediately after being created, as shown by the following `ifconfig` output.

Before:

```
# ifconfig -a
eth0      Link encap:Ethernet  HWaddr 00:16:3E:1E:99:EB
          inet addr:192.168.0.128  Bcast:192.168.0.255  Mask:255.255.255.0
          inet6 addr: fe80::216:3eff:fe1e:99eb/64 Scope:Link
          UP BROADCAST RUNNING MULTICAST  MTU:1500  Metric:1
          RX packets:311843 errors:0 dropped:0 overruns:0 frame:0
          TX packets:11734 errors:0 dropped:0 overruns:0 carrier:0
          collisions:0 txqueuelen:1000
          RX bytes:95789093 (91.3 MiB)  TX bytes:2229498 (2.1 MiB)
lo        Link encap:Local Loopback
          inet addr:127.0.0.1  Mask:255.0.0.0
          inet6 addr: ::1/128 Scope:Host
          UP LOOPBACK RUNNING  MTU:16436  Metric:1
          RX packets:0 errors:0 dropped:0 overruns:0 frame:0
          TX packets:0 errors:0 dropped:0 overruns:0 carrier:0
          collisions:0 txqueuelen:0
          RX bytes:0 (0.0 b)  TX bytes:0 (0.0 b)
```

After:

```
# ifconfig -a
eth0      Link encap:Ethernet  HWaddr 00:16:3E:1E:99:EB
          inet addr:192.168.0.128  Bcast:192.168.0.255  Mask:255.255.255.0
          inet6 addr: fe80::216:3eff:fe1e:99eb/64 Scope:Link
          UP BROADCAST RUNNING MULTICAST  MTU:1500  Metric:1
          RX packets:305518 errors:0 dropped:0 overruns:0 frame:0
          TX packets:8140 errors:0 dropped:0 overruns:0 carrier:0
          collisions:0 txqueuelen:1000
          RX bytes:95242213 (90.8 MiB)  TX bytes:921368 (899.7 KiB)
eth1      Link encap:Ethernet  HWaddr 00:16:3E:33:4F:CC
          BROADCAST MULTICAST  MTU:1500  Metric:1
          RX packets:0 errors:0 dropped:0 overruns:0 frame:0
          TX packets:0 errors:0 dropped:0 overruns:0 carrier:0
          collisions:0 txqueuelen:1000
          RX bytes:0 (0.0 b)  TX bytes:0 (0.0 b)
lo        Link encap:Local Loopback
          inet addr:127.0.0.1  Mask:255.0.0.0        inet6 addr: ::1/128 Scope:Host
          UP LOOPBACK RUNNING  MTU:16436  Metric:1
          RX packets:0 errors:0 dropped:0 overruns:0 frame:0
          TX packets:0 errors:0 dropped:0 overruns:0 carrier:0
          collisions:0 txqueuelen:0
          RX bytes:0 (0.0 b)  TX bytes:0 (0.0 b)
```

You can obtain detailed information about the virtual network interfaces associated with different domains using the `xm network-list` command, as discussed later in this appendix.

network-detach: Destroy a Domain's Virtual Network Device

The xm network-detach command enables you to remove a virtual network device from a domain.

The basic syntax of the xm network-detach command is as follows:

```
xm network-detach DOMAIN DEVICEID [-f]
```

This command removes the virtual network device identified by the device identifier DEVICEID from the domain DOMAIN. The -f (or equivalent --force) option removes the interface regardless of whether the interface is up or there is active traffic on that interface.

You can identify the DEVICEID for a given network interface using the xm network-list command or, unless you manually specified the vifname when creating a virtual network interface, from the name of the interface. See the "network-list: List Virtual Network Interfaces for a Domain" section later in this appendix for more information about the output of that command. For an example of inferring DEVICEID information from the output of the brctl command, consider the following brctl information:

```
# brctl show
bridge name       bridge id              STP enabled      interfaces
xenbr0            8000.feffffffffff      no               vif0.0
                                                          peth0
                                                          vif31.1
                                                          vif31.0
                                                          vif24.0
```

In this case, the virtual network interface vif31.0 probably has a DEVICEID of 0, and the virtual network interface vif31.1 probably has a DEVICEID of 1.

The xm network-detach command does not display any output when it completes successfully. An example of this command is as follows:

```
# xm network-detach 31 1
```

After issuing this command, you can re-run the brctl command to see that the network interface is no longer associated with the bridge.

network-list: List Virtual Network Interfaces for a Domain

The xm network-list command provides detailed information about all of the virtual network interfaces that are associated with a given domain.

The basic syntax of the xm network-list command is as follows:

```
xm network-list DOMAIN [--long]
```

This command displays the virtual network interfaces associated with the specified *DOMAIN*, as in the following example:

```
# xm network-list 31
Idx BE     MAC Addr.     handle state evt-ch tx-/rx-ring-ref BE-path
0   0  00:16:3e:1e:99:eb    0     4     8      768  /769       \
          /local/domain/0/backend/vif/31/0
1   0  00:16:3e:33:4f:cc    1     4    10     1280  /1281      \
          /local/domain/0/backend/vif/31/1
```

The first column shows the ID of each device. The rest of the per-interface information includes a count of the packets transmitted and received by this interface, the event channels used to exchange information to and from the virtual device, and so on.

The optional `--long` argument causes the output of the `xm network-list` command to be displayed in SXP format, as in the following example:

```
# xm network-list 31 --long
(0
    ((backend-id 0)
        (mac 00:16:3e:1e:99:eb)
        (handle 0)
        (state 4)
        (backend /local/domain/0/backend/vif/31/0)
        (tx-ring-ref 768)
        (rx-ring-ref 769)
        (event-channel 8)
        (request-rx-copy 1)
        (feature-rx-notify 1)
        (feature-sg 1)
        (feature-gso-tcpv4 1)
    )
)
(1
    ((backend-id 0)
        (mac 00:16:3e:33:4f:cc)
        (handle 2)
        (state 4)
        (backend /local/domain/0/backend/vif/31/1)
        (tx-ring-ref 1344)
        (rx-ring-ref 1345)
        (event-channel 10)
        (request-rx-copy 1)
        (feature-rx-notify 1)
        (feature-sg 1)
        (feature-gso-tcpv4 1)
    )
)
```

new: Add a Domain to xend Domain Management

The xm new command enables you to register a domain configuration file with the Xen daemon in a persistent fashion that will be preserved across any restarts of a domain0 system.

The basic syntax of the xm new command is as follows:

    xm new CONFIGFILE [variable=VALUE] [Other Options]

This command creates a XenStore entry for the domainU guest defined in *CONFIGFILE*. This command accepts the same variable=*VALUE* pairs and most of the same options as those for the xm create command, with the exception of console-related options. The xm new command does not start a domain, and therefore the console-related options are irrelevant. See the description of the xm create command earlier in this appendix for more information about the options and variable=*VALUE* pairs that you can use with the xm new command.

pause: Pause the Execution of a Domain

The xm pause command pauses the execution of a domain, making it unavailable to be scheduled for execution.

The basic syntax of the xm pause command is as follows:

    xm pause DOMAINID

This pauses the execution of *DOMAINID*. A paused domain retains all of the memory that was originally allocated to it. Remote service requests to a paused domain, such as HTTP or SSH requests, will either time out or be unable to locate the paused host until it is unpaused.

reboot: Reboot a Domain

The xm reboot command reboots all active domains or a specified domain.

The basic syntax of the xm reboot command is as follows:

    xm reboot DOMAINID | -a [-w]

Specifying a single *DOMAINID* reboots only that domain. Specifying the -a option reboots all domains that are active on the current domain0 host. The optional -w parameter causes the xm reboot command to wait until all reboots have completed before returning, which makes it convenient for use in scripts that need to reconnect to the restarted domains.

rename: Rename a Domain

The xm rename command enables you to rename an active domain or one that has been registered with Xen's lifecycle management.

The basic syntax of the xm rename command is as follows:

```
xm rename OLDNAME NEWNAME
```

The xm rename command renames the domain OLDNAME to NEWNAME. The new name must follow standard domain name conventions, such as not containing whitespace or non-alphanumeric characters (except for ., _, and -).

resources: Show Information for Each Labeled Resource

The xm resources command displays summary information about each labeled resource. Labeled resources are listed in the file /etc/xen/acm-security/policies/resource_labels.

The xm rename command takes no arguments:

```
xm resources
```

Sample output from this command is as follows:

```
# xm resources
file:/home/xen/PARAVIRT/fc6/fedora.fc6.img
    policy: example.chwall_ste.vonhagen
    label:  WordSmiths
file:/home/xen/PARAVIRT/fc6/fedora.swap
    policy: example.chwall_ste.vonhagen
    label:  WordSmiths
phy:/dev/VM/F7
    policy: example.chwall_ste.vonhagen
    label:  vonhagen
phy:/dev/hdb
    policy: example.chwall_ste.vonhagen
    label:  vonhagen
```

restore: Restore a Domain From a Saved State

The xm restore command restores a suspended domain from a specified checkpoint file, reallocating all of the resources that the domain was using when it was suspended. By default, the xm restore command also unpauses the restored domain, leaving it running.

The basic syntax of the xm restore command is as follows:

```
xm restore CHECKPOINTFILE [-p]
```

The xm restore command uses a *CHECKPOINTFILE* created by the xm save or xm suspend command to restore a domain. The optional -p argument leaves the restored domain in a paused state — by default, domains are unpaused and made active when they are restored. Domains that are restarted using the xm restore command do not need to be registered with Xen's lifecycle management.

The checkpoint files created by the xm save command can be located anywhere on your system — their location is one of the arguments to the xm save command. Domains that have been suspended with the xm suspend command are checkpointed to subdirectories of /var/lib/xend/domains. These subdirectories are named based on the UUID of the suspended domain, and contain a checkpoint file and a configuration file for the suspended domain. (See the description of the xm suspend command later in this appendix for more information.)

In general, domains that have been checkpointed using the xm save command should be restarted using the xm restore command. Domains that have been suspended using the xm suspend command should be restarted using the xm resume command.

resume: Resume a xend Managed Domain

The xm resume command restores a suspended domain using the information about that domain that is stored in the appropriate subdirectory of /var/lib/xend/domains, reallocating all of the resources that the domain was using when it was suspended. By default, the xm resume command also unpauses the restored domain, leaving it running.

The basic syntax of the xm resume command is as follows:

```
xm resume DOMAINNAME [-p]
```

This command looks up the UUID for the domain *DOMAINNAME* in the XenStore and uses the UUID to identify the subdirectory of /var/lib/xend/domains that contains information about the suspended domain. It then uses the checkpoint and configuration files in that directory to reallocate resources and restart the domain. The optional -p argument enables the xm resume command to reallocate memory, but remains paused. By default, domains are unpaused after being resumed, and are therefore instantly available.

In general, domains that have been suspended using the xm suspend command should be restarted using the xm resume command. Domains that have been checkpointed using the xm save command should be restarted using the xm restore command.

rmlabel: Remove a Security Label from a Domain

The xm rmlabel command removes the specified security label associated with a domain or resource. Security labels support the Xen/sHype access control framework that was discussed in "Xen Access Control and Security Policies" in Chapter 9.

The basic syntax of the xm rmlabel command is as follows:

```
xm rmlabel dom CONFIGFILE | res RESOURCE
```

When working with domains, the xm rmlabel dom CONFIGFILE command removes any security label that is present in the domain configuration file CONFIGFILE.

If no security label is present in the specified configuration file, the xm rmlabel command displays an error message, as in the following example:

```
# xm rmlabel opensuse.cfg
Error: 'Domain not labeled'
```

When you're working with resources, the xm rmlabel res RESOURCE command removes any security label associated with the RESOURCE, as in the following example:

```
# xm rmlabel res phy:/dev/VM/F7
```

Note that the RESOURCE must be fully qualified, exactly as it is in any configuration file that describes that resource. If this syntax is incorrect, the xm rmlabel command displays a somewhat cryptic error message, as in the following example:

```
# xm rmlabel res opensuse.img
ACMError: Resource spec 'opensuse.img' contains no ':' delimiter
Error: "Resource spec 'opensuse.img' contains no ':' delimiter"
```

save: Save a Domain State to Restore Later

The xm save command suspends the execution of a domain (specified by name) and writes the memory and configuration of the domain to the specified checkpoint file.

The basic syntax of the xm save command is as follows:

```
xm save DOMAINID CHECKPOINTFILE [-c]
```

This command writes the entire contents of memory for the domain identified by DOMAINID to the file CHECKPOINTFILE, which can be a relative or full pathname. By default, the domain DOMAINID terminates once the checkpoint is complete. Specifying the optional -c argument keeps the domain running after the checkpoint has completed.

In order to be checkpointed, the domain DOMAINNAME must be running. Only domainU guests can be saved.

sched-credit: Get/Set Credit Scheduler Parameters

The xm sched-credit command enables you to fine-tune the relative priority of a domain by adjusting its relative weight and the maximum amount of a processor that the domain can use. The Credit Scheduler is the default scheduler used by Xen.

The basic syntax of the xm sched-credit command is as follows:

```
xm sched-credit [-d DOMAINID [ -w[=WEIGHT] | -c[=CAP]]]
```

When executed with no arguments, the xm sched-credit command lists the current WEIGHT and CAP for all running domains, as in the following example:

```
# xm sched-credit
Name                          ID Weight Cap
Domain-0                       0    256   0
FC6-IMG-PV                    10    256   0
FC6-YUMIMG-PV                  6    256   0
XP-LV-HVM                      9    256   0
```

The weight of a domain is a relative number that effectively prioritizes a domain. WEIGHT values are not scalar, but are comparative. For example, a domain with a WEIGHT of 1024 will get four times as much CPU time as a domain with a WEIGHT of 256. The default value is 256. Valid values range from 1 through 65535.

The CAP on a domain determines the maximum percentage of a CPU that a domain can consume, and is expressed in terms of a percentage of one CPU. For example, a value of 50 means that a domain can use, at most, 50 percent of one physical CPU. Values over 100 mean that the domain can use more than one physical CPU (assuming that you actually have multiple physical CPUs). The default value is 0, which means that there is no limit.

Consider the following example:

```
# xm sched-credit -d 61 -w 512 -c 75
 # xm sched-credit
Name                          ID Weight Cap
Domain-0                       0    256   0
LAMP-VM                       61    512  75
Ubuntu                        59    256   0
```

In this case, the domain LAMP-VM gets twice as much CPU as other domains, but is only able to use, at most, 75 percent of one physical CPU on the current domain0 system. This enables other processes to co-exist and still get some processing cycles.

See "Controlling Hypervisor Scheduling" in Chapter 2 for more information about the schedulers used by Xen.

sched-sedf: Get/Set SEDF Scheduler Parameters

The xm `sched-sedf` command enables you to modify the scheduling parameters used by Xen's Simple Earliest Deadline First (SEDF) scheduler when scheduling various domains. The SEDF scheduler is not used with Xen by default. In order to use the xen `sched-sedf` command, you must modify your GRUB configuration file so that the Xen hypervisor uses the SEDF scheduler, as described in "Controlling Hypervisor Scheduling" in Chapter 2.

The basic syntax of the xm `sched-sedf` command is as follows:

```
xm sched-sedf DOMAINID [Options]
```

The options available for the xm `sched-sedf` command are as follows:

- ❑ `-p MS,--period=MS`: The maximum scheduling period (relative deadline) in nanoseconds.

- ❑ `-s MS,--slice=MS`: The time slice that should be associated with each request in nanoseconds (must be less than the scheduling period).

- ❑ `-l MS,--latency=MS`: An optional scaling value for the period if heavy I/O is in progress.

- ❑ `-e FLAG,--extra=FLAG`: A flag (`0-=false, 1=true`) indicating whether a domain can extend the time slice.

- ❑ `-w FLOAT, --weight=FLOAT`: The relative weight of the virtual CPU for the specified domain for this time slice. This setting is mutually exclusive with specifying scheduling parameters using the period/slice values. This is rarely used, but can be used to set relative weights as opposed to explicit period/slice values.

If you attempt to use the xm-sedf command on a domain0 host that is running a different scheduler, you will see a message such as the following:

```
Error: Xen is running with the credit scheduler
```

See "Controlling Hypervisor Scheduling" in Chapter 2 for more information about the schedulers used by Xen.

serve: Proxy xend XML-RPC over stdio

The xm `serve` command proxies XML-RPC traffic to the Xen daemon via standard input, enabling tunneling via SSH for secure communication with the Xen daemon.

The xm `serve` command takes no options, and therefore looks like the following:

```
# xm serve
```

To enable XML-RPC traffic to the Xen daemon without using this command, uncomment the following statement in the Xen daemon's configuration file (/etc/xen/xend-config.sxp):

```
#(xend-unix-xmlrpc-server yes)
```

This command and the associated client-side protocol via URLs of the form ssh://[user@]hostname [/path] are primarily designed for use with administrative utilities that use the xmlrpclib2 library.

shell: Launch an Interactive Shell

The xm shell command provides an interactive, command-line, shell-like environment in which you can sequentially execute multiple xm commands.

The xm shell command takes no arguments, and is executed in the following way:

```
# xm shell
The Xen Master. Type "help" for a list of functions.
xm>
```

Once the xm> prompt displays, you can enter xm subcommands and associated arguments without needing to enter the "xm" prefix, as in the following example:

```
xm> list
Name                         ID   Mem VCPUs      State   Time(s)
Broken-LAMP                 256    1                        0.0
Domain-0                      0 1400    2      r----- 254747.6
Foresight                    24  384    1      --p---   5694.3
LAMP-VM                      61  256    1      -b----    894.9
Slackware-11.0              128    1                        5.2
Ubuntu                       59  256    1      -b----     35.0
centos.5-0                  256    1                        0.0
xm>
```

To exit from the command-line environment provided by the xm shell command, press Ctrl+ d (hold down the Ctrl key and type d).

shutdown: Shutdown a Domain

The xm shutdown command initiates an orderly shutdown in a domainU, and is the equivalent of initiating a shutdown from within the domainU guest.

The basic syntax of the xm shutdown command is as follows:

```
xm shutdown DOMAINID [-w] [-a] [-R] [-H]
```

This command initiates a shutdown within the domain identified by *DOMAINID*. This command ordinarily returns immediately after sending a shutdown signal to the specified domain, but the -w option can be used to prevent the xm shutdown command from returning until the specified domain has completed the shutdown process. The -a option can be used to simultaneously send a shutdown signal to all running domains. The -H and -R options are the equivalent of the shutdown -h (halt after shutting down) and shutdown -r (reboot after shutting down) commands.

start: Start a xend-managed Domain

The xm start command enables you to start a domain that has been registered for Xen lifecycle management, has persistent entries in the XenStore, and is being managed by the Xen daemon.

The basic syntax of the xm start command is as follows:

```
xm start DOMAINNAME [-p]
```

The domain identified by *DOMAINNAME* must have already been registered for Xen lifecycle management via the xm new command, and must not be running or paused. Specifying the -p (or equivalent --pause) option causes the domain to remain paused after being started.

suspend: Suspend a xend-managed Domain

The xm suspend command suspends the execution of a domain (specified by name), writes the memory and configuration of the domain to checkpoint and status files, and relinquishes the resources associated with that domain.

The basic syntax of the xm suspend command is as follows:

```
xm suspend DOMAINNAME
```

In order to be suspended, the domain *DOMAINNAME* must be running, must be managed by Xen's lifecycle support, and must therefore have a persistent entry in the XenStore. Only domainU guests can be suspended. Trying to suspend a domain that was started using the xm create command or through an administrative tool that does not use the XenStore results in an error message such as the following:

```
# xm suspend 31
Error: Domain is not managed by Xen lifecycle support.
```

Information about suspended domains is written to subdirectories of /var/lib/xend/domains. These subdirectories are named based on the UUID of the suspended domain. Each subdirectory contains a checkpoint file that contains the complete contents of memory for the suspended domain, and a configuration file in SXP format that describes the configuration of the virtual machine and provides a variety of status and address information for the domain.

sysrq: Send a System Request to a Domain

The xm sysrq command enables you to send a special system request to a domain. This command is essentially identical to the use of the alt-SysRq-KEY sequence on a standard x86 Linux system, often referred to as the use of the "Magic SysRq key," which is the Linux kernel configuration option that must be set in order for this function to work. This capability is enabled by default in Xen kernels, as it is in most modern Linux kernels.

The basic syntax of the xm sysrq command is as follows:

```
xm sysrq DOMAINID LETTER
```

This command sends the system request *LETTER* to the domain identified by *DOMAINID*, where *LETTER* is one of the following:

- ❑ b: Immediately reboots the system without syncing or unmounting filesystems.

- ❑ c: Executes a kexec reboot in order to generate a crash dump. Your kernel must have been compiled with the CONFIG_KEXEC configuration option enabled, which is enabled in the default open source Xen source code distribution.

- ❑ e: Sends a SIGTERM signal to all processes except for the init process.

- ❑ f: Calls the kernel's out-of-memory killer (oom_kill) to terminate a process that is hogging memory.

- ❑ h: Displays a help message listing supported sysrq commands (as will any key that is not in the list of supported sysrq keys).

- ❑ i: Sends a SIGKILL signal to all processes except for the init process.

- ❑ k: A secure attention key (SAK) that kills all programs on the current virtual console. This sysrq can be quite useful if, for example, an X server has crashed on your console and you can't get a login or shell prompt there, but you can still connect to the system in some other fashion.

- ❑ l: Sends a SIGKILL signal to all processes including the init process, which will hang your system.

- ❑ m: Displays information about the current state of memory.

- ❑ o: Turns your system off. Your kernel must have been compiled with CONFIG_IMPI_POWEROFF enabled or as a module, and the IPMI management controller must be working on your system. This option is enabled as a module in the default open source Xen source code distribution.

- ❑ p: Displays the current registers and flags.

- ❑ r: Turns off keyboard raw mode. This sysrq can be quite useful if, for example, an X server has crashed on your domain0 system and you can't interact correctly with the current virtual console.

- ❑ s: Attempts to sync all mounted filesystems.

- ❑ t: Displays a list of current tasks and related information.

- ❑ u: Attempts to remount all mounted filesystems in read-only mode.

- ❑ 0-9: Sets the console log level to the specified level, controlling which kernel messages will be sent to your console. This can be used to temporarily lower or raise the log level so that you can see more or fewer error messages when debugging a problem.

The xm sysrq command is often used to shut down unresponsive domainU guests. The most common sequence in this case is to send the unresponsive domain the s, u, and b system requests to try to force it to sync all pending writes to disk, unmount all mounted filesystems, and then reboot.

For more detailed information on sysrq operations, see the file Documentation/sysrq.txt in any set of Linux Kernel sources. You can also find this file online, at sites such as www.mjmwired.net/kernel/Documentation/sysrq.txt.

top: Monitor a Host and the Domains in Real Time

The xm top command executes the xentop command, which was discussed in the "XenTop" in Chapter 7. The xm top command does not accept any arguments or pass them to the xentop application.

trigger: Send a Trigger to a Domain

The xm trigger command enables you to send a specific signal to a domain and (optionally) a specific VCPU used by that domain.

The basic syntax of this command is as follows:

```
xm trigger DOMAINID nmi | reset | init [VCPU]
```

This command is currently under development, and may not be available on the version of Xen that you are using.

unpause: Unpause a Paused Domain

The xm unpause command enables you to unpause a specified domain.

The basic syntax of the xm unpause command is as follows:

```
xm unpause DOMAINID
```

This command unpauses the domain specified by DOMAINID. You can identify paused domains by executing the xm list command and looking for the p flag in their State field.

uptime: Print Uptime for a Domain

The xm uptime enables you to display information about the amount of time that one or more domains have been running.

The basic syntax of this command is as follows:

```
xm uptime [DOMAINID] [-s]
```

With no arguments, the xm uptime command displays uptime information for all running domains, as in the following example:

```
# xm uptime
Name                              ID Uptime
Domain-0                           0 3 days, 16:01:18
FC6-IMG-PV                        10 23:36:14
FC6-YUMIMG-PV                      6 1 day,  2:20:34
XP-LV-HVM                          9 1 day,  1:38:21
```

Specifying one or more domain IDs restricts the output of the xm uptime command to providing information about only those domains, as in the following example:

```
# xm uptime 10 9
Name                              ID Uptime
FC6-IMG-PV                        10 23:36:14
XP-LV-HVM                          9 1 day,  1:38:21
```

The optional -s argument displays the current time and summary uptime information for all (or specified) domains, as in the following example:

```
# xm uptime -s
 12:25:34 up 3 days, 16:01, Domain-0 (0)
 12:25:34 up 3 days, 16:01, FC6-IMG-PV (10)
 12:25:34 up 1 day,   2:20, FC6-YUMIMG-PV (6)
 12:25:34 up 1 day,   1:38, XP-LV-HVM (9)
```

vcpu-list: List the VCPUs for a Domain or All Domains

The xm vcpu-list command enables you to determine the usage of the virtual CPUs that are available on your system.

The basic syntax of the xm vcpu-list command is as follows:

```
xm vcpu-list [DOMAINID]
```

With no arguments, the xm vcpu-list command shows virtual CPU usage for all domains, as in the following example:

```
# xm vcpu-list
Name                   ID  VCPU   CPU State   Time(s) CPU Affinity
Domain-0                0     0     0   r--   48456.9 any cpu
FC6-IMG-PV             10     0     0   -b-     300.2 any cpu
FC6-YUMIMG-PV           6     0     0   -b-     373.8 any cpu
XP-LV-HVM               9     0     0   -b-    1253.8 any cpu
```

Of course, the output from the xm vcpu-list command is more interesting on systems that have multiple cores or physical CPUs. Output on such a system looks like the following:

```
# xm vcpu-list
Name                    ID   VCPU   CPU State   Time(s) CPU Affinity
Domain-0                 0     0      0   r--     46.3 any cpu
Domain-0                 0     1      1   -b-     21.1 any cpu
WinXP-LVM-HVM            3     0      1   -b-     45.5 any cpu
```

Note that Domain-0 is listed twice because domain0 on VCPU 0 is assigned a dedicated thread in order to improve I/O performance and general responsiveness to administrative commands.

vcpu-pin: Assign VCPUs to a CPU

The xm vcpu-pin command enables you to assign virtual CPUs (VCPUs) to a specific CPU. This is only meaningful on systems with multiple cores or physical CPUs.

The basic syntax of this command is as follows:

```
xm vcpu-pin DOMAINID VCPU CPU | all
```

This command pins the *VCPU* for a specific domain identified by *DOMAINID* to run on a specific CPU. Specifying the keyword all instead of a specific *VCPU* enables the *VCPU* for a domain to float across all available CPUs.

The following output shows *VCPU* usage before and after using the xm vcpu-pin command:

```
# xm vcpu-list
Name                    ID   VCPU   CPU State   Time(s) CPU Affinity
Domain-0                 0     0      0   r--     97.6 any cpu
Domain-0                 0     1      1   -b-     31.5 any cpu
WinXP-LVM-HVM            3     0      0   -b-    121.8 any cpu
# xm vcpu-pin 3 0 1
# xm vcpu-list
Name                    ID   VCPU   CPU State   Time(s) CPU Affinity
Domain-0                 0     0      1   r--     98.1 any cpu
Domain-0                 0     1      0   -b-     32.0 any cpu
WinXP-LVM-HVM            3     0      1   -b-    122.3 1
```

In general, this command does not need to be used for load-balancing purposes if you are using the Xen credit scheduler (the default Xen scheduler at the time that this book was written). The credit scheduler automatically balances guest VCPUs across all available physical CPUs on an SMP host, based on the system load. You can still use this command to restrict the CPUs on which a specific VCPU can run, but note that any value set using vcpu-pin will not persist across migrations.

vcpu-set: Set the Number of Active VCPUs Allowed for a Domain

The xm vcpu-set command sets the maximum number of active VCPUs that a domain can use.

The basic syntax of this command is as follows:

```
xm vcpu-set DOMAINID VCPUS
```

This command enables you to modify the number of *VCPUS* that are available to a domain identified by *DOMAINID*. The number of available VCPUs is typically set in a domainU configuration file using the vcpus=*VALUE* name/value pair, but can be temporarily overridden when a domain is running by using the xm vcpu-set command.

vnet-create: Create a vnet from a Configuration File

The xm vnet-create command enables you to create a vnet based on a vnet configuration file. vnets are persistent virtual networks to which domains remain connected even after migrating to other physical hosts.

The basic syntax of this command is as follows:

```
xm vnet-create VNETCONFIGFILE
```

A *VNETCONFIGFILE* is a text file in SXP format that looks like the following:

```
(vnet (id VnetID)
       (bridge bridge)
       (vnetif vnet-interface)
       (security level)
)
```

The keywords and their required parameters are as follows:

❑ VnetID: A non-zero 128-bit vnet identifier, specified as eight colon-separated, four-digit hex numbers, or as a single four-digit hex number. The latter form is the same as the long form with 0 in the first seven fields. ID 0001 is reserved.

❑ bridge: The name of a bridge interface to create for the vnet. Bridge names are limited to 14 characters.

❑ vnetif: (optional) The name of the virtual interface to the vnet. The interface encapsulates and decapsulates vnet traffic for the network and is attached to the vnet bridge. vnetif names are limited to 14 characters.

- ❏ level: (optional) Security level for the vnet. The level may be one of the following:

  - ❏ none: No security (default). vnet traffic is in the clear on the network.

  - ❏ auth: Authentication. vnet traffic is authenticated using IPSEC ESP with hmac96.

  - ❏ conf: Confidentiality. vnet traffic is authenticated and encrypted using IPSEC ESP with hmac96 and AES-128.

The auth and conf security levels are still under development and therefore can use only built-in keys at the moment. See the tools/vnet/examples subdirectory of any Xen source code installation for some examples of vnet configuration files.

vnet support for Xen is not built by default. You can build it by cd'ing to the tools/vnet directory of a Xen source code installation and executing the make command. vnet support requires a kernel module and a user-space daemon named varpd.

I have been unable to use vnets in most Xen distributions. See the Xen User's Manual provided with your Xen distribution for more information about the status of vnets in the version of Xen that you are using.

vnet-delete: Delete a vnet

The xm vnet-delete command enables you to delete an existing vnet. The syntax of the xm vnet-delete command is as follows:

```
xm vnet-delete VNETID
```

The VNETID is the identifier that you provided in the configuration file when you created the vnet. You can also locate vnet identifiers by running the xm vnet-list command.

vnet-list: List vnets

The xm vnet-list command lists all available vnets on your local network. The syntax of this command is as follows:

```
xm vnet-list [-l]
```

The -l (or equivalent --long) option displays as much information as is available about the vnets that your domain0 can locate.

vtpm-list: List Virtual TPM Devices

The xm vtpm-list command lists the virtual Trusted Platform Module (TPM) devices that a domain can locate. TPMs are normally hardware devices used for privacy and authorization when verifying system identity for secure computing environments. Because different virtual machines may have different TPM requirements, Xen provides a mechanism for using different virtual TPMs with different virtual machines.

The syntax of the `xm vtpm-list` command is as follows:

```
xm vtpm-list DOMAINID  [-l]
```

This command lists the virtual TPMs that are recognized by the domain specified by *DOMAINID*. The option `-l` (or equivalent `--long`) argument displays a long listing with additional information.

Virtual TPM support is enabled in the open source version of Xen by default, but the tools to create and manage it are not built automatically. To build Xen with TPM support, you must set the `VTPM_TOOLS` variable to `y` in the `Config.mk` file in the root of your Xen source code distribution, and then rebuild Xen. See Chapter 9 for more information about TPM support in Xen.

The TPM specification is sponsored by the Trusted Computing Group. See `www.trustedcomputinggroup.org` for more information.

B

Xen Virtual Machine Configuration File Reference

As discussed in Chapter 6 and touched upon elsewhere in this book, Xen supports a number of different mechanisms for defining virtual machines and storing their configuration information. Most commonly, Xen virtual machine configuration information is stored in text files in Python variable format, making it easy to examine and update that configuration information. Links to these configuration files can be placed in `/etc/xen/auto` to automatically restart specific virtual machines whenever you restart a domain0 system.

If you are using Xen's lifecycle management (discussed in Chapter 9) the configuration information in these files can be loaded into the XenStore and preserved there, making this configuration information persistent and simplifying scripted system restarts. Once in the XenStore, virtual machine configuration information can also be displayed in standard formats such as SXP and XML. Distributions such as Fedora and Red Hat provide utilities such as virt-manager for graphically defining, storing, and editing configuration information for Xen virtual machines. As with Xen's lifecycle management, virt-manager stores this configuration information in the XenStore.

Regardless of how you define your Xen virtual machines and where their configuration information is stored, the configuration parameters that are supported by Xen are the key to your Xen virtual machines. This appendix discusses all of the virtual machine configuration parameters that Xen supports, any arguments they require or accept, and any default values for the parameters or their arguments. Some sample Xen configuration files in Python variable format are provided in the directory `/etc/xen`. These files have names beginning with `xmexample`, and show a variety of different paravirtualized and HVM configurations and suggested variable settings.

> Many statements in Xen configuration files, such as disk definitions and network interface configuration information, can be repeated to simultaneously configure more than one device, interface, and so on. When using SXP or XML format configuration files, multiple instances of these elements are inherently scoped by nested parentheses or XML elements (respectively). When using multiple instances of a single statement in a configuration file in Python variable format, they must be enclosed within a set of square brackets, each instance must be enclosed within delimiters (typically single quotation marks), and they must be comma-separated.

❑ `access_control='policy=POLICY,label=LABEL'`: Associates a specified security policy and label with the domain. When starting, restoring, or migrating, the local ssid reference is calculated when starting or resuming the domain and the specified policy and label are checked against the active policy. This ensures that local labels are created correctly for the system where a domain is started or resumed. See "Xen Access Control and Security Policies" in Chapter 9 for more information about security policies and labels.

❑ `acpi=0|1`: Disables (0, default) or enables (1) ACPI (Advanced Configuration and Power Interface) in an HVM domain.

❑ `apic=0|1`: Disables (0, default) or enables (1) APIC (Advanced Programmable Interrupt Controller) mode.

❑ `blkif=0|1`: Disables (0, default) or enables (1) a domainU guest's ability to export block devices to other domains. Domains that export block devices to other domains must have both frontend and backend block device drivers. By default, domainU guests have only frontend drivers, and only domain0 systems have both and can therefore export block devices to other domains.

❑ `boot=a|b|c|d`: Identifies the default boot device for HVM domains. If more than one letter is specified, this option identifies the sequence in which devices should be searched for a boot image.

❑ `bootargs=NAME`: Enables you to specify arguments to pass to the boot loader used on an HVM.

❑ `bootentry=NAME`: (Deprecated) This option formerly identified the entry that the boot loader should boot. This has been replaced by the `bootargs` configuration file entry.

❑ `bootloader=FILE`: Identifies the path to the boot loader for an HVM system. If this option is not specified, the kernel option is used to identify the program to use to simulate a BIOS.

❑ `builder=FUNCTION`: The function to use to build the domain. HVM domains should specify `hvm`, whereas paravirtualized domains typically use `linux` (which is the default if no value is specified for the builder configuration option).

❑ `cpu=NUM`: In a multi-CPU or multi-core system, this option specifies the number of the CPU on which to run VCPU0.

❑ `cpu_cap=NUM`: Sets the maximum amount of allotted CPUs that the domain can consume.

❏ `cpu_weight=NUM`: Sets the relative weight of this domain in terms of the amount of CPU time that it can consume.

❏ `cpus=CPUS`: Specifies the CPUS on which to run the domain. If this configuration option is absent or set to an empty string, Xen uses available CPUs, as needed. This option can be set to a single integer (identifying a specific CPU), a comma-separated list of CPUs expressed using integers, ranges of integers (1–3), and negated integers (such as ^2, meaning, not on CPU 2), or even based on the virtual machine identifier if it is specified as a value that is passed to the virtual machine startup script and can therefore be used internally (as in '"%s" % vmid', which means use the CPU corresponding to the vmid modulo of the number of physical CPUs).

❏ `device_model=FILE`: The full pathname of the device model program used for HVMs. This is typically expressed as '/usr/' + arch_libdir + '/xen/bin/qemu-dm', where `arch_libdir` determines whether the device is a 32-bit or 64-bit system using the following Python function:

```
import os, re
arch = os.uname()[4]
if re.search('64', arch):
    arch_libdir = 'lib64'
else:
    arch_libdir = 'lib'
```

❏ `dhcp=0|dhcp`: Determines whether the domain should find its IP address using DHCP (`dhcp`) or not (`0`). This option is only relevant for paravirtualized domains.

❏ `disk='phy:DEV,VDEV,MODE[,DOM]'`: One or more triples that define a disk device for a domain. The first value, `DEV`, consists of a variable:variable pair. Default device types are `file` (deprecated, referring to a partition image mounted as a loopback device), `tap:aio` (referring to the blktap driver), and `phy` (a physical device). `DEV` is exported to the target domain as `VDEV`. The `MODE` is specified as `r` (read-only), `w` (read-write), or `w!` (forced read-write). The `w!` should be used with extreme caution because it forces Xen to be able to write to the device, and should rarely be necessary. An optional fourth value, `DOM`, defines a specific backend driver domain to use for the disk. Multiple devices can be defined in a single disk statement.

❏ `display=DISPLAY`: The name of the X11 display on which to display a graphical console. This is only relevant for HVMs.

❏ `extra=ARGS`: Enables you to specify extra arguments that should be appended to the kernel command line when booting the virtual machine. This is only relevant for paravirtualized systems.

❏ `fda='FILE'`: The device name of floppy drive A or the full path to a floppy image that should be used as floppy drive A.

❏ `fdb='FILE'`: The device name of floppy drive B or the full path to a floppy image that should be used as floppy drive B.

❏ `features=FEATURES`: (Deprecated) Identifies features to enable in guest kernel.

❏ `gateway='XXX.XXX.XXX.XXX'`: Sets the IP gateway for the kernel to the specified dotted-quad IP address. This is only relevant for paravirtualized domains.

❏ `hostname='NAME'`: Sets the hostname for the system. This is only relevant for paravirtualized domains.

❏ `interface='DEVICE'`: Sets the name of the Ethernet device used by the kernel. This is only relevant for paravirtualized domains.

❑ ioports='*FROM-TO*': Adds an I/O range, defined by hexadecimal values, to a (for example, ioports=03f8-03ff). The option may be repeated to add more than one I/O range. This is only relevant for paravirtualized domains.

❑ ip='*XXX.XXX.XXX.XXX*': Sets the IP address for the system to the specified dotted-quad IP address. This is only relevant for paravirtualized domains.

❑ irq='*NUM*': Adds a specified IRQ (interrupt line) to a domain. This option may be repeated to add more than one IRQ, and is rarely necessary unless your hardware explicitly assigns fixed IRQs.

❑ isa=0|1: Simulates (1) an ISA only system. The default value for this configuration option is 0, which simulates a modern, PCI-based system.

❑ kernel='*FILE*': Path to a kernel image or an application that can locate it for paravirtualized domains, or the path to an application that simulates a BIOS for HVM domains. For paravirtualized domains, this option is usually either the full pathname of a kernel image, or pygrub, which is a utility written in Python that can locate a kernel image inside a QEMU-format partition or file. For HVM domains, this is typically hvmloader, which is a 32-bit application that simulates a generic BIOS to boot an HVM from the boot sector of the partition or QEMU disk image in which it is located.

❑ keymap='*FILE*': Sets the keyboard layout used. The default is a standard US English keyboard, type en-us. Valid keymap values are da (Danish), de (German), de-ch (Swiss-German), en-gb (English, UK), en-us (English, US), es (Spanish), fi (Finnish), fr (French), fr-be (French, Belgium), fr-ca (French, Canada), fr-ch (French, Switzerland), hu (Hungarian), is (Icelandic), it (Italian), ja (Japanese), nl (Dutch), nl-be (Dutch, Belgium), no (Norwegian), pl (Polish), pt (Portugese), pt-br (Portugese, Brazil), ru (Russian), and sv (Sweden).

❑ localtime=0|1: Enables you to specify whether the Real-Time Clock (RTC) is set to local time (1) or not (0, default). If it is not set to local time, the RTC is based on Universal Time Coordinated (UTC). UTC is the mean solar time for the meridian at Greenwich, England, and is used as a basis for calculating standard time in most of the world.

❑ maxmem=*NUM*: Specifies the maximum amount of memory, in megabytes, that can be associated with the domain.

❑ memory=*NUM*: Specifies the initial amount of memory, in megabytes, that is associated with the domain when starting it. Specifying a value that is too low prevents a domain from starting. Values lower than 32MB are not recommended.

❑ monitor=0|1: Specifies whether to disable (0, default) or enable (1) any monitor that is available for the specified device model. This is only relevant to HVMs. You should usually set this option to 1 for HVMs to provide access to the QEMU monitor, which you can use for various device-related tasks, such as enabling and directly attaching USB devices. When this option is enabled, you can connect to the QEMU monitor by pressing the Ctrl+Alt+2 keys simultaneously.

❑ name=*NAME*: Specifies the name of the domain. This must be a unique text string, and can either be explicitly specified or can be calculated using Python expressions and variables.

❑ netif=0|1: Disables (0, default) or enables (1) a domainU guest's ability to export network interfaces to other domains. Domains that export network interfaces to other domains must have both frontend and backend network device drivers. By default, domainU guests have only frontend drivers, and only domain0 systems have both and can therefore export network interfaces to other domains.

❏ `netmask='`*`XXX.XXX.XXX.XXX`*`'`: Sets the netmask for the system to the specified dotted-quad IP mask. This is only relevant for paravirtualized domains.

❏ `nfs_root='`*`PATH`*`'`: Specifies the full pathname for the NFS directory containing an NFS root filesystem. This is only relevant for paravirtualized domains. Using an NFS root directory also requires changes to the default kernel configuration used to build the Xen domainU kernel, as discussed in Chapter 3.

❏ `nfs_server='`*`XXX.XXX.XXX.XXX`*`'`: Specifies the IP address of the NFS server, in dotted-quad notation, that hosts the NFS root filesystem. Using an NFS root directory also requires changes to the default kernel configuration used to build the Xen domainU kernel, as discussed in Chapter 3.

❏ `nics=`*`NUM`*: (Deprecated) Specifies the number of network interfaces available to the virtual machine. Network interfaces are now defined using the `vif` keyword, discussed elsewhere in this appendix. Specifying multiple, empty `vif` entries will create the specified number of network interfaces using default configuration values.

❏ `nographic=0|1`: Specifies that the virtual machine does not (`0`, default) have graphical console capabilities. Specifying `1` identifies the virtual machines as having the graphical console capabilities provided by its device model. The use of 0 and 1 here is somewhat counter-intuitive, but reflects the correct syntax.

❏ `on_crash='destroy'|'preserve'|'rename-restart'|'restart'`: Specifies the behavior of a virtual machine when a domain exits with the reason `crash`. Possible values are `destroy` (the domain exits and Xen structures allocated for that VM are reclaimed), `preserve` (any console or SDL/VNC console associated with the virtual machine is preserved until the domain is manually destroyed), `rename-restart` (the old domain is not cleaned up, as if the `preserve` option was specified, but is renamed and a new domain is started in its place, as if the `restart` option was specified), and `restart` (a new domain is started to replace the one that terminated).

❏ `on_poweroff='destroy'|'preserve'|'rename-restart'|'restart'`: Specifies the behavior of a virtual machine when a domain exits with the reason `poweroff`. Possible values are `destroy` (the domain exits and Xen structures allocated for that VM are reclaimed), `preserve` (any console or SDL/VNC console associated with the virtual machine is preserved until the domain is manually destroyed), `rename-restart` (the old domain is not cleaned up, as if the `preserve` option was specified, but is renamed and a new domain is started in its place, as if the `restart` option was specified), and `restart` (a new domain is started to replace the one that terminated).

❏ `on_reboot='destroy'|'preserve'|'rename-restart'|'restart'`: Specifies the behavior of a virtual machine when a domain exits with the reason `reboot`. Possible values are `destroy` (the domain exits and Xen structures allocated for that VM are reclaimed), `preserve` (any console or SDL/VNC console associated with the virtual machine is preserved until the domain is manually destroyed), `rename-restart` (the old domain is not cleaned up, as if the `preserve` option was specified, but is renamed and a new domain is started in its place, as if the `restart` option was specified), and `restart` (a new domain is started to replace the one that terminated).

❏ `on_xend_start='ignore'|'start'`: Specifies the action that should be performed for the domain when the Xen daemon starts. Possible values are `ignore` (the domain remains in its current state) and `start` (the domain is started, as if the `xm create` or `xm start` command had been executed). The default value is `ignore`.

❑ on_xend_stop='continue'|'shutdown'|'suspend': Specifies the action that the domain should perform when the Xen daemon is stopped. Possible values are ignore (the domain continues to run), shutdown (the domain is shut down, as if the xm shutdown command had been executed), and suspend (the domain is suspended). The default value is ignore.

❑ pae=0|1: Specifies whether the domain supports (1) or does not support (0, default) the Physical Address Extensions (PAEs) that enable 32-bit machines to access more than 4GB of memory.

❑ pci=BUS:DEV.FUNC: Identifies the bus address of a PCI device that should be exclusively available in a domain, which is then known as a "PCI driver domain." PCI devices are identified by their unique slot definition that is typically of the form bus:device.function, in hexadecimal. This option may be repeated to dedicate more than one PCI device to a given domain.

❑ ramdisk='FILE': The full path to the RAM disk used by a domain. This option is only relevant for paravirtualized domains.

❑ restart='always'|'never'|'onreboot': (Deprecated) Used in pre-3.x Xen releases to specify how the system should respond to various exit codes from a domain. The configuration file settings on_poweroff, on_reboot, and on_crash should be used instead of the restart configuration parameter on 3.x and newer Xen distributions.

❑ root='DEVICE [MOUNT]': Specifies the name of the device containing the root filesystem for a domain, and how it should initially be mounted. This is equivalent to the root= parameter and associated mode than can be specified on a kernel command line. The specified device should be the root filesystem identified in your disk configuration file variable, or /dev/nfs when you are using a NFS root filesystem.

❑ rtc_timeoffset=NUM: Specifies the offset between local time and the time specified by the real-time clock.

❑ sdl=0|1: Specifies whether the graphical console of a machine should be available via Simple DirectMedia Layer (SDL) graphics (1) or not (0, default). This option is only relevant for HVMs. Using SDL graphics simplifies displaying the graphical console for an HVM, but requires that X11 be running on domain0 or that the display variable is used to specify the graphical X11 host on which the SDL console window should be displayed. Using SDL graphical console displays can be problematic when migrating HVMs from one system to another.

❑ serial='PATH': Specifies the path to the serial, pty, or vc device to which serial console output should be redirected.

❑ shadow_memory=NUM: Specifies the amount of memory, in megabytes, that should be reserved for the shadow pagetable, which is used to map domain memory pages to domain0 memory pages. This value should be at least 2KB per MB of domain memory, plus 3MB per VCPU. For example, a system with a maximum of 1GB of memory and two VCPUs should specify a value of at least 8 MB of shadow memory.

❑ soundhw='DEVICE': Identifies the type of sound card support that should be provided by the underlying device model used by an HVM. Possible values are all (all supported sound hardware) es1370 (Ensonic 1730), none (no sound support), or sb16 (SoundBlaster 16). The default is none if this option is not specified. This is only relevant for HVMs.

❑ stdvga=0|1: Specifies whether the graphical console for a domain should support standard VGA (1) or Cirrus Logic graphics (0, default) adaptors.

❑   `tpmif=0|1`: Disables (`0`, default) or enables (`1`) a domainU guest's ability to export a Trusted Platform Module (TPM) device to other domains. Domains that export TPM devices to other domains must have both frontend and backend TPM device drivers. By default, domainU guests have only frontend drivers, and only domain0 systems have both and can therefore export TPM devices to other domains.

❑   `usb=0|1`: Disables (`0`, default) or enables (`1`) support for USB devices. This is only relevant in HVMs.

❑   `usbdevice='NAME'`: Specifies the USB mouse model used in the graphical console for an HVM domain. Valid options are `mouse` (for relative, PS/2 mouse support) and `tablet` (for absolute positioning mouse support).

❑   `usbport='PATH'`: Specifies the path to a USB device that should be associated with the domain. This option can be specified multiple times to identify more than one USB device to pass through to the domain. This option is only relevant for HVM domains.

❑   `uuid=UUID`: Specifies a Universal Unique Identifier (UUID) to use for the domain. If no UUID is specified, the Xen daemon will automatically generate one when creating or starting a domain. This value must be unique across all domains running on a class C subnet.

❑   `vcpu_avail=NUM`: Enables you to specify the maximum number of virtual CPUs to make available to the domain.

❑   `vcpus=VCPUS`: Enables you to specify the number of virtual CPUS to initially allocate to a domain.

❑   `vfb=type={vnc,sdl},vncunused=1,vncdisplay=N,vnclisten=ADDR,display=DISPLAY, xauthority=XAUTHORITY,vncpasswd=PASSWORD`: Enables the use of a virtual frame buffer in the domain so that it serves as a framebuffer backend. The backend type should be either `sdl` or `vnc`. If `type=vnc`, the domain automatically spawns an external vncviewer that displays the graphical console of the domain. If `vnclisten` is specified, the VNC server listens on ADDR (default `127.0.0.1`) on port n+5900. If `vncdisplay` is not specified, `N` defaults to the domain ID. If `vncunused=1`, the server tries to find an arbitrary unused port above 5900. (The `vncdisplay` and `vnclisten` option are mutually exclusive, and should not be used together.) Specifying `vncpasswd` and a password value overrides the default password VNC password configured in the Xen daemon configuration files. For `type=sdl`, a viewer is started automatically using the given display and xauthority files, both of which default to the values associated with the current user.

❑   `vif=type=TYPE,mac=MAC,bridge=BRIDGE,ip=IPADDR,script=SCRIPT,backend=DOM, vifname=NAME`: Creates a virtual network interface with the specified (or default) values, which are configured and specified by the script. If no values are provided (`vif = [ '' ]`), this statement creates a virtual network interface using default values. If `TYPE` is not specified, the default is `netfront`. If `MAC` is not specified, a random MAC address in the range 00:16:3E:XX: XX:XX is generated. If `bridge` is not specified, the first bridge found is used (xenbr0 by default). If `script` is not specified, the default script specified in the Xen daemon's configuration file is used to configure the new virtual network interface. If `backend` is not specified, the default backend driver domain is used. If `vifname` is not specified, the backend virtual interface will have the name `vifd.n`, where d is the domain ID and n is the interface ID. This option may be repeated to add more than one vif.

❑   `vnc=0|1`: Specifies whether the graphical console of a machine should be available via Virtual Network Computing (VNC) (`1`) or not (`0`, default). This option is relevant only for HVMs.

❏ `vncconsole=0|1`: Specifies whether the domain should automatically spawn a `vncviewer` process for the domain's graphical console (1) or not (0). This is only relevant for HVMs, and then only when VNC is being used to access the graphical console (`vnc=1`).

❏ `vncdisplay=NUM`: Specifies the number of the VNC display to use for the graphical console for this system. Any user attempting to display the graphical console in VNC needs to specify the `vncdisplay` number, as in the command `vncviewer 127.0.0.1:2` if `vncdisplay` is set to 2.

❏ `vnclisten='XXX.XXX.XXX.XXX'`: Identifies the IP address on which the VNC server should listen.

❏ `vncpasswd='PASSWD'`: Specifies the password for the VNC console on an HVM domain. The passwd is an unencrypted text string, so you must ensure that your Xen configuration files are not publicly readable on your domain0 system.

❏ `vncunused=0|1`: Tells (1) the VNC server to find an unused port on which the VNC server will listen. By default, VNC servers listen on port 5900+n, where n is the domain ID. This option is only meaningful if `vnc=1`.

❏ `vncviewer=0|1`: Tells (1) the Xen daemon to automatically spawn a `vncviewer` that is listening for a VNC server in the domain. The address of the `vncviewer` is passed to the domain on the kernel command line using `VNC_SERVER=<host>:<port>`. The port used by VNC is 5900 + n, where n is the domain ID. This option is meaningful only when `vnc=1`.

❏ `vtpm='instance=INSTANCE, backend=DOM, type=TYPE'`: Specifies that the domain should create a Trusted Platform Module (TPM) interface. The specified instance is used as the virtual TPM instance on domain0. If you specify an instance, that value is used as the number of the preferred instance — the hotplug script determines which instance number is actually assigned to the domain. The VM/TPM mapping that is used is in `/etc/xen/vtpm.db`. The `type` parameter specifies the specific driver type that the VM can use, which can be set to `paravirtualized` to prevent an HVM from being able to access an emulated device model. For more information about TPMs, see Chapter 9.

❏ `xauthority='XAUTHORITY'`: Specifies the full pathname of the X11 authority file to use. If no value is specified, the name of the X11 authority file to use is taken from the xauthority environment variable of the user who started a domain.

Index

C